KATHLEEN DAYUS

OMNIBUS

KATHLEEN DAYUS

OMNIBUS

Her People
Where There's Life
All My Days
The Best of Times

A *Virago* Book

First published by Virago Press 1994

Published by Virago Press 1998

Her People
Published by Virago Press 1982
Copyright © Kathleen Dayus 1982

Where There's Life
Published by Virago Press 1985
Copyright © Kathleen Dayus 1985

All My Days
Published by Virago Press 1988
Copyright © Kathleen Dayus 1988

The Best of Times
Published by Virago Press 1991
Copyright © Kathleen Dayus 1991

A CIP catalogue record for this book is available from
the British Library

ISBN 1 86049 599 0

Printed and bound in Great Britain by Mackays of Chatham plc,
Chatham, Kent

Virago Press
A Division of
Little, Brown and Company (UK)
Brettenham House
Lancaster Place
London WC2E 7EN

CONTENTS

List of illustrations

Family photographs reproduced by kind permission of Kathleen
Dayus. 'Hop Pickers' reproduced by permission of the Reference
Library History & Geography Department (Stone Collection),
Birmingham Public Libraries. All other photographs reproduced by
permission of the Reference Library Local Studies Department,
Birmingham Public Libraries.

HER PEOPLE

To Christina Rainey,
my granddaughter

Contents

Our Yard

O
ne day, a few years ago, I found myself walking through a part of Birmingham I hadn't seen for a long time. Hockley is an area of warehouses and factories today and I shouldn't think anybody lives there except the landlords of the pubs that are dotted about here and there on corners. It was a different story seventy years ago, though. Then this whole district was so crammed with humanity it was more like a rabbits' warren. There were still factories and lots of small workshops and foundries and the same pubs were crowded all day long, not just at lunch-time when the workmen were having a break like today. Then, this was what people today would call a 'slum' I suppose, and the people who lived there would be pitied as the 'have-nots', but then there was no pity and we were left to sink or swim, rise or fall, as best we could. Yes, this was where I was born in 1903 and the poor people who struggled to live until that struggle killed them were my people.

So as I was walking by the George and Dragon where I had shivered on Christmas Eve singing carols for a few pence to buy a small treat that my mother and father couldn't afford, I thought, these people may have had nothing, but they don't deserve to be forgotten. My people; my parents and their friends and my brothers and sisters and the rest of us who fought for a crust here ought to be remembered now that the National Health Service, council houses and colour television have clouded our memory of where we came from and who we are.

People then were superstitious. They had no education and some couldn't even read and write: they never had the chance to learn like everyone has today. What we didn't have we had to do without, and what we didn't know we had to find out the hard way, although more often than not it was the wrong way! The menfolk were mostly out of work and the women had to earn a living by taking in washing, or carding linen buttons, or sewing on hooks and eyes by the light of a piece of candle. There was never much of a fire in the grate but plenty of ashes from old boots or anything else that could be found to burn to warm ourselves. When we were fortunate enough to have coal, every lump was counted! Us kids would run a mile for a farthing or a piece of bread and dripping which we'd have to share with the rest.

The grown-ups always tried to help each other the best way they could, but they found it very hard, for some had large families to feed and clothe; ten, twelve and even sixteen in one family was not uncommon. Sometimes their language was terrible but they had harsh conditions to put with. Consumption was well known in our district and there were plenty of burials. The only people who did a good trade were the undertaker and the midwife. However, if you couldn't afford a midwife one of the neighbours would oblige, which resulted in many a baby dying before it had even opened its eyes and many a young mother as well. They were worn out and old women at forty, with children dragging at their dry breasts, a practice which was prolonged because they believed that if they kept a child to the breast until it was three years old they wouldn't become pregnant again. However, this rarely stopped them producing a large family despite the warnings they were given. I can recall many young children pulling at their mothers' skirts, crying to be picked up for a feed. You would hear the child cry out, 'I'm 'ungry, I want some titty.' Then the mother would lift her child up and pull out a breast while she walked along or sat on a step. There was often no milk there nor the bosom there used to be, only an empty flat piece of flesh, but this comforted the child and the mother, who hoped that the child would get something out of it even if it was only wind. Still most of these women wanted a large family, 'the more the better', they used to say. I imagined the reason for this was because they were jealous of the others having more than themselves, but this was not always so; and as I grew older I learned that the true reason for having a large family quickly was to replace the children that died, which many did, sometimes at a very early age. Diseases that were common at that time were rickets, 'wasting disease', fever, consumption and the rest. Those who did survive had to begin work at a very early age to help feed themselves and their parents, otherwise it was starvation or the workhouse.

Our street was called Camden Street. Along one side of this street facing the high school wall ran ten terraces called 'groves'. Ours was called Camden Drive. There were five houses or hovels with five more back-to-backs to each terrace. They were all built the same; one large living-room, one bedroom, and an attic. There were also cellars that ran under each house, damp, dark and cold. Here was where they kept their coal, 'slack', or wood when they had any, which was never very often. For this reason there was usually some rubbish tipped in the cellar ready to be put on the fire for warmth or for cooking. I don't suppose this habit would be regarded as altogether healthy today but then it was essential.

Sometimes the shopkeeper down the next street would leave an orange-box with a few specked oranges left in it outside the shop, or a soap-box or perhaps a wet-fish-box. Then there would be a mad rush of us kids and many a fight would ensue as we dragged the box home for our parents to put on the fire. We'd skin away the mould on the oranges and share them out with those not lucky enough to grab a box.

My mum and dad slept in the main bedroom over the living-room and my brothers, Jonathan and Charlie, slept in another bed in the same room. My other brother, Francis or Frankie, and my sister, Liza, and I slept in the attic over the bedroom and my eldest sister, Mary, had her bed in the other corner of the attic facing ours. Mary was twenty and was going to be married soon, when she was twenty-one. She had to wait because Mum and Dad would not give their consent until she was of age. In 1911 my brother Jonathan (Jack) was nineteen and Charlie was eighteen, Liza was eleven, Frankie was ten and I was eight years old. Us younger ones slept three in a bed; Liza and I at the top and Frankie at the bottom.

One night I asked Mary if I could sleep with her in the big bed but she told me, 'No! It's for me bottom drawers.' Now this puzzled me somewhat because I couldn't see how she could get a big bed like that in her bottom drawers.

We all lived in the first house in the fifth 'grove' which we all called 'our yard'. Next door lived Mr and Mrs Buckley and their six boys and one girl. In the third house lived Mr and Mrs Huggett with ten children: five boys and five girls. Next door to the Huggetts lived Maggie and Billy Bumpham. They had no children, or none that I knew of anyway. The neighbours used to say they weren't married and I could never understand this because I used to watch them undress and get into bed together – they never drew their blinds because they had none. What they did have that I loved was a little bull-terrier called Rags. Mrs Taylor lived in the last house in our yard. She had seven children and as many cats of both sexes who were continually producing offspring of their own: Mrs Taylor gave them to neighbours who needed them, to eat or clear away the mice. Everybody in our district had plenty of these. What she couldn't give away she drowned in the maiding-tub. No one knew what had became of Mr Taylor. Some people said she was so expert in drowning cats that she must have drowned him too.

At the end of the yard stood three ashcans and five lavatories, or closets as we called them. These each consisted of a square box with large round hole in the middle. Us children had to hold the sides of the seat otherwise we could have fallen in. These were dry closets. You can imagine the stench in summer! Next to the closets were two wash-houses where every washday everybody did their weekly wash. Like all the outhouses they were shared between the five houses in our yard and the five that backed on to us. There were always rows over whose turn it was to clean the closets so to save further quarrels Dad put a big padlock on one and gave Mrs Buckley next door a key to share. We kept our key on a cotton-reel tied with string behind our living-room door. The other closets were left open for anyone to use and they were filthy. We had to hold our noses as we passed by, but Mum and Mrs Buckley always saw to it that ours was kept clean: her girls and Liza and I had to do it in turns while the women looked on. Finally, there was a gas-lamp in the centre of the yard and also a tap where everybody got their water for all household uses.

No one had a garden, not a blade of grass. There were cobblestones everywhere. If we wanted to see any flowers we went to the churchyard to play. We were often sent there, out of the way of our parents. We would take a bottle of tea and some milk for the younger ones who were transported in our go-cart. We nicknamed the churchyard 'Titty-bottle Park', a name that stuck with us for years. We'd tie the go-cart to a tree or a tombstone and play at hide-and-seek or perhaps some of us would change the stale water in the jam jars and rearrange the flowers. We'd be happy for a while playing at our games until the vicar appeared with his stick to chase us away. But try as he might he could never get rid of us; we always returned the next day.

All our homes were in old buildings that were tumbling down. The rent was usually three shillings a week; that was when the landlord was lucky enough to be paid. I've seen him wait until his tenants came out of the pubs at eleven at night. Often he wasted his time and if they couldn't pay their arrears he'd send along the bailiffs, but as often as not they'd already done a 'moonlight flit'. Down the street some one would borrow a hand cart, on the chattels would go and into another house they would move, for empty houses were common at that time. They were still the same old sort of hovel, though. The landlord rarely did any repairs, as the reader can imagine. So people did their own after their own fashion. When Christmas was drawing close they scraped together a few pence to buy some fresh wallpaper to brighten up the walls. I remember Dad used to paste ours with a mixture of flour and water and when Mum wasn't watching he'd mix in a bit of condensed milk. He swore it stuck the paper better but Jack said it only gave the bugs a good meal. Dad never stripped the old paper off. 'I daren't. It's only the bugs and the paper that's holding the walls up.'

They were dirty old houses; everyone had vermin or insects of some description. There were fleas, bugs, rats, mice and cockroaches – you name it, we had it. But I'll still say this for our mum; although we were as poor as the rest, she always kept us clean. Many times we had to stay in bed while she took the clothes from us to wash and dry in front of the fire so that we could go to school the next day looking clean.

Our mum was also very cruel and spiteful towards us, especially to me, and I could never make out why until I was old enough to be told. I can picture her now as I write. She was a large, handsome woman, except in her ugly moods. She weighed about sixteen stone and always wore a black alpaca frock, green with age, which reached down to her ankles, and a black apron on top. On her feet she wore button-up boots, size eight, which it was my job to clean and fasten with a steel button hook that hung by the fireplace. Mum always pretended she couldn't bend when she wanted her boots buttoned. She had long, black hair which she was always brushing and combing. She twisted it round her hand and swung it into a bun on top of her head. Then she'd look in the mirror and plunge a long hatpin through the bun. She called this hatpin her 'weapon'. Sometimes when she went out she'd put Dad's cap on top which made her look taller. She was always on the go, one way or another. I felt sorry for her at times and I tried my best to love her but we all lived in fear when she started to shout. When she did start you knew it. You had to move quickly, for it was no sooner the word than the blow!

Many a time we felt the flat of her hand, Liza, Frankie and me. We never knew what for at times, but down would come the cane from its place on the wall. If we tried to run away then we really had it. Neither our parents nor the neighbours had any time to give us any love or affection and they didn't listen to our troubles. We were little drudges and always in the way. You may ask who was to blame for us growing up like this in squalor, poverty and ignorance. We were too young to understand why then, and I don't think I understand yet, but there it was, we had to make the best of it. My dad would listen to us sometimes but only when Mum wasn't about, or if he'd had an extra drop of beer. It was at these times that I liked him best because sometimes, not always, he was jolly. This wasn't very often because he was out of work, and had only Mum or his pals to rely on to buy him a drink. He had to do an odd job or two before Mum gave him his beer money. Sometimes he did odd jobs for other people on the sly, before the relief officer made his visit.

Our dad never hit us. He would tell us off and show us the strap but he left the correcting to Mum, and she did enough for both. So we young ones tried very hard to behave ourselves when Dad was out and he was more times out than in. He always said he couldn't stand her 'tantrums' but my brother Jack took over when Dad was out, pushing us this way then that and giving us the occasional backhander if we didn't do what he told us.

We saw very little of my brother Charlie; he only came home to sleep. Mother's tantrums got on his nerves also.

Frankie and I were the best of pals. He always tried to get me out of trouble, but he often got me into some. But I still loved him.

My sister Liza was very spiteful to me as well as being artful and although I tried to love her she pushed me away and pinched me on the sly when she had the chance. I couldn't do much about this because she was bigger than I was and very fat besides. When she did give me a sly dig I just had to grin and bear it and keep out of her and Mum's way. I still had to sleep with Liza and if she didn't pinch me she'd kick me out of bed. It was no good complaining, because Liza was always telling lies and Mum would believe her: she couldn't do wrong in Mum's eyes.

I remember one night very clearly. It was about one o'clock in the morning. I woke very thirsty so I crept quietly out of bed so as not to wake Liza or Frankie and went downstairs to get a drink of water. There wasn't any in the house, only a drop of warm water in the kettle. After satisfying my thirst I tiptoed back upstairs but when I got halfway up I heard Mum say, 'No! You can put it away! I've already had a baker's dozen. I'm 'avin' no mower so yow can get to sleep!'

I was always a very inquisitive child so I sat on the stairs to listen for more but I only heard the bed creak, so off up to the attic I went. I was feeling cold in my torn and threadbare chemise, one of Mary's cutdowns. I lay awake that night trying to puzzle out what my mum meant. I thought maybe she had eaten too much and wasn't feeling well so next morning when I came downstairs I said, 'Don't you feel well, Mum . . . have you eaten too much?'

At once she glared down at me and shouted, 'What do yer mean . . . 'ave I eaten too much?'

'Well, I heard you say to Dad you'd already had a baker's dozen,' I answered, trembling a little.

Mum went red in the face and cried out, 'And where did yer 'ear that?'

Then timidly I explained how I came down the stairs for a drink of water but before I could finish she slapped me across the face and shouted, 'That'll teach yer ter sit listenin' on the stairs!'

I moved back quickly as she lifted her hand once again so I was quite surprised when she seemed to have second thoughts.

'I'll get yer dad ter settle with yow.'

Whether she told him or not I never found out but I was determined to find out one way or another what was meant by a baker's dozen. So that same night I waited for Mary to come up to bed and after Liza and Frankie fell asleep I crept over to her bed.

'Are you awake, Mary?' I whispered in the dark.

'Yes. What do yer want?' she snapped. She didn't usually snap at me, but I could see why she didn't want to be bothered at that time of night. I began to tiptoe back to bed when she lit the candle and called me.

'Come on, Katie. What is it you want?' she asked more pleasantly.

Just then Mum shouted up the attic stairs. 'Let's 'ave less noise up theea!'

Mary smiled as she put her finger to her lips. 'Hush,' she whispered. 'Come and get into bed beside me and get warm then you can tell me all about it.'

I snuggled up close and felt very comforted. I could have gone straight off to sleep, but Mary wanted to know what was troubling me.

'Can you tell me what a baker's dozen is, Mary?' I managed to ask between yawns.

'Why? Where did you hear that?' She sat up in bed looking at me quizzically, and as I told her a broad smile spread across her face.

'You were lucky to get away with only your face slapped.' I was wide awake by now.

'Well, what does it mean?'

'It means Mum didn't want Dad to love her and to have any more babies. She's already had thirteen which is what's called a "baker's dozen" and you being the thirteenth, Mum calls you the "scraping of the pot".'

I could still see her smiling in the candlelight as she whispered to herself, 'I must tell Albert about this when we meet.'

'But if I'm the last, what became of the others in between?'

'They all died before you were ever thought of,' she answered sadly. 'Now lie down and go to sleep.'

We both snuggled up to keep warm after she blew out the candle. Although I was warm and comfortable I couldn't help but think about those other seven who had died. Maybe they were happier in the other world, I thought. There wouldn't have been room for them here, and Mum and Dad wouldn't have been able to feed us all. And with all these thoughts in my mind I eventually dropped off to sleep.

The Pig's Pudding

Everyone in our district was more or less poor. They never knew from where or when the next meal was coming. Most of them had to have parish relief but what they received was insufficient to feed us growing children, let alone our parents as well. Each Friday morning or afternoon, according to their surname, they queued up for their rations. Each person had a card for coal, bread, margarine, a tin of condensed milk, tea and sugar. They received more and some less according to their circumstances and the size of their family. No one was given any money. The officers in charge decided this would be spent on beer, tobacco, snuff and other unsuitable commodities. Therefore those that didn't indulge in those habits had to suffer for those that did, but everyone did little odd jobs on the quiet to get some extra coppers. Some didn't care, as long they could manage to borrow or beg a cup of sugar, a piece of soap or half a loaf until they could collect their next ration card. They were artful: they never returned the same quantity. It was a smaller cupful or less than half a loaf and no soap. They said the kids had left it in the water and it had melted away or they had thrown it down the 'snuff' with the water. Thus they wore out their welcome. It only happened once to Mum – 'once bitten twice shy', she used to say. No one ever came to borrow at our house a second time.

She was independent-minded and, although we too had to have parish relief sometimes, she wouldn't ask a neighbour for anything. She used to say, 'What we ain't got we'll goo without.' Nor would she have any neighbours in our house unless it was essential. She said they only came to see if you'd got more than them. If anybody did call and ask Mum to help them out, her reply would be blunt.

'I don't arsk yow fer anything so don't arsk me! I don't borra and I don't lend!'

13

With that they'd get the door slammed in their face for their pains. Mum was very hard, but then the neighbours said she could afford to be because they thought she had more coming in than they did. Perhaps they were right: Jack was at work as was Mary, but Jack didn't give Mum much and nor did Mary, who you'll remember was saving to get married. At this time Charlie had already left home and Dad was unemployed like the other men. So we can't have had it much better than other families in our yard.

We were forbidden to play with the kids who had dirty heads but how we were to know they had dirty heads I never understood. We saw more scratch their heads and others were sent home from school, but they were our friends, so we still played with them despite what our mum said. I came indoors one day with one of my girlfriends and Mum pounced.

'Come over 'ere, yow! What yer doin' with yer fingers in yer 'air?'

I walked slowly towards her. I was afraid. She knew and I knew that I had disobeyed her. Suddenly she slapped me across the face and grabbed me by the hair.

'Kneel down 'ere and put yer 'ead between me legs!' she shouted.

I did as I was told and she combed my hair so hard with the steel comb that I began to scream.

'That'll teach yer ter defy me . . . And if I do find anything 'ere I'll cut the lot off!'

I hoped she wouldn't because a previous occasion was fresh in my memory. I had come home with a note and Dad had held my head down over a piece of newspaper and after pouring paraffin over my hair he had cut the lot off. I wasn't allowed to grow my hair long after that. I had to have it in two plaits but on this day they survived. Mum found nothing to tell Dad about. I would still rather lose my hair than my little friends so I continued to play with them. However, I kept my distance just in case.

Later that evening I waited for my sister to go to bed first, then I lit my candle and crept up the stairs so as not to wake her. I checked to see that she was asleep then I blew out the candle and slipped into bed beside her, but as usual she was only catnapping and all of a sudden she kicked me out of bed.

I fell with a bang on the floor.

'You ain't sleepin' with me! You've got ticks in yer hair!'

'No I ain't! You ask Mum!' I shouted back at her with tears in my eyes.

At that moment the attic door flew open and in came my brother Jack.

'What's all this bloody racket about?' He bawled. 'I carn't get any sleep!'

'Liza's kicked me out of bed,' I cried, hoping to get a few words of comfort from him, but all he said was, 'Shut yer cryin', yer big babby.'

He struck a match and gazed down at Liza who was pretending to be asleep again.

'She's not asleep. She's only pretending,' I cried.

'Don't you dare to answer me back!' he said sharply, and he pushed me into the corner between the bed and wall and left me there and returned downstairs.

During all this commotion Frankie had lain quietly at the bottom of the bed but, when Jack had gone, he jumped out of bed and pulled all the clothes off Liza.

'If you don't keep yer hands off Katie and give her more room in bed I'll pay you out when I get you on yer own.'

Liza was afraid of Frankie when he was in one of these moods so she moved over without saying a word and I climbed back into bed. She still gave me a couple of sly digs but I didn't care while Frankie was there to protect me. So it just my luck and his when the very next morning he should feel ill and so wasn't able to go to school. Dad told Mum, 'Polly, I'll light a fire in the attic grate so Frankie can stay in bed.'

'You'll do nothing of the sort! I carn't spare the coal,' she shouted.

'Oh well,' replied Dad, 'he can sleep down on the sofa in front of the fire. Anything for a bit of peace.'

Mum went mumbling out of the room. She always sulked when she couldn't have her own way. So Liza and I had to leave for school without Frankie. Liza never spoke to me all day. She pushed past me in the playground and ignored me. When I returned from school Frankie was huddled by the fire on the sofa. I asked him how he was but he could hardly speak, he had such an awful cold. Dad asked me to get the blue paper sugar bags which we always saved for slack or tea leaves to bank up fire. Mum was out, so Dad gave us our tea. Then we did our jobs. I didn't want to finish because I was afraid to go to bed. Frankie wouldn't be there to protect me from Liza and when she went to bed first I stayed up to give her plenty of time to get to sleep. To kill time I looked for things to do. I washed all the crocks twice over, very slowly, then I went up the yard to fill the kettle for the next morning. I even went down the cellar again to fetch up another bucket of slack. I searched around the room for more to do but I hadn't escaped Mum's notice. She turned round in her chair.

'Why are yow still up?'

'I was wondering if you want anything else done, Mum,' I said nervously, with my back to her.

'No, there ain't. So yer can get up ter bed!'

'Can I stay up a bit longer, Mum? I'm not tired.'

But I was tired, very tired; I was only making excuses and I guessed Mum wouldn't let me stay up any longer.

'What ain't done tonight yer can do tomorra night! Now be off with yer,' she shouted.

She always frightened me when she shouted. I wished her and Frankie good-night, but only Frankie answered. I prayed God that Liza would be asleep. I prayed also that the stairs wouldn't creak, but they were like everything else in the house, very old, so I wasn't surprised when they did. When I reached the top of the stairs I knew my prayers hadn't been answered. There was Liza wide awake, sitting up in bed, waiting for me.

I crept into bed beside her, afraid to speak and scared of what she would do now Frankie was not there to defend me. Suddenly she sprang on me.

'You ain't got yer pal tonight, have yer?' she hissed in my ear. I didn't answer, thinking it was best not to, but she continued louder, 'Did you hear what I said?'

I still didn't answer, I was too afraid. Then she grabbed hold of my two plaits and shouted in my ear again, 'Get out of this bed. There's no room for two of us.'

Then I finally lost my temper and cried out, 'If you wasn't so fat there'd be room enough for the three of us!'

But I knew I'd get the worst of it for calling her 'fat' so I crept down into Frankie's place. Then she pushed her feet out and I fell with a thump on to the floor and there I stayed. I sobbed quietly to myself, afraid Mum would come up to see what all the noise was about and I knew I'd be blamed. After a while, I pulled one of the coats off the bed and crawled into a corner to cry myself to sleep. I don't know how long I had been asleep when I awoke with a terrible fright. Something warm and soft brushed against my face. My first thought was that it was a mouse; we had plenty and they always came out at night, but when I put my hand up to face I could feel that it was our cat, Pete. I pulled him to me and hugged him tightly and like that we slept right through the night.

Next morning Liza went down first and we washed for school. I looked for Dad but he wasn't around, only Frankie who was sitting up on the sofa.

'Are you better, Frankie?' I asked.

'Yes,' he replied.

Before I could say another word Mum beckoned me over.

'Come 'ere, yow!'

I went slowly towards her, thinking to myself what have I done wrong now.

'What was all that bangin' I 'eard larst night?'

'It wasn't me, Mum, it was Liza. She kicked me out of bed again.'

'What do yer mean, "again"?' She shook my shoulders roughly.

'I never did, Mum.' Liza lied. 'Katie's telling lies.'

I was surprised when Mum turned to Liza and said, 'You speak when yer spoken to . . . I know who's telling lies.'

Then turning to me again she spoke angrily, 'I'll put the cane across yer backs if I 'ear any mower from either of yer! Now get yer-selves off to school.'

I was always glad when she stopped shouting. When she started you never knew when she was going to stop and her language was usually terrible. I remember Mary telling her to be quiet.

'Oh, shut yer face! You like to hear the sound of yer own voice.'

Mary and Jack were the only two who could speak to Mum this way and attempt to put her in her place. What they said usually quietened her because they threatened to leave home if she kept on with her tantrums, but we all recognised that Mum changed her tone and moods when it suited her.

Frankie got off the sofa and got himself ready for school. His job every day was to take the tin bowl to the tap in the yard and fetch our washing water. But on this morning the tap was frozen when he went out. The Jones and Buckley kids were already there waiting for the water to thaw. I took a burning piece of paper which I pushed up the spout. It started to trickle and eventually Frankie managed to half fill the bowl. We took it inside and stood it on the stool.

'Can I have a drop of hot water in here, Mum?' he asked. We were both shivering with the cold.

'No yer carn't! I ain't got none till the fire's lit, so hurry yerselves or yer'll be late agen fer school and miss yer breakfast.'

On and on she went, jumping off the chair and she was sitting on and pulling Frankie by the ear and holding his head over the bowl and rubbing his neck with carbolic soap so hard that he began to cry. Frankie was a tough lad and it took a lot to make him cry; even when Mum caned him he would grin. But on this occasion he wasn't well and if Dad had been there he wouldn't have allowed him to go to school. Mum was only stopped by the sound of the school bell. We dashed out of the house and arrived just in time to receive our 'parish breakfast'.

All the poor children in our school were provided with a breakfast, so when the bell rang out at five minutes to nine we had to be ready and waiting. The kids from our yard would rush up the street like a lot of ants because if you were not in line when the bell stopped you would be lucky to get any at all. The breakfast consisted of an enamel mug of cocoa and two thick slices of bread and jam. The bread was usually stale or soggy. Dad would get up very early some mornings and earn himself a few extra pennies fetching the big urn which contained the cocoa, and the bread and jam. He had to wheel it along to the school in a basket carriage and when he passed our yard Mum would be waiting with a quart jug hidden underneath her apron. When she could see no one about, Dad used to fill it with cocoa. She would have helped herself to the bread and jam too but Dad stopped her because they were all counted. Mum and Dad would have been in trouble with the authorities if they'd ever been found out; but they never were. Our parents were both too cute to be caught, and although I knew what they were up to I never told anyone. I was too afraid in case they were sent to prison.

One morning we were dashing up the lane to get there in time for breakfast but the bell stopped ringing. Frankie grabbed my hand and dragged me along.

'Come on! We can still make it, Katie!' But I started to cry.

'We're too late now and I'm hungry!'

18

We hadn't had anything to eat since tea-time the day before, and then only a piece of bread and dripping.

'Shut yer blarting!' Liza hissed as she pushed us inside the door. Our teacher was calling the last name from the register when she saw us come in.

'I see you three are late again. I'm afraid you are too late for your breakfasts.'

'But we're hungry, miss!' pleaded Frankie.

'Well you can stand at the back of the line. You may be lucky,' she answered sharply.

We reached down a mug each from the ledge but when it came to our turn all we had was some warm cocoa, watered down, but no bread and jam. There was none left, and by the time our lessons were over at twelve o'clock we were very, very hungry.

On our way home from school we had to pass a homemade cook shop where we always paused to look through the window at all the nice things on show. This particular morning we stayed longer than usual, pressing our noses to the pane of glass, saliva dripping down our chins. There was pig's pudding, hot meat pies, hocks, tripe and cakes of every sort staring back at us. Worse than the sight of this potential feast was the smell. It was too much for Frankie who burst out: 'I'm so hungry I could smash the glass in and help myself.'

'And me!' I said.

'Don't you dare,' said Liza, who was afraid he would.

'Well, why should they be on show when we're so hungry?' asked Frankie.

Liza had no answer; she too was dribbling down her chin and she didn't stop Frankie who glanced quickly up and down the street to see who was about and hissed: 'If you two look out for me and as soon as "Skinny Legs" goes around the back of the shop I'll nip in quick and help myself to a few.'

Every one called the shopkeeper this because he gave short measure and he never gave you a stale cake or a loaf like other shops did. Anyway, it seemed ages before Frankie did anything but at last he saw 'Skinny Legs' go through to the back of the shop and he dived in whilst Liza and I watched the street to warn him if anyone came along. I saw his hand in the window as he grabbed hold of a roll of pig's pudding and several hot meat pies. He came out, stuffing them under his gansey, and the three of us ran off down the street as fast as we could but before we had gone many yards Frankie stopped.

'Catch hold of these pies, Liza, they're burning my belly!'

'No,' she replied, 'I don't want any part of them!'

'No? But you'll take your share to eat 'em, won't you!' he snapped.

I was sure someone would come along and overhear us so I put my hands up his gansey and pulled down the pies. He wasn't kidding, they were hot, but my hands were so cold I was glad of the warmth.

'Did anyone see me?' he asked anxiously.

'Yes. He did.' Liza was pointing at Jonesy, one of the lads from our yard. 'Hello, how long have you been there?' said Frankie.

'Long enough, and I seen what yer bin dooin' an' all, an' if yer don't give me some, I'll snitch on yer.'

We all knew he meant it, so reluctantly Frankie pulled down the roll of pudding from his gansey and handed it over to Jonesy who dashed off home after saying he wouldn't tell anyone. But I knew he'd snitch all right. His mum went out cleaning on a Tuesday, so thinking she wouldn't be at home and he'd enjoy himself with his pudding he ran indoors. However he was unlucky: she was there.

'Where ever 'ave yer 'ad that from?' we heard her shout.

We heard his cringing explanation and Frankie shouted in the door, 'Yer traitor.'

Then the three of us ran down the yard to the wash-house to eat our pies. I don't think I ever tasted anything like that meat pie. It was delicious. Afterwards as we came from the wash-house we saw Mrs Jones walking towards our house. We knew we were in trouble but we didn't care now that our appetites were satisfied. Mrs Jones didn't like our mum, in fact I don't know who did, so I wasn't surprised by what happened next. Mrs Jones knocked loudly on our door and Mum lifted the corner of the curtain to see who was there. Seeing Mrs Jones she opened wide the door and shouted for all to hear, 'What do yow want?'

Mrs Jones stood on the step with her hands on her hips, grinning like a Cheshire cat. She always liked to get a dig at Mum, so she shouted louder so the neighbours could hear. 'I've got news for you, Polly. Your kids 'ave pinched some of "Skinny Legs"' pies.'

She didn't mention the pig's pudding though.

'I don't believe yer and get away from my dower, the lot on yer! Goo an' look after yer own kids.' And Mum slammed the door shut.

I thought, one day the door is going to fall off.

When Mrs Jones had gone away she came out again to call us in. Mrs Jones was still gossiping with the others.

'Come in, yow three. I want some explainin'.'

We went in timidly, but before we could utter a word she began angrily, 'An' what's this I 'ear about some pies?'

Liza quickly unburdened herself about how Frankie had stolen the pies and the pig's pudding.

'Pig's pudding. She never said anything about any pig's pudding.' She was furious.

'Frankie gave it to Jonesy,' said Liza.

'Well, we'll see about that!' said Mum.

She was fuming. She couldn't get out of the house quick enough. On went Dad's cap, off came the apron, and round the backyard she marched. When she got to Mrs Jones's door she banged twice, as hard as she could. All the neighbours lifted their windows and popped their heads out while some of them crowded round to watch developments more closely. They knew Mum was big enough to eat Mrs Jones. There was no answer so she knocked again, louder and shouted, 'Yow can come out. I've seen yer be'ind the curtin.'

Slowly, Mrs Jones opened the door a little way to face Mum standing there, hands on hips, chest puffed out.

'Yer crafty old sod! Yow never told me that my Frankie giv' your lad a roll of pig's pudding. Now what about it? An' I ain't gooin' from 'ere till I get it.'

Mrs Jones was scared now, thinking what Mum might do, so she shut the door quickly and we all heard the bolt rammed home. But Mum wasn't finished. She banged again, louder than ever.

'Yer better 'and over that puddin' or else!' demanded Mum, her fist in the air.

Then suddenly the window shot up and the pig's pudding came flying out. It caught Mum on the head and everyone began laughing, but Mum ignored them and grabbed hold of us and the pudding and marched us indoors. She never bothered about what the neighbours thought or said as long as she didn't hear them. Woe betide them if she did.

21

'Get yer clo's off and get up them stairs. I'll get yer dad ter deal with you two when 'e comes 'ome.'

She pushed us towards the stairs and Frankie and I ran quickly up to the attic. We didn't go back to school that afternoon because Mum kept us up there until Dad returned in the evening and all we had to eat that day was the meat pie each.

It was late when we heard Dad come up the stairs so we pretended to be asleep. We knew he wouldn't wake us. Sure enough we soon heard his receding footsteps on the stairs. In the early hours of the morning Frankie crept downstairs and brought a cup of water and a thick slice of bread and lard. We shared this between us while Liza slept on. Then we climbed back into bed and finally fell asleep.

Saturday Night in Our Yard

⌖

T he next afternoon Dad came home pleased and excited. This
was pleasing for us as well because he wasn't often happy.

'Where's yer mum, Katie?' he asked.

'Down in the wash-house, filling the boiler,' I answered.

'Well, go down and tell her I've got a lovely surprise for her.'

I hadn't seen Dad so cheerful for a long time so I ran down the
yard and, seeing Mum through the steam in the wash-house, I called
out to her, 'Come quickly, Dad's got a surprise for you!'.

'What's 'e want now? Mower money for beer I suppose,' she
snapped.

'No, Mum. I don't think so. He's too excited.'

'Hm . . . we'll see,' she mumbled.

She stopped to put some more slack under the boiler, then, with
me trailing behind, marched down the yard. She never walked like
other women, she always seemed to stride along, taking big steps
with her back straight and her head held high. When we were
indoors she took Dad's flat cap and her hessian apron off, then
staring at Dad she said, 'Now, what do yer want this time?'

'Give us a kiss first, then I'll tell yer,' he replied, putting his face
forward close to hers.

'Don't be daft!' was her reply to this show of affection. 'I ain't
got time any mower fer that sort of thing.' She turned her back on
him.

I felt so sorry for Dad; he looked so dejected as he stood looking
at her. I can never remember Mum and Dad kissing each other: they
were always snapping or not on speaking terms. I stood by Dad,
watching and waiting. I, too, was eager to know what the surprise
was, but Dad didn't say a word. He just flopped down in his chair
and lit his pipe. Then Mum raised her voice and shouted at him.

'Well, come on, Sam! Let's know what it's all about.' She was getting impatient.

Dad turned around in his chair and told her he'd got a job. 'It's hard work, and it's only twenty-five bob a week. I don't mind the hard work, Polly, but it's long hours, six in the morning until six o'clock in the evening.'

'That ain't much money for all them hours,' was all she said.

Then she turned and went out again to the wash-house with her apron over her arm. I stood there waiting for Dad to say something more, but he just got up from his chair and walked out.

'Can I come with you, Dad?' I asked.

He just nodded, so along I went, walking behind him. I knew he was going to the Golden Cup to have a drink. He met Mr Taylor inside, and thanked him for getting him the job. Mr Taylor bought Dad a pint and a pop for me. I sat just inside the door, filling a Woodbine packet with sawdust from the floor, when I noticed four navvies stroll in. I could see they were already well oiled. They called for a pint each and then began a song. Some of the songs they sang I knew so I joined in.

'Come and give us a song, littl' 'un,' said one. But I was too shy, so Dad came over to me, picked me up and sat me on the counter.

'You want to hear my Katie sing?' Dad asked proudly.

'Yes, mate,' they replied.

Dad knew when I sang someone always gave me a halfpenny and sometimes a penny, so with this in mind I burst forth with my favourite, 'Mid Pleasures and Palaces'. Everyone in the pub joined in after I had sung a few lines, including the publican and his wife. When I had finished my song I heard one of the navvies say to Dad, 'That kid's got a sweet voice, yow ought to get her trained, mate.'

They each gave me a penny. I felt like a queen when they applauded me and asked me to sing some more, but Dad lifted me down from the counter.

'You better be off now before yer mum sees yer.'

He took threepence from me and left me with a penny and the excuse that I could have the rest when he came home. I never did, but I went home happy knowing that Dad had the threepence instead of Mum.

Monday morning came and Dad rose early to start his first day at the casting works. He had to get himself up because Mum said it was too early and too cold for her to get up first. When Dad returned home that evening I thought he looked miserable, tired, dirty and wet through: it hadn't stopped raining all day.

'It's hard and dirty work in that casting shop, Polly,' he sighed as he flopped into his chair. Mum was preparing supper, but she appeared not to hear him.

'Shall I pull your boots off, Dad?' I asked.

He neither said yes or no, nor did Mum, so I bent down on the floor and untied the laces, pulled off his boots, stood them on the fender to dry and passed him a torn piece of towel to dry off his hair.

'I don't mind the hard work, Polly,' he continued at last. 'But last night I couldn't sleep.'

'Why? I dain't keep yer awake,' was her sharp answer.

'Oh no,' replied Dad. 'I was afraid to get to sleep in case I overslept on my first day. Anyhow, where's the alarm clock gone from off the mantel-shelf?'

'Why ask? You know it's in pawn with the rest of the things. I'll get them out at the end of the week.'

'I carn't wait until then,' he pleaded.

Mum went on preparing supper which was bread and cheese, a pint of ale and a bit of Spanish onion.

'I know what I'll do,' he said, jumping up from his chair and reaching for his cap.

'Now where yer gooin'?' Mum shouted across the table.

'I'm going to ask Fred the lamplighter to tap his pole on the bedroom window when he comes in the mornings. Keep my supper till I get back.'

He swallowed three parts of his pint and, as he dashed out to see the lamplighter, Mum finished the rest. Fred happened to be coming down the yard to light the gaslamps when Dad bumped into him.

'Hello, Fred,' Dad said. 'You're just the chap I'm looking for. I've got a job for you. Will you tap my bedroom window every morning?'

'Why, Sam, you've got a job then?'

'Yes,' said Dad.

'It'll cost you a tanner a week and a pint,' said Fred, scratching his head.

'Very well, you old fraud,' smiled Dad. He knew very well what the charge was.

'That's what all the others pay me,' said Fred, a bit indignant. 'But don't tell anyone, Sam. If the Gas Department find out I'll lose my job.'

'You can trust me,' Dad told him, and they shook hands and wished each other good-night.

So each morning at break of dawn Fred did his job as promised. Then on the following Saturday night Dad met him in the pub. Fred was about to take his sixpence when Dad pulled him to one side and whispered in his ear, 'Fred, I want a few words with you.'

'Make it quick, Sam, I've got me rounds to do.'

'You'll have to tap our window a bit harder. Some mornings I carn't hear yer.'

'I'm sorry, Sam, but yer know how it is. If the others hear me knock your window loud they won't want to have theirs tapped and I'll lose their tanners. You know what I mean?' he said slyly, and winked at Dad.

'Yes, I know what yer mean. You're a crafty old sod,' smiled Dad, returning the wink. 'But you'll do till the missus gets the alarm clock out of the pop-shop.'

I was an inquisitive child and always followed Dad or anyone else I knew to find out what was happening, but on this occasion they turned and noticed me drawing in the sawdust behind the door.

'You'd better be off before yer mum comes after yer,' the lamp-lighter said, pressing a halfpenny into my hand as I followed them out. Reluctantly I walked home with the coin safely hidden down my stocking.

When I arrived at our house I noticed Mum was standing on the step with her arms folded across her chest and looking like thunder. Now what have I done, I thought to myself. She was glaring all the while as I approached her, then she bellowed, 'Where 'ave them two gone?'

I acted as though I didn't know, hoping I would not be forced to tell her.

'Who do you mean?' I asked.

'Yer know who I mean! That Fred an' yer Dad.'

'They went in the Cup, Mum, but they've left now and gone down the street,' I answered truthfully.

'I think I know where they are. If there's any treatin' to be done they can treat me.'

She mumbled to herself as she went inside, snatched down a flat cap from the back of the door and slapping it on top of her bun, she marched down the street. I trailed behind her as usual to watch developments. She arrived at the King's Head, flung wide the door and shouted, 'Anybody seen my Sam?'

Everybody looked round, but no one answered; they only shook their heads.

'I'll find 'im if it's the larst thing I do!' she fumed, as the door banged after her.

I looked up the street and saw Dad walking towards the Cup. He didn't see Mum, but she saw him just as he was going inside. Her strides grew bigger and when she reached the pub door she pushed it wide and entered. Kicking the sawdust out of her path she went up to the counter.

'Mine's a pint!' she called out to Dad.

Everyone stopped talking, and a hushed quiet descended. They all knew what Mum was like when she was in one of her moods. I watched her bosom heave up and down as she breathed heavily. Then she flopped down on one of the benches, all sixteen stone of her. Little me climbed up beside her, hoping she wouldn't have another of her tantrums.

Dad came over to her and gave her a pint. Poor Dad, I thought. She tipped her head back and drank it down. Dad was always giving into her when she was in a bad mood. He tried not to answer her because we all knew she would have the last word. It was the only time we got any peace when Dad took no notice of her. I often looked at the picture of Mum and Dad that hung on one of our walls. Mum had been quite a goodlooker and Dad was handsome when he was young. Dad was still handsome, despite his years of worry and toil, but Mum looked older than her years. Today I realise why she was like she was. It must have been a terrible ordeal for her and the rest of the women who had to live in one room and two bedrooms and bring up thirteen and even more children. They had no bathrooms, no hot or cold water in the house and had to live on relief when they could get it. These women were tired and worn out when they reached the age of forty. Some never lived to that age; many were claimed by consumption, childbirth or plain hard work.

Now that Dad had started work we all had more to eat. He would bring in a joint of meat for Sunday, whereas before I used to fetch fourpenn'orth of pieces. Our clothes and knick-knacks started coming out of pawn, and life in general at our house seemed more pleasant for a time. However, Dad still collected the relief without telling them he was working. Then one day I remember Mum warning him, 'I think yer better sign off, Sam, before they find out.'

'I'll stay on a bit longer, Polly. I don't know how long me job's going to last.'

'Oh, well! Please yourself. If yer goo ter prison, don't say I didn't warn yer,' was her only answer.

No matter how bad our neighbours seemed, they always tried to help one another in their own kind of way. They would never 'snitch' on each other, because they were all doing odd jobs on the side without reporting them to the relief officers. They had to do this; it was the only way to make ends meet. But they had to be extra careful to hide things away when the visitor came to call because they were always poking around to find out what was happening. With that in mind, Dad signed off after having two free weeks.

Saturday dinner-time, Dad had his first wage packet and, after giving Mum hers, he went off down the pub to get his quota. Later, when he came back, he lined us up. There was Frankie, Liza, several of our school friends and me and he took us to the Saturday afternoon matineé. We used to make an awful clatter in our clogs and Dad in his heavy boots, and even the horses turned their heads to see where the noise was coming from. Along the cobbled street we marched in a line like little soldiers, so proud were we to be treated to the pictures. Up the stone steps to the top of the gallery we climbed, then rushed madly to get a good seat on one of the low forms. It was wonderful to watch the silent films and hear the pianist banging away at the piano. We were sad when it was all over because we never knew when we'd get another treat like this. As we went out the 'chucker-out' who stood on the door gave each of us a bag of sweets.

'You've been behaving yourselves, haven't you?' he said.

We couldn't do anything but behave with Dad with us. When we got home it was growing dark and Mum was waiting for Dad to take her out for the usual Saturday-night drink. I can see her now, standing on the doorsteps in her white starched pinafore which she kept especially for these Saturday nights, with her arms folded across her huge bosom and Dad's flat cap stuck on top of her head.

'And about time too! I've bin waitin' for yer this larst 'arf 'our, and I want these kids in bed!'

Dad didn't answer, so she turned to me. 'There's tea in the pot an' bread an' drippin' on the table and when you've 'ad it get up to bed. An', yow two . . .!' she called out to Frankie and Liza.

Dad had walked off while she was giving us our instructions but she didn't let him get far before she caught him up. Frankie and Liza didn't drink their tea. They said it tasted like old boots, and no wonder, the enamel teapot was chipped and cracked through being stewed on the fire so often. I was too thirsty to care what it tasted like; I even drank Frankie's and Liza's share. After feasting on the bread and dripping, we lit our piece of candle and went up to bed. However, we didn't get undressed that night: this was the Saturday night and we were going to be entertained.

We all looked forward to these Saturday nights when we saw Battling Billy, as he was universally known, who became a little peculiar when he'd had to much to drink. He would then offer to fight anyone in sight. Our parents never took any notice of him. They understood why he was like he was: Dad said he was more to be pitied than blamed. He'd fought alongside Dad in the Boer War and was shell-shocked.

None of the pubs would serve Battling Billy because of his antics, so his wife Maggie used to fetch drink in bottles from the outdoor for him and he always seemed to have plenty on a Saturday night. Downstairs we hurried and when we emerged into the yard we saw some of our neighbours already there. The children were sitting on old mats and coats on the wall, waiting for Battling Billy to appear. Our friend Jonesy and his mum kept our places. We hadn't waited long when Billy dashed out of his house, just like a bull at a gate. He was only a small man, but he had a lot of strength, the more so when he'd had too much to drink. He was swearing and performing worse than ever, and soon everyone was laughing at him. He looked very comical, running back and forth in bare feet and red flannelette combs. He reminded me of one of the warriors out of our school history books. The cats flew in all directions to get out of his way. He stared to the right and left and with the yard broom in one hand and a dustbin lid in the other he yelled at the top of his voice, 'Charge!'

Using the lid for a shield, and thrusting the broom handle forward, he yelled again, 'Charge! . . . Let 'em all come!'

Suddenly, he shot a glance up at the wall and saw us sitting there. He put the shield up to his face and peeping round its edge he shouted at us, 'Come on down, all you bloody Boers!'

Then we all began to scream. We'd never seen Billy in such a fierce mood before. But Maggie and his bull-terrier were used to him and they both stood on the step waiting for him to tire himself out so that he could be put to bed. To us he seemed worse than ever and we clung to our places on the wall for all we were worth. He was going strong. He ran down the yard, yelling, 'Charge!' again and this time thrust the broom handle through Mrs Taylor's only unbroken window. As the glass shattered, someone shouted down the yard that the cops were on their way. But Billy was too wrapped up in what he was doing. In fact he was enjoying himself so much that he was oblivious to our warnings. We all managed to scramble off the wall and run indoors, from which place of refuge we watched the finale from our bedroom window. Billy was still peering over his shield, waving his broom about and shouting as four burly policemen came marching towards him. Two stood at the entrance to the yard and the other two tried to catch poor Billy, but he was like an eel slipping between their legs. After a lot of struggling, Billy tired, and the policemen managed to hold him down so that they could talk to him quietly.

'Now come along peaceably, Billy, and in the morning when you've sobered up you can be bailed out.'

All the police in the local lock-up knew Billy, and they never took him to the cells unless he became too dangerous.

'If you don't behave yourself we'll have to drag you there.'

We'd all heard this but he continued to kick and struggle so that the other two policemen had to help take him away. By this time Billy's dog Rags had seen what was happening and he too joined in. He grabbed hold of Billy's combs and tried to prevent him being carried off. During all this performance Maggie still stood on her doorstep watching. However, when she saw that things were threatening to get out of hand she walked over to Billy and spoke to him.

'Go along quietly, Billy, and I'll bring the rent book in the morning to bail you out,' she said, soothingly.

Then she gave him a kiss, picked up the dog and walked away, but before she could get to her door one of the policemen called out, 'I'd like a word with you before you go.'

'I ain't done nothin',' she answered, scared.

'Maybe not, but he's worse than ever tonight. Why's that?'

'Well, it was his birthday and I bought him a drop of the best.'

'You should be ashamed and have more sense. But I'm warning you now, next time he may go to prison for a long time and you with him!'

She didn't answer. She probably thought it better not to, and her eyes were cast down to the floor, but she did have a last word with Billy.

'Good-night, Billy, love, and behave yourself now. I'll be round in the morning, early, and I'll bail you out.' She didn't seem to care whether he went or not.

Then he was taken away, with crowds of people following behind to see the poor chap taken to the station house.

As Maggie walked towards her door with the dog still under her arm, Mrs Taylor shouted from her attic, 'You ought to be ashamed of yourself, Maggie, letting the cops take your Billy away. And remember, I want me window mended.'

'Push your head back in and look after yer own! I'll look after mine,' she yelled back. 'Anyway, if you want ter know it's the only time I get a wink of sleep when the cops tek 'im in.'

Then she went off and we heard the door slam behind her. I often wondered why some of the doors did not fall off, the way everyone slammed them shut? Tempers were always getting frayed because things never seemed to go right for these people. They skimped and saved to make ends meet, but they knew it was hopeless, so they gave up trying, or, worse, caring. Many's the time I've heard and seen them quarrelling with each other and coming to blows over the least little thing, but they didn't mean to say or do these things. They would be friends again the next day, and meet in the pub to discuss their troubles again.

The following morning, after putting Mrs Taylor in her place as she put it, Maggie knocked on her neighbour's door to ask her if she could take her rent book along to the station to bail poor Billy. In the end she had to ask Mrs Taylor for her book because she was the only one with a clean sheet. So they forget their argument of the previous night and hurried along to the lock-up. They were not alone. Nearly the whole street had risen early to meet Billy. We had hoped to see him appear in his combs but after confessing to the officer in charge that she'd forgotten to bring Billy's clothes, one of her friends volunteered to lend some of her own husband's. After a brief delay while the garments were found and handed over, Billy emerged from the station. We couldn't see his hands or feet the borrowed clothes were so large; we could only make out the top of his tousled head and part of his dirty face. Maggie grabbed him to her, hugged and kissed him, then we all trooped off to the Cup to celebrate his release. Everyone crowded in round him and pushed through the door so Billy could be smuggled in, but unfortunately the publican spotted him and rounded angrily on the crowd.

'I ain't servin' 'im! I'll lose my licence!'

'Well, if you don't serve 'im yer don't serve us!' was the reply, and there was a general movement towards the door.

The landlord couldn't afford to offend so many customers so he called them back.

'All right, he can have one pint but no more.'

They sat Billy down and warned him to be quiet while drinks were called for and Billy given his. There was quite a crowd round him waiting to hear what he had to tell them about who else had been in with him. Billy was reluctant to divulge his exploits. 'If you buy me a drop of the best, I'll tell yer what happened.'

But the landlord heard this and adamantly refused, and Maggie backed him up. 'No!' she shouted. 'He ain't 'avin' any mower! I want 'im back 'ome, not back in the lock-up!'

Somebody had already slipped him a couple of whiskies which he drained quickly before the barman could jump over the counter to prevent him.

'Right! That's it! Clear out! Clear out, the lot on yer, before I call the cops.'

The pub emptied in no time but it was too late for Billy. When he emerged he started to rave again and wave his arms in the air. Maggie pleaded for help and between several of them they managed to carry him home where Maggie put him to bed and locked him in the bedroom before returning to the pub to continue the days gossiping.

My Brother Jack's 'Ghost'

It was the middle of winter and our boots were letting in water. It was no wonder we had snotty noses, coughs and colds. Each winter all our parents put in applications for boots and clothing. Our teachers would inspect us then, after giving us each a form for our parents to fill in, she would warn us that everything must be written down correctly. If not, our parents would be in trouble.

I always read our leaflet to Mum and Dad and explained what it was all about because Mum couldn't read or write, and although Dad could write, he could only manage to read the newspaper (when he could afford to buy or maybe borrow one). Some people tried to claim what they were not entitled to, but the teachers could tell who was in need just by looking at us all. In our street alone there were at least sixty or seventy poorly clad children and most of them were at our school.

The annual distribution used to be an exciting day. We went along to the supply office to be fitted out with clothes, boots or clogs, as well as being given a mug of hot soup which the Salvation Army supplied. The girls were fitted for woollen combs or vests and bloomers, navy blue woollen slips or jerseys, and thick black woollen stocking. The boys had vests or combs, navy-blue woollen ganseys and trousers that hung over their knees, because most of these clothes were ill-fitting. We had to wear them or go without. I told my teacher once that I didn't like any of the clothes because they were so coarse and rough to wear and she shouted at me, 'You should be very grateful. Beggars can't be choosers.'

When we emerged from behind the screen in our clobber, Frankie and I had clogs, and Liza had boots. Mum asked us why we didn't get boots. Frankie lied and said there were no boots left to fit us, but really we preferred clogs. We loved dancing a clog dance on the cobbles down our street. These articles all had to have holes punched in them or be marked with an arrow so that our parents couldn't pledge them. If they had done, they could have been fined or sent to prison. Everything else of any value went into pawn, sometimes for food, but mostly for beer. There were pots, pans, clocks, kettles and umbrellas, if you were lucky enough to own one. Everything went to the pop-shop, or 'uncle's', as we called it. I used to hate the pawnshop as much as I did washdays, because there were always rows on these occasions.

Mum always did the washing on Monday morning, wet or fine, and when she was finished in the wash-house she left the hot suds in the boiler for the next woman. This went on day after day, each one leaving the soapy water for the next in order to save buying extra soda or Hudson's Powder, Lively Polly or Rickett's Blue. There was always plenty of blue in the water because it was thought things looked better blue than grey: they never managed to get clothes really clean or white. Some women would scrub their wash until nearly dark, sometimes by the light of a piece of candle or the glow of the boiler fire. On a rainy day this washing would be taken indoors to dry, ready for the pawnshop. I remember two lengths of rope nailed across our kitchen as a permanent fixture. We had many a back-hander off Mum if we didn't duck our heads low enough under the washing. The washing had the distinctive smell of carbolic soap. It took up every available space – hung over the fireplace, draped on the fire guard, on the pictures, in fact anywhere where there was space to be found.

When it was fine Mum and Mrs Buckley from next door would be up very early before anyone was awake to get their washing done and hung out on the clothes line in the yard. Nobody got any extra sleep when it was Mum's washing-day Bang! Bump! Bang! Bump! The maiding-tubs made a dreadful noise as they rolled them round to the wash-house. Then they would start agitating the washing with their dollies, singing at the tops of their voices in time to the rhythm. Mum had a powerful voice and she knew it. She always let rip for anyone to hear and Mrs Buckley tried to keep up with her. It was always the same song and Mrs Buckley always sang it off-key, but Mum's rendering of 'My Old Man Said Follow the Van' drowned Mrs Buckley out. Then when they'd eventually finished and the clothes were pegged out on the line, the next two neighbours would begin theirs. Mum used to fold and squeeze the washing through the mangle to remove the water and to press it if the iron was being used by one of the other women. The old mangle squeaked and groaned each time the handle turned. The cogs wanted oiling but we had no oil, so Dad poured paraffin over it.

'It helps,' he maintained. He also sewed rags round the rollers to stop the rotten wood getting into the clothes, the mangle look as if it had come out of hospital. Then when everything was folded up and ready for the pawnshop, Mum would called out down the yard, 'Maggie! Nell! Liz! Are yer ready?'

'Yes, we're ready.'

Then down the street they'd go with their bundles under their arms to the three brass balls. I followed, as usual. They knew I was following behind but they never took any notice of me. They never did, unless it was to run their errands for them. When they arrived at 'uncle's' Mum was the first, as usual.

'Can yer loan me fower and six? I've put in extra today.'

He gave the washing a good going over before he replied, 'I'm sorry, these are getting a bit worn but you can have three and sixpence.'

Mum gave him one of her dirty looks, but he wasn't afraid of her and just glared back.

'Take it or leave it! Next one.'

So Mum quickly grabbed what was offered, less a penny for the ticket, and went down the entry to wait for the others. They came, all moaning and saying what a skinny, bloody Jew he was. Then off to the local they went to wet their whistles. This routine was repeated week after week. In, out, in, out, more often in than out, it was never any different.

It was on a washday like this when Mum gave me sixpence wrapped up in paper.

'Katie!' she called down the yard. 'I want yer to goo down ter Longman's and tell 'im I want a fresh rabbit. Tell 'im it must be fresh or else! And 'urry, I want to get it in the pot.'

I did as I was told, but when I got there he just glared down at me.

'Does she want it skinned?'

'I don't know,' I answered timidly.

He left the skin on, wrapped it up and I ran back with it clutched under my arm. It didn't smell very fresh to me, and when Mum took it from me she sniffed it, then threw it across the table and began raving.

'Now yer can tek it back right now! It stinks!'

I picked it up. On dear! It smelled awful but I wrapped the newspaper round it as best I could and took it back to the butcher's. When I arrived Mr Longman was still standing outside in his blue and white striped apron with his straw boater on the back of his head. I peered up into his huge, round face trying to appear confident as I timidly spoke to him.

'Mum says you've got to change this rabbit.'

'What's the matter with it?' he bawled at me.

'It stinks!' I bawled back, and pushed it under his nose.

'I'm not changing it. What's yer mum want for a tanner?'

But I was feeling courageous now, and I attacked him.

'I don't know. I know this though, Mum'll give you what for if you don't change it.'

'Be off with yer, yer cheeky little sod!'

Next then I knew he hit me across the head with the rabbit and it fell to the floor. After this I was afraid to go home but I knew I had to face Mum with an explanation, so I picked the rabbit up off the floor and wrapped it up in the newspaper and off home I went.

'He won't change it,' I wailed, hardly before I had entered the door.

''E won't, won't 'e. Well I'll see about that!'

The neighbours heard Mum shouting, and came out to their doorsteps to see what it was all about. Mum went in and on went Dad's cap, offcame the apron and, holding the rabbit at arm's length, she marched down the street. Some of the neighbours with their children followed. So did our cat, Pete, and some of his friends. Mum knew they were all behind her to see the fun but she didn't mind, She enjoyed having an audience and encouraged her followers.

'I'll show 'im.'

When she saw Mr Longman she flung the rabbit across the counter and shouted for all to hear, 'What yer mean by sayin' you ain't changin' this? I asked for a fresh one and I want a fresh one!'

'But I ain't go another one,' he replied nervously.

Mr Longman saw the size of Mum and how angry she was, and hurried back into his shop. Mum glanced up and saw a large rabbit hanging from his wall on a hook. She didn't need prompting, and stretched up on her toes and reached it down and call into the shop, 'Then I'll tek this one.'

This brought him running after Mum, but she was striding back up the street with her prize.

'Come back here!' he shouted. 'I'll call a copper.'

Mum looked back over her shoulder and, to the immense amusement of the crowd that had gathered, yelled back at him, 'Yow do! An' I'll 'ave yer pinched for sellin' rotten meat!\

With her head held high she marched back home with the parcel under her arm, smiling all over her face.

'It's a woppa,' she kept saying to herself.

I watched the crowd dwindle by the time we were home. We entered and Mum kicked the door shut. Dad was there to greet us.

'What's all the commotion about? You've had the bloody street in uproar again.'

Then she told him the story.

'But 'e dain't get the better of me. An' 'e 'ad the cheek to say 'e'd call a cop.'

She tossed the parced on to the table for Dad to see and when he saw what it contained he was first surprised, then angry.

'It would've served you right if he had called a cop. This ain't a rabbit, it's a bloody hare!' He glared at her.

''Are or no 'are, it's goin' into the pot,' she replied, and began to skin it. Dad knew it was no use arguing, so he stamped out of the house leaving Mum to prepare our dinner.

I helped scrape the carrots and peel the onions and when everything was ready Mum put all the ingredients into the pot which was like a witch's cauldron hanging over the fire from a hook that swung out from the grate. This completed, she went out mumbling about the day's washing and how it would never be done.

'Come an' tell me when it starts to boil an' I'll be back to mek the dumplin's,' she called back to me.

Just then Frankie came in and I told him about the commotion. We both laughed uncontrollably about Mum's behaviour. I didn't want to fetch Mum so I asked Frankie if he thought she'd be pleased if I made the dumplings. I'd often watched them made so I foresaw no problem. Frankie agreed and stood up on Dad's chair, reached up for the mixing bowl for me and fetched the flour from the cupboard over the sink. I rolled the flour up into balls after pouring the water on. They were big and looked good enough to eat before they saw the pot but I'd forgotten to mix in the suet. Anyway, it was too late and Frankie thought they would not taste too rubbery. I felt proud of my handiwork and could hardly wait to call Mum. After moving Mum's bloomers and Dad's pants further along the fireguard we leaned over and dropped the dumplings into the pot. The pot was boiling merrily away over a fierce fire and Frankie and I stood back to admire our workmanship. The flames licked round the pot and before our eyes the dumplings seemed to rise. We looked at each other: we couldn't believe our eyes: the dumplings grew too big for the pot and continued to swell! It was then that we realised what we'd done. We'd made them from self-raising flour and we hadn't allowed room for them to rise.

We were frightened. How big were they going to become? Then, all at once, they rolled out of the pot into the fire. The chopped hare and carrots followed. Steam and ashes filled the room as the stew boiled over into the fire, putting it out. Frankie turned and dashed out of the house. He'd heard Mum coming up the path.

'I'm off! he shouted.

'Wait for me!' I cried, grabbing hold of the back of his gansey.

We were scared but we didn't get far: as we ran round the corner we collided with Dad. Now we're really for it, I thought.

'Well, well, well, and what's this all about?' he asked, looking down at us both.

'I told him breathlessly how we'd tried to help Mum with the dinner. Frankie didn't say a word, he just looked at the floor and kicked the stones. Then I began to cry. But Dad only smiled down at me.

'Come along now, and you, Frankie.'

I felt a bit safer now my dad was there. The three of us went inside the house where Mum was standing by the wall with the cane at the ready.

'Not this time, Polly,' Dad said, taking the cane away from her. 'They only wanted to help you and give you a surprise.'

'Surprise? Surprise!' she blustered. 'Yer call this a surprise? Look at all the mess they've med.'

She was waving her arms about indicating the state of the room. She didn't stop yelling.

'No dinner fer anybody today. I've got no mower money to buy any.'

'I have,' said Dad gently, in an attempt to calm her down. 'I've had a sub off the gaffer.'

This seemed to please Mum, at least she altered her tone and set to to clean up the mess while Dad lit the fire again. Then Mum took the pot and the remains of the hare and swilled it under the tap to save what she could: she didn't believe in wasting anything.

'Wasn't we lucky we run into Dad?' Frankie whispered to me.

I nodded in reply and we began to see the funny side of the affair but we didn't laugh for long. Mum and Dad had fish and chips while Frankie, Liza and I had to eat the hare that had been rescued from the floor.

When Mum's birthday came round Dad told her to put on her best bib and tucker and took her out. She was dressed in her stiff white pinafore that was kept for such occasions. I'd cleaned and polished her button-up boots and fastened them for her. Dad had his white muffler on. Off they went, leaving us with the warning to behave ourselves while they were out. We watched them go out of sight, then called some of our friends in to play at shop. We had nothing to sell, but it was fun just to wrap nothing up in newspaper and pretend to buy. Little Maudie Taylor made us laugh when she mimicked Mum.

'I'll 'ave a rabbit, an' see it's fresh or else!'

All too soon it was time for our parents to return, so they all scattered. It was very late when Mum and Dad arrived home and Liza and Frankie had already gone up to bed, leaving me to let them in. We always put the bolt on the door when we were alone. I jumped off Dad's chair when I heard their footsteps.

'Why ain't yow in bed?' Mum managed to say.

I didn't answer: I could see it was no use.

'Don't stand and stare at us. Mek yerself useful an' pour me out a drink.'

Dad took four bottles from his jacket pockets and banged them down on the table. I looked from one to the other and thought how stupid they both looked. They were really well oiled.

'Come on. Do as yer told, yer know it's yer mum's birthday.'

I knew, and I was thankful it was only once a year. After helping them to their 'lunatic soup' (this was Charlie's phrase), I sat down on the stool listening to their patter but I couldn't make out what they were whispering about. They'd forgotten that I was still there when just a few minutes later Jack came in. He glanced at Mum then at Dad, and tutted. He didn't see me at first but then I coughed. He put his finger to his lips for me to keep quiet and then he beckoned me over.

'Katie, I want you to do me an errand,' he whispered.

'Where to?' I was alarmed. 'It's late.'

'Shush,' he hissed. 'I'll give yer a penny if you'll go.'

But he needn't have whispered because Mum and Dad were asleep.

'I want yer to take a note round to Lil's house.'

'But it's late, Jack, and I'm tired and sleepy.'

'I'll come part of the way with you. How's that?'

I didn't mind when I knew he was coming with me. He handed me the letter and a penny which I slipped down my stocking, then I put on my coat and off we went. It was nearly midnight as we hurried down the narrow streets. I wasn't very brave, even with my big brother, because the moon was casting weird shadows everywhere as the clouds scudded over it. I pulled at his coat.

'Jack,' I pleaded. 'Can't the letter wait until tomorrow?'

'No!' he snapped. 'She must get it tonight. I don't want to see her tomorrow.'

'But it's late, and I'm cold.' I clung to his coat tail and shivered.

'Oh, let go and give me yer 'and. We'll go through the churchyard for the quickest,' he said impatiently and pull me along.

When we reached the other gate at the opposite end of the church-yard, Jack pointed across the road.

'That's the house. Number seventeen. Just push the note under the door and I'll wait for you here.'

When I'd delivered the message I ran back to my brother as fast as I could.

'Are you sure you pushed it right under the door?'

'Yes, Jack, I'm sure.' I was trembling.

'Come on then. We can get back home before Mum and Dad miss you if we go back the same way.'

I felt braver now because Jack held my hand as we hurried along. The church clock struck twelve. The moon was so bright it lit up the whole cemetery. You could read the words on the tombstones. Everything was still and quiet as we scurried across the grass. Jack started to whistle a tune and then suddenly a body popped up out of a hole in the ground and spoke in a deep voice.

'Hello, mate.'

At that Jack took to his heels and ran for dear life, leaving me to escape as best as I could. I ran screaming. Then I tripped over a jar of flowers on one of the graves but Jack turned and dragged me along. We couldn't get home quick enough. We fell inside the door, waking up Mum and Dad as we flopped on to the sofa.

'What's all the bloody noise about?' Dad shouted.

'And why ain't yow in bed?' Mum cried out to me, as I edged towards the stairs and began to cry.

'I went an errand for Jack,' I managed to blurt out. But Jack wouldn't let me finish.

'I've seen a ghost tonight, Dad,' he said, still shaking and pale.

'What yer mean? You've seen a ghost. Where?' Then Jack told all.

'You had no right to take Katie through the churchyard at this time of night. Do your own dirty work!' Dad spluttered angrily. 'And another thing I want to say. I'm sick and tired of these girls you love and leave coming up to ask me if I've seen yer. If you have seen a ghost it's yer sins finding you out!'

By now Mum was fully aroused.

''E must 'ave seen a ghost. Look at his face.'

Jack was pale with fright and so was I, but no one seemed to notice me on the stairs, until suddenly I let out a loud scream as I felt a hand on my back. I needn't have worried though, it was only Frankie who'd crept downstairs, dressed only in his nightshirt.

'What's the matter, Katie?' he asked.

But I was hysterical and couldn't speak. Anyway, you couldn't have heard your own voice with Mum, Dad and Jack arguing.

'Be quiet, all of you!' Dad shouted. 'Now, Jack, I want the truth. Did you really see a ghost?'

'Yes. It came up out of a grave and spoke to me, didn't it, Katie?' I nodded my agreement.

'Are you sure you ain't had too much drink?'

'No. I've bin playing cards with my workmates.'

'I believe 'im,' Mum said. 'Just look at 'is face. 'Ere, tek a drop of this.' She handed him a mug of beer which he drank down in one gulp.

'If you don't believe me,' he said, 'you come with me now and I'll show you the grave he popped out of.'

'All right. I could do with a breath of fresh air,' Dad replied.

Frankie got his trousers on quicker than I'd ever seen him, and followed Dad out of the house. Determined not to be left out, I followed behind.

'I'll come as quick as I can,' said Mum.

She wasn't afraid of anyone or anything and neither was I now that Dad was with us. It was nearly one o'clock in the morning but the moon was bright enough for us to see all we wanted as we walked through the churchyard.

'Which hole is it? Is it this one?' asked Dad, pointing to an open grave.

'No,' whispered Jack. 'That's the one, next to it.'

'You must be mad!' Dad replied. 'There's no one down there.'

Dad turned to go back when suddenly a body clad in a white coat popped out of the grave behind Dad and spoke in a rough voice.

'What do you lot want at this time in the morning?'

Jack nearly fell into the open grave with the shock. Frankie and I stood petrified, but Mum and Dad didn't turn a hair. Dad burst out laughing.

'It's all right, Jack. I know 'im.'

We all collapsed on one of the tombstones to recover our breath, and Mum turned to go home without a word. I think she was disappointed.

'You're working late, ain't yer, Arthur?' said Dad.

'I've got to. I've got a busy day tomorrer. Another four to dig yet,' replied the ghost.

'Would yer like me to fetch yer a jug of 'ot cocoa?' Dad asked.

'Thanks, Sam,' he replied. 'It's getting a bit chilly in 'ere.'

Dad said he hadn't got anything warmer to give so we returned home where Mum had already gone to bed. Frankie and I crept quietly upstairs after wishing Jack good-night. We heard him and Dad tittering as we climbed into bed. News always travelled fast round our district and everybody pulled Jack's leg about his ghost. But Jack had a sense of humour, so each time he told the story he stretched it a bit longer.

Christmas 1911

When Christmas came, Frankie, Liza and I went into the 'better' district which was not far from our school where there was a pub called the George and Dragon. This was a large public house with a long mixed bar, a gentleman's smokeroom, a bottle and jug department, and a 'snug' for ladies only.

We all knew when Dad went there to have a drink with his mates because I always had the job of pressing his best suit and his white muffler. When Mum went there with any of the neighbours she always wore her Sunday best, a stiffly starched pinafore which she took great pride in ironing, especially the lace edges. Her hair would be plaited round over each ear, instead of the usual bun on top. She always tried to make an impression. I can remember her saying, 'We're as good as this lot 'ere, even if we ain't got much.' The kind of people Mum was talking about were mostly shopkeepers and independent, but the folk who lived in our district were happier in their own little local, the Golden Cup. They used to say, 'We feel at home here; the gaffer and the missus are like us.' How true that was: they both drank like fish too! Their moods were unpredictable, though. They would sometimes join in with their customers and sing, or alternatively throw them out if they'd had enough. This usually happened on Saturday night when a burly, punch-drunk barman was employed for the purpose. Then there'd be a free-for-all – spittoons and saw-dust flying everywhere. You never saw a pub empty so quickly as when someone peeped round the door and warned them that the cops were on their way.

The night before this particular Christmas Eve it was snowing and freezing hard when Frankie, Liza and I hurried along the street to sing carols. The shopkeepers were busy in their windows putting up their decorations ready for the Christmas spree. While this was going on, Frankie nipped smartly up the baker's entry and helped himself to a large, empty flour sack. This was to keep us warm while we waited for the shops to close and the pub across the street to fill with customers. The three of us sat on an empty shop step, huddled up close together wih the sack over our heads to keep us warm. Although we were covered in flour we didn't mind as long as we didn't feel the cold. I was lucky; being the smallest, I sat between Frankie and Liza. Even so, my feet were cold and wet because my clogs were split at the sides and my clothes were threadbare.

At last we saw the lights go out in the shop windows. The street was deserted and dark now except for the lights that shone from the leaded windows of the George and Dragon, the knight in his brightly coloured armour making red, blue, green and yellow lights that glistened on the snow. We were just about to cross the street when we saw two shadows coming towards us. Quickly we dashed back to our hiding-place, but it was too late. Before we could hide our heads underneath the sack again, a man's hand dragged it from us. He struck a match and peered down at us.

'Well, well, well and what have we here? Three little orphans of the storm?' he chuckled.

We were too scared to move. We just sat there looking up at him wide-eyed. He called back over his shoulder, 'Aggie, is there any port left in the bottle?'

Aggie brought the bottle and said, 'It's time they were in bed and dreaming about Father Christmas.'

'Here, drink this.' He offered the port. 'It'll warm yer up.'

Frankie quickly took the bottle. I thought he was going to drink the lot but he gave Liza and me the bottle, and between us we finished the rest. There was only a drop for each of us which was a good thing because otherwise we'd have been tiddly. Anyway I felt warmer. Frankie gave him back the empty bottle after draining the dregs and saluted him gratefully.

'Thank you, sir. And a merry Christmas.'

The man put his hand into his waistcoat pocket and pulled out three pennies which he dropped in my lap.

'Do you want us to sing some carols?' I asked, hoping to return his kindness.

'Don't be silly; of course he don't!' said Frankie, giving me a nudge which nearly pushed me off the step.

His lady companion walked away as the man warned us to get off home before a bobby came along. But we had no intention of doing that.

'We ain't sat on this wet step just to go back home,' muttered Frankie.

So we pulled ourselves up off the step and walked a little way to hide in a doorway until they were out of sight. Then we dashed back to sing outside the George and Dragon. We were happy to have threepence and grateful for the port wine. It gave us Dutch courage. We could've faced anybody or anything that night, we felt so happy and warm inside. The other kids at our school never sang carols here, they weren't allowed to go near this pub. Their parents used to frighten them by saying the owners were wicked people who, just like George and the dragon and the Mormons who came along our street, carried little children off. I asked Frankie if it was true about the Mormons.

'You don't want to believe everything people say. Anyway, our parents don't want us, yet they don't want the Mormons to have us either. It don't make any sense to me.'

'Shut up!' spat Liza. 'Let's get on with the carols. It's getting late.'

We stood just inside the doorway out of the snow, wiped the snow and flour off our faces, and began to sing. But we couldn't hear ourselves above the noise of merriment going on inside, so Frankie pushed open the door a little and kept his foot there. We waited until the sound had died down, then we burst with 'Hark, the Herald Angels Sing'. We sang at the top of our voices to drown Liza who was off-key as usual. Then someone shouted from inside, 'Some bloody angels!'

'Close the door,' somebody else cried.

This dampened our spirits. Frankie retrieved his foot and we walked away. However, before we'd got out into the street a kindly little lady came up behind us and gave us a silver sixpence. She told us to return on Christmas Eve, then she popped back inside, leaving us dumbfounded.

'Who was she?' asked Frankie.

'She's George's dragon we've heard so much about,' said Liza.

I was a bit disappointed. I'd imagined her to be a large woman something like our mum. We were happy, though. We ran to the fish shop to buy a pennyworth of fish and chips which we thought was plenty to share between the three of us. We ate it as we walked slowly back home. When we arrived, Frankie ran straight upstairs and put the rest of the money in a tin box which served as our savings bank. He had a good hiding-place, no one knew where, not even Mum.

The table was strewn with coloured papers which Mum had left for us to make our paper trimmings that night. We cut them all into loops and Liza made the paste with flour and water. If this failed, Frankie said he would get a tin of condensed milk to mix it with. Frankie took a little, not enough for Mum to notice, and this did the trick, and it was nice to lick our fingers each time we stuck one loop inside another and so we made the decorations for the walls and pictures. We didn't have a real Christmas tree. We had to beg two wooden hoops off a cheese tub from the grocer's. We fitted these one inside the other and covered them with different coloured tissue and crepe paper.

When Dad came home he said we'd done a good job and helped us hang the streamers across the room, high up above the clothes line: and to let people see we had some sort of tree, the paper Christmas tree was hung in the window from a nail. Every time we had a farthing or a halfpenny given us for running errands we bought white sugar mice and little chocolate Father Christmases and shiny, coloured balls and tinsel or any little thing we could afford. After we'd trimmed up the room, Dad gave us a penny each to buy extra gifts for the tree. Then, after drinking our cocoa, we went off to bed, happy and contented, knowing we had some money to spend and that we were going carol-singing again the next night to earn some more. We got up early in the morning to do our errands and daily chores around the house, then when it got dark we got ready to go out to continue our carolling. Mum watched us with keen eyes as we donned our coats and scarves.

'And where do yer think you three are gooin' this time o' night?' she asked, sternly.

'We're going carol-singing,' Frankie replied, defiantly.

'That's all right,' Dad said, 'but be back in bed before we get home.'

'Yes, Dad,' we replied in unison.

We ran out and turned up the street towards the George and Dragon. I was glad Mum and Dad hadn't asked what part we were going to because this street was forbidden territory. When we arrived we started 'Hark, the Herald Angels Sing' again, but we only got as far as 'Hark' when I felt a hard thump on my back.

'Don't sing that one,' Frankie said. 'You know what happened last time. Let's sing 'Noël'.'

Halfpennies and pennies came flying through the door and when I picked them up I counted tenpence ha'penny in all. We showed our gratitude by singing it again, only louder. But when Liza reached the high notes she gave out an off-key shriek which brought George out with the warning to 'clear off'. Frankie turned on Liza as we walked away.

'You spoil everything with yer cracked voice. I wish I'd brought one of Mum's gob-stoppers along for you.!'

She walked on, but never answered. We turned into our street where we thought we'd try our luck again. When we got to the Golden Cup, Frankie warned Liza to keep her mouth shut and pick up the money instead. We were unlucky this time, though. While we'd been up the street the other kids had been here, so we sang in vain. Next we tried the Mermaid, then the King's Head, but they told us the Salvation Army band had already called. We were reduced to singing for the passers-by, a few of whom gave us a penny. By now it was getting late and we remembered we had to be in bed before our parents returned, but we decided to satisfy our hunger first. We went to the cow heel and tripe shop and bought three pig's trotters. Frankie hid the rest of our earnings while we sat munching away. Then suddenly I remembered that Mum had told me that morning to mend a hole in my stocking.

'Don't forget to sew that 'ole or Father Christmas will leave yer nothin',' she'd said.

But I was too tired now. Anyway, I thought, perhaps she'll forget about it.

'Ain't yer going to hang up yer stocking?' asked Frankie as we were undressing.

'In a minute,' I yawned.

'Never mind. I'll hang it up,' he said, as I climbed into bed. Liza and I watched him hang three stockings over the bedstead. Then he jumped into bed and after blowing out the candle we fell to sleep.

Next morning we woke early and wished each other 'Merry Christmas' before looking to see what we'd been given. Liza jumped off the bed and grabbed her stocking while Frankie looked to see what was inside ours. Liza had an apple, an orange, some mixed nuts and a bright new penny. Frankie had the same, but when I looked in mine there was nothing, only the hole. In the dark Frankie had hung up the wrong stocking.

'Never mind.' Frankie was trying to be sympathetic and wiped my tears away. 'You can share mine.'

'But that's not the same. Mum's never loved me. I don't know why, Frankie, I always do as she tells me and I always try to please her,' I cried.

'Come and dry your eyes. It's Christmas Day. Anyway we've got our money-box hidden away for the holidays,' Frankie said cheerfully.

Liza didn't say a word. She was busy sucking her orange, sitting up in bed. So I sat up beside Frankie at the foot of the bed and he shared what he had with me. He nudged, winked and smiled at me with his big blue eyes. Then I returned his smile because his mirth was infectious.

This was the one morning in the year we had to stay in bed until Mum called us downstairs. So after eating our Christmas fare we got back under the bedclothes to keep warm, planning what we were going to do with our savings. All of a sudden we were startled by Mum's voice.

'Yer can get up now!'

We dressed quickly and went downstairs. Mary, Jack, Dad and Charlie were sitting at the table ready for us to join them. Mum was standing over a big fire frying eggs, sausages and bacon in a big pan.

'Merry Christmas,' we called out to them all. They each returned the greeting except Mum. She turned round to face us and waved the fork at the bowl of water for us to get washed.

''Urry yerselves. We're waitin' to 'ave our breakfast.'

After falling over each other to get to the bowl first, we sat down in our usual places on the sofa which was drawn up to the table. Dad, Jack, Mary and Charlie each had an egg, two sausages and a rasher of bacon. On our enamel plates was half a sausage, half an egg and a piece of fried bread. By the side of my plate was a small packet wrapped in tissue paper. I smiled across at Mum. I thought, she's not forgotten me after all.

'Thank you, Mum,' I said as I opened it.

She didn't turn an eye, only said, 'Yer can look at it when you've 'ad yer breakfast.'

I didn't want any breakfast, I was too anxious to see what was in the small packet. So while Mum wasn't looking I slipped my fried bread and sausage under the table to Frankie. Then I finished my half egg but I daren't leave the table until everyone else had finished. I looked at Mum and smiled.

'Can I please open it now, Mum?'

She didn't answer, so I presumed she meant me to and I eagerly unwrapped it and dropped the paper on the floor. It was a match-box but when I opened it and saw what was in it I burst into tears. Inside was a little ball of black wool and a darning needle. I stared hard at it. My sister Mary came round the table and picked it up.

'How could you do such a thing to her?' she said. 'What's the reason?'

All eyes were on Mum now as I blubbered.

'That's 'er punishment fer not doin' as she was told!' Mum answered sharply.

Then Mary and Mum started to quarrel, and between my sobs I heard Mary accuse Mum.

'You've never loved her. But she'll know why some day!'

Mum walked over to the fireplace and Dad joined in.

'Now, Mary, let's have no more of this. It's Christmas Day, remember?'

Jack went out and Charlie followed behind him, banging the front door behind him. Dad patted me on the head and said softly, 'I'll be back when you've settled your arguments.' Then he too walked out.

Frankie and Liza just looked at Mum. I didn't know what they were thinking but I knew why she'd given me the needle and wool. I went upstairs and took off my stocking and began to darn it when Mary came in to see me. She unfastened her trunk and took out a box of lace handkerchiefs. 'Here you are, Katie,' she said. 'Here's my present for you.'

I thanked her with a sob and a smile.

'Don't take Mum to heart too much, Katie. She didn't mean anything.'

I knew she was making excuses for Mum. I knew Mum didn't love me from piecing together bits of conversations I'd overheard, and now this morning I'd heard Mary say so to Mum.

'Mary,' I asked as I put on my stocking, 'do you know why Mum doesn't love me?'

'She does, in her funny way,' she said gently.

'She can't do or she wouldn't do and say the things to me that she does. Won't you tell me why?' I sobbed.

'When you're older,' she said. Then she went downstairs.

'That's all I get off you grown-ups; "when yer get older",' I answered angrily, following her down.

Mary whispered something to Mum and then got her work-box out. She called me over to show me what was inside. I soon forgot my troubles as she showed me the presents the friends she worked with had given her. I couldn't believe my eyes: there were two rows of pearls, a row of blue glass beads, some more hankies and lots of other trinkets. There were also pretty Christmas cards with real lace round the edges. Before Mary closed the box she put the pearls round my neck. I saw Mum look, so I unfastened them quickly and gave them back.

'Now you just put them back on. They're yours, from me to you,' Mary said to my immense surprise and joy.

'Thank you, Mary.' I threw my arms round her neck and hugged her.

During all this time Mum never said a word until Mary went back upstairs with the box.

'Come on. 'Urry yerselves up, the three of yer. Yer gran'll be waitin' for yer.'

I was eager to go, so was Frankie, but Liza couldn't care less one way or the other. Anyway, Mum made her come along with us whether she wanted to or not. Frankie and Liza had Christmas cards in their hands to give their school friends, but I had mine in a surprise parcel for Granny. Our granny lived about twenty minutes' walk from our house – that was if we ran all the way, which we had to do that day because the snow was freezing underfoot and we wanted to keep warm. Her house was built on the same pattern as ours which meant there were no repairs done and she couldn't afford to improve it herself. Anyway, she used to say, 'I ain't spendin' any of my money to clean this place: it's the landlord's job.' She was a stubborn old woman, but I loved her. I believe if the house had fallen down she wouldn't have cared. She was very defiant and independent. When we arrived, Frankie knocked on the door with his foot and we heard the heavy bolts being pulled back. Then she peeped round the door.

'We've come to you a Merry Christmas, Granny.'

She glared at us. She didn't look very pleased when we handed our Christmas cards to her.

'What's there for me to be merry about?' she shook her head and dislodged some paper curlers which whirled to the floor. 'Anyway, come inside an' warm yer feet, yer must be afreezin',' she said hobbling over to the fire.

I looked round the room. There wasn't much fire in the grate to warm us and there was nowhere to sit. Frankie rushed to sit on the only, backless, chair. Granny sat in her rockingchair, and Liza dashed for the stool.

'Yoo ain't sittin' theea!' she screamed out at Liza. 'That's Katie's seat.'

'You don't like me, do yer?' Liza put out her tongue at Granny.

'No, I don't! Yer a little tell-tale,' she said, looking away.

'An' I don't like you!' said Liza, shrugging her shoulders.

But I don't think Granny gave Liza another thought because she turned to me. 'You sit in me rockin'-chair, Katie.'

It was a big old chair. It had to be big for Granny because she was a large woman like Mum, and when I sat down in her chair I felt lost. Whenever Granny sat in it the chair creaked, squeaked, rocked and rolled as she hummed to herself. I always expected her to tip over backwards, but she never did: she must have timed those rusty old springs to a fine point. All in all she was a very funny old granny. Sometimes she would be very kind to us, and other times her entire manner would change. She had her moods, just like Mum.

I sat trying to rock myself, but the chair was too heavy for me to get even a squeak. She stood by the table trying to untwist the paper curlers from her black hair. Then I remembered her present.

'Here you are, Granny, I've bought you some real hair curlers for Christmas.'

'Thank yer, I'm glad someone thinks about yer old granny.'

She took the box from me. Then she looked up at the alarm clock, which had only one hand and half a finger.

'Ain't it about time yer went now? It's getting late.'

We'd only been there about five minutes, but she could see we were already fidgety to be going. As we made for the door she said to Frankie and Liza, ' 'Ere y'are. 'ere's a new penny for yer.'

I felt dejected again when she said she'd not got one for me, but then, as if from nowhere, she produced a cardboard box tied with real pink ribbon.

'And that's for you,' she said with a smile.

A lump came to my throat and tears started to flow, and I threw my arms round her waist.

'Be orf with yer at once. I'm 'ungry now and me cat wants 'is breakfast too. An' don't untie that ribbon now. Wait until yer get 'ome. 'An yer can tell yer mum yer old gran don't forget yer, even if she does.'

I wondered then if she knew about the hole in my stocking, for Mum had always said she was an old witch. I felt sorry for Granny living in that old hovel all alone with her mangy old cat.

We ran all the way home, eager to see what was in the cardboard box. When we got indoors I untied the ribbon carefully because I wanted it for my hair. Then Frankie and I tore the wrapper to see what the present was. When I removed the lid there inside lay the biggest golliwog I'd ever seen, a lovely Christmas card and a note which read, 'This is for Katie which have made all myself.' I hugged it and kissed it and tears of delight ran down my face and dropped on to the golly's.

'She might have put a few marbles in the box for me,' said Frankie, beginning to sulk. But when Liza saw my present she just said, 'Phew,' and walked away with her head in the air.

'She's only jealous,' said Frankie, smiling.

The golliwog was made out of a black woollen stocking and filled tight with straw. She, for I had decided that it was a lady, had red wool for her lips and two linen buttons for her eyes and on the top of her head was real, curly black fur. I was proud to think that Granny had made this with her own two hands. I carried her nearly everywhere and I treasured her for years.

That was one Christmas I never forget. Frankie even said I could have his new penny, but although I was grateful for his offer I only wanted my golliwog because this was the first one I had ever had of my own. I hadn't even had a doll to play with when I was younger. Liza told Mum later that afternoon what Granny had made for me but she didn't ask to see it, and I could tell she wasn't interested. All Dad said was 'That's very kind of her.'

Christmas afternoon, Frankie, Liza and me went to a teaparty at the Salvation Army Hall where there were other little girls like me with real dolls, but theirs weren't as big as mine, so there and then I decided to name her Topsey.

The Free Samples

A fter our Christmas holiday we started back to school. Each day when lessons were over and it was time to go home I would look out for the welcome sign of smoke coming from our chimney. Then I'd know Mum had lit the fire to warm us. One particular day I remember glancing up and being surprised to see that the expected trail of smoke was absent. In fact none of the chimneys was smoking. I pointed this out to Frankie.

'Did you fetch the coal up from the cellar this morning?'

'You know I did,' he answered. 'Why?'

'Well, look, there's no smoke coming from our chimney nor any of the others.'

He agreed that this was funny and so did our friends when we showed them. It was very quiet and there seemed to be no adults about either. Then somebody noticed that some little packets had been left on each of our steps. We all made a mad dash to pick them up. Each little packet consisted of a little silver paper parcel labelled 'Ex-Lax'. We didn't know what this meant so we opened them and found five small tablets of chocolate which we pocketed, promising to say nothing to our parents. It was not long before Mum and Dad and the rest of our neighbours came walking down the yard with blankets under their arms. Then I realised where they'd been. Once a year the poor went to the church to be issued with bedclothes.

As soon as Frankie spotted Mum he cried out, 'We're hungry, Mum, and we'll be late back to school.'

'Well you'll 'ave to wait! I've bin to the church to get me issue. I couldn't miss them, could I?' she answered with a glare.

So while we waited for something to eat we slipped the chocolate into our mouths while Mum wasn't looking. She gave us each a slice of bread and lard and told us to clear off back to school.

'I'm already be'ind with me washin'.'

I thought how wicked and crafty our people were: they only went to church when something was being given away free. Then of course they would smile and say, 'Oh, well, we'll 'ave to go.' The only other time they went was for weddings, christenings and funerals.

At five to two we all hurried up the street to get back before the bell stopped ringing. When we arrived we all took our places, the boys in their classroom and the girls in theirs, separated only by a glass partition so that we could see the boys and they us, if we stood on tiptoe. We had to be careful that the master or mistress didn't catch us, otherwise we had the cane or the ruler across our knuckles.

Lessons began, and after a while my tummy began to rumble as the Ex-Lax began to do its work. I started to wriggle about in my seat and when I looked around the other girls were wriggling too. Then, while the teacher was writing on the board, I stood on my toes to look for Frankie. He was also moving uncomfortably, as were the rest of the boys. I whispered to Liza, 'Liza, I got an awful pain in my tummy. I think I want to go to the lavee. It must have been that chocolate I ate.'

'And me!' she hissed back.

'Me too,' Sarah Taylor said, looking pale.

Then all the girls who'd eaten the Ex-Lax joined in.

'Oh-er, and me.'

Miss Frost, our teacher, couldn't understand why we were whispering and wriggling in our seats.

'What's wrong there?' she called out sharply, the cane at the ready.

Up shot our hands in unison as we chorused, 'Please, miss, may we leave the room?'

She looked at us over the top of her spectacles and spoke firmly. 'No you may not!'

Then the cane came down hard across the desk with a loud swish. We flinched, and practically jumped out of our skins. Matters were getting no better and we remained with our hands in the air, afraid to move in case of an accident.

'What is this?' she repeated harshly. 'Some new joke you're playing? Put your hands down at once and sit down!'

Slowly our hands dropped halfway at least. But we didn't sit still. We couldn't.

'Very well,' she said deliberately. 'I haven't the time to cane you all, but you will stay in and write two hundred lines on how to behave in class.'

Then she wobbled out, locking the classroom door behind her. Liza and I managed to look over the partition to see how the lads were behaving. Although we couldn't hear them, we saw they too had their hands raised high while the master's face was getting redder and redder. I turned to Liza.

'What are we going to do? I'd do it in my bloomers if I don't go soon.'

'I've already done something in mine,' she answered, beginning to cry.

Some of the other girls were weeping too, and others were trying the door but it wanted a battering-ram to make that door yield: it was made of oak. We were all more or less in an awful mess and lessons hadn't even begun. Just then we heard the heavy tread of our teacher in the corridor. She unlocked the door and stood still. I saw her nose twitching like a rabbit's.

'What an awful smell!' she managed to say, before turning back down the corridor, leaving the door open.

This was our chance. We knocked each other over as we made a mad dash for the exit. We ran headlong down the passage, pushing past the master and mistress who were standing at the end and tearing out into the street. Once outside, we scattered in all directions towards our homes. When we got inside the door Mum was about to ask why we were home so soon when her nostrils also twitched and she sniffed at us.

'Blimey! What a pong!'

Frankie and I tried to explain, but we were sobbing by now and she wouldn't listen anyway. She pushed us away and asked Liza to explain. Usually when she had to explain anything it was a twisted version to lay the blame on us two. This time, however, she had to tell the truth. Mum went out and dragged back the big tin bath that always hung on the wall outside the door and filled it full of water.

'You sit on the stairs while I strip these two, and close the dower,' she told Frankie, pushing him in the direction of the stairs.

After our clothes were stripped off we stood up naked, waiting for some hot water to be added to the cold, but Mum was too impatient to clean us for niceties like that. She pushed us roughly towards the bath. We had to get in even though the water felt freezing. Then Mum poured in disinfectant and began to scrub us with carbolic soap. She dipped us up and down like a couple of yo-yos, swearing at us all the time. When we were dried she threw one of Mary's chemises at me and one of her own at Liza. We looked like Marley's ghost! Then we were sent straight to bed without a drink or anything to eat.

Frankie's turn was next but he had to help Mum lift the bath of dirty water into the yard and wait for it to be filled before he was performed upon. In the meantime, instead of going up the stairs as we'd been told, we sat on them and peeped through a crack in the door. We watched Frankie stripped and bundled into the bath.

'Come on! Jump in!' Mum shouted at him in exasperation.

He jumped out a lot quicker than he jumped in, and stood beside it naked and shivering, complaining that it was too cold.'

'It'll be colder still if yer don't get back in!' She was growing angrier by the second.

However, Frankie was made of different stuff from us. He had that extra bit of nerve. He refused to do what Mum told him. Liza and I looked at each other, then back at Frankie, and began to titter. We put our hands across our mouths to stifle any noise but it was too late. Suddenly the door was flung open and Mum chased up the stairs bringing the cane across our bottoms as we fled. When we tripped over our long nighties she was able to give some more. Luckily, however, she tired after the first flight and descended again, puffing and blowing. We crawled into bed, sore and sorry. I still managed to say my prayers through the tears, though. Just as I was saying, 'Amen,' Frankie came into the room dressed in one of Dad's shirts. He stood there like a third Marley's ghost, all shirt and no legs. Liza burst out laughing when she saw him, but I was crying. I was too sore even to smile.

'I'm hungry,' I cried to Frankie, as he climbed in the bottom with me.

He said he was too. Then we heard Mum's footsteps on the stairs.

'Yow can stop yer cryin' or I'll come up an' give yer some mower . . . an' 'urry up an' blow out that candle!'

We heard her close the stair door but Frankie didn't intend going to sleep. He sat up and turned to me.

'Don't cry, Katie. I've got some bread and jam hidden away in the tuck-box.'

I looked at him, somewhat surprised. 'Where've you had that from?'

'Bertha Marpley gave it to me for some marbles, but you can win them back for me tomorrow.' He winked and smiled.

He knew I could and so did I because I was the champion marbles player in our neighbourhood. So the three of us sat quietly in bed while Frankie shared his swap. I didn't know how long it had been in that tin box but the jam had soaked through the bread and the whole thing had set rock hard. However, we were so hungry it seemed to taste wonderful. We finished our feast and happily settled down to sleep. I was still tired and sore but I had Topsey to cuddle. Just then Mum called out, 'Liza, are yer awake?'

'Yes, Mum,' she replied.

'Come down 'ere. I want yer.'

'I'm coming.' Liza sounded fed up.

I wondered what Mum could want, but Frankie was already asleep and I soon joined him in the land of nod. So I didn't hear Liza return, which was unusual because when she got in it always tipped up, catapulting us out.

Next morning we couldn't go to school nor could the others who had eaten the free samples. None of us had any clothes to wear until the wet ones dried, so we had to stay in bed until they were. We weren't bothered because our attic was bedroom, prison and playroom as well as anything else that was necessary. We started to play 'I spy with my little eye' but that proved too easy so we moved on to a spelling game. This also bored us quickly so we took to gazing listlessly out of the window. We saw in the yard below our bloomers and the boys' trousers billowing in the breeze on the clothes lines. Then we spotted Dad coming down the yard so we pulled our heads back inside. We'd forgotten Dad came home early when he was working the nightshift. We crept to the top of the stairs to hear what Mum had to say about us.

'An' thay ain't getting nothin' to eat till their clothes are dry.'

'But, Polly, you can't leave them kids up there without anything to eat. Don't you think they've been punished enough? I'm having my way, just for once.'

We dashed into bed as we heard him coming upstairs. He entered the room and looked at us sitting up in bed with the bedclothes wrapped round us, then he turned without a word and returned downstairs. He was soon back, this time with a large jug of hot cocoa, some bread and dripping and our three enamel mugs on a tin tray.

'Get this down yer while it's hot,' he said jovially.

He left us again without a word of sympathy, but before he could get downstairs I called out to him, 'Thank you, Dad. We're sorry we caused Mum so much trouble but we thought the Ex-Lax were chocolates.'

'Well, perhaps this'll teach you a lesson not to touch free samples that are left on doorsteps until your mum comes home.'

If only he'd forgiven us we'd have felt happier, but he never said another word. But we heard Mum carry on at him when he got downstairs.

'Yer too easy with 'em!'

'Yes, and you're too 'ard on 'em and don't you dare hit them kids again today, otherwise you'll answer to me!'

Then we heard Dad go out, banging the door to behind him. As soon as he'd gone Mum came bounding up into the room.

'You don't drink that until you drink this!'

Then she held our noses in turn and poured a large spoonful of castor oil down our throats 'to bind you up'. I swallowed mine. So did Liza. We had no option, but when she left us Frankie spat his into the chamberpot. He warned Liza with an unnamed threat.

'If you dare tell Mum . . .'

While we were drinking our cocoa I thought over what Dad had said about Mum hitting us.

'Frankie. I think our dad does love us in his funny kind of way. Don't you think so?'

'Perhaps,' he grunted.

Frankie's Illness

I used to like helping people, running their little errands for them or doing small jobs, but the farthing or halfpenny or piece of bread and jam that I usually received as a reward was an added incentive. Better than these, though, was a little love, a kind word or small affection, that was all I needed really. I remember one day Dad sent me to the homemadesweet shop to fetch a pennyworth of pear-drops. Eager to please and hopeful of reward I ran all the way there and back. I even left Topsey behind. When I returned, breathless, he gave one to Frankie, one to Liza and one he placed in my pinafore pocket, or so I thought. Then we dashed off to school. During break I put my hand in my pocket for the sweet but I was surprised to find that there were two. I ate one and although I was tempted to eat the other I didn't. I wanted to impress Dad with how honest I was. When I returned, Dad was dozing by the fire. So I tiptoed up to him and pushed the pear-drop under his nose, waking him up. He sniffed and opened his eyes.

'Dad, you gave me two pear-drops by mistake, so I've brought you the other one back.'

He yawned lazily and pushed my hand away.

'Go out and play.' He seemed unconcerned at my exemplary behaviour.

I felt dejected. If only he'd thanked me or given me a pat on the head or just a kind word I would have been proud and happy. I didn't realise that Dad didn't want to be woken up when he'd just returned from a hard day's work. It was really no wonder he was irritable, but it took me some time to forget that incident and my childish hurt. I still ran his errands when he asked me, though. I was too young to understand my own feelings and the strange ways of adults so I bestowed my love on Topsey.

I wandered out, hugging my golliwog, to look for Frankie. I found him sitting on the pavement with the other boys and girls. I soon won him the marbles he'd swopped and a few more besides. I even won some 'glarnies', larger and brighter than ordinary marbles, much to the delight of my brother who squatted nearby, watching me beat the boys and hugging my Topsey. When I'd cleaned out the opposition and we were about to leave, Jonesy and Freddie who lived in our yard began to jostle Frankie.

'Look at 'im. The silly little Topsey,' they taunted.

This angered Frankie who flung Topsey at me and jumped up so violently that one of his braces snapped. The other boys backed away apprehensively. They were alarmed because they knew what Frankie might do. He was a tough lad, not easily frightened, and on this occasion his tormentors thought better of their challenge and ran off, which was just as well because no matter what the result of the fight, their mothers would have got us into further trouble. Frankie never looked for it, he didn't have to, trouble found him. Frankie's annoyance subsided and then I noticed that he was shivering. His trousers were wet through from sitting on the moist pavement and he began to sneeze. I told him I thought he'd caught a cold and that, worse than that, Mum wouldn't like the look of his trousers. But he wasn't worried about that.

'Well, she ain't going to see them, is she?'

Nor did she. Each time Mum was about he contrived to face her and edge about backwards which aroused no suspicion because there was precious little room to do anything else in our tiny room. The following morning he was slow to get up, but when Mum called him the second time and warned him that she was coming to get him with the cane he responded. He looked very pale when he came down, but he assured me he was all right when I inquired how he felt. So off to school we went and after eating our school breakfast we parted to go to our separate classes.

Out of all the girls in my class I was the one picked to do odd jobs. I suppose I was thought to be trustworthy and reliable. Anyway, each Friday afternoon I had to wash out all the inkwells ready to be filled on Monday morning. I did other jobs as well, and the one I preferred was emptying the flower vases ready for the fresh ones our teacher brought each Monday morning from her garden. Secretly I thought it was a wicked waste to put them in the dustbin when some were still fresh and I sorted out the best ones and hid them behind the school door until it was time for me to go home. Mum was usually pleased with the flowers when I gave them to her for her to put in a jam-jar and stand them on the windowsill for the neighbours to see.

On this Friday afternoon I was taking the ink-wells to wash when I happened to look over the partition to see what Frankie was doing. As soon as I saw him I could tell something was wrong. He was sitting at his desk with his head on his arms. I was so alarmed that I forgot for the moment where I was and gasped aloud,

'What's the matter, Frankie? Are you ill?'

I dropped the ink-wells with a tremendous clatter, which I was oblivious of and strained to see Frankie whose head was being lifted by his teacher. My own teacher had come over and was trying to drag me away but I resisted her defiantly and remained looking through the glass partition. Frankie's face was covered with what looked like bright patches and he looked quite ill. By this time Liza had come over to see what the matter was and the rest of the class took the opportunity to break our regimented routine. They crowded round, standing on tiptoe, craning their necks to see Frankie and pulling faces at the boys. Liza and I were too upset to join in the noisy chaos. We were intent on watching Frankie who was being carried out to the corridor by the master. Our teacher was totally preoccupied, trying to restore order, so Liza and I took the chance thus offered to run out to where he was.

'What's the matter with my brother?' I wept.

'I believe he has a fever. Is your father at home?' he asked.

'Yes, sir, I think so. If he isn't, I know where I'll find him.'

'Run along then and tell him to come at once!'

I was off like a shot. I didn't need telling twice.

I only paused to pick up the flowers, then off I ran home, leaving Liza to wait there. I burst into the house, throwing the flowers on the table and breathlessly pouring out my story to Dad. He hurried along to the school as soon as he heard what was up and I trailed behind, trying to keep pace with him. I noticed that all the boys and girls were seated and quiet when I entered. The schoolmaster had a few words with Dad who picked Frankie up in his arms and then carried him home while I was sent to fetch the doctor.

When he arrived the doctor examined Frankie and said he would have to go to the hospital at once because he thought it was scarlet fever. We waited anxiously for the ambulance and I cried bitterly as he was driven off with Dad. I had to wait for Mum to come home and tell her what had happened, but she eventually came in just as Dad returned alone. I just sobbed as Dad told Mum that there had been no empty beds in the hospital and that Frankie had been taken to the infirmary instead. The worst news was that nobody would be allowed to visit him for a week, until it was discovered whether he had scarlet fever or not.

Dad called at the infirmary each time he passed on his way home from work to inquire how Frankie was. He was eventually told by the matron in charge that he had a very bad chill and that he still had to stay in their care for at least two weeks because he had a high temperature and other complications. I missed having Frankie around very much indeed. I prayed and cried for him every night.

When it was clear Frankie's illness was not infectious, Liza and I had to attend school again, but I wasn't able to concentrate on my lessons. Every time we went out into the playground the other children crowded round to ask about Frankie but Liza had to answer because I was so upset. I was glad when the following Friday, as I was gathering the ink-pots, my teacher put her hand gently on my shoulder and told me she'd given this job to Minnie Taylor. I wasn't sorry; it was a dirty job anyway and I always received a scolding from Mum when I came home with ink on my pinafore and all over my hands. I looked up into her glasses, perched on the end of her nose, and asked about the flowers. She looked surprised, but agreed.

'Yes, you may do that if you wish,' she answered kindly. 'And how is your brother getting along?' she added.

'He's still very ill, miss.'

'Never mind, we'll all say a prayer for him. Now run along and change the flowers.'

Off I went to pick over the flowers and discard the dead ones. I returned home with the others and gave them to Mum for her and Dad to take to Frankie with a get well note from me when they visited him on the next Sunday afternoon. On Sunday I waited at home and prepared the tea for Mum and Dad when they returned. When I looked out of the window, I saw them returning and Mum still carrying the wilting flowers. Why were they home so soon, I thought? I imagined all kinds of things had happened to Frankie in the few seconds before they came in and I was afraid of hearing their answer when I managed to ask how he was.

'He's been put outside on the verandah,' Dad replied.

Apparently he was very pale and the matron had said he needed plenty of sun and fresh air. When Mum had gone indoors the neighbours began to flock round, asking Dad all sorts of questions about Frankie and the infirmary and the nurses and if he had seen so and so in there. Dad elbowed his way through them muttering that Frankie was clean and comfortable. He never had much to do with our neighbours because he thought they gossiped too much, which was the truth, and on this occasion they wandered up the yard noisily speculating on matters of health and illness. With their shawls pulled tightly round their heads and shoulders they formed a ring, and I hovered on the periphery to listen to them, and you should have heard them, nodding their heads and thinking the worst.

''E ain't got enough flesh on 'is bones to keep 'im warm,' said one.

'Poor lad. I don't think 'e'll come out agen, do you?' said Mrs Taylor to Maggie.

'I don't know,' she answered, shaking her head.

'Oh!,' wailed another, ''e must be a-dyin'.'

I couldn't bear to hear any more from these ragged, ignorant women. The tears ran down my cheeks and I put my fingers in my ears and screamed at them, 'You're a lot of wicked old witches!' then ran indoors.

'What's the matter with 'er?' Mum asked Dad, and I told them.

When she heard what they were saying, Mum made to dash out into the yard but she was restrained by Dad who told her not to be a fool and that it didn't make any difference. Fortunately, when she did get the door open they'd scattered.

Not much was said that night. We had a late tea but I wasn't hungry and Dad didn't go out but read his paper while Mum sat stitching a patch on a sheet. After Liza and I had washed the dishes, I took my candle and went to bed and prayed as I had never prayed before.

'Please, Jesus, save my brother. Don't let him die and please show me a way to go and see him and also forgive these wicked people who are telling lies. Also forgive me if I have sinned. Good-night, O Lord, and God bless everyone. Amen.'

I crept into bed but I couldn't sleep. I kept thinking of a way to see Frankie. I knew children were not allowed in the wards but I also knew that Frankie would be missing me. Whatever would I do if he died, I thought. I imagined the worst. I felt so sad when I pictured him lying at the bottom of our bed. Then I pretended he was still there and I shook up his pillow and tucked him in. Just then Liza came into the room. She too was weeping as she knelt down to pray for Frankie. I looked at her with some surprise. I hadn't thought she cared, but apparently she did because when we got into bed we threw our arms round each other and cried ourselves to sleep.

Next morning, very early, I awoke and lay there puzzling how I could get inside that infirmary when suddenly I remembered the gully that ran along one of its walls. If only I could climb that wall I'd be able to see him and then he'd feel better, I said aloud. I told no one about my plan, not even Liza.

The next afternoon, when teacher let me out early, I made my way to the infirmary. Before I got there I remembered the flowers I was going to give Frankie and I ran home to fetch them. I was lucky, and there was no one in. I sorted out the best ones from the wilted ones but all I found were six daffodils. I didn't want to be seen carrying them because I'd be asked where I was going, so with them under my pinafore I hurried to the infirmary. I found the gully, but each time I tried to climb the wall I slipped back again, taking the skin off my knees. I made several attempts, but my clogs wouldn't grip. I took them off and walked along to where the wall was lowest and, leaving my clogs at the bottom, I scaled the wall in my stockinged feet. Then I was inside the grounds.

I could see several beds outside on the verandah, so I crept over and peered at the faces of the people lying there, but I couldn't see Frankie's until I came to the last bed outside the ward. I stood and looked at his pale face.

'Frankie,' I whispered. 'It's me, Katie.'

But he didn't hear me because he was fast asleep. I was just about to kiss him when a nurse appeared from nowhere and saw me.

'What are you doing here?'

I was afraid then. I threw the six daffodils on the bed and ran towards the wall. I climbed back over as quickly as I could, put my clogs on and ran home. I was disappointed but determined to try again.

The following afternoon I asked my teacher if I could leave early.

She said I might but only after I had got all sums correct. This seemed like an impossible task but with the help of an older girl who sat next to me I did. So off I went to try my luck again at the infirmary. First I peeped over the wall to make sure no one was about, then I took off my clogs once more and climbed over. I couldn't see Frankie anywhere and had no idea where he could be. I was beginning to worry when a young man in bandages on the verandah hailed me.

'Who are you looking for, my dear?'

'My brother. He was here yesterday and now he's gone.' I was almost in tears by now.

'Oh, you're the little lass that was here yesterday. He's been taken into the ward. If you peep round the door quietly before the sister comes you will see him. He's in the last bed on the right.'

'Thank you, sir.' I replied with pleasure.

I wiped my eyes on my sleeve, and peered into the ward. There were about a dozen beds on each side but Frankie's didn't seem to be there. Men and boys were sitting up in bed blocking my view so the only way to see if he was there was to pluck up courage and run down the ward. I saw no nurses or doctors about so I ran in. As I did so my stockinged feet slipped on the polished floor. I skidded, bringing a screen down on top of me. I struggled to push the screen aside and getting to my feet I saw that I was next to Frankie's bed and I slipped quickly in. As I pulled myself together I heard the man in the next bed say, 'Poor little sod,' and he smiled at me as I turned in his direction. The rest of the patients were laughing at my comical entrance but I only had eyes for Frankie, who was sitting up in bed sucking an orange. In my excitement to see that he was well, I jumped on to him, hugging and kissing him. He was happy to see me, too. But the sister and matron were not; they had come to see what the commotion was all about. They had to drag me away from him: I wouldn't let go. Eventually each took an arm and hustled me along the ward. As I was ejected, I could hear Frankie's voice. 'Don't worry, Katie. I'm coming home tomorrow.'

They pushed me outside without saying a word. It wasn't the way I'd come in, but through the front gates. I didn't care. I was happy now. God had answered my prayer and Frankie was coming home again. I still had to walk round to pick up my clogs from where I'd left them, but when I got there, I couldn't find them. Someone had stolen them. So it was with tears in my eyes that I slowly walked home in my stockinged feet. I knew Mum would cane me hard for this. I would make no difference explaining. Still, I thought, it would have been worth it, so it was an added bonus when I met Mrs Taylor.

'Whatever are yer doin' with yer clogs off?' She smiled when I told her what had happened. 'You'd better come with me and see if our Min' s old 'uns' ll fit yer before yer mum finds out.'

'Thank you, Mrs Taylor,' I said, and followed her.

She sorted them out from a lot of other clogs and boots in the bottom of her cupboard. I tried them on but they were too big, so she packed the toes with paper and that did the trick. Then she gave me a sweet and sent me off.

'Yer better get 'ome now before yer mum misses yer.'

I thanked her again and asked if she wanted any free errands run for her. I don't think anyone ever found out about the clogs: it remained a secret between us.

The next day was Saturday and Mum and Dad got themselves ready to fetch Frankie home, but at the last minute Mum complained of a headache and told Dad he would have to go without her.

'Can I come with you, Dad?' I asked eagerly.

'Yes, but you'll have to wait outside the gates, and you can't take that with you,' he said, pointing at Topsey.

I laid her down on the sofa and tagged along with Dad. He gave me Frankie's clogs to carry, wrapped up in an old comic while he took the clothes. He stopped to have a quick one at the pub, not long, though it seemed like hours to me. I kept looking through the door and calling to him to hurry, but he just ignored me. At last we were on our way and it was not long before we arrived. Dad took the clogs while I waited outside the gates. I walked up and down the pathway to keep warm. I felt tired and hungry but excited in anticipation of seeing Frankie. People passed in and out of the hospital but no one spoke to me. I wished Dad had let me bring Topsey, I thought, at least I'd have been able to talk to her. The waiting seemed to last for ages then eventually I heard the familiar sound of Dad's hob-nailed boots and the clatter of Frankie's clogs coming down the path. I ran towards him as he came through the gates. The visitors turned to look at us and smiled as I threw my arms round his neck and kissed him several times.

'Come on, don't eat him,' Dad said kindly.

I asked Frankie if I could carry his parcel and was curious as to what was inside. 'I'll show you when we get home.' he told me, winking.

It seemed a long walk home from the infirmary and Frankie began to lag behind. Dad looked back and when he saw how pale he was he put his hand into his waistcoat pocket, took out two pennies and we boarded a tram: a penny fare for him and a halfpenny each for us two. Mum was waiting indoors with a roaring fire and the kettle singing on the hob. She greeted Frankie gruffly.

'Well, and 'ow did yer like the nurses looking after yer?'

'Smashing! It was better then here,' he replied without thinking. Mum and Dad glared at him.

'Well, you know what I mean,' he added quickly.

'Yes, we know what you mean,' replied Dad.

As Frankie was untying his parcel I heard Mum whisper to Dad, 'We'll 'ave to get 'im a bed of 'is own now, 'e's too big to sleep with the girls, Sam.'

'Yes. I see what you mean, Polly!'

And so did I and I turned to him. 'Did you really like being in the infirmary, Frankie?'

'Yes, everybody was kind. I didn't have to bath myself and even the patients gave me sweets, fruit and comics. And the nurses tucked me up!'

I asked him what happened to the comics and he reached down his trousers and pulled them out.

'Put them under the bed with the others,' he hissed.

As I went upstairs Mum shouted, 'What 'ave yer got there?'

'They're only my comics,' replied Frankie.

When I returned, Mum and Dad had gone out so we sat in their chairs. They wouldn't be home again until late, so we kicked off our clogs and pushed our feet towards the fire. Then Frankie told me all about what went on in the infirmary. Frankie wanted to be a doctor when he grew up. I told him I thought that would be great, if I could be a nurse too. At least I wouldn't have to climb the wall to get in, I said, and we burst out laughing again at my antics. We were so happy to see each other. We wanted things to stay like that for ever. We had no idea then what the future would hold for any of our generation.

I told Frankie about the wilted flowers and the loss of the clogs, and then our elder sister came in. Mary picked Frankie up and hugged him. 'I'm so glad you're home again.' She had tears in her eyes: in those days hospitals were places to fear.

Frankie had never had so much fuss made of him in his life before. He was lapping it up. I asked Mary where Mum and Dad were.

'They're down the local. We're all going to celebrate your home-coming tonight, Frankie.'

'Where's Liza then?' I asked.

'She's down at Granny's but she'll be home later.'

She sat down in the armchair with Frankie on her lap and began to sing in that sweet voice of hers which we all loved to hear, except Mum of course, who was jealous because Mary could reach the top notes and she couldn't. She was too illeducated to know that Mary was a soprano and that she was a contralto. Mum was a good singer, but when she tried to reach Mary's top notes she made an awful noise. Mary stopped singing soon after because Liza had come in and she was always off key when she joined in. She too only had eyes for Frankie.

'Hello, are you better?' she asked, and kissed him too.

He looked surprised and so did Mary. They hadn't expected any fuss from Liza but I thought that perhaps she'd changed for the better. Then Mary began to tell us about what had happened to her when she'd been in hospital herself, but before she'd finished Mum and Dad stumbled in.

'You can all stay where you are,' Dad managed to say as we all jumped up in surprise. Then we all experienced something new. They stood up while we sat down. 'We're all going to have a sing-song tonight,' Dad said.

Dad gave us children some port wine and we all waxed happy and merry. Mary drank stout and Mum had gin. Dad poured himself some ale. Then we each had to sing in turn. It was only on very rare occasions that we sang together – at weddings or christenings and sometimes when our aunty came to visit us, which wasn't very often. On this occasion Mum and Dad were so pleased to have Frankie back that they declared a general celebration. Mum got out the gob-stoppers that were kept on the shelf for special occasions and gave one to Liza in case she joined in.

Mum did 'Nellie Dean', and we all joined in the chorus. Liza joined in as well, off-key. Mum stopped at once and shouted at Mary, 'Give 'er another gob-stopper. I don't know who 'er teks after. Not me!'

As Mary pushed it into her mouth, Liza grinned at Mary and sucked away to her heart's content. Mum gave Liza one of her hard stares before she started again. We all sat quiet while Mum finished her song, then Dad said it was time for Mary to sing a duet with him. She sang her favourite, 'Annie Laurie', and Dad harmonised. It was beautiful to hear their rich voices, Dad's baritone and Mary's soprano. When they'd finished, I asked Dad to sing my favourite.

'What's that?'

'You know, the one you sing in the pub, "A Soldier and a Man".'

I always called it 'my song' because I knew the tune and most of the words. I'd heard Dad sing it so often when he wanted a few coppers for a pint.

'Very well,' he said and cleared his throat with a swig from the bottle. Then he thrust out his chest and was about to begin when Mum's fist came down with a bang on the table, causing everything to shake and rattle.

'Now give order! All on yer, while yer Dad sings 'is war song.'

Mum sat down at once. So did Mary. Frankie and I were still sitting on the horsehair sofa and Liza sat on the stairs sucking her gob-stopper. Dad looked at each of us in turn, then rose to his feet, and with his back to the fire he began to sing. I gazed at him, fascinated. He gave the song all he'd got. I would have liked to join him but I didn't dare. I knew what Mum would do to me if I did, so I contented myself with listening to the stirring song.

'A solider stood upon the battlefield,
His weary watch to keep,
While the pale moon covered his mantle o'er
A soldier who needs a sleep.
"Ah me," he cried,
With tearful eyes,
As he called to God above.
"I am far away from my children dear
And the only ones I love."
But as the bugle sounds
He turns once more, amid the shot and shell.'

But he never finished the rest of the song that night. He said it was too sad and brought back too many memories. I always pictured Dad in the Boer War standing on the top of a mountain, alone and sad, and I loved to hear him sing because it always made me weepy. Dad's song ended our evening because Frankie and I were sent to bed. Liza was still sucking her sweet when she joined us soon after. As we climbed into bed Mum shouted up to us, 'Yer can 'ave a lie-in later, being' it's Sunday.'

Then the stairs door closed with a bang. Our privilege was a mixed blessing because if we made use of it we'd miss our meagre breakfast and have to wait until dinner-time to eat.

Next day we went to Sunday school. They were kind and asked Frankie if he was better, making a fuss of him and giving him sweets and cake. I could never understand why people were so generous when a person was ill and had such short memories when they got well.

Monday morning came all too soon and we had to return to school. I watched Frankie with envy as he cleaned his teeth and washed himself with scented Erasmic soap someone had given him while he was in hospital. I was proud, though, to think he looked and smelled better than anyone else in our school. We settled down into our different classrooms, but halfway through lessons I was eager to see how my brother was faring on his first day back. So while my teacher was writing on the board I tiptoed to the glass partition and peeped through. His teacher was making a fuss over him. I asked myself why he was having all the attention. I felt sorry for myself because I was always ignored. Then I heard my teacher's voice boom out so loud that it startled me. I walked slowly back to my place and sulked.

'Sit up straight!' she cried out. 'I'll settle with you after class.'

She turned once more to write on the board and I was aware of the class's eyes on me. It was then that I had an idea.

'I don't feel well,' I whispered to Nelly, who sat in the next desk.

'What's the matter, Katie! You look pale.'

I didn't answer. I just lay my head on the desk and pretended I was ill. I thought that if I could convince my teacher, I might get a little affection and perhaps go to the infirmary. I lifted my head and whispered to Nelly to tell the teacher I was feeling sick. I sprawled back on the desk and waited.

'Please, teacher, Katie's ill.'

However I began to be afraid when I heard the heavy tread of the teacher's feet coming down the classroom towards me.

'Sit up and pay attention,' she said angrily.

I didn't move a muscle. I meant to carry out my plan now at all costs but when she caught hold of my hair and lifted my head up roughly, I began to tremble inside. I must have turned pale in earnest then.

'What's the matter with you!' she asked sharply.

Then I put my hand to my forehead and lied for all I was worth.

'Please, teacher, my head and throat hurt.'

I tried to squeeze out a few tears but none came. I was even more frightened now, in case she found out that I'd lied. I must have been pale because the next thing I knew she called out to Liza to come to me. She saw that by now I was trembling all over but she did not realise the cause. I wished I hadn't started the deception.

'Take her home, and if she's no better your mother had better call in the doctor.'

With that she turned to the rest of the class and brought the cane down with a loud swish and screamed at the rest of the girls who'd turned round to see what was happening. It was difficult to remain calm and take no notice as I walked slowly out of the classroom with Liza. I must have put on a good show because Liza appeared to believe that I was ill and she put her arm around my shoulder and helped me home. She'd never shown such kindness before. I hoped Mum would be home and I was pleased when I could see the welcoming smoke from our chimney. Then I remembered that today was the day for scratching stew and I began to anticipate it with pleasure. When we entered Mum's first reaction was to ask why we were home so early. I just looked at her, feeling sorry for myself, while Liza told her about my sudden illness and being sent home to see a doctor. When she'd heard all this she turned on me and let fly.

'An' now what's the matter with yow? Don't yer think I've 'ad enough with yer brother being ill an' only one pair o' 'ands 'ere ter do everythink?'

Oh dear, I thought to myself, when's she going to stop. My head really was beginning to ache now and I wished I hadn't started this pretence. But I'd gone this far and had to continue. I began to whimper.

'My throat's sore, Mum, and my head aches.'

'Sit down theea!' she cried out and pushed me down into Dad's armchair. 'An' open yer mouth wide! Wider.'

Trembling with fear I slowly opened my mouth a little way as she returned with something from the cupboard. I regretted trying to deceive everyone, it wasn't worth the trouble.

'Come on, open up agen!' she screamed in my face as she leaned over me. I opened wide, there was no escaping.

'I feel better now, Mum,' I cried, and struggled to get up from the chair. But she prevented me.

'"Old 'er 'ands down," she told Liza.

Then I was told to open my mouth again as wide as I could but she had to slap my face before I'd opened it wide enough. I watched her make a funnel with a piece of newspaper; then she emptied some sulphur powder from a jar and blew it into my throat. I coughed and spat it out immediately but she made sure the second time. She held my nose with her finger and thumb, squeezed hard and blew down again. I had to swallow it this time. She blew so hard I was knocked breathless and I thought I was going to choke.

'That'll learn yer a lesson not to play the fool with me. Now get yer dinner 'an then get ter school before I blow some mower down yer.'

I couldn't eat a bite; my throat was really sore and felt like sandpaper. My head hurt terribly and I had to admit to myself that my plan had failed miserably. I determined there and then to run away from home and become a nurse when I was old enough.

Granny Moves In

Each Friday night Liza, Frankie and I had to stay up later than usual. This was not a treat, far from it. We had to blacklead the grate and the big, iron kettle that stood on the hob, as well as rub off any soot on the enamel teapot that stood beside it. On the other hob was a battered copper kettle which had a hole in the bottom; Mum never threw anything away. She said Dad would mend it one day, but he never did, and we still had to polish it. Jutting out from the top of the grate was a large meat jack which always held our stewpot. I called it a witch's cauldron. We had to scrub the deal-topped table, the stairs, chairs and the broken flag-stones, brown as they were from years of hard wear. The soda we used hardly touched them, the only things that were cleaned were our hands.

Standing each side of the fireplace were two wooden armchairs, one for Mum and one for Dad. We children were never allowed to sit in these unless given permission to do so, but we did make good use of them when Mum and Dad were out at the pub. Our usual seat was the old horsehair sofa under the window. Someone had given this to Dad in return for doing odd jobs. It replaced the old wooden one which was chopped up for firewood. Only the legs were spared because Dad said they might come in handy for something one day. Every corner of the house was cluttered up with odds and ends. Our sofa was moulting badly and had bare patches all over. We nicknamed it 'Neddy'.

Beside the table were two ladder-backed chairs, one for my brother Jack and the other for Mary. There had been three but after Charlie and Dad had a row over money, Charlie left home, and Dad burnt the chair. There was also a three-legged stool under the table; on its top stood our large, tin washing bowl. Set into the wall beside the fireplace was a long, shallow, brown earthenware sink. We only used this for putting dirty crocks in because we had no running water indoors. On the other side of the fireplace was an alcove behind the stairs door where the old, rotten mangle was kept; this was a permanent fixture. We had orders that if anyone called we had to leave the stairs door open to hide our laundry from view.

The fireguard, round the fireplace, was always covered with things airing or drying, especially when the lines across the room were full. Around the mantel-shelf was a string fringe with faded, coloured bobbles and on the shelf were two white cracked Staffordshire dogs and several odd vases which contained paper flowers and pawn tickets. Hanging high on the wall above was a large photograph of our granny. We'd have loved to have got rid of it, but didn't dare. When you stared at it, the eyes seemed to follow you round the room. The effect was heightened at night when the paraffin lamp was lit. This was the only picture in the room with the glass intact. Mum in particular objected to it.

'I carn't see why yer don't 'ave a smaller picture of 'er. It takes up too much room.'

'No!' Dad would reply. 'Nothing's big enough for my mother. It stays where it is.'

'It'll fall down, you'll see, one of these days!' Mum replied.

'Not if you don't intend it to. But I'm warning you, Polly!' He wagged his finger at her in admonishment. So there the picture stayed.

We also had to dust all the pictures and knick-knacks that hung over the walls. There were three pictures, 'Faith', 'Hope' and 'Charity', as well as a print of 'Bubbles' – the advertisement for Pear's soap – and many photographs of Mum's first-, second- and third-born, all dead and gone. Underneath these were the death cards and birth certificates of the others, and photographs of relatives framed in red and green plush. They were so faded you had to squint to recognise who they were. There were even paper mottoes stuck to the wall which announced such sentiments as 'God Bless This House' and 'Home Sweet Home'. I could never understand why they were there, our house or home was far from happy. They were supposed to be Christmas decorations but they were not taken down until Easter, when Mum folded them up and put them away for next year.

On the wall opposite was a picture of Mum and Dad taken years ago on their wedding day. Mum looked happy, wearing leg o' mutton sleeves with her hair parted in the middle. She was smiling up at Dad who stood beside her chair. Dad had one hand on her shoulder and was standing erect like a regimental sergeant-major. His hair was dark like Mum's and was also parted in the middle, with a kiss-curl flat in the middle of his forehead. His moustache was waxed into curls at each end. He held a bowler across his chest. Now as it happened this was the very same hat which had pride of place on the wall, just low enough for me to dust. One night I happened to knock this hat on the floor just as Mary entered. As I stooped to retrieve it she said, 'You'd better put that back on its nail before Mum comes in.'

So I snatched it up and, as I put it back, I replied, 'It's no good. It's going green. About time Mum got rid of it, like most of the relics here.'

'You'd better not let Mum hear you. She happens to be proud of that. It has a lot of memories for her.'

I went on working around the room; then I noticed that Mary was smiling. 'What are you smiling at, Mary?'

'Come and sit down and I'll tell you about it.'

I sat on 'Neddy', but before Mary sat down she peeped round the curtain to see if anyone was coming. Then she began her story.

'Now that billy-cock –' she pointed towards Dad's delapidated hat, '– that hat has sentimental value for Mum. About the time when she started having the family . . . I'll tell you all about it, but only if you don't laugh and can keep a secret. Every twelve months Mum gave birth to a baby and when it was a few weeks old Mum and Dad went to church to have it christened. They thought they'd gone on their own. They never saw me watching them. I used to hide behind the pillar.'

Her face was beaming and I was intrigued to hear what was coming next.

'Now when the parson took the child off Mum he'd sprinkle water on its forehead and then it would cry and water would come out the other end. When the parson had finished the christening and handed Mum the baby she'd sit down in her pew and change its nappy. Well, it was then that Dad was at the ready. Taking off his billy-cock he'd take out a dry nappy and put the wet one inside the

76

hat and then when he replaced it on his head, they'd leave the church and go in the pub to celebrate. You see I always followed them, just like you do.'

She gave me a sly wink and we both burst out laughing.

'Phew!' I cried, holding my nose.

Then she left and I finished my chores and although the house looked and smelt better it was not fresh air, it was carbolic soap and Keating's Powder. In the end I was almost too tired to crawl up the attic stairs and fall into bed. I just peeled off my clothes and was asleep immediately. I didn't even say my prayers.

Friday wasn't the only day I had chores to do. Saturday mornings was my day to get up early and be down to riddle the overnight ashes and place the embers in the steel fender ready to place on the back of the fire when it was lit. It was also my job to make a pot of tea and take a mug for Mum and Dad.

Now as the reader can imagine, Mum's temper wasn't always at its longest first thing in the morning. She'd yell at me, 'The tea's too 'ot!' or 'It's too cold!' or 'Not enough sugar in it. You ain't stirred it up!' She'd find fault with anything. This particular morning I was saved from her nagging, but only for a short time. Just as I was about to take the mug of hot tea upstairs, a loud knock sounded on the door. I lifted the corner of the curtain and peeped out. It was only the postman, who was a cheery man with a smile for everyone he met.

'Good morning, Katie, and how are you this bright, cheery morning?'

'Very well, thank you, Mr Postman,' I replied.

If only everybody in our district was as pleasant, life would have been much happier. He asked me to give a letter to Dad and returned down the yard. He'd only just stepped down from our door when Mum shouted, 'Who's that bangin' on the dower this time of the mornin'? Carn't we get any sleep around 'ere?'

She'd forgotten that she woke everybody, singing and banging at the maiding-tub at six o'clock every Monday morning.

'It's the postman, Mum. He's brought a letter for Dad,' I called back from the foot of the stairs.

I put the letter between my lips and turned to get the mugs of tea. It was then that I saw the postman standing under the window, shaking his head from side to side. I heard him tutting to himself as he walked down the yard. Mum shouted down again for the letter, so I hurried up to the bedroom where I found her sitting up in bed. I put the mugs down on the cracked, marble-topped washstand and had the letter snatched from my lips.

'An' about time too!'

'It's for Dad,' I said, loud enough to wake him.

'I know, I know' she repeated. 'An' where's me tea?'

'On the table,' I answered timidly.

I made to go downstairs, but she called me back to read the letter. Mum couldn't read or write. She couldn't even count, except on her fingers and then it always took a painfully long struggle. I always did any reading or writing when Dad wasn't about. Dad could correct my spelling because he was more literate than Mum and he spoke better too. I watched him stir and yawn as I fumbled with the envelope. I was glad he was awake; it was his letter anyway. But he waved me away.

'Oh, read it, Katie, and let's get back to sleep.'

I was anxious myself now to find out what the letter contained but when I'd opened it and read it there was no extra rest for anyone that morning. It was from Granny and although her spelling was bad I managed to read it out.

'"Sam an Polly,"' I read aloud, '"I'm not well in elth me ouse as got ter be fumigated The Mans bin an ses Ive gotter move for two weeks so Im coming ter you Ill bring wot bitta money I got an Im goin ter joyn the salvashun army an Ill bring me rockin chare an me trunk so Ill see yer all tomorra so be up early. Hannah."'

She didn't ask if she could come, she just assumed she could. When I'd finished reading the jumbled and nearly illegible writing, Mum jumped up with a start.

'Good God above!' she cried, waving her arms about. 'We ain't 'avin' 'er nuisance agen, are we?'

She glared at Dad, who was still lying on his back. He wasn't asleep. Who could be, the way Mum was raving? But he did have his eyes closed. He was thinking about how to deal with Mum.

'Yow asleep, Sam? Dain't yer 'ear wot I said?'

'I heard yer,' he shouted back and opened his eyes wide. 'The whole bloody town can hear when you start.'

'Well, what can we do?'

'It's only for two weeks. Nobody will take her, so we'll have to do the best we can,' Dad replied.

They must have forgotten that I was still standing at the foot of the bed. I watched them both lay back again and stare up at the ceiling deep in thought. Then suddenly Mum shot up out of bed. I'd never seen her move so quickly, nor look so misshapen as she did then, standing beside the bed in her calico chemise all twisted up in the front. I'd never seen her undressed before, or without her whalebone stays. She used to have them laced so tightly she used to look like a pouter pigeon with her heavy breasts pushed up high. I never knew how she got all that flabby flesh inside those stays. She looked so comical that I had to put my hand over my mouth to keep from laughing out loud. As she leant over the bed and shook Dad, her belly wobbled and her bare breasts flopped out of the top of her chemise.

'Sam!' she shrieked. 'Wake up!'

'Stop bawling. I'm not deaf.'

'I wanta knoo where 'er's gonna sleep.'

I thought it was about time to go downstairs before they noticed me giggling.

'Shall I go and make some more hot tea, Mum?' I managed to say.

Suddenly she realised that I was still there and she yelled at me to shut up and clear off as she tried to cover herself with her shift. This was the chance I'd been waiting for, so I fled downstairs, but still strained to hear what was being said.

'Now listen, Polly, and calm down. You know she'll help. She'll bring you some money for her keep and if you don't tell the relief officer we'll be all right.'

'But where d'yer think she's gonna sleep? She carn't sleep with us. It ain't decent.'

'I'll sleep on "Neddy" for the time being so don't worry about me.'

This arrangement must have pleased her because I heard a change in her voice.

'Orl right, just as yer like, Sam.'

Now the shouting had died down, I took two mugs of tea up to find that they were still discussing Granny. I stood the mugs on the table and stood anticipating the usual grumbles from Mum but she and Dad just lay there looking snug and warm. She pulled the clothes around her and turned to Dad.

'Do yer think the bed'll 'old us two? She's sixteen stone. I'm sixteen stone an' that meks us . . . er . . . er . . .'

I could see she was trying to puzzle out how many stones they would both be. Suddenly she sat up in bed. Sticking her two hands in front of her face and spreading her fingers apart she began to count. 'I'm sixteen and sixteen makes seventeen, eighteen, nineteen . . .'

'Sixteen and sixteen makes thirty-two,' I said, trying to help.

'I count my way then I know I'm right,' she snapped.

Dad lay back smiling and let her get on with it. Up went the fingers again and she counted on each finger again and again until eventually she yelled, 'The bed'll never 'old us!'

Dad and I collapsed in laughter as she tried with her hands to demonstrate the combined weight.

'Well,' Dad replied, still smiling, 'if you both come through the ceiling we'll have to do a moonlight flit.'

This was not the first time a flit was threatened, but we never did.

'Well, we'd better get up an' goo downstairs an' 'ave an 'ot cuppa. This is stone cold.' She handed me the mugs of tea which they'd forgotten to drink.

I found Frankie and Liza washed and dressed when I got downstairs. I was pleased because I could see that my brother had lit the fire and had put the kettle on to boil. Mum and Dad were not long following. We pulled our chairs up to the table and waited for our breakfast which turned out to be a burnt offering of toast; however, the tea was fresh, as I'd just made some more. Usually the leaves were used over and over again until they were too weak to stand the strain, then they were thrown on the back of the fire. Nothing was ever wasted if it could be reused, not even water or paper. We seldom had enough to eat. Sometimes we sat like three Oliver Twists, although we didn't dare ask for more. In fact, if we ever refused to eat anything that was placed in front of us, it was taken away and we had to eat it next mealtime, by which time we'd be so hungry we'd be glad of it. After our burnt toast, Dad told Mum to get the bedroom ready and he pinched her bottom as she rose from the table. She waved his hand away and warned him not to do it in front of us children. They both seemed happier. He pushed her gently up the stairs and turned to wink at us. I thought, if only they were always smiling or acting this way our lives would be much happier.

As we stood washing up the mugs and enamel plates we could

hear the iron bedsteads being dragged along the bare floorboards towards the wall so that Granny wouldn't fall out of bed. This was only the preliminary to a hectic tidying up operation and although we'd cleaned the night before, we had to get out the carbolic soap and begin again. Mum was always one for making an impression when Granny called, but I couldn't see why because Granny's house was far more cluttered than ours. Dad cleared out and Frankie and I were left singing as we dusted and scrubbed. When Liza joined in Mum yelled at her to stop her 'cat warlin'. I think she was expecting another gob-stopper but if so she was unlucky. We all fell silent and I thought maybe Granny would bring a little cheerfulness into our home now she was going to join the Salvation Army.

Very early next morning, before anyone was awake, I heard a loud knock on the downstairs door and before I could get out of bed a louder knock and three taps on the window pane. I woke Frankie and Liza with a good hard shake and told them what was happening. We three got out of bed and dressed quickly. Then we lifted the window to see what the racket was all about. As we leant over the window sill to look down into the yard below we saw Granny at the door, calling and waving her arms in all directions.

'Ain't nobody awake yet! 'Ave I gotta stand 'ere all day? I'm freezin' an' if nobody lets me in I'm comin' through the winda.'

She sounds just like Mum, I thought. Then, before anyone could get down to let her in, she tried to push up the window. Turning to the little man who'd brought her things on a hand cart, she shouted for assistance. He looked too scared to move. Then Granny saw the bucket of rainwater that Mum kept for washing her hair. She promptly tipped the water away and turned the bucket upside down. Then she pushed the window up and stepped on to the bucket to aid her entry. The reader can imagine what a funny sight sixteen stone Granny was, standing on a rusty old bucket. We were not used to the capers that Granny cut. Suddenly, just as she was halfway through, disaster struck. The sash cord broke and the bucket slipped, leaving Granny pinned half in, half out, by the window frame. She began to kick her legs in a vain attempt to free herself but she only succeeded in showing the neighbours her pantaloons. For the first time we experienced a temper worse than Mum's. She swore till the air was blue. Proof, I thought, that she needed to join the Salvation Army. Then Dad popped his head out of the window and called down angrily, 'You'll have to wait, Mother, while I slip me trousers on.'

When he came downstairs and saw the plight she was in, he lifted the window but he was too quick. Granny fell out backwards, rolled over the bucket and landed in a puddle of rainwater.

'An' about time too,' she bawled while he struggled to pick her off the floor.

'I'll get meself up,' she muttered.

By this time Mum's head had appeared at the window and the neighbours too were peering down at the commotion.

''Annah!' Mum shouted. 'Yer'll wake up all the neighbours.'

'Wake 'em up! Wake 'em up!' she shrieked, struggling to her feet.

She turned round and waved her fist at the amused onlookers and bellowed at them, getting redder and redder in the process.

'Look at 'em! The nosy lot of idle sods.'

All the time she'd been carrying on, the little old chap was standing still, waiting to be paid for his labours. Suddenly she turned on him, leaned against the cart and sniffed.

'Don't stand there all day. 'Elp me off with me trunk an' me rockin'-chair. An' mind 'ow yer 'andle me aspidistra.'

He couldn't manage the trunk nor the rocking-chair, but Dad soon came to the rescue. Meantime Granny felt inside the bosom of her frock, sniffed a couple of times and pushed a silver sixpence into his outstretched hand. He looked down at it disdainfully and mumbled a barely audible 'Skinny old Jew.'

'What did yer say?'

'I said, "Thank you",' he answered meekly.

'Dain't sound much like "thank yer" ter me,' she retorted.

Scratching his head, he wheeled his empty cart away and said to Dad in a louder voice, 'I feel sorry for yow, mate,' but Dad ignored him.

The neighbours closed their windows. The fun was over for them but for us the trouble was only just beginning. We dressed hurriedly and dashed down to see Granny. She looked huge standing beside the trunk. We hadn't seen her for some time and it was easy to forget her size. She wore a black taffeta frock almost to her feet, black elastic-sided boots and a battered black woollen shawl. Her lace bonnet, also black, was hanging from ribbons on the back of her neck where it has slipped while she'd been trying to climb through the window.

Her hair, too, was dishevelled, but what I noticed most was the large raised lump on her behind. I poked Frankie and he whispered, 'Ain't she got a big bum.'

'That ain't her bum. It's a bustle,' I replied as he started to snigger.

Liza too stared at Granny, but Granny paid us no attention until she suddenly straightened herself up to her full height of six feet, pulled her shawl around her and addressed us. 'Don't just stand theea gorpin'. Come an give yer ol' gran a kiss.'

I closed my eyes and lifted my face up sideways for her to kiss my cheek. She must have read my thoughts because she just pushed me roughly away, with a slap and bent to peck Liza and Frankie's cheeks. As I walked off clutching Topsey she asked what I was holding.

'It's the golly you made me, Granny,' I replied.

'I don't remember mekin' that.' She shrugged her shoulders and dismissed me.

'Now, now, Mother. You gave it to her last Christmas. You must have forgotten.' Dad attempted to pacify her.

'Er's always forgettin',' Mum piped up from putting Granny's plant away.

'Put the kettle on, Polly, and we'll all sit down and have a cup of tea.'

This was Dad's favourite tactic when he saw a quarrel brewing. He drew Gran's rocking-chair towards the fire. Granny sat down and rocked in the creaking chair. With hers in the middle and Mum's and Dad's chairs on either side of the fire-place no one else could feel or see the flames. I picked up Topsey and sat with Frankie on 'Neddy' to await my tea. When it was made, Granny's was the first cup to be filled. Then she took a sip and without warning spat it back out.

'What yer call this?' she spluttered, pulling a face at Mum.

'It's yer tea. Like it or lump it.' This was a favourite retort.

'Tastes like maid's water ter me.' Granny could give as good as she got.

We looked at each other; we all knew what Mum's tea was like. The pot had been stewing all morning. Dad told me to make a fresh pot. As I squeezed past Mum to empty the tea leaves into the spare bucket, I heard her whisper to Dad, 'Thank the Lord we've only got 'er fer two weeks.'

During Granny's stay the gas-fitters came to connect the place to the mains. We'd already had the enamelled iron stove and the gas mantle fixed to the wall weeks before. They'd also fitted a slot meter to the wall at the bottom of the broken cellar stairs. It was lovely to see the lighted gas mantle after the paraffin lamp. We still had to keep this relic, along with the others, in case Mum ran out of pennies. We also had to have a candle to light us to bed because, as Mum said, 'It's not safe to have gas upstairs.' I thought it was much more likely that she objected to gas in our bedrooms because she had candles free from Jack's works. He always brought a couple home in his pockets every night. He supplied Granny too. She didn't believe in having gas installed at all, and said, 'When I die I wanta goo ter me Maker in one piece, when me time comes!'

The following Saturday afternoon Mum said they were going to the Bull Ring to do the shopping. This was our marketplace, where everything was sold cheap. There was the fruit and vegetable market, the fish market, the rag market and the flower market, all next to each other; and on each side of the street were barrow boys shouting their wares.

Dad asked Granny if she would like to go as well, but she said, no, that it was too noisy, and that there was too much swearing for her liking. I could tell by the look on Mum's face that she didn't want Granny to go but Dad asked anyway.

'No. I can find summat betta to do with me time. Anyway I'm gooin' ter see the Captain of the Salvation Army,' Gran replied when pressed.

'Come on, Sam, before she changes 'er mind,' Mum said irritably.

As he was leaving the house, Dad said, 'Now if you kids behave yourselves I'll bring yer back a little present from town.' Then off they went, slamming the door behind them.

'Things must be looking up,' said Frankie, 'Dad's getting generous.'

'Well,' I answered, 'he's better than Mum.'

'Perhaps.' He shrugged his shoulders.

Granny put on her bonnet and shawl and went off to the Salvation Army Hall without a word to us. We were at a loss for something to do: then our eyes alighted on Granny's trunk. Frankie heaved open the rusty tin lid and we peered eagerly inside to see what secrets it held. We were disappointed to find only a pair of white pantaloons, a long, black lace frock with a bustle, a pair of button-up boots and a pair of whalebone stays like Mum's. We lifted them out to see what was underneath. It was then that we discovered Granny had been in the Army before. There was a tambourine, a uniform, and a bonnet with a red ribbon with 'Salvation Army' written on it. Underneath these was a bundle of old papers tied with string. We were about to start returning these things to the trunk when I hit on an idea to amuse ourselves until the grown-ups returned.

'Let's dress up and pretend we're in the band,' I said. The other two agreed.

Frankie fetched Mum's broom handle and tied the pantaloons on to it to represent a flag. Liza put on the bonnet and carried the tambourine and I put on the long black frock with the bustle. When we were ready we marched up and down the yard. Frankie waved the flag, Liza banged the tambourine and I dragged the bustle behind me. We sang 'Onward, Christian Soldiers' as we marched back and forth. All the neighbours turned out to see what all the noise was about. They joined in too. People sang a lot in those days. The children joined our band and we paraded up and down. Frankie's pantaloons bellowed out in the breeze as Liza's tambourine kept the beat. We were having great fun until Liza gave one hell of a scream, dropped the tambourine and ran into the house. Frankie and I were scared stiff, thinking it was Granny or our parents come home early. Frankie dropped the broom and followed Liza into the house. I tripped over the long frock in my anxiety to follow them. Everybody was giggling, thinking it was all part of the act. When I did manage to get indoors I saw Liza was standing on 'Neddy' still screaming and pointing at the bonnet. We couldn't understand what she was screaming about until she flung the bonnet violently at Frankie. I stooped down to pick it up when I was startled by a mouse which suddenly ran out across the floor. Liza was still hysterical but Frankie and I tried to catch it; the mouse was too fast for us. Like a flash it ran down a hole under the stairs and was gone. We must have caused quite a commotion because people had gathered round our door to see what all the fuss was about. They disappeared quickly enough when I told them what it was though. I couldn't understand why they were so squeamish; they had plenty of mice of their own.

We managed to quieten Liza down eventually. Then we packed Granny's belongings back into the trunk, but we had a good look to see if we'd left any other little friends behind. Then we fastened down the lid just as we'd found it.

Now perhaps the reader will remember what I've written about Liza telling Mum tales about Frankie and me, so we warned her that if ever she said anything about what had happened we'd put the mouse down her frock while she was asleep. Liza knew that whatever Frankie said he meant, so she promised not to say a word. We'd only just put the things away and set the kettle on the stove when the door opened and Dad walked in.

'Yer been good kids?' were his first words.

Frankie said we had, and warned Liza with a look.

'Well, here you are.' Dad handed me a box. I couldn't believe my eyes when I opened it. There, sitting on some straw, was a tame white mouse with tiny pink eyes.

'Oh, it's lovely,' exclaimed Frankie.

'Thank you, Dad.' I was overjoyed, but Liza didn't look or speak. Frankie stared at her in a meaningful way and she said nothing.

'You're not to let it out of the cage,' Dad told us. 'We don't want any offspring. We've got enough already.'

'I don't know why yer bought it,' Mum snapped.

'I didn't buy it. It was given me,' Dad replied.

'Hm . . . hm . . .' She obviously didn't believe him. 'I've 'eard that before.'

Just at that point I opened the cage to stroke it. Liza gave an enormous scream when she saw, and jumped on a chair.

'Don't be a babby,' Dad told her. 'It ain't going to hurt yer.'

'It ain't going to get a chance,' she retorted, climbing gingerly down from the chair.

I really thought she'd tell Dad our secret now so, as Dad turned to the fire to light his pipe, Frankie whispered in her ear, 'I'm warning you. If you let on, this is the one I'll put down your neck.'

She went pale and we didn't hear another word from her for the rest of the day.

'Where shall we keep it?' asked Frankie.

'We'll keep it on the attic shelf, away from Pete,' I answered.

We asked Dad what sex it was, but he said he didn't know so we called it Snowy to be on the safe side. Each night before we went to bed we fed it on breadcrumbs we'd saved and watered it on cold tea in a cocoa-tin lid. Frankie and I were so proud of our little pet and we showed it to all the kids in the yard, but we didn't let them touch it. As the days went by, Snowy looked well and happy running up and down his cage, standing on his back legs or washing his face; until one morning when we went to give him his tea and crumbs the cage was no longer on the shelf. There was a scuffle on the floor and there we saw the cage with Snowy still inside and Pete trying to get his paw between the bars. I shouted in alarm to Frankie but before I could rescue the mouse a clog came flying across the room. Pete was not deterred by this though. He only retreated under the bed from where he watched, ready to pounce again if the opportunity offered. As I bent down to reach for the cage I caught Liza out of the corner of my eye grinning all over her face. She lay back quickly and hid under the bedclothes. Then I guessed how the cage came to be on the floor. Frankie had guessed, too. He snatched at the cover and dragged her out and accused her. He was just about to strike her when we heard Mum's heavy tread on the stairs.

'What's all that racket and what yer all doin' out of bed?' she demanded. 'Get back, the three o' yer, before yer feel the back of me 'and!'

I crawled out from under the bed where I'd been keeping Pete at bay. Liza lay on the floor whimpering and although we tried to explain, Mum wouldn't listen. She made us bare our bottoms and slapped us hard and pushed us on to the bed. She seemed to have the strength of a tiger when she was roused. We were really scared and so was Snowy, who was running madly round inside his cage. We sat watching Mum nervously, wondering what she was going to do next. She struggled to get down on her knees to reach under the bed for the cat.

'Come on out. I know yer theea!'

But Pete sensibly stayed put. He was used to Mum's rough handling so he remained where he was hiding under our comics. However, after fumbling around she eventually managed to grab his tail. Then, as she tried to pull him out, we heard hissing and spitting. This had its effect on Mum who was afraid he would fly at her. So she let go and Pete, his fur standing on end, flew down the stairs. Mum heaved herself off the floor with considerable effort and, seeing Snowy's cage, she snatched it up.

'Not another word from any of yer!' she yelled, and with that marched downstairs.

We knew very well what Mum's temper was like and we were sure she'd get rid of the mouse. Without waiting to dress, Frankie and I ran down the stairs two at a time and peeped round the corner into the living-room. Mum was nowhere to be seen but there on the table was the cage with Snowy still tearing round inside it. Pete had also plucked up his courage to make another attempt to catch him and was sitting glaring at the mouse. We made a dash for the table but Mum must have loosened the catch because, when Pete clawed at the cage, the door flew open and like a flash Snowy fled down the same hole as Granny's mouse before either of us could grab him. I began to sob, but I stifled my crying when I saw Mum standing in the doorway. Silently she reached for the cane but we were saved from a thrashing when the door opened and Dad walked in. 'Now what's going on here?' he asked. 'What yer doing standing there in yer underclothes.'

We didn't get a chance to explain. Mum told the story her way and ended by pointing out the hole that our mouse had disappeared down. 'An' that's the larst of that,' she added. 'Yow never ought to 'ave bought it. I'll get rid of the cat as well, fer all the good 'e is.'

'All right. Calm down. Don't keep on about it. Anyway it'll be happy enough down there with the rest of them. And get back upstairs, you two, and put some clothes on before you catch yer death. Go on, GET!'

There was nothing else to do but obey, but as we climbed slowly up the steep flight Liza pushed past us on her way down, fully dressed.

'I'll pay you out for this, you wait and see,' Frankie hissed.

'It's all her fault,' Frankie grumbled as we were dressing.

I agreed with him, and tears began to trickle down my cheeks again.

'Even Granny pretends to be deaf when we tell her anything.' I nodded my agreement.

For weeks after, when nobody was about, we'd wait by that hole in the hope of catching a glimpse of our Snowy. We even pushed scraps into the hole so he wouldn't be hungry. Little did we know it was the worst thing we could have done. Still, we were happy knowing he would have Granny's mouse down there to play with. Each night I mentioned Snowy in my prayers and asked Jesus to watch over him because Frankie and I missed him so much.

Mums Decides to Take Us Hop-picking

Almost everyone in our neighbourhood thought it was best to steer clear of Granny when they saw her coming towards them down the street. She was a holy terror! But all the kids, especially her grandchildren, loved marching along with her when she was in her Salvation Army uniform singing in the band. Sometimes she let me carry the tambourine while she waved the banner and we all sang 'Onward, Christian Soldiers'. You'd have thought that Granny really was marching as to war'. Everybody looked out to see her with her head held high and her voice above all the others. She knew they were watching, but didn't care a jot, she just gave them a haughty stare and sniffed between hymns.

I was never able to keep pace with Granny's big strides and when I fell behind she'd snatch the tambourine from me and urge me on. 'Sing up, little soldier,' she'd cry and tap me on the head with the tambourine.

Soon, I'd grow too tired to stay in the band, and cold and hungry as a rule, I'd wander back home. On this particular occasion it was getting dark, and when I got indoors I found Dad dozing in his chair by the fire. There was no other light in the room, just the flickering flames of the burning coals. I tiptoed quietly towards him and whispered in his ear. 'Are you awake, Dad?'

He sat up and yawned. 'I've been waiting for one of yer to come and put a penny in the meter.'

I was scared to go down the dark cellar, but I asked him for the penny and tried to be brave. As soon as I reached the meter and heard the penny drop I was up those stairs three at a time. I lit a paper spill Dad always kept in the fender for lighting his pipe, then lit the gas.

'Where's the other two?' he asked, meaning Liza and Frankie.

'Still with Granny in the band,' I answered.

He twisted round in his chair and told me to get the bottle off the shelf and fetch him a pint of beer.

'And hurry yerself before yer gran comes home. You know how she sees the beer bottles about.'

'Yes, Dad,' I replied. He handed me tuppence and I ran off to the pub. The lamplighter was just about to enter and noticed me.

'That for yer dad?' I nodded. 'Very well, I'll get it, littl' un.'

I waited outside and kept a look-out for Granny but there wasn't a soul about. At last he emerged with the pint bottle. I thanked him and he gave me a humbug and told me to hurry home before the froth went off it. I hurried, but it was for a different reason. However, as bad luck would have it, I spotted Granny in the distance. My heart nearly stopped beating. I doubled back around the square to get indoors first. I stumbled inside the room, nearly dropping the bottle which must have had a good head of froth by now.

'Quick, Dad!' I blurted out, 'Granny's coming up the street.'

He snatched the bottle from my hand and took a quick gulp, then hid it in the sink behind the curtain. He flopped down in his chair and I sat cradling Topsey on 'Neddy'. We were both hoping and praying that she hadn't seen me, but she had eyes like a hawk's and must have spotted me in the street because she came into the room sniffing the air and made a dive straight for the sink, hauled out the bottle and held it away from her as though it were about to explode.

'What's this?' she cried out and waved the bottle with the remainder of its contents under Dad's nose. Dad just shrugged his shoulders and said it was cold tea.

'Don't yer tell me more of yer lies!' she shrieked. 'Yer wicked, the lot on yer. Yer'll never goo ter 'eaven. 'Ell's the place fer yow.'

She kept on and on, still waving the bottle at him. Dad let her carry on. He never said a word until she began pouring the beer down the sink. Then he lost his temper. Jumping up from his chair he stood beside her and shook his fist.

'Now look here, Mother, I've just about had enough of your tantrums. Now I'm warning you. While you're in my house you'll behave or you can go back to your own bloody house now!'

All the time Dad was shouting at her she kept marching up and down, waving her arms in all directions and knocking over everything in her way. I thought she was going out of her mind, but she stopped dead in her tracks when Dad caught her by the shoulders and began to shake her. When he released her, she straightened her bonnet and walked to the door with her head thrown back.

'I'm gooin' back ter the Mission Hall and pray ter the Lord ter wash yer sins away,' she declared.

'Yer better ask Him to wash away yours too while you're at it. Don't think I ain't seen yer sitting on the stairs having a sly drag from my pipe. Mission Hall my foot!' he shouted after her as she disappeared into the yard.

I felt sorry for Granny because I'd seen tears in her eyes while Dad was shouting at her, so I ran outside and caught her up.

'Where're you going, Granny?'

'In the churchyard an' wait fer me Maker,' she replied.

'Can I come with yer, Granny?' I pleaded.

'No yer carn't. Yer as bad as 'im for fetchin' it,' she said, pushing me to one side, and looking down her nose at me.

But that didn't deter me, I intended following at a safe distance. She turned down the street, passing the churchyard and the Mission Hall. I packed quickly into a dark doorway when I saw her look back. Then I couldn't believe my eyes – she marched straight into the pub! I was really surprised at Granny going into such a place, particularly after her recent argument with Dad, as she always condemned pubs. Anyway, I waited for about half an hour for her to emerge but I was shivering with cold, and when it began to rain I returned home to tell Dad.

As soon as I got indoors I blurted out what Granny had done, that she hadn't gone to the churchyard or the Mission Hall but to the Golden Cup instead.

'Yes, I know,' he answered calmly. 'She's there washing away her sins with gin.'

'But Granny's religious, Dad.'

'You'll understand one day. Now get the bottle and fetch me another pint before she comes back.'

Just at that moment Frankie and Liza returned home and Frankie volunteered to get it. When he came back, Dad gave us our lighted candle and told us to get to bed before Mum or Granny came in. We took our bread and dripping and did as we were told. We ate our supper as we were undressing and jumped into bed. I was too tired to say my prayers even. It wasn't long before we were all asleep.

Next morning I told Frankie about the quarrel and how I'd followed Granny and what I'd seen. But Frankie only smiled.

'She carn't help what she says or does. Not really. She's a bit doo-lally, tapped,' he said.

'What's that mean?' I asked.

'Don't yer know? It means she's a bit funny in her head.' He pointed his finger to his temple.

'I don't believe yer.'

'You ask Dad, then. Mum knows too. That's why she keeps out of Granny's way when she can. But you carn't help laughing at her some of the time.'

I couldn't see anything to laugh about and I didn't really believe him. I still made up my mind to ask Dad about it the first chance I found.

When Dad had an extra drop of drink he always talked to himself. Two nights later my opportunity arose. Dad was sitting in the chair by the fire dozing off, when I whispered nervously, 'Can I fetch you another drink, Dad?'

'No,' he mumbled between yawns, 'I've had enough tonight.'

I could tell by his voice and the smell on his breath that now was the time to ask about Granny.

'Why is our granny like she is? You know, quarrelsome all the time.'

I edged away from him in case I was sounding too inquisitive. He started to mumble under his breath but I couldn't catch all the words because he kept nodding off to sleep. But I nudged him and kept him awake.

'What yer standing there for?' he asked, smiling at me.

'I was listening to you talking about Granny. Did you have a dad?'

He stared hard at me, no doubt wondering whether to tell me about his family or not. He could probably see how interested I was, and after a bit he said, 'Make me a nice cup of tea.'

I made the two mugs of tea and watched Dad light his pipe, then he told me to sit on Granny's rocker. I was pleased with myself. I hadn't annoyed him and when I handed him his tea he told me the story in between puffs of his pipe.

'Now, Katie, I hope you'll understand why your granny is like she is. Your mum knows, but she loses patience with her. My father joined the Salvation Army band when we were very young.'

'Who's "we", Dad?'

'Me and my two brothers. Now don't interrupt.'

He stopped to yawn before continuing. 'He asked your granny to join with him but I remember her saying she didn't believe in "blood and fire" praying. She was just happy to stay at home and look after us. But one night he went out and never came back.'

He sounded sad and his voice drifted away and began to nod off to sleep again. So I gave him another nudge to rouse him once more and he opened his eyes blankly. 'Oh yes,' he said, 'you might as well know the rest. Anyhow you'll find out one day. Your granny went to the Captain and asked if anyone had seen him. But he told her the sad news that Dad had run away with a Sister called Agnes. My mother never really got over the shock. She loved Dad and so did us three boys. He was our only breadwinner and although the Captain came round to try and help us, yer granny was very proud and stubborn. She wouldn't accept charity from no one. So when her savings had gone she had to let us go to the workhouse. She even joined the Salvation Army and travelled from town to town trying to find him, but she never did.'

'What became of your brothers, Dad?'

'Arthur went to Australia, and George died when he was ten,' he answered sadly, and a tear appeared in the corner of his eye. I had tears flowing from my own and I couldn't ask him anything else. We were both upset but I hoped he would tell me more some other time.

'Now think what I've told you and be kind to your gran. And you'd better clear the table and get up to bed before she or Mum come home.'

I kissed his cheek after fetching him his tea and wished him goodnight. Frankie and Liza were still out playing so, as I had the bedroom to myself, I decided to say a private prayer. I prayed, 'Dear Lord, please find my Dad's brother and Father for Granny.' I also asked Him to make her better and help her mend her ways, then I crawled into bed and cried as I tried to picture my grandfather and piece together what Dad had said, but I was too young to grasp what it all meant.

By the following morning I'd forgotten the previous evening; it was Dad's pay night and he gave us each a penny to buy sweets with.

Dad and Granny must have settled their differences because they seemed to be in a better mood when we sat down to breakfast. Mary and Jack had already left for work when there was a loud knock on the door.

Mum jumped up from the table exclaiming loudly, 'Now who can that be this time a mornin'? Bloody pest, whoever it is.'

'Well, go an' see,' Dad told her.

Shrugging her shoulders, she shuffled to the window and lifted the curtain to peer out. 'It's Mrs Nelson, Sam.'

'Well, call her in then, don't leave her standing there.'

Now Mum was a real artist, she could change her mood whenever it suited her. She opened the door and greeted Mrs Nelson cheerily, 'Good mornin', Mrs Nelson. An' 'ow are yer? Come in.'

As she came in Granny called out, 'An' who's Mrs Nelson?'

'I don't think yer know 'er, 'Annah. This is the kind lady what organises trips an' outin's.'

'Oh,' said Granny, and carried on munching her toast with toothless gums.

Mrs Nelson lived over near the churchyard and did a lot of work for local charities. She was also better off than most and helped those in need. She was small and round as a barrel.

'Good morning, everybody,' she bellowed to us in her deep, manly-sounding voice.

We all returned the greeting, except Granny who looked up and merely grunted. Dad drew up my brother's chair and wiped it with his newspaper.

'Please sit down,' he said.

Mum smiled at her and asked if she'd like a cup of tea, 'just med it 'ot'.

'No thank you, I carn't stay. I have more calls to make.'

'Suit yerself,' Gran piped up, but Mrs Nelson ignored her.

'Would any of you be interested enough to go hop-picking for a few days in the country? I believe the change and the fresh air will do the children good while they're away from school. Transport's laid on and meals and sleeping accommodation's free.'

We all looked at each other, but I could see that Mum had already made up her mind. 'I'll 'ave ter let yer know,' she answered pleasantly. 'An' thank yer fer askin' us,' she added.

'I must have yer answer this evening at the latest,' Mrs Nelson told her, and then rolled out.

As soon as she'd gone, Mum turned to Dad, beaming all over her face. 'It'll do us the world of good. Don't yer think, Sam?'

'You can go, and the kids, but not me?'

'Well, yer carn't, can yer? You've got yer job ter goo to.'

Then, banging her mug on the table Granny exclaimed, 'An' who d'yer think's gonna look arta 'im an' me?'

'Now, now, Mother, don't worry.' Dad reassured her, patiently. 'Mary'll see to our needs. Anyway, it'll do us good to have a change.'

'Yes, you can come too, 'Annah. You can earn as well as mek yerself useful.'

Granny mumbled under her breath, but Mum ignored her and rushed out of the house without stopping to take off her apron or put Dad's cap on.

'I shan't be long. I'm gooin' ter tell Mrs Nelson we're gooin',' she called back over her shoulder.

While she was out Dad gave us three a lecture. 'Mind yer manners, and don't forget to address the farmer as "sir", and no climbing trees or scrumping apples. Anyway, I don't have to tell you how to behave. Yer mum and granny'll see to that. And, you, Katie, if you don't like it, just write me a note and I'll fetch you back.'

'Yes, Dad. But I wish you were coming.'

'Some other time. Anyhow, I might jump on the train and come and see how you're all getting along. The country air will put some colour in all yer cheeks. Now be off and play, the three of yer, while I have a talk to yer gran.'

He didn't seem too cheerful. In fact he looked a bit down in the mouth as we ran out. We rushed along the yard to tell the other kids we were going hop-picking with them. They'd all been before, either potato-, pea- or hop-picking, but this was a new experience for us. I used to envy the kids when they went away each summer and returned with lovely brown complexions. They always bragged about what good holidays they'd had.

All our neighbours and their kids were busy as bees, dodging from place to place, getting the clothes off the line and fetching their buckets and bowls from the wash-house. Everything in our district was done on the spur of the moment; you were never given a date. It was 'make up yer mind' or 'it's now or never'. That was why

Mum dashed out of the house the way she did. However, we weren't sure whether we were going or not until we heard Mum call us indoors to tell us we'd have to start getting things together for ten o'clock in the morning.

'She might have given yer more time,' Dad said.

'She couldn't, Sam,' Mum replied, 'Mr and Mrs Goode 'ad a bad cold an' she 'ad ter 'ave somebody ter fill their places.'

'Oh, I see, a makeshift. Well I hope yer know what yer doing. And I'm warning you – look after them kids!'

And so with those sharp words Dad went out, slamming the door behind him. Mum began at once snatching down the clean clothes from the line around the room and giving out orders to us to fold up what we needed.

'Come on, 'Annah, get a move on,' she shouted at Gran, who was trying to do her best but badly.

'Oh, back-peddle!' Granny shouted back, and threw down the towel she was trying to fold and stormed upstairs. Mum retrieved the towel and threw it to Liza.

'Silly ol' fool. I s'pose she'll tell yer dad I've bin on to 'er agen. Mek a cup of tea an' tek it up to 'er, Frankie.'

While Frankie put the kettle on to boil Mum handed me the list Mrs Nelson had provided, with all the instructions printed on it. First on the list was a towel, followed by soap, clean clothes, cups, frying-pan, bucket, bowl and other articles that we'd need. And underlined at the bottom was 'NO PETS, CATS OR DOGS'. We were happy tying labels on each article with string to identify them as ours. Just as we were doing this, Granny came downstairs.

'I thought we goin' 'op-picking!' she said when she saw the jumble of utensils on the floor. 'I ain't carryin' none of them,' she added, pointing to the bucket and bowl.

'Don't worry yerself, Granny. The kids will carry 'em.'

Just as that moment Mrs Taylor called in the door. 'What time are we going, Polly?'

'Ten o'clock in the mornin', prompt. An' if yow ain't ready, Mrs Nelson said she'll leave yer be'ind,' Mum replied.

'We'll be ready.' She ran off to tell the others.

While us children were doing our best to help, Mum was losing patience with Granny. She wanted to wear her uniform and take the tambourine along too. But after sharp words, Granny got her way.

I managed to smuggle Topsey inside the bucket and covered her with Liza's clean knickers. When everything was ready and pushed into a corner for us to pick up next morning, Mum flopped down into her armchair.

'I'm done in,' she puffed.

Just then Dad and Mary came in. I could see Mary was upset and so could Mum. 'What's the matter with yow?'

'Nothing's the matter with me,' Mary answered. But she glared at Mum. 'It's what's the matter with you. Dad says you're taking the kids hop-picking. You must be mad. It's no place for them.'

'Now, now, Mary,' Dad said calmly, 'It's all arranged, so calm down. Anyhow, I'll be able to get a bit of peace when they're gone.'

'They won't like it, Dad. They'll soon want to come back.'

'If they do, Katie will write and let me know. Now let's have something to eat. I don't want to hear any more about it.'

But Mary wouldn't have any supper. She gave Mum one last frozen stare and flounced up to bed. Frankie, Liza and late our pig's trotter and followed her. Mum was not the only one 'done in' and we soon fell asleep.

Dad, Mary and Jack had left the house early before Mum called us downstairs.

'Come on, get a move on. An' yow, 'Annah. Unless yet want ter stay be'ind.'

We jumped down the stairs two at a time. A few minutes later Granny came down already dressed in her uniform and bonnet with her tambourine clutched in her hand.

'I said I'd wear 'em, dain't I, Polly?' She grinned, and gave Frankie a tap on his head with the instrument. Mum didn't answer but Frankie yelled, 'Save it for the trip, Granny, we'll need a bit of community singing.'

We each had something to carry. I hung on to the basket and Frankie and Liza carried the tin bowl and the other odds and ends. Granny, true to her word, just carried the tambourine. We had our mugs tied with string round our necks. We each had the labels I'd written round our necks as well, in case we lost them.

After Mum had taken a last look around to see if we'd forgotten anything we were ready to join the others in the yard to wait for the cart to pick us up. With us was Mrs Taylor and the little twins, Joey and Harry, wearing their everyday suits which had been starched and mangled. Mrs Buckley was dressed up to kill in her dusty, black velvet coat with a hat that looked more like a plate of withered fruit. Every time she moved her head, I thought it would fall off. She had her eldest girl and boy with her who were busy scratching their heads. Then there was Mrs Jones and 'Pig's Pudding Face', her son. She was gossiping with Mrs Phipps who was one of Granny's neighbours. She kept getting out of line to show off her moth-eaten fur coat which she always wore on special occasions, no matter what the weather. This day promised to be hot, the sun was already shining and Mum saw an opportunity to get in a dig.

'Where yer think yer gooin', ter the North Pole?'

They all turned to stare at Mrs Phipps's coat, but she threw her head back proudly and breathed defiance.

'It's real skunk!'

'Smell's like it, an' all,' Mum shouted back in triumph, and held her nose.

'Yer only jealous!'

'Jealous? Of that? I wouldn't be seen dead in it.'

Just then Mrs Nelson intervened. 'Now then, you two!' she yelled out like a sergeant-major. 'Get in line, all of yer, and let's have some order!'

But they went on pushing and shoving although after a bit Mum's temper cooled off and she helped Mrs Nelson form some sort of straight line. Granny helped too by tapping the kids' heads with her tambourine and shouting, 'Get in line, little soldiers, get in line.'

Mum smiled at Granny and said, 'That's come in useful after all.'

Then Mrs Nelson spotted little Billy Bumpham and Maggie. She hadn't noticed him before, as he was hidden from view behind Maggie's large, battered and well-worn picture hat.

'In line, you,' she bawled, but when he didn't move she grabbed hold of his shoulders and shook him. As she did so his little terrier jumped out from under his coat where he'd hidden it.

'Didn't you read the list I gave out? No livestock!'

"E carn't read. Please let 'im tek 'is little dog,' Maggie pleaded.

'No. *You* know the rules even if 'e carn't read.'

As she walked to the front, Billy came running forward with the dog in his arms. 'Can I tek 'im?' he pleaded, pushing the dog into her face. 'Look, 'e's a nice little dog. Ain't yer, Rags? 'E'll be no trouble I'll promise yer.'

'I'm sorry. No.' She'd calmed down by now and told him that there were two sheep-dogs on the farm.

'You wouldn't like them to eat him for their supper now, would you?' she said kindly, but Maggie shook her fist and shouted, 'Well, if Rags ain't gooin', we ain't gooin'.'

'Please yourselves,' replied Mrs Nelson as Maggie and Billy walked off.

Everybody was feeling a bit down in the mouth by now because we all knew Billy would have entertained us after his fashion. Mum and Granny pushed everyone closer together and got us three to the front of the queue so that we'd get in the cart first. Just then we saw two shire horses pulling a farmer's cart down the street. I wondered how we were all going to get in but we did, with a squeeze. Mrs Nelson urged us to hurry and the driver dismounted from his high perch and tied the reins to a lamp post. He looked a typical farmer with a old dusty cap, corduroy trousers, a fat face and wiry, grey hair like a halo. He gave a jolly laugh and scratched his head as he spoke to us.

'Well, what a motley crew.'

He dropped the back end of the cart which looked like one I'd seen in a book describing the French Revolution. Some sat on the floor, some stood. It smelled like a pigsty and he apologised for not having had time to clean it out. I don't think any of us minded much really. We were all too happy to be on our way to the country. Granny was the last on board and stood looking at the cart sniffing.

'I ain't gooin' in theea,' she protested to the driver.

'Well, by the look of yer, you'd better sit up front with me.'

This pleased Granny. She beamed, but when she tried to climb up, she slipped backwards.

'Let me help,' the driver said, and got down to assist her.

'I can help meself up,' she snapped back.

Everyone was tittering as they watched her capers. Several times she tried to lift herself up into the passenger's seat, but failed.

'Come along, Grandma, we'll be here all day,' he said, getting behind her and heaving her bottom up with his shoulder. Eventually she flopped on the seat, and the farmer got back into the driver's seat. Granny gave him a dirty look for pushing her that way, but he just sat there gathering the reins and the whip.

At last we began to move. The rest of the people in the yard

waved us goodbye and shouted ' 'Ave a good time,' and 'We'll look
after yer animals,' and we in turn waved and shouted our farewells.
By the time we'd reached the end of the street we'd begun to sing,
even Liza. And Mum only put her hand on her shoulder and said,
'Yer'll 'ave ter yell, I'ain't gooin' back for no gob-stoppers.' Everyone seemed happy, even Granny who was banging her tambourine.
As we passed the Golden Cup the draymen rolling the barrels off the
drays turned and waved, and the shopkeepers swilling the pavements stopped to cheer us on our way. Even our local bobby turned
to smile as we sang merrily along into the unknown.

It seemed hours before we saw any country lanes or green fields
and, when we did, I thought it was a wonderful sight. I wished I
could go on riding forever. However, our journey nearly ended in
tragedy. As the horses trotted along, they relieved themselves and
Mrs Phipps remarked what a waste it was and how she could have
done with that on her window box. At this, Granny turned round
from her high seat to register her disapproval and was only just
saved from falling into the road by the driver grabbing her coat. He
pulled the horses up and after seeing that Granny was all right he
climbed down to retrieve her tambourine, mumbling grumpily all
the while.

By this time we were getting restless. Most of us thought it was
time we got down to stretch our legs, or that was what we said!
However, the driver wouldn't stop till we reached a water trough
where we could water the horses. Luckily we rounded a bend and
came upon a public house which had a trough outside. The farmer
spurred the horses on with the whip which made Granny hold on
for dear life, because when the horses saw the water glistening in the
sunlight they broke into a gallop, throwing us all on top of each
other. Mrs Phipps and Mrs Jones swore at the driver when he came
round to unfasten the chain, but he ignored them and dropped the
side of the cart for us to tumble out, much relieved, or about to be!
The little twins began to bawl as they'd wet their trousers but
nobody paid them any heed. They were too concerned to rush
behind a hedge to do what nature intended. Granny, I noticed,
looked down at us in disgust but even she had to join us eventually.
I saw the driver glance back and indicate to the boys to follow him
into the inn, but they couldn't wait either, and peed up the wheel of
the cart. When our immediate needs had been satisfied, we stood

around on the grass verge waiting for the farmer to come back. It wasn't long before I saw him returning, carrying a large enamel jug.

'Get this down yer!' he cried, and handed us the jug filled with cider. 'Then let's be going.'

Mum was the first to drink. Then the other women followed and finally it was the turn of us children. I noticed that the farmer didn't give the jug to Granny who was staring hard at him all the while. We kids unfastened our mugs from round our necks and had them half-filled in turn, but when Frankie's had been filled Granny snatched the remains of the cider from his hand and, pointing at her Salvation Army uniform, said angrily, 'Don't let these fool yer, mista. I've gotta swolla as well!'

And with that she emptied the rest of the jug.

Frankie was told to take the jug back to the inn and when he returned we were pushed back into the cart and Granny was once more heaved up next to the driver; and so we continued our long, cramped journey. I was hot, hungry and drowsy and before long I began to nod but I couldn't sleep. I was restless like everyone else. Joey, one of the twins, was tugging at his mother's skirt.

'I wants me titty. I'm 'ungry,' he protested.

'Later,' his mum snapped back.

'Gi' 'im some an' shut 'im up,' Mrs Buckley retorted.

Everyone was getting on each other's nerves. I looked down at Mum dozing on the floor with Liza's head in her lap, thankful that, for a change, she wasn't interfering with me. Then Mrs Taylor managed to squeeze down between Mum and Mrs Jones and, pulling the twins towards her, exposed her breasts for all to see. Harry decided he wanted some too and she lay there he and Joey helped themselves to whatever they could get. It was a pitiful sight to behold. There was nothing there to satisfy them, but they sucked away and hoped. After this slight comfort they fell asleep.

After a while everybody had dozed off, doubtless suffering from the effects of the cider. I strained to keep awake, because I was inquisitive to know what was happening and where we were going. After a while the driver turned the horses sharply to the left and they broke into a trot and we rocked from side to side. I held on to the open lathes until the driver pulled the horses to a dead stop and I could see we'd arrived at our destination. We were in a farmyard.

'We're here!' I screamed. 'We're here!'

There were ducks and chickens running in all directions to avoid the rattling wheels of the cart. I noticed the pigs and cows in the field had stopped to stare, wondering, no doubt, what was happening. We all tumbled out of the cart, dishevelled, dirty and hungry, with an avalanche of tin bowls, mugs and buckets. We were glad to roll out of the old jalopy after our tiresome journey. Mum, Granny, Mrs Buckley, Mrs Phipps and Mrs Taylor with the twins dragging behind made a dash to sit on a low wall that ran along the side of the farmhouse. Frankie, Jonesy and Annie ran off to explore, with Liza tagging behind. I was too bewildered to move. I'd never seen a farmhouse or a farmyard – especially one with live pigs! The only ones I'd seen were dead ones hanging outside the pork-butcher's shop. Then there were the cows, which I was pleased to see were in the distance because I was more afraid of them than I was of the horses. I watched the driver lead the horses to the water trough, then he went off across the field to look for the farmer. I was fascinated by everything. I spotted a water pump and realised how thirsty I was. I ran towards it, took the mug from round my neck and pumped for dear life. But when it came, the water gushed out so quickly that I was soaked to the skin. I put the mug on the ground and held my head under the tap so that trickles ran into my mouth. It tasted like wine. When I'd had enough I pumped again and again until the stone basin was full. Then, taking off my woollen stockings and clogs I stood in the water, happily bathing my feet.

I looked round to see if Mum was watching but everybody was fanning each other with their hats and paying me no attention. I was so happy jumping up and down in that cool, clean water that I didn't notice two black and white sheep-dogs and several ducks waddling towards me, followed by a lame pig. They'd decided that they were thirsty too. When I saw them I hopped out of the basin, afraid of what they might do to me, but they were friendly enough and seemed more interested in drinking than they were in me. So I helped them and pumped some more. Then suddenly they scattered. They'd seen the farmer and our driver coming towards us. I had no time to dry my feet or put my stockings and clogs on before Mum came running towards me.

'Goo an' find yer brother an' Liza!' she shouted, and pushed me along.

I ran down the yard. The cobblestones were hot and covered with the muck of farm animals, and I slipped as I tried to find the clear spots to put my feet on. When I eventually got to the end of the lane, I saw Frankie and the rest coming along.

'Come on, you lot!' I yelled. 'Mum's sent me for yer. The farmer's here an' yer know what that means.'

But they weren't interested in what I was saying. They were only interested in telling me where to go scrumping later!

Our First Day
in the Country

We all gathered round the farmer to hear our instructions. I realised from the likeness that he and our driver were brothers. Later, we found out that the driver had a farm a mile down the road. The farmer introduced himself as Farmer Onions which caused some tittering amongst the boys. Mum soon put a stop to that by giving them one of her black looks and raising her hand. But it didn't fall because the farmer gave a warning glance and told us to go and wash ourselves before going to the kitchen.

I'd never seen them move so quickly. We all took turns pumping, but most of them only splashed their faces. Granny was last but she was too busy shooing away the ducks to have much of a wash. Master Harry, Farmer Onions's brother, came over and told us we would find his brother a good man to work for if we did as we were told. However, he said his wife was a tartar who we ought to steer clear of. With that, he gathered his horse and cart and went on his way. We didn't see him until a month later under very different circumstances.

Farmer Onions emerged from the house just then and told us our meal was ready. We followed him into the kitchen where the first thing we saw was a large, stony-faced woman of middle age staring through us all as if we weren't there. But she couldn't outface Mum who went boldly up to her and, putting on her best tone of voice with aitches in the wrong places, said, 'Good hafternoon, Mrs Honions.'

Jonesy started to giggle. 'What's the matter with 'er? Showing off agen? Silly old fool.'

His answer was a resounding slap across his face from his mother. Mrs Onions said nothing, but her eyes spoke volumes. She beckoned us to follow her into a larger kitchen where we could smell bread baking. I glanced around and saw several hams and strings of onions hanging from the ceiling. The shelves around the kitchen were full of all kinds of stone jars of homemade jams, honey and preserves, labelled with dates written on. There were slabs of cheese and butter and lots of other good things to eat. In the middle of the red-tiled floor stood a white wooden table with cheese scones, chunks of new bread, butter, pickled onions, cakes and buns together with a large jug of cider. We stood drooling as we waited for the word to start. First, Mrs Onions dragged a long wooden form from beside the wall and gave the boys an icy stare. They understood and jumped to help her. At last in a gruff voice she spoke.

'Be yer gypsies?'

'No, we ain't!' piped up Granny and gave her a filthy look.

'Well, whatever yer be, I hope yer be better than the others we've had here.'

We all wished she'd hurry up and tell us to sit down and eat, but Granny would have the last word.

'What yer staring at? Me uniform? Or me? 'Cos I'm as good yow any time!'

'Now, now, 'Annah. Mrs Onions is only being kind,' Mum chimed in.

Mrs Onions said no more but beckoned us to be seated and left us to help ourselves.

'An' about time too,' Granny said ungratefully.

We all made a mad dash for the food. We didn't even wait to sit down. We were ravenous, for we hadn't eaten all day and it was now late afternoon. We soon made up for lost time, though. What we couldn't eat we filled our pockets with for later. Mrs Taylor even found room for some down the twins' trousers.

Shortly after we'd cleared the table, except for a few crumbs. Mrs Onions came back carrying a large enamel jug of warm milk, straight from the cow. It was delicious. I'd never tasted anything like it before, neither had the twins. Their mother had to take it away from them when she thought they'd had enough, but they wouldn't let go until she had given them a couple of smacks. The farmer's wife looked on and frowned as she stood beside the table with her arms folded across her heavy bosom.

'Well if yer be ready, farmer is outside waiting to give ye all the instructions.'

We all filed out. I was fascinated by the kitchen and the food and because I was looking round I was the last to leave. Just as I was going through the door I turned round and looked into that stern face and said, 'Thank you, Mrs Onions,' and ran out scared.

The farmer gathered us altogether and asked us all if we'd had enough to eat.

'Yes, sir. Thank you, sir,' we chorused.

'Now it's too late to go picking tonight so I want each of yer to take a sack, and two for you,' he said, pointing to Mrs Taylor who had the twins. 'Then follow me.'

We picked up our sacks from a pile that stood against a wall and followed behind. Frankie and I looked at each other wondering where he was taking us. We had the idea we'd be sleeping on the logs in the farmhouse, but he was leading us to a large barn across the meadow. Inside it was very warm and stuffy. There was only one small window to let in the light, which was dusty and dirty and covered with cobwebs. At the top end of the barn were piles of clean straw, a broom and a long, heavy rake. There was also a clock and a ladder which hung from hooks on the wall. Overhead was a loft with more hay and straw.

'Now, Sunny Jims,' the farmer yelled out to Frankie and Jonesy, 'get the broom and clear a space for yer mothers and fill yer bags with straw.'

They fetched the broom and swept the dust from the stone floor into the corner while the others began filling their sacks. We were bustling about merrily until Granny turned to the farmer.

'What's the bags gotta be filled for?'

'They're yer sleeping bags to sleep on,' He snapped. 'An' that's where yer sleep!' he added, pointing to the bare floor and snatching the broom from Jonesy who was leaning on it like a crutch. But Granny grabbed it from him at once.

'I ain't sleepin' on no straw. I'm gooin' 'ome.'

'Please yerself, old woman,' he answered, and walked out and left us to our fate.

This was our first disappointment. We all thought we were to sleep in the house but we were a long way from the farmhouse and miles away from home. I was getting homesick already. I wanted to see Mary, Jack and my dad and all my friends I had left behind. This was the first time in my life I'd been away from home. But I tried not to dwell on these thoughts and busied myself helping people fill their sacks. It was too light to sleep, although Mrs Taylor had already bedded the twins down, fully clothed, and they were soon asleep. I sat on my straw bed beside them and remembered what Dad said before we left.

'Yes,' I said to myself. 'I'll write tonight when they're all asleep and I can post it in the morning.'

Suddenly I heard Granny throw her tambourine at a mouse that scurried across the corner where the rubbish had been swept.

'I never ought to "a' come,' she sobbed.

Mrs Jones and Mrs Phipps went over to her and tried to comfort her, but she pushed them away.

'It's all yower fault. Yower used ter this. I ain't!'

They shrugged and left her to it, but Mum managed to calm her down by telling her that things would seem better in the morning and that the country air would do us all good. I hoped so too. However, as it turned out things didn't get better. In fact they got worse from that night onwards. By this time it was six o'clock by the dusty clock on the wall and the sun still hadn't set. We'd all been so busy picking out our places to bed down that we'd forgotten we still had our hidden surplus food. Then Mum took charge and called us together, all except Granny, who was snoring loudly.

'Now,' Mum began, sitting on an upturned bucket, 'I want yer all ter be 'ave yerselves, an' let's 'ave no mower arguments.'

I smiled to myself for it was always Mum who started the arguments and the present occasion was no exception. She stood up and went across to Mrs Phipps and Mrs Jones who were always in league together.

'I wanta ask yow two what 'appens now?'

'Whatya mean, Polly?' returned Mrs Phipps.

'Yow know what I mean!' Mum flared. 'Yow've both bin 'op-pickin' before, ain't yer?'

'Yes, but not on this farm,' answered Mrs Jones meekly.

'But yer know the ropes, don't yer?' Mum snapped angrily. 'What I mean is, when do we start eatin'? An' 'ow do we get our grub?'

'The farmer will tell yer that when he wakes us up in the mornin'. I know we'll 'ave ter mek our own tea an' buy our vittles from the stores.'

'What with?' Mum interrupted sharply, losing her temper.

'With the money we earn pickin' the 'ops,' Mrs Jones yelled back equally annoyed. 'An' if yer wanta know any mower ask the farmer!'

Mum cooled down for a while, but not for long.

'Don't we get any grub from the farm'ouse?'

'Oh, no,' Mrs Phipps replied. 'Only yer first meal, what we've already 'ad.'

Mum looked amazed. So did Mrs Taylor. Then all of a sudden Mum burst forth, hands on hips.

'Then in that case yer betta empty yer pockets an' let me 'ave the grub yow all 'elped yerselves to.'

'What d'yow want it for?' Mrs Phipps ventured meekly.

'What d'I want it for?' Mum was getting angrier. 'It's to keep it safe in case we goo 'ungry.'

'Why carn't we keep it?' asked Mrs Buckley, who'd been quiet until now.

'No! An' above all not yow!' Mum snapped back.

'Oh, very well,' she grumbled. And she began to empty her pockets.

'An' the other one!' Mum said waiting beside her.

Reluctantly she emptied them both and so did Mrs Jones and Mrs Phipps, for they were really afraid of Mum. We were hoping she'd let us keep ours, but she didn't wait to ask us; She helped herself. When she'd collected the broken buns, cakes and lumps of cheese, she placed them on a towel which she'd laid on the floor. Then Mrs Phipps piped up, 'What about Mrs Taylor and 'Annah?'

'Gimme time. I'm coming to them next,' Mum snapped back.

She went across to Granny who was still snoring on her straw bed. She bent down quietly to see if she was really asleep. Then, she lifted Granny's frock and from the secret pockets sewn inside she took lumps of cheese, buns, cakes and a lump of butter. Granny had good pickings. I sat with bated breath in case Granny woke up and caught Mum robbing her of her treasures. However, Mum took everything and then pulled down Granny's frock, and Granny still continued snoring. Then Mrs Taylor handed Mum her share but Mum told her to keep it.

'Yow keep yowers. Yer'll need it fer the babbies.'

'Thank yer, Polly,' she replied and after putting the food in a box, she lay down beside the twins.

Then Mum gave Granny a couple of pokes and rolled her on to her side to stop her from snoring. It didn't work for long.

Mrs Taylor was a meek and mild woman and always fell in with other people's plans whether they suited her or not. So Mum knew she'd have no trouble there. Freddie and Annie Buckley were timid too, and scared of their mum and ours, but when they were out with us they let themselves go. However, I couldn't abide Jonesy or Pig's Pudding Face. He was cheeky and always swearing. The twins were different, though. I loved them. They were only a little over three years old and although Joey was bow-legged and Harry was cross-eyed I took them nearly everywhere with me.

We pushed all our utensils into a corner until we'd sorted ourselves out and, while I was shaking out the worn, grey army blankets to cover us, everyone shook out their straw beds.

'Frankie, bring me that bucket an' bowl,' called Mum.

Suddenly I thought of Topsey hidden beneath the clean knickers inside the bucket. Before Mum saw me I snatched her out but then Jonesy grabbed the bucket and bowl and threw them across the floor to Mum. They clattered to her feet and Jonesy shouted, ''Ere y'are, yer greedy old sod!'

At this Frankie gave him such a hard clout that he fell over backwards, nearly landing on top of Granny.

'Shut yer mouth, Pig's Pudding Face!'

This started a wrestling match. His mother didn't take an eyeful of notice, but Mum came to the rescue at once and parted them. As she did so, she gave Jonesy a sly dig in the ribs with her elbow.

'That's fer yer cheek,' she hissed in his ear.

Just then Granny woke up and moaned about getting no sleep and the twins began to cry. I lay down beside them and gave them my Topsey to hug it and it wasn't long before they dropped off to sleep again. I sat up and watched Mum untie the bowl from the bucket. All eyes were on her. She was in a real temper and doing things at double pace. She threw the clean knickers across to Liza who could take the credit for thinking of packing them. Then she gathered all the broken food together and rolled it up in a towel, placed it in the bowl and stood the bowl in a corner of the barn, away from us all. She took the bucket and placed it upside down over the bowl of food. Next she marched off into the yard and returned a few minutes later with the biggest and heaviest stone she could carry. This she dropped heavily on top of the bucket. Then she slapped her hands together with satisfaction.

'That'll keep the grub safe from the rats until we need it.'

We all smiled at Mum's performance, and she smiled too when she surveyed her handiwork.

'Now I think we all gotta goo out an' explore. It's too light yet an' too early ter get ter bed.'

Granny was first to respond, for she was wide awake now.

'Yow ain't leavin' me be'ind.'

Mrs Taylor said she couldn't leave the twins in case the rats nibbled them.

'Rats don't eat everything that's moovin',' Granny replied. 'Any'ow, what's the other kids dooin'? Carn't they mind 'em?'

So us kids were left behind to look after them. In any case we all knew where our mums were going to 'explore'. They were looking for the nearest pub which, as it turned out, was the one our driver had stopped at earlier, the Pig and Whistle.

Granny, still clutching her tambourine, marched out on Mum's arm. I'd hoped she'd leave it behind so that I could play with it and use it to scare the rats and mice away. But I had to settle for a rake to shake at them. Mrs Jones and Mrs Phipps followed them out with their heads together and fell in step with Mrs Buckley and Mrs Taylor. They soon caught Mum and Granny up and I watched them all go arm in arm down the lane and out of sight. After they'd gone the boys decided they were going to scrump some more apples. This left only Liza, the twins and myself. So Liza and I decided to look around outside while the twins were asleep. It was still very light. According to the clock, it was seven o'clock, so there was plenty of time to explore.

When we got outside we noticed a large shed with a stove-pipe coming out of the roof. We looked inside and saw a rusty, round iron stove in the middle of the floor. Against the wall was an old, worn, marble-topped table and an earthenware sink like ours at home. In the opposite corner were a lot of baskets piled one on top of the other. There was dust and bits of straw everywhere. Someone had been here recently, as the kettle on the stove was still warm and there were half-burnt pieces of wood in the tin at the bottom.

'This must be the place where we've got to cook our meals,' I said to Liza.

'Well, let's clean it up,' she replied.

Liza began sweeping and I looked around and found a rusty tin bowl behind some baskets, and a wet rag, and then ran down the yard to the pump. I kept my eyes on the cows across the meadow while I filled the bowl and then hurried back. When we'd finished sweeping the dust away, we decided we'd better look for Frankie and the others. However, I remembered the twins and decided to stay with them while Liza went off. The twins were still sleeping, and I was scared to be left on my own, and was startled by noises like the rustle of Woodbine packets in the rubbish so it was with great relief that I heard Frankie and the rest running along the gravel path. I was never so happy to see them and threw my arms round my brother and burst into tears.

'What yer cryin' for?' he asked. 'Look what I brought yer.'

I wiped my eyes on the back of my hand and watched him pull up his gansey to reveal several red, waxy apples. His pockets were bulging fit to burst. The others had plenty too, which they shared out. What we couldn't eat there and then we hid under our straw beds for later.

By this time it was beginning to grow darker. The night was very warm and still, and Liza said she thought we were in for a storm. We searched around and found a piece of candle but we had no matches. I started to get nervous again and imagined all sorts of things that could happen to us. Then I heard the sound of heavy footsteps on the path outside. I crouched behind Frankie who'd taken hold of a rake in readiness. At that moment a deep voice boomed out, and into the barn strode the farmer.

'No need to be afraid of me. I've brought you a lamp.'

We watched him light it and climb the ladder to fix it high on the wall, out of reach. Then he asked where our mothers were.

'Gone for a walk,' Frankie replied quickly.

'Well, Sunny Jims, tell yer mums or whoever's in charge, there's only enough paraffin in the lamp to last another two hours. See you're all up early in the morning,' he said abruptly. He paused as he went off and called back, 'I see someone's been busy in the shed next door. And mind yer all behave until yer mums get back.' Then off he went into the darkness.

We could only just see our beds in the dim light. I glanced up at the clock again. It said five past nine and Frankie, Liza, Annie and

Jonesy had all stretched out for the night, fully clothed. I was hoping and praying Mum and the others would return soon. I was so afraid I dared not go near the door to listen for them now that the others had gone to sleep. So after a while, tired of listening for any kind of sound outside, I lay down beside the twins hugging Topsey for comfort. As I nodded in the dim light, all I could hear was the tick of the clock and the rustle of paper beneath the rubbish. I suppose I dozed off at last. Suddenly I was awake again, and could hear voices in the distance. Plucking up courage, I got up and felt my way quietly to the door. I opened it a little way and put my head outside into the darkness. To my great relief I heard Mum's voice singing above all the others.

'My ole man says folla the band', rang out, followed by a chorus of 'An' don't dilly-dally on the way.' I could hear Granny's tambourine distinctly, keeping the beat. They were all drunk; I could tell by the way they were all laughing. I'd been amused by their capers when I was younger, but now I was nearly ten years old, and I no longer found them funny. They all looked stupid, and I hated to see people like this, especially Mum.

I quickly rushed back inside the barn and lay on my straw bed, pretending to be asleep, because I knew if Mum found me awake she'd have pestered me with all kinds of questions and given me odd-jobs to do. I wasn't going to tell her how long the paraffin in the lamp would last. Fortunately, there were no arguments. They were all too drunk even to undress and they just picked their places and went to sleep.

Mum lay at the top end of the barn, Granny next, then Mrs Phipps, Mrs Jones and Jonesy, Mrs Buckley and Annie and Freddie, Frankie and Liza, Mrs Taylor and the twins, and finally me. It was very warm and stuffy and there seemed to be no air at all. I closed my eyes and tried to sleep but Mrs Taylor woke me up to look at the twins who were still asleep. Then she turned over on to her side and it was not long before she too was snoring. I wept. I felt so unhappy and miserable. I wanted to be home with my dad and Mary. Then I remembered what Dad had said to me about writing. I determined to write a letter and with that thought in mind I felt better and, hugging Topsey, I fell asleep.

I was woken by a loud crash of thunder and several flashes of lightning which illuminated the whole barn. Mrs Phipps and Mrs

Jones sprang up at once. Mrs Jones was evidently frightened because she ran round the barn crying and crossing herself.

'Mother of God, save us all!'

'Shut up, yer stupid fool. Yer wanta wake up all the rest?' yelled Mrs Phipps.

'Let's get some sleep! We gotta goo ter work in the mornin',' Mrs Buckley cried out and pulled Mrs Jones back on the bed.

Everybody was restless now. They tossed and turned but eventually when the thunder died away they all fell sound asleep again. Mum and Granny took up their snoring in contest where they'd left off and I lay back with an arm across the twins and tried to sleep. However, the storm returned with a vengeance. There was lightning and thunder, and hailstones that hit the corrugated roof so hard that I thought it would fall in. Mrs Taylor was wide awake now, and I was very happy to hear her voice.

'You afraid, Katie?'

'Yes,' I replied. And I meant it.

'Never mind. You'll feel betta in the mornin'.'

There was another loud crash and a third which seemed to shake the barn – at that point everybody woke up. I watched Mum between the flashes of lightning as she fumbled around for the candle and matches. Swearing, she lit the candle and placed it on the stone that stood on the bucket. Granny too was cursing and saying she wished she hadn't come. Mrs Phipps were feeling all over her body to find her sleeping pills.

'I know I 'ad 'em. Yow seen 'em, Mrs Buckley?'

'No! But I could do with one meself.'

'I'll gi' yer all one when I can find 'em. Then p'raps we can all get some sleep.'

'That's a good idea,' Mum said, and joined in the search.

Frankie and Liza got up and took the ladder down from the wall, propped it against the loft and climbed up into the darkness out of everybody's way. Then, after knocking the candle over and nearly setting fire to the straw, Mum found the bottle of sleeping pills.

'I'll tek charge of these,' Mum said. 'Or you might tek too many. Anybody like one?'

So Mrs Buckley had one, Mrs Jones followed suit and so did Mrs Phipps, but Granny refused. She said she wanted to 'die natural'.

Then Liza shouted down from the loft, 'Can I 'ave one?'

'I know what you'll get one of if yer don't goo back ter sleep!'
Mum shouted back crossly.

Mrs Taylor didn't want one in case she was asleep when the twins
needed her. Mrs Phipps was watching Mum hide the bottle down
the front of her blouse but she couldn't argue with her because
Mum's word was law. She stepped over everyone and blew out the
candle and lay down once more. After a while the storm abated and
all that I could hear was the sound of snoring once more. I lay there
thinking about Dad and what I should put in the letter, and what
with these things on my mind, the heat and the lack of air, I couldn't
sleep until Mrs Taylor turned over and whispered that she'd open
the barn door to let a little cool air in. I didn't answer, but she knew
that I was awake. She opened the door a few inches and lay down
again with a sigh. Soon she too was snoring and with the light
breeze on my face I finally drifted into an exhausted sleep.

Settling In

It was just breaking dawn when I heard a cock crowing in the distance. I sat up and rubbed my eyes and looked up into two big brown doleful eyes looking down at me. I fell back and screamed for all I was worth, waking everybody. Mum was the first to my rescue, treading over everyone, before she could push the cow through the door. But it wouldn't leave. I clung to Mrs Taylor who was guarding the twins. She was as scared as I was. We stared, horrified, as Mum tried to get the cow to budge but it only glared at her and mooed loudly. I started to cry, trembling with fear.

'Shut yer blartin'!' Mum yelled, and began rolling up her sleeves as if she really meant business. 'I'll soon settle 'im.'

She wasn't afraid of the cow but nor was the cow afraid of her. They faced each other. Mum 'shoo-shooed', and the cow 'moo-mooed' back. They were holding quite a conversation but the cow had the advantage of size and with an extra loud moo it stepped closer. Mum ran back to the corner of the barn and grabbed a rake. By now the rest of us were giggling, but I didn't think there was anything to laugh about. I was too frightened of what the cow might do to her and me if she used the rake. Luckily, she didn't have the chance because just as she was about to attack, the barn door was flung wide to reveal the farmer standing there with a stout stick in his hand. Glaring angrily at Mum, he snatched the rake from her and bellowed, 'Cows won't hurt yer!'

Then he hit the beast hard on its rump and it backed slowly out to rejoin the others. The farmer looked around the barn and informed us gruffly that he'd lit the fire in the shed and told us we could get water from the pump and milk from the farm. The baskets for the hops were in the corner of the shed and we were

116

expected in the field 'when yer ready'. With that he turned and stalked out.

Mum told me to follow him to make sure he was out of sight, then she really took over. She called the boys down from the loft and we got ready to leave. She gave us orders to pile up our straw beds on top of each other in the corner ready for the evening. By the time this task had been accomplished we were beginning to get fidgety for the toilet but no one seemed to know where one was. Little Jonesy was crossing his legs and Joey pulled the hem of his mother's dress and complained, 'Me wants a two-two.'

Frankie and Jonesy had already vanished after complaining of belly-ache, evidently the result of all the sour apples they'd eaten the previous evening. Mrs Taylor picked up the twins, one under each arm, and went outside. I followed. There, at the back of the barn, we found a long wooden shed which I hadn't noticed before. There was a door at each end of this structure with a wet cardboard notice on each which read 'MEN' and 'WOMEN'. These must be the toilets. I looked round to tell the boys but they were nowhere to be seen. So while Mrs Taylor was holding out each twin in turn over a piece of newspaper, I entered through the door marked 'WOMEN'. There was a stone floor covered with wet lime, the result of water leaking through the roof. From one end to the other was a long wooden seat in which were three round holes. Behind the seats was a tarpaulin sheet which, although I didn't realise it, parted the three holes on our side from the three holes on the other. Curious, I lifted the sheet to see what was behind it but I dropped it quickly with shock because what I saw were the two bare bottoms of Jonesy and my brother. They both turned round and, when they realised that it was me, burst out laughing. I went all hot and felt so ashamed. I ran out, nearly knocking Mrs Taylor over. She was on her way to dispose of the newspaper parcel. I watched as she disappeared through the door of the boys' side but I was too late to tell her. I waited to see what would happen, when all at once I heard Jonesy say in loud voice, 'Yer can come an' sit on the 'ole next to me if yer like.'

'Yer cheeky bleeda,' was her startled reply.

The next thing I heard was a loud slap. Then she chased him outside, still with his trousers round his ankles. Needless to say, he made his escape. I held my head with shame as Mrs Taylor came over to me.

'Come now, Katie.' She took my hand. 'There's nothing to be ashamed of. We've got to put up with what we find on a place like this.'

'I wish I was home,' was all I could say.

'I wish I could goo 'ome too. I wish we'd never come,' she answered sadly.

I told her I was going to write to my dad and tell him everything and that when he collected us perhaps she and the twins could come too.

'We'll see,' she whispered softly.

I liked Mrs Taylor. She was the only one who ever really talked to me and she'd helped me when I'd lost my clogs.

As we made our way back we could see the others waiting their turn. Mum was first as usual. She announced that she was closing the door and that they'd have to wait. However, Granny managed to squeeze past her sideways. At this further example of high-handedness, the others began to grumble. I felt very uncomfortable and hoped Mum and Granny would hurry. I couldn't see Liza or Annie anywhere and hopped from foot to foot.

Then Mrs Taylor whispered in my ear, 'You go through the men's door. I'll watch out fer yer.'

Reluctantly, I entered. I thought no one would see me but there, sitting on the same two holes as Frankie and Jonesy, were Liza and Annie. So I lost my embarrassment and dropped my bloomers and with great relief sat next to them on the vacant hole. They were giggling and whispering together but I didn't know what about until they stood down from the seat, pulled their bloomers up and then deliberately lifted the sheet and pointed to Mum and Granny sitting next door. But when Mum turned and saw them they dropped the flap and it swung against Mum and Granny's bare bottoms with a thwack. I sat there, afraid to move in case I was blamed. Meanwhile, Liza and Annie rushed outside. I could hear Mum after them. When I'd fastened my bloomers I ran out too. Liza was halfway across the meadow with Mum calling after her, 'I'll deal with yow later! Yer brazen little bugger!'

As Mum turned she saw Annie hiding behind her mother's skirts and she was promptly dragged out with cries and yelps. Granny began laying down the law to Annie's mum but she didn't bat an eyelid. Mum put Annie's head between her legs, pulled down her bloomers and gave her three hard slaps on her bare buttocks in front of all of us.

'Now, 'ow d'yer like everyone ter see yower bare bottom?'

Annie went screaming to her mother.

'Serves yer right fer bein' cheeky. An' stop yer snivellin' or yer'll get some mower off me!' And she pushed Annie away.

At last the commotion died down and they got their turn in the toilet. We then went into the shed to wash and get something ready to eat. But before we could do this, Mum said we had to pool what little money we had. I gave the only penny I'd been saving for some sweets. Mrs Taylor said she'd only got the rent which had to be paid when she returned home, but she would willingly give some of that until they did. However, Mum restricted her levy to half a crown whilst the others placed a few coppers on the table. Granny hesitated to give her share until she saw Mum glaring at her, then she threw a shilling down on the table.

'An' I want it back!'

Altogether there was four shillings and twopence three farthings. Mum called Annie to her because I was busy washing little Joey, but Annie, remembering their recent confrontation, backed away. However her mother pushed her towards where Mum was sitting by the table.

'She ain't gooin' ter bite yer,' she snapped.

Mum gave Annie a pencil and paper and told her to write down what we wanted from the general stores down the lane.

''Alf a pound a cheese, 'alf a pound a marg, three loaves, an' don't forget the mek weights. A quarter a bacon, an' see it's lean. Two ounces a tea, a pound a sugar, an' a tin a 'andy brand.'

'What yer want tinned milk for when we can 'ave fresh from the farm'ouse?' Granny wanted to know.

'It's ter shove on the twins' dummies ter keep 'em quiet,' Mum snapped back and she began to count on her fingers how much the food would cost: but after getting herself into a muddle she pushed Annie away and called for me to reckon it up. I told her it all came to one shilling and three halfpence.

'That's right,' she answered, defying the others to deny her ability to add it up herself. But she hadn't a clue whether it was right or wrong: she could only trust to her fingers. I was still standing, waiting while she sat fumbling with the money in her lap as though she didn't want to part with it; then after a while she told me Annie could fetch the food while I went to the farmhouse for the milk. I didn't wait for any more orders. Grabbing hold of the twins, I dragged them after me as I rushed out of the barn.

It was a lovely, warm, sunny morning and the cobbled path looked clean and fresh now that the heavy rain had washed all the animal dung away. I skipped along happily with the twins following closely behind. Turning round to check on them I saw Frankie and Jones at the water pump. I hoped the twins hadn't seen them, but they had, and Joey called out, "Ello.' I shook him because I wanted to avoid the boys, but Frankie called me over. He looked rather shamefaced, no doubt remembering the toilet incident. I walked over to him.

'What yer want?'

'Here, take these apples and 'ide 'em.'

I took them and turned away. I put them down my bloomers but I hadn't gone more than a few yards when the elastic gave way and the apples rolled down into the gutter, I looked around for my brother but he had disappeared. Before I could pick them up I felt a tug at my frock and when I turned round the twins were trying to attract my attention to a little pig with a limp and some ducks approaching us. I became nervous again for I remembered what Granny used to say when we ate pigs' trotters at home.

'Kids who eat trotters or cows' meat are 'witched. An' animals are like elephants, they never forget.'

She often said she never ate meat of any kind but we knew she did if she thought no one was watching. She also used to frighten me with the story that cows tossed you in the air if you wore red drawers. As a result, I was terrified of almost any animal with four legs. With this in mind, I picked up one of the apples and threw it at the pig. It was a good aim and while the pig stopped to eat the missile I grabbed the twins and ran towards the farmhouse as fast as I could.

However, it didn't take the pig long to swallow the apple and come running after me for more. I quickly lifted the twins on to a wall and pushed their dummies into their mouths, and told them to sit still until I returned with the milk. Then I dashed off, only slackening my pace after I'd run some distance. When I looked back I could see the pig had dropped behind, so I reached the farmhouse safely. I knocked on the door, and the farmer's wife came almost at once.

'Please. My mum has sent me for some milk,' I said timidly.

She looked down at me and asked if I had something to put it in. I'd forgotten to bring any kind of vessel, so I told her Mum hadn't got a jug and would she please lend one. She disappeared into the dark depths of the kitchen and returned a few moments later with an enamel jug filled with milk, still warm from the cow.

'Here yer be,' she said, handing me the large jug. 'And tell yer mum to let me have the jug back.' She didn't seem to look as stern as when I had first seen her. She really smiled broadly and asked if I was getting on all right. I nodded, and then asked her boldly what was wrong with the little pig's trotter.

'Yer mean Hoppity. There's nothing wrong with his leg now, but he did cut it on some barbed wire. My little granddaughter plays with him sometimes and wraps a rag round it.'

'What for?'

'She thinks his leg still hurts and that's why he hops.'

'Is that why he's called Hoppity?'

'Yes. Now be off with yer before the milk gets cold,' she said, returning to her sharp manner. 'I'm busy.'

I thanked her for the jug and went off to pick up the twins but when I looked over to the wall they were nowhere to be seen, nor were the ducks and nor was Hoppity. I thought the worst. There was only one place to look: the pigsty. And that is where they were. They were sitting in the midst of the filth, still sucking their dummies and stroking Hoppity. I rushed in and hauled them out and dragged them across to the shed where I knew Mum would be waiting impatiently for the milk. But before we'd gone three strides Hoppity began to follow. I picked up one of the previously discarded apples and threw it at him but he merely swallowed it and continued to wobble after us. We ran and arrived back to find Mum in an awful temper. She scolded me for being so long but I knew it was hopeless trying to explain. I glanced across at Liza and could see from her red eyes that she'd had her punishment. I was lucky to have avoided a similar fate!

Mrs Taylor snatched the twins away from me and began to wash them down while the others sniffed the air. This didn't stop them continuing to eat their bacon sandwiches. Mum was cooking my pieces of bread in the bacon fat. Mrs Taylor filled the twins' titty bottles with the rest of the milk. I was surprised that they guzzled it so readily because I wasn't aware that they'd ever tasted cow's milk before. I thought it would be a good idea for us to have a cow, but I knew this was only wishful thinking. Anyway, where would we keep it? I knew Mum wouldn't keep it in the yard for the neighbours to help themselves, and it was probably as well we couldn't afford one because I always wore red flannelette bloomers.

When we'd all finished eating, the farmer came along with his horse and cart to take us to the hop field. The cart was similar to the one we'd come in, but larger, with plenty of room for us and all the baskets. The farmer threw the baskets in first and then told us to jump up after. We all climbed in one by one, except Granny. She wanted to ride up on top with the farmer, but he wouldn't hear of it and insisted that she had to ride with the rest. So after a few moans and groans Mum pulled her inside and they embarked on their first trip to pick hops.

It was decided between Mum and Mrs Taylor that Liza and I should stay behind to look after the twins. So we waved the others out of sight and returned to the shed to clean away the crocks. While we were busy, Liza told me how Mum had taken down her bloomers and smacked her bare bottom in front of everybody.

'Not in front of Frankie?' I said, shocked.

'Yes. And Jonesy,' she replied. 'They didn't even look away. They just laughed. But I'll get my own back when they return,' she said darkly.

I could see plainly that she was still upset but I was soon able to cheer her up when I told her about the twins and Hoppity.

'I'd forgotten until now about writing to Dad so while Joey and Harry were playing around on the floor, I turned to Liza and said, 'I don't like it here, do you, Liza?'

'No. I wish I could go home,' she answered.

Then I told her I was going to write to Dad to fetch us home.

'When?'

'Now. As soon as I can find the pencil and paper he gave me.'

After fumbling in my pockets I found the paper and envelope and a stub of pencil. While Liza was getting the twins to sleep, I began to write. My letter went something like this.

Dear Dad,

We are all very unhappy here. Will you come and fetch us home? Mum and Granny and Frankie and the rest have gone to the hop field and left Liza and me to look after Mrs Taylor's twins. Liza is trying to comfort them while I write this letter. Please, please fetch me back home or I shall run away. I'm afraid of the cows. One came in the barn this morning and if the farmer hadn't come in when he did, the cow would have tossed Mum in the air. And there's a little pig here called Hoppity and he follows me everywhere I go. So please come and fetch me home as soon as you can. I don't know this address, only that the farmer's name is Onions. Mrs Nelson will give you our address.

love, Katie

This was the first letter I'd ever written and I was hoping it sounded convincing. Liza read it and put in the envelope and addressed it.

'Where's the stamp?' she asked.

I fumbled around again in my pockets. Then I realised Dad hadn't given me one. 'Now we carn't post it,' I told Liza.

'Yes we can,' Liza said. 'But we'll have to take a chance whether Dad gets it or not.'

She held the envelope and in the top right-hand corner she pressed her wet, dirty thumb.

'There you are,' she said, smiling at her handiwork. 'The postman will think the stamps's fallen off. If he don't, Dad'll have to pay when he gets the letter.'

We were both pleased with this idea, and hoped it would work.

'We'd better not tell Mum you've written to Dad or we'll cop it,' she warned me.

'I'll have to, Liza. She'll find out soon enough.'

'Well, we'll wait until she's in a good mood before we decide, then maybe if she's had a few drinks . . .'

So we decided on our approach, gathered together Joey and Harry, and went off to post the letter in the letter-box outside the stores. We'd only gone as far as the toilets when Joey decided he wanted to go.

'Yow would, yer little pest,' Liza snapped and began to shake him.

'I want a two-two,' Harry joined in.

We both lost our patience then and pushed them into the lavatory, but they couldn't reach the seat and we had to help them. We took their ragged trousers down and held them over the holes. I had to put the letter in my pocket until Harry had finished. Then, as he was pulling his trousers back on, I saw that Liza was holding her nose and had released her grip on Joey. Quickly I grabbed him by the feet just as he was vanishing down the hole. Liza came to the rescue and we hauled him out just in time. I shudder to think what he would have looked or smelled like if he had fallen in. We started on our way again down the lane, then suddenly we looked at each other and burst out laughing, hysterically.

'Oh, what a calamity that would have been. He nearly went down the hole,' Liza giggled.

'Yes. And it could have been worse,' I answered.

At last we reached the collection box and I slipped the letter in. Then we gazed into the shop window. There was almost everything imaginable there to make your mouth water, or so it seemed – cakes, jam tarts and all kinds of sweets. But we hadn't got a halfpenny between us – at least we thought we hadn't until Joey said, 'Me got penny, Tatie. To buy yoo sweeties.'

We didn't bother to find out where he'd got it from, but grabbed it from him and entered the shop. Once in the stores, we had no hesitation in asking the lady behind the counter for two liquorice laces.

'Let's see the colour of your money first,' she said, peering accusingly at us.

Liza showed the penny and she promptly gave the two long strips of black liquorice. She glared at us all the while.

'Where yer from?'

'Onions's farm,' snapped Liza. 'An' we want a coupla bull's-eyes with the change.'

Bull's-eyes were what Mum called gob-stoppers, and gave to Liza when she tried to join in the singing. When we left the shop, the twins were chewing on the black strips and we followed behind sucking a bull's-eye each. I always liked these sweets because they lasted a long time. While we sucked them we took them out of our mouths now and again to observe their changing colour. So we left the shop a lot happier than when we entered. Liza and I skipped merrily down on the lane and the twins followed up behind with more liquorice around their mouths than in them.

It was a very hot day and the bad weather of the previous night had quite disappeared. We didn't know what to do or where to go, so Liza suggested we go exploring. We walked along the quiet lanes for about a mile and didn't meet a soul, only the cows in the fields. Soon the twins grew tired and decided that they'd had enough so down on the grass verge they flopped. I must say I was surprised Joey's little bowed legs had carried him that far. Liza and I wanted to go on, but we couldn't leave them behind to get lost. So we pick-a-backed them, but we soon wearied of this. They were small for their three and a half years, but they were still heavy if you tried to carry them as we were doing. We decided that we'd have to return to the barn. Just then we heard a lot of hammering and saw sparks flying overhead from somewhere nearby.

We sat the twins on the verge and told them to stay put. Then we went to investigate the noise. As we rounded the corner of the lane we saw a large, well-built, muscular man outside what we realised was the blacksmith's. He was hammering out a red-hot horseshoe on the anvil. The red sparks were shooting in every direction as he hammered out the metal. We didn't speak to him, and as he had his back to us, he didn't see or hear us. We stood fascinated by his movements and the sweat dripping from his body. After watching for a while we remembered the twins and wandered back to collect them and make our way back to the barn.

The Hop-pickers

After our long walk we were tired and beginning to feel hungry. On top of that, we realised that we hadn't allowed for the return journey. The twins were still sitting where we'd left them, sucking on their dummies, which always conveniently dangled from strings round their necks. We took them by the hand but still had to carry them at intervals. Unfortunately, we were too young to have much sense of direction, and instead of keeping to the same lane, we must have turned off at some point. All the lanes looked the same to us. There was nothing but fields and meadows – not a house or a human being in sight. Soon we were completely lost, afraid and on the verge of tears. My clogs had rubbed holes in my stockings and made blisters on my heels. Liza was complaining about the heat. We decided to sit down by the wayside, remove our clogs and rest. Perhaps someone would come along and show us the way. The twins began to grizzle.

'Me is 'ungry, Tatie.'

'An' me's wet me trousers.'

Soon we were all in tears together. We were hungry, tired, lost, and not a little miserable. We endeavoured to pacify the twins with a lullaby but they continued to sob until eventually they fell asleep. Then Liza decided to take a look to see what was round the bend in the lane. I didn't want to be left because I was still afraid the cows might come and I was beginning to panic. Liza promised she wouldn't go far, but I was determined not to be left alone. But Liza pointed to the twins who were still sleeping and told me not to leave them. They soon woke up though, they must have sensed we were considering leaving them. Just as I got to my feet, they stirred. So it was impossible for me to leave. I stayed, but I was praying Liza wouldn't stray off for long.

While she was gone, I was more scared than ever. I was aware of every little sound and I imagined everything I heard was a cow or a pig that was about to pop out of the hedge. What would I do? 'Please, Lord,' I prayed out loud. The twins renewed their wailing and we hugged each other for comfort. I hummed a tune to them and they fell back to sleep and I dozed off myself after a while. I don't know how long the three of us slept, but we were awakened with a start by Liza's voice.

'Wake up! Look what I've got!'

I rubbed my eyes and rose to my feet and looked at what she was carrying in her pinafore. I could hardly believe my eyes. Her pinafore was full of rosy red apples. She must have been running because she was out of breath, but when I looked up the lane I could see no one had been chasing her.

'Where did yer get them from?'

'Shush,' she whispered. 'Never yer mind. Yer 'ungry, ain't yer? Well, eat.'

We all made absolute pigs of ourselves. Then, when we'd devoured the lot, we huddled together on the verge and slept. We must have been there for hours because the next thing I knew was a horse neighing and loud voices. Then somebody was shaking us.

'What yer all doin' 'ere? Wake up. Wake up, the pair on yer.'

I can't remember being so happy to see and hear my Mum bawling at me. Liza and I quickly got to our feet and the twins were snatched up by Mrs Taylor.

'Oh, my poor little babbies. Whatever are yer dooin' 'ere?'

But we were too relieved to answer her and we just gazed at Granny and the rest of the hop-pickers who were standing among the baskets on the cart. They all looked surprised to see us, even the farmer.

'Come on,' he called. 'Jump in, all of yer. I'm late already.'

So Mum pushed us roughly aboard the cart and told the farmer that she'd walk, and off she went with Mrs Taylor and the twins. It was then that it dawned on us. We were only a few yards from the farm and we hadn't realised it. In our panic we must have walked round in a circle.

The farmer dropped us off, and then went over to Mum and paid her the hop-picking money for her and the rest of the women. This provoked a lot of grumbling from Granny and the others because

Mum was in charge. But they needn't have worried. She shared it equally amongst them – all except Annie and the boys, who had to be content with a penny each for their troubles. Mum called me over to do the counting. When I'd completed this by a feat of mathematics, she wasn't satisfied with her share which she'd already calculated on her fingers, so I was ordered to do it all over again.

'All bloody day for two bob each?' she asked Mrs Phipps.

'Well, we do get twopence more than the other farm we worked at, dain't we, Mrs Jones?' she asked. 'An' we do get paid every day.'

Mrs Jones nodded her head in reply, but Mum wasn't satisfied. She shouted across the barn to Granny and the rest, still glaring at her two shillings.

'We worked like bloody Trojans for this!' She spat her words out with contempt. 'If that bloody farmer thinks I'm pickin' 'is 'ops all day for two bob, 'e's off 'is rocker.' She was livid, and paced up and down.

'Yow tell 'm, Polly, I ain't doin' any mower! I want ter goo back 'ome,' Granny sobbed, and sniffed and blew her nose.

'We'll think about that, 'Annah, after we've 'ad summat ter eat.'

Mum collected sixpence off each person to buy some food from the stores and Mrs Taylor walked over to get some food from under the bucket for the twins. When she yelled out in surprise we all went to look.

'It's gorn. The rats 'ave 'ad it.'

Mum pushed us all out of her path and strode over to see for herself. She examined the bowl and then turned and glared at us each in turn. Placing her hands on her hips, she snarled angrily, 'They're two-legged rats 'ave 'ad it. Come on, who's the varmint?'

We looked from one to another, waiting to see who was going to own up. I knew it wasn't Liza, the twins or me. But all eyes were on us because we were the only ones left out of the hop-picking party. Mum dragged Liza and me over to the corner where the bucket and bowl were. She raisd her hand high but we both vehemently denied having been in the barn. Then, just as she was about to bring down her hand, Mrs Phipps piped up.

'Wait a bit, Polly. What about them two? They dain't pick 'ops all the time. They ran off part of the afternoon.'

Mum turned to question Frankie and Jonesy but there was no need. They had both fled. Mum and Mrs Jones made a dive for the barn door but Granny cried out, 'Yer won't catch them two. Send somebody to the stores and let's 'ave summat ter eat. I'm clammed. I wish I was back 'ome. I was allus sure of a pot of stew.'

'Oh shut up, 'Annah! We're all clammed,' Mum snapped back. 'Anyway, let's goo to the shed an' 'ave a cup a tea while one of yer fetches some food.'

'I'll goo,' Mrs Jones volunteered quickly.

'No!' shouted Mum. 'I don't trust yer.'

So Liza and I had to go instead, and by the time we returned the tea was ready in the pot. I still had to go to the farmhouse though, as we had no milk. I'd hoped to avoid the twins but they tagged along behind before I could fetch the jug and dash off. Most of the time I loved their company, but other times they could be a couple of pests. They dragged along after me and there was nothing I could do without hurting their feelings. Before we'd gone very far we saw little Hoppity in front of us. I tried to edge past him because I was still nervous, but Joey and Harry ran up and stroked him. They thought he was a kind of dog and they tried to climb on his back. I tried to call them away because I was afraid the pig might turn nasty. But they didn't turn a hair; they were enjoying themselves and so apparently was the pig. It was then I found enough courage to stroke him myself. He was just a friendly little pig. I noticed that the dressing had come loose so I wrapped it back on for him and from that moment we became friends. He trotted along behind us and when we got to the farmhouse the farmer's wife told us not to encourage him or he would follow us everywhere. I smiled, and thanked her for the milk and the pig followed us back along the path towards the shed. But didn't come in. He stood outside and, would have nothing to do with anybody else, only the twins and me. In the end the only way I could get rid of him was to throw an apple as far as I could and hope he wouldn't return for more.

It was about eight o'clock and the evening was still warm and light. We had our share of fried bacon, mugs of cocoa and fried potatoes. Mum, Mrs Phipps, Mrs Jones, Mrs Buckley and Mrs Taylor washed and combed their hair ready to go to the pub again. The other kids had already vanished across the field to do their scrumping. I knew I would be left alone, but I didn't mind being left with the twins as long as someone else was there in the barn with me. Mrs Taylor could see that I was apprehensive and on the verge of tears so she agreed to stay behind with me. I threw my arms round her waist and almost cried for joy. She bent over me.

'Come on now. Wipe your eyes and we'll go back to the shed and clear up the crocks and pans and then we'll go for a walk.'

I felt happy then, but not for long. Mrs Taylor was the only one who seemed to notice me when I was unhappy or miserable, and I was too young to realise that she was only using me. She washed and cleaned up the shed and I helped her to wash and dress the twins. Then, while she took them into the barn, I filled their two empty medicine bottles with what was left of the cow's milk and fastened the teats on the ends. I took them to the twins who were already bedded down for the night. I lay down beside them and they sucked their milk while I sang a lullaby until they fell asleep, then I rose to my feet and crept quietly out of the barn so as not to disturb them.

Mrs Taylor was already standing outside and I could see how restless she was to be off. She took me by the hand and quickly hurried me along the lane. I felt that the twins shouldn't be left, but when I told her Mrs Taylor snapped, 'Don't worry yerself. They'll be orl right.'

I could see that she wasn't happy either, but I was too innocent to realise that it was the pub she was eager to get to, I asked where she was going.

'Only to the pub. I'm garspin' for a drink,' she replied.

But I wasn't prepared to accompany her.

'I'm going back to the twins. They might wake up and cry for us.'

'Please yerself,' she said smiling, and left me to return to the barn by myself.

She hurried off in the opposite direction and I retraced my steps. The twins were still asleep, sucking their empty bottles. I tried to remove them but they held them too tightly, so I gave up and flopped down beside them. I felt so unhappy and miserable that I considered running away. But where could I have gone? I was miles from home and I couldn't even walk to the farm to ask the farmer's wife if I could stay with her because I was too afraid of the cows. I could still hear their lowing in the fields. All kinds of things crowded into my mind, but above all I thought I must not leave the twins. I put my arm round them and cuddled them until we all dropped off to sleep. This didn't last long. Liza and Annie and the lads woke me up when they came bounding in and dropped their pile of apples and carrots on the floor. I heard the farmer approaching with his dogs and we pushed the loot under some straw. When he'd gone by we retrieved the fruit and vegetables, and gorged ourselves before our mothers returned. But I knew they wouldn't be back before closing time.

When the boys had had their fill they climbed the ladder to the loft and settled down for the night. Liza and Annie made their beds on the other side of the twins. It was really dark now and I could only just make out the time by the dusty clock on the wall. It was ten thirty. Soon after this I heard the farmer enter and hang the lamp on the wall but he didn't bother to check who was there.

His departure marked the beginning of a night I shall never forget.

It was very warm in the barn with the door closed and very humid as well. So I tiptoed to the door and opened it to let in some air. As I did so I heard singing in the distance, and I was relieved to hear Mum's voice way above the others. But as I stood in the doorway waiting for them to arrive I became aware of male voices too. For some reason I assumed that it must be my dad and felt immensely happy that he'd come in response to my letter. However when they all drew nearer I could see, in the dim light of the lantern, Mum, Granny and the rest arm in arm with four men we'd seen earlier in the other hop field. I was disappointed and frightened when I saw the state they were in. The smallest of the four was holding Granny up, while the other three were trying to push past Mum into the barn. They were dishevelled, ragged and swearing loudly and they each brandished a bottle of beer. I was scared when they tried to get into the barn, but Mum pushed the first one outside.

'Thank yer fer seein' us 'ome. But that's as far as yer goo,' she said firmly. But they wouldn't budge. The leading one stood there and seemed most aggrieved. 'What d'yer tek us for, missus? We've treated yer all night. Come on, let's open a bottle inside.'

Then he pushed his way inside and the other three followed, waving their bottles in the air. I ran to the twins to protect them in case they were trodden on, but they were difficult to miss because they were screaming their heads off. Liza and Annie were awake too, and seemed to be perplexed about what was happening. Then the little bearded man grabbed Granny round the waist and dragged her on to the straw, nearly landing on the girls as they rolled about.

Mrs Phipps, Mrs Jones and Mrs Buckley were also struggling to free themselves from the other men and Mum was giving a right and a left to the other fellow's belly. Before he could get a grip on her, she lifted her heavy foot and landed a kick in his groin. He let out a yell and fell to the floor, clutching his private parts and, as he laid there groaning, the contents of his bottle poured out beside him. Mum clapped her hands and grinned.

'That's number one settled.' She smiled, as she stepped over him to help the others on their way out.

Mum was really enjoying herself and so were the boys, who were laughing fit to burst in the safety of the loft. However, Liza and I were scared. We were in the thick of the skirmish and didn't think it was funny at all. We crouched in the corner with Mrs Taylor and the twins, who were still crying loudly, and watched as Mum caught hold of the little man by his beard and dragged him off Granny, down whose throat he'd been trying to pour more beer, Mum held him firmly and then threw him through the door. He was probably glad to leave! While Mum was dealing with these two, Mrs Phipps, Mrs Jones and Mrs Buckley were still struggling with the other two burly fellows. These blokes obviously had no intention of leaving the women and things seemed to be getting rougher. As Mum made to help, the men lashed out at her and she fell over Granny who was lying on the straw exhausted, but with sufficient energy to cry and swear at the interlopers. Mum was unable to get to her feet. Each time she got up she was pushed down again. I shouted out to Frankie to come down and help, but he was already sliding down the ladder with Jonesy and Freddie close behind. They jumped on to the largest fellow's back and pummelled him and they were soon joined by Mum who'd struggled to her feet. Meanwhile Mrs Jones was standing in the corner, crossing herself and praying. 'Mary, Mother of God, save us!' she kept crying out.

Meanwhile the second man was chasing Mrs Phipps and Mrs Buckley round the barn, when suddenly we were all plunged into darkness. The lantern and our supply of paraffin had burnt itself out. Liza, Annie, Mrs Taylor and I were still crouching out of the way, afraid for our lives. But as the man chasing Mrs Phipps passed us for the second time I lifted my foot and kicked for all I was worth. Unfortunately I missed my target. Mrs Phipps yelled out and fell, with the man on top of her. When I realised what I'd done I dodged behind Mrs Taylor, out the way of retribution. Just then the big fellow shouted, 'Come on, George. We'll settle this lot tomorrow night.'

Mrs Buckley crawled to the up-turned bucket and lit the only piece of candle we had left. When we could see where we were and what we were doing we could see George getting to his feet. Mum rushed at him, but his friend came to his rescue; but Mum was afraid of no one, not even the devil. She lunged at them both but we could see that she was getting the worst of it. However, we were too frightened to interfere. She knocked one fellow down and then Frankie tried to come to her aid with the hay-fork. He rushed at them but the fork was too heavy an he tripped over the chap on the floor. He pulled himself to his feet and when he saw that Mum was not going to stop he dashed outside and at last the big fellow decided he'd had enough, too. He helped the first fellow Mum had floored, who appeared to have fallen into a drunken stupor, to his feet, and they limped out. Mum slammed the door and pushed its wooden bar into place, and slapped her hands together, in a gesture of having polished them off.

'Well, that's the end of that!' she cried in triumph.

Frankie and Jonesy climbed back into the loft and we emerged from our hiding-place. The barn was a shambles. Straw and empty bags were strewn about amongst the broken beer bottles. We all set about refilling our beds but it was impossible to see, so we girls clambered up to join the lads in the loft. The women below began to quarrel. I could still hear their efforts to scrape together some straw when I heard Mum's voice.

'I wish to God we 'ad a light in 'ere to see what we're doin'.'

Suddenly her prayer was answered. The farmer stood in the doorway with his lantern lighting up the whole barn. He gazed at the scattered straw and then looked at us all hard in turn.

'What's been going on here?'

Mum put on her look of surprised innocence.

'Nothin', sir,' she replied, giving him the benefit of one of her smiles.

'What do you mean nothing? I want an explanation!' He was angry. 'The place is a shambles and I could hear the noise all the way down the lane. Come on, who's going to own up?'

No one spoke. We all stared at him, afraid of what he might do. Then after a few seconds he spoke.

'Very well. You all leave in the morning.'

But as he turned to go, Granny burst out with sobs.

'It worn't us, sir. It was them men from the other field who followed us 'ere.'

Mum stood in front of Granny and said she didn't know what she was saying. 'A bit funny in the 'ead, sir,' she said, putting her finger to her forehead. He glared at Mum and passed out of the way.

'I'll talk to you lot tomorrow. And see that you've all got yer belongings ready to clear out!'

When he went off, leaving us in the dark again, the quarrelling started in earnest.

'Yer dain't 'ave ter tell 'im, 'e'd 'ave found out anyway. The way yow carried on with all yer 'ootin' an' ravin'.'

'Oh, lie down, yer silly ole fool, an' get ter sleep!' Mum yelled.

Then Granny laid down on the straw again and Mrs Phipps asked, 'Do yer know who kicked me on the shin, Polly?'

''Ow do I know? I was too busy tryin' to defend yow lot! Get ter sleep, all on yer. Any'ow, I'm tired if you're not.'

I was pleased to know that no one had seen me kick out in the dark and I was not fool enough to own up either. Soon everybody was snoring but I just lay there praying that my dad would fetch me home as quickly as possible. It was pitch dark now and quiet but for the sound of a steady succession of women using the bucket. Then I resolved to run away as soon as it got light and with that thought I must have drifted off to sleep.

Our Last Day on the Farm

I was woken by Frankie shaking me. I looked around sleepily and realised that it was long past dawn, in fact it was ten o'clock by the clock on the wall. When I was fully awake I could hear that there was a storm overhead. It was thundering and lightning and raining in buckets. All thought of running away was out of the question. We couldn't even get to the shed to see if there were any scraps or leftovers from the previous evening. Instead we set about rousing our mother who made loud complaints about the weather and their headaches. Granny was the last to rise and was the loudest complainer.

'I want ter goo 'ome. If nobody comes ter fetch me I shall die 'ere!' she sobbed.

'Don't cry, Granny. I've written a letter to Dad to come and take us home,' I confided in her. This seemed to pacify her and she pulled me to her.

'God bless yer, me wench.'

But I recoiled from her. The smell of stale beer on her clothes made me feel sick. I felt miserable because the rain had prevented me from running back to Birmingham, but I consoled myself with the thought that Dad might come after it had stopped. By now everybody was up and the twins were yelling to be fed, but their mother couldn't be bothered with them. I looked away. I knew how they felt; I was hungry too. It was then that I remembered the apples and carrot I'd hidden under the straw the night before. However, when I looked the apples had gone and only the carrot remained. I could see no sign of rats or mice so I guessed that the culprits must have been of the two-legged variety, but it would have been no use arguing about it. Nobody would have owned up. Anyway, I felt too drained to pursue it so I took the carrot and after wiping it on my frock, I bit a piece off and gave the rest to the twins.

'Do 'em good, Mrs Taylor. 'Elp 'em see in the dark,' Frankie piped up, when he saw them munching their carrot like human rabbits.

She was not in a pleasant mood, however.

'They've seen an' 'eard enough, yer cheeky little sod!'

Mrs Taylor was not the only one in a temper. Everybody was in the same mood. They were getting in each other's way as they tried to clear away the half-empty bags of straw. We were really fed up, particularly with the rain, and every few minutes someone would stick their head out the door to see if it was easing off.

After a while Mum asked Granny and the rest to pool what money they had left to buy some more food from the shop.

'I carn't, Polly,' said Mrs Jones, 'I've only a few coppers left.'

I saw Mum, hands on hips, glaring at Mrs Jones and it was then that I noticed for the first time that Mum had the biggest black eye I'd ever seen – and I'd seen a few in my time! There were always drunken brawls in the street. I don't think Mum herself knew that she had it, because there were no mirrors in the barn, and although the others had seen it they were too afraid to mention it, but I couldn't stop myself glancing at it every now and then. Mum grew red in the face giving out instructions.

'All on yer!' she commanded. 'Yer'll 'ave ter doo yer share! There's no 'ops ter be picked terday in this rain. An' another thing. We've got ter get our chattels together. Yer knoo what the bloody farmer said.'

To which Granny responded, 'Talk a the bloody devil an' 'e'll be bound ter appear.'

At that, all eyes turned to the barn door and everyone lost their tongue in amazement as they saw the farmer standing there. He gave them all an icy stare before he broke the silence.

'Well? And what have you all got to say for yourselves?'

No one answered. Not even Mum. They were all looking very sheepish and feeling sorry for themselves. Then he called us to him and continued in a gentler tone.

'Now I want you to listen carefully. All of yer. I been over to my brother's farm and I've found out what happened last night. Now if you'll promise not to go to the local I'll let things pass. But I warn you all, if you do go you'll be sorry! The men you tackled last night said they won't forget you lot in a hurry, so I'm putting you on your guard to keep away.' It was then he caught sight of Mum's face and saw her black eye and his face broke in a broad smile. 'Well, I see you won a medal too!'

Mum smiled, but she didn't know what she was smiling at until Granny told her later. The farmer gave us another black look and stroked his whiskers.

'There'll be no picking today. The ground's too wet. But see you're up bright and early in the morning. I want double-pickings tomorrow.'

As he reached the door he turned and looked at Frankie and the boys.

'And you lads don't sleep in that loft any more. You'll sleep on the floor with the rest.'

With that, he picked up the ladder and took it out with him.

We felt a bit happier now we knew we weren't going to be turned out in the rain. Mum turned again to collect the few coppers the others had placed on the table. Liza and I knew we'd have to go to the shop, so we went out to the closet and as we went we could hear Mum shouting, 'Don't yer be all day. We're starvin'.'

When we got back, Mum and the others were waiting for us. I jotted down the items as Mum dictated them, and Liza found an old basket to carry them in. We also took two sacks to cover our heads and shoulders from the rain. Then, carrying the basket between us, we skipped along the lane. When we arrived at the shop we peered through the window and saw two gaunt-looking women and a down-and-out-looking man inside. The man was small with a goatee beard. I immediately recognised him as the man who'd held Granny down on the straw bed the previous evening. I was scared stiff and too afraid to go in but I had to, or face Mum. Liza wasn't frightened though.

'Come on,' she whispered, 'follow me.'

She pushed open the door. The bell tinkled overhead and all eyes turned towards us. We edged to the counter. They'd stopped talking and backed away from us as though we had some kind of disease. Liza glared boldly at them and pulled me after her.

'I want these,' she said abruptly to the women behind the counter, and put the note down in front of her.

Timidly, the shopkeeper asked the man something but we couldn't make out what she said. We felt sure that they were talking about the events of the night before, and we could tell by their attitude that they were hostile.

'Yow ask 'em, missus.'

So the shopkeeper asked us who we were.

'Be yer 'op-pickers from Onions's farm?'

'Yes,' said Liza, imitating the woman, 'we be the hoppickers from Onions's farm. So what about it?'

At that the man and the two women left, giving us extremely hostile looks and leaving the woman behind the counter to serve us. She seemed to be very nervous and apparently wanted to serve us quickly and get rid of us because she didn't take the list to reckon up the goods, she just slapped them down on the counter and when she weighed the bacon it bumped the scales but she didn't stop to take any off like she had before, so we got good measures. She didn't even count the money Liza gave her. She put it straight into the drawer.

'Thank yer,' she managed to mumble. 'Will that be all?'

We could see that she was on edge, wanting to be shot of us, but Liza nudged me and then gave her a hard stare before replying, 'Where's the jar of jam?'

Down came a two-pound jar of blackcurrant jam which Liza put in the basket with the other things. We'd no sooner got outside than we heard her shoot home the bolt and saw her pull down the blind. We took the sacks off our heads and I turned and said, 'Why did you ask for jam? That wasn't on the list.'

She smiled artfully. 'She was too nervous to see the list or count the money, so it was payment for talking about us.'

'But what will Mum say?'

'She ain't ter know. I'll tell her she gave it to us for being good customers.'

'But that's a lie, and you're sure to be found out.'

'Not if yow don't tell 'er. Anyway it's the truth. She did give it to us, didn't she?'

I thought for a moment. 'Yes, I suppose you're right.'

When we got back to the shed everybody was doing something, even the kettle was boiling on the stove and the pan was ready with a lump of lard melting, to fry the bacon. The table was laid ready with tin plates and mugs. The twins were seated on up-turned boxes, rattling away at the mugs with their spoons. After a while we sat on the floor – there wasn't enough room to sit at the table – and our meal, which Mum had rationed out, was presented to us. There was only enough food for breakfast and we still had the rest of the day to get through before we could pick more hops and earn more money. Liza explained to Mum about the jam and it was put with the leftovers for later.

It was still raining hard and so there was nowhere any of us could go. We couldn't even play outside and the only time our mothers ventured out it was to make a journey for some straw.

'I hope they don't get splinters in their bottoms,' someone said.

After a while everybody, except Mrs Taylor, the twins and me, left the shed to return to the barn. I stayed behind because I wanted to wash the boys. I was glad when I'd finished because while I was drying their pants in front of the stove the wind blew the smoke down the pipe into the shed nearly choking us. At last we went into the barn and sat with the others. Mum, Granny and the rest were stretched out taking an early nap, and Liza and the children were playing a guessing game. At about seven o'clock it stopped raining and since it was still light we decided to end our boring game and go out while the adults were still sleeping. We didn't get far enough, because Mum woke up and called to us, 'Where do yer think yer all gooin' to?'

At that the other kids ran off, leaving me. I only wished I had the courage to follow them, but I was timid and very afraid of Mum so I stood still.

'Yer better goo to the farm'ouse an' get the milk,' she ordered.

I collected the jug from the shed and looked around to see if I could see Frankie and the others but they'd fled. I was feeling very miserable. None of them seemed interested in me until there was a job to be done. I took the jug and trudged reluctantly to the farm-house, hoping that at least I might meet Hoppity, but he too appeared to have forsaken me.

Mrs Onions was sweeping pools of rainwater away from the door as I approached. She looked up when she was aware of me and fixed me with a glare.

'Well!' she said sharply, 'I see you've come for some more milk.'

'Yes, please,' I replied timidly, and handed her the jug. I didn't like the look of her when she returned with the jug full.

'This is the last yer get without money. Yer better tell yer mother I want paying at the end of the week.'

'Thank you,' I whispered, but as I was creeping away she called me back and was smiling.

'Just a minute. You wait there while I wrap a parcel for you.'

I wondered whatever it could be. Some leftover clothes, I supposed, and while I was guessing she returned with a parcel wrapped in newspaper inside a large paper bag. She also gave me two rosy red apples which I was tempted to eat there and then. However, I put them in my pocket for later. I couldn't really understand Mrs Onions. One minute she snapped at me, the next she smiled and handed me a present. I thought I'd never understand grown-ups.

'Off yer go now and don't forget the money for the milk.'

I thanked her again and hurried back to find a bustle of activity as the table was prepared for tea. Mrs Taylor took the milk from me and I handed the parcel to Mum.

'What yer got there?' she wanted to know.

'I don't know. Mrs Onions gave it to me and she says she wants paying for the jugs of milk.'

'Well she can wait till we goo to work tomorra,' she snapped and the rest, who'd gathered round to watch her unwrap the parcel, nodded in agreement.

'If it's 'er left-off clothes, she can keep 'em,' Granny grumbled.

Everybody's face changed and their eyes lit up. So did mine as Mum placed on the table a dozen buns, a big lump of cheese, a lump of best butter, a slab of currant cake and a piece of fat bacon.

'She ain't so bad after all,' Mrs Phipps said as she stared hungrily at the contents of the bag.

I thought so too. Grown-ups were changeable creatures when they wanted to be. They all bustled about like busy bees, getting everything laid out in apple-pie order. Mum told me to call the other kids in and while she wasn't looking I managed to grab one of the buns for my trouble and contrived to find a corner to gobble it down. I spotted the other kids coming over the field, their pockets bulging with booty which they'd managed to hide in the barn before we left. They could hardly believe what they saw on the table. It was laid out with everything we had, even the jar of blackcurrant jam was there. And when we'd eaten, we thought it was the best feed any one of us had had for a long, long time. We even had the best butter on our bread with thick jam on top, and a bun each as well. The adults had fried bacon and cheese sandwiches. They'd been warned off the Pig and Whistle, so the kettle was boiling and the pot brewing all night. It was still light and Mrs Taylor asked me to go for a drop more milk. I told her what Mrs Onions had said about paying but she insisted.

'Well yow tell 'er it's for the twins. They won't sleep without their bottles. I'm sure she'll let yer 'ave some till I can pay 'er.'

With that she pushed the empty jug into my hand. I looked up at Mum for some support, but she only stared blankly back at me.

'Goo on! Do as yer told. An' 'urry yerself!' she bawled.

I began to weep. How could I ask for more milk when the woman had been so kind and given me all that food? I was too ashamed to go to her door. In the end I decided what I'd do. I'd take my time and pretend I had been and tell them a lie and say that there was none left. So I began to walk slowly when I noticed a van drive up towards the farmhouse and stop near the door. I stood and waited to see what was happening but when I saw who got out I dropped the jug and ran as fast as my thin little legs would carry me; because it was my brother, Jack.

'Jack! Jack! Oh, you've come to fetch us back home!' I cried out and tears welled up in my eyes.

'All right, let goo.' He smiled at me clinging to his trouser-legs. I let go and hung back while he knocked on the door.

'Anybody in?' he called out, but there was no reply.

He knocked again to make sure, but there was no one about but Hoppity who came running towards us on his three legs. I was happy and excited, telling my brother that this was Hoppity who followed me wherever I went.

'Funny little pig,' he said, lifting his flat cap and scratching his head in wonderment. 'What's the matter with his leg?'

I told him the pig had been cut on barbed wire while he petted it.

'You've got him tamed all right,' my brother said, smiling.

Nevertheless I didn't like the look he gave Hoppity when he said, 'You'd look nice on the table, Hoppity.'

I was very shocked when I realised what he was saying.

'Don't look so worried. I'm only kidding. You know I wouldn't do that.'

But you never knew with my brother Jack. However, I was so happy to see him that I forgot how he looked and what he'd said for the time being anyway.

'Jump in the back and show me where you're staying,' he said.

'It's the first big barn at the bottom of the field,' I replied, and leapt in the back of the van.

Hoppity followed along behind us. He knew I had another apple, but when I saw that he couldn't keep up with us I threw it back to him and watched him stop and munch it.

As Jack drove up to the barn I jumped down and while he parked it at the back I ran to tell Mum the good news. Mrs Taylor was the first person I ran into, but she wasn't interested in Jack. She only wanted to know about the milk. I was glad I didn't have to lie as I told her nobody was in. Then I ran to Mum who was sitting on a box near the table.

'Mum, Mum!' I cried excitedly. 'Our Jack's outside. With a van. He's come to take us home!'

Mum jumped up, knocking the box flying against the wall and rushed outside to meet Jack. She threw herself at him and, with her arms round his neck, almost smothering him, she kissed him. But he tried to hold himself aloof. He always did when she tried to kiss him.

'Where've yow sprung from?' she cried out.

Jack replied in his usual joking vein, 'Well, old 'un. I've come ter fetch yer 'ome.' He very seldom called her Mum or Mother.

'Thank God y've come. I've 'ad anough of this 'ole,' she declared, indicating the farmyard in general with an expansive gesture.

It was then that he noticed her black eye.

'Who give yer that?' he asked, pointing at her face.

'I fell over in the dark an' 'it it on the wall,' she lied.

Granny jumped up and screamed out, 'No she dain't! Tell 'im the truth!'

Mum walked away, giving Granny a filthy look, but Granny always had to have the final word.

'Yes. I'll tell 'im an' all. An' why dain't 'e come? 'E never answered Katie's letter.' She paused to draw breath. 'Any'ow, it's about time too. Somebody's come to fetch us at last.'

I was scared now and hoped Mum hadn't heard Granny mention the letter but she'd began quietly putting things away. She seldom listened to Granny's outbursts. Then Mrs Buckley asked how everybody was at home and if her husband and children were all right, but before Jack could answer Mum butted in, 'How's yer dad, Jack? An' 'ows Mary an' Charlie and 'ow's everybody coping with the rest of the kids?'

'They're all doing fine. Maggie an' Billy have been looking after 'em,' Jack replied, 'but Dad wants you all back 'ome.'

While they were all trying to get a word in edgeways, I put the kettle on to make Jack a cup of tea but when he noticed what I was doing he said he had something better in the van. He went out and came back with a pint bottle of whisky. All eyes were on him now. So were Frankie's and Liza's. They'd only just entered and were obviously surprised to see him. The women's eyes were glued to the bottle. Nobody wanted tea now. He poured them half a mug each but there wasn't enough to go round so, to our surprise, Jack went out to the van and returned with another bottle. Frankie and Jonesy were hoping Jack would give them some too, but Jack was adamant. They were too young and the whisky was too precious to be wasted on them. So the tea came in useful after all. We kids drank it.

I noticed Mrs Taylor putting some of her whisky into the twins' milk and when she saw me watching her she put her finger to her lips and whispered, 'Shush. It'll mek 'em sleep. They was awake 'alf the night with the row.'

After a while, when all the chatter had died down and the crocks had been cleared away we retired to the barn.

'Mower room ter move about in theea,' Granny said.

We led the way and when Jack entered he began fuming. 'What a bloody place to sleep. I'll have a bloody word with the farmer.'

'It's better than some barns we've slept in, ain't it?' said Mrs Phipps.

'Yes, that's right,' Mrs Jones replied, trying to look indignant. 'Anyway we ain't gooin' 'ome till the end of next week.'

'You please yerself what yer do.' Jack was annoyed. 'I'm teking my family out of this place first thing in the morning.'

Frankie piped up. 'I want to stop with Jonesy. I like it here.'

'You'll do as you're told.'

With that Jack gave him a good back-hander that made him sulky for the rest of the evening. I would have loved to tell Jack a lot of things that had been going on, but I knew I'd better be quiet while Mum was around, so I cuddled up next to the twins and watched Mrs Taylor making their bottles up. I knew that whisky was the wrong thing to give them, but I could do nothing; I had to do as I was told. Anyway, I thought, they'll get a good night's sleep. She handed me the bottles and I gave them one each to suck and soon they slipped into sleep. It was not long before the others were dozing off too. What with the commotion the night before, the slap-up meal, and the whisky, it was no wonder they all slept so soundly. Just as I was dropping off, I heard Jack and Mum talking.

'Where yer gooin' ter sleep, son?'

'I'll muck down in the van. Now, don't forget.' His voice dropped to a whisper. 'I'm going to have a drink at the Pig and Whistle. Get some sleep and I'll wake yer when I get back.'

'All right, son, an' mind 'ow yer goo,' she whispered in reply.

I heard the van drive away; then Mum lay down and went to sleep. Everybody was quiet now. I got up off my bed and tiptoed over to Frankie and whispered in his ear, 'Are you awake, Frankie?'

'What yer want?' he mumbled, and struggled up.

'Shush,' I hissed, looking around to see if anyone had heard him, but they didn't stir.

'Jack's gone to the Pig and Whistle and I'm afraid the men might set on him, Frankie.'

'Oh, go to sleep! He can take care of himself. Anyhow I don't care about him any more.'

And with those words he turned his back on me. I could see there was no use arguing with him while he was in that mood, so I curled up beside the twins again. I took Topsey from them. I felt so unhappy I wanted to cry. My mind was like a maze. I imagined all sorts of things were going to happen before Jack could get us safely home. I tortured myself, asking all kinds of questions and getting only black answers. What if he didn't come back? But he had promised and although he didn't always keep his promise I hoped he would this time. Anyway, Frankie was right. He could take care of himself. He was six feet tall and as strong as three men. I still wished I was back in my bed at home. Dad had said the country air would do us good but it only seemed to have made us all quarrelsome and miserable. That was how my mind wandered. Then after I'd said a little prayer, I drifted off into a troubled slumber.

I don't remember how long I slept, but I woke up and could hear voices in the barn. I thought my prayer had been answered. I could see Jack lighting the candle and crossing the floor to where Mum was sleeping.

'Are you awake, old 'un?' I heard him whisper.

'Is that yow, son?' she replied.

'Yes. Are yer dressed ready?'

He wasn't to know that none of us had been undressed since we arrived. It was cold at night and we only had sacks to cover ourselves. I watched Mum get up and, carrying her button-up boots, she followed him outside in her stockinged feet. I closed my eyes quickly when they turned to see if anyone was awake. They needn't have worried, the women slept on, snoring in different tones. I was fascinated to discover what was going on and why they were acting in such a conspiratorial way, so I got up and crept to the door to listen to what they were saying.

'Come on, old 'un. We ain't got all night. I want to get away before it gets too light.'

I could tell he'd had plenty to drink by the tone of his voice.

'There's only a few more things to get out in the van now,' I heard Mum reply.

I ran back quickly and lay down again and only just in time because they came back to collect the rest of our chattels. They seemed to be a long time whispering together but I didn't dare listen again. After a while, they both came back and looked around to see if anyone was stirring. Then I heard Jack tell Mum to get some sleep and he'd wake her up at dawn – and not to forget the pills.

'Yer betta 'ave 'em now,' Mum whispered, and I saw her take Mrs Phipps's sleeping pills from her pocket.

'Only give 'im one,' I heard her say.

'All right. Now get some sleep before the others wake up,' he answered.

Then he put the candle out and disappeared. I couldn't think what was going on. What were they plotting? I tried to puzzle out what they'd been talking about, but I couldn't. My eyes ached and at last I fell asleep again. It was just breaking dawn when I woke again in time to see Mum and Jack carrying armfuls of straw and empty sacks out to the van. Then they returned and whispered to Gran to get up and go to the van.

'What's 'appenin'?' she mumbled as Mum led her outside still half asleep.

'Hush. We're tekin' you 'ome. We don't want to wake any of the others.'

I jumped out of bed quickly, thinking they were leaving me

behind. I grabbed Topsey in one hand and my clogs in the other and ran outside and stood by the van. They weren't leaving without me, even if I had to hang on the back. Even though Granny was only half awake, she still made sure she had plenty of room and she stretched out on the straw to finish her sleep.

'I'm glad you're up and ready,' Jack said. 'You can keep an eye on Gran while we go and get Liza and Frankie.'

There was no great need to watch Gran: she was already snoring. After a couple of minutes, Jack came out with Frankie who was still protesting about having to leave, but when Jack raised his hand to him he soon scrambled aboard. Mum and Liza were the next to climb in and I followed before Jack closed the door. Then he mounted the driver's cab and we slowly pulled away. Only Mum and I were awake but I closed my eyes and tried to let the rocking motion of the van going over the ruts send me to sleep. We hadn't gone far when Jack stopped the van and opened the doors and Mum got out. I pretended to be asleep.

'Come on, old 'un,' Jack hissed, 'we'll have to hurry up before it gets too light.'

Mum jumped down and followed Jack in the direction we'd just come from.

They've just gone for a wee, I thought. But after they'd been gone quite a time I began to worry. Then at last I heard their footsteps and I feigned sleep again. When the door opened I could see Jack with Hoppity in his arms fast asleep.

'Where yer found him?' I managed to splutter.

'I've bought 'im off the farmer for yer.'

I stared at him wide-eyed as he continued, 'He told me he was always running away and getting lost and said you might like him. Now move over while I put him down.'

I moved across to accommodate the pig and Mum, but apparently she was riding up front with Jack. I was glad of that. But I wasn't very happy about the pig beside me. I liked him well enough when he ran to me for apples, but I couldn't bring myself to be too friendly because I was really nervous of him. However, I consoled myself with the thought that I would now have the opportunity to become more fond of him. Anyway, Jack placed him on the straw and whispered, 'Now listen carefully. I don't want anyone to know I've bought him. Not even Liza, Frankie or yer gran. This is our secret. I'm going to hide him until he wakes up. Then we'll make him a sty in the yard. Promise me now that you'll keep our little secret.'

I believed every word he told me and crossed my heart and hoped to die. Still I couldn't make out why we had to keep it secret and as Jack swung the doors shut I whispered, 'Jack, I wasn't asleep last night when you and Mum were whispering. Did you give Hoppity a pill?'

'Yes, two. To keep him from waking all the other pigs up. Now lie down and don't forget your promise.'

I nodded my reply but I still couldn't understand why it was necessary. He started the van and when we reached the open road we speeded up. I tried to sleep, but between dozing off I could hear Granny's snores and the pig's grunts. Liza and Frankie slept on like the babes in the wood. It was still very early in the morning and the lanes were misty and quiet. All I could hear was the occasional noise such as the bellowing of cattle, and later the clanging of a tram bell in the distance. At last the van halted in our yard. Jack opened the doors and whispered instructions to me to make no sound. I watched him lift the sleeping pig in his arms and carry him into the house. Mum followed behind with an armful of straw. Jack lifted the old bit of sacking off the cellar grating and carried the pig down into the darkness. I stared and wondered. Why were they hiding him in the cellar if they'd bought him? It didn't make sense. I assumed they'd explain to me later, and in any case the cellar was the only spare room we had.

Our Homecoming

T here was no other at home when we arrived and the house was cold, so I was soon busy chopping sticks to make the fire with. Then I put the kettle on to boil while Mum covered the cellar up with the sack and woke the others up. They rushed in to the fire to warm themselves. I was itching to tell them what Jack had bought for me, but Jack guessed that I was about to tell Frankie and he shook his head at me. I didn't have time to say anything further because Mum began bustling about, making a meal. She asked Jack to reach up to the cupboard to find out what was there. He found some eggs, cheese and sausages but this didn't please Mum. She moaned at the way Dad had spent all the money so there was none left for other household expenses. But, as Jack pointed out to her, there was nothing we could do now except eat what he'd purchased. So we sat down to our breakfast – all, that is, except Granny. She was sniffing and sneezing in the corner and seemed to have a bad cold.

'Come on, Gran,' Jack chivvied her, 'yer breakfast's ready.'

But as she tried to stand up, she swayed and was only saved from falling into the fire by Jack's timely intervention. We were concerned, but Mum, predictably, was unmoved.

'I 'ope I ain't gooin' ter 'ave 'er bad on me 'ands. I've enough ter do round 'ere as it is.'

'Don't be too hard on her, old 'un. She's caught a chill,' Jack said, as he steered Granny to bed.

'I know I ain't wanted,' Granny cried between sniffs. 'I'll be gooin' back to me 'ouse in the mornin'.'

But she didn't leave the next day, nor the next, nor the one after that. Jack was firm with her and Dad told her she was to stay until she felt well again. Jack had changeable moods, like Mum.

Sometimes he'd be kind and jolly, and others he would be bad-tempered. A lot liked him though, especially the women. He always seemed to be pestered with lady friends wanting him to take them for walks, and of course he always tried hard to oblige! On Saturdays and Sundays he looked very smart with his freshly pressed suit, highly polished boots, flat grey cap and white starched muffler. He looked extremely handsome, or so I thought, particularly when he brushed down his sideburns with burnt cork. It was my job to procure these on my numerous errands fetching and carrying. Jack would give me a penny for every six I collected, and cheap they were if you remember the number of errands I had to run to get them.

Granny was quite ill and I was given the job of looking after her, but she was far from being an ideal patient. One time when I took her bowl of gruel she refused to eat it. When Mum found out, she determined to see that she did eat it, cold for her next meal if necessary. I was only too happy to let Mum take over.

Anyway, to return to the day of our return – we finished our meal, and Frankie and Liza went out to play and Jack returned the van after I'd helped him clean out the bits of straw. I could see he was in one of his better moods when he smiled at me and handed me a silver sixpence. I could hardly believe my eyes and stared at the coin in amazement.

'That's for being a good girl,' he told me. 'But don't forget our secret.' He winked. I nodded but I wanted to tell someone, Frankie for example, because I knew he could keep a secret. But I had crossed my heart and promised. I dropped the sixpence down my stocking and went indoors. I knew it was no use asking Mum to explain why it had to be a secret. She was busy combing her hair and arranging it in different styles to hide her left eye, which had now turned yellowish. She turned round from the cracked mirror and glared at me.

'Don't stand gorpin'! Call Liza to come an' 'elp fill the copper. I want ter get the washin' done before yer dad gets 'ome.'

Liza was nowhere to be found as usual, so I took the bucket and went to the tap in the yard to fill it. This was Monday morning – Mum's washday, and most other women's too. Maggie was standing by the tap with her own bucket as I approached.

''Ello, Katie,' she greeted me – in some surprise I thought. 'When did yer come 'ome?'

I told her we'd arrived early that morning.

'All on yer? But where's Mrs Taylor and the others?' she asked. 'They ain't bin ter collect their kids they left be'ind yet!'

I explained that we'd returned alone, and this aroused her curiosity.

'How's Jimmy?' I said to change the subject.

'Oh, 'e's bin as good as gold. But I carn't say the same fer the other little varmints.' She didn't say any more because she'd seen Mrs Huggett hurrying down the yard. 'What d'yer think, Nell?' she said. 'The others ain't come back yet.'

She turned to me again for an explanation as though it was my fault. I was about to reply when I saw Mum dashing towards us. I could have laughed out loud. She looked so comical, marching along with Dad's flat cap pulled well down over her left eye. She just snatched up the half-filled bucket and marched back towards the wash-house, glancing back over her shoulder and calling out, 'They're stoppin' a few more days if yer want ter know. We've 'ad enough of it!'

'An' so 'ave we 'ad enough!' Maggie shouted back at her. 'It's took me an' Billy, an' the rest of the good people round 'ere to feed 'em. Let alone tryin' ter keep 'em out of trouble,' she continued, looking to Mrs Huggett for support.

But Mum wasn't listening. So they went off to the neighbours to spread the news and gossip about it. 'Never agen!' I heard one of them say. 'The little buggers 'ave eat us out of 'ouse an' 'ome.'

This was the first Monday I'd seen Mum washing alone at the washtub. The women always did their washing in pairs, but on this day the rest were too busy pulling everybody to pieces. Mum was pleased because it gave her more time to get the clothes dried and into the pawnshop before Dad returned for his meal. Once or twice I went upstairs to keep an eye on Granny, but she was fast asleep and peaceful. I also ventured down the cellar stairs to see how Hoppity was. He too was asleep and although I did think he might be dead I could see the rise and fall of his belly and knew he was sleeping peacefully. Then, just as I was about to return upstairs, I heard Liza above. She was looking for her whip and top and when she'd found them she left, and I re-emerged into the room. But I had a sudden thought. What if my little Hoppity woke up and wanted a drink? So I emptied the soapy water out from the only tin bowl we had, and filled it full of fresh water for him.

Later, in the warm of the late evening, I helped Mum fold and mangle the dry clothes and while she was away at the pawnshop I set to and peeled the potatoes. We were having a treat that night – corned beef and mash. I placed a clean newspaper on the table and arranged the tin plates. The potatoes were already cooked when Mum came in with her apron full of goodies. Two loaves, margarine, a tin of condensed milk and, of course, the corned beef.

Mum counted the plates and then said to me, 'Mek yer gran some more gruel. Do 'er more good while she's in bed.'

I made it, and when I took it upstairs I found she was still sleeping soundly. So I left her meagre meal on the marbletopped table in case she woke and was hungry. I felt sorry for my gran. She seemed to be unloved, just like me. I could see that Mum was going to send her packing when she was well and I hoped she would send me away too. But I knew that this would never happen, not yet anyway, not until I was older. At the moment I was too useful. Someday, I thought, when I'm older, I'll alter things around here or clear out completely. I was in the middle of these musings when I heard Jack's footsteps outside the door.

'Wipe yer feet!' was Mum's greeting.

When Jack saw the cap over her eye he burst out laughing.

'Yer better put it on straight before the old man comes in. He'll notice it anyway. Yer carn't hide an eye like that.'

'Sit down, an' stop yer staring, all on yer!'

She was in an awful mood. Mary wouldn't be home till late, so I sat on her chair next to Jack. Frankie and Liza sat on the other side of the table and we waited for Dad to come in. We were never allowed to have our meals without Dad because he always said grace. Soon we heard him scraping his boots on the mat and Mum began slapping mashed potatoes and paperthin corned beef on to the plates. When Dad entered he looked at Jack first and said, 'Have much trouble getting home, Jack?'

'No, Dad,' he answered, smiling.

Then Dad looked round at us all and said, 'I'm glad you and the kids are home, Polly. I've missed you all.'

Mum was careful to present her unbruised cheek for him to kiss for obvious reasons, but his attention was caught by the cap. 'Yer want to get yer cap straight, Polly. You look like an out-a-work navvy,' he teased.

'Navvy am I now?' She straightened herself to her full height but her quick temper had found her out again because Dad saw her eye for the first time.

'How did yer get that?' he demanded.

'I fell down,' she snapped back at him. 'Now sit yer down an' get yer supper before it's cold.'

He left it at that, and went to the sink to wash his hands.

'Where's the bowl, Polly?' he asked.

'On the stool under the sink where I always keep it,' she answered impatiently.

It was then that I forgot my promise and blurted out 'I'm sorry, Mum. I took it down the cellar to give Hoppity a –' But I didn't get any further. Jack gave me such a hard dig with his elbow that I screamed with pain.

'What's going on here?' Dad demanded of Jack as I began to weep.

Mum tried to change the subject and told Dad to get on with his dinner while she fetched it.

'No yer don't! I want to know what's going on first.'

He stood beside the table in his shirt sleeves waiting for an answer. He was in a temper by now. His face was red and he banged down his fist like a crack from a gun. The potatoes jumped into the air and rolled on to the floor. Mum moved away from the table and sat in her chair beside the fireplace weeping into her apron. She realised, and so did Jack, that I'd given the game away. I hadn't meant to, but it was too late now. Dad was waiting for an answer but no one spoke. Frankie and Liza looked puzzled but they didn't know what the row was all about. At that moment there was a knock at the door and voices called for Frankie and Liza. They could see that something unpleasant was about to happen, and although they were curious they guessed that they were better off out of it, so they ran out before anyone could stop them. I stayed behind because I wanted to see what Dad was going to do with Hoppity when he found out about him.

'What's all the secrecy about the cellar, and why did Katie take the bowl down there? You may as well tell me because I intend to find out.'

Jack and Mum looked at each other, but neither of them said a word. Dad could see that they weren't going to speak so he went to the door and peered down into the murk.

'What's that down there?' he asked. 'It lookes like a pig!'

'That's right, Dad, but it's all right,' Jack began to explain.

'Now don't yer soft-soap me.' Dad was still overcome with surprise.

'Well, Dad, it's like this.' Jack kept stealing a glance at Mum for support. I could see how nervous they looked. 'I was going along the lane to have a drink at this pub, the Pig and Whistle, when I saw this little pig.'

'So it is a pig then, is it?'

'It's only a little one. He was hurt. Some one had put a rag around his leg so I picked him up and put him in the van and drove down towards the farmyard and left him there. But when I came back he was standing outside the barn, and when I called Mum out we decided then to put him in the van and bring him home with us. But when he started to scream I decided to . . .'

'Go on. You decided what?'

'To give him a couple of sleeping pills. You know the rest.'

I jumped and began to pummel him furiously with my fists.

'You lied to me! You lied to me! And I promised . . .' I screamed. And the tears streamed down my face. Dad lifted me into the air and flopped me back into the chair.

'Now you be quiet. I'll hear what you have to say later.'

I'd never seen Dad in such a bad temper, but after he'd paced up and down a few times he seemed to calm down and then he turned on Jack.

'And what do you intend to do with it?'

'I thought we 'aye 'im for the table or sell him.'

At this, Dad brought his fist down again with a thump and Jack and Mum went visibly paler. 'Have yer gone mad?' he bawled. 'I don't want any part of yer thieving ways. I'm warning you, if that pig or whatever you call it ain't out of this house when I come home tomorrow night I'll throw you out with it . . . for good!'

'Don't be too 'ard on 'im, Sam. 'E was only thinkin' of us,' Mum said, weeping some more.

'You can turn yer tap off, Polly. I suppose you've lied as well about that black eye,' Dad said. He turned his back on her.

Then Jack promised he would ask his gaffer to lend him the van again and make some excuse to take the pig back as soon as it was dark.

'Who else knows about this, Polly?' Dad asked.

'Only me, Jack and Katie.'

'What about Frankie, Liza and Mother?'

'No. They don't know. They just slept in the van,' she replied, wiping her eyes on her apron.

'Well, where's Mother now?' Dad wanted to know.

'She's upstairs asleep.'

Dad stared at her. 'I suppose you've given her a tablet, too?'

'No,' Jack answered for her, shaking his head. 'I took her upstairs. She's got a bad cold.'

'I don't wonder at it. I warned yer not go in the first place, but I never thought you'd do this.'

Jack tried to calm him down and repeated that he'd sort things out. Dad was still very angry. 'Don't yer forget what I've told yer. That pig goes back to the farm.'

Dad didn't say another word but sat down in his chair and, picking up his glasses and paper, began reading. Jack didn't say anything. He just gave me a look good enough to kill, then banged the door behind him, and rattled the window frame. This demonstration had no effect on Dad, who read on. Mum told me to fetch the bowl up from the cellar. The water was untouched and Hoppity was still sleeping, so it seemed I'd taken the bowl and the row had happened to no purpose. I bent down and spoke to the pig.

'Poor little Hoppity. I thought you was mine for keeps. What's going to happen to you? Anyhow, you'll be happier with the other pigs.'

But I had my doubts about his future. My brother Jack had lied to me before, and he could easily lie again. I thought how foolish I'd been to believe him. I could only console myself with the thought that he'd promised Dad he'd return him to the farm. I picked up the bowl and climbed back up the stairs. I went into the yard for some clean water and put it in the sink for Dad to wash his hands. As he was doing this, he turned round and looked at me. His face was still grim and he told me to sit in the chair.

'Now, Katie, I want to hear what you know about this.'

I was facing Mum, but Dad had his back to her. He turned and told her to bolt the door. 'What for?' she asked, surprised.

'I don't want Frankie or Liza in until I've got this trouble straightened out.'

Mum sat back in her chair facing me after she'd shot the bolt home. Dad asked me again what I knew.

'I don't know much, Dad. Only what Jack told me.'

'That'll do for a start,' he said, keeping his voice low. Then I began my tale.

'That's all, Dad. I only know what Jack told me.'

'How did yer mum get that black eye?'

I began to weep and looked across at Mum. The sight of her screwed-up lips and warning eyes made me very careful about what I said.

'Well, I'm waiting,' he said slowly.

'She fell down,' I answered, and the tears flowed faster.

'Where? In the street?'

'In the barn. It was dark.'

'Very well,' he said more gently. 'Dry yer eyes.'

I felt enormously relieved when he didn't ask any more about Mum because I wasn't very good at lying, especially to Dad.

'Now, yer sure Granny nor Frankie nor Liza don't know about the pig?'

'Yes, Dad, they were fast asleep.'

Dad unbolted the door and called out for Frankie and Liza to come indoors. They both looked puzzled and wondered what had been going on, but they were used to quarrels and few secrets remained secrets very long in our close little yard so they weren't very bothered.

I got the small brush and shovel that were kept in the fender and cleared up the mess. There was only a bit of potato mash left. Our cat had eaten what was left of the corned beef. While I emptied the remains of our meal on to the fire, Liza helped Mum to prepare some cheese and onions. Mum didn't say a word but instead she slapped everything down on the table until Dad could stand it no longer and warned her to make less noise and let him read his paper in peace. Liza was treated to his watchful eye to make sure she did her share, and Frankie was given some hard looks as he dragged the chairs about noisily. When we'd all eaten our supper of dry bread and cheese Frankie and Liza went to bed, leaving me to clear away the supper plates and lay the table for the morning. I was about to reach for my piece of candle and follow the others when Dad stopped me.

'Before you go I want another word with yer.'

What does he want now, I thought? I stood at the foot of the stairs wishing I was in bed. Butterflies fluttered about in my stomach and I was scared.

'Don't look so frightened,' he said. 'I'm not going to eat yer.'

I walked across to his chair.

'Now, Katie,' he said quietly, 'you're sure that no one knows about this pig?' I could see that he was really worried.

'Yes, Dad. Cross my heart.'

'No need for that. Now sit down and listen to what I have to say.'

Mum sat down too but I had my back to her this time and I was glad. I couldn't face her again without getting frightened. Dad stood over me and told me to say nothing of what he was going to say nor to repeat it anywhere. 'Now, Katie, I want you to keep this a secret – about your brother and this pig.' I kept nodding my head as he continued, 'Jack'll take it back to the farm where it came from or he'll be put in prison if he's found out. So you understand why you're not to tell a soul, then no one will be any wiser.'

'Yes, Dad,' I nodded. Then suddenly I remembered how Hoppity was always getting lost.

'Dad, I think Jack'll get him back before he's missed because he was always wandering off and getting lost.'

'How do you know?' Dad asked.

'Mrs Onions, the farmer's wife, told me.'

Dad smiled and said he hoped Jack would get him back in time. Then he told me once more to remember what he'd told me and with that I was told to go to bed. I turned to bid them good-night and Mum actually smiled as she wished me good-night, and reminded me to take Gran her gruel. When I was halfway up the stairs I could hear her talking to Dad but I couldn't catch all she said. I only heard Dad reply, 'Yes, she's the best of the bunch. At least she can be trusted to tell the truth and I believe her.'

I didn't hear any more, but took the gruel in to Gran, who was fast asleep. I peered at her and thought to myself, I wonder if Mum has given her a sleeping tablet? She was sleeping so soundly it didn't seem natural. Then I spotted that her bowl was empty so she must have wakened at some stage. So I put the other bowl on the table and after kissing her lightly on the forehead I made my way to the attic.

Frankie and Liza were asleep. I sat down on the bed to undress. Then, as I removed my stocking, I discovered the tanner Jack had given me. I placed it on my hand and wondered if I should give it back. But I took a second look at it and resolved to keep it as payment for the lies I'd been told. As bad luck would have it, as I was blowing the candle out the sixpence fell and rolled down a crack in the floorboards. There was nothing I could do in the dark, so I crept into bed and wept. I felt sorry for myself; everything seemed to happen to me, but I consoled myself with the thought that I might find the sixpence in the morning.

I was first down in the morning after Dad and Jack had gone to work. I lit the fire and filled the kettle ready to put on the hob. Then I went down to the cellar to take a last look at Hoppity. I was sorry for the little pig and wondered what would happen to him. When my eyes grew accustomed to the dark I could see that Hoppity wasn't there. All that was left was the straw he'd lain on. Jack must have taken him in the middle of the night, and I was glad really for all our sakes. Perhaps there would be no more rows now. And there was none, for a while at least. No more was heard of Hoppity and, as Dad and Jack weren't on speaking terms, it made two less to snap at each other. I was glad about this. Anyway, we carried on as though nothing had happened. Mum carried on with her normal moaning and Granny with her aches and pains. Evidently she was recovering. So life went on until the return of the hop-pickers.

Along a little alleyway, not far from our house, was a small white-washed house which had been turned into a fish and chip shop. It was owned by a Mr and Mrs Gingold, who were Jews. Everyone on our yard used to heave their shoulders and call them 'skinny'. But I didn't think so, neither did Liza. Mum had a little job there once a week for two hours in the afternoon, helping to clean out the stale fried batter from the chip pan. When it was time for Mum to finish, we always found our way to play outside the shop window, hoping Mrs Gingold would see us. Then she'd give us a paper of scratchings. She even put salt and vinegar on them as though she were serving a customer. We'd sit on the step of an empty house and crunch away to our hearts' content and when we'd finished we'd drink the vinegar from the paper so as to get the last drop of flavour. After that we waited for Mum to catch us up.

It was on an afternoon such as this, not long after our return from the country, that we entered our yard to be greeted by a tremendous commotion. There in the middle of the yard were Mrs Phipps, Mrs Taylor, Mrs Jones, Mrs Buckley, Mrs Huggett and Maggie and a few more besides from the next yard, all nattering away, nodding their heads together. Jonesy and Freddie, the twins and Annie, were running around listening to the conversation as they played. However, as soon as they heard Mum's heavy tread they turned their heads and stared at us. Mum seemed to know at once that they were talking about us. They moved away when she marched up to them. Standing with her hands on her hips, her head thrown back, she shouted out for them all to hear, 'What yer gotta say, yer say it to me face!'

All the kids scattered when they saw Mum but none spoke. Everything went dead silent as Mum waited for someone to speak. Then Maggie moved away from the rest and said from the safety of her doorstep, 'Do yer really want ter know, Polly?'

'What yer think I'm waitin' for?' she replied angrily.

'Well, these lot 'ave told me yow've pinched a pig but I don't believe 'em, Polly,' she stammered.

Mum glared at her, knowing she was as big a gossip as the rest, but Maggie went on to finish what she had to say. 'An' the farmer's goin' ter 'ave yer all arrested.'

It was clear that Mum had to deny it there and then to save us from prison.

'Yer must be mad, the lot on yer! They can come an' search my 'ouse as soon as they like. We ain't got no pig. 'Ave we?' she said turning to me.

I noticed how pale she'd gone but I kept up the act.

'No, Mum,' and Frankie called out, 'Yow lot 'ave pinched it and are trying to blame us.'

Mum shut him up with a clout across his face but that didn't stop him sticking his tongue out at them. Then Mrs Phipps spoke up for all the others.

'Well, Polly,' she began timidly, 'what was we to tell the farmer? You left while we were fast asleep. Dain't they, Mrs Jones?'

'Yes,' came the reply. 'And yower Jack made sure we would get to sleep when he give us that whisky.'

'Believe what yer like!' Mum shouted back.

But as we turned to enter our house, Jonesy shouted out, 'I bet it's yower Frankie that's pinched the pig!'

At this there was a scuffle and a fight broke out, as Frankie pitched in and soon they were rolling on the ground. Mum stepped in and dragged Frankie off because he was holding Jonesy down and it was obvious he'd had enough. But that didn't stop her giving Jonesy an extra sly dig before parting them.

The reader will no doubt remember that neither Frankie nor Liza knew what all the fuss was about. They had no idea why we should be accused of stealing the pig, but they were too frightened to ask Mum while she was in such a temper. I was glad they didn't ask me, but then they had no reason to suspect that I knew any more than they did.

News travelled quickly in our neighbourhood and when Mum gave me sixpence to go to the grocer's to get some vegetables everyone glared and whispered as I passed. When I entered the shop it was full of women chatting about this and that. I stood just inside the door and watched them and listened to snatches of their conversation. No one saw me, they were too busy talking to each other and I soon gathered what the subject of conversation was.

'Common lot, them 'op-pickers,' I heard one say.

'Wonder who they were?' said another.

'Don't yer know? They live up the top end.'

'I hear they stole a pig.'

'Yes, an' it only 'ad three legs.'

'Somebody told me they'd tried to chop the other one off!'

'Did yer know the police are goin' ter arrest 'em?'

'Shame.'

'Serves 'em right. They ought to get life.'

I was so scared I didn't wait to hear any more but backed quietly out of the shop and, still clutching the bag and the six-pence tight in my hand, I ran crying back home. I tumbled through the door and began gabbling my story. Mum looked pale when I told her word for word what had been said.

'It's that Mrs Phipps and the Joneses that's got all this about.'

She was wiping the tears from her eyes. This was a great surprise to me because I'd never seen Mum so upset. I noticed how calmly and quietly she was talking to me, which also surprised me.

'Now listen to me, Katie. Jack's took the pig back during the night. The farmer is sure to find 'im an' nobody will be any the wiser. So if anybody asks yer about it, yer don't know anythink. Understand? If you don't we'll all goo ter prison.'

'I won't say a word, really I won't. Really,' I sobbed.

'Now wipe yer eyes before the others come in. And give me the sixpence. I'll goo ter the shop meself.'

I noticed that she didn't snatch the money away from me or dash out of the house as she normally would've done, but moved slowly and told me to make two cups of tea. Then she went off with the bag under her arm. I hoped and prayed that afternoon that my brother really had taken the pig back to the farm, but I had my doubts. You could never tell if he was telling the truth, he had such a way with him when he turned on the charm. Nevertheless, I kept my promise and no one ever knew the truth except Jack, Mum and Dad.

Two days later, Mum said she had to do some shopping. This made me curious because she always asked me to run errands. She saw the look of surprise on my face and said she'd fetch things until the trouble had blown over. I didn't know whether she was trying to be kinder to me or whether she couldn't trust me to remain silent if I was questioned. She asked me to write down the article she wanted and how much they'd cost. Then she left, leaving me alone in the house. Frankie and Liza were out playing somewhere and Granny was at the Salvation Army Mission practising for the Sunday afternoon march. I busied myself tidying up the house when I became aware of Mrs Jones talking outside the door.

'That's the house. They live there, mister.'

There were three loud raps on the door. I went to the window and lifted the corner of the curtain. I saw a policeman and a man in plain clothes who I later discovered was a detective. He wore a collar and tie and a bowler hat, like Dad's on the wall. I trembled when I realised who they were. Slowly, I dropped the curtain and crept down the cellar to hide, but they continued knocking. I was terrified they'd find me and take me away, so I crouched in the darkest corner I could find. I was so scared by now that I'd wet my bloomers. Then I heard the door open and a deep voice above.

'Very well. We'll call again.'

I heard the door close and their heavy tread on the cellar grating as they walked away from the house. After a while I came out of the cellar and could hear the neighbours and their kids outside our door. Off down the broken stairs I went again, too scared to cry. I crawled to the far end and peered up the grating and saw Mrs Phipps looking down at me.

'There's someone down theea,' she squealed.

'I bet they're too frightened to come out,' Mrs Jones suggested.

Yes, she was right. I was frightened and I wasn't coming out not until Mum came back home. Soon I heard the door open once more.

'Are yer there, Polly?' Mrs Jones called.

'I wonder where she's gone?' Mrs Buckley said.

Just then, I heard Mum's voice bellow out, 'What's gooin' on 'ere?'

'Two policemen 'ave been to see yer,' Mrs Buckley informed her, smugly.

'What yer bawling about? Clear off before I throw this bucket of water over yer all.'

There was the sound of general scattering footsteps. They knew well that Mum meant what she said. Then the door slammed and I came up to find Mum slumped in the armchair, crying into her apron. I felt so sorry for her because she wept so infrequently. I asked her why she was upset and when she heard my voice she sprang up from the chair with fright.

'Where've yow sprang from?' she asked. 'Yer nearly frightened the daylights out of me.' I backed away from her immediately. Then, quite unexpectedly, she did what I'd always wanted her to do; she drew me to her and hugged me, and with our arms round each other we both wept. I was weeping because I was happy and felt safe at last in my mother's arms, but I knew she was weeping over Jack. She told me he'd been arrested and would be tried the next day. I plucked up courage and asked what was going to happen to us. I pressed her to assure myself that everything would be all right.

'But, Mum, he did take Hoppity back to the farm, didn't he?'

'I don't know,' she replied. ''E said 'e did when I spoke to 'im last night.'

'What are we going to do to help him, Mum?'

''E's goin' to deny 'e ever seen the pig, and I think that's the best way out.'

I looked at her, surprised.

'But, Mum, he did,' I exclaimed. 'You know he did and I know he did. It will be worse if he tells lies.'

Then she sat me down in Dad's chair and faced me. 'Now, Katie, listen to what I'm goin' ter say. Jack is your brother and my son an' we've talked this over before he was arrested. That's the best thing to do an' he might well get away with it.'

Yes, I thought, he could, knowing how he could turn on his charm when it suited him. What I couldn't understand was why Mum was making so much fuss of me. She'd never spoken this way to me before, nor could I remember her ever taking me in her arms.

'Now, Katie, promise me you won't say a word about this to anyone.' Her eyes were full of tears as she pleaded, but I didn't ponder too much on the significance of what was happening. I was too happy and felt on top of the world at the thought that Mum really loved me, so I promised. Then she sat me on her lap once again and kissed me.

'Yes,' I said again. 'I'll even lie if I have to.' I felt I was really wanted at last and would have done anything. 'Shall we have a cuppa, Mum?' I asked, as though we had been this close for years.

'Yes. Mek a pot. Yer gran'll be in soon.'

While I was busy humming a tune and waiting for the kettle to boil, Granny came in. She flung the door wide open and demanded in a loud voice, 'What's all this I've 'eard about our Jack's stole a pig? Is it true, Polly?'

'No it ain't! An' don't yer start yer tantrums. I've 'ad enough from the neighbours,' Mum shouted, her face going red.

Granny could see what a bad temper Mum was in, so she went out, saying she'd come back when Dad was in. At the tender age of nine I couldn't understand the moods and foibles of grown-ups. If I ever asked for an explanation I was told that children should be seen and not heard. I think that's why I was so nervous and afraid of adults.

Dad came home later that evening looking like thunder. He neither spoke nor appeared to notice us, but flung himself into his chair. When I went out into the yard for a bowl of water for his wash they must have started arguing. I heard, 'It ain't my fault the gaffer's put our wages down and put us on short-time,' then I entered. 'Anyhow,' he continued, 'I'm luckier than some. They've been stopped altogether.'

I stood back and watched Mum's eyes raised to the ceiling. Then she erupted.

'Oh my God! Double trouble!'

Dad sat down calmly, lit his pipe, then asked me to give him his specs and began to read his paper. Mum went red in the face as she tried to control her temper.

'Yer don't care, do yer? An' what about poor Jack?'

'Poor Jack!' he burst out. 'I've heard all I want to hear about poor Jack from my workmates. I hope they send him to prison for life. And I'll tell you another thing. He don't darken this door again while I'm here. Now, I don't want to hear any more about poor Jack.'

'But, Sam, he took the pig back,' she pleaded.

'Hmm . . .' was all Dad said.

I thought how unkind and hard he was to talk to Mum this way. I felt so sorry for her, she was very upset. She'd been crying on and off all day. I tried to say something, hoping it might elp, but I couldn't get my words out and began to cry too. My eyes were sore and my head ached and I didn't want to be around when Granny returned home because I knew there'd be more trouble. So I told Mum I didn't feel well and asked if I could go to bed.

'Yes, Katie. An' be up early in the morning,' she replied pleasantly.

Then I wished them both good-night. I saw Dad glance at Mum over the top of his paper. He looked surprised when he heard Mum's soft words instead of her usual bawling. I went upstairs and began to undress. Then I realised that my bloomers had dried on me. It was just as well. I couldn't have a clean pair until the end of the week.

I lay on my back staring at the ceiling wondering why Mum was being so kind to me. Things were suddenly changing in unexpected and inexplicable ways and I was no longer being beaten and shouted at. I tried to fathom it out, and then suddenly everything fell into place like pieces of a jigsaw puzzle. I sat up in bed. Yes, that's it, I thought. Mum knew I'd been awake that night in the barn when they were planning what to do and that I'd heard them scheming to drug Hoppity with sleeping pills. Then I felt very miserable again. I also knew how she'd come by that black eye. Yes, that was why she was so nice to me. She was afraid I might tell

Dad the truth. But while I kept my promise she would think twice now before hitting me again. The knowledge of this secret between us made me feel happier and with this comforting thought I fell asleep.

Our Jack's Trial

After Dad had gone off to work next morning we got ourselves ready to go to the courts to see my Jack's trial. I watched Mum in the mirror putting on her Sunday best, her stiff, starched pinafore, over her shabby alpaca frock. Then she twisted her hair into a bun on top of her head and reached for Dad's flat, grey cap that was hanging behind the door. She put it on the bun and glanced in the mirror to see how she looked. All at once she snatched the cap off and slung it across the room.

'That don't look right,' she said, completing her preening.

Granny too was busy getting dressed. After she had put on her uniform she tied on her bonnet. Mum saw what she was doing. 'Yow ain't gooin' in that get-up. Put summat else on.'

'No!', Granny shouted back, 'An' yer carn't mek me. An' I'm gooin'. I'm one of the witnesses.'

Mum didn't answer, she just shrugged her shoulders, tut-tutted and shook her head. Liza and me were already waiting to go, but Frankie too had to give a finishing touch to his wiry hair with a dab of dripping from the basin. Then off we went, closing the door behind us.

The reader will appreciate that we knew everyone in the district, and they knew us, so the incident of Jack and the alleged theft of the pig was the topic of the hour. However, we never expected the scene that greeted us outside. All our neighbours were there dressed to kill and waiting to follow us to the courts. There was Mrs Phipps with the same old moth-eaten fur coat which was supposed to be real skunk. She also had a flat cap on. She was talking quietly to Mrs Buckley who had her black, dusty velvet coat on which brought her in steady income from the tuppence fee she charged when she loaned it out for funerals, and she had her old, flat straw hat with the wax fruit on top. Mrs Jones wore a boater on her red hair and a brown, coarse-looking frock which dragged to the floor. All the while she chatted with her two friends, she kept swinging an orange coloured boa round her neck, and the loose feathers flew everywhere. They stopped whispering when they saw us. Mum stared at them.

'Yow lot ain't comin' with us,' she cried out haughtily, throwing her head back.

'But we're witnesses. Yer carn't stop us. The copper came an' told us 'ad to goo an' give information on what we know. Dain't 'e, Mrs Jones?'

'Yes,' said Mrs Jones meekly. 'An' if we don't 'urry we'll be late.'

'Plenty a time,' Granny told them. 'Yow can goo in front.'

I could see she didn't want to walk with them either. Nor did I. It wasn't because they looked like freaks – they thought they looked lovely. But to my mind they were three gossiping, spiteful old women and I was scared to think what they might say if they were called to give evidence. So off they went, leaving us behind. I tugged at Mum's pinafore and whispered, 'Mum, do they know?' She just looked at me. I knew what she was thinking.

'No. They're only busybodies an' want ter 'ear everything so they can 'ave a good old gossip. An' don't yer forget what yer promised to say if anybody asks yer.'

When we arrived at the courts, Granny and Mum were out of breath. We struggled up the steps and entered a spacious hall. I was surprised to see so many people and all with such sad faces. Some were sitting on a long bench and others were gathered together in groups. It all seemed very strange. I'd never been inside this place before and I was afraid. I looked around and noticed four glass doors leading into different courtrooms. Mum was already peeping through the first one when a policeman crept up behind her and tapped her on the shoulder. She turned round and told him who we were and whose case we were concerned about. He asked us to follow him and he ushered us into courtroom two. We trailed in, in single file, with Granny bringing up the rear. When the policeman saw Granny's uniform he spoke to her very politely.

'This way, madam.' And he took her arm and let her to a seat.

The seating was just like the pews in our Mission Hall. The trial was in progress, but I didn't listen to what the judge was saying because I was too busy looking at the people round me. On the left side was the farmer and his wife and the farmer's brother, the man who'd taken us to the hop fields in his hay cart. Next to him sat a middle-aged man, very smartly dressed, in top hat, black cape and silver-topped cane. Then I saw my brother, looking as charming as ever as he stood in the dock. My gaze settled on the judge who peered sternly over the top of his spectacles. He towered over us in an upright, high-backed chair. Below, sitting at a long, oblong table, were several sombre-looking men, writing down what everyone was saying. The voices seemed to echo in this dismal, dark, dusty room with its oak-panelled walls. Mrs Phipps, Mrs Jones and Mrs Buckley sat in the row behind us. I'd never seen them sit so quietly. After a while my eyes were drawn to the gentleman opposite. My curiosity got the better of me and I whispered my question to Frankie, but before he could answer Mum hissed, 'That's Jack's boss. Now 'ush!'

However, when Frankie saw Jack he jumped up, waved and called out, 'Hello, Jack.'

Everybody turned their heads just like they do when watching a tennis match. It went dead quiet for a couple of seconds. Then the judge broke the silence. His voice boomed out to the constable standing by the door.

'Remove that lad at once!'

Frankie didn't wait to be removed. He ran out, and Liza followed him. I would've liked to have gone too, but I couldn't move. Once more there was silence, but just as the judge began to speak again Granny decided she wanted to go to the lavatory. She moved towards the door quickly and asked the constable where it was and I saw him smile as he whispered loudly that she'd find it in the hall. It was clear that the judge was not amused. He sat bolt upright in his chair and frowned at us over his glasses. I followed Granny out. The hall was nearly empty now, apart from the old policeman darting about from one room to another. Frankie was sitting on a bench reading a comic. We couldn't see the lavatory anywhere. Then Granny spotted another door tucked away in a dark corner.

'What's it say on theea?'

'Private Chambers,' I answered.

'Well goo an ask 'em if I can borrow one of 'em or I'll burst in a minute,' she complained, holding herself.

I was just as ignorant as she was. I thought they were chambers like the one we had under our bed. I was just about to ask a policeman, when a young lady came out of the courtroom. She could see Granny crossing and uncrossing her legs and said, 'It's over there in the corner. Mind the steps.'

Granny dived down the half-dozen steps for dear life, but when she tried the door it was locked from the inside and smoke was coming over the top of the door. Granny banged on the door and yelled out, "'Ow long yer gooin' ter be?" She was hopping from one foot to the other, but there was no reply. 'If yer don't 'urry up I'll do it on the floowa.'

I was scared stiff in case she did and I knew Granny might. Then the door opened and Granny rushed past the previous occupant, nearly knocking her over, flopped down on the seat and kicked the door shut. I couldn't look at the woman, I was so ashamed. When she started to ascend the steps I looked at her and saw the back half of the prettiest drawers I'd ever seen. I was fascinated by this but felt too shy to tell her. Yet if I didn't she'd be out of the door and it would too late. When she reached the top step I ran up after her and cried out, 'Lady, you've tucked your frock into the back of your drawers.'

Like a flash, she pulled the remainder of the dress out and when she turned to thank me I could see it was Mr Skinny-Legs's wife, I hadn't recognised her at first, she looked so pretty in her blue dress with matching gloves and a pretty blue picture hat with lace trimmings. She thanked me kindly and asked how Jack's case was going. I said I didn't know and then, struck with curiosity, asked why she was here too.

'I came to see Jack, but I'm afraid I'm too late. Anyhow, I'll wait outside until we know the result.'

I was just going to ask how she knew about our troubles when Granny emerged from the cubicle.

'Don't yer let me see yer talking to that brazen 'uzzy,' she said, dragging me out of the door.

I had to obey and we returned to the courtroom, Granny to be escorted by the policeman to her seat, and me making my way as best I could to my place on the bench. Mrs Jones was in the witness-box giving evidence. There seemed to be something different about her, but I couldn't put my finger on it. It wasn't her clothes because I'd seen her dressed in these same clothes as far back as I could remember. She looked pale against the orange boa.

'No, sir,' I heard her saying to the judge.

'But you said you saw the prisoner that night with the van.'

She didn't answer, but began to fidget. Then she burst out, 'Phew! It's 'ot in 'ere!'

She pushed her boater back on her head and I could see why she looked so strange. She was wearing a big red wig and as she pushed the boater back the wig went with it. People in the court began to titter. Even the judge smiled, but he was obviously losing his patience and drummed the desk with his fingertips.

'Silence!' he boomed out again.

Everyone obeyed, but they continued to grin broadly. The judge turned once more to Mrs Jones and told her to listen to him.

'Now, did you see the prisoner at any time with the pig?'

'No, sir. After I 'ad the whisky I fell asleep. Yer see I was worn out an' tired. I'd bin . . .'

'That will be enough,' the judge interrupted, still drumming his fingers. 'We're getting nowhere. You may stand down.'

'Thank you, sir,' she said, getting down from the box. 'I wish I could tell yer mower but the truth is I don't know mower.'

He waved her away and called out sharply to the constable at the door.

It was Mrs Phipps's turn. All eyes followed her as she made her way noisily towards the witness-box. She climbed the steps and stood waiting. She looked very frightened, and held the rail to steady herself. I'd seen her and Mrs Buckley having a nip or two of gin from a medicine bottle before they went in. They needed Dutch courage, no doubt. The officer handed her a Bible and asked her to read the words that were written on a card. Everyone was so quiet now you could have heard a pin drop as he waited for her to begin.

'I carn't read,' she said in a hoarse whisper.

'Very well. Repeat after me.'

She repeated what he said word for word. Then she kissed the Bible and handed it back and looked across at the judge.

'You are Amelia Emily Phipps?'

'Yes, sir.' She nodded vigorously.

'Now, did you, on the night in question, see the prisoner with –'

'Can I sit down, sir?' she interrupted. 'Me legs are killin' me. Yer see I've got varcus veins an' if I stand too much they'll bust. I'll show yer if yer don't believe me!' she babbled, hitching up her frock at the same time.

The judge looked across at her and cleared his throat noisily. Everyone started to laugh at the sight of Mrs Phipps holding up her dress, showing all the holes and tears in her black woollen stockings.

'Sit down and answer the questions.'

He was red in the face and as he frowned his shaggy eyebrows pushed his glasses to the tip of his nose. He looked over the top of them at us lot in the court.

'Silence!' he almost shouted. 'Or I'll clear the court.'

Silence descended once again and he began slowly and deliberately:

'Now, Mrs Amelia Emily Phipps, I want you to tell me in your own words, and truthfully, what you saw on the night in question. Did you see the prisoner with the pig?'

'No, no. I dain't. I only told 'im I thought Jack 'ad took it.'

'You're a liar,' the farmer shouted across to her.

Suddenly there was a sharp crack as the judge brought down his gavel on to the desk in front of him. He banged it down several times before he got any kind of order.

'Now,' he said, addressing Mrs Phipps. 'I want you to tell me in your own words, and truthfully, what you saw on this particular night. Did you see the prisoner or anybody else with the pig?'

'No, sir! No, sir!' she repeated, and shook her head so fiercely that the cap seemed about to fly off.

'Did you tell the farmer that you knew who had stolen the pig?'

'No! No! I dain't. I only told 'im I *thought* Jack 'ad took it.'

Again the farmer called her a liar. Again the judge struggled to re-establish order.

'Now,' he said to the farmer, 'if I don't get some kind of order I shall dismiss the case at once.'

There was dead silence once more, not a whisper from any one. Then glaring at her, with the gavel still clutched in his hand, he waved Mrs Phipps from the witness-box.

'Step down! I'll question you again later.'

He blew his nose hard, making a noise like a trumpet. Then he called the farmer to the witness-stand but, before he moved, Jack's boss asked the judge for permission to speak. He said he could but to make it brief. Jack's boss said he had found my brother honest and trustworthy all the time he had been in his employ. He added that Jack was truthful and that he didn't believe that Jack had stolen the pig.

'I'll be the best judge of that,' the stipendiary replied.

I looked at him again – in fact I very seldom took my eyes away from that hard-looking old man while we sat in court. I was so afraid. I hoped and prayed that he'd dismiss the case so that we could all go home. The farmer mounted the witness-stand. Again the judge blew his nose and cleared his throat.

'Are you Mr Henry William Onions?'

'Yes, sir,' he answered.

'Now do you recognise the prisoner?'

'No, sir,' he answered at once.

'No? You mean to say that you don't know him?'

'I've never seen him before.'

The judge started drumming his fingers hard, with obvious impatience.

'If you say you have never seen this man before, how is it that he is charged with stealing the pig?'

The farmer jumped up and pointing across at Mrs Phipps shouted, 'She told me. She said she saw him put it in the van.'

All eyes turned in her direction as Mrs Phipps jumped up and denied his accusation. Once more the gavel banged down with enough force it seemed to split the desk.

'Put that woman outside!' he instructed the constable at the door.

She was led out and Mrs Buckley and Mrs Jones walked out in sympathy. Mum, Granny and I sat very still, too scared to move. I was trembling and so afraid that I might be called next to answer their questions. How could I lie to such a flint-faced man? His eyes penetrated you when he looked at you. I was fascinated by his face. He returned to question Jack. He asked several questions and told him to explain how he came to be at the farm. Then he sat back in his high chair and fixed my brother with his cold stare.

'Now, begin at the beginning.'

Jack looked handsome as he stood up to his full height and began. 'My father received a letter from my sister Kathleen to say would he fetch them all home as they were sleeping all together on bags of straw and they were all hungry. This is the letter, sir,' Jack said, and handed it to the constable to give to the judge. He read it and placed it on the desk and then spoke slowly.

'You were saying?'

'They were very short of money and food and –'

'That's a lie!' the farmer shouted. 'The missus gave –'

Down came the gavel again.

'Silence!' the court resounded. 'If I have any more interruptions I shall close the case.'

The farmer sat down, looking furious. Then the judge told Jack to continue. He sounded to me as if he'd rehearsed the answer over and over again. He spoke easily, without hesitation.

'My father asked me to fetch them home. I asked my boss if he would kindly lend me the works van, which he did. So that same night I drove to the farm, but when I knocked at the farmhouse door there was no answer. Then I drove up to the barn and found my mother and her friends. I told my mother I had come to take them back home.'

'Go on,' the judge said, looking Jack squarely in the eye.

'I drove the van along to the Pig and Whistle to have a drink of cider, and to see if I could find out where the farmer was, but when I inquired no one knew. The first time I saw him was when I was arrested, sir.'

'What happened after you left the public house?'

'I drove back. Everyone was asleep bar my mother. I asked her to wake my granny and my two sisters and brother. Then we all got into the van. That's the God's truth, sir.'

I waited for him to explain how the pig came to be in the van but he didn't mention it.

'Why didn't you wait to see the farmer and explain why you were taking these people away?' the judge asked.

'I hung about until after midnight, sir, but we had to go. I had to be in work by six o'clock the next morning and I'd promised to take the van back.'

The men in black who sat round the table were writing down what he said, word for word. Then the judge stopped drumming his fingers and stroked his chin. He looked first at Jack, then at the farmer and then round the room at the rest of us. I knew, and so did my mum, that Jack had lied and that if he were ever found out we would all go to prison. If only my dad was with me I would have felt safer. I knew I wouldn't be able to face that man's steel-grey eyes without speaking the truth. So I made up my mind to dash out, but just as I started to get up off the bench Mum caught hold of my plaits and pulled me down again. I prayed to myself and began to cry.

The judge was speaking again. 'Do yo wish to question the . . .'

The farmer was angry now, and he interrupted the judge again. 'If he ain't had my pig, well, who has? Tell me that!'

Once more I put my hands to my ears as the gavel banged loudly. The judge had finally snapped and he was furious.

'Case dismissed. Clear the court!'

My prayer had been answered and I didn't have to give evidence. I didn't stay to see the people leave. I flew out of there as fast as I could. I saw Frankie in the hall talking to the woman with the pretty frilly drawers and when she saw me she asked how my brother had got on. I told her the case had been dismissed. She smiled at me and sat down beside Frankie who was more interested in his comic than in Jack's fate. Then I saw Jack, Mum and Granny, beaming big smiles, coming towards us. Jack had eyes for no one but his fancy piece, as Granny called her. Almost at once I felt that I never wanted to see him again and couldn't stop myself tugging at his coat tail and upbraiding him.

'You lied, Jack. I won't ever believe you again.'

But he only grinned at me and put his hand in his trouser pocket and drew out a handful of change and selected a silver sixpence for me. He pushed it into my hand and it occurred to me that this was the second sixpence he'd given me. The other one was still under the floorboards beside my bed. This second gift made me even madder. To think he couldn't trust me to keep his secret without bribing me. I looked down at the sixpence in my hand and wondered what I could do with it. Then I heard Jack say, 'Come on, Lil. Let's go across the road and have a drink.'

Then I decided. I threw the sixpence down and called after Jack, 'I don't want yer sixpence, and you can have the other one back when I find it!'

I watched it roll across the floor and before Mum could stoop to retrieve it, Frankie had beaten her to it. He put it quickly in his pocket and ran off. Granny, who hadn't noticed what had happened, said she was going after Jack to have a gin to warm her up. However, Mum wasn't interested. She dragged me by the hand down the street. Passers-by could hear every word she uttered in her harsh, loud voice.

173

'What yer do that for? Come on! You bin 'iding money away from me, ain't yer?'

'No. I ain't yer,' I mimicked.

By now people were stopping and staring at Mum who was shaking me violently. But I didn't care any more what she said or did because I'd found the courage to answer her back. Suddenly I broke away from her and shouted that the sixpence was under the floorboards and then I took to my heels and tore down the street. Mum didn't follow me, but turned and marched off into the pub.

It was late in the afternoon by this time and I was hungry. I regretted throwing the sixpence away. Still, I think I'd have tossed a sovereign back at him, if Jack had given me one. Anyway, it was idle speculation to think about the tanner because Frankie had probably spent it by now. Then I had a thought, I would stand outside Mrs Gingold's window and if she saw me she might give me a twist of batter scratchings. I hurried along and turning the corner, I came face to face with Frankie eating fish and chips which he'd bought with the sixpence. My eyes fixed on them and my mouth began to water.

'Here, have a chip.' I grabbed a few before he changed his mind, and stuffed them in my mouth. He was annoyed.

'Here, have 'em all,' he said handing me the remains. 'I'll go back and get some more.'

I sat down and finished them off and It didn't take long either. I was so hungry I even licked the vinegar off the paper. Then Frankie came back and let me help him with the second lot. What a lot of fish and chips you could buy then for tuppence!

Frankie still had tuppence left and that he shared with me too. I felt better when my belly had stopped rumbling. We strolled along together and Frankie didn't say a word. I was glad, really. I thought that at any moment he would ask me about the pig, but my brother was no fool, he knew when it was best to say nothing. Just as I was thinking what to say if he should ask, Jonesy ran up and they went off together, leaving me standing alone. There was nothing left to do except return home to face Mum. If there had been any other place to go I would have gone willingly. But I knew that wherever I went in our district people would ask me all sorts of questions, and I had no idea how I would answer them. I'd always tried to tell the truth and grown-ups had a way of getting round a child. So reluctantly I returned home. When I got indoors there was nobody there, so I sat down to wait for Mum. I'd only been there a few moments when I heard a noise like boards creaking and I dashed upstairs.

'Is that you, Mum?'

'Yes,' she called back. 'Come up 'ere. I want yer!'

When I reached the attic door I wasn't surprised to see that she'd lifted the boards.

'Where did yer say it was?'

'There.'

I pointed to the one beside the bed where there was a large crack. I knew she wanted the sixpence badly. She went on her hands and knees as best she could. The loose board came away in her hand when she tugged at it, for it was rotten and half eaten away. She felt around in the open gap but didn't find the tanner until she'd placed several piles of fluff and dust beside the bed first. I went back downstairs, wondering if all mothers were like mine. I knew we were living through very hard times, but we were a little better off than some. My dad was working, after all, but you only had to mention money and Mum was all ears. She counted every penny on the fingers of her left hand. When it came to farthings I always did the reckoning, but the Lord help me if she discovered I'd made a mistake. She followed me downstairs and when I looked at her I could see she was pleased with herself.

'Get the bag and fetch some stewin' meat and vegetables. We'll 'ave a nice pot o' stew fer yer dad when 'e comes 'ome.'

She never bothered about us kids all day but it was always the same, 'yer dad must 'ave this', and 'yer brother must 'ave the other', until I was sick and tired of the sound of her voice.

Then I saw her self-satisfied grin and I said defiantly. 'No! I'm not going! That sixpence belongs to me.'

Like a shot she raised her hand to strike me, but before it came down I backed away.

'If you dare hit me again, I'll tell Dad, Mary and everybody else about that night in the barn and about the pig!'

She turned pale and her hand droppped to her side. Flopping down in the chair, she demanded, 'Come 'ere!'

'No!' I gripped the door knob, ready to run out.

'Come 'ere,' she said, 'I'm not gooin' ter 'it yer any more.'

I wasn't sure what she was going to do, so I left the door ajar, ready if I needed to make quick getaway and slowly I edged towards her. She changed her tone of voice and smiled at me.

'Get me yer dad's cap off the door, an' the bag. I'll goo meself.'

I couldn't believe my ears. I had actually defied her and she'd done nothing to me. Quickly I reached down the cap and handed her the shopping bag and, keeping my distance in case she changed her mind, I watched her push the cap on the back of her head and march out without another word. I was sure she was going to punish me when she returned but I determined to disappear until Dad came home. Frankie and Liza always did that and got away with it. Then I thought, if I don't have my punishment she'll never forget. She always said, 'There, that's what I owe yer,' when you were least expecting it. That was one reason why I was always nervous. I was sure she didn't love me, and at times I think I hated her, although at others I was sorry for her. After all, I was lucky to have a mum of any kind, some kids round our way had no mother at all. They were welcome to mine at times, though. I tried too hard to make her love me and I always did the wrong thing, the result was that I was afraid.

After she'd left for the shop, I tried to think what I could do to please her. Then it dawned on me that I needn't bother. I had the secret of why she had a black eye and I knew all about the pig. It was this secret that stopped her from hitting me and she was afraid I would break my promise and tell Dad. I realised that I had a weapon to defend myself with and I made up my mind to use it whenever I needed to.

I jumped up from the chair but I sat down again quickly. I could hardly see. There were little flashes of light in front of my eyes. I was afraid. This had never happened to me before. I felt sick and there was a nasty taste in my throat. I rushed for the bowl but it had dirty clothes in it. I couldn't use the sink either, it had the crocks in it, so I rushed outside with my hand to my mouth. I didn't want to retch in the yard in full public view, so I ran down toward the lavatory. But Frankie and his friends were kicking a can about and I felt too weak to brazen my way past them. I leant against the wall and Annie Buckley approached me.

'What's the matter with yower Katie, Frankie?'

'Yow ain't 'alf white!' I heard someone say.

I felt dreadful and didn't want them around me.

'Go way! Go way! All of yer!'

Then the gang round me parted and Maggie Bumpham pushed her way towards me.

'My God!' she said, but her voice sounded far away. 'Yer look as if yer dyin' an' yer white as a ghost! What's the matter with yer?'

'I think I am dying, Mrs Bumpham, and I can't see either!' I cried out in what must have been a pitiful voice, and my eyes filled with tears.

She put her hand on my forehead and roughly pulled my eyelids apart and peered into my eyes. She propped me against the wall and fetched out a backless chair for me to sit on. The flashes subsided and I became aware of my surroundings. Maggie pushed my head back and tried to pour salt water down my throat. The kids crowded round to watch the performance. I lurched out of the chair and tried to spit it out but I'd already swallowed most of it. I tried to run away, but before I could, she grabbed me and told Jonesy and Frankie to hold me down. Then, while I struggled, she pushed her grimy fingers down my throat as far as she could. I thought I would choke. I heaved twice. The the only meal I'd had that day slid down the drain. I felt better when my stomach had emptied and the flashes subsided. I dashed for a drink of water.

I looked to Frankie for sympathy but got no support.

'You shouldn't 'ave bin so greedy with the chips,' was all he said.

They continued playing their game and I walked indoors. I looked in the bit of cracked mirror on the wall. I was still very pale but I felt better when I sat back in Dad's chair. Soon after Mum walked in. She looked tired and harassed and she didn't look my way. She knew I was there but she didn't speak, and had her back to me. She tipped the food on to the scrubbed table top. I watched her sorting things out. She looked pathetic, and I felt sorry I'd made her go to the shop.

'Mum,' I said. But she didn't answer.

'Mum,' I repeated. 'I'm sorry. I won't tell anyone or say a word to Dad. Really I won't, Mum.'

Then she turned and faced me.

'What yer bin dooin'?' She saw how pale I was. 'Are yer sickenin' fer summat?'

'I've been sick, Mum,' I said.

But I said nothing else, only that I was feeling better.

'Very well. You can 'elp me get yer dad's tea ready.'

I wrung the clothes out and emptied the bowl, then I took it down the yard to fill it with clean water. The yard was deserted. The kids had gone off to play in another – they always fled when they saw our mum. When I returned, Mum had aready got the pot on the fire in readiness for the stew. I placed the bowl on the table.

'Can I peel the potatoes, Mum?' I asked, eager to make it up with her.

'No! I want 'em cut thin. Yer can scrape the carrots while I skin this rabbit.'

I watched her hang the rabbit by its two back legs from a convenient nail and with two deft tugs she had it skinned. I began scraping the carrots at one end of the table while she chopped up the rabbit into small portions at the other. I didn't look at her, but I could feel her eyes on me all the time. When she'd completely dismembered the rabbit and it was in the pot she sat down and called me over to her. 'Now I'm for it,' I thought.

'But I haven't finished the carrots yet.'

'Never mind about them. I want ter talk ter yer.'

I slowly edged round the table towards her.

'Now,' she began looking me straight in the eye. 'Yer remember what yer said this afternoon? About 'ow yer was gooin' ter tell yer dad?'

I was too afraid to answer, so I nodded several times and all the time she fixed me with her stare.

'An' do yer remember yer made me a promise not ter tell yer dad?'

I nodded again.

'Well,' she continued. 'I'm gooin' ter promise yow this. If yer'll keep yer promise not to say a word to 'im or anybody else about the pig or anythink what's 'appened, I'll never 'it yer again.'

I threw my arms round her and said all in a rush, 'I'll never tell a soul, cross my heart, Mum, and hope to die!'

'All right! All right! she answered and impatiently pulled my arms from round her neck and waved me away.

So, I thought, while she keeps her promise I'll keep mine. After that day she never did hit me again – with the cane or her heavy hand. But there were times when I would rather have felt either than the lashings she gave me with her tongue.

I finished scraping the carrots while Mum put them in the pot with the rabbit. I wiped down the table and spread a sheet of newspaper over it. It was not many minutes before Dad came in, closely followed by Frankie, Liza and Granny. Dad washed his hands as usual, picked up his newspaper, took the spectacles I handed him, and proceeded to settle in his chair without a word. I could see he wanted to be left alone but Mum was very fidgety and kept glancing across at him. Then she could contain herself no longer and she burst out with the news.

'He got off, yer know!'

Dad carried on reading.

'Sam!' she persisted, 'Our Jack got off, yer know. I told yer 'e never kept that pig. 'E took it back ter the farm.'

Dad slowly looked up over the top of his glasses and stared coldly at Mum.

'I don't want to hear another word about Jack or the pig.'

Then, pushing his glasses back on to the bridge of his nose, he recommenced reading his paper. But Mum couldn't leave well alone. She thought Dad should hear about the court hearing. When Mum was excited about anything she kept on and on until she got every little detail off her chest.

'But, Sam,' she began, but got no further. Dad slapped the paper down, pushed his chair back, and went across to her.

'Now look here, Polly. I don't want to hear any more. I've already heard enough from outsiders. Now get my supper ready, I'm clammed.'

I watched him take down the lavatory key and go out into the yard to find a refuge. Just after he'd gone out Granny came in and started questioning Mum.

'What's all this fuss about? I knew Jack wouldn't pinch a pig. That farmer's took 'im for somebody else. Still, I'd like to know who did take it, wouldn't you, Polly?' She rambled on and on.

'No I wouldn't!' snapped Mum. 'An' don't yow start!'

Then Granny's temper really exploded.

'Nobody tells me anythink that goos on in this 'ouse. I'll be glad when I can goo back to me own place. An' yer keep yer supper. I'm goooin' ter bed!'

'You're not going anywhere, Mother!' Dad said as he entered. 'You'll sit down with the rest of us and eat. Now, let's not hear another word. And you, Katie, call Liza and Frankie in. It's about time they were here.'

Then we all sat down round the table and while Mum dished out the food, Granny sat with a self-satisfied smirk on her face. Not another word was spoken and later, when Jack came in, Dad didn't even look at him. In fact he didn't speak to him for days, and each time he returned Dad would deliberately walk out and go to the local for a drink.

How Things Turned Out

O ur neighbourhood soon settled down again to the dismal daily struggle for a crust. Although we didn't know it then, the world was about to be shattered by the Great War but looking back I doubt if it made much immediate difference to many of us – except the young lads who enlisted for the Front. Our brother Jack was one of these, and I well remember taking my first job cleaning the school corridors for money to buy khaki wool to knit him a pair of socks.

The circumstances in which I started work were typical of my sort of people. Mum wanted to make me useful so she asked Mrs Morton, the caretaker's wife, and it was agreed I should get half a crown for Friday night and Saturday and of this Mum would be given one and sixpence. I didn't relish the thought of this job much because I was terrified of Mr Morton. He was a weedy little man who had an unsavoury reputation in our neighbourhood. I suppose today 'Weary Willie' would be regarded as a pervert, but then his peculiar antics were accepted as ordinary enough.

On my first evening, Mrs Morton left me to get on with my cleaning while she carried on with other jobs. I took off my clogs and knelt down to start scrubbing. I hadn't been long working when I was startled by the sensation of heavy breathing down the back of my neck. I sprang to my feet and found Weary Willie grinning at me and leering through his pebble-thick glasses. I was scared stiff wondering what he wanted. Then I felt his hot, smelly breath on my face and he squeaked in his peculiar high-pitched voice, 'The missus ses yer carn't clane the flowa without this.'

With that he slapped a big gob of soft brown soap into my hand. It felt and looked repulsive and I let out a scream. At that sound Mrs Morton appeared and inquired if he was bothering me. I could only nod dumbly. She just pushed a paraffin rag into my hand and told me to rub down the benches. Meanwhile Weary Willie had vanished. I was still frightened though, and I decided to turn the gaslights up to brighten the corridor more. As I was standing on the bench, stretching to reach the brass tap, I felt a cold, clammy hand on my bare thigh. In my shock and fright I fell off the bench on top of him and we both landed on the floor in a heap. His head hit the bucket and the soapy water gushed all over him. I found my strength and pushed the rag I was still clutching into his face and as he lay there spluttering I escaped down the corridor. I ran home as fast as my legs would carry me and fell through the door into our kitchen sobbing, 'Mr Morton . . . Mr Morton . . .!'

Mum knew at once what was wrong. I can see that now. She probably knew what to expect from him. 'What's 'e done to yer?' she demanded, shaking me.

I couldn't explain clearly, partly because I wasn't sure myself exactly what had happened, but what I did say was enough for Mum. She grabbed my wrist and dragged me back up the hill. When we entered the school corridor Weary Willie was having his hair dried by his wife. When Mum saw him her jaw set and she strode towards him in her familiar determined manner. Mrs Morton could only look on helplessly as Mum grabbed him by the shoulders and shook him violently.

'Yer dirty little ram!' she shrieked. 'If I ever catch yer pesterin' my child agen, or anybody else's kids, I'll swing fer yer! An', yow!' she added, rounding on his wife.

''E dain't mean any 'arm, it's the only little comfort 'e gets, teasin' little girls,' she whined.

'Comfort!' Mum was furious. 'Comfort? 'E betta watch out or next time I'll cut 'is bit a comfort off!'

With that Mum strode out, hauling me with her. When we got home I was sent to bed and Mum threatened to tell Dad what had happened, but I knew she wouldn't. He had said I was not to help the caretaker and that it was a job she could do herself. However, I never earned those few coppers and Jack didn't get his khaki socks, but fortunately he survived without them.

This incident happened when I was eleven, just after the outbreak of war. I didn't earn any more until I left school at fourteen, except by begging or running little errands. It was 1917 that I finally started work, and lots of girls and young women were earning good wages. My first job paid twelve shillings and sixpence for a 48½ hour week. I pressed and drilled brass army trouser buttons. It was an easy job to learn, but after deductions for cleaning, tea and overalls I received only ten shillings. Later, I went into piecework and could earn fifteen shillings, but when piecework rates were reduced I moved on.

I lived on the edge of the Jewellery Quarter and it was in one of the many jewellery trades that I worked next. This area was, and still is, one of Georgian and Victorian residential houses centred on St Paul's Square which today is Birmingham's only remaining eighteenth-century square. The individual rooms of the houses are still rented off to craftsmen and small manufacturers who ply their various trades. In my young days many houses were still occupied by families but, as they left, the landlords would encourage jewellers to come in, so that eventually there was a different trade thriving in each room. They were mostly outworkers making jewellery of every description – gold watches and chains, diamond rings, wedding rings and gold bracelets.

My first job was in a room which had obviously been somebody's kitchen. On the gas stove were pots of bubbling glue and I was shown how to make jewel boxes from plywood, cardboard and velvet. Although it was not hard work and I received fifteen shillings a week in wages, I left after a month because I was expected to carry packages containing what I discovered were illicit diamonds. When I realised this I left in a hurry. I stayed in the Jewellery Quarter though, and eventually settled down to work as an enameller, enamelling small brooches which were very popular then, and later badges and motor plates. I wasn't able to become skilled immediately because, in common with most employers then, my first boss would teach me one process only and that was how to 'lay on' enamel. In order to learn all the other processes I had to move from firm to firm, and pick up the trade bit by bit.

My skill as an enameller was very valuable to me after my husband died and I had to bring my children up alone. We'd married in 1921 and were very happy together, but married life was very different form being single. I had to give up work whenever I was pregnant, and being pregnant made it hard to keep accommodation because we could only afford to lodge in rooms, and landladies weren't keen on children. We had four at that time, two boys and two girls and all the while they were young we had a struggle to make ends meet. My husband, Charlie, was out of work most of the time and made a paltry living buying sawdust from the sawmills and selling it to pubs and butchers. This brought in two shillings or half a crown a day, but it was miserably insufficient and he became depressed and gradually took to drink. My father's health declined and he died in 1927, broken by a life of hard work and poverty. I managed to work intermittently as an enameller between pregnancies and I worked up to two days before my fourth confinement. In general, though, I couldn't keep a job because I had to look after the children and found time-keeping difficult.

Bad luck seemed to haunt us then. My father died, as I've said, soon after the birth of Jean, my second daughter. Then, not long after that, my eldest son, Charles, was knocked down and killed by a meat van on his way home from school. After that my husband's health seemed to deteriorate but he managed to do odd jobs and seemed to be drinking less. For a short period after this things went well. I managed to find a job with a Mr Brain who allowed me to bring my baby to work so I could feed her during working hours and while John, my other son, was at school my mum looked after Katie. However this good fortune didn't last. Mr Brain closed down because he had so little work and I was out of a job.

I had to look for work, it was either that or parish relief, and rather than this I took in washing and mending, but the earnings from this were nothing like sufficient. In common with most women then I knew nothing about birth control and I became pregnant again at about this time. This meant I was less capable of the heavy work involved in washing and mangling but I had to struggle on. The illness which Charlie suffered from became much worse as well. He was doubled up with stomach pains for which the doctor gave him injections and tablets and I nursed him, but his condition steadily deteriorated. The doctor returned and when he saw how Charlie was he ordered an ambulance to take him to hospital. That same night I went into labour and I gave birth to a baby girl, my third. Poor Charlie did not live to see his daughter though, he died three days later on 26 April 1931.

I was shattered. I had no real home, no job and no money. I was turned down when I applied for a widow's pension because Charlie didn't have enough insurance stamps on his card. How could he, when he'd been unemployed most of our married life? I had to turn to the parish and I'll never forget the humiliating and degrading way that the stern-faced inquisitors treated me. I determined that if the Lord gave me strength again I would do something better with my life than, sitting there helplessly begging for a crust.

I was given food and coal vouchers eventually, but not before I had pawned everything except the clothes we stood up in. Still, what was given was not enough for us and I had to moonlight as an enameller in order to survive. Even then I couldn't cope. Life was unbearable with Mum, and I was at my wits' end. Finally, I had to let my children go into a Dr Barnardo's home. I was heartbroken, but what could I do? We were starving and helpless; there was only Mum and me and so I decided to let them go where they would at least be clothed and fed. The home turned out to be better than I had expected. It was in Moseley which was still quite rural then, and the matron was a kindly soul. I still wept bitterly when I had to leave them there, but they were laughing and chatting with the other kids soon enough, and I knew I'd done the right thing. That was not what my Mum and the neighbours thought. I was the worst woman in the district!

I went back to work full-time and moved to a furnished room. I visited my children regularly, but it took years for me to fulfil my promise to myself and to them to have them home and they were growing up and away from me. It was not until the Second World War broke out that my chance came. My boss offered to supply me with outwork if I could find suitable premises. This I did eventually. It was a top-floor room and rat-infested, but that didn't deter me, Mr Butler kept his word, and I began enamelling red and green Castrol badges at seven shillings and sixpence a gross.

After a while work began to pour in. Other firms called to see if I could help them complete their orders, and I had to take on young girls to help me. I soon had a thriving business.

All my spare energies and money went into providing the home that my children had never had. I rented a three-bed-roomed house with a large garden and was in seventh heaven furnishing it. Then I applied to have my children back. By this time they had been evacuated and I had to wait, but they eventually returned – the girls that is, because John was a naval cadet on HMS *Ganges*.

Later I bought a house and a small car and we went to see him. We moved just in time because our rented house was bombed soon after we left. My mother and my sister Mary were not so lucky. They were killed in an air raid which completely destroyed our house in Camden Drive and those of the old neighbours from my childhood who still remained there. My son was luckier, though. He survived the war on HMS *King George V.*

Today, although they are widely scattered, I've a large family of whom I am very, very proud indeed.

WHERE THERE'S
LIFE

Contents

Granny's Funeral

It was a cold, wet, wintry day in November 1913 when the undertaker brought the coffin with Granny inside it to our house. Before he arrived Mum made us children bustle about making the place 'spic an' span' to create a better impression on the visitors who were expected to drop by to pay their last respects to the memory of a notable local character. I was then aged ten and we lived in a 'yard' of back-to-back cottages in the Jewellery Quarter of Birmingham. My brother Frankie and sister Liza were a little older than I was, so perhaps it was for this reason that I seemed to end up doing most of the chores. I didn't mind; it kept my thoughts off morbid fancies about Granny in her wooden box. The house was buzzing from early in the morning. Mary, my eldest sister, had taken the day off work and had washed the curtains but for lack of time to dry them properly had hung them back up wet. The blinds were drawn to darken our downstairs room where the coffin rested on the table in front of the range. My oldest brothers Jack and Charlie had turned up and were shuffling about, getting in everyone's way, and Dad lit the candles so that the flickering glow shed an eerie light. My attention was attracted by Granny's big black eyes staring down from her photograph on the wall. To my childish imagination it seemed as if she was still alive to what was happening and was showing her disapproval. I hadn't noticed this picture much while she was alive, but now she was dead it seemed as if her eyes sparkled with the same vitality that they had appeared to possess when I had seen her lying cold on her straw mattress a few days earlier.

Granny had been living with us for some time. She was a contrary old woman and a match even for our Mum, with whom she was continually arguing. She was Dad's mother and I suppose there was a certain amount of rivalry between them. So it was little surprise to me when one evening after a skirmish Mum had blown up at Dad with more than her normal vehemence.

'I can't stand any mower of 'er. She 'ave ter goo,' she stormed as soon as he got through the door. As usual he tried to smooth things over, but Mum was adamant.

'I mean it this time. I can't stand 'er. If 'er don't goo, I goo!'

Looking back with seventy years' hindsight, Dad might have been wiser to have accepted this offer, but things were different before the First World War and couples might quarrel and argue all their married life as Mum and Dad did but rarely separated and never divorced. As bad luck would have it, just as Mum was shouting, Granny walked in and surprised them.

'What's all the row about? 'Ave yer med up yer minds ter be rid of me?' she demanded. Dad must have recognised the inevitable so he began gently.

'Polly an' me think it's best fer yer ter go ter yer own 'ouse now it's ready,' he told her firmly. Granny had originally come to stay with us while her house was being fumigated but that had been months before and there was no excuse for her to continue living in our overcrowded home. But I could see he looked sad as he added, 'I think it'll be fer the best fer all of us.'

'Oh!' she cried, beginning to gesticulate as she did when excited and then to square up like a boxer. She did calm down shortly, though.

'I know when I ain't wanted. No, I can 'elp meself.'

She turned round and stormed out and I followed her as she marched down the street to Mr Kiniver's 'hire shop' where you could rent a horse and cart for two hours for one shilling. The boy in the stable said that Mr Kiniver was out at a funeral and was not expected back until late.

'Can't wait!' Granny told him. 'I want a loan of one of the 'orses and a cart, now.'

The lad was obviously frightened and backed away from her.

'Giss yer shillin' then,' he managed to mumble. He came forward warily and took the coin she offered and then he went off to one of the stables to fetch the horse and cart. I was glad when we were able to leave that yard. It reeked of wet straw and stale horse manure, and the old nag the lad fetched smelled sweaty. The flat cart was none too clean but Granny didn't seem to mind and was only anxious for the horse to be hitched to it. When this was accomplished she took the reins and walked the old horse down the street. This was by no means an easy feat and she soon attracted an interested audience who speculated loudly about her intentions.

'Where's 'Annah gooin'?' asked one of another.

'I bet yer that Polly's told 'er ter goo,' said another.

'Where's 'er got that old nag from? It oughta be in the knacker's yard,' exclaimed a third.

As they gossiped noisily I followed Granny who was pulling the reluctant animal towards our house. The horse's hooves and the iron cart rims made a terrible clatter on the cobblestones but at last silence fell as she came to a halt outside our door. The neighbours and their children crowded around to see what was going on and to hear the conversation between Granny and Dad.

'There's no need to get that old nag, mother,' he said. 'I would 'ave helped yer move yer trunk and chair if yer'd waited.' He spoke quietly, but Granny wanted to create a scene.

'Get me things on the cart,' she ordered him loudly.

Dad went indoors and brought out her belongings and placed them as she directed. He looked sad and I knew he didn't want her to leave but I also knew that he hated the constant uproar of quarrelling, so what was he to do? All he wanted was a bit of peace and quiet.

'Well, I'm off now,' she yelled and glared round at the neighbours with her finger on her nose. Then she tried to heave herself up onto the driving seat but couldn't manage without Dad's help. However, when he tried to assist her she pushed him away indignantly.

'I don't need any 'elp from yow. I can get meself up.' And she did, by pulling herself up backwards.

Dad returned to the house but I remained to watch her, seated now erect and looking proud, whip in one hand and reins in the other, for all the world the expert driver as she prepared to move off.

'Gee up now,' she cried, clicking her tongue at the old mare. But she just turned her head and stared at Granny.

'Gee up! Gee up!' she repeated but it was no good, the horse stood still.

Crowds were gathering by now, and many were laughing with amusement. Granny paid them no heed. She reserved her temper for the horse. She yanked the reins and brought the whip down hard upon its bony rump. The toothless old mare only turned her head and gave Granny what seemed like a horsey laugh too.

Granny decided to dismount which she did with some difficulty on account of having to keep her frock pulled down to hide her torn drawers. Once on the ground again she tried pulling the horse, but still it would not budge an inch. At that moment I spotted Jonesy, the son of a neighbour, throw a stone which caught the animal on the rump and caused it to rear up. Jerking the reins out of Granny's hand, it galloped off, leaving Granny standing in the road waving the whip and cursing.

She appealed to the onlookers for help. I would have given anything to have been able to do something, particularly since nobody else seemed interested in assisting, but Granny was a difficult person to help and I was young and afraid of horses. Then Mr Mitchell the muffin man came to the rescue. He jumped off his cart which was nearby and ran after the runaway. He soon had it back with Granny's belongings intact, and I could hardly believe my ears and eyes when I heard her thank him and allow him to lift her back onto the driver's seat, in gratitude for which she kissed him on the cheek. At this Mr Mitchell may have regretted his generosity for he coloured, but nothing could stop Granny when she wanted to create a drama.

'Yer'll be all right now mother, off yer goo.' He gave the horse a gentle slap and the old grey mare, the cart, Granny and her possessions went slowly on their way. However, before she'd gone many yards she recollected herself and turned to the bystanders.

'Yer a lotta nosey parkers. Yow'll never goo ter 'eaven. None on yer!'

I watched her go with sadness in my heart because I felt for some inexplicable reason that I would never see Granny again.

When I returned indoors Dad asked me if Granny had got off all right. I thought he looked upset, so I didn't mention the pantomime I had just witnessed and instead offered to make him a cup of tea. He nodded and returned to his chair while I stoked the fire.

'I want yow and Frankie ter pay yer Granny a visit every Sunday and let me know how she is. Do you understand?' he said, and I replied that I would.

However, each time we called she wouldn't answer the door

although we could see the curtain move so we knew she was at home. I told Dad and suggested that if he called she would open up, but he said, 'No. I don't think so. She'll come round if she wants anything.'

So our house got back to normal and our life carried on as before. Then one cold afternoon later that winter when we were all huddled round the fire for warmth from the snow falling outside, Dad sighed, looked at his mother's photo and said, 'I wonder how yer Granny is faring in this cold weather?'

'Perhaps you could take her a lump of coal in yer cart, Katie?' he suggested.

'Goo on then get yer coat on,' Mum told me. Dad said I should wait until it stopped snowing so hard, so I watched from the window, and before very long it did ease and I was sent down the cellar for the fuel. One lump Mum told me to fetch. But I thought to myself, I'll take two when she isn't looking, which I did. Dad saw what I had done but he covered the coal with an old sack, winked and whispered, 'Good girl.'

Mum had a habit, whenever she sent me any distance on an errand, of insisting that I had clean bloomers on, 'in case yer get knocked down by a 'orse', which was why I was scared of them. But for some reason she forgot on this occasion and I did not stop to remind her.

Granny lived about half a mile away, in a narrow street with drab shops dotted between the houses, which were one down and two up, like ours. I was walking down the street, singing happily to myself, when I was startled to hear the sound of hooves on the cobbles. The first thought that came to me was that I hadn't got my clean bloomers on. I looked round to see how far away the horse was and saw there were two galloping towards me. I ran onto the pavement, dragging my cart after me. There was a wet fish shop just there and in my eagerness to escape I darted in. But the floor was wet and I slid along before colliding with a slab of sprats, cod and ice which showered over me. I began to cry. I couldn't pick the fish up because they were slippery and eluded my grasp, and when I tried to stand up I'd slip back again amongst the icy cold debris. I had just succeeded in sitting upright when the fishmonger appeared.

'What yer think yer doing down there?' he asked, looking at me quizzically. I was frightened and began to sob.

'I'm very sorry but I'm afraid of horses and my Mum forgot to change my bloomers,' I blurted out in confusion.

'Well I never!' he exclaimed, laughing. 'I've 'eard some things in my life but that beats 'em all.'

And with that he bent over and lifted me to my feet and told me to be off, which I did not need to be told twice to do.

A few minutes later I arrived at Granny's where I found a crowd of people outside her door. In the middle of them were Mrs Phipps and Mrs Taylor, our neighbours, sitting on the step crying. I couldn't tell what was happening so I asked them to move so I could take the coal into Granny's house.

'Yower Granny won't need that where 'er's gone to,' Mrs Phipps said.

'Where's she gone to then?' I asked, wondering what she meant.

'She's dead. Don't yer Mum know? Everybody else does,' Mrs Taylor replied.

'That's right. She's 'ad 'er chips this time,' Mrs Phipps added.

'I don't believe yer,' I exclaimed.

'Come 'an see fer yerself. I'll tek the coal.' And so saying she helped herself.

I didn't want to go in. I was so shocked I just turned tail and ran home as fast as I could. I stumbled across the threshold but before I could say anything Mum shouted at me, 'Where 'ave yow bin all this time? An' what yer cryin' for now?'

'Granny's eaten some chips and now she's dead,' I stammered, tears dripping off my nose.

'What yer talkin' about? An' where's that lump of coal?' she yelled, shaking me.

'Mrs Phipps took it. She said Granny wouldn't need it where she was going.'

'Oh! She did, did she? Well, we'll see about that.'

She slapped Dad's flat cap on the top of her bun and marched out of the house. She thought more about losing the coal to Mrs Phipps than about Granny, it seemed to me then, but I expect it was the shock that caused her to react in that way. She wanted me to accompany her but I hung back, afraid that she'd find out that I had taken two lumps of coal, and Dad had gone out, so he was not there to protect me.

'Come on. An' don't 'ang back theea. An' bring yer cart along with yer. I might need it fer summat else beside the coal.'

I snatched up my doll, Topsey, and laid her in the cart and ran after Mum who was half way down the street before I caught her up. I was confused and still worried that there might be horses and that I had not changed my bloomers which were wet from where I had fallen in the icy fish. When we arrived at Granny's house Mrs Phipps and Mrs Taylor were still standing outside gossiping with the neighbours. Mum went straight up to Mrs Phipps and demanded to know what she meant by saying Granny had had her chips.

'She's dead Polly. I come in this mornin' to see if she wanted anythink, an' there she was, stiff an' cold.'

This made me shudder but I was brought back to my own worries when I heard Mum demand that she gave the lump of coal back. At that Mrs Phipps began to back away from Mum's fierce stare.

'Oh, I forgot about that. Now she wunt want it will she?'

'No, she wunt, will she,' mimicked Mum. 'Well goo on 'an fetch it.' Mum was insistent.

I watched and held my breath, but to my relief she only brought one lump out of her bag, and that the smallest of the two, which she gave to me and I put it quickly into my cart.

Granny's neighbours were still looking on, watching for further developments, because they all knew Mum's temper. But Mum just gave them one of her black looks and elbowed her way past the two women and went into Granny's house. I followed and peered round. Everything was so still and quiet and there was dust everywhere. I wondered why this should be when Granny was so particular, but I was soon roused from my thoughts by Mum.

'Katie, I want yer ter stay 'ere with yer Gran while I goo out an' get Mrs Taylor. An' don't let anybody in. I don't trust 'em.'

To make doubly sure of this she turned the key in the lock as she went out. At this I was more frightened than ever. Granny was seated in her rocking chair facing the fireplace, but her back was to me and I could only see the paper curlers she had in her hair. There was something strange about these and they seemed to scare me though I could not take my eyes away. I put my hands over my eyes to shut out my fears: I'd never seen a dead person before. But after a bit my curiosity got the better of me and I spread my fingers slowly to peep through. Then I crept forward to look at Granny. I wished I hadn't. I started back petrified. Granny was staring at me with her eyes wide open. I never wanted my Mum so much in my life as I did at that moment. I wanted to run out and scream, but Mum had the key and all I could do was stand stock still, listening to the thumping of my heart. I literally jumped for joy when I heard that key turn in the lock and saw Mum and Mrs Taylor enter with another woman. As they banged the door shut, the vibration set Granny's chair rocking and I put my hands over my eyes. But Mum wouldn't have that.

'Yer don't 'ave ter look if yer don't wanta,' she said sharply, pulling them away.

'We're gooin' ter tek 'er upstairs an' lay 'er out,' she said.

I felt safer now that they'd arrived and I was curious to see what she meant by 'laying out'. So, avoiding Granny's staring eyes, I watched Mum, Mrs Taylor and the big-bosomed woman they called Aggie lift Granny with some effort out of her chair and up the creaky stairs. I stood engrossed by this until I heard the rocking chair creak behind me, and at that I scampered up after them. They stripped off Granny's clothes and then washed her all over. Then Aggie dressed Granny in a brown calico shift which she had brought with her. Then they laid her back on the straw mattress and covered her with a sheet. When this had been done they made to go downstairs again, but I was in front of them going down two at a time. Mum flopped into Granny's chair, heaved a sigh and exclaimed, 'My God, she was 'eavier dead than alive.' And her companions nodded in agreement.

Then Mum thanked them and said she would pay them later for their trouble and invited them to the funeral. Then she showed them to the door. When they had gone I was surprised to see her lock the door again. Then she returned upstairs with me close behind. We entered the room and Mum began to look round, but my eyes were drawn to the bed. I let out a shriek. The sheet had slipped off Granny's face and I was horrified to see that her eyes were still open.

'What's the matter with yer now?' she demanded, shaking me.

'I want to go home.' My voice was trembling now.

'Get outa me way. An' wait,' she muttered irritably, pushing me to one side.

I walked over and looked out of the window into the yard below where several of the neighbours were looking up at me. They must have heard my scream. I couldn't look at them; nor could I look back into the room. I wanted to run away, and if that window had not been so high I believe I would have jumped through it. But I turned round and watched what Mum was doing, avoiding looking at the bed. Then Mum went over and I gazed on as she replaced the sheet and then rolled Granny onto her side and began feeling under the mattress. At last she found what she'd been looking for. It was a small, battered tin money-box. She opened it and took out several half crowns, silver threepenny pieces and some pennies. There were some faded letters but she wasn't interested in those and shoved them back in the tin, unopened. Then, pocketing the money, she placed the box back underneath the straw mattress and rolled Granny onto her back again.

I squatted on the stool at the foot of the bed while Mum searched the drawers, from one of which she pulled a bottle of gin. She consumed the contents quickly before replacing it as she had the box. Amongst the assorted contents of the other drawers she found another small box. Her eyes lit up when she opened it and found it full of farthings. These she slipped in her pocket, then she tidied the stuff away. As she was poking about for more loot I glanced back at Granny and saw that the sheet had moved again.

'Mum, Granny's watching you,' I sobbed.

'Don't be silly. It's only the sheet that's slipped. I'll soon fix that.'

And with that she took two of Granny's pennies from her pocket, put her fingers on Granny's eyes to push her eyelids down and placed a penny over each eye.

'That'll keep 'em shut,' she said with satisfaction and replaced the sheet.

At last she stopped searching and said, 'Come on, there's nothing mower 'ere.' But I was already fleeing downstairs to the door.

When we emerged we found the neighbours still standing around discussing what had happened, but Mum just pushed her way through them without a word. However, we hadn't gone more than a few yards when she stopped and turned around.

'Where's the cart with the coal in? Yer betta goo back an' fetch it. 'Ere's the key,' she said, fumbling in her pocket.

I stood and looked at her, petrified. I could no more return to that house alone than face the devil.

'No! No! No!' I screamed and ran off down the street.

I turned to look back once but Mum was nowhere to be seen.

When I got in I found the house was empty and the fire nearly out. I felt so miserable. I was cold and wet. I pulled down my damp bloomers and changed them for a warm, dry pair that were hanging on the line over the fire. Then I just sat on the floor and wept for Granny, and for myself.

When I recovered myself and controlled my weeping, my attention was attracted by Granny's photograph hanging over the mantelshelf. She seemed to be glaring down at me with her deep-set, black eyes. I thought about the chips that Mrs Phipps had spoken of and remembered that I had nearly choked on them once. No more chips for me, I vowed. I didn't want to die like Granny had. I was deep in such thoughts when I heard Mum's unmistakable heavy tread coming towards the door. I thought, I'm for it now, but all she said when she'd bustled in and taken the coal from the cart, was, ''Ere yar. Tek 'old a this an' mek tha fire up before yer Dad comes in.'

I was only too happy to be busy breaking the coal up with the hammer, pulling out the drawer pan and stoking up the fire with the bellows. Soon Dad returned. I could tell immediately by the look on his face that he knew about Granny, for news travelled fast in our district and nothing was secret for long. I ran over to him.

'Dad!' I cried. 'Granny died from eating chips. Mrs Phipps said so. Shall I die too?'

'No,' he replied. 'It's just a saying.'

'How did she die then?' I asked.

'She was just getting old,' he said sadly.

Now I was talking to Dad I wanted to tell him about how Mum and I had found Granny and what wicked things Mum had done, but I knew Mum's eyes were on me so I thought better of it. Whether she ever told what she'd found I never discovered, but for my own part I only wanted to forget the whole frightening incident. But I never did. That episode has lived with me all my life.

When Dad had eaten his tea I heard him ask Mum if she'd kept the payments up on the insurance policy.

'Course I have,' she told him.

I knew this was right because every Saturday I had the job of taking the insurance book and sixpence along the street to the insurance agent's house. Mum didn't believe in paying any premiums for herself, though. 'Why should I waste a penny a week?

I shan't be 'ere ter spend it,' she always said.

No matter how Dad tried to explain the principles of insurance to her she didn't want to know. That was how she was. She always looked at every farthing twice before parting with it.

Later, when Frankie and Liza, my brother and sister, came in from playing I told them the sad news, but they didn't seem very upset. This was no surprise: neither of them cared much for Granny.

Mum got me to reach down a tall vase from the mantelshelf. From this she drew the policy and with its lots of pawn tickets. I was given the job of going to fetch the agent, but Dad offered to go and so I went with him. When we got to his house we found he was out so Dad poked a message under his door. Then he told me to go back home and explain to Mum.

'Aren't you coming back with me, Dad?' I asked, surprised that he was leaving me.

'No, I'm going down to the pub,' he answered and he wiped a tear away from his eye.

I felt very sorry for him then. If I'd been older and known the words to comfort him . . . But I was only a child, so I just stood and watched him out of sight and turned reluctantly to deliver his message.

When I entered our room I found Mum had down two more vases and was sorting out a pile of pawn tickets. Some she discarded and threw into the fire, others she kept.

'I'll be able ter get some of these things out,' she mumbled. 'An' I must set a good table for the funeral.'

Just then there was a knock on the door. Mum lifted the corner of the curtain and peeped out to see who it was. It was Mrs Jonesy, Mrs Phipps and Mrs Taylor.

'An' what der yow three wanta borra?' she inquired sarcastically.

'Can we speak to yer, Polly?' Mrs Phipps asked, ignoring her last question.

Mum opened the door to them. 'Well? Spake up then.'

'We're very sorry about poor 'Annah passin' on, so we thought we 'ad better come to pay our respects.' They stood there with their aprons to their eyes. But Mum knew them for crafty rogues and she hadn't forgotten the coal. She probably knew too that they had been none too fond of Granny when she'd been alive. She made to close the door on them when Mrs Phipps added, 'We're gooin' from dower to dower ter get a collection up for a few flowers. Is that all right with yow, Polly?'

'That's the least yer can do!' Mum replied and stared at them hard and long.

'Well,' Mrs Taylor said. 'We'll do our best, Polly.'

Then off they went but I had noticed that Mrs Taylor was really crying. I liked her. She was always kind to me and she was the only neighbour Mum could really trust.

When Dad returned he didn't speak a word to either of us. He just sat in his chair and gazed up at Granny's picture in its faded gilt frame.

'May God rest your soul, Mother,' I heard him say to himself at last. 'If only I'd 'elped you more you might still be 'ere.' And he put his face in his hands and sobbed. Mum went over and tried to console him but he pushed her gently from him. I suppose his grief was a personal thing which he could not share with anybody.

So that was how we came to be sitting in the darkened room with Granny's coffin on the table, waiting for the neighbours to come and show their last respects. I remember the undertaker asking if anyone wanted to see her before she was screwed down and the people filing past one by one, their heads bowed. Some shed real tears too. Some of them I had never seen before and some were there to satisfy their curiosity. Wreaths and flowers were piled up outside in the yard, waiting to be heaped on the coffin. I remember going upstairs while they were looking at the corpse and writing a note with trembling fingers. It went something like this:

Good bye Granny and God bless you. And please forgive my Mum.

I really did love you and so did my Dad. XXX

I rolled this message into a little ball and returned downstairs. Dad was still standing by the coffin and I whispered to him, 'Dad, can I have another look at my Granny?'

He nodded and turned away, and while the others' attention was elsewhere I put my hand down inside the coffin until I felt Granny's cold fingers. My stomach went all queer inside but I managed to push the message between her icy fingers and kiss her forehead before I pulled my hand away.

'Good bye, Granny, I'll try to be a good girl,' I sobbed before I stood back for the undertaker to screw down the lid.

I was pleased he hadn't seen the note or the tears that I left behind on my Granny's face. I wiped my eyes and felt a bit better, knowing that Granny was taking my message with her to heaven. Then I wandered outside to look at the wreaths and the Salvation Army Captain touched me on the shoulder.

'Katie, will you tell your father I'd like to speak to him?' he asked me.

'Yes,' I said. 'Will you come inside?'

I thought I ought to ask him. I could see the neighbours looking curiously at the big box he had with him. I heard him say to Dad how sorry he was about Sister Hannah and how he'd have liked to have seen her before she was screwed down. Then he handed the box over, saying, 'Here's the crocks I promised to lend your wife . . . and some extra food. It's not much but it'll help.'

It was amazing how people did rally round at times like this. They didn't bother much at other times unless asked, and then they often had to think twice. But now the Captain was on his knees beside the coffin praying. When he'd finished he stood up and asked Dad the time of the funeral so, he said, he could be there with the other brothers and sisters and the band. Mum kept out of sight until he had left, then down the stairs she came, all dressed up in a long black taffeta dress, which rustled when she moved. She wore new black buttonup boots and on her head was perched the largest black hat I had ever seen with a black bird on top.

'Now 'ow do I look, Sam?' she asked as she stood preening herself. Dad didn't take a bit of notice but Mary stared at her.

'Anyone would think you was going to a weddin' instead of a funeral,' she let out. 'Disgustin' I call it.'

I looked at Mum and thought if only she was as nice as she looked maybe all our lives would have been better. But I knew this was wishing for the impossible.

Mary was dressed as usual, for she always wore a black tam-o'-shanter and a black coat. Dad, Jack and Charlie just wore a black armband each with their Sunday suits, and I was dressed in a white lace dress with a wide black sash of silk ribbon. I also had real boots for the first time. I remember the argument there had been too between Mary and Mum over keeping her wages back that week.

'What about buying the kids some clothes?' Mary had said. 'Instead of spending all the insurance money on yerself.'

But Mum's reply had been, 'I'll see what I've got left when I've got the grub in.'

'I shouldn't bother yerself if I were you,' had come the reply. 'I'm keeping my wages to buy them some myself.'

So that was how I came to have a new dress and boots and a real ribbon for my hair instead of the usual string. She also bought Frankie new clothes and Liza too, but neither of them was able to attend the funeral: they both had bad colds. Liza had to stay in bed and Frankie was downstairs in front of the fire. Mum said he had to watch the house and the food in case anyone slipped in while we were out and helped themselves.

By this time there was quite a crowd gathered in our little room. There was Mr Phipps, Mr Jones, Mr Smith, the lamp-lighter and another of Dad's drinking pals, all having a drink and talking quietly. They were to be the pall-bearers. This was all new to me and interesting for that reason. I'd seen plenty of funerals, but this was the first I'd been involved in and I was fascinated by the splendid flowers and the well-groomed horses of the hearse and I forgot, for a moment, my fear. Anyway I had my clean bloomers on.

When we went out the sun had come out and the horses' coats shone like black silk. They were so different from the dustman's horses and those that pulled the water carts. Then the bearers carried the coffin out and the Salvation Army band struck up with 'Nearer My God to Thee' just as we climbed into the carriage.

We passed along slowly so that the corte[grave]ge could be seen and all could have a last look at the coffin. I looked through the window and there were people lined up on both sides of the street, the women with black aprons and the men with their caps and hats off, bared heads bowed as we passed. Even the dustcart and the draycart pulled over to one side. Shops had their blinds drawn down and the shopkeepers stood in their doorways as a mark of respect. I saw some of my school friends on tiptoe, straining their necks to see.

'Hello Katie,' Annie Buckley called out and waved.

'Hello Annie,' I called back from the half-open window.

At this my sister Mary slapped my face. 'Behave yerself,' she whispered. 'This is a funeral not a wedding.'

But this did not deter Mum who leaned out of the window.

'Some people 'ave got no respect for the dead.' Mary pulled her back from the window and closed it. She was obviously disgusted. 'You're as bad as the rest!' And after that no more was said. Dad sat there quietly throughout.

The church bell was tolling mournfully as the carriage entered the cemetery gate. We stopped outside the church door and the driver handed us down. There seemed to be crowds of people lined up on each side of the door and lots were already seated inside the church waiting for the coffin to enter. Just inside the vestibule there was coconut matting, and seeing this Mum looked about then began to wipe her feet. I thought she was never going to stop until I heard a woman say, 'I see 'er's still showin' off.'

At this Mum turned round and gave her a dirty look before she moved along with Dad, followed by the rest of us. However, it was obvious that she was intent on making a spectacle of herself. She wanted to be noticed in all her finery and as she walked up the aisle she kept stopping to give a little cough on the back of her hand and looking from side to side. Dad simply pushed her forward but I heard him whisper, 'Move along, yer 'olding up the service.' She moved but she still kept glancing about. She would touch her hair then fiddle with her hat and pretend to straighten her dress.

Everybody's eyes were on us, especially on Mum. Then I heard someone say, 'It's disgraceful the way she keeps standin' there preenin' 'erself.' Then another joined in. 'Who does she think she is? The Queen of Sheba?'

All at once people began 'shushing' and those who were not 'shushing' were commenting on Mum's behaviour. Finally Dad pulled her down into her seat. Then everyone fell silent as the preacher entered and the service began. When it was over we filed out to the accompaniment of the organ. It seemed all were anxious to see Granny's coffin lowered into the ground. There were people from everywhere in the district standing around that wet, muddy graveside that day. Some of them wept as the preacher opened up his prayer book and the coffin was gently lowered into the grave. He delivered a sermon during which everyone stood still, until he picked up a handful of earth and spoke in a deep voice: 'Ashes to ashes. Dust to dust.' Before he could continue little Jonesy chipped in: 'An' if God don't 'ave yer, the devil must.' All heads turned as his father gave him such a clip that he landed in the muddy, freshly dug grave behind him. The preacher held his hands together and looking skywards said, 'Forgive them Lord, for they know not what they do.' Then, walking away in disgust, he said, 'I've never come across such a disgraceful congregation in all the years I've given burial services.'

Jonesy was still struggling to get out of the grave, and this he managed only with his father's help, after falling back in once. By now some were laughing openly, but Mrs Jonesy did not think it was funny. She turned round angrily: 'It's no laughin' matter. We might 'ave 'ad another funeral,' she wept.

Then we were walking back towards the carriage, and as we passed I heard Mr Jonesy say to the preacher, 'I'll give 'im the devil when I get 'im 'ome.' But the preacher just walked slowly away, taking no notice of anyone.

When we arrived home Frankie was still sitting by the fire with a coat round his shoulders and Mrs Taylor was there in Mum's starched white apron ready to serve. Mum had given her permission to wear her pinafore. At that time it was a tradition that when someone in a family died there was always a bow of black ribbon draped over the top of their photograph frame. But we had had to make do with black crepe paper, which was the next best thing. It was also said that if the bow should move of its own accord after it had been draped it was a bad omen. While we had been out Mrs Taylor had placed the paper in position.

Then we squeezed round the table – Mum, Dad, the bearers, and several neighbours who had been 'helpful in her hour of need' as they called it. I had never seen such a mouth-watering display of food on our table. There was cheese, pickled onions, corned beef, cottage loaves, pig's pudding and even a gallon jug of ale. However, Mary, Jack and Charlie didn't stop but made the excuse that they had to go back to work. They left, and while the adults were talking and stuffing themselves, I picked up a piece of pig's pudding for Frankie who was still huddled by the fire. I found it was stale so I replaced it and was about to make him a corned beef sandwich when Dad asked, 'Where's Pete?'

'Who's Pete?' the lamplighter asked.

'Our cat. He's usually waiting here for scraps.'

All at once Frankie jumped up, knocking over the stool. 'Oh dear, oh dear!' He sounded worried. 'I forgot 'im, Dad. He went out in the rain and I put 'im in the oven to dry!'

'Yer what?' Dad gasped, dashing to the oven door.

Pete shot out with his hair standing on end like the bristles of a brush. This proved to be only a minor diversion and they quickly settled down to their food and drink again. Frankie did not escape though. Mum went over to him and delivered a hard slap then ordered him off to bed.

After they had consumed all they could the guests began to leave, saying what a good send-off Mum had given Granny. Mr and Mrs Jonesy apologised to Dad for their son's behaviour and promised that he would get 'what's comin' to 'im when we get 'ome'. After they had all left – Dad too – Mum hung Granny's death card beneath her picture then went off to join the others in the local. Now that the house was quiet I filled a plate with some of the leftover food and took it up to Frankie. I found him with Liza sitting on the edge of the bed fully dressed reading a comic.

'Have they all gone?' Liza asked.

'I thought you was ill.' I glared at her. But I suppose she had pretended to be ill because she didn't want to be at the funeral. I turned my attention to Frankie, who still looked pale but who insisted on going downstairs. We sat round the fire with our leftovers and I answered their questions about the day's events. Then I thought of a way to cheer them up.

'Tell yer what. I'll bring in some of the kids who were there and Jonesy can imitate the preacher.' To this they laughingly agreed.

I went into the yard, rounding up those I could find. I knew Mum and Dad would be out until late drowning their sorrows. The pubs didn't shut until eleven o'clock so we would have a good three hours' fun.

I had to go to the next yard to fetch Jonesy. I didn't like him much because he was a terrible liar but it wouldn't have been fun without him. I knocked on his door and when he answered I could tell from his face that he'd been crying. I told him our plan but he was none too eager until I told him we were going to play at funerals and that Frankie wanted him to imitate the preacher; then he came along at once.

When we were all seated in our kitchen Frankie wanted to know who was at the graveyard and what had happened.

'Well I'll tell yer what the bloke said if yer'll all be quiet,' said Jonesy.

With that he pulled Dad's shirt off the line, put it over his head and, pushing his arms through the sleeves, picked up the Bible which was on the sideboard.

'Ashes to ashes, dust to dust,' he intoned, just like the preacher had. We roared with laughter. Then he put his hands together and continued.

'Forgive them Father, for they know not what they do. But my Dad said, "I know what I'm gooin' ter do when I get 'im 'ome."' He changed into an imitation of his Dad. But Florrie Mitchell from the next yard was not convinced.

''E dain't say that did 'e?'

''E did!' he replied angrily. 'An' I've got the marks to prove it.'

With that he replaced the Bible, tore off the shirt and dropped his trousers. We could see the red marks when he bent over but that was not all we saw. We burst out giggling at the sight of his bare bottom and we were still tittering when the door burst open and Mrs Taylor entered. Seeing Jonesy she cried out, 'Pull yer trousers up yer dirty lad.' But he was out the door, tripping over them in his anxiety to avoid another whack.

'What d'yer want?' Liza asked in her surly way.

'Yer Mum asked me to call in and clear away the crocks and tek the chairs outside ready ter goo back ter the mission 'all.' Then she added, 'An' why ain't yer all in bed? Yer'll catch it if yer Mum knows yer've 'ad that Jonesy lad in.'

'I'll 'elp yer ter move the chairs if yer don't tell ower Mum,' pleaded Frankie.

'Very well then,' she conceded. 'But see that yer behave yerselves in future, or I might.'

We were happy helping Mrs Taylor tidy up. I liked her: she was different from the other women. She was always ready to do odd jobs for anyone in need.

She bustled round finishing her jobs and was just about to leave when she noticed that the crepe paper had slipped from Granny's frame. She stood on the stool and reached up to replace it, and when she stood back down again she bent over and whispered to me, 'That's a bad omen, luv. I should get up ter yer bed before there's any more trouble.' I was really scared at this. 'An' remember to be careful what yer say or do, fer yer Granny's eyes will be on yer in the future.' Then she went off.

I tried to remember what my sister Mary had said about ignoring old wives' tales and I tried to put them from my mind, but after that I often caught myself glancing at Granny's picture and it seemed to me that her black eyes came alive and followed me round the room.

Mary's Wedding

One day, a few weeks after Granny's funeral, Mary came home earlier than usual from work. I heard her tell Mum the news that she was getting married.

'Why dain't yer tell me before?' Mum said loudly.

'Yer don't 'ave ter shout so loud. I can 'ear yer. You knew I was getting wed. I told Dad weeks ago.'

'Yower like the rest on 'em,' Mum replied irritably. 'Yow tell yer Dad everything but I'm the last to be told.'

'Oh be quiet and sit down,' Mary yelled back. 'I tell yer lots of things but you never even listen. You always say "shut up" or you've got no time or "tell me later". You aren't interested.'

I could see they were losing their tempers and I wished Dad would come home.

'Don't yer give me any of yer lip!' Mum started going red in the face. 'Yow ain't too old ter 'ave yer face slapped!'

I was afraid, waiting for Mum to raise her hand, but she did not move. Mary was no longer scared of Mum; she stood up to her and matched her temper.

'Strike me if you dare! I don't fear you any more. You can't push and slap me around like you do her,' she said, pointing her finger at me. 'But don't forget, she'll grow up one day too and then yer'll be sorry.'

Mum went quiet for a moment but then she started on Mary again.

'I suppose yower in the family way, is that it?'

'That's 'ow your dirty mind works. Yer'll 'ave ter write the date down and wait an' see won't yer?' Mary must have forgotten that Mum couldn't write.

They were still arguing when Dad came in.

'What's all the shouting about? I could 'ear yer 'alf way down the street.' He loathed the constant uproar of our house and only wanted peace and quiet when he was in the house.

'It's 'er,' Mum told him, pointing at Mary. 'She wants ter get married.'

'Well, what about it?' Dad answered. 'She's old enough to make up 'er own mind.'

'But 'er Gran's only bin dead a few weeks. And I shall miss 'er wages when she goes,' moaned Mum.

'That's all yow ever think of,' Mary retorted. 'Money! Money! Money! Yer'll 'ave ter drink less beer then, won't yer.'

Dad put his hand on Mary's shoulder. 'Now, now Mary. You mustn't talk ter yer Mum like that. Anyway we'll try to manage. I'll put a few more hours in at work.' Mary shook her head, obviously upset, and rushed out into the yard. Dad followed her and I slipped out as well and heard him talking softly to her.

'Don't tek any notice of yer Mum's tantrums, Mary. You know she'll always 'ave the last word, so please come back and tell 'er yer sorry fer yer 'arsh words.'

'No, never,' she told him firmly. But Dad pleaded with her and this had its effect.

'All right,' she sulked. 'But only fer your sake, mind,' she told him.

So we went back in and things were patched up and Mum made a pot of tea and tried to make amends by promising to do her best to make the wedding the best in the district. However, Mary was still upset and sulking and wouldn't have any tea, and with a 'so long' to Dad she walked out, head held high, just like Mum.

I didn't want to stay so I followed her and asked if I could go along with her. After some hesitation she agreed, and taking my hand we went off to her young man's house. Albert his name was, and he greeted her with a kiss when he opened the door to us. He didn't give me so much as a glance. He only had eyes for Mary, especially as she immediately burst into tears.

'Now what's the trouble?' he asked, getting out a white handkerchief. When she'd finished telling him he went wild.

'You're not to go back to that place any more! An' I don't want anything from that house or yer mother,' he told her.

'But I've already bought the new bed, Albert,' she sobbed.

'Never mind about that. You can leave it. We're going to start afresh. My mother will take care of you while I get the house together,' he said, embracing her gently before taking us into the house.

Albert's father was a bookmaker and they were partners in the business. Sometimes Albert's mother helped with the book-keeping in a side room she called 'The Den'. She was a kind woman and whenever I called with a message she would sit me down and fetch me a biscuit or a glass of milk. They were a happy family and very hospitable, but Mary told me I was not to call too often or I would wear out my welcome. So I would walk down Mrs Lewis's street in the hope of bumping into her. Once I met her carrying several parcels and she called to me. I didn't answer at once, pretending to be surprised.

'Oh, hello, Mrs Lewis. Can I carry your parcels?' I asked her.

She smiled at me and gave me two small ones and I followed her to their house. She fumbled in her pocket for the key then let us in the side door. She was a smartly dressed woman, different from the other women in our district, but then she could afford to be because they were very comfortably off. She was generous, though, and helped anyone that was really in need – if she liked them, that is. Our Mum was not one of these and she knew it, but the knowledge didn't bother her; she couldn't care less whether she was liked or not.

I placed the parcels on the table and Mrs Lewis gave me a piece of cake and a penny. I thanked her and left after slipping the coin down my stocking for safe keeping.

When Mary came in from work the day after the row she told Mum that she and Albert had had a talk and that she was going to stay with his parents for a bit while Albert sorted out a house and furniture and the paraphernalia of married life.

'That's nice,' Mum said sarcastically. 'They can afford it with all the money they tek off people, can't they?'

Mary resisted the temptation to answer her back and after a moment's silence Mum continued.

'Yer won't want yer bed then, will yer Mary?' she spoke slyly.

'No, I won't. Albert's told me to leave it.'

This pleased Mum, until I made the mistake of asking Mary if I could sleep in it. Mum scowled at me when Mary said I could have it.

'Huh, we'll see!' Mum shrugged noncommittally.

I vowed to do anything to please Mum so I could have that bed, but I should have known better: it was impossible to please her. I went over to the range to get the kettle and make a pot of tea and listened to their conversation.

'When's the 'appy day then?' Mum asked.

'It'll be soon. I'll let yer know in plenty of time,' Mary answered.

'But yower gooin' ter get wed from 'ere, ain't yer?' Mum asked anxiously.

'Yes. That's the usual thing isn't it?' said Mary, gulping down her tea. I could see she wanted to leave and soon she pushed her chair back from the table and stood up to leave. But Mum put her hand on her arm.

'Will yer 'elp me out? Yer know what I mean. With a little money, so's I can give yer a decent wedding.'

Mary knew what she meant all right. She wanted to show off in front of the neighbours. Mary didn't want the wedding from our house, but she was prepared to concede to get away from Mum as quickly as possible. She even promised she would speak to Albert and see what could be done in the way of money. With that she lifted the latch, but before opening the door she turned to me and asked if I would like to go shopping with her.

'Can I, Mum?' I asked eagerly.

'I s'ppose so, but don't be back late,' she said grudgingly.

I was really glad to be going out with Mary instead of Mum; I don't think Mary had ever asked if she could take me with her before. We boarded a tram which was a treat on its own for me. Finally we got off in a street with enormous shops with beautiful window displays: I could have stood gazing at them for hours, but Mary pulled me away. Liza and I had wanted to go into the big shops in New Street and Corporation Street for ages but we'd never dared to pass the attendant who stood in the doorway ready to shoo small children off. But I wasn't afraid now with my big sister, and while Mary tried on garments I stood gazing in awe at all the sumptuous clothes that hung in the display cases. I would have loved to touch them to see what they felt like but I could see out of the corner of my eye that I was being watched. So I sat down on a chair that stood by the counter and looked around the shop while waiting for Mary to emerge from behind the colourful painted screen where she was trying things on. I was fascinated by the nearly naked figures of ladies in different positions that were painted on it. Some wore only frilly drawers and black camisoles so you could see their bare thighs on which they wore fancy garters and suspenders. It seemed quite shameless to me then but it would probably seem tame to today's youngsters. I sat there imagining all the pretty clothes I would have when I married a rich husband, but then Mary appeared with the assistant. Mary was carrying a long white veil and dress over her arm. These were wrapped up together with a pair of white satin shoes. Then we left the shop. By now it was getting late and I began to worry. Mary must have noticed my changed mood because she asked why I was so miserable.

'We told Mum we wouldn't be late and it's getting dark,' I mumbled.

'Never mind about Mum. You're with me and you'll go home when I take you.' She was firm. 'Would you like to come with me to Albert's and see his Mum?'

I forgot my fears when she said this and we went off. When we arrived, Mary let herself in the front door and we entered the dining room. My eyes were immediately attracted to the table and my mouth started watering when I saw the homemade cakes and jam tarts laid out on a white lace tablecloth. I was starving; it was hours since either of us had eaten but Mrs Lewis made me wash my hands before sitting at the table. When I sat down I was handed a plate made of real china which had bread and butter and cakes on it. We only had enamel plates at home and never had food like this. I wished this could go on for ever but I realised that all too soon I would have to return. Just as I was thanking Mrs Lewis and getting ready to leave Albert came into the room.

'Hello littl'un and how are you?' he asked pleasantly.

'Very well, thank you,' I answered shyly as he patted me on the head.

'I think you'd better stay a bit longer and Mary and I will take you home.'

I was only too glad to sit down and wait. Mrs Lewis left the room and Mary and Albert talked.

'Well love,' I heard him say. 'Did you tell your mother?'

'Yes,' said Mary. 'I've explained everything. But you must understand, Albert, I must get married from my home. And we must both help Mum to do the honours. I promised, so if we give my parents some money towards the expenses it will make me very happy.'

'Say no more about it now. We'll both see your Mum and Dad together and make all the arrangements.'

They hugged each other, and then taking me by the hand we went into the street and made our way home. When we arrived they kissed each other good night and Albert kissed me on the cheek before he turned and walked off.

Mum was waiting up for us when we got indoors, but before she could speak Mary began telling her about the agreement she had with Albert to pay for the wedding and this took the wind out of her sails.

'You'll see Albert when he calls tomorrow and he'll give you enough money to get the food and whatever you want to get.' So saying, she turned abruptly to go upstairs. Mum was satisfied with this. She started talking excitedly.

'I'll mek this the best weddin' in the district,' she blustered, but Mary wasn't interested and climbed the stairs without another word.

Next day Mary took Frankie, Liza and me to the shops to buy us some new clothes for the wedding. Liza and I had white satin dresses and shoes with bows on, and Frankie had a suit of small grey and white checked material with a cap to match and a pair of new boots. After the shopping spree Mary took us to a little tea shop for tea and cakes and then we returned happily with our presents.

Mum was pleased as punch when she found that Mary had bought us new clothes, but she was not so pleased when Mary told her she couldn't see them until the day of the wedding and took them straight up and locked them in her trunk. We all knew why: left with Mum they would have been in pawn before we had the chance to wear them.

One afternoon the following week, Mary was coming into the yard having been to hear the banns read for the last time, when she came upon a group of local women standing around gossiping about the wedding. I was sitting on the wall between our yard and the next, so I could hear every word. So could Mary; they hadn't noticed either of us.

'I wunda if 'er is?' asked one.

'An' 'er's gooin' ter get married all in white, orange blossoms an' all,' said another.

'I bet 'er's in the family way. 'Er's deep like 'er mother,' added a third.

I jumped down off the wall and joined my sister who was standing behind them listening. Then she elbowed her way through them with her head high.

'You'll all have to do the same as me and put down the date and see, but if yer want ter know it's the first of May.'

They went quiet at that and moved away. I put my tongue out at them as far as it would go. Mary never liked our neighbours and she seldom even spoke to them, but she knew Mum had invited them all. Even so, she wanted to keep the peace so she said nothing when she got indoors.

I never knew how much Albert and Mary gave Mum and Dad, but they threw money around like water; as Mum had said, she was going to give Mary the best turn-out in the district. She and Mrs Taylor went around the shops ordering what they thought was necessary and Dad and his cronies, Fred the lamplighter and his workmate Willie Turner, went along to The Golden Cup to order the drink. When she returned from the shops, Mum told me to accompany her to the Captain's to ask if we could have the Mission Hall for the wedding. She was disappointed when he told her he was sorry but it was being used for band practice that day. This put Mum in a terrible temper and to make matters worse, when we got home Dad and his friends were there pouring out beer from bottles. I could see at once that they had all had a skinful. This made Mum livid.

'It's all right fer yow. Leavin' me ter do all the dirty work,' she wailed, appearing to burst into tears.

'Now what's wrong with yer? Can't a man 'ave a drink ter celebrate?' Dad asked, continuing to pour the beer. ''Ere, 'ave one an' shut up.' He pushed the mug under her nose.

Mum took the mug from him but she didn't drink it. She slapped it down on the table, spilling some of its contents.

'I wanta know whater we gooin' ter do. The Captain can't let us 'ave the 'all for me daughter's weddin'.' She sagged into her chair and sobbed.

Fred went over to her. 'Can I make a suggestion missus?' he asked.

'Anythink as long as it'll 'elp us out,' she wailed through her apron.

'Why don't yer 'ave yer celebrations in the yard? It's big enough and besides yer'll be near the closets when yer need 'em.' He laughed, as did Willie and Dad, but Mum wiped her eyes and smiled.

'Now why didn't I think of that?'

On reflection, though, she doubted if she'd got enough crocks or cutlery and 'what was they going ter sit on?' After a pause for thought she told Dad that he must go and ask the Captain if he could let them have some cups and saucers and whatever else was available, even if they could not have the hall. Dad was less than enthusiastic about this suggestion.

'No, no, go yerself if yer want 'em. Yer never took the last lot back. 'E 'ad ter come an' fetch 'em.'

'Oh well,' she answered, 'I'll goo meself. Yow carn't do anything in that state any'ow.'

She drank down the remains of the mug of beer and off we went again to see the Captain. Mum pushed the door open wide and marched up the room as if she owned it. I hung back and watched to see what was going to happen. I could see Battling Billy Bumpham, a well-known local 'character', and the Captain seated facing each other at the other end of the room, deep in conversation. At the sound of footsteps the Captain looked around, and frowned when he saw it was Mum bearing down on him.

'What's 'e doin' 'ere?' she demanded, pointing at Billy.

'He's come to sign the pledge and become one of us,' he replied. 'I wish more would do the same.'

Then Mum changed her tone, as she always did when she wanted to wheedle something out of somebody.

'I've come ter ask yer, if we carn't 'ave the 'all, would yer be kind enough ter lend us some crocks an' chairs? Yer see, we're gooin' ter 'ave the party in the yard after the weddin'.'

'I'm very sorry,' he answered sharply. 'I shall be needing them all for the meeting.'

'But what am we gooin' ter do?' she wailed tearfully.

After pausing for a second he must have relented, because he told her that if it was any help she could borrow benches and trestle tables.

'That'll do.' She brightened up visibly. 'I'll send somebody to fetch 'em in the mornin'. Yer see it's tomorra the weddin'. An' yow come yerself if yer like.'

But the Captain didn't reply. He just waved her away and turned his back on us, and while he wasn't looking Mum whispered in Billy's ear: 'Yer wunt ter keep that up fer yer bung!' And with that she dug him in his ribs so hard that he nearly fell off his chair. Then she turned on her heel and we marched back down the hall. When we reached the door Mum called back, 'Good afternoon Captain', as though nothing had happened.

When we got back home Dad's mates had left and he himself was snoring in the chair. Mary was there too. She'd washed her hair and was drying it on the hessian towel. Mum told Mary about the changes in the arrangements but Mary wasn't at all pleased. She threw down the towel and turned on Mum.

'Whatever are yer talking about? I thought everything was arranged for using the Mission Hall?'

Mum tried to calm her but Mary was not impressed by the thought that the money for hiring the hall had been saved. In the middle of the fuss Dad woke up.

'What's all the bloody shouting for now?'

'We carn't 'ave the use of the 'all Dad, and we carn't 'ave the celebrations in the yard neither! Whatever will Albert's people think?' Mary sobbed.

Mum chipped in with, 'They'll 'ave ter think what they like. The stuck-up lot!'

Mary was now in tears. 'I wish I hadn't agreed ter get married from 'ere. In fact I wish I wasn't getting married at all.'

Mum made a half-hearted attempt to calm her daughter down, but Mary shrugged her off and continued sobbing bitterly. Then Dad tried. He told Mary that it would be all right and that anyway it was too late now to do anything else. He put his arm around her shoulder and she wept some more. I could see that it was time for me to make the tea. While I busied myself, I listened to what Dad said to Mary.

'Now Mary,' I heard him say, 'dry yer eyes and listen ter me. It's yer weddin' day termorra and we all want ter see yer 'appy. Yer Mum's done the best she can under the circumstances.'

'But Dad, I feel so ashamed to think that Mr and Mrs Lewis will 'ave ter mix with our kind of neighbours, and you know what Mum's like when she's 'ad a few drinks.' Mary glared at Mum who was pretending not to listen.

'Leave everything to me, Mary. I'll keep yer Mum and everyone else in order.'

But I knew that was easier said than done. It would be as much as Dad could do to keep himself in order after he'd had a drop too much. Dad was a jolly chap sober, or could be, but when he'd had a few he thought himself a bit of a lady-killer. Mum knew this too, which was why she always kept an eye on him when he was the worse for drink.

I handed Mary and Dad their cups of sweet tea and they both smiled. Mum picked up hers as well and we drank in silence. Then when they'd finished Mary and Dad went out together. Mum followed them and I too decided to find Frankie to tell him the news after I had cleared away the crocks. When I got outside I found Mum in the yard, waving her arms about and giving directions to the neighbours whom she was organising for the party.

'I want this 'ere,' she said, pointing. 'An' I want that there,' she said, indicating where the chairs and tables were to go. 'An' bring some crocks, an' knives, an' forks an' anything else we can use.' She was not asking, she was demanding; but they were all used to her ways and were probably scared of upsetting her in case she changed her mind about the invitations.

I slipped away before she spotted me and renewed my search for Frankie, but I could find neither hide nor hair of him, or of Liza either. I finally came to the churchyard, 'Titty-Bottle Park', where there were literally dozens of kids running about the tombstones. Frankie and Liza were there with some of our friends, who gathered round to hear me excitedly telling my tale.

'Better than the Mission Hall,' Frankie said. The others agreed that it would be more fun to eat in the yard.

We wandered back home and when we entered the yard we were called in to go to bed early so we could get up to help in the morning. So it was bright and early when, with a clatter of buckets and bowls, we started to swill down the yard. The lavatories also had a birthday, and Dad left ours unlocked with plenty of fresh newspaper on the nail. The women even cleaned their windows. This was a red-letter day indeed. The clothes lines were taken down and rolled up by the dustbins, together with the props. I couldn't remember such a bustle and hubbub in our yard before. Everyone was singing a different song out of tune and taking no notice where they were throwing the water. Several people ended up with wet feet and all the cats vanished and even the kids who were trying to help got the odd clout for 'gettin' under our feet'. Eventually Frankie and I were called in by Mum and told to get a wash and change as it was nearly time to go. But it was worse in our house than in the yard. We were all at sixes and sevens, getting in one another's way. Mum and Mary kept calling for this, no that, yes that, to be brought upstairs. It was pandemonium. Then to top it all, two of Mary's friends squeezed in with several more parcels. They were what were then called 'buxom young women' and I thought them very pretty. They had come to help Mary dress but there was no room at all when they started busying themselves. Still, they were efficient. They put the parcels on the table and tidied the room while Frankie and I sat on the sofa and watched. Then brother Jack strolled in and he wasted no time in chatting them up. He joked and playacted, then put his arm round one's waist and kissed her on the cheek. This started them both giggling and they fled upstairs in hysterics. But they were no strangers to Jack because he called out 'See yer later Molly' as took his leave.

I was expecting that at any minute Mum would shout down to find out what was going on but she must have been preoccupied, trying on her new frock. Just then the postman called with more packets and greetings cards, amongst which was also a letter. I recognised the handwriting. It was from Auntie Nellie. Although she was Mum's youngest sister she always addressed her letters to Dad. Mum couldn't read anyway but she always seemed to know when Auntie Nellie wrote and Dad made it my job to hide these letters and give them to him when Mum was out of the way. I never read any of them although it was not for want of trying. But once I'd given them to him I never saw them again so I imagine he must have burnt them.

Auntie Nellie only came to visit on special occasions so I expect Dad must have written to invite her to the wedding. I knew Mum would not have done so because they didn't get on, although I never found out why. Dad had a soft spot for Auntie Nellie and perhaps Mum had something to be jealous about.

I surveyed the scene around me and vowed that when I grew up I would marry a rich man who would carry me away from all this noise and squalor. I little knew then what the future held for me and looking back I can see what a lot I had to learn.

After a while Mary came down with her two friends. Molly removed the rags that Mary had put in my hair and it fell down in ringlets. Then she helped me put on my white satin dress, after which I pulled on my shoes. Frankie dressed himself, and he looked smarter than I had ever seen him in his check suit, waistcoat and matching cap. Liza looked good too. Then Mum came rustling down the stairs in her almost-new taffeta dress with its leg o' mutton sleeves. I could hardly believe my eyes. She looked years younger. Her hair was done on top like a cottage loaf with bits dangling around her ears, in which she had long red glass earrings, and peeping out from under the long russet-coloured dress were her brand new button-up boots. She twirled around the room but Mary wasn't interested and returned upstairs with her friends to complete dressing. Mum kept preening herself in the glass until Frankie could contain himself no longer.

'If yer don't watch out yer'll crack that mirror.'

Mum scowled at him and slapped him hard across the face. However, he wasn't bothered. He'd expected it and just shrugged his shoulders and sat down on the stool. Mum returned to the mirror and replaced strands into the bun which had become dishevelled during the twirling. Then, looking satisfied with herself, she marched out into the yard to see how well her orders had been carried out and incidentally, to show off her fine clothes. We followed. All eyes turned, filled with admiration and envy. Even Dad looked at us proudly as he paused in his job of putting up the bunting. All our playmates crowded round to marvel at our get-up and touch our finery, but Mum soon put a stop to this and sent us indoors.

'Goo inside, we don't want their dirty maulers on yer clothes.'

We were disappointed but we could still watch through the windows as Mum gave her final instructions to Mrs Taylor and Mrs Buckley. Then we stood down when Mum and Dad came to the house. The young women had come downstairs and Dad, who had already had a skinful, addressed Molly in a jovial manner.

'Why 'ello Molly. I didn't know yow'd bin invited.' Then he pulled her towards him and asked her to give him a kiss, but she pulled away quickly when she saw Mum's scowl.

'No yer don't! I ain't 'avin' none a that in my 'ouse. An' yow,' she turned on Dad, ''ow long 'ave yer known them two?'

Just then Albert put his head round the door and I could see that Dad was relieved that he did not have to go into explanations. Mum turned her wrath on Albert.

'Out! Out! Get out! Don't yer know it's bad luck ter see yer bride before yer married?'

He was probably as glad as Dad to do as he was told and leave and I noticed that Mary's two buxom friends slipped out after them. But Mum's attention was elsewhere. She was upstairs at once to tell Mary what had happened, though I don't suppose Mary paid her much heed. In any case, Mum was soon down again in front of the mirror. She didn't say anything to me and I was too scared to speak in case she started on me, but her mood changed in a flash when Mary came down, and she was all smiles.

'Are yer ready now Mary me luv? We'll be late if we don't 'urry.'

Mary ignored Mum and just smiled at me. I could hardly believe my eyes. She looked a picture, radiant, all in white. Over her orange-blossom headdress she had a long flowing veil which flowed down her back; her dress of white satin rustled and crinkled as she walked. She seemed to glide on her little satin-shod feet. As I watched her I thought Granny would have been proud if she'd been alive to see Mary now. I glanced up at Granny's picture and for once she seemed to be smiling.

Dad came in and I was struck by how handsome he seemed with his moustache freshly waxed and his hair brushed flat and parted in the middle. He wore his best suit which had been redeemed from the pawnbrokers and was freshly cleaned and pressed. He even had on a collar and tie, which I'd never seen before and which he would tug at every now and then as if it were too tight. When he had finished looking in the mirror to put in his buttonhole rose, it was time to go.

Mary picked up her bouquet of white roses from the table and placed her hand through Dad's arm. He looked at her proudly then they turned and we walked out into the crowd. Confetti showered down on us and congratulations were shouted from all directions. Then the people moved aside and we passed through the smiling, cheering crowd, some of whom I noticed had tears in their eyes. I wondered where all that confetti came from; knowing Mum I guessed she must have supplied it, but none of us children were given any. But we'd anticipated this. One night we had sat up late while Mum and Dad were at The Golden Cup and had cut up old Christmas decorations into tiny squares and diamonds and then hidden them in envelopes. Now we hung back and got them out of our pockets and joined in with everyone else. Mary and Dad ducked their heads to avoid the waving arms as they walked along and everyone was smiling, including Mum.

This was not a wedding such as we see today. This was an old-fashioned wedding. There were no wedding cars nor yet carriages. The church was within easy walking distance of our street so everyone went on foot. It was a warm May day and everybody seemed to be out in the street or standing on their steps. There was quite a procession by the time we got to the church, St Paul's, and as we entered the organ played 'Here Comes the Bride'. We walked down the aisle and the church seemed really awesome. I looked from left to right to find somewhere to sit and could see nowhere. Then before I had gone a few yards I felt a tug on my back. It was my friend Nellie who lived in the yard next to ours. She pointed to the pulpit where the parson was beginning the words of the service. Suddenly I was frightened because he had once caught us playing in the churchyard and had shouted at us and chased us out. Nellie and I tiptoed quietly back down the aisle and out of the door. While we waited for the service to finish we amused ourselves rearranging the flowers on the graves. Some had no flowers at all so we shared the flowers out more equally. When we ran out of jam jars we pressed the daffodils and tulips into the earth. I don't suppose that that graveyard ever looked prettier than on our Mary's wedding day.

Then the people came streaming out of the church. We joined the crowd before our handiwork was noticed and watched as Mary and Albert had more confetti thrown over them as they stood on the threshold of the church. Mary was kissed and hugged by her workmates and Albert's back was slapped and his hand shaken by his friends. Mum and Dad and Mr and Mrs Lewis entered into the spirit of the occasion but I thought I could see some sadness in Mrs Lewis's eyes. She didn't smile and this perplexed me because I knew she liked our Mary. But I also knew that she was far from pleased with the arrangements. I heard her say so, though she would not interfere in anything Mum had organised.

When we reached our yard again I could see that Mrs Taylor and her friends had worked hard. The trestles had been put up and were covered with white tablecloths of American oilcloth. They were piled with corned-beef sandwiches, cheeses, sausage rolls, sliced pickled onions, beetroot, all kinds of pickles, watercress, pig's pudding and every mouthwatering delicacy you could think of. And standing in the centre was a two-tiered, iced cake. At one end of the table there were four stone gallon jars of ale, bottles of stout, gin and whisky. There was room on the benches for twenty guests each side, facing each other. We children had a table to one side to ourselves on which were laid out bottles of pop, cakes, buns and bread and jam.

While the adults sat on their forms we sat ourselves down on an assortment of broken chairs borrowed from the neighbours. There was a plate, knife and fork and a paper napkin for everyone. Some, the lucky ones, had a glass for their drink but the rest had to make do with a cup or a mug. After we had settled down, brother Jack stood up and banged the table and called for order for Dad to say grace. Everybody bowed their heads, then as he said 'Amen' they dived into the 'eats'. You would have thought some of them hadn't eaten for days, but then perhaps they hadn't. Many seemed not to know what the knives and forks were for and took the napkins for handkerchiefs.

Mrs Taylor kept an eye on us, ready to rap our knuckles if we got too greedy. As everyone feasted themselves Mum went round with the drink, pouring out gin and whisky or stout as they preferred, making sure to test them all as she did so, while Dad and Fred did the same with the ale. Even the newly converted Battling Billy broke the pledge that day. His wife Maggie kept on eye on him but said it was all right for a special occasion and that he could rejoin the pledge tomorrow. Things were beginning to hum when I noticed Mrs Lewis get up from her seat and go over to Mary. Mum was out of earshot but I could hear. She said, 'Fred and I will have to leave now as we have to catch the early train in the morning, Mary. But we'll see you as soon as we get back from our holidays. In the meantime, I hope you and Albert will be very happy. You have my blessings, my dear.'

'Thank you, mother,' replied Mary with tears in her eyes. 'I didn't want the weddin' this way.'

'I quite understand,' Mrs Lewis assured her. 'But I've never liked your mother and I never shall.' They embraced briefly and I heard her say quietly, 'Remember I shall always love you and if there's anything I can do or that you want, don't be afraid to come to me.' And with that she and her husband left.

Soon after this Mary and Albert got ready to follow his parents and depart. They slipped away unnoticed except by me. I didn't want Mary to go because I thought I wouldn't see her for a long time, and I ran over to her and pleaded. 'Where are you goin'? Ain't you stayin' till the end of the party?'

'No, Katie,' they answered in unison. 'But,' Mary continued, 'you can come and visit us when we've got settled in.'

'But remember,' said Albert, 'only you and Frankie, mind.' And they picked me up in turn and gave me a kiss.

Nobody seemed to miss them, only me. I tried to get Dad to tell me where they'd gone but he was tipsy and only laughed and said they'd gone on their 'funnymoon'. They were all pretty well oiled by then so I went back and sat with the other children. Battling Billy was attempting to sing one of his war songs and Maggie was merry too; if he went too far she would have to help him indoors. Mum was leading the chorus and us kids were singing our own dirty ditties. By now the barrel organ was in action, belting out 'Down at the Old Bull and Bush'; the noise was tremendous. When that number was over people started calling for order so that Mrs Buckley could do one of her songs. Unfortunately Mrs Buckley couldn't sing a note in tune; her throat sounded like it had gravel down it. There was nearly a fight when her husband heard Fred the lamplighter say to Dad that she sounded like 'a constipated canary'. The adults were beginning to get out of hand: some were dancing, having a 'knees up'; others were arguing with the organ grinder about what should be played. Then the men got round to the subject of politics. 'Asquith should be shot,' someone suggested. 'This government's never bin any good,' another agreed. Others sprang to the defence of their rulers and the argument became furious until a heavy fist banged down on the table and bottles and food went flying. This started a real rough and tumble, with people falling or being pushed to the ground amongst the debris.

Us kids were highly amused at all this, but I was distracted from the fun by Frankie who suggested that we gather up the bottles and hide them in the washhouse before they all got broken. We ended up with about a dozen assorted gin, whisky and stout bottles. We hid them in the copper, closed the lid and crept back into the yard, shutting the door carefully behind us. When we emerged the women were still at it. Two were pulling each other's hair and screaming at each other while the men tried to part them. Mum was not taking part. She stood there with hands on her hips, glaring with a face like thunder. However, the disturbance didn't last long because just then there was a cry of 'Hey up! Here's the cops!' They were not joking. It was not only the cops but the Black Maria as well. Dad pushed Mum indoors and Frankie and I followed quickly. Then Dad shot home the bolt, though this didn't stop us opening the window to see the end of the rumpus. We saw Maggie drag Billy from under the table where he was on his knees praying for 'the good Lord to send down lightning and scatter all these wicked people'. The police took one look at him and decided to leave him for later. But while they were hauling various protesting individuals off to the police wagon Maggie got him indoors. Then in a few minutes they were gone and quiet descended on our yard – but not for long.

Just as we'd closed the window and were breathing a sigh of relief there was a loud knock on the door. We looked at each other, scared, thinking it was the police come back for us. Dad whispered to us to keep quiet and not to answer it but then there was an even louder bang and then more knocking. The door rattled and the pictures shook. Granny's crepe paper slipped over one eye and she seemed to be saying 'Serves them right.' Mum whispered, 'That's another bad omen.' Then Dad decided that the banging had gone on long enough.

'I don't think it's the police, Polly. Yer better see who it is.'

Mum was taking no chances. She lifted a corner of the curtain first to make sure it was safe. It turned out to be Mrs Taylor.

'Yer tryin' ter knock our bloody door down?' she shouted. 'What yer want?'

Mrs Taylor stood there sobbing. You could hardly make out what she was saying.

'P-Polly, S-Sam, 'ave yer seen me three young uns? I carn't find 'em. I've looked everywhere. Whatever shall I doo?' she wailed.

'Come on Polly, we better help look for 'em before it gets dark,' Dad suggested.

'Not me,' Mum replied, 'I'll mek yer all a cup of tea when yer get back. They carn't be far.'

Dad and Liza went inquiring door to door while Frankie and I used this opportunity to see if our bottles were safe in the washhouse. They were, and so were Mrs Taylor's twins, Joey and Harry, and little Billy. I tried to lift Joey into my arms but he wriggled onto the slack and ashes on the floor and started giggling. I couldn't understand what was wrong with him until Frankie pulled out the other two from behind the boiler and found them in a similar state.

'They've bin drainin' the dregs outta the bottles. They're drunk!' he cried.

We stood them up. They were filthy with coal dust. We tried to get them to the door but they kept falling about. They looked really comical, and Frankie and I were in fits of laughter trying to help them. Then I spotted Dad down the yard and called out to him. He and Mrs Taylor came tearing down the yard to see what was up.

'Whatever's up with 'em? They're filthy!' he said.

'Yer'll 'ave ter carry 'em, Dad. They're drunk,' Frankie told him.

Then he caught sight of the empties and saw what had happened and began laughing as well. But Mrs Taylor began crying even more, this time with tears of joy and relief that her babies were safe. Dad tucked a twin under each arm and took them home, where we helped to wash and clean them before they went to bed. Mrs Taylor gave Frankie and me a piece of bread pudding each but we didn't like the smell of it so we threw it over the wall on the way back to our house. When we got in there was no tea waiting for us. Mum was asleep in her chair, snoring. Dad motioned us not to disturb her: 'She's 'ad a busy day.' But so had we all. However, we were not hungry for once, so we didn't mind going to bed. Besides, we had plans to make about how to spend the money we'd get for the empties. It was therefore with some disappointment that we faced Dad's inquiries about them next morning.

'How did those bottles come to be in the copper?' he asked. We were afraid to tell Dad the exact truth so we said we'd put them there to prevent them getting broken.

'Good idea,' Dad replied with a twinkle in his eye: he knew why they were there because he went out and fetched them in and later took them back himself. So we ended up with nothing for our trouble.

Thus ended Mary's wedding day. The party did not continue after the police raid. I can't remember who did the clearing up. I suppose the adults must have attended to it. I suppose you could say that the occasion went with a bang.

When Dad went off to the pub with the bottles the following day I followed him. I thought he'd send me home but he didn't.

'Here's a penny,' he said. 'I want you to sit on the step and watch out fer yer Mum and come in and tell me when you see her.'

I sat there a long time, bored, with a cold bottom, and I was about to open the pub door to tell him I was going home when I saw the organ grinder trundling his barrel-organ down the street. He stopped outside the pub and started turning the handle. The music burst forth. I was delighted and decided to stay and watch a while. Then the pub door burst open and two women tumbled out, drinks in their hands, and began dancing and singing. Dad poked his head round the door to see what was going on and to ask if I'd seen Mum. When I told him I hadn't, he disappeared inside again.

After he'd played a couple of tunes, the organ grinder took off his old frayed cap and handed it round the crowd that had gathered. At this the women stopped their knees up and went back in without a look at the man. A few pennies were dropped into it but he didn't look very pleased. I looked at my penny in the palm of my hand. I wondered if he would let me turn the handle if I gave it to him. So timidly I approached him.

'Please, will you let me turn the handle for you?' I asked.

'No!' he snapped. 'Little kids should be seen an' not 'eard.'

How many times had I heard that remark? But I persisted because I loved the sound of the old organ.

'If yer'll just let me play a tune I'll give yer me penny.' He peered down at me and scratched his head as he replaced his cap on his bald head.

'Well littl'un, yer'll 'ave ter stand on yer toes if yer want ter reach the 'andle.' Then he took the proffered penny and went inside the pub, leaving me to get on with it.

He was right, I did have to stand on tiptoe and even then I could hardly reach. I couldn't move the handle and yet it looked so easy when the man did it. I didn't give up; I wanted to get my money's worth. I pushed with both hands but I wasn't strong enough to get a squeak out of it. Then with a renewed effort I managed to get it to moan like a person in pain. I knew that if the handle moved faster it would sound better, so I really exerted every ounce of my miserable muscle power and the handle jerked forward with such force that I was lifted clean off the ground. So with a series of jerky motions I pumped that handle, but all I succeeded in producing was the sound of a set of bagpipes. The noise must have attracted the attention of the people in the pub because the next thing I heard was Dad's voice booming above the bedlam.

'What d'yer think yer tryin' ter do?' he asked. 'I thought someone was bein' murdered.'

Then the organ grinder pulled me away and I began to cry and pull at his coat.

'I want me penny back. It wouldn't play a tune for me.'

At that Dad grabbed the man. 'What's this? Did you tek 'er penny?' he demanded.

The organ grinder, however, did not have time to answer, because the drunken women had pushed his organ which began to roll down the hill. He shook himself free and ran after it.

'Don't yow ever show yer face round 'ere agen,' they shouted after him. Then they drifted back into the pub and left me standing alone. We never did see that organ grinder again and I felt sorry about what had happened. But I really wanted my pennyworth.

Our New Neighbour

In the yard next to ours was a tiny cottage squeezed in the corner. It must have been built to fill a space that was left after the five houses had been completed. It had just one room up and one down, big enough only for two people to live in. It was unoccupied, but whether that was because it went unnoticed or because every family was so large it was never taken by anyone, I don't know. So I was surprised when one morning, while filling the kettle at the tap in the yard, I noticed some of our neighbours looking across at this cottage where a painter was taking the 'To Let' sign out of the window.

It was a novelty to see a painter in our district. The landlords didn't bother and people had to look after their houses as best they could. So it was to be expected that this sight should arouse some curiosity, and after putting their heads together the women put down their bowls and kettles and went over to ask the painter who was coming to live there. But he couldn't enlighten them: he only had orders to 'paint the place up a bit'. They wandered back to their chores, clearly dissatisfied with this answer. Here was a new topic for gossip.

I must confess I was as curious as they were so I kept an eye on the cottage to see who came. But it was not until three mornings later that I spotted a horse and cart arrive. I knew then that it must be someone special to have their furniture brought in a van. Everyone in our district used flat hand carts when they moved house – unless they were 'doing a moonlight', when their chattels went on a push cart, pram or whatever else was handy. I dashed back in to make Dad his sandwiches and pour his tea into his billy can. I saw him off to work impatiently, then over the wall I went to see who our new neighbour was.

I watched with growing amazement a succession of beautiful old pieces of furniture go into the cottage. There was a new straw mattress and brass bedsteads on which the morning sun glittered like gold. There were real carpets, not like our old rags. There was a leather armchair and kitchen chairs which matched, and brass firedogs and a fender – in fact things that you never saw under the same roof in our district. However, what caught my eye most was a highly polished harmonium. How I would have liked to play that, I thought, but chance would be a fine thing.

I gazed at this scene thinking that of all of the things I wanted when I was grown up, the one I wanted most was to play a harmonium. Little did I think I would soon be playing, or trying to play, this one. Then the removal men came out of the house for the last time, wiping their brows on their once-white aprons, and then they helped down from the van a little old lady. She was not a lot taller than me. She had wisps of grey hair poking out from under a black lace bonnet and wore a long black lace dress down to her feet. Her face was wrinkled with age but she looked friendly and her voice was pleasant when I heard her talk to the men. She thanked them for their efforts but although they waited for a tip it was not forthcoming, so they went off grumbling. Then she went into the cottage and closed the door and I came out of hiding.

She hadn't noticed me, but she had seen the neighbours hanging out of their windows, spectating. When she'd gone I approached the door timidly. I wanted to ask her if I could run her errands before the other children had a chance. So I plucked up my courage and tapped gently on the door. It opened almost at once and I was confronted by the old lady. I was nervous but she put me at ease immediately.

'Well dear, and what do you want so early in the morning?' she asked, rubbing her hands together.

My voice trembled as I answered. 'I live over there,' I said, pointing to our house on the other side of the low wall. 'I've come to see if yer want any errands fetched.'

She seemed to look straight through me when she continued. 'And what's your name?'

'Kathleen, but everybody calls me Katie,' I told her.

'Well Katie,' she said after a pause. 'If you come back tomorrow I may have an errand for you.'

'But I can help yer now if yer want me to,' I said eagerly. I was anxious to get inside and nose around her furniture.

'No thank you,' she said abruptly. 'My brother will be here later and we shall be busy arranging the furniture. Now run along like a good girl and don't be late tomorrow.'

I walked away disappointed but I was glad I'd found someone new whom I could confide in. I was also excited at the prospect of earning some reward, and I couldn't sleep that night for thinking about visiting her in the morning. But it wasn't till after school the following afternoon that I found time to go. I washed and combed and plaited my hair and rubbed my clogs, then I went round and knocked on the door. I had to stand on tiptoe to reach the brass knocker, which had appeared since the previous day. Then I heard a voice call me to come in so I turned the door knob and entered.

'Come along in Katie and sit yourself by the fire. You must be cold,' she said, but I just stood and warmed my hands: I didn't dare sit down. She picked up a brass poker and stirred up the fire which already burnt brightly in the grate. However, I was too excited to notice the cold or the warmth; I was too excited by the sight of all the beautiful objects that filled the room. There was a copper kettle boiling on one hob and a china teapot on the other and the stove shone clean. Set out on the white lace tablecloth were matching cups and saucers, and a plate with bread and butter and teacakes on it. The old lady made me jump when she told me not to stare but to sit down and not be nervous. I sank into the leather armchair and thought to myself that this couldn't be real; I would wake up soon.

'Now come along, Katie.' Her voice brought me out of my daydream. 'I want you to meet my brother.'

It was only then that I noticed the small man seated in the armchair next to mine. Anyone could tell they were brother and sister they were so much alike, except that he had a little goatee beard on his chin. Like his sister he too was dressed all in black and he had the same habit of rubbing his hands together.

'This is my little friend Katie,' she told him. 'She's going to be my little errand-girl.'

'Good afternoon, Katie.' And he put out his hand, but I quickly wiped mine on my pinafore before I shook hands.

'I like the look of her, Louise,' I heard him whisper to her. 'But the poor little mite looks half-starved.'

She indicated the pretty flower-patterned basin for me to wash my hands in, then I joined them at the table. But I was too excited to eat much. I'd never been surrounded by so many nice things before, not even at the Lewises'. The old lady spoke to me occasionally, but I noticed that she seemed to lapse into quiet moods. This didn't bother me. I just felt this was too good to last and I was right. I had no idea she was using me for a purpose of her own: I was too naive to realise until it dawned on me what it was, a few weeks later.

After tea she wrapped up some fruit cake for me to take back home. With that she saw me off with an invitation to visit her the next day after school but that I was to tell my parents in case they were worried where I was. As if they would be, I thought.

When I got indoors Mum was out but Frankie was sitting in her chair by the fire warming his toes on the fender.

'Where 'ave yow bin?' he inquired moodily. 'I've bin lookin' fer yow everywhere.'

I sat down in Dad's chair and told him all about the old lady and her brother, or at least what I knew, which wasn't much. But before I'd got very far with my story he shrugged his shoulders and said he didn't believe me.

'Any'ow what's 'er name?' he asked suspiciously.

'I don't know, I never asked 'em.'

'Yer tellin' lies,' he said triumphantly.

'I'm not! But I did hear 'er brother call 'er Louise. But if yer don't believe me I'll take yer tomorra to see 'er,' I told him angrily. I felt close to tears to think he doubted my word.

'Is that on then?' he asked, getting excited.

'Yes it is,' I said, although I had no idea what the old woman would say. We shook hands on the promise anyway.

The next afternoon couldn't come quick enough. No one was at home when we came out of school so we didn't have to explain where we were going. I made sure Frankie washed himself and warned him to behave himself as well.

'I still can't believe you,' he remarked, but he washed anyway and he dried himself on the piece of hessian and then spat on his hands and flattened his hair. I couldn't understand why he did this because his rebellious hair always sprang up like bristles on a brush and never stayed flat like Dad's. I plaited my own hair and then I straightened my ink-stained pinafore and we were ready to go. We had soon reached the old lady's house and rapped on the door.

'That won't be there long,' said Frankie. I gave him a frown and told him to mind his manners because I wasn't sure what the old lady's reaction would be to my brother.

'I don't like you when you're like this,' he said sulking. 'You sound just like our Mum.' But I had no time to reply because just then the door opened and there stood the old lady in her black lace dress.

'Good afternoon, Katie,' she said to me but she frowned at Frankie and said, 'And who is this boy?'

"E's my brother, miss, and 'e's come to pay yer a visit,' I answered nervously.

'You should have asked my permission first before bringing him along. I'm not keen on little boys,' she snapped back.

I could tell she was angry and I was ready to cry, but Frankie pulled me roughly back off the step and we turned to leave. She must have changed her mind because she called us back.

'Well, you may as well come on in now you're here.' And we turned and followed her in. Frankie's eyes nearly popped out of his head when he clapped eyes on the room and its contents, especially what was laid out on the table. It was all neatly laid out as it had been the day before.

The old lady fetched out another plate and cup and saucer, then she checked that our hands were clean and told us to sit down. Frankie, however, flopped into the leather armchair, and putting his hands behind his head lay back like a grown-up.

'This is the life for me,' he said. I was so embarrassed by his behaviour.

The old lady frowned at him and asked him sharply what his name was and he sat up straight but he answered cheekily.

'My name's Francis William Samuel after me Dad ... but everybody calls me Frankie, except me school mates and they call me ...' But I kicked his shin before he could finish the sentence. To my relief the old lady smiled and said, 'Never mind what they call you, Frankie. But remember not to call here again unless I ask Katie to bring you. Now come along, sit up at the table and have your tea.'

We sat down then and all the time he was eating Frankie couldn't keep his eyes off her or the things that surrounded him. When we'd finished I asked if we could wash up and run the errands but she said she'd already been to the shops with her brother. I was disappointed at this and was afraid she was still vexed at me for bringing Frankie.

'Don't look so sad,' she said softly. 'I shall still want you to come the day after tomorrow.'

'But that'll be Sunday and all the shops'll be closed,' I replied.

'Yes, I know, but if you call early we can have a long talk.' And with that she said 'Good afternoon' and saw us out. As we left I thanked her for the 'nice tea' and off we went.

'I don't like 'er,' were Frankie's first words when we were out of earshot. 'But I loved all that beautiful furniture and the tea she gave us. What about that brown leather armchair? I'll 'ave one o' them when I go to work and don't forget to ask 'er if I can come again. And don't tell Liza!'

'I won't,' I promised and he went off to find his mates while I made my way home to start the chores. For once I was happy doing them because I had the thought of Sunday to cheer me up.

When I returned from Sunday school the following Sunday I wrapped up in my scarf and tammy because it was a chilly day.

'An' where do yer think yer gooin'?' Mum asked when I came downstairs.

'Back ter Sunday school, I've forgotten me test card,' I lied.

'Well, see that yer come straight back. I want ter talk with yer.'

This worried me because I could not make out what I had done this time to annoy her. So I decided to return to Sunday school to fetch my card. I ran all the way there and back and handed my test card over.

'Sit in that chair an' listen ter what I've got to say.' She paused for a moment before continuing. 'I 'ear that you've bin runnin' errands an' payin' visits to the new neighbour across at the cottage.'

'Yes Mum,' I answered truthfully. 'I was goin' ter tell yer about that but I thought you wouldn't be interested.'

'I'm only interested in who she is, an' what she does for a livin',' she said sharply.

So I had to explain. I told her the old lady was rich and that she had done the cottage up beautifully. I had found out that her name was Miss Vulcan and I gave her this information as well as telling her that Miss Vulcan had a brother named Freddie who visited her and that he was a little old man who wore a black cap on his head and sported a goatee beard.

'Sounds like they're Jews ter me. I'll 'ave ter pay 'er a visit,' she said more to herself than to me.

'I'm goin' this afternoon, Mum. Shall I tell her you would like to call?' I asked.

'Yes, yer can tell 'er I'll be callin' on 'er tomorra. No, tell 'er I'll come Tuesday, it's washin' day Monday.'

'Yes Mum,' I replied dutifully and left before she changed her mind.

A few minutes later I was standing on Miss Vulcan's doorstep. Before I lifted the knocker I gave my clogs an extra rub on my stockinged calf, then I rapped on the door.

'Come along in, Katie,' I heard her voice from inside, so I entered. This time I went straight to the pretty china bowl and washed my hands. As before the table was laid out for tea, but instead of bread and butter there were toasted muffins oozing butter. We seated ourselves and I watched her cut her muffins into quarters. This was a real treat for me. I could hardly remember having muffins before, although I'd seen the muffin man in his white apron, a towel over his arm and a tray of muffins every Sunday afternoon. But we never saw them in our house.

I picked up my knife and attempted to copy the old lady but I soon got into difficulty. The old lady only smiled and leaned over to show me what to do. Thus at my ease, I ate my tea and then I washed up the dirty crocks. After this I was told to sit by the fire beside my benefactor. I sat quietly trying to work out how I was going to give her Mum's message.

'You're very quiet. Is there anything you want to tell me?' she asked me.

'It's me Mum,' I blurted out. 'She's coming ter pay yer a visit and she wants ter know all about you before I can come here again. I don't think you'll like my Mum, Miss Louise, nobody does.'

'Don't worry your little head about me. I'll see your Mum and whatever she wants to know I'll be only too pleased to tell her.' She smiled archly. 'But,' she added, 'would you like me to tell you what I do and how I come to be here?'

'Yes, I would,' I answered, perhaps a little too eagerly.

'First make me another cup of tea and hand me my knitting.'

I did as she asked then settled down again. Then as she knitted she began to relate her life story from when she was a young girl. She went rambling on much as I am doing myself now. She seemed to be talking to herself as she gazed into the fire. I listened, all ears, to hear what she was saying.

'I was only a small child when my parents sent my brother and me to an orphanage. I was twelve and Freddie about fifteen. I was very unhappy after this because I did not want to be apart from my Momma. At first they came to visit us once a month but then the visits became few and far between. I wanted to go home so eventually I ran away. By this time Freddie had already gone home. But I had no idea where I was going. I left early before the nuns were awake but I only got as far as Glasgow before I lost my way.'

I sat stock still, hardly breathing, my chin cradled in my hands. When I looked at her her eyes had tears in them like my own. Her story was like a tale from a book. Then after a pause she started again.

'A young man came along on a bicycle and asked me if he could help but I refused his offer. I didn't like the look of him. Just then two policemen rode past and stopped. They said they were looking for me and I had to go with them back to the convent.' She wiped her eyes with her dainty lace handkerchief and I wiped my own on the back of my hand. She told me how she wrote several letters to her home complaining of the punishment she was given and begging to be taken away but she received no reply until one day her brother paid her a visit and gave her the news that their parents were both dead. After that she went into service and there she stayed until, when she was about twenty-two years of age, her brother came to tell her he was married and to ask her if she would leave her employer and come to look after his wife who was expecting a baby.

I felt very sorry for her by now and for want of knowing how to express my sympathy I offered to make another pot of tea. This broke her train of thought and she brightened up. I made the tea and she drank it, then she continued her story.

'I was surprised to hear that he was married but I wanted a change of surroundings so I packed my few belongings and went with him there and then. He told me he was a money lender in a small way and that he lived in London now. I thought London was a wonderful place but I was disappointed when I saw what a small, tumbledown house my brother and his wife lived in. And to make matters worse I took an instant dislike to the wife. When we were introduced she turned to Freddie and said haughtily. "So this is your sister. Well, she'll have to make herself useful while she's here." Freddie took my few belongings up to the garret where I was to sleep and spend most of my time until the baby was born. I was so unhappy but I had nowhere else to go so I stayed until the baby was born. But it died within two weeks.'

I was fascinated by her story and waited impatiently while she refreshed herself with tea before continuing.

'She blamed Freddie and me for what went wrong but within two weeks she'd died herself; she had never recovered from the birth.' A flicker of a smile passed across her face as she said this. 'Freddie was not sorry and neither was I. I stayed on with him to keep house. I did all the cleaning, cooking and kept his books in order, which was no mean feat because he had a lot of clients call and all the money passed through my hands.'

'Didn't yer want to leave 'im then?' I interrupted.

'No,' she snapped. 'I loved my brother and he needed me, and you must care for people,' she insisted.

'But I do try.' Her words seemed like an accusation. 'But no one seems to be bothered with me. An' when I ask questions no one listens and Mum says I always get under 'er feet,' I added.

'Never mind. I expect she does love you in her own way,' she said gently.

I wanted to hear more of her life so I asked her why she had left London to come to Birmingham.

'My brother's married again now,' she continued, frowning. 'I didn't like his second wife either. She's taken over the household and the book-keeping too. I was treated like a servant so I asked Freddie to find me a place of my own. He wanted me to stay but I'd made up my mind. So when he was in Birmingham he bought me this house, which was going cheap, so that I could start a money-lending business here for him. I have looked after his books for forty years and that's all I know, so he gave me the capital to start and here I am.' She paused. 'You see there's lots of shops and businesses here and we think it's a good place to begin.'

I didn't know what she had planned for me but I understood well enough her meaning.

'But most of the people round 'ere are very poor,' I pointed out. 'They 'ave ter go ter the pawnshop.'

She smiled. 'I can lend them money instead of going to the pawnshop. And that's where you can help,' she said archly.

'But I don't see 'ow I can 'elp,' I mumbled innocently, waiting to hear her reply.

'But you can help me, Katie; I'd like you to spread the word around and tell people what my business is, and that if they need me I'll be able to help and charge only a little interest.'

I didn't understand what 'interest' was but she'd been kind to me and I thought she would be kind to others and help them. She was – but only to suit herself. I learnt this later. At that moment all I wanted to hear was more of her story, but she'd lost interest in that now.

'Off you go now,' she said, 'it's getting dark.'

With that she got up, put her knitting away and said she would go with me as far as our house. She put on a coat, took down her walking cane which hung behind the door and then we left. She held my hand and we walked slowly up the yard. She reminded me what she wanted me to do, then as we neared our house I became frightened that she would fall foul of Mum. So I stopped and turned to her.

'Me Mum won't let yer in,' I blurted out.

'Maybe not, but she will one day,' she said, very sure of herself. Then with a queer, knowing smile on her face she made to go.

'Goodnight, Miss Vulcan,' I said.

'You may call me Miss Louise,' she replied, and with that walked slowly back to her cottage.

It was only after she had gone that I started to ponder why she had confided so much in me. This was most unlike adults of my previous experience. But I dismissed these thoughts from my mind and entered our house. Only Frankie and Liza were in so I decided to tell them both what had happened. I was too excited to bother about my sister's listening, all ears. Anyway, I thought, Liza would do my job for me.

'Where's she going ter get 'er money from?' asked Frankie.

''Er brother,' I replied. 'She says he makes 'er an allowance.'

'That won't last long when the vultures round 'ere get their 'ands on 'er money,' he said. 'Some people are good at borrowing but she'll have to watch them to pay back.'

'Well we'll 'ave to wait an' see. She's kind anyway,' I said.

'I hope our Mum don't start borrowin' off of 'er or she'll never get it back.'

'I don't think Mum will,' I told him. 'I don't know about the rest but anyway I've got to pass the word around.'

'What 'ave you got ter do it for? They'll find out soon enough,' he said.

'I promised,' was my reply.

Next day it was the usual Monday routine: washing, maiding, singing and sharing the gossip of the day. The news soon went round the district about why Miss Louise had come live there. Liza took care of that before I had a chance, but I didn't mind this; she was better at it than me. I was fetching a tin bowl of water from the tap in the yard when I heard Mum call out, 'Katie, fetch me a bucket of slack before yer goo ter school.'

I was scared stiff of going down those cellar steps but Frankie wasn't around to do it so I had to do as I was told. As I was struggling down the yard with the fully laden bucket a few minutes later a neighbour, Mrs Woods, saw me. I tried to walk past her but she caught hold of the bucket.

'We want yow in the wash'ouse,' she insisted. I followed, and on reaching the door I saw Mrs Jonesy, Mrs Phipps, Maggie and Mum, together with two or three more from the other yards, in animated conversation. It was cold and snowy outside so I squeezed in with them. They were chattering like a lot of parrots but I listened to what was said.

'Well fancy that.'

'I carn't believe it.'

'T'ain't true.'

Mum broke in decisively. 'It might be a good idea an' find out,' she said.

'It'd be betta than gooin' ter uncle's,' one said. With this it dawned on me what they were talking about so I became more attentive.

'Well goo on then ask 'er,' said Mrs Woods.

'Well goo on then.' Mum shook me. 'Tell us. Is that the truth? Is she a money lender?'

'Yes Mum,' I told her.

'Right. That's all we want ter know. Yer can get off ter school now before yer late.' She spoke sharply and pushed me outside where it was snowing hard.

In school the girls kept whispering and turning round to look at me; Liza had told everyone. But it was not until we were in the playground that they could tackle me.

'Make way for Miss Louise,' they chorused, but I was not bothered by their sarcasm: it was the snowballs that some threw that mattered. I was alone; even Liza looked on as the snowballs rained down. I turned to run but slipped over, and that was too much even for my sister who came to my rescue and dared them to throw any more. They did not.

'What's wrong with 'em?' I cried. 'What 'ave I done?'

'I told 'em about you an' the money lender but I didn't know they were gooin' to snowball yer,' she said, pulling me to my feet.

I rather liked the name 'Louise' but not the snowballs, and from that day on until I left school the girls who didn't like me called after me: 'There goes Miss Louise.' It was jealousy, I suppose; the fact that I had spotted a chance they had not, although I couldn't get over the suspicion that their reaction to me had something to do with how Liza had told the story.

When I returned home that afternoon I was surprised to find Dad already sitting in his chair by the fire.

'Aren't you at work, Dad?' I asked him.

'No I ain't,' he answered sharply, which was strange for him. 'An' where's yer Mum?'

She must have been upstairs because almost as if in answer to him we heard her heavy tread on the stairs. I could see the mood Dad was in and all I wanted to do was to make myself scarce before they started to quarrel.

'I don't want any tea Mum,' I called out quickly before she was down the stairs. 'Miss Louise will be waitin' for me.'

'What's all this about?' inquired Dad grumpily. 'What yer mean yer don't want any tea?'

'It's all right Sam, she's fetchin' errands fer the old lady that lives in the cottage.'

Dad stared at her hard before he replied. 'It seems to me that she's always over there.'

'I've told yer Sam,' snapped Mum, 'she's outa mischief, an' besides, it's one less ter feed.'

I didn't realise that Dad was home early that afternoon because he had been put on short time and had had to take a drop in wages in consequence. I was too excited about my new job to stop and think. I made myself scarce as quickly as I could. When I arrived at Miss Louise's door, out of breath from running, I kicked the snow off my clogs and went straight in. The first thing she asked was if I had done what I promised.

'Yes,' I replied. 'Everyone knows.' She seemed pleased with my reply and smiled that crafty smile of hers. Then when we had eaten tea she said she was going to play the harmonium. This pleased me very much because I was longing to hear her play the instrument. Quickly I tidied away and washed the tea things, then she seated herself in front of the harmonium, pulled out the stops and began to play. But after a few notes she stopped and turned round on her stool to face me.

'Would you like to sing for me? I hear you've got a good voice.' I knew there were no flies on her but I wondered how she'd found that out.

'But I only know the songs I sing at school,' I told her warily.

'Well, would you like me to sing for you then?' she asked. I nodded.

She arranged herself in front of the harmonium again and after pulling out more stops began to sing 'On the Banks of Allen Waters'. She played and sang so plaintively that I almost wept, the song was so sad. She taught me the song later, and showed me how to control my voice, open my mouth wide and sing loud or sing softly. I can picture her now sitting at the harmonium in her black lace gown, me standing beside her as we sang together. Another time I was so fascinated by her clicking needles that she offered to teach me to knit as well. That afternoon she took me upstairs to her small bedroom for the first time. I was spellbound by the brass bedstead and all the knick-knacks, but what held my attention most were the knitted bedspreads that were on the bed and draped over the chairs. They were made out of small, knitted squares, all the different colours of the rainbow. What I wouldn't give, I thought, to be able to lie down on that bed, just for a minute. But I was awoken from my daydreaming by her calling me over to the large chest which stood beneath the window. She told me to lift the lid, and there inside were packed hundreds of balls of different coloured wool. She directed me to take as many balls as I could carry and put them downstairs. As I rummaged through the chest, gathering up as much as I could carry without dropping any, I found knitted scarves, blankets, gloves, socks and all sorts of garments of varying sizes. I picked out as many balls as I could manage, then she closed the lid and we returned downstairs.

When we were seated facing each other again she gave me a ball of pink wool and a pair of knitting needles and I had my first lesson in how to knit properly without dropping stitches. As I struggled to follow her directions my natural curiosity overcame me and I asked her how she came to have all that wool and all those knitted garments which were obviously not for her.

'Well,' she said, with a twinkle in her eye, 'if you'll keep a secret, I'll tell you, but first you'll have to promise to keep it a secret.'

'I'll promise,' I said, offering my hand for her to shake, but she only smiled and replied, 'I think I can trust you.' Then she told me about her knitting sideline.

'When I go to my clients to collect I always ask if they have any hand-knitted woollen garments they don't need, and if I'm lucky they give me some. Then I bring them home to wash and I unravel them before they dry. Then I wind them into balls and put them in the oven to dry, and that's how I come to have all those woollen articles to sell.' I thought what a good idea it would be for me to do the same and I kept this in mind.

After a while she examined what I had done. 'You're getting along fine. Keep up the good work.' The more she praised me the quicker the needles clicked. I had soon knitted all sorts of things for her, such as hats, teapot cosies and iron holders. I would have been pleased to own any of these, but after they were finished she told me they were all ordered. All I received for my labour was my tea. I didn't mind this; I was happy just to be there, hoping that one day she would give me some of the pretty wool to make something for myself but she never did. I was afraid to ask in case she said I wasn't to come any more. She was moody at times and easily irritated. Soon she took my visits for granted and I was given the spare key to let myself in the door. I was surprised at this.

'Why do yer want me ter have a key?' I asked her.

'Well, I always take a nap of an afternoon and when you rap the knocker it startles me, which is bad for my nerves.' And she stretched out her hand for me to see it shake.

'I hope you ain't gonna have a fit. I wouldn't know what ter do.' I was frightened.

I don't believe she heard me because she yawned, handed me the key and told me to hang it round my neck so that no one could take it from me. I was very honoured and proud to think she could trust me.

Another afternoon she took me with her to deliver the knitted garments. She said that everything was ordered, and that pleased me because I had to carry it all. We called at several small shops and houses in the better-class district which we called 'the kippers and curtains'. I did not find out how much she sold the garments for because she left me standing outside, but she always looked pleased when she emerged from these visits. When we got back to her cottage she put her hand in her bodice and pulled out a string with her key and a whistle attached to it.

'What's that for?' I asked, pointing at the whistle.

'That's a police whistle in case I'm attacked while I'm collecting the week's takings.'

'But nobody would attack yer round 'ere. At least I don't think so,' I told her, but she just smiled and told me she had no further use for me that day and to call the next day which was to be a school holiday. The following morning I asked Mum if I could spend the day with Miss Louise.

'Yow can, as long as yer do yer usual jobs 'ere first,' she said grudgingly. Although I was helping out Miss Louise I had to get up at six o'clock in the morning to do all the chores before school. I had to fetch the coal up from the cellar, chop the wood, light the fire, make the tea and then take up a mug each for Mum and Dad. Then I went skipping round to the cottage to see Miss Louise before I went to school.

That holiday morning I found Miss Louise waiting for me just inside the door with a pair of old shoes and a pair of slippers in her hands.

'I want you to try these on,' she said, handing them to me. I did as she said but they were two sizes too big for me; they fitted better after she had packed the toes with scraps of wool. She wrapped up

the clogs and gave them back to me with the instruction that I was
only to wear the shoes when I came to call.

'What about the slippers?' I asked, delighted by these gifts, tatty
as they were.

'I'll leave them on the mat inside the door so you can change into
them, then your clogs won't wake me up from my nap.'

As I was pulling on the worn satin slippers I thought of the
new ones my sister had bought me for her wedding. It was no use
thinking about them; they were in the pawnshop with the rest of our
wedding clothes. We sat down to knit, but before we had settled
there was a loud knock on the door. When I opened it I was
surprised to find Mrs Phipps and Mrs Woods.

'Is Mrs Vulcan in?' they chorused, peering past me into the room.

'It's not Mrs Vulcan, it's Miss Vulcan ter you,' I told them
haughtily.

'Huh! Puttin' on airs an' graces ain't yer?' Mrs Phipps said
sarcastically, looking me up and down. Before I could reply Miss
Louise called out, 'Who's that at the door?'

I thought of what my Dad called them and replied over my
shoulder, 'It's them two vultures.'

'Now, now,' Miss Louise called back sharply, 'mind your manners
and let them in.'

I disliked these two intensely and didn't like being told off for
being rude to them, so I told her peevishly that I wasn't staying while
they were there and kicked off the slippers, put on my clogs and ran
out banging the door behind me. I went home sulking and was still
in a mood when Frankie returned.

'What's the long face for? 'Ave yer worn yer welcome out?' he
asked none too sympathetically.

'No!' I snapped, with tears welling up in my eyes.

'Why are yer cryin' then?'

I tried to explain that Miss Louise was always short with me when
anyone called.

'I s'pose she don't want yer knowin' what's goin' on,' he
suggested wisely.

'I know what's goin' on so that's not the reason she sends me
away. She said she trusted me but I don't think I like 'er any more,'
I said, pursing my lips. 'But I'll miss the teas an' my knittin' lessons
so I'll 'ave to go back.'

'Oh you go back if yer want to, but it seems ter me that yow've served yer purpose now an' she don't want yer any more. Does she ever give yer any money for what yer do?' he asked.

'No, she only gives me money ter do the errands an' then I 'ave ter go back twice because I carn't carry them all in one go. She reckons up the change over an' over like she don't trust me,' I admitted reluctantly.

'You know, Katie, she's an old miser and everyone borrows money off her or else they buy the things you knit off her. I even 'eard Mum say the other day she was goin' over there to get a loan. Dad 'eard 'er an' 'e told 'er that while 'e 'ad two 'ands she was not to borrow money off 'er. So I'd stay away from 'er if I was you an' come an' play marbles with me like you used to do.' I knew he was trying to cheer me up but I was determined to go back to my knitting lessons when the vultures had gone.

'Please yerself.' He shrugged his shoulders and went off leaving me to ponder what he had said.

I plonked down on the hard wooden sofa and began musing: was he telling the truth? Would Mum borrow off her? Mum always bragged about never borrowing off anyone but I had noticed that since Dad had been on short time she seemed to have more money than ever to spend and was getting more friendly with the neighbours she could not stand as a rule. Then I remembered an incident not long before. I'd been taking a bucket of slack to the washhouse where all the women were gathered gossiping. They dropped their voices to a whisper when they saw me but I'd seen them taking nips from a bottle of gin. I didn't think too much about this at the time, although I knew they usually only had money for their 'little pleasures' after they'd done the washing and pawned it. Now I understood and I put all the blame on Miss Louise. I determined to discover if Mum was going to Miss Louise like the rest.

I was unsure of my welcome when I visited the cottage the next afternoon. The door was locked but I got out my key and let myself in. She'd placed my slippers in their normal place on the mat so I slipped into them and crept quietly to her chair. She sat very still, her eyes closed, breathing softly and regularly. On her lap lay a large ledger, wide open. I was tempted to look for Mum's name so I checked that she was really asleep, although I didn't care if she woke up or not. Gently I lifted the ledger and placed it, still open, on the table. I looked up again to see that she was still asleep and then I began leafing through the pages, curious to see whose names were entered there. Most of it was double-dutch to me but I could make out the names entered in columns. Some I knew, others I didn't. Beside each entry was the money lent and paid, with the interest and the date. I felt relief when I couldn't find our name, but then I turned a page and there it was, together with those of Mrs Phipps, Mrs Woods, Mrs Buckley and several more of our neighbours. My heart sank. What Frankie had said was true. Mum was as bad as the rest. Sadly I turned back the pages and returned the ledger to Miss Louise's lap. She moved a little but I couldn't have cared less if she awoke. I slipped off the slippers and quietly left the cottage.

As I walked slowly back I kept asking myself what Dad was going to say when he found out. I consoled myself with the thought that he wouldn't find out from me; there was enough trouble at home already. That night as I lay in bed I prayed that it was not our name, only one like ours; I still couldn't believe it. I thought, I'll ask Miss Louise the truth tomorrow, and I drifted off to sleep.

Next afternoon when I let myself in Miss Louise was not asleep; she was seated, upright in her chair, eyes wide open. She looked as if she was waiting for me so before she could say anything I spoke.

'Does my Mum borrow money off you?' I blurted out.

'Yes, you know she does. You saw her name in my ledger yesterday, didn't you?' She snapped angrily and frowned fiercely at me.

I went very hot and felt myself redden. She couldn't have been asleep when I lifted the ledger from her lap and scanned its pages: she must have been watching me all the time. I began to feel ashamed of my nosiness but I hadn't intended to be nosey: I was just curious. I began to dislike her; she looked sly and I felt indignant that she'd spoken to me like that. I replied boldly, 'Yes, I did see our name in that book, along with a lot of others.' Then, placing my hands on my hips like I had seen Mum do many times when in a temper, I looked her straight in the eyes.

'You'll never get paid, yer know, and if my Dad finds out there'll be trouble!' I shouted.

'Well, if yer Mum don't pay yer father'll have to. My brother will see to that.' She answered calmly and shuffled over to the fireplace, but I hadn't had my say yet.

'I don't know 'ow because my Dad's on short time now. My

brother Charlie's left 'ome an' sister Mary's married an' Mum 'as to go out cleaning the fish an' chip shop to make ends meet.' I paused to get my breath and this gave her an opening.

'Have you quite finished?' she yelled. 'If so, you may go. I'm very vexed with you!'

'An' I'm vexed with you too!' I retorted and pushed past her to the door. Then, as I turned before leaving, I saw she was grinning at me. I hated her then. I felt that her character had been revealed and, what was more, that she'd been using me.

I went home feeling miserable and ashamed for being such a fool but I didn't have long to indulge my self-pity, for when I entered our house I found my brother Jack and Mum quarrelling loudly. They didn't notice me so I made myself unobtrusive and listened.

'But where're yer gooin'?' Mum wailed, putting on her tearful act and flopping into the chair as if exhausted.

'Not far away. If yer really want ter know I've been courtin' a widow for some time an' we're thinkin' of settlin' down tergether,' he replied.

'Don't goo yet Jack,' pleaded Mum. 'I'm in a lot of trouble with some debts I owe.'

'What debts?' demanded Jack, getting excited again. 'You always said yer never borrowed off anybody.'

'I couldn't 'elp meself,' she confessed tearfully. 'An' I don't know 'ow I'm gooin' ter pay it back if yer leave 'ome now.'

'Pay what back? An' 'ow much? 'Oo d'yer owe this money to, anyway?' Jack was confused but I was not. I knew what Mum was talking about. Then they really went at it, hammer and tongs – so loudly, in fact, that neither of them heard or noticed Dad enter the room. I coughed loudly and scraped my foot on the floor to draw their attention to who was standing quietly listening to them rowing.

'I owe five pounds an' some interest if yer must know,' Mum shouted.

'Oh blimey, whatever'll the ole man say when 'e finds out?' Jack whistled through pursed lips. He always called Dad 'the ole man' when we wasn't about. They finally became aware of Dad and as the penny dropped they both stared at him speechless.

'What's this yer don't want "the ole man" ter know? Something about owin' five pounds, is it?' he inquired quite calmly.

Mum covered her face with her apron and cried noisily, but she got no sympathy from Jack who pushed past Dad and left, leaving her to face the music. Dad slammed the door behind him with an 'An' good riddance!' Then he strode over to Mum and pulled her to her feet, although her face was still buried in the apron and she was wailing louder than ever. He shook her violently by the shoulders and then pushed her roughly back into the chair. 'You can turn yer waterworks off now, Polly. Let's 'ave the truth.'

I was standing mouth wide open afraid of what was going to happen next, but I practically jumped out of my skin when he yelled at me 'to stop gorpin' an' fill the kettle'. I was shaking so much that I had to lift the kettle with two hands when I staggered down the yard. Outside there were several neighbours obviously listening to what was going on in our house, but I just pushed through them. Frankie appeared as I was filling the kettle and offered to do it for me. When we got back to our door Mrs Jonesy and Mrs Phipps were still loitering, all ears, so Frankie deliberately poured some of the icy water on Mrs Jonesy's feet.

'Yow did that on purpose yer cheeky little sod!' she cried out in surprise.

'If yow'd done that ter me I'd ave wrung yer bloody neck,' Mrs Phipps chipped in, but Frankie only grinned and dropped the kettle, contents and all, on her foot. That did the trick! She ran off screaming and hopping down the yard. Frankie picked up the empty kettle and went to refill it but I noticed that none of the onlookers tried to wring his neck while he had the kettle in his hands. He poked his tongue out at them and entered the house in triumph. Indoors Mum was still crying into her apron and Dad was pacing back and forth, fuming.

'I warned yer what would 'appen if yer got into 'er clutches. Yow'll never be able ter get out of 'er debt now,' he stormed.

'But I ain't the only one,' Mum managed to blurt out. 'They all borra off 'er.'

'Never mind the others! It's this family I'm thinking about. Do yer know she can send yer ter prison if yer don't pay? Did yer think about that?' He glared angrily into her face.

'I thought I could pay a bit each week outa yower wages and Jack's, but now 'e's leavin' us,' she wept even louder.

'And a bloody good job!' answered Dad. ''E's gettin' too big fer 'is boots, demandin' this an' that every time 'e enters the 'ouse. I only 'ope 'e finds time ter marry this 'un, whoever she is.'

All the while I stood listening and Frankie sat calmly on the sofa reading his comic as though nothing was happening. During a lull in the shouting I made the tea, and as I was pouring the cups out Mum asked Dad what she should do.

'Goo ter bloody prison with the rest of yer croonies yow've got yerself mixed up with for all I care,' he bawled in reply, and with that he stormed out slamming the door behind. I looked up at Granny's picture and saw the black crepe paper had slipped again – but then it always did when the door was slammed. Mum jumped up straight away and began rear-ranging the furniture which had been upset in the commotion. Then she forgot her tears as Jack came back into the room. She pointed at the crepe paper and told Jack it was another bad omen, but he only scoffed at her superstitions and went upstairs to collect his belongings. I poured four more mugs of tea. Mum didn't touch hers and when he came down neither did Jack. He had a parcel under his arm, and much as Mum pleaded with him he wouldn't stay.

'Carn't yer try an' 'elp me out Jack?' she wheedled.

'No! I'm off fer good this time. Yow've drove us all away. Them two will be the next.' He pointed at us kids. Then he paused, put his hand in his pocket and threw four half crowns on the table.

'That's the last yer'll get off me an' don't forget I want my suit from the pawnshop when I come back ter fetch me other things.'

And with that he left, making sure he gave the door a good hard slam as well. The pictures shook and one fell, just missing Frankie's head, but he didn't bat an eyelid and just kept on reading his comic. As I reached for the fallen picture he said to me, 'That door's gooin' ter fall off its 'inges one of these times.'

I looked at him and wished I could be so unconcerned. Frankie always got away with cheeking his elders but I never did. Mum was crying as she picked up the money and slipped it into her purse which she kept down her bosom. I went over to comfort her but she shooed me away. I might as well not have bothered, but then I was too young to know what to do anyway. Tears came to my eyes as I thought that this was my and Miss Louise's fault. If she had not lent Mum the money none of this would have happened. I blamed her and the fact she was a Jew for how she had used us all. Most of the moneylenders and pawnbrokers were Jewish and they had a reputation for meanness. I vowed to have no more to do with her but thought I ought to return her shoes and her key, so I snatched Frankie's comic and tried to persuade him to come with me. At first he refused, then he softened and consented.

'You know I will,' he said and jumped up ready.

We walked together over to the cottage. I had already made up my mind what I was going to say by the time Frankie had rapped on the door. He must have liked the sound it made because he gave it another couple for luck; my courage rising, too, I gave it two more. However, there was no reply, so I opened the door with the key and we entered. I kicked the slippers that were there waiting for me out of the way and then we saw her standing with her back to the fire.

'What's all that noise for?' she asked. 'Why didn't you just use your key, and why have you brought him?' she demanded, pointing her bony finger at Frankie.

''E's my brother an' where I go 'e goes,' I replied defiantly.

Frankie asked why she didn't answer our knock but she ignored this.

'We've come ter bring yer shoes back. We don't want anything more ter do with yow,' I told her.

'Well I never,' she exclaimed, advancing towards us. 'I never heard such cheeky kids in all my life. Get out of here at once.'

'Well, yer 'earin' 'em now!' put in Frankie. 'An' do yer know what ower neighbours an' the kids in the street call yer? An old blood sucker.'

She gave a sly grin at this. 'Oh that's mild. I've been called worse than that round here. Now clear off the pair of yer.'

'Here's yer key.' I flung it on the open ledger on the table. I thought if only I could steal that some time and destroy it, maybe she'd have no proof of what was owed her. But I knew this was a vain hope because the house was always locked securely. I walked over to the door before I spoke to her.

'I'm not coming any more for yer ter use me. It's all your fault. You've upset Mum an' Dad, an' ower Jack's left 'ome. So now I know yer won't be paid, so there!' I put out my tongue and Frankie did likewise, but before we had got out she said, 'You can tell your mother and father that I shall be calling at the usual time on Saturday. And I expect to be paid.'

I'd never seen her look so evil before. This was a side of her nature that she'd kept hidden from me but it made me realise my feelings were justified. I had no regrets as I slammed the door behind me and left the cottage for the last time.

Dad's Business Venture

When we got home I was surprised to see Dad sitting in his usual seat because he should have been at work.

'Katie,' he said to me. 'I want you ter take this letter ter your sister Mary. 'Ere's a penny for the tram fare and try to be as quick as you can.'

'Yes Dad,' I answered eagerly. I was glad of a reason to visit Mary in her new home.

I combed my hair, then quickly snatched up Topsey, my rag doll, and took the letter from Dad and went off. The ride on the tram was not far; only a halfpenny each way. When I arrived and rang the bell it was Albert who showed me in. I told him I had a letter from Dad for Mary. But Mary was out so I gave him the letter and began to tell him about the trouble at home.

'I'm not surprised,' he said. 'It's been going on for a long time, but yer Mum's bin very foolish an' so have the rest. Getting into the clutches of a money lender!' As if bookmakers were much better, I thought. I gave him a hard look. I could see there'd be little sympathy here.

'I'll give Mary the letter when she comes 'ome. 'Ave you got your fare back?'

I told him I had and left without saying any more. When I returned home I told Dad what had happened and what Albert had said.

'Good girl,' he said. 'Put the kettle on, I expect she'll have a cuppa when she gets 'ere.' But we waited and waited all that afternoon and saw neither hide nor hair of Mary. I could see Dad was worried so after a couple of hours of hanging about I offered to return to Mary's.

'No,' he replied sadly. 'She don't seem to bother about us any more.'

'I can run there and back in no time if you ain't got the money for the tram,' I said eagerly.

'It's not the penny I'm bothered about,' he mumbled almost to himself, gazing into the fire. I wished I could help him then; he looked so down in the mouth hunched up by the stove.

'Can I do anything else for yer Dad?' I asked quietly.

'No, I don't think so. Anyway it's getting late. Yow better get off ter bed before yer Mum comes back.'

I said 'good night' and kissed him on his cheek but he didn't respond. He just sat there, his thoughts miles away. I wept a little as I climbed the creaky stairs, and when I got into the attic I knelt down beside the bed, put my hands together and prayed. I asked Jesus to help us, and to forgive Jack and me and to make Dad happy. I felt exhausted when I climbed into bed and I fell into a deep sleep from which I awoke next morning refreshed and happier. I went down to put the kettle on and while I was doing so in walked Albert.

'Good mornin' Katie,' he greeted me cheerily. 'Is yer Dad in?'

I told him they were in bed and I dashed up the stairs, two at a time, to fetch them. I leant over Mum and whispered to Dad.

'Dad, Albert's 'ere. 'E wants ter see yer.'

I could tell Mum was awake but she didn't offer to move or say anything. She wasn't on speaking terms with Albert.

'Tell 'im I'll be right down. As soon as I've slipped me trousers on.'

When Dad joined us Albert greeted him just as pleasantly as he had me, and I thought at least they're all happy this morning.

'I'm sorry,' Albert began, after clearing his throat. 'Mary couldn't come over last night. She was too upset when she read your letter, Sam. We talked it over and I've decided to let you 'ave five pounds. Yer can pay me back when yer can.' He concluded his speech.

'I don't know 'ow ter thank yer,' Dad said, grasping Albert by the hand. 'I'll see to it that Polly don't get into any debt again, don't you worry.' Albert nodded.

'Remember Sam,' he lowered his voice. 'I'm doin' this for your sake. Not your missus's.' He stroked my head and said as he was about to go, 'Be a good girl Katie, you've got a good Dad under the circumstances.' Dad thanked him again and he left, shutting the door quietly behind him.

I thanked God then for answering my prayer. Dad kissed me on the forehead and asked me to make another pot of tea and he sat down in his chair and smoked a quiet pipe of tobacco looking happier than he had for days. When Mum came down he told her about Albert's offer and she perked up, too. Dad told Mum that Miss Louise would be calling later for her money.

'You'd better be out when she comes,' he told her, but she didn't want telling twice. Soon after breakfast she was off. The rest of us settled down to wait. Dad warned us to be seen and not heard but we didn't need telling either. Frankie read his tattered old comic and I busied myself with the crocks. Just then there was a tap at the door.

'Come in,' Dad called out sharply. The door opened slowly and there stood Miss Louise.

''Ere's yer bloody five pounds,' he said, throwing five gold sovereigns on the table. She stooped and scooped them up. Dad was angry. I suppose he must have resented giving this much money to her; it was a large sum after all.

'Now get out!' he shouted at her. 'I don't want ter see yer round 'ere any more an' I don't want Katie to come near yower place either!'

She just glared back and said acidly, 'What about the interest?'

'Yow can wait fer that. Now get out of my house, you bloody old bugger.'

Frankie peered over the top of his comic, unable to resist the temptation to join in. 'That's tellin' 'er,' he said.

'That's quite enough lip from yow,' Dad snapped at him. 'Get yerself washed an' put that comic on the fire. It's filthy.'

Reluctantly he did as he was told. The comic wanted burning anyway; it was torn and the print was totally obscured by the grimy hands of its previous owners. Miss Louise stood quietly observing this domestic scene, grinning. Dad was furious by now. He made a move towards her and bawled at her to 'get out', which she did but not without slamming the door for all she was worth behind her. Amazingly this must have been the final straw for it, because its top hinge broke and it swivelled on the bottom one, narrowly missing Miss Louise before it crashed to the floor. With that she marched off, and after we'd got our breath, I made the usual cup of tea while Frankie went to fetch nails and hammer from Dad's tool box so he could fix the door before Mum returned and explanations were necessary. In fact the door was mended, and we were drinking our tea when she came in. Dad told her that it was settled but he warned her she must never borrow again. He warned Frankie and me as well. Just then brother Jack came strolling in to collect the rest of his clothes. He went straight up the stairs and a few minutes later came down carrying a parcel of his things. Mum looked pleadingly at him but not a word was said between any of us until he was opening the door to leave and Dad said, 'Bloody good riddance, an' don't bang the door when you go, I've only just mended it.' But he did and once again the pictures on the walls quivered in fear. After that things went more smoothly for a few days, at least until the following Monday.

I got up as usual at seven o'clock to make Dad his cup of tea and his bread and cheese for dinner. We never normally talked in the morning: he got up at the last moment and rushed out without a word. But this morning he spoke to me. He told me to be a good girl for Mum, and that he would give me some money to go to the pictures. I said I would be good and thanked him, and then quite unexpectedly he bent down and kissed my cheek and turned and abruptly left. I loved it when he did that. I couldn't remember the last time he'd shown me so much affection. I pitched into the chores with a light heart, singing to myself as I worked. Then after about an hour I heard the familiar heavy tread of Dad's boots on the cobbles. The door opened and there he was looking pale and worried.

'Did you forget something Dad?' I asked, though I knew he hadn't.

'We've all bin laid off work,' he said simply.

'Oh, dear, whatever will Mum say?' I burst out. Her reactions in situations like this were never predictable.

'Matter a damn what she says,' he muttered almost to himself. 'We'll all 'ave ter go on the parish relief again.'

Just then Mum, half-dressed, came into the room, but Dad had hardly got a word out before she cut him off.

'I know. I 'eard yer. Whatter we gooin' ter do?' she demanded.

'I'll think of something don't worry, but in the meantime we won't starve. We're all goin' along to see the relief officer,' he soothed her.

'When?'

'Now if yer like,' he said impatiently and went out. I followed him and saw him join some of his mates who were waiting on the corner. Then they all turned and went in a group to the Welfare Offices. This was the same old tumbledown mission hall which the Sally Army used and which all the neighbours used when there was a wedding or some other big function to be held.

I hung back and watched what would happen. The men went in and stated their case to the man in charge, but he merely informed them that they would get nothing immediately and that they were to come back when their money had gone. So there was nothing to be done. The men drifted away and I returned home. By the end of that week things were looking grim around our way. Things were particularly bad for the people who owed Miss Louise because the interest was growing all the time. The women were to be seen hanging around in the yard talking quietly or trying to wash to get a few more rags to the pawnshop. The men idled their time away on street corners or outside the pub, cadging a drink or a smoke. There were more quarrels than usual. We never had much to eat in ordinary times, but we had less now and us kids were really glad of the extra slice of bread and jam that we were given for our school breakfast.

The Monday after the men were laid off I came home from school to find crowds of people gathered outside Miss Louise's door chattering excitedly. There was a buzz of expectation about them and quite a few seemed to be smiling and jolly. Mum was amongst the crowd; Frankie and Liza too.

'What's the matter?' I asked Frankie when I had pushed through to him.

'Don't yer know? Miss Louise has died,' he answered.

'That's nothing for them to smile about,' I said, quite shocked at their callousness.

'But they won't 'ave ter pay 'er what they owe 'er now she's dead, will they?'

I had no time to answer; I spotted Dad edging his way through the throng. He must have heard what was being said because he rounded on them.

'Don't yer kid yerselves, yer stupid women. Yow'll still 'ave ter pay. Yow'd better clear off before 'er brother comes.'

At that they began to disperse, chatting and nodding all the time. Mum, Frankie and Liza had been the first to go, before Dad saw them. I was glad he hadn't seen me either as I hurried away in the opposite direction.

This news provided ample scope for gossip in the next few days. Next day Mr Vulcan arrived and the first thing he did was to call on everyone who owed money to his sister. I bumped into him and told him I was sorry to hear about his sister, which I was, despite how she'd treated us. I also hoped she hadn't told him about Frankie's and my rudeness although why I should have been bothered about him I can't think. He smiled, thanked me and patted me on the head before knocking at our door. Dad invited him in and I followed.

'I suppose yow've come for yer interest?' said Dad sharply. 'Well, I ain't got it yet. I'll bring it when I can. No need ter call.'

Dad sat back in his chair, expecting Mr Vulcan to leave, but he paused a moment, looking first at Dad then at me, and I thought, This is it, now what'll he say?

'You have a good girl here,' he began, much to my relief. 'She was good to my sister. I'll forget the interest you owe and cross it off the book as paid.'

'That's very kind of you,' Dad muttered grudgingly, but Mr Vulcan carried on without listening.

'I've locked up the cottage and when I come back in a couple of days I shall sell up my sister's belongings. So if there's anything Katie would like, she can have it.'

'Thank you, Mr Vulcan,' I said as he turned and left. After he'd gone Dad said he would consider what Mr Vulcan had said but I knew already what I wanted and I knew Dad wouldn't object. Those two days couldn't pass quickly enough. Then Mr Vulcan returned from London as he said he would to arrange the funeral.

Everybody in the district came out to watch the coffin being carried away. It was not a grand affair like Granny's. There appeared to be only one wreath. The neighbours didn't have the usual collection for flowers either. Some had tried but the general feeling was that she wasn't one of us. The hearse took her to St Paul's churchyard where the service was to be held. I waited around to watch the burial. I wept when they lowered her coffin into the ground. I'd liked her until the money lending began, and I was sorry for being unkind to her. Then Frankie saw me.

'No use cryin', 'er's dead an' that's that.' And in that breath I thought how like Mum he sounded.

He left me to walk home alone. Later that afternoon I saw a horse-drawn van pull up outside the cottage and soon a burly fellow was fetching furniture out and loading it into the van. I waited for Mr Vulcan to come out with a group of our evercurious neighbours. At last he emerged and called me in. This caused a murmur of surprise amongst the onlookers. I pushed past them and went in with him.

'I want you to look around, and if there's anything you'd like, don't be afraid to say. I know Louise would like you to have something,' he said quietly.

I hesitated for a while. Then I overcame my shyness and said I would like the coloured wool from the trunk upstairs.

'Very well, go up and help yourself,' he replied. He gave me a pretty cane basket to put it in and I went upstairs, opened the trunk and loaded all the balls I could get into the basket. I looked for the knitted garments that I used to help her with but they must have all been sold. Just then I glanced through the little bedroom window and saw all the women and kids still hanging about outside. Then I closed the lid of the trunk and returned downstairs, tears of happiness in my eyes. As I wiped them on my pinafore Mr Vulcan asked what was wrong with me. I found myself gazing at the harmonium and my memories of the happy times I'd spent listening to Miss Louise play came flooding back and I wept more. Mr Vulcan handed me his black-edged handkerchief.

'I'm happy to have these,' I said truthfully. 'But I was thinking about how we used to sing together.' He looked at me awhile before he said.

'Would you like the harmonium? I have no use for it.' I didn't know what to say: I couldn't believe that I'd heard him correctly. My mouth fell open and I must have stared wide-eyed at him. But I hesitated only a second before I accepted his gift excitedly.

'Run along home then and tell your Dad to come and wheel it away.'

I elbowed my way through the nosey parkers gossiping in the yard and ran home to tell Dad my good news. I fell indoors and crashed into Mum.

'What's the matter with yer? What's in that basket?' she demanded.

'It's a present from Mr Vulcan. Where's Dad?' I blurted out.

"'E's down the pub with 'is mates. Why?' She was curious now.

I didn't stay to explain. I dashed out down the street to the pub to get him round to the cottage before Mr Vulcan changed his mind. I'd only gone part of the way when I collided with Dad.

'Well, well, well, an' what 'ave yow bin up to now?' Excitedly I told him what had happened and begged him to let me have the harmonium.

'We'll see,' he answered calmly. 'Don't rush me. If 'e says you're ter have it, it'll still be there.' Then he took my hand and we walked round to the cottage. There the loading was still underway and the women were still hanging about. Dad and I went in and Mr Vulcan explained that he wished to give me the harmonium and that there was a clean bed upstairs if we wanted it. Dad thanked him and said he would return for the bed after he'd wheeled the instrument to our house. Mr Vulcan wouldn't hear of this but offered to send the removal men over with it. I was in tears of joy. I kissed Mr Vulcan: I was overwhelmed. I was the owner of a harmonium as well as the basket and the wool. Then we returned to our house under the gaze of the neighbours.

'I wonder where they got the money to buy them?' I heard Mrs Woods say.

Then Mrs Jonesy replied. 'That Polly's a dark 'orse if yow arsk me.'

Mum was pleased as punch when she saw what we'd got, particularly when the men arrived with the brass bedsteads and a red striped flock mattress. However, she wasn't so pleased with the harmonium.

'We ain't 'avin' that contraption in the 'ouse. We ain't got no room fer it,' she told Dad. Dad scowled at Mum when one of the removal men said to him, 'Yow've got a right one theea mate. I know what I'd do if she was my missus.'

But he ignored the remark and concentrated on bringing the things in. He hauled the harmonium into the room past Mum, pausing only to wink at me. That meant it was mine for keeps. Mum was right though; there was very little room for it and Dad had to move the mangle to fit it in. Mum was furious at this and demanded to know where her mangle was going.

'Inside the pantry,' Dad snapped back. 'An' yow can come an' give me a hand. An' shut that door too before all the neighbours come nosing in.' But Mum didn't lift a finger to help and gave as good as she got.

'Do it yerself. I'm gooin' ter put the kettle on an mek a cuppa tea.' This was a ploy she always resorted to when she wanted to avoid doing something. Dad knew it was no good arguing with her and he carried on with the job.

'That's where the mangle is and that's where it stays,' he told her when he'd done. Mum ignored him. He pushed the harmonium into the place where the mangle had stood, then sat down to sup his mug of tea. He finished before Mum who was still sulking.

'When yow've drunk yer tea, we'll get the mattress and the bedsteads in,' he said impatiently.

'I s'ppose that's for Katie an' all,' she snapped sarcastically.

'No, it's fer Frankie. He's gettin' ter be a big lad an' he's noticing things.'

No more was said except for Mum's moans and groans as she struggled to get the bedding upstairs to the attic. Now there were three single beds in our small room; I had Mary's old one, Liza had the one we all used to sleep in and Frankie had Miss Louise's. I was thrilled with these gifts, especially to have a bed to myself.

When the house was empty I would take the key from round my neck, unlock the harmonium and experiment with pulling out some of the stops. I began trying to play 'God Save the King', but after tapping away for an hour with one finger I hadn't made much progress. Later I improved and graduated to two fingers, and eventually learnt to play the tune using all my fingers. I thought I was ever so clever and I wanted everyone to hear me, so each time I spotted one of the neighbours near our house I would bang out the tune. The noise must have been awful but it was sweet music to my ears.

I was not allowed to play when Mum and Dad were in because they couldn't stand the din, so I had to wait until they were down the pub to enjoy myself. We used to invite in the other children from the yard and I would pretend to be our music teacher and conduct a lesson. One night I dressed up in one of Mum's frocks and Frankie donned Dad's billy-cock hat but in the middle of 'Rock of Ages' Dad returned. The kids scattered quickly and Frankie and I had to explain ourselves; he ignored Liza as usual. We were warned not to dress in our parents' clothes and he threatened Frankie with his belt, but nothing more was said about it.

After a few weeks all our money was gone and everything was in pawn so Dad had to go to the relief office. When he returned Mum asked what they had said.

'They're sendin' the visitor termorra to see if we've got anything we can sell. In the meantime they've given me this to go on with,' he answered, throwing our ration card across the table. When Mum had looked at it she cried out.

'We carn't live on that!'

'We'll 'ave ter manage,' Dad replied calmly. 'Other people 'ave to, an' they 'ave more kids than us.'

'That's their bad luck,' screeched Mum. 'I'd 'ave 'ad mower, if yow'd 'ave 'ad yower way.'

Dad was not prepared to stand any more and got out of the chair into which he had just flopped.

'Talk ter yerself, Polly. I'm off out.'

'Where do yer think yer gooin'?' she demanded, but he'd closed the door behind him and left.

The next day the visitor came. He didn't even knock but just walked right in and went through the house looking to see if we had anything of value to part with before we could receive any relief. Dad didn't object to him nosing around but I wondered what Mum would have said if she'd been home; she was out cleaning at the fish shop. Dad looked as if he didn't care what happened any more.

'Is there anything you haven't told me?' the visitor asked Dad, his eyes settling on my harmonium.

'No,' he replied at once, defying him to look under its cover.

'Then what's this?' he said, lifting the cloth.

'That's my Katie's,' Dad told him, snatching the cover off him. 'I ain't partin' with that. It was a gift ter the child.'

'Well,' the man replied. 'I'll have to report it. That's my job and I doubt whether we can grant you anything until it's sold. Good day.'

He went and Dad slammed the door after him. 'Good day and good riddance to you too,' he said angrily.

The next day another visitor called but he said the same as the first. Dad looked sad and worried. I didn't like to see him like this so when the second man had gone I turned to Dad.

'You can sell the harmonium, Dad, if it'll 'elp. I can't play it properly anyway and I know the sound of it gets on Mum's nerves.'

He looked at me with a gentle, sad expression on his face.

'Do you really want me to sell it?' he asked.

'No, Dad,' I answered truthfully.

'Then it stays where it is. I'll think of something else ter 'elp us through. Now put the kettle on an' we'll 'ave a pot of tea an' think.'

A cup of tea was our universal cure-all and comforter. We sat and drank our tea in silence then Dad stood up and told me to tell Mum, when she returned, that he'd gone to have one last talk to the relief officer. He'd never told Mum about the words he'd had with the relief officers, which was a blessing really because she would never have shut up about it. I don't know what was said at the relief office but when Dad came back he just threw the ration card on the table in disgust. Mum snatched it up to see what we had got but Dad forestalled the outburst he knew was coming.

'Now don't go off the deep end. I've thought of an idea to bring some extra money in the house.'

'What? Not another one of your bright ideas.' And with that she went off to the shop to collect the miserable amount of provisions that were due.

Dad sat poking the dead ashes in the grate and sucking on his empty clay pipe. The tea caddy was empty too. I had to make do with stewing the old tea leaves. When Mum returned and saw the teapot on the hob she flared up.

'Yow can throw that down the sink! It's bin stewed I don't know 'ow many times. 'Ere's some. An' goo careful with it.' She tossed a two-ounce packet on the table.

This was how we went on then. It was winter and the weather was wet and cold and our life was hard; we survived only on hand-outs from the parish. Soon we were down to our last lumps of coal. Although Mum was working at the fish shop she didn't get much for her labours, sometimes only some fish and chips. Still they helped, especially if we had a loaf of bread to go with them. Dad would go out very early each morning, without even a cup of tea inside him, to tramp round looking for a job – anything to tide us over. Plenty of times I'm sure he stayed out only to avoid Mum's sharp tongue because there was no work to be had for any of the men.

Late one afternoon as I was packing some old boots I had begged with wet slack and tea leaves to use as fuel on the fire the door was flung open and Dad stumbled in. I saw at once he'd been drinking.

'Yer won't 'ave ter do that much more,' he said. 'You'll see. I've got a good idea and this time it'll work.'

I didn't understand what he was mumbling about. He was looking round with a vacant look on his face and I was frightened. Then he suddenly told me to fetch the chopper from the cellar.

'What for?' I managed to ask.

'What for? Never mind what for, just do as yer told at once before I change me mind.'

I fled down the cellar and returned with the chopper. I handed it to him at arm's length, not knowing what he was about to do. He snatched it and I watched, terrified now that something awful was about to happen. He turned and went upstairs muttering to himself. I wished somebody else was at home because I was afraid to be in the house with him in this mood. Loud bangs started upstairs and I imagined all kinds of things were happening. Then I heard him call down from the attic for me to open the stairs door wide. I was too scared to reply but I opened the door anyway and hid behind it. The next moment something heavy came clattering down the stairs. I wedged myself further out of sight. My first thought was that this was Dad lying at the foot of the stairs having killed himself. I clasped my hands tight over my eyes and scarcely breathed. But I knew I had to look, so slowly I peeped round the door. Then I opened my fingers wide and peered down at the floor. With a sigh of relief I dropped my hands, because instead of Dad lying there there was the attic door which had fallen in such a way that it was wedging the door back, trapping me where I was. I called to Dad but he didn't hear me; instead he sent another door crashing down. Then he came down himself, managing with difficulty to negotiate the obstacles on the floor.

'Well I never!' He smiled when he saw where I was. 'I told yer ter open the door wide, not ter get behind it,' he chuckled.

'Katie,' he said when he had released me. 'You know what I'm gooin' ter do? I'm gooin' to sell firewood an' these doors are gooin' ter give me a start.'

'But what's Mum goin' ter say when she sees what you've done?' I began to get worried again.

'Never mind what yer Mum says. Any'ow it'll be all cleared away by the time she gets 'ome.'

He was looking pleased with himself as he dragged the table to the side of the room to make space to work in. He set to with a will and soon the doors were reduced to kindling. After I'd got used to the idea I helped to count the sticks and tie them up in bundles. He tore one of Mum's dusters into strips for this purpose and we busied ourselves counting out sticks and piling up bundles. Then the door opened and Mum walked in. She saw the mess and flew off the handle at once.

'Whatcha dooin'? What's all that wood on me clane flooar? Ain't we got enough broken quarries without yow cracking any mower?' she demanded.

'Sit down and keep calm,' Dad told her. 'Listen ter what I 'ave ter say. I've 'ad this idea for a long time an' if I can get a few customers, we'll be able ter buy some extra food an' we'll be able to rent a better 'ouse, with good strong doors not like these rotten ones.' He waved his hand at the firewood.

'Oh my God!' she shrieked, not waiting for Dad to finish. 'Where's these dooars come from?'

'The attic an' our room. They were hangin' off anyway,' he told her matter-of-factly.

'They wouldn't 'ave bin 'angin' off if yow'd 'ave put a nail in 'em. I don't know what the landlord will say or do when 'e finds out,' she wailed.

''E won't find out if nobody tells 'im and 'e ain't likely ter goo upstairs in any case,' Dad pointed out to her. 'Now put the kettle on Polly an' we'll 'ave a nice cuppa tea then Katie an' me'll get cracking.'

By the time we were drinking it Mum had calmed down considerably. Then she had to go back to the shop to get our fish and chips, so we bundled up the rest of the wood and, as it was dark, ventured out to see if Dad could find some customers for his new business. We couldn't have gone in daylight for fear that Dad would be spotted and reported to the reflief officers; then as now claimants were not allowed to earn money. I pushed the go-cart with the bundles inside covered with a cloth, and Dad strolled behind looking nonchalantly about him. The first shop we stopped at gave Dad an order right away, providing the wood was dry and clean. It couldn't have been anything else but Dad had put out the best wood the first time; some of the rest was rotten.

Dad's business prospered. Frankie helped with the chopping and I went with Dad when he delivered the orders. When the doors were sold Dad went out and bought soap boxes, orange boxes, even smelly fish boxes to use, and Mum was happy with money coming in again. He always said he did best when I was with him.

One day Frankie was chopping a particularly springy orange box when suddenly the head flew off the handle and cracked our only mirror.

'Now look what yer've done!' yelled Mum. 'Another bloody seven years' bad luck!'

'Rubbish!' he snapped back and ran out. He didn't come back for several hours, afraid of Mum's temper but Dad said he would replace the mirror and this seemed to pacify her.

Another day we nearly came unstuck altogether. The previous day the proprietor of a little paraffin shop had asked Dad to deliver the sticks in the afternoon because she was closing early; and to oblige and keep a customer Dad agreed. Off we went the next day and had nearly got to the shop when Dad spotted a relief officer. He pushed me into an entry and we hid there until the man had passed by. Then we hurried to the shop, delivered our wood and hurried back home.

Another day we returned to find an empty space where my harmonium should have been. I burst into tears because I was sure Mum had pawned it or sold it. Dad moved slowly towards Mum and I could see by the look of him that he was furious.

'Now I warned yow, Polly,' he began. 'Where's it gone?'

She turned round without betraying a sign of understanding what he was on about.

'What're yer talkin' about? Where's what gone?' she asked mildly.

'Yow know very well what I mean!' he shouted. 'Katie's harmonium. If ever yow've parted with that, I warn yer, I'll kill yer!' And I believe he would have too.

'Oh that,' she replied. 'Well we had the visitor call about four o'clock. Frankie warned me he was comin' down the street so we wheeled it into the pantry until he'd gone. But we couldn't get it back agen 'cause one of the wheels 'as come off.'

'Oh, I see,' said Dad, calming down. 'I'll soon fix that.'

Dad fixed it by removing all four wheels and with an effort we dragged it back into position.

'That stays as a permanent fixture from now on,' Dad said. I could have hugged my Mum that day for saving the harmonium but I was afraid if I did she would push me away.

We were all made very wary by this brush with authority and Frankie even refused to go out with Dad that night in case they were spotted by the parish man.

'Yow'll do as yer told!' he was told. 'It's only for another few days then I'll sign off,' Dad promised.

Towards the end of that week the visitor called on us again. We knew he was coming because we could see him calling at our neighbours in the yard first. This gave us enough time to cover the harmonium and clear away any telltale signs of wood.

'Come in,' Dad called out as the knock was heard, but the man was already in the room. Without any preliminaries he began interrogating Dad.

'What's this I hear about you selling firewood?' the man demanded.

'An' who's told you that?' Dad looked the man straight in the eye.

'I cannot divulge any information. You were seen one afternoon this week and I've made inquiries.' His voice tailed off. Dad just turned away and didn't reply. When he could see he would get nothing out of Dad, the visitor continued.

'You know you can go to prison for failure to report a source of income like this?' he said.

Dad turned to the man, head bowed. 'I'm very sorry,' he said humbly. 'I was goin' ter call terday but it's bin snowin'.'

We children were huddled together, scared of what would happen. We knew only too well what could happen to Dad and we were afraid. I began to weep and so did Liza.

'Please don't take our Dad away,' I pleaded with him, and Frankie too chipped in, 'That's quite so sir, he said he was going to sign off.'

We must have looked pathetic because the man paused, looking at us, then he turned to Dad and said if Dad promised to call at the office he wouldn't report the matter.

'I'll come now,' Dad said, obviously relieved. However the offices were closed so he said he would call first thing in the morning. Dad thanked the man several times but he just grunted and left.

'Phew, that was a close shave,' Dad said, flopping into the chair wiping his brow. True to his word Dad signed off the next day and we heard no more about it.

In the weeks that followed he built up a regular round of customers and boasted that it was better than going to work, especially on cold winter mornings. But it was not good enough for Mum. She always had to find fault with everything; she wouldn't have been our Mum else. As the days went by she moaned more and more about the mess the wood caused.

'I ain't 'avin' this mess under me feet every day. Yow'll 'ave ter doo summat about it,' she told him.

It put him off his stroke and the chopper slipped, cutting his finger. Blood spurted and he swore.

'No? But yer 'old out yer bloody 'and when the money comes in, don't yer?'

'Now Mum's goin' ter spoil everything,' I whispered to Frankie.

'No, she ain't!' Dad shouted, having overheard my remark. 'I'm thinkin' of buildin' me a shed where I can work in peace,' he added, sucking his bleeding finger.

'The landlord ain't goona allow it. We owe too much rent,' she replied.

'I'll get round ter that when he calls,' said Dad not to be outdone. Mum didn't bother to reply but went off mumbling to herself, not forgetting to shut the door with a bang after her.

The next day, as it happened, was rent day. No firewood could be chopped up until after the landlord had called so the room was clean and tidy, all except for the odd quarry tile Dad had broken during the wood-chopping. Eventually there was a knock on the door and Dad called out to the landlord, Mr Priest, to enter. Mr Priest looked like an undertaker, dressed in his long black frock coat, top hat, long sideburns and grey whiskers. Dad paid over the four shillings and while he was entering it up in the book said, 'Mr Priest, I was wondering if yer could give me permission to build a small wooden shed facing the house?'

Mr Priest looked up and stared at Dad for a while and Dad stood there waiting for a reply.

'What will you be wanting it for?' he inquired.

'Well, you can see,' Dad replied, waving his arm. 'We have no room for everything an' I thought the place would look brighter if the missus 'ad somewhere to put her buckets an' brooms.' The landlord thought for a bit, stroking his beard, before he gave his decision.

'Now if you'll promise to pay off some of the arrears you can build your shed. But I'll have to raise the rent one and six a week.'

Dad gave his promise and he kept his word. He built his shed which, made as it was of old floorboards from a couple of hovels that had been empty for years, resembled a shack. He was no carpenter but he did his best and he began to sell wood on a larger scale. He supplied shops with the best quality wood which he bought cheap from sawmills; he even sold sawdust to pubs and butchers' shops to sprinkle on their floors. When any of our neighbours wanted firewood theirs was from old fish boxes, but they had it cheap at a penny a bowlful, and 'no tick', 'cash on the nail,' as he said firmly.

Now he was at home more Dad and I became closer. He listened to me more and had time to answer my questions. He still didn't know whose side to take when Mum carried on at us but she never came to the shed while we were chopping wood with him, so we had a retreat. He took us to the pictures sometimes and we shared his intimate refuge from Mum. Each night when we'd finished our various tasks he would look at our hands by the light of a candle and probe with a needle for splinters. We didn't like him doing this for he was rough, but we got used to it and our hands became tough. Kids like us had to be tough in those days.

Liza was like Mum; she never came into the shed to help. She only came to fetch wood for Mum or bring us our cocoa. Dad never bothered about her. He said she was more trouble than she was worth. One night she brought in the usual cocoa and watched while Dad removed a splinter from my palm. Dad looked up and caught her grinning.

'What are yer waitin' for?' he asked her, but she just shrugged her shoulders and held out her hands.

'I ain't got splinters in mine.' She turned to leave, but Dad got off his orange box and grabbed hold of her hands and proceeded to prod her palms with the needle.

'How do yer like that? That's took the smile off yer face,' he told her. 'Now goo an' tell yer Mum that!' She ran off screaming but she never pulled faces at us again if Dad was around.

When we'd finished that night Dad gave us tuppence to go the first half at the Queen's Hall. He told us to hurry back home after the picture had finished because it might get foggy later. He told Frankie to take care of me and so we went off hand in hand. When we got there the chucker-out told us to go in quickly because the film had started. The board over the door proclaimed that it was *The Clutching Hand*. Frankie had seen it before and thought I wouldn't like it and tried to dissuade me from going in. I was determined to see it and I pulled away from him and went up to the box office to pay my penny, hoping he would follow. I started up the cold stone steps to the gallery. It was dark and dismal. There were only two dim lights flickering from two iron brackets high up on the wall. They made weird shadows on the cracked plaster of the walls. I was beginning to get scared even before I'd seen the film. My clogs clattered on the steps and I looked back over my shoulder a couple of times to see if Frankie was following me, but he wasn't. When I eventually reached the gods I hesitated, afraid to push the door open, but after a couple of minutes I became too frightened to stand there in the dark any longer. I pushed the door and went in. I could see that the picture had only just started. Then quietly I walked down the steps and felt for a seat on one of the wooden forms; after being hissed at by several people I found one empty, next to an old woman. She smelt of snuff when she leaned over and said, 'Sit down dearie, yer blockin' me view.' I flopped down in the seat but missed and landed on the floor. This provoked more disapproval.

'Shut yer row down theea,' a voice boomed out from the darkness. This brought the chucker-out to see what the commotion was about, but luckily he couldn't tell what row it had come from because the old woman snatched me up by the hem of my frock and sat me on the seat. Then everything went quiet apart from the piano which was played slower and slower and quieter and quieter as a hand moved across the screen. Then the fingers began to move and the piano got louder and stopped with a final note as the hand fell on to the floor. Everyone was glued to their seats in anticipation of what was to happen next. I was almost too scared to look. I hoped and prayed that the lights would come on so I could fly down those steps. Then the woman took a paper bag out and I thought she had some sweets and might give one to me. But she dipped her thumb and forefinger into the bag and took out a pinch of snuff. She saw me looking at her and thrusting the bag under my nose invited me to take a pinch. I jumped up in fright and in the process knocked the snuff out of her hand. It went all over us. I began sneezing and couldn't stop; nor could several of our neighbours who'd shared in the shower. Someone called out, 'Turn that woman out, an' that brat.' In the confusion that followed the form tipped up propelling us all on to the floor. Then the lights went up and I saw the chucker-out standing over us.

'Who's mekin' all this racket?' he bawled in a thunderous voice.

'Me,' I called out. I would have been only too pleased to be thrown out, and to no one's surprise with a poke and a shove I was. He conducted me back down the cold stone steps by the scruff of my neck and soon I found myself back in the street again.

'Don't let me see yer here agen,' he warned me, but I was off at a run.

Dad had been right; it was foggy and getting thicker so I had to slow down because I couldn't see where I was going. I started to sing to give myself courage and to avoid running into someone. Ghostly shapes loomed out of the fog and then disappeared again. A cat dashed over my feet at one point and I began to think about the disembodied hand in the film. Eventually I reached our yard safely and entered the house breathless. The gas was unlit and the only light was the feeble glow of the coals. Mum and Dad were dozing in their chairs but Dad opened his eyes as I sat down and asked if I'd enjoyed the picture.

'Yes Dad,' I lied. I thought that if I told him what had really happened he might not let me go again and I wanted to see Charlie Chaplin and the Keystone Cops ones that were coming soon.

'Where's Frankie?' Dad continued, scratching his head.

'I don't know, Dad,' I told him. 'He said he'd seen the film once an' didn't want to see it agen.'

'I'll give 'im a feel of my belt when he comes in. I told 'im ter look after yow.' He was annoyed and I had not wanted to get Frankie into trouble. 'Eat yer bread an' drippin' an' drink yer cocoa. Then get up ter bed.'

I was not keen to go yet because I still had a vivid memory of that hand. I offered to do some jobs until the others returned. But Dad told me Liza had already done them, which struck me as a miracle. I asked if I could wait for Frankie but Mum, who I'd thought was asleep, piped up at that.

'No!' she shrieked. 'Tek yer piece of candle an' do as yer told.'

So I took my time over the bread and dripping and I spilt my cocoa on the floor in an effort to play for time.

'That's the last of the cocoa. There's no mower in the jug. An' wipe that mess up,' Mum snapped at me.

In the end I gave in and reluctantly mounted the narrow stairs. The candlelight on the peeling walls made scary shapes that I'd never noticed before. I tried to look straight ahead until I reached the top, then I entered our attic room and stood there as my eyes accustomed themselves to the dim light. My eyes fell on the bed and to my horror something began slowly to stir under the blanket. I let out a terrified scream and scuttled down the stairs. But in my hurry to get away from whatever it was in the bed I missed my footing and fell. As I did so I grabbed the banister to save myself. It broke my fall but the strain of this was too much; it ripped out of the wall and landed on top of me at the foot of the stairs.

'What the devil's the matter?' I heard Dad ask as he jumped up off his seat.

'There's something in my b-b-bed,' I stammered as he bent over me. He sat me down roughly on the sofa and Mum said she was going to find out what I was on about.

'I wonder if it's that Jack the Ripper,' she laughed, and followed Dad out to the shed, leaving me with Liza who had just come in. We clung to each other, the only time I ever remember this happening. Mum came back with the chopper and Dad brandished a heavy lump of wood. They crept up the stairs but can't have got more than half way up when our cat, Pete, came scurrying down followed by the chopper and the lump of wood. Dad stamped back down, leaving Mum to get her second wind.

'No more bloody pictures fer yow me girl,' he said angrily. 'Yow've frightened the life out of yer mother.'

I was so relieved that I began to weep tears of joy but Liza was not similarly affected. She pushed me over and said, 'I knew it wasn't nobody, yow great big baby!' I knew she was just as scared as I was when we heard the cat on the stairs.

Mum flopped down in her chair and didn't say a word but by her look I could see I would suffer for it later. Just then Frankie walked in. He couldn't have returned at a less opportune moment.

'An' where do yer think yow've bin till now?' Dad was in a right lather.

'I got lost in the fog,' Frankie said, looking at his feet.

'An' where's the money I gave yer fer the pictures?' he demanded. 'An' look at me when I talk to yer.'

'Spent it,' Frankie said at once.

'Right! Get up them stairs. There's no supper for yow me lad.' And with that Dad thrust him roughly towards the door. But Frankie didn't care; he always had something hidden away in his tuckbox for occasions like this.

Finding Out the Facts of Life

Our next-door neighbours, Mr and Mrs Buckley, had a daughter named Sally who had been staying with an aunt for a year or so. I didn't realise why she'd been away, but when she returned I soon found out. She was three years older than I was. She was mysterious about herself but had plenty to say on the subject of her boyfriends. I was impressed by her self-confidence; I'd never had one boyfriend, let alone as many as she'd had. She used make-up and bleached her hair and was a very attractive girl. The neighbours held their noses in the air when she went out dolled up. Everybody seemed to shun her but I felt sorry for her and we became close friends. However, she didn't suit Mum. The first time she found us chatting in the yard she rushed up and dragged me away.

'Don't yer 'ave nuthin' ter do with that brazen 'uzzy!' she warned me, and when we were indoors she rounded on me. 'Don't yer dare let me catch yer even lookin' at 'er agen.'

'Why? What's she done?' I asked angrily.

'Never yow mind what she's done. Yer'll find out when yer older,' she ranted. 'She's the talk of the district. After anythink with trousers on, or off!'

'I don't believe it,' I said, although I knew she had boyfriends.

'Whether yer believe it or not, don't ever let me see or know yer've 'ad anything to do with 'er agen,' she concluded.

Saying this to me was like holding a red rag to a bull: the more anyone told me not to do a thing, the more I tried to do it. So we continued to meet on the sly. I bumped into her one evening when I was out fetching Dad twopenn'orth of twist. We greeted each other and were soon chatting. She asked me if I'd like to meet her current boyfriend and I agreed.

'There's two really,' she said winking. I didn't understand what she meant by this but she smiled and asked if I would like to go to the 'flicks' the following Saturday. I agreed and we arranged to go to the second house. I would have to wait until Mum and Dad went out to the pub so we couldn't make it to the first. The second house finished at ten so that would give me plenty of time to get home before my parents.

Saturday afternoon arrived and I had the house to myself to get ready. I sorted through my frocks but could find none that fitted me; I'd outgrown them all and was waiting until I'd grown into Liza's castoffs. I tried hers on anyway and after rummaging about for a bit I found one I liked. But it was too big in the bust and too long. I put it back in the trunk, disappointed that there was nothing right for me to wear and wondering what I was going to do, for I wanted to go out with Sally. I decided to go round to her place to see if she had anything I could borrow. Sure enough she offered straight away and gave me some lipstick as well.

'Yow 'ave ter look nice for the boys.' She nudged me, and I, innocent enough to think I could have a boyfriend like her, accepted the dress and the make-up. She was combing out her blonde hair and pouring a colourless liquid from a bottle over her head. She noticed my interest and offered me some.

'It'll make your hair blonde like mine.'

I thought her hair was a lovely colour so I took the remains of the bottle and the other things, thanked her and returned next door. There was still no one home so I was safe to carry on with my experiments in dressing like an adult. The dress was a little too long, but they were worn long at that time so with the help of a pin or two I was able to achieve the desired effect. However, it fitted tight across my bosom. My breasts were developing fast and I was ashamed to see that my nipples showed through the material. I couldn't wear it so I returned to Sally's. When I showed her she lent me a silk shawl to drape round my shoulders and over my breasts. I returned home to admire the effect. I thought I was the cat's whiskers. Then I began combing my hair, wondering if I dared use the peroxide. I'd look better blonde and I assumed that I could wash the colour out before my parents saw: I must have been naive to think that bleach would affect my hair differently from anything else. I was engrossed in these thoughts and just about to drip it on the top of my head as I had seen Sally do when, from nowhere, a hand knocked me to the floor, spilling the contents of the bottle. I was taken completely by surprise to find Dad standing over me. I was petrified; I'd never seen him like this.

'Don't yow ever let me catch yow using that terrible stuff agen!' he bawled.

With that he snatched up the bottle and flung it through the open window into the yard. I was too scared to cry out as he hauled me roughly to my feet and shook me violently. I was in floods of tears. This seemed to calm him down and he spoke more quietly.

'I'll forgive you this time but I'm warnin' yow, my gel, if I catch yow with that stuff agen I'll cut all your hair off an' leave yer bald, and I'll put this strap across yer back!' He pointed to the large brass buckles on his belt.

'I'm off now,' he continued, 'ter meet yer Mum, so when yer've cleared up the table yer can get ter bed.' With that he left, slamming the door behind him. This meant that they wouldn't be back before the pubs closed, but I also knew that if they knew who I was going out with they would have locked me in. I suppose I was kicking over the traces a bit and parental authority seemed as irksome to me then as it does to teenagers today. I fussed about, preparing myself, washing, combing my hair and putting on my borrowed finery. When I'd completed this process I turned to the mirror to look at myself for a last time. Then I received a shock. When Dad had knocked the bottle out of my hand some of the bleach must have spilled down my face because my right eyebrow was blonde. No doubt this would be considered fashionable today but the thought of going out like that mortified me. I'd no idea how I was going to deal with this until my eyes settled on the grate. Then it came to me. I spat on my finger, rubbed it in the soot, then applied it to my eyebrow so that although it was not too convincing at close range, from a distance it looked natural enough. Then, after I'd made sure that I'd left no telltale traces, I was off. There was nobody about to see me knocking on Sally's door. When she came out I stood there waiting to see if she noticed anything but she didn't seem to. Then we took off down the back alleys in case someone saw us and told our parents.

Finally, by the roundabout route, we reached St Paul's churchyard where we were to meet the boys. Sure enough they were there and the smallest was introduced as my date. He was not a bad looker, I thought, and shook hands as he told me his name was Freddy. 'Frederick the Great, that's me,' he said with a chuckle. He placed his arm round my waist, which gave me a pleasurable feeling I'd never experienced, and then we set off to the picture house. He did all the talking. I was very shy but his mischievous grin put me at my ease and we strolled along behind Sally and her beau. We'd hardly gone half way when it began to rain and we had to run the rest of the way to queue under shelter. Just inside the foyer there was a long narrow mirror with an almost naked woman painted on it. How shameful, I thought. I glanced at my reflection to admire the effect and then I got my second shock that evening. The rain had smudged my sooty mascara and it was streaked down my cheek. I looked away quickly. Frederick the Great had been straightening his tie but now he turned round to look at me and after registering a look of surprise he called to Sally and her friend and they all burst into laughter. I was angry and embarrassed in equal measure and hated them. I just turned and ran off. They deserved each other, I thought.

When I got indoors I was still so upset that I tore off the frock, ripping a sleeve in the process, but I didn't care; I was so angry. I rolled it up into a ball and pushed the shawl and lipstick inside the bundle, then I went to put it on Sally's step. As I dodged down the yard I noticed the broken bottle lying in the drain. Picking it up, I rolled that up with the bundle too. I put it on the step, knocked on the door and ran back home. I closed the door behind me then heard the door of the Buckleys' open and close. Nobody saw me, I'd been so quick. With that I washed my face and went to bed.

I was surprised to find Liza sitting up in bed reading one of her romances. She hid it away quickly as I entered the room.

'What's the matter with yow?' she said when she saw my tears. I had to tell someone so I told her. When I'd finished we began to see the funny side of it and ended up laughing. Liza laughed so much she rolled off the bed onto the chamber pot, spilling its contents on the floor. This caused more hilarity and we ended in hysterical fits.

My first experience with boys was not a great success but it wasn't the last, and later I found myself in worse scrapes than on that first occasion. I had nothing further to do with Sally but she didn't seem to be bothered when I passed her in the street without speaking. In the end I thought it was a good job that I'd cut her dead because I began to pick up the gossip about her and found out that she'd left home when she did because she was pregnant and had had a baby. She was what was known as 'a bad lot' and several times later I saw her standing in alleyways, always with a different man. Mum summed her up when she said, 'Any man can have her, with or without his trousers down.'

This experience renewed my curiosity about the facts of life. All I knew were the half-truths and lies that children were told in those days. I was afraid to ask Mum any details of where babies came from and the word 'sex' was considered a dirty word in our house.

When I saw my first period I was scared to death. I ran all the way home from school thinking I was going to bleed to death. I burst into tears when I saw Mum, and told her what had happened. But all the explanation she gave me was, 'Now yow keep away from the lads an' never let 'em kiss yer or the next thing yer know yer'll be 'avin' a baby. Then God 'elp yer.' I pointed out that I kissed Frankie but she dismissed my puzzlement.

'That's different. 'E's yer brother, ain't 'e. Now be off with yer, I'll see ter yer later. An' don't forget what I've told yer! Keep away from the lads.'

I couldn't make head nor tail of this. Why was Frankie different? I knew he had something more than Liza and me because we'd seen him when he had his bath and when he lay in bed in his short shirt. I was perplexed. If only someone would explain these things to me, but I was too shy and scared to ask. When Mum had left I determined to overcome my embarrassment and go and ask Mrs Taylor. Perhaps she could tell me why I was bleeding. When I told her what was troubling me she just gave me a piece of clean rag and said more or less the same as Mum had.

'Is it true?' I asked her. 'Will I have a baby if a boy kisses me?'

'Well, it's a start,' she answered, smiling, 'but when yer grow older you'll find out.' This was clearly little help either.

I knew when people were married and slept together a baby usually followed, but this didn't enlighten me about the facts of life. In fact, for a while I was almost as afraid of boys as I was of horses and cows. As far as my education on the subject was concerned I was reduced to listening to gossip in the hope of learning more.

I was in the yard one day when all the women were gossiping and Mrs Smith from the next yard happened to pass.

'Hello Nell, I see yer've bin eatin' new bread agen,' Mrs Phipps called to her.

'Yes, an' it's all me own,' she replied, smacking her belly as she walked by.

Then Maggie said, 'Did yer know Mrs Buckley's balloon's up agen?'

'Yes, we 'eard,' replied Mrs Jonesy.

Mrs Phipps gave Maggie a cold look and said, 'Why is it yer've never 'ad your balloon up, Maggie?'

'That's my affair,' Maggie replied. 'Any'ow my Billy ain't got much, an' what 'e 'as got 'e's keepin' it fer 'imself.' And they all burst out laughing.

I didn't make much of this but Mrs Smith's daughter was a friend of mine. Her name was Nellie and she was in the same class as me at school and her family had not long moved into the neighbourhood. Nellie was not a bit shy or timid like I was, and I was attracted by her outspoken ways. Sometimes after school we would visit their house and she would show me all her nice clothes. Nellie promised me one of her old dresses when she had a new one. Then one afternoon Mrs Smith came in and found us and asked who I was.

'It's Katie, my school friend,' Nellie replied.

'Well, sit yerself down Katie. Don't be shy, I'm not going ter eat yer,' she said, busying herself untying the parcels she had with her.

She was a pretty woman and would have had a good figure had she not been pregnant. She had a pleasant dispositon and always had a twinkle in her eyes. She had a soft voice and always put me at my ease. We watched her untie the parcels which turned out to contain pretty blue woollen baby clothes. When Nellie saw them she asked, 'Why 'ave yer bought blue?'

'Because I know it's goin' to be a son . . . Anyway,' she said 'I'm 'opin' it is.'

The next parcel contained a new dress for Nellie. It was bright pillar-box red with a white lace collar and cuffs. When her Mum undressed her to try it on I couldn't take my eyes off the lovely white underclothes she wore. I turned my head away then, because Mum always said it wasn't decent to watch people undress. Evidently Mrs Smith thought differently

'Don't be shy, Katie,' she said. 'Yer can turn round now.'

Nellie looked sweet in her new frock. Then she asked her Mum to find something for me. She was the same size as me so I knew that her clothes would fit me. Mrs Smith went to the wardrobe and brought out a yellow dress with pretty flowers and leaves all over it.

'Take your dress off and try this on. It should fit.'

I must have looked embarrassed when she handed it over because they both turned their backs while I slipped my old dress off and slipped the new one on. After fastening all the buttons up the front I said meekly, 'You can turn round now.' I felt great when Mrs Smith said I looked pretty and that I could keep the dress. I was so overwhelmed that I started to cry.

'What's all this for?' she asked kindly.

'Mum will never let me keep it. I've only got old ones an' this one will go to the pawnshop.' I wiped the tears with the back of my hand.

'Never mind that. Wipe yer eyes and then we'll go upstairs and see what else we can find,' Mrs Smith soothed me.

Nellie had a pleasant bedroom all to herself. If I had a room of my own, I thought, I would knit and knit to make it as pretty as this or as Miss Louise's had been. We girls sat on the bed while Mrs Smith sorted out some underclothes for me.

'Now, don't be shy. Yer can undress in front of Nellie and me,' she said. 'But if yer like we'll go downstairs.'

'I'd like Nellie to stay,' I whispered. I was shy of undressing in front of adults. So Mrs Smith left us alone and I stripped off in front of my friend although I made her turn away when I came to my combs. Then I dressed in the vest, bloomers, camisole with pink ribbon threaded through the top and bottom, a pretty lace underskirt and finally the yellow dress. I felt like a princess.

'You look lovely, Katie,' Nellie said. 'Let's go an' show Mum.'

They both enthused over my new look and I became weepy and wailed that I couldn't keep them.

'But they're yours to keep, like I told you,' Mrs Smith said gently.

'No, they'll end up in the pawnshop,' I sobbed.

'Oh, no they won't. Nellie, you go upstairs and bring down Katie's clothes,' she said.

What was she up to, I thought. She wrapped them up in a parcel and took them out to the dustbin. She was about to pop them in when we heard the strains of the rag and boneman's cry. Round the corner he came, pushing his handcart with balloons flying high. She gave him the bundle and he opened it to examine the contents.

'What yer want fer these, Mrs?' he inquired.

'Oh, just give the kids a balloon each,' she told him.

'They're only worth one,' he grumbled.

'Right! I'll put them in the bin then,' she replied, but before she could get them off the cart he handed us the balloons.

We went in and I stayed a bit longer; then, with many thanks to Mrs Smith, I left for home, anxious to tell Mum about my good fortune. When I entered our kitchen Mum stared at me, dumfounded, until she recovered and found her voice.

'Who's got yow all dressed up?' she demanded, shaking me.

'Mrs Smith gave them to me,' I told her.

'An' where's yer own?' she snapped.

I was too scared to admit to her what had happened to them, so I said Mrs Smith would tell her. Now our houses backed on to each other, with only the party wall between, so she just picked up the poker from the fender and started banging on the wall so that the plaster showered a cloud of dust in the room.

'Are yow theea, Mrs Smith, cos if yow are I want some words with yow!' she bellowed.

Mrs Smith came immediately, with Nellie behind her. Neighbours who had heard the noise were gathering round the door and chattering noisily. However, Mum had found her mistress in Mrs Smith. She drew herself up to her full height, hands on hips; quite a figure.

'An' what's the matter with you?' she asked sarcastically. 'Yer tryin' ter knock the 'ouse down?'

'Where's me daughter's clothes yer've took off 'er? I want 'em back.'

Mrs Smith was unimpressed by Mum's overbearing manner but simply grinned and replied calmly, 'Sorry my dear, you'll have to ask the rag an' boneman for them.'

'WHAT!' yelled Mum.

'Yes,' Mrs Smith nodded.

Mum knew then she had met her match and tried to retreat indoors, but Mrs Smith left her foot in the door so that she had to listen.

'They weren't worth keeping so I swapped them for a couple of balloons.' Mum's face reddened visibly.

'Oh, I could tell all yow a thing ter shock yer,' she said wagging her forefinger. She continued to splutter and threaten. 'An' don't let me catch yer layin' another finger on 'er,' she said, pointing at me. 'I'll 'ave the law on yer.'

'Let me tell yow if you ever lay a finger on her yerself, I'll 'ave the authorities on yer,' Mrs Smith was not to be bested. 'And don't yow take them clothes away from her either,' she concluded, just as Mum saw her chance and slammed the door shut, leaving me standing there with Mrs Smith, Nellie and the neighbours.

'Come on you two,' she said to us. 'I never 'ave anything to do with trash if I can 'elp it.'

I went round to their place again and we had toast and tea with real cow's milk, not the Handy Brand condensed milk we always had at home. After tea we went out to play. I was afraid to go back home for fear of the trouble I'd be in from Mum. When I left Nellie I hung about waiting for Dad's protection but he didn't appear. I went to several pubs looking for him but nobody had seen him, so, as it was getting late, I turned to go home to face the music. As I dragged reluctantly along past Mrs Smith's house who should come out, deep in conversation with Mrs Smith, but my Dad. They were smiling and when Mrs Smith saw me she called out cheerily. 'It's all right Katie, I've explained to your Dad.'

I ran up to him and took his hand in mine. He said 'goodbye' to our neighbour and thanked her for 'everything', and he squeezed her hand. 'That's all right Sam, any time you're passing,' she told him. I was puzzled about what had been going on but was pleased that Dad, at any rate, was in a good mood.

'Come on Katie,' he said. 'Let's face the music.'

Before we'd set foot over the doorstep Mum had started. 'What yer think about 'er round the back? Tellin' me what ter do with me own kids. She wants ter look after 'er own.' She stopped to draw breath which gave Dad his opportunity.

'Now yow be quiet, Polly. Yow don't want all the neighbourhood round yer door do yer?'

'Oh, she's told yow the tale 'as she?' Mum didn't miss much.

'Only the truth, and I admire her for it. She's one person yow can't push around like the rest of yer cronies.'

Mum could see she was getting nowhere so she tried shedding a tear or two. This was an old ploy when she couldn't get her own way. Dad was having none of this.

'Yow can turn yer tap off, I'm going up to bed and you, Katie, better get off too,' he said, handing me a saucer with a stub of candle on it. I didn't wait to be told twice and I made myself scarce.

After that Nellie and I became close friends and so did her Mum and my Dad. Mum never said a word when I invited Nellie into our house but I could tell she didn't like her. We played the harmonium and sang together and Dad sometimes gave us money to go to see a picture at the Queen's Hall. When Nellie's Mum was very large and the baby was due she wouldn't let Nellie go far in case she needed to fetch the midwife. All this time I still wondered about the origin of babies, and one night I raised the subject with Nellie. I began by asking her if she like boys. She said she did 'a bit' but she was also afraid of them 'a bit' as well. I asked why and she gave me a reply I hadn't expected.

'Well, my Mum told me not to let boys fondle me or kiss me now I've started me periods, otherwise, if I did, I'd soon be having a baby.'

I told her that I was surprised at that because my Mum had said the same and I hadn't believed her. Was that how Nellie's Mum came to be having a baby, I wondered?

'But I like it when boys whistle at me,' she continued.

'Me too,' I agreed, 'but my Mum says she don't want me growing up like Sally Buckley.'

'Do you know 'er?' she asked in apparent surprise.

'Everybody knows 'er,' I said.

Then I offered to tell her my secret if she didn't tell anyone else. I told her about the date at the pictures with the two boys and about the disaster with the bleach.

'How lucky you were,' Nellie laughed. 'Yer never know what would 'ave 'appened if it 'adn't rained.'

'Nellie,' I said, 'd'yer know where babies come from?'

'Course I do, silly. Don't you?'

'No.' I shook my head, a bit shyly.

'Well you know when mothers get fat and their stomach sticks out like a balloon? Well, they carry that for nine months, don't they? Then when the time comes their belly goes pop with a bang and the baby pops out.' That seemed to make sense to me.

'I wondered what the belly button was for,' I said. Nellie was always right about things.

'Tell yer what,' she offered. 'When my Mum's about to have her pains I'll call for yer and we'll sit on the stairs and listen.'

Although I was anxious to be there I didn't get the chance because Mrs Smith gave birth to a baby girl in the early hours of the morning later that week. We were both disappointed but Nellie said we could wait until the next time.

I also wondered about why we never saw Nellie's Dad and eventually I asked her about him. Nellie rounded on me angrily and asked me why I wanted to know. Then I told about the tales the neighbours were telling about her Mum and her men friends. She replied that she knew where he was but she didn't want to discuss it. 'What my Mum does is her affair.' She was adamant. She must have know what her Mum was up to but I didn't question her any more on the subject.

We were still at school when, later that year, the First World War broke out. We were in standard seven, the highest class, which meant we could leave school early, when we were thirteen, which would be another eighteen months at least for me. We were both monitors and I helped the teacher with the younger children, teaching them how to knit socks and balaclavas for the soldiers at the Front. We put little messages wishing the Tommies 'good luck' in them to cheer them up. I loved knitting and do to this day. I won first prizes for the best garment and for the most knitted in my class. The only thing I didn't like was the monotonous khaki wool. One day I asked the teacher if it wouldn't be more patriotic to knit some items in red, white and blue. She smiled at this and said if I wanted a change I could knit up navy blue wool for the Royal Navy, which I did. I won another prize for this as well, and I was presented with a beautiful work basket lined with red satin by the headmistress, Miss Ford. I had to stand in front of the whole school which gave me ample opportunity to observe the envy on some girls' faces because knitting for the troops was a popular pastime then. In fact, everybody seemed to be busy finding some job to help with the war effort, except Mum who continued to clean at the Gingold's chip shop.

My two eldest brothers, Charlie and Jack, volunteered for Kitchener's army as most boys of their generation did. Even Dad tried to enlist. He told the recruiting officer that he'd been a sergeant in the Boer War and boasted that he knew more about the Army than all these whipper-snappers who were waiting to join with him. He was told to strip for a medical examination but he wasn't up to scratch and failed, and so never got his chance. Nevertheless he was determined to do his bit, so he gave up the firewood business and went back to the casting shop to make shell cases. This was more patriotic than wise because he had to work long hours and came home coughing; you could smell the sulphur on his clothes. But he said he didn't mind as long as he was helping the war effort, and anyway it would all be over in six months and he could go back to selling firewood. Little did we imagine then that the war would last until November 1918.

Frankie left school and Dad found him a job with him, fetching and carrying sand for the men. He was a strong, healthy lad and as pleased as punch to be working with Dad. He began to put on airs and think he was a grown-up who could boss us around until Dad checked him for it. Liza left as well and got a job on the munitions with Sally Buckley, which boded no good. There were rows at night over her staying out late with Sally. Mum always stood up for Liza, her longtime favourite, telling Dad she had enough sense to know what was right and wrong, but I doubted she did. Dad wasn't convinced either.

I wanted to help too but I was still too young to leave school. There was work for everyone. People were doing all kinds of jobs to earn money; even the married women who could get nothing before were able to take in washing for the posh folk whose maids were earning more in a week in the munitions factories than they could in a month skivvying. Mum would have none of this: she was not going to do other people's dirty washing and she stayed at the fish shop all the war years.

It was ironic that now everybody in our district had plenty of money for food they couldn't obtain it because everything was rationed. Still, this left all the more to spend on drink. The pubs were doing a roaring trade, what with this new-found prosperity and the constant flow of soldiers on leave with money to spend and precious little time to get rid of it. There was plenty of scandal about the Australian and Canadian troops being out with other men's wives or, worse, being seen in doorways or entries with them while the blackout was on. Women whose men were away at the war were still having babies. Several times I was given money to go to the chemist's for bitter aloes or penny royal or a bottle of gin from the outdoor. Miscarriages procured in this way often led to death or malformed births.

Brother Jack wrote each week while he was in training on Salisbury Plain with the Royal Field Artillery. Mum always opened the letters but I had to read them for her. He would write that he was 'doing fine' and that the war would be over soon. He also asked her to keep an eye on his widow because he had heard about the carrying-on with the women-folk. 'And', he underlined the 'and', 'keep an eye on our Liza.' I always wrote the replies and told him the news and reassured him that Mum was watching his widow, which it gave her great pleasure to do. I knitted him socks as well and slipped packets of Woodbines in with them. It was through the need to obtain money for this that I took the part-time job with Mrs Morton and her husband, Weary Willy. They were the school caretakers but my job helping them didn't last long.

Another incident which sticks in my memory from those final years at school concerned a friend of mine, Nelly Mitchell. I'd discussed the mystery of child birth with her as well and she'd offered, like Nellie Smith, to call me when her mother, who was pregnant, was about to give birth. I was playing jackstones in the street when Nelly Mitchell ran up with the news that she was going for the midwife. We ran and knocked on the midwife's door and Mrs Bullivant seemed to know who it was without looking, for she called out for Nelly to run and get newspapers and hot water ready.

When we got to Nelly's the fire was low, but while she was collecting newspapers I filled the kettle and using the old leather bellows stoked up the heat. Mrs Mitchell called out for Mrs Bullivant from upstairs and at that moment in she came. She was the only midwife in our district and if the women couldn't afford her the neighbours helped, a practice which often ended in tragedy. As Mrs Bullivant, carrying her bag of instruments, mounted the stairs, Nelly's Mum began to cry out in agony. We looked at each other, scared stiff, but we followed Mrs Bullivant upstairs. She was a small, round woman with eyes that seemed too small for her face which was flushed red; it was as much she could do to struggle up, rolling from side to side and, I noticed, smelling of drink. When we followed her into the bedroom she ordered us out, saying it was no place for kids. We went outside but could still see because the door didn't quite close. As soon as she thought we were out of sight she reached under her apron and produced a small bottle from which, tipping back her head, she took a swig. Then she replaced it and went over to see to Mrs Mitchell who lay on the top of the bed dressed only in a calico nightgown groaning as she writhed about. Then the midwife lifted up the gown and rolled her roughly on to her side. I almost screamed out but Nelly's hand stifled any sound. I saw the largest bare belly I'd ever seen in life. The belly button was protruding and it looked ready to burst. I'd seen enough. I didn't want to wait for the baby to appear through the navel. I tried to back down the stairs but Nelly kept hold of my frock and prevented me. Just then the midwife told Mrs Mitchell to get up and pace the room and simultaneously we crashed against the door and ended in a heap on the floor. I expected a slap but Mrs Bullivant just stepped over us saying she'd be back later, after she'd attended Mrs Groves who was having her first. Then she was gone.

Nelly begged me not to leave her, and plucking up courage I stayed. Nelly held her Mum's hand while I dipped a sponge into the cold water jug and mopped her brow which was sweaty from the pain she was in. I became frightened; I thought she was going to die and I felt sick. It was the first time I'd seen anyone in labour and I made a silent vow that when I was married I wasn't going to have any babies if this was how you had to suffer. A few minutes later, when Nelly was preoccupied, I'm sorry to say my cowardice got the better of me and I crept out of the room, down the stairs and ran off home.

For hours I couldn't put those dreadful cried out of my mind and I imagined that with every breath my own stomach was swelling and about to burst. I had a nightmare that night which ended with me rolling out of bed and landing on the floor where I was sick. Next morning I cleaned up the vomit and got myself ready for school but I still had a nasty taste in my mouth and I was hot and achey. When I peered at myself in the mirror I screamed. My eyes were puffed up and my face was covered with red spots. My scream brought Mum up to see what was wrong and when she saw my face she ordered me back into bed. I had measles and had to stay isolated in the darkened room for two weeks.

I was dosed with saffron tea which tasted foul and I couldn't see anybody. By the time I'd recovered I was skinnier than ever, having been rationed to an orange a day. After a few days I was allowed downstairs and began to eat proper meals again, and two weeks later I started back at school.

On my way there the first morning I noticed that Nelly's house had a 'To Let' sign in the window. I ran to catch Liza up and when I asked her where they were she hesitated before replying.

'She's dead,' she said. I was dumbstruck.

'Who? Nelly?' I stammered. Then Liza told me that Mrs Mitchell had died in childbirth and that Nelly herself had been taken to Wolverhampton to live with an aunt and uncle. I felt miserable and blamed myself even more for not staying that night or fetching a doctor, but I didn't realise and I was so scared. I was too upset to go to school. I went and sat in the churchyard and wept for Mrs Mitchell and Nelly and prayed for myself to be forgiven and for them to be looked after. I was not missed that day either at school or at home. I didn't forget Nelly who had been a good little friend to me, and eventually we did meet up again, several years later.

The World of Work, 1917

A t Christmas 1916 when I was nearly fourteen I was preparing to leave school. The Great War was still going and there was still plenty of work for young people in our district. I got an inkling of what was in the wind when I came home early from the Band of Hope and overheard a conversation between Mum and Dad.

'She don't look strong enough ter work on a press,' said Dad.

'But that's where the big wages are, on munitions,' Mum told him. 'Anyway,' she continued, 'we'll soon fatten 'er up if we give 'er plenty ter eat.'

'All right,' Dad said, 'I s'ppose yer know what's best for 'er.'

'She's gotta earn 'er keep like the rest of 'em,' Mum concluded.

I was amused when I was given two thick slices of bread and half a cow heel before I went to bed but I didn't take long to devour it. This was a treat and no mistake and I sucked all the bones clean I was that hungry. I was even offered more, and I could see the writing was on the wall. Every mealtime for the next few weeks it was as if I was being fattened up for the slaughter. I had as much as and more than I could eat for a change. And I was putting on weight so fast that my clothes wouldn't fit. I was also getter taller. Mum said she couldn't afford to buy me a new frock and that I would have to have one of Mary's old ones cut down. She cobbled it together which black thread so I felt a proper charlie, but she said it would have to do until I earned my first week's wages.

I wasn't going to wait until then. I'd been saving pennies and half-pennies up for ages for this moment. Next day when the house was empty I bolted the door and ran upstairs to the attic. Pushing the iron bedstead across the room I got on my knees and with a knife prized up the floorboard and pulled out a mice-nibbled newspaper package. I emptied its contents on to the bed and counted out three shillings and ninepence-halfpennny, all earned running errands. I put it in my rag purse, replaced everything, unbolted the door and went off down the street to an old woman who sold second-hand clothes from her front room.

When I got there I looked through the window and there as luck would have it was the prettiest pink crepe-de-chine blouse I had ever seen. It had lace trimmings on the cuffs and round the high collar, and down the front it was fastened with six round pearl buttons. I had to have it. I pushed open the door and went in, a rusty bell clanging a warning to the owner. At first I couldn't see her and assumed she was in the back but then I saw her sitting on a stool sewing, amidst heaps of old clothes. Suddenly she looked up, glared at me and shouted, 'What der yer want, comin' in 'ere like that?'

'H-how much is that blouse in the window?' I managed to stammer.

'Who wants ter know?' came the reply.

'Me,' I said. 'I want ter buy it.'

She stared at me in disbelief until I shook my bag and she heard the chink of coins. That livened her up and she grinned a gummy smile and said, 'Ter yo' it's 'alf a crown.' She then proceeded to extol the garment's virtues and the 'fine lady' who originally owned it. However, I had to explain that although I liked it I couldn't afford that much because I wanted to buy a pair of boots as well and all I had to spend was three shillings and nine-pence-halfpenny. I explained that I wanted it for an interview for a job because I was leaving school and she began to soften.

'All right,' she grinned, 'yer can 'ave a pair of second 'and button-up boots an' the blouse for three an' ninepence an' I'll throw in a camisole. Now come on through the back so's yer can try 'em on.'

I held on to my money though until I'd satisfied myself the clothes were worth what she wanted for them. She handed me the camisole which was frayed and yellow with age but which looked clean, then she shuffled through to the window to fetch the blouse. I was pleased when she handed it to me to see how nice it was, and when I tried it on it looked better on me than it did in the window. So she wrapped them both up in some newspaper. I next tried on several pairs of boots until eventually I found a pair that fitted. They were a bit down at heel but with blacking I could see they would look better than the ones I was wearing.

'Yer got a bargain,' the old crone cried, counting the pennies. 'Now be off with yer before I change me mind!'

All I had left was a halfpenny, but I was pleased with my purchases which I hid under the straw mattress until I needed them. The following Friday I shook hands with my teacher for the last time, listened to her lecture on 'my new life', was handed a book for good attendance and walked home feeling grown up, at the tender age of fourteen.

When I got in I showed Mum my book and told her what the teacher had said but she didn't seem interested. All she said was that my sister was coming to tea and she wanted me to fetch some errands.

'I want yer ter go ter Jefferson's an' fetch two ounces of tea, two pounds of sugar an' a tinna condensed milk. Oh, an' 'alf a loaf, an' see it's new. An' don't forget me change.'

I remember Mr Jefferson vividly. He was a short, fat man with a red face and a bald head. He reminded me of Humpty Dumpty. He kept a well-stocked, tidy shop where you could buy almost anything. I ran all the way to the shop and rushed in, pushing open the frosted-glass door and making the bell clank noisily. I went straight up to the counter. I climbed on the hot-water pipe that ran along the floor and peered over the top where I could see Mr Jefferson's bald head. I blurted out my order without drawing breath and jumped down to the floor.

He glared at me over the counter and said, 'Be quiet, an' wait yer turn.' Then for the first time I noticed three well-dressed women looking daggers at me. Then they began whispering and looking down their noses at me.

'Serve her, we can wait,' one said.

While he was fetching Mum's order I had time to observe the women as they dithered over the glass cases of biscuits, trying to make up their minds which to have. Then I remembered the blacking I needed for my boots and I picked some up. That I paid for with my halfpenny. When I got back Mum was in a lather again. 'About time,' she said and snatched the bag off me and started checking it was all as she had asked for, even squeezing the bread to check it was fresh. Just then Mrs Taylor tumbled into the room and Mum looked up with a glare on her face.

'Yower Mary ain't comin' terday, she told me ter tell yer 'er mutha-in-law's took bad.' She collapsed breathlessly into a chair.

"Er thinks mower of 'er than she does of me,' Mum fumed, sitting down in the other chair. I could see signs that they were going to be some time nattering so I crept up to the attic and rummaged through Liza's trunk. I found an old, long black hobble skirt which I knew she didn't want because she'd grown out of it.

With the hem turned up and some elastic in the waist I thought it would be just the thing to go with my blouse. When I heard the two women leave a little later, I went down and set to with a needle and thread. I took some elastic from a pair of bloomers and pretty soon had a serviceable skirt to go with the other things.

On the following Monday morning Mum gave me two-pence for a bath at the public ones in Northwood Street where I went now that I was 'a big girl', and sixpence for my medical which I had to have before I could work in a factory. I bundled up my new clothes and set off. It was heavenly to stretch out in such a big bath and soak in gallons of hot soapy water; I could have stayed there all day, but I knew I had to go out and look for a job before long. I stepped out of the bath and dried myself and admired myself in the mirror; I'd certainly filled out. I felt so clean and fresh. I put on my stockings, clean bloomers, my camisole and skirt then my blouse. It felt a bit tight when I fastened all the buttons up but I thought, I won't burst open if I don't breathe too deeply or thrust my chest out. Then I buttoned up my boots which were now polished and I felt ready to face the adult world. I folded the old clothes into a bundle and standing on the lavatory seat I pushed them behind the iron cistern. Then I walked out into the street. Imagine my surprise when the first person I bumped into practically on the steps of the bath, was my old friend Nelly Mitchell.

We threw our arms round each other and exchanged greetings. She told me she was in lodgings round the corner. I asked her why she hadn't been to see me before but she said she'd only been there a few days and had only just moved from her aunt's in Wolverhampton. Her aunt had died and now she was with a friend and looking for work like I was. We walked along arm in arm exchanging news, oblivious of anything else. Then I noticed how well dressed she was and she told me about the good times she had with boys. It seemed so exciting, but my first thought was to find a job and I began to miss what she was saying. Then as luck would have it we turned a corner and saw a notice on a factory gate which read: 'WOMEN AND GIRLS WANTED TO LEARN PRESSWORK'. I knew it was heavy, manual work, swinging the handles of the heavy mechanical presses which were used to stamp out metal components, but many young girls like us were doing this sort of work because so many men were away at the Front.

'You go in and ask first, Katie, while I wait here. Then you can let me know how you got on and I'll go in after.'

I agreed as long as she waited for me, because I didn't want to lose contact with her again. Up the narrow stairs I went, trying to avoid slipping on the grease which covered them. I reached the top and pushed open the door and found myself inside a small cubicle just big enough to hold two people. I tapped the wooden panel and suddenly a small trapdoor shot up and I jumped with fright as a woman's face and shoulders appeared in the gap.

'What yer come for? The job is it?' She had to shout to make herself heard above the noise of the presses in the room behind her.

I was suddenly nervous. Why, I wondered, didn't Mum come with me for the interview like other mothers did? Now I was fourteen I had to stand on my own two feet, she'd said. I stared at the woman's stern face until I found the courage to speak.

'Yes, ma'am,' was all I could manage. She eyed me up and down and asked me my age.

'Fourteen. I left school last week,' I told her.

'An' yer sure yer want ter work on a press?' she asked.

'Yes, we do,' I answered without thinking.

'We, who's we?' she snapped gruffly.

'My friend Nelly. She's downstairs.'

'Well, send 'er up. Let's take a look at 'er.' Then the trapdoor slammed shut.

I ran and fetched Nelly and we both returned to the cubicle. Up shot the door again.

'So you're Nelly?' she snapped. 'Well, yow'll do.' She had to bellow.

She gave us a note pad to write down our names and addresses and when we handed it to her she told us to return at eight the following morning with our birth certificates and medical certificates. 'An' I mean eight, not five past!' she shouted.

'Yes ma'am,' I replied while Nelly tried to peer over her shoulder into the workshop beyond.

'Yower ter call me Madam. I'm the forewoman,' she snapped.

'Yes Madam,' I replied timidly. With that the trapdoor shut again and we were alone in the cubicle.

'I don't like 'er, she's an old battleaxe,' said Nelly as we made our way down the iron stairs and back into the street. Then Nelly asked about the pay.

'Didn't she tell you 'ow much the wages are?' she asked and I had to admit that I'd forgotten to ask.

'Well, you'll 'ave ter go back and ask 'er then, won't you,' she snapped.

'You go!' I retorted.

'Anyway I didn't ask for the job an' if you don't want ter go I'll look round for something else that pays better. She don't look like she pays much,' she pouted.

'Oh, all right.' I sulked my way back up the stairs again. I noticed it was always me who had to do things.

When I entered the cubicle the trap sprang and Madam appeared wanting to know what I wanted.

'Please Madam,' I asked, "ow much will the wages be?'

'Twelve an' six a week, eight o'clock till six and one o'clock on Saturdays. Yow get fifteen minutes for lunch and one till two dinnertime and yow'll clock in and out. I'll put yow right, an' if yer be'ave yerself an' work 'ard you get a rise to thirteen shillings at the end of the month.' And with that the trap closed again and her hard face was gone.

I thought on twelve and six I would be rich in no time. Mum could have ten shillings and I could have the half crown for myself. I could do a lot with that much. But when I told her Nelly didn't seem very pleased and suggested that it was not wise to take the first job that offered itself but to look around for something better.

'But Nelly,' I told her. 'She's got my address an' if my Mum finds out I'll be in trouble.'

'Yer Mum won't find out an' anyway she won't mind more money.' With this I had to agree.

We went off down the street in high spirits, looking in all the shop windows, planning what we would spend our money on. Then we thought we'd better look for an alternative job. By now it was one o'clock and the boys were coming out of the factories. They began to whistle at us and although I didn't want anything to do with them, Nelly stopped to talk to them. I was so scared I ran round the corner and hid. Eventually when Nelly appeared she said she'd made a date with one of them. I was shocked at her brazenness. How could she? I thought. She was only the same age as me but a lot more forward.

We stopped at several other workshops that were advertising for women and girls, at each of which I had to make inquiries. Nelly was not so forward at this, it seemed. None of them wanted to pay more than ten or eleven shillings and one small place only seven and three pence with overtime. So we decided to take the first job at the factory in Vittoria Street.

Then we thought about going for our medical. We walked along the street, arm in arm, as the trams clanged past, their bells ringing. Posters were pasted up everywhere there was room. Life-size posters of Kitchener looked down on us proclaiming 'Your Country Needs You'. There was the odd Union Jack, and hand-painted slogans saying, 'Down with the Hun', and 'Votes for Women', and rude ones like, 'Fuck the Kaiser'. I was shocked when I saw this. Bad language was frowned on even in poor households and you didn't see the graffiti you do today. Finally we arrived at the clinic. There were several women waiting with their children. Nelly and I sat down on the bench beside them to wait our turn. The women and girls stared at us; we were the only ones without our mothers. We watched the steady stream go in and come out until it was our turn, when Nelly pushed me in front as the voice called loudly, 'Next!'

I steadied myself and entered; I was very nervous. The doctor was sitting at his writing table. Without looking up he said, 'Sit down!' I sat down on the chair and took the opportunity to have a good look at him. He was a thick-set man, very dark-skinned with wavy black hair. I couldn't make up my mind what nationality he was but he wasn't English. When he'd finished writing he suddenly swivelled round in his chair and stared at me, and his black eyes seemed to look through me. He stood up and bent over me and with his pen he lifted up my plaits.

'I ain't got ticks in my hair, doctor,' I told him, but he didn't answer but instead shone a little light in my ears. 'Hm, hm,' he repeated. 'Hm, open your mouth and put out your tongue.' I did as I was told. When he was satisfied with that he took his stethoscope and put it to his ears. Nobody had told me there'd be all this rigmarole. I thought he just asked you questions and you paid the sixpence for your medical certificate; I had already put it on the table. I was beginning to wonder what he was going to do next when he snapped at me:

'Open your blouse!'

I was rooted to the spot with fright; I wanted my Mum or Nelly to walk in to come to my aid.

'Come along, open your blouse. I can't stand here all day,' he said becoming impatient.

Slowly I fumbled with the first button, then the second, but for the life of me I was not going to open my blouse any further than that. I felt unclean as he looked at me and the next thing I knew he had pulled my blouse open wide and the lovely pearl buttons had gone pop, pop, pop and were rolling about the floor. I was unable to move, terrified of what was to come next. Then he put his cold hands down inside my camisole and lifted out my bare breasts. He felt them for some time, then with another 'hm' slowly returned them – but not before he'd smiled and squeezed them. I slapped his hands as hard as I could, and clutching my blouse fled out of the room with 'Next!' echoing in my ears. I had no time to tell Nelly who was through the door in a flash and I collapsed on the bench in tears over my beautiful pearl buttons. In no time at all Nelly emerged, all smiles.

'He's nice ain't 'e?' she said.

'No! 'E's not an' I don't ever want ter go through that again,' I replied still sobbing.

'Yer too modest,' she laughed. 'Anyway, 'ere's yer buttons an' yer medical certificate 'e gave me ter give yer.'

Birmingham's Jewellery Quarter near where we lived was an area of old Georgian and early Victorian houses that had once been fashionable but were now run down. As the tenants left the landlords would rent off the rooms singly to craftsmen in the many trades of the area. Workshops were built at the back of these houses and the whole area was a warren representing many of the city's 'thousand trades'. Some people in the district I knew let off their front room, undertaking outwork for the jeweller who moved in. All kinds of gold and silver objects were made there: diamond rings, tableware, anything you could think of in that line; it still is to this day.

When I was a bit older I would go on a Friday night to a pub called The Jeweller's Arms with some of the girls I worked with. Many's the time I have watched the gaffers of these thriving little businesses exchanging hundreds of pounds or packets of diamonds in corners of this and other pubs in the area. The factory where Nelly and I started work was not far from this pub. It was called The Birmingham Brass Works. The front door led to a small office and the workshop was down the entry.

At five minutes to eight the next day we were standing outside the gate with several roughly dressed women. They pushed Nelly and me to one side when the gate opened, clocked in and went off up the yard, disappearing up the steps without exchanging a word. We were standing there, hesitant, when a voice boomed out 'Follow me'. It was Madam, the forewoman, dressed in a khaki overall. She was elderly, tall and straight and very serious: I never remember her smiling. She showed us how to clock in with our timecard and then we followed her along the cobbled yard and up the greasy steps into the workshop.

The women who we'd seen previously were already busy operating the presses. At the end of the shop were smaller machines driven by an electric motor on the wall which worked the leather pulleys that ran along the ceiling. The workshop was dirty and reeked of oil. In the centre of the room was a large, battered pipe stove filled with glowing coke, the smoke from which went up the pipe and out through a hole in the roof. Every now and then smoke billowed into the room and when it did Nelly and I began to cough, but no one else seemed to be affected. They just sat there busily swinging the handles of the presses.

We were each handed khaki overalls like the rest had on; mine came almost to the floor and my cap, when I tried it on, kept slipping over my eyes. The forewoman told me it was the smallest they had. Nelly was taller than me and had more hair to fill her cap with.

'Come along you two,' she snapped at us. 'You can work the guillotine,' she said to Nelly.

As soon as she had Nelly settled in she came back to me and showed me how to use the press to cut brass blanks from strips of scrap metal. I soon picked the job up but she came several times that morning to see how I was getting along.

'We don't want any scrap left,' was all she said. She examined the blanks that I had made and seemed satisfied, and that made me work harder. Then I noticed the other women along the bench were giving me black looks but I had no idea why.

At break time when I was standing eating my corned beef sandwich, one of the women shouted over to me.

'Yow've got my job, an' it's the best in the shop!'

They were all about to join in when Madam appeared and warned them if there was any more trouble they would be reported to the gaffer. They went on eating in silence. One of the women came over and offered me her place by the fire but I was too scared to move and anyway it was too late because just then the bell rang for us to start work again. I hadn't finished my sandwich so I wrapped it up and put it in my overall pocket. I was surprised I hadn't seen Nelly but I found out later that she'd walked out because she didn't like the place or the work. But I did. It was satisfying work cutting out the shilling-sized blanks and stacking them in three dozens. Afterwards I took them to the drilling machine where Minnie, the woman who had offered me her place, showed me how to drill four holes in them. I was proud to be doing my bit for King and country when I was told they were brass trouser buttons for the Army.

When one o'clock came and I was clocking out, Minnie came up to me and spoke. She was a small, thin woman, very pale, and came, she told me, from the Black Country. I asked why she couldn't get a job nearer home but she said she had seven children and a husband to keep and this was the best-paid job she could find. We became very friendly. She looked as old as my Mum with her lined face but she told me she was not yet thirty. She explained why the other women were nasty to me. Apparently they were on piecework, although I hadn't realised this, and I had one of the best jobs. That made me work harder. But when I got my first week's wages I received a shock. Instead of the twelve and six I expected there was only ten shillings and ninepence. I was too embarrassed to ask the other workers why so I plucked up courage and tapped on the office door.

'Come in!' came the voice of the Battleaxe from within.

I edged in timidly and asked if there had been a mistake in my wages.

'No!' came the reply. 'If you read the notice, you'll find it's correct.'

'What notice?' I asked; this was the first time I had heard about a notice.

'The girls will show you, now be off. Can't you see I'm busy?'

I went over to Minnie and asked her and she pointed to a notice on the wall at the end of the machine shop. It was small and splashed with oil and almost illegible but I could make this out:

STOPPAGES EACH WEEK
TO BE COLLECTED FROM WAGES

6d. FOR XMAS FUND
3d. FOR THE SWEEPER
3d. FOR THE LAVATORY CLEANER
6d. FOR THE TEA LADY
3d. FOR THE LOAN OF OVERALLS AND CAP

I thought about it and reasoned that since we all had to take our turn sweeping and cleaning the lav then next time it was my turn I would receive my fair share. When my turn did come I found that they were dirty, smelly jobs but I did them anyway thinking of my reward at the end of the week. But when the wages arrived I found the same amount as usual. I demanded an explanation from the other women but they just laughed.

'Silly girl. All the money's pooled together for our outing and Christmas party.' Unfortunately for me I went on neither.

When I returned home with that first week's wages I was afraid to tell my Mum because I knew there would be hell to pay. She would have turned workshop and the forewoman inside out, so I gave her the ten shillings that she expected and made do with the ninepence: not much for a hard week's work.

I went back on the Monday after I'd discovered my error over the deductions but I was determined to find myself another job. However, during the morning the forewoman came over to where I was pressing the brass buttons and offered to put me on piecework like the others, although I hadn't been there as long as you normally had to have been for this to happen. She told me I could earn more money and I deserved it because I was a good little worker. When she'd gone the other women sent Minnie over to find out what she'd wanted and when Minnie told them they started to laugh and titter. I ignored them and set to as hard as I could; so hard that by the end of the week my fingers were bleeding from many cuts I had from the sharp brass discs. The others tried to compete, I suppose because they still resented me, but I worked even harder. I even slipped back in, unknown to them all including the forewoman, and worked through my dinner hour; at the end of that week I'd earned fifteen shillings and fourpence clear. I didn't tell the others but the following Monday the forewoman told me how pleased she was with my 'output'. I didn't tell Mum either; she still had her ten shillings and the rest I hid under the floorboards.

The following week the pace began to tell and I had to slow down because I was tired and lifeless. All I wanted when I finished work at six o'clock was my bed. I was in more trouble at work as well. The women crowded round me, jostling me and shouting, making all kinds of threats. I had no idea why until Minnie told me that the piece rates were being cut and it was my fault. And sure enough at the end of the week all I had earned was seven shillings and threepence. It was not even the day rate. That was it! I decided there and then to leave, and I did. I was only glad I had enough to make up Mum's ten shillings.

I didn't move far because my next job was at a firm only a few doors away where they were advertising for a young girl to learn case-making. I went along the next Monday and rang the bell of the workshop which had been someone's front room. It was opened by an elderly man, small with a grey, pointed beard. On his head was a black velvet cap and round his waist a long, well-worn leather apron. He smelled horribly of glue, as did his little workshop. I told him why I'd called and after looking me up and down while he fingered his beard he took me inside where there was a long bench from one end of the room to the other on which were laid sheets of red and blue covered cardboard and plywood. Sitting at the bench with their backs to me were two women and a young man busily making boxes out of the cardboard. These, he told me, were jewel cases. I didn't get much chance to see what was going on here because he led me into a smaller room at the back which I could see had been somebody's kitchen. There was a gas stove with two pots of molten glue on it, and on the other side of the room was a bench with scissors, a tape measure and a small roll of velvet.

He told me I was to work here and that my job was to cut out the pieces of velvet and pass them through to where the women sat glueing. I enjoyed this job because although it was smelly it was clean and wasn't hard work. He said my wages would be fifteen shillings a week if I could be trusted and I did what I was told. I spent a happy month there until an incident happened that scared me off.

It happened one Friday night. The boss asked me if he could trust me to take a packet to a woman who would be waiting outside The Rose Villa, a nearby public house, which stands on the corner of Vyse Street. With that he brought a Bible out of his desk and asked me to swear on it that I would not tell anyone what I was carrying or where I was going. I agreed and after I'd kissed the Bible he handed me a small leather 'dolly bag' which he said I was to give to a tall woman, dressed in a fur coat, who would approach me and say, 'I'm Di.' In return she would give me a packet which I had to bring straight back. I must, he emphasised, be very careful that nobody saw me hand the bag over. My immediate reaction was to be thrilled to be trusted with this important errand and when I said I would hide the leather purse round my waist under my apron he just smiled and told me to be off. Before I had even reached the pub the woman approached me and said the password. Then taking me by the hand she led me up an entry. I retrieved the purse from underneath my frock and in return for this she handed me a large flat envelope which I could feel contained banknotes. Then she was off, without saying another word. I retraced my steps as quickly as I could and found my boss waiting for me outside the workshop door.

'Good girl,' he smiled and whispered, taking the packet. 'Now come in an' warm yer 'ands while I make up the wages.' As soon as he'd disappeared upstairs one of the other women came over to where I was warming myself by the stove.

'I want ter warn yer,' she whispered, glancing towards the stairs. 'Yer don't want ter goo on them sorta errands.'

'Why?' I whispered too although I had no idea why.

'Yer know what yer was' carryin?' I shook my head. 'A bag o' diamonds. He's too scared ter tek 'em 'imself in case 'e gets caught or somebody knocks 'im down. Tek my advice, yow leave before it's too late or yow'll get caught or worse!' she hissed.

I was terrified. I didn't want to go prison or get killed, and as soon as he gave me my wage packet I was off, never to return there again.

When I'd calmed down enough to open my wage packet there was the fifteen shillings I had been expecting and in addition a ten-shilling note and a message which read, 'Thank you, this is for you.' I wasn't sorry to be clear of whatever racket it was that they were up to, but the ten shillings helped me over the time until I found another job. I couldn't be out of work and I couldn't tell anyone why I'd left my last job.

I went to several factories asking for work; I'd decided I would be safer working with lots of people. I had a couple of jobs at factories in Frederic Street and Vyse Street, still in the Jewellery Quarter, but I spoilt the work, not being very experienced, and was given the sack. Eventually I settled for a job learning to enamel brooches and badges and motor plates at Fray's in Tenby Street North. It was an interesting job although all I was doing was learning how to 'lay on'; that is, apply the powdered glass on the metal prior to firing in the kiln. I wanted to learn all the other aspects of the process from grinding the enamel to firing, filing and polishing. I suppose I was impatient and there was a kind of informal apprenticeship system in operation in the trade to prevent somebody like me learning enough to set up in competition with the existing gaffers. I found out that I would have to spend three years laying on before I was likely to move on to anything else, and at that rate I would be middle aged before I was expert in all the processes of enamelling. However, I was not to be deterred so easily and I decided that if I couldn't learn everything at one firm then I would move on and learn more somewhere else. That, in fact, is what I did. I changed jobs, making sure that when I moved I was taken on to be trained in a process that was unfamiliar to me, and in that way I picked up the entire trade bit by bit. In no time at all I knew it inside out, but I'd learned enough to make sure that it was never me who was responsible for getting the piece rates reduced again.

Love and Marriage

I had steady work in the enamelling trade until 1920. By then the War to End all Wars was over, but so too was the boom in the metal trades of Birmingham. It was no longer easy to flit from job to job until you settled for something you fancied. Plenty of people were laid off and many girls, particularly married women who had found no difficulty getting jobs in munitions and such like a year before, were now reduced to whatever odd jobs they could find. In short this was the beginning of the Depression which, unlike what many people think, began then and went right through until the Second World War brought another period of full employment to Birmingham. That time too it brought destruction of life and property in the Blitz. It was during those two decades of grinding poverty between the wars that I grew to womanhood, experienced love and marriage and children and had it all taken away, all my hopes dashed. I was brought to the very edge of complete and utter despair before I was able to drag myself back from the abyss of sorrow and re-establish myself and my family. But this is jumping the gun, and a lot happened to me and to Birmingham before that came about.

Mum was not so strict with me now I was contributing to the household. I placed my wages beneath the faded, bobbled mantel fringe every Friday night and I was free to go out to the pictures with the girls I worked with.

'Keep away from the boys,' she would warn me, wagging a finger at me as I was leaving. 'An' don't forget if yer bring any trouble 'ome 'ere I'll 'ave ter put yer in the workhouse.' She still enjoyed ranting, but I would shrug my shoulders now: it was an old record I had heard throughout my childhood. I needed maternal love and affection and I needed to understand what really happened between men and women, and what it was I was to avoid, but I didn't learn any of these things from Mum.

I worked with a lot of pleasant girls mostly my own age and I suppose you would say I was enjoying life. I was young, had money in my purse if I needed it and a sort of independence. I remember Christmas Eve 1919; Florrie, a girl I worked with, had invited me to a party at her mother's house. I agreed and when I told Mum she said it was all right, although not without the usual cryptic warnings. I'd saved a few pounds over the years since I'd left school and this particular Christmas I decided to celebrate be ceasing to be a regular customer of second-hand shops and splash out on some brand new clothes. As Christmas Eve approached I began to look around the shops for something suitable for the party, but then as now with my grand-daughters, the clothes I wanted were too expensive. So this particular evening, since I could find nothing in the shops in town and it was near to closing time, I decided to go to the Bull Ring markets where the shops kept later hours to try my luck. I caught a tram into the city centre and alighting from it bought a twopenny bag of roast potatoes to eat as I went along. The streets were crowded with late-night shoppers, young couples and the inevitable drunks weaving along the pavement. Eventually I arrived at the Bull Ring where the barrow boys lined the pavements, naphtha flares casting an unnaturally bright light on their wares. There were crowds of people pushing and shoving, trying to get a bargain, and the noise was like a fairground on a Saturday night. The barrow boys shouted to outdo each other and the Salvation Army band was there too, competing for the attention of the people.

One of the barrow boys shouted at me, 'Come on duckie, fower a penny oranges, all sound', but I moved quickly on, clutching my purse tightly. When I reached the open-air fish market I saw two down and outs, disabled soldiers still in their khaki overcoats. One, a man with only one arm, had a card round his neck saying that he had a wife and six children to support. The other was trying to play his concertina above the hubbub. These men were not unusual then. There were several disabled soldiers in our district alone who were reduced to busking for a crust. When these two saw me stop and stare, the one pushed his cap towards my crying pitifully, 'Please 'elp an old soldier, missy.' I dropped a coin into the cap, wishing it could have been more, and then I went on my way to the little clothes shop I was heading for.

It was in Moat Row, near the Rag Market, and when I arrived I found the woman closing up. I pleaded with her to serve me, telling her what I wanted, but she said she was sorry but her 'ol' man' had taken all the best stuff home. However, when she saw my tears she relented.

'Oh all right, wait 'ere while I get me basket carriage an' lock up, an' then yer can come 'ome with me an' try a few things on.'

I knew she only lived round the corner because Mum had taken me there one Sunday morning. The proprietress was a small woman, not much bigger than me. She had untidy hair and a dress that dragged on the floor, and around her shoulders she swung a black knitted shawl while on her head she slapped a flat black straw hat. Then she set off wheeling the basket carriage full of clothing in front of her. I offered to help but she said she could manage. We were soon at her house and she kicked open the door and pushed the carriage inside. I followed her into the room which was piled so full of clothing old and new that you could hardly move.

'Come on in the back,' she said as she made her way through a pile of coats strung across the room. We entered the back which was only slightly less crowded, and there she introduced me to her husband who I could see was in a drunken sleep in a chair. I was glad she didn't wake him because I knew I would be there ages talking about my Dad and Mum who they'd known years ago when they lived in Deritend near the Bull Ring. She asked me what I wanted and how much I had to spend. I had three pounds fifteen shillings and sixpence and I wanted a skirt, blouse, stockings and a coat.

'Can't let yer 'ave all them for three poun's fifteen,' she said.

'Well, that's all I've got. I haven't bin able ter save more,' I told her.

'Oh well, let's see what we've got,' she said, rummaging through things.

So instead of new I had to be content with nearly new, which is little different from second hand but sounds better. I tried on several pairs of shoes until eventually she let me have a new pair of black patent leather which were the only ones that fitted. I'd always wanted a pair of these since I'd seen a woman wearing some in

Jefferson's years before. I also chose two pairs of lisle stockings, a black hobble skirt, a white satin blouse with a frill down the centre and a brown velvet cape. She threw in a dress that was frayed along the edge saying that if it was cut and hemmed I'd be able to wear it for work. I was very pleased with my purchases, which she folded up for me and put in my string bag.

While she was doing that I opened my purse to pay her but when I did I couldn't believe my eyes. Inside there were only three pounds, two half crowns and a sixpence. Where was the half sovereign? She saw me fumbling and stopped what she was doing.

'What, yer mean yer ain't got the money?' she demanded.

Then I remembered. 'I must have given the half sovereign to those two soldiers,' I said, getting very upset.

'What soldiers?' I could see that she didn't believe me. I tried to explain between sobs that I must have dropped that coin into the man's cap instead of the sixpence I'd intended.

'Yer wunt see that or them again. They're more likely ter be in the pub now suppin' ter their good fortune. Anyway dry yer eyes an' give me the three pounds. Yer can pay the other after Christmas.'

I gave her the money, and the two half crowns I slipped back in my purse. Then after thanking her I made my way back through the heaps of clothes towards the door. She warned me not to stop or talk to anybody on my way home.

'Pretty little thing like yow shouldn't be down a rough quarter like this at night. I'd send the ole man along with yer but yer can see 'e's in a drunken stupor.'

I was glad. I thought I'd be safer without him. Her last words to me were, 'Now off yer goo, an' mind what I said, an' a merry Christmas.' I returned the compliment and hurried off with my bag on my arm. I returned the way I'd come. The barrow boys were thinning out by now, sweeping their speckled oranges and apples into the gutter along with the other rubbish. I thought of when I was little when I would have been glad of these, and indeed there were some small children scavenging. But now I could afford to turn up my nose at this scene. I half hoped that I would see the two soldiers still begging when I reached the fish market but they were nowhere to be seen. I guessed they were in the nearby pub and I was debating whether I dared go in to look for them when I was startled by a gruff voice behind me.

'Want ter buy a coupla puppies missy?' it said.

I turned round and saw a man I took to be one of the barrow boys holding a straw basket with two black and white puppies in it.

'It's me last sale, three bob the two,' he told me, lifting them out of the straw. I was fascinated by them. They licked my fingers and looked like they were saying 'please take me'. But even if he'd given them to me I knew that I couldn't take them home because Mum would have turned them out into the street. While I was thus occupied he thrust them into my arms and said, "Ere tek 'em. Yer can 'ave 'em fer 'alf a crown.'

I've always been soft-hearted and I could not resist them, so I gave him the money, hugged them to me and walked off thinking I could find someone to give them a home. A few yards down the street I saw two lads sitting on the edge of the pavement sorting through the rotten vegetables that the stall-holders had left there. These are two likely lads I could give them to, I thought.

'Here, would you like these?' I asked them, holding out the puppies.

"Ow much?' the taller of them asked.

'You can have them for nothin',' I replied.

'Goo-on, we don't believe yer, do we Jimmy?'

'No we don't,' Jimmy replied and continued sorting the rubbish.

I bent down and handed them over. "Ere,' I said, 'if you'll promise to give 'em a good home and be kind to 'em you can 'ave 'em for nothin'.'

'Really missus? Yo' ain't kiddin' us are yer missus?'

With that they tucked them under their ragged waistcoats and darted off down the street with a 'thank yer an' a merry Christmas'.

I had some misgivings about letting them have them but it was no good my keeping them. By this time I'd missed the tram so I set off to walk home and by the time I got there it was past eleven o'clock. The house was deserted and the fire only embers. It seemed damp and cold and I set to to put some life into the fire with some wood and coal from the cellar. I found a penny and put that in the meter and got the kettle going and then went up and put my purchases in my trunk. I had very little money left but I reflected I'd bought all my Christmas presents so there was nothing else I needed. I had got Dad a new clay pipe and an ounce of twist, a black apron for Mum, two packets of Woodbines for Frankie and a box of chocolates for

Liza. For Mary I had a box of white handkerchiefs. Just as I was about to sit down Mum and Dad appeared, both well oiled. They pulled their chairs up to the fire and began singing 'Only a Rose'. I'd heard enough drunken singing on my way home so I went to go to bed. But before I'd got to the door Mum called me back and told me to hang up some holly she had bought and some 'mottoes'. As I was sticking the oval mottoes up I thought what it was to put up the message 'GOD BLESS THIS HAPPY HOME' in our house. There were not many happy homes in our area now that the war was over and there were so many unemployed. When I'd done this I grabbed some bread and pickled beef from the table and tiptoed up to the attic where I sat on my bed eating my meagre supper, listening to Mum and Dad's feeble attempts at harmony before getting undressed and popping into bed.

I was too old to hang up my stockings now I knew who Father Christmas was, but even though he was out of a job Dad gave me a shilling and kiss. 'Thank yer me wench, just what I could do with,' he said next morning when he saw his present. Mum gave me a pair of fawn-coloured lisle stockings and a Christmas card with lace edging. Frankie had a tin of toffees for Liza and me. We thanked each other with kisses that were only exchanged in our house at the festive season. After breakfast Dad went out to find his mates and us three helped Mum clean the house and prepare for dinner. We had a stuffed goose and sausages and roast potatoes with Christmas pudding to follow. Mum couldn't afford to put silver three-penny bits in that year but I'd made the pudding and had slipped in four anyway. This meal was what passed for a real 'blow out' in 1919, but it wouldn't rate much for Christmas today.

After we'd washed up the dirty crocks Dad produced half a bottle of rum from the cupboard. He said he'd won it at a fair but I could see Mum didn't believe him. That didn't stop her from helping him empty the bottle though. Then they went upstairs to have a 'nap' as they termed it. As soon as they'd gone Frankie and Liza went out, leaving me alone, but I didn't mind; I went up to get out my clothes in readiness for Florrie's party that evening.

I bolted the door then stripped and began putting them on. First I put on the camisole, then clean bloomers, stockings and so on, until I was competely ready. Then I combed my hair, parted it in the middle and tied it up in a bun on top. I was ready to face the world.

I looked in the mirror and thought I looked just 'swell'. My cheeks did look a little pale and since Liza always hid her carmine away I spat on my finger and rubbed some red off the wallpaper and rubbed it gently into my cheeks and lips. At last I had it right, I thought.

It was a cold frosty night that Christmas but I hadn't far to go. I was hurrying along past The George and Dragon when I heard the strains of 'The First Noel', and looking towards the pub doorway I saw six small, ragged children, four boys and two girls, trying to reach the top notes. I stood at a little distance – they hadn't seen me – and listened. It brought tears to my eyes, recalling as it did the night when Frankie, Liza and I, equally ragged and runny nosed, had sung carols on those very steps. Like us they were not having a lot of luck. So I opened my purse and gave them all I had with me, sixpence; a penny each I thought, not much. But I was late so holding my hobble skirt above my knees I hurried on. Lights were on in many houses and the sounds of jollity drifted on the night air; somewhere a gramophone crackled out a popular tune.

I could hear that Florrie's party was going with a swing before I reached her house. I knocked on the door but no one heard over the noise so I walked in boldly. As soon as I entered a churus of voices sang out, 'A merry Christmas, Katie.' I knew most of the boys and girls from the works and I felt relaxed and at home in no time. Florrie introduced me to her Mum, who was sitting at the piano about to play.

'Hello,' she said cheerfully. 'Go an' 'elp yerself to the eats and have a glass of port.'

Mrs Chatwin, Florrie's Mum, was a youngish woman with fair hair done in a bun on top. She had a pleasant smile and made me feel welcome. As the notes of 'Hearts and Flowers' sounded from the piano I helped myself to sandwiches and a glass of port as she'd directed. I stood by the piano listening to the tune and reflecting that Florrie was lucky to have such a nice Mum and homely home. I thought, I can never ask her to my home, I'd be too embarrassed. I moved across to stand by the log fire which was blazing in the grate. After a minute or two Florrie's young man came up and invited me to have another glass of port, but before he could take my empty one, Florrie had whisked him away.

'Come on, we haven't finished our dance,' she pouted. I saw at once she was jealous but he ignored her for the moment and fetched me my drink. Then I was left to drink alone. Everyone was paired up and I began to feel left out. They were all dancing and nobody had asked me but I couldn't dance anyway, so I made the best of it and enjoyed the scene. I couldn't dance because I'd never been taught and was definitely not allowed to go to dancehalls. The second glass of port I could feel warming me, and I had another for 'Dutch courage'; then I had a fourth because by now I was beginning to feel merry. After that I became bright and gay and finally tipsy.

'I'll show 'em,' I thought, 'they'll regret ignoring me.' I walked boldly, not a bit unsteadily, over to the piano and requested Mrs Chatwin play 'Annie Laurie' and I would sing. I had a good voice and as she called for quiet and the first notes sounded I let rip. When I had finished there were calls of 'encore', and as they pressed round me I felt dizzy and faint. One of the girls took me outside for a breath of fresh air and a glass of cold water. I couldn't go home looking and feeling like I did, so I was taken back in and made to sit on the plush green sofa.

My first party was not turning out to be a success and I determined to leave as soon as I felt well enough. I was making my way over to the door when a young man in soldier's uniform came in.

'Don't go yet, Katie,' Florrie urged me as she dashed over to greet the newcomer. 'I want you to meet Harry's friend, Charlie.'

I looked up into his face and I knew in that instant that I didn't want to leave. As soon as he'd entered he removed his cap, showing his dark auburn hair. He had light blue eyes and a fresh, ruddy complexion and a few freckles. I thought him most handsome. I must have stood there staring, too shy to speak, but he soon put me at my ease.

'So, your name's Katie? I've seen you lots of times coming home from work but I didn't like ter speak to yer when you was with the other girls.' I felt myself go hot all over and blush at this.

'Don't be shy,' he said gently.

'She's just leavin', Charlie,' Florrie called out, but I didn't want to leave now. I wanted to stay.

'Would you like me to see you home then?' he offered.

'I only live two streets away but if you don't mind you can see me part of the way.' I didn't want him to see the yard where we lived; I would have been too ashamed.

I said my good nights to everyone and as I did so noticed that Florrie seemed to be fuming, but I couldn't have cared less about her. When we got into the street we found it freezing hard and icy. Neither of us spoke as we walked along the pavement. I was too shy and perhaps he had nothing to say but every now and then when I slipped on the ice his arm went round my waist to steady me. To tell the truth I slipped purposely a couple of times so that I could feel the slight pressure as he gripped me. If it had been anybody else's arm I should have knocked it away, but each time he tightened his hold I experienced a certain thrill that I'd never known before. All too soon we reached the corner at the top of the hill which led down to Camden Drive where our yard was. He was as keen as any young man ought to be to see the girl he is escorting right to the door. However, I dissuaded him by telling him that I was not quite eighteen and that my parents would object if I was brought home by a boy.

'Can I see you tomorra night then?' he asked me and without hesitating I replied, 'Where?' We were looking straight into each other's eyes, the way only people falling in love do, as he replied, 'Outside the Mount Zion, seven o'clock.'

I knew the chapel in Graham Street he meant; I'd gone to Sunday school there as a child.

'Now, you're sure you'll be all right?' he asked, bending to kiss my cheek.

I felt a little disappointed he'd not taken me in his arms and kissed me properly but as I walked down the hill I heard his footsteps behind me, and as I turned he took me in his arms and squeezed me so hard I thought he would squeeze me to death. I was thrilled; I wanted to stay like that for ever. At last he released his grip and whispered, 'Good night, and don't forget your promise or I'll come knocking on your door.' With that he hugged me again and kissed me full on the lips, then turned to walk away. As I walked down the hill towards the Drive I felt I was walking on air; I was in love for the first time in my life. I had had a few boyfriends but nothing that felt like this.

The next night, Boxing Night, Charlie looked so handsome in his navy blue civilian suit, white shirt and dark tie, and as he doffed his cap to greet me I noticed his auburn hair highlighted under the street lamp. He kissed me on the cheek and took my hand. We walked and talked as young people have done since Adam and Eve. He told me he was twenty-two and lived with his sisters nearby in Nelson Street and that we were going there to meet them. I was too shy to meet any of his relatives and so he agreed I should meet them after Christmas. In any case he knew of a party in Nelson Street so we decided to go there.

He introduced me all round but he could see I looked uncomfortable so we didn't stay long and, having one port (I had learnt my lesson of the previous evening), we left. We strolled along the Sandpits and went into a pub called The Stores. He knew some of the customers there who asked me to have a drink, which I did though I stuck to lemonade. Everyone was singing and making merry and we joined in. Then all too soon it was eleven o'clock and 'Time gentlemen, please!'

We stopped on the way home to kiss and cuddle and parted with a promise to meet again outside the Queen's Hall, off the Parade. Before meeting Charlie the next night I took special pains with my dress and my hair, parting it down the middle and pinning it back into a tight bun. I kept looking in the mirror and back at the clock whose hands seemed to be standing still. At last it was time to leave. We met as planned and it was then, sitting in the dark, that he told me he loved me.

In the next few weeks we went for walks or to the pictures and each night before we parted we stopped to kiss and cuddle in an entry. In fact we stopped in one regularly near Stern and Bell's in Arthur Place, which was lined either side with larger, bay-windowed houses. It was an alley between two of these houses and at its end was Moseley's toffee factory. There was nowhere else to go and it was at least warm and out of the wind. One night we were seen together by my sister Mary who questioned me later. She wanted to know if I was going with Charlie steady. So I told her. I wasn't like Liza; I love him, I said, and when I was older I would marry him. She tried to warn me, tell me the facts of life, but I was too much in love with love to listen or care.

We were invited to a New Year's party where we both drank too much but we were so happy and so terribly in love nothing seemed to matter. Going home he stopped me and, putting his hands on my shoulders, sang, 'I'll take you home again, Kathleen'. He had a good voice and I shall remember his singing that song to my dying day.

We sang together and laughed and giggled all the way to our courting place. That evening I forgot my sister's warning and we made love for the first time. We stayed there for a long time after, our arms around each other, huddled together until the thin light of dawn began to streak the night sky. Eventually we did part and I floated home without a care whether my parents were waiting up for me or not. When I got home and tried the door I found it bolted on the inside. They must have assumed I was already in bed so I was left with only one alternative; I had to lift the cellar grating and get in that way. I slid down the heap of slack on my bottom and landed amid the cobwebs on the floor. I pulled myself to my feet, felt for the stairs, climbed up and entered the living room. I dusted the cobwebs from my hair, took off my shoes and crept up the bare wooden staircase, hoping it wouldn't creak too loudly and wake them. I could hear Mum and Dad 'sending the pigs home to market', as they used to say, and reaching the landing I felt safe. I quickly undressed and jumped into bed and had hardly hit the pillow than I was waking up the next morning.

As I awoke what had happened the previous evening came flooding back to me. Now I finally knew the facts of life: there was no doubt in my mind at all where babies came from now, and I felt ashamed and worried in about equal measure. What if I have a baby and he won't marry me, I thought. There were girls in our neighbourhood who had babies and were not married. Would Mum turn me out into the workhouse as she'd always threatened she would? All that day I was worried sick and when I met Charlie that evening I was that upset I broke down and cried. I hung my head, I was too ashamed to face him. But Charlie lifted my face to his and kissed my wet cheeks and smiled.

'Don't get upset Katie. I really do love you an' as soon as we can save enough money, we'll put up the banns and in the meantime we'll save 'ard an' look for a 'ouse.'

Of course, then as now, this was easier said than done. We met only at weekends, when Charlie took me to lodgings where he was staying since he had left his sisters'. That was only temporary while he sorted himself out after his discharge from the Army. I cleaned and cooked for him and was happy that we had things worked out between us. I managed to save a pound a week and Charlie likewise. I put it away safely and our savings began to grow. The first of

February was my birthday: I was eighteen. I told Charlie I was going to tell my parents that I was courting but he dissuaded me, saying he would tell them himself in a while. I was reassured by this and each time his landlady was away at the weekend we made love. Towards the end of March I felt out of sorts, and one morning couldn't face my breakfast. I felt nauseous and frightened. I pushed my food away untouched and Mum noticed I'd turned pale.

'Wot's the matta with yow? Ain't it good enough for yer or summat?' she said.

'Yes, but I feel sick.'

'Sick or not yer betta 'urry yerself fer work or yow'll be late agen,' she yelled.

I knew that I was pregnant. I'd missed my period and now I was feeling sick in the morning. I wanted to confide in Mum but I was too scared: I knew she wouldn't understand. I should have brought Charlie home before so she could have got used to the idea of my getting married.

When I returned from work that evening Mary was waiting for me. Straight away she said. 'Mum says yer've been outta sorts the last few mornin's. What's the matter with yer?'

I just broke down and cried. 'I think I'm going to have a baby, Mary,' I wailed.

'Oh, my God! Are you sure?' she gasped.

'I hope not, but I think I am,' I sobbed.

'You'd better come upstairs an' let me see,' she told me. She made me strip, and when she felt my breasts and belly, sure enough, the evidence was there.

'Is it the young chap I've seen you with?' she asked, and I nodded my tearful reply.

'Then he better marry yer before Mum finds out. Or anyone else round 'ere for that matter, yer know how the tongues wag,' she added.

I got dressed, feeling miserable, and followed her downstairs. She made tea and we drank it.

'Now we'll talk,' she said sharply. 'An' stop yer snivelling.'

I told her all that had happened and when I'd finished I could see she was not impressed.

'You should both be ashamed! If it had been Liza I could understand but not you!' she said harshly. 'I warned yer, didn't I.' At that I flared up.

'Yes, you warned me, but too late!' I snapped back. 'I was always asking you an' Mum to explain things to me years ago, but no, you never did!' "Yer'll 'ave ter wait until yer older", that's all I ever heard from Yow. 'Ow old 'ave I got ter be, tell me that?'

'Well, why didn't you bring 'im home?' she asked.

'What! Bring 'im ter this hovel!' I shouted at her.

'Oh, well, I'll see what I can do to 'elp,' she said, getting up to leave.

Next night I came home from work to find Charlie, Dad and Mary already there, discussing me. I looked from one to the other, shaking in my shoes, wondering what was going to happen. But Charlie came over and put his arm round me.

'It's all right, don't worry Katie. Your Dad's given 'is consent, so we can get married in a few weeks' time.'

Hearing that I threw my arms round my Dad and hugged him. There was no one like my Dad.

'Be good to 'er lad,' he told Charlie. 'She's a good girl. But I don't know 'ow her mother is goin' ter tek this,' he added.

'You leave 'er ter me,' Mary said firmly. She was quite strait-laced was Mary. She was married for the second time now and also a bit of a snob.

'Come along, lad. Let's go out an' 'ave a drink an' leave these two to sort things out,' said Dad.

As soon as they had left I asked Mary how Charlie came to be here.

'I thought it was about time he found out what his responsibilities were and had a talk with Dad, so I made it my business to find out where he was lodging.'

'But Mary, I can't face Mum. What am I goin' ter say?'

'You should 'ave thought of that before getting into this trouble! Any'ow you better slip upstairs and wait there while I try to explain.'

I rushed out of the room and hid. I was so confused and upset I just lay down and wept. I would sooner have faced the devil than face our Mum. It wasn't long before I heard her voice below.

'Oh my God! Oh my God!' she shrieked. 'Whatever will the neighbours think?'

Then I heard Mary's voice very angrily. 'Never mind the neighbours as you call 'em. It's your daughter upstairs you've got to think about now, and stop crying. That won't mend matters.'

'I warned 'er, I warned 'er wot would 'appen if she brought disgrace on us,' she wailed.

'Don't be stupid, mother. And wipe your eyes. We're to blame really for not explaining the facts of life to her years ago when she asked us. Anyway it's too late now; she's getting married in three weeks' time.'

'Who ses so?'

'Dad and the young man she's been going with. He seems a nice fella, Mum, and I know you'll like 'im too.'

'We'll see,' I heard her say more quietly before adding, 'yer betta call 'er down while I mek a cuppa tea.'

When I heard Mary's voice from the foot of the stairs I felt too ashamed to come down to face them. But I knew I would have to sooner or later; better face Mum now while Mary was present, I thought, than wait till we were alone. Slowly I crept down the stairs and finally stood facing Mum. It was then that I got the biggest shock of my life. She threw her arms around me, drew me to her bosom and wept.

'Why did yer do it? Why?' she sobbed. I was in tears now as well, thinking I'd been forgiven. I should have known better: Mum was never one to forgive or forget. She was like the weather and whenever we were alone together she kept harping on about the disgrace I'd brought to the family, and each night I cried myself to sleep. I felt I could never be happy there any more and on the following Friday, after placing my wages as usual under the mantel fringe, I put some of my belongings in my string bag and prepared to leave the house. There was only one place where I'd be welcome now, I felt. Then, just as I was opening the door, in walked Mum.

'An' where do yer think yer gooin'?' she demanded.

'Charlie's. He's made arrangements for me with his landlady,' I replied at once.

'All right!' she snapped as she pushed past me. 'Yer can please yerself but wotever yer do from now on I wipe me 'an's on yer.'

I walked down the hill in tears. If only she'd offered to forgive me, taken me in her arms and meant it. That was the impossible, and it was not until later when I was raising my own family that we came to understand each other better and became closer as mother and daughter.

Married Life

Charlie and I were married on 25 April 1921, by which time I was three months' pregnant. I would have loved to have been married in white with a flowing veil like Mary, but she had said that it would be a 'sin' and 'a mockery' and no matter how tightly I laced my whalebone stays, she said, the neighbours would know the truth when they recollected the date of the wedding. So I was wed in a pale blue frock and coat, both much out of date, with a blue straw picture hat and white shoes and stockings. I had begged Mary to lend me some money which I'd promised to pay back from my wages each week so that I could put on a better show on my wedding day. However, she refused, saying she'd enough money owing to her already. It was then she told me she was going to America to make a fresh start, and this was another reason, I suppose, why she wouldn't lend me anything. Perhaps she thought I should be punished as well. In any case we quarrelled and were never truly close after that.

They did do us the courtesy of coming to the church though: Dad, Mum, my brothers and sisters, as well as a few of the neighbours and some of my friends from work. After the ceremony we received the usual congratulations and Mum was the last to kiss me. I noticed a real tear in her eye, but I was past caring then; I was what is known as 'a happily married woman'.

Charlie and I returned to our lodgings to pack our weekend case ready to catch the early train to Blackpool next morning. I'd saved the money to do this in a 'diddleum' club, run by a Mrs Chapman with whom I worked. I'd never seen Blackpool so we thought this would be a good idea for a honeymoon: we couldn't afford anything better.

The following morning, Saturday, found us waiting on the platform for our train when several women from my works, together with their men friends or husbands, appeared. They were already the worse for drink, rolling around and looking bedraggled, as if they'd not been to bed. Had the train not drawn up when it did we would have foregone the diddleum money and returned home.

'Good 'ealth, me wench,' one of the women cried out to us as she tipped back the contents of a bottle.

'Mind wot yer doin' ternight,' another shouted, amid howls of raucous laughter. The only two who were sober, I noticed, were two spinster sisters who lived in Sloane Street.

When the train stopped we jumped on and found an empty compartment. We pulled the blinds down, then we were alone and happy. We could still hear the off-key singing from along the corridor, but we weren't disturbed.

When we arrived at the boarding house we had to be shuffled about because there were too many guests and some had to go next door, but our landlady had the pick of the bunch before sending the others off. In our group there were the two maiden sisters, prim and proper, two women friends, Mr and Mrs Chapman and Charlie and I. The landlady was a small, plump, middle-aged woman; a typical seaside landlady. She motioned us upstairs and off we trooped. Our rooms were on the first floor; small bedrooms made from partitioning one large room into four with plywood walls. Although our room was virtually empty apart from the bed it was clean. The bed was only three-quarter size and stood in the middle of the room. There was a washstand by the window with a crock bowl and water jug on it and there was also a small piece of Sunlight soap and a threadbare towel. There were only nails on which to hang our clothes and no carpet or lino, just bare floorboards. Yes, and beneath the bed there was the regulation china chamber pot. Pinned to the door were the house rules regarding lights out and breakfast time which was 'nine o'clock sharp'. Over the bed was another handwritten message: 'Please Be Quiet As Other People Want To Sleep'.

Before she left us she said, 'I'll send Fred up with your bag,' and as she opened the door she paused and said, 'You're the newlyweds?' We nodded and she left, smiling.

There was a strong smell of disinfectant about the room which seemed to emanate from beneath the bed. I turned down the bedclothes and the mattress to check for flea or bug powder but everything, though threadbare, was clean. Charlie and I sat down on the edge of the bed and giggled. We'd expected something better than this but would make the best of it.

'When am I going ter see the sea?' I asked him.

'As soon as we're ready ter go downstairs,' he replied.

'No, it's too dark now. Anyway, the landlady says its about fifteen minutes' walk unless we go by tram. We'll wait till morning and we'll go an' explore before the others are awake,' I told him.

So we settled down to wait for the supper bell, and while we sat there we became aware that every movement and word that went on in the rooms adjacent to ours was distinctly audible. Then the bell sounded and we went downstairs to see what was in store for us. We entered a large kitchen where the landlady was standing beside the large, black range ladling out soup.

'Sit yerselves down.' She motioned with the ladle when she saw us standing, politely waiting.

We all found seats at a large table covered with American oilcloth and waited while Fred served us plates of thin, watery soup and chunks of dry bread. The two old maids sitting across from us whispered, 'Is this all we're gooin' ter get?' This produced a black look from Fred but we did get a good meal of roast mutton, carrots, cabbage, peas and roast potatoes. Fred and his wife sat down and had their meal with us and we had a pleasant conversation. When we'd finished the other guests asked us if we'd like to join them for a drink in a nearby pub but we couldn't afford to go drinking. Fortunately, before we could refuse Fred came to the rescue.

'You young 'uns don't want to start drinkin' your time o' life. Anyway if yer like ter stay in an' keep me an' the missus company we've got a drop in,' he offered.

Charlie and I were happy to accept this offer because apart from anything else it was now raining heavily. Fred and his wife turned out to be a jolly couple and they made us feel very welcome, and as we sat round the range supping stout and ale we became very talkative. Fred regaled Charlie with his exploits in the Navy and Charlie in turn talked about his time in the Army while 'the missus' and I talked of our families and what I was going to do when I got a home of my own. We seemed to chat like this for hours until, when it was time to go to bed, I felt quite dizzy, not being used to drinking much. Charlie too, I could see, had had enough but we thanked them without difficulty and said 'good night'. However, when it came to the stairs I needed some gentle pushing from Charlie to get up. As soon as we had entered our room and lit the gas jet I flopped down on the bed. The others were already in their rooms, as the laughing and giggling we could hear testified, and when Charlie had removed his boots and trousers and was standing beside the bed in his shirt I was infected with the giggling too: I could see all he'd got.

'What's there ter giggle about?' he asked huffily. 'Get me the pot, I want ter mek water.' But before I could reach it he bent down and we both somehow managed to topple over. We lay there giggling hysterically as the floor began to resound with thumping on the ceiling of the room underneath ours.

'What's goin' on up there?' we heard Fred shout.

'Sorry ol' man,' Charlie replied, 'I 'appened ter fall over.'

'All right, but think of us what wants ter sleep,' came the annoyed response and we could hear our neighbours laughing at this exchange.

'I wonder just what they think we're up to,' Charlie said close to the partition.

We sorted ourselves out and I held the pot for Charlie to stop his making too loud a noise. I was embarrassed. I closed my eyes and turned my head and giggled and while he made water I must have raised the pot higher. I'd forgotten there was disinfectant in it and I suppose his penis must have dangled in, because the next thing I knew the pot and its contents went flying across the room.

'Oh my God! Oh my God!' he kept screaming as he shook it and chased me round the bed. 'I'll kill yer,' he shouted, 'I'll kill yer!' By the look on his face I could believe him.

Before I could reach the door it was flung open and there were Mr and Mrs Chapman and the two old maids, their eyes almost popping out as Charlie showed them what I'd done. I fled down the stairs and fell into the landlady's arms. She had to sit me down and administer whisky before I could explain coherently what had happened. Then she and Fred began to laugh but I'm afraid I couldn't see the funny side of the situation so she sent Fred up to see what could be done. He took a bowl of cold water and a sponge. When he returned, still smiling, he said there was no real damage done, only that the pot was broken and Charlie was a bit sore but that it was safe for me to go back upstairs. I was scared, though, and the landlady had to go with me to see that all was all right. She pushed me through the door and I sat on the edge of the bed while she cleaned up the floor and removed the broken pot. Charlie all the while lay in bed, staring up at the ceiling. Not a word was spoken for a long time until he began to cough. I threw my arms round him and whimpered.

'I'm sorry Charlie, I forgot there was disinfectant in the pot.'

'No good bein' sorry now. It could 'ave bin worse. Now get undressed an' get inter bed before yer catch cold, an' stop yer snivelling.' He sounded far from pleased.

I undressed slowly and lay nervously beside him. Then he took me in his arms and kissed my wet cheeks and I knew I was forgiven. That's how we lay, in each other's arms, until we fell asleep.

The next morning the landlady knocked on our door and brought our breakfast in on a tray.

'I thought you'd like ter say in bed late. 'Ow is it this morning?' she asked Charlie, who replied sheepishly. 'Not so sore this mornin', thanks.'

'Well, you can stay in bed an' I'll call yer later, 'ows that?' she told us.

We thanked her as she left the tray on the foot of the bed. We sat up and I poured the tea as well as I could without spilling it, but before we'd begun to drink it Fred arrived with a wooden stool and another chamber pot.

'Yer won't be able ter break this un, it's enamel,' he informed us jovially before leaving us to our eggs, toast and marmalade.

After putting the dirty crocks and tray on the stool Charlie decided to slip his trousers on and go downstairs to the outside toilet, and when he returned I asked him if he was still sore.

'No, it's wearin' off a bit now, but we won't be able ter mek love until I've seen the doctor,' he said.

'But I wasn't thinkin' about that,' I replied angrily.

'Now, now don't lose yer temper. Let me get back inter bed, it's freezin' out 'ere.'

And there we lay just huddled together to keep each other warm until the dinner bell rang. Then we hurriedly washed and dressed and went down to the dining room, not the kitchen as before, where we found that the others had already started theirs. I could see by their exchanged glances that they knew what had happened the previous night. So we finished the meal in silence and then it was time to get our things together to catch the train back to Birmingham. We'd not seen a great deal of Blackpool on our honeymoon except what we'd glimpsed after our arrival the previous afternoon.

We were lucky enough to have a compartment to ourselves again for the return journey and as the train puffed slowly out of Blackpool station I observed to Charlie, 'We never did see the sea, did we?'

'Never mind,' he answered, putting his arm round me. 'We'll come next year an' stay a whole week. I promise yer we'll 'ave a real good 'oliday.' But I was to be thirty years of age before I ever saw the sea: the only water I saw till then was the canal. However, we both looked forward to a happy future that spring day and perhaps it was just as well that we didn't know what fate had in store for us because neither of us would have had the strength to face it.

When we arrived home late that Sunday night our landlady greeted us with bad news.

'Yer'll 'ave ter find yerselves new accommodation,' she said. 'I'm sorry but I let the 'ouse ter me brother an' 'is family an' they want ter move in next week.'

Charlie called her a liar. 'Yer want ter get rid of us because my wife's 'avin' a baby,' he told her and she didn't deny it.

'Well, yer've got till next week anyway,' she conceded. All that week we searched desperately but we had no furniture to put in a house even if we could afford one which we couldn't. Furnished rooms were difficult to come by as well, particularly when the landlady found out I was pregnant. By the end of that week we were at our wits' end and there was only one thing to do as a last resort. We went to see Mum and Dad together and explained that in a few days we'd be out on the street. Mum said she knew a Mrs Larkins who lived on the corner of Arthur Place next to The Leopard public house who had a furnished room to let. Mum thought that Mrs Larkins would give her first chance of the room because she'd often cleaned for her.

We were able to take the room, which was very scantily furnished, for eight shillings and sixpence a week, but while we were there we saved enough to buy some second-hand furniture including a couple of chairs and a large oak wardrobe. There was a bed and a table and odd crocks that belonged to Mrs Larkins and we had to manage without other things until such time as we could afford them.

Mrs Larkins was soon to go to Australia to visit her son and it was arranged that I should pay the rent to Mr Dykes at The Leopard Inn. In the basement of the house there lived Mr and Mrs Penny. She was a small woman and although she had very little herself she was always kind to me and gave me what she had. She often came up for a chat, a cup of tea and sometimes some cake if she'd been cooking. Soon, however, they had to leave because they couldn't pay the rent and the room was taken by a couple I hardly ever saw.

Now that I was living just a stone's throw from Mum and Dad they came to visit us often. Dad would call in at The Leopard for a pint and a game of dominoes while Mum dropped in to chat and tell me what to get for my confinement. We were closer now than we'd ever been and I was glad, because now I was going to have a baby I needed her more than ever. She told me she'd booked a midwife, who turned out to the same Mrs Bullivant who'd attended Nelly's mother. When I told Mum she'd died Mum sprang to Mrs Bullivant's defence.

'Yer carn't blame the midwife fer that. Any'ow yow ain't gooin' ter die, yer too young an' 'ealthy, an' another thing, she's brought 'undreds o' babbies inter the world. It ain't 'er fault if any died,' she concluded.

She convinced me and I ceased worrying and set to to knit the little garments the baby would need. With Mum's help I washed and ironed the nappies, nightgowns and 'belly binders' that would be needed.

When my labour pains started Mum came at once while Charlie ran for the midwife. Mum was right. I had a troublefree confinement and on 7 October 1921 my first child, a boy, was born. He was a fine, healthy baby weighing in at 6 lbs 12oz. It was the custom then to bind babies and after he'd been washed Mum fastened his belly binder round him before she put on his nappy and wrapped him in his nightgown. Then she held him close.

'My little gran'son,' she whispered, and as she put him on my breast there was a tear in her eye. She bent over and kissed me too. At that moment I felt the happiest woman in the world; I had my son, my husband, my Dad and finally my Mum.

Charlie and I had our son christened Charles Samuel, after his father and grandfather, at St Paul's Church when he was a month old. By then I was back at work, doing press-work, with Mum looking after little Charles, but I had to pay her five shillings a week for his milk and rusks. My husband was now on short time and we were very hard up. Between us we were earning two pounds ten shillings a week which had to cover rent, food, coal, lighting and the boy's food, as well as 'club money' for sheets and blankets which I was buying on hire purchase, the 'never-never'. I'd scarcely stopped breast feeding my first and my milk had only just dried up when I found I was pregnant again. Mrs Larkins, who had returned from Australia, found out from the neighbours' gossip and she told us we would have to look for other rooms.

Mum had angry words with her but Mrs Larkins was adamant. So Mum said I'd better get my few 'traps', as she called our belongings, and move in with her and Dad until Charlie found a better job. Dad agreed with this but it was the last place I wanted to live. Liza was the only one still living at home and Mum said she could sleep in their room and we could have the attic. When Charlie returned footsore from looking for a place we discussed Mum's offer and reluctantly decided to accept the room, at least for the time being. When he heard, Dad said that we should have all our belongings in our room to avoid any arguments with Mum. I was happier living up there, out of Mum's way, but first I had to scrub and disinfect the room which was filthy. I paid Mum eight and sixpence a week for that small room, plus the coal which she rationed out and the washing.

I worked until a week before the baby was due and my second son was born eleven months to the day after my first, on 7 September 1922. He was christened John Ernest after my eldest brother and my husband's brother. Charlie was out of work altogether by now and we were in terrible straits with two small babies to look after. With no money coming in I had to go back to work a few weeks after my baby was born and leave my two sons with Mum. How hard I persevered to get us away from that hovel no one knows; I even went office cleaning after I'd finished my press-work at the factory and had fed and put the boys to bed. I literally worked all hours God made to earn a little extra to take care of their needs, but as hard as I worked we seemed to be no better off; it was like treading water to stay afloat, we were always short of money. We tried to find our own place but that was just as hopeless; nobody wanted two small children.

Charlie tramped the streets day after day looking for a job but to no avail. Finally in desperation he decided to go to the timber mills and buy bags of sawdust to sell to pubs and butchers' shops. This he did, but it was an ill-fated venture because he made very little profit from it, only managing to give me two shillings or half a crown a day. And, more important in the long run, he started drinking heavily. I suppose visiting all those public houses to sell sawdust presented too much temptation and he would have a drink in each; by the time he rolled home he was very much the worse for drink. This went on for two years, during which time things went from bad to worse. It was more than anybody could stand; our situation never seemed to improve, and we seemed destined to a life of grinding poverty – what would be called 'deprivation' today. For me and those who lived through similar experiences it was just plain misery.

Dad was out of work as well. He was ill and at home with asthma, the legacy of his years in the casting shop, and Mum was at her wits' end. In the end there was no alternative: she went on the parish again and when the visitor came to inspect the house we had to hide because Mum had told them that she and Dad were living alone. She got away with this subterfuge and no one in the yard split; how could they when they were in the same boat themselves? As the reader can imagine I was utterly exhausted each night after leaving my second job and I would crawl into bed with the babies and pray to the Lord to get us away from all that poverty. I cried all the time. I suppose in retrospect that I was emotionally as well as physically drained.

Dad was not one to give up, though. He bought himself a last and mended the boots of everyone who could afford to pay, even some of the firemen at the Albion Street Fire Station. This helped us for a while, but soon Dad became too ill even to do this. Then to cap it all I became pregnant again and had to give up my job and fall on the parish. Needless to say when they found out that Charlie was selling sawdust I was refused help. This time I had a daughter, christened Kathleen like me, born on 13 March 1925.

It was during this period that I had two lady visitors from the welfare call with clothes for the children and blankets and sheets for the bed. Later we became entitled to Salvation Army soup and bread, sometimes a meat dinner, but you had to be in the queue early or the food would be cold. To me at that time all this seemed like history repeating itself, and I could see no way that I could do what I wanted most which was to ensure a better future for my children. Charlie had lost his spirit and seemed content making the sawdust rounds for a few coppers a day, most of which went to finance his heavier and heavier drinking. It was enough to break your heart. We quarrelled often but the rows did no good and only increased the bad feeling. I threatened to leave him but then what would become of my babies? Charlie himself stayed out more and more and we seldom saw him, and then rarely sober. There was only one alternative for me. I would have to go back to work and hope that the children would be all right without me.

One day not long after Kathleen was born I was taking the children for a walk when I happened to spot what I'd been hoping for: a notice in a window that read, 'EXPERIENCED ENAMELLER WANTED, YOUNG AND MUST BE USED TO BADGES AND MOTOR-PLATES'. I could hardly believe it: it was just up my street. I left the two boys sucking a toffee apple on the step and, carrying the baby in my arms, I went in. The boss, a Mr Butler, looked me up and down and asked me how old I was. I told him twenty-three, though I was a year younger than that. He asked what experience I'd had and I told him that I'd worked at B. H. Collins, Frederic Street, and Joseph Fray's, Tenby Street North, but I didn't tell him about all the other jobs I'd had. He seemed satisfied with this and fetched out a motor-plate and asked me how I would enamel it. I showed him, and with that he said I could start the following Monday morning at thirty shillings per week. I couldn't get home quick enough to tell Mum the good news, and later that week I pawned my wedding ring and with the money I bought coal and extra food. Mum too was glad of the money I gave her for looking after the children while I was working, and Mr Butler was pleased with my workmanship and I received two increases in wages in consequence. I was able to save, after all was paid for, about five shillings a week, but I should have known that this was too good to last.

When I found out I was pregnant with Jeanette I was afraid to tell Charlie and I certainly didn't want any more babies. I couldn't adequately feed and clothe the children we had already, and in the absence of child benefit and family income supplement and the other support that the Welfare State provides, another child was simply another mouth to feed, reducing a family's ability to care for the children it had already. I was so desperate that many times I made up my mind to ask one of the neighbours to abort me, but fear rather than conscience prevented me – fear of what would become of little Charles, John and Kathleen if I should die. I knew of many young women who had died through trusting the ignorant old women of the neighbourhood to terminate their pregnancies. Abortion was also a crime, and prosecution would surely follow if you were found out.

The reader is probably asking at this point why Charlie and I hadn't taken precautions to prevent another pregnancy, and the answer is simple: I had no idea that contraception existed, nor did I until after my fifth child was born. It is not appreciated today when the pill is so universally available to young women such as I was then that the subject of sex was completely surrounded by ignorance, myth and misunderstanding throughout the working-class community. I cannot speak for those who were better off and better educated, but in our neighbourhood these things were never spoken of.

Despite the poverty-stricken circumstances of my early married life there were some happier moments. I remember Dad and Charlie spending many happy hours with the children when I was at work and Mum was too lazy to see to them. They organised games for the kids in our yard like 'kick the can' and 'tip cat' and if the weather was fine and windy Dad would make a kite from newspapers and take them all to the recreation ground in Goodman Street where they would take turns in flying it. I also remember young Charlie worrying us because he'd not got a ball to play with like the other boys at his school; he must have been five then, and he couldn't understand that we couldn't afford to buy him one. So one day his Dad brought him home a golf ball he'd found or been given. My son treasured that little white ball, even putting it under his pillow at night. Then one day the inevitable happened and it was kicked through the window of a nearby shop and we had to pay the proprietor half a crown we could ill afford. A crying match followed and eventually Charlie promised to get him a ball that would do no damage. How he managed this shows the lengths parents had to go to then to provide even the simplest toys for their children. One of Charlie's customers on his sawdust round was Knight's, the pork butcher, on the corner of Great Hampton Row and Tower Street, Hockley, and he asked the butcher there for a pig's bladder. What fun we had trying to inflate it! In the end we succeeded and Dad, Charlie and my two sons had many happy hours playing football with it in the yard.

Those were the good times, when I or one of the neighbours was able to play with Kathleen and the other little girls in the yard. We would hold the skipping rope for them or they would play at marbles or with their spinning-tops or else draw a grid with chalk on the bricks and play hopscotch, games that children of this present generation seem to have forgotten. The pig's bladder football was not to Mum's liking though. When she first saw young Charlie bring it indoors she exclaimed, 'I ain't 'avin' that stinkin', greasy thing in my 'ouse an' if I see it about it'll goo on the fire.' So to avoid his grandmother's wrath Charlie dropped it down the cellar grating at night before coming in to bed and then retrieved it to play with the next day. Until one afteroon when he returned from school and went down the cellar to fetch it and found it had gone: the rats had eaten it. There was another tearful scene before his Dad brought home another one. To avoid a similar fate Charlie hung this one high up on a nail outside the attic window where it was safe from the rats' gnawing teeth.

My fourth child, Jeanette Elizabeth, was born on 3 Septembe 1927 after I'd been rushed by ambulance to Dudley Road Hospital. There I experienced a proper childbirth with real medical attention and I was well looked after, even being given a bottle of stout every evening. This would give me strength while I was breastfeeding I was told. While I was there I was very concerned about my other children and received a reprimand from the matron for worrying. 'You'll lose your milk,' she warned me. She was right because when I returned home I found that the neighbours had each taken it in turns to look after them. We were all in the same boat and there was always help at hand if needed.

I was shocked to discover that Dad had been taken into the poorhouse on Western Road while I'd been away. As soon as I could I went there to see him. The workhouse was a forbidding-looking building and I shuddered as I walked through the heavy wrought-iron gates and across the cobbled yard. I was standing not knowing where to go when an old man in grey corduroy trousers and heavy boots approached me and asked who I was looking for. When I told him he led me into the building and up several flights of steep stone steps to the second floor. When I entered the ward and looked around I saw that it was filled with men of all ages lying on their beds in an eerie silence. They stared at me and looked so dispirited that I felt like bursting into tears. I searched down the ward for my Dad but couldn't see him. Then a male nurse came up and showed which bed he was in. When I reached his bedside I couldn't believe my eyes; he'd changed so much in the ten days since I had seen him last. He looked old and drawn and had a faraway look in his eyes, as if he was looking at something a long way away. I just broke down and wept; I was so shocked to see him like this. I took his hand which seemed pitifully thin and wasted in my own and kissed him.

'Dad,' I managed to say, 'it's me, Katie, I brought you some oranges and some twist.' But he didn't answer or move at all but continued to stare into space as if I wasn't there. The male nurse, seeing my distress, told me that he'd had a stroke, and as he led me away, still crying, I wondered if Dad knew what a terrible place he had come to.

I couldn't believe that my father would end his days in the poorhouse when he'd been good, honest and kind and had always worked hard when there were jobs to be had. I visited him several times but his condition didn't change. I have often wondered since if he was conscious of what was happening but had simply suffered a temporary paralysis. Either way, his suffering, if suffering it was, didn't last long and a few days later a policeman called at my mother's house with the news that Dad was dead. My mother began to wail and cry when she heard this, and soon a crowd of our neighbours had gathered round to offer their sympathies, but to me these were only crocodile tears and I couldn't believe she would mourn his loss long. Dad had always been my favourite. I loved him and came to rely on his kindness and sound advice and I never forgave my Mum all the pain and suffering she'd caused him over the years. After Dad's death she took to drinking more heavily, which she was able to do because she was receiving ten shillings a week widow's pension. As we laid Dad to rest I reflected on my own life: twenty-four years old, I'd seen nothing of life, only poverty and hardship, and it seemed to me then that I'd been born simply to breed. Yet I couldn't afford the luxury of self-pity for long; life had to continue and my four little ones had to be cared for.

By now both Charles and John were at school. I'd refused to send them to St Paul's School in Camden Drive, the school I'd gone to myself, but had insisted instead that they go to Nelson Street, off the Sandpits, where the school had a better reputation and I hoped they might get a better start in life than I had had. While I was at work and the boys at school, Mrs Taylor, my long-time friend, looked after the girls and we were able to cope sufficiently for me to cast aside the *Daily Mail* boots that were always blistering the children's feet and buy them ones that fitted properly. Again things were looking up for us – if only I didn't become pregnant again.

Each Saturday evening Mrs Taylor would look in – Mum was hardly ever at home any more – and when I'd put the children to bed she would keep an eye on them so that Charlie and I could go out together.

'If yer want me ter mind 'em, it's no trouble, as long as yer bring me back twopenn'orth o' snuff,' she would say.

I always cherished these Saturday nights when Charlie would embrace me and say, 'Get yer togs on, I'll tek yer out.' I knew well enough where we would be going. We would take a penny ride on the tram to the terminus at the top of Snow Hill, outside the railway station, now sadly demolished. Our first stop would be to buy a tuppenny bag of baked potatoes or roast chestnuts, then off we'd stroll, arm in arm, to the Bull Ring markets where we would haggle with the barrow boys for our fruit and vegetables or whatever we needed. Then when we had made our purchases we'd call in The Nelson where Charlie would have a pint of bitter and I would have a stout, sometimes two if we had the money to spare.

We had the house to ourselves more now as well, including the room downstairs. Mum was often away. She took trips to Gloucester, she said to visit relatives, but I knew of no relations there. However, I did not ask questions, being only too glad she was out of our way. I'd lost whatever interest I had had in her, and despised her for the drunkard she was turning into. When she'd collected her pension and our rent money she would disappear for days at a time. Things went more smoothly then. I even managed to save a few pounds without Charlie knowing. This was for a 'rainy day' or, perhaps, my dream – to get away from this bug-infested hovel I'd lived in all my life. I imagined being able to bring my children up properly, without their arses hanging out of their trousers and in a clean, tidy house in a pleasant district. But this was just not to be.

The next blow came just as things were beginning to look up for us. One Monday afternoon there was a knock at the door and there stood a policeman. He had come to break the news of my son Charles's death. Even now, nearly sixty years later, I cannot describe how I felt and feel about the loss of my eldest child. He'd been knocked down by a butcher's delivery van on his way home from school at lunchtime, and I never forgave myself for the foolishness of insisting on his going to that school in the Sandpits rather the close, safe school at the top of the Drive.

I was out of my mind with grief and guilt and although people were kind in their sympathy, nothing seemed to help. I kept breaking down and crying, and I suppose I had what today would be classed as a nervous breakdown but then was not understood as other than a mother's natural grief. People came from all over the district to his funeral but this simply made me worse. I couldn't face them without breaking down and I isolated myself from contact with people. I experienced frightening nightmares and refused to allow my children out of my sight lest something should happen to one of them too. I suppose I was trying to give them the protection that I felt in my misguided way I hadn't been able to give Charles. Looked at rationally I had nothing to reproach myself for, but logic is not what guides one's actions or thoughts in the state of shock following bereavement. Eventually, I had to send John back to school because the man from the school board threatened us with a summons if I didn't. Still I hid indoors with the girls, more mad than sane. Each time I looked out of the attic window and saw the old pig's bladder hanging there it started me off. Then one day it was no longer there. I asked Charlie what he'd done with it and he said he'd buried it next to our son's grave in Warstone Lane cemetery. Strangely enough, that act was like laying a ghost, because although I still grieved after that I began to pull myself together. I realised that I was making Charlie suffer, and the children whom I was neglecting, to indulge my own feelings. I still had a heavy heart but I determined to get on with life which did, after all, have to go on. I went back to work and resumed my role as the main support for my family.

Charlie was still out of work. He did have a few odd jobs but nothing permanent, and he continued with his sawdust round. In truth his health was not good. The doctor had warned him, but every penny he could lay his hands on he drank. He had spells when he drank less but often he came home raving and would fall asleep at the foot of the bed. I think he was probably just as upset about little Charlie as I was and his drinking was a form of escape for him.

This was how the first few years of married life went for me, hardly fulfilling the childish fantasies of a bright prosperous future that I'd cherished when Charlie and I had met that Christmas only a few short years before. Since then it had been a seemingly inevitable cycle of pregnancy, hard work, poverty and grief, but although, by today's standards, life for me was rough, it was no rougher than it was for thousands of other people like us in Birmingham in the 1920s.

The World Collapses Around Me

After my son's death I returned to work. I couldn't return to Butler's because my timekeeping was not up to standard, so I applied for a part-time job with a Mr Brain in Tenby Street North. He took me on at once and I joined his workforce, which consisted of his two elderly daughters. His workshop was an old converted redbrick house, and his business was enamelling the round, metal Union Jack badges for Standard cars.

After working there about a week I confided in one of the sisters that the job was getting me down because I had to rush home to breastfeed baby Jean. She must have mentioned it to her father because Mr Brain told me that if I still wanted the job I could bring the baby along and feed her during my working hours. Creches are by no means a normal facility today and then they were unheard of, but this arrangement suited me perfectly; John was at school, so Mum had only Katie to take care of.

I borrowed a pram from a neighbour and was then able to push Jean to work and leave her in the pram in the entry beside the workshop. I could work and listen for Jean's cries to tell me she was ready for her feed. The sisters were kindness itself to me. Each day they would bring a little something in the grocery line for me to take home for the other children. Often they would change Jean for me if she was wet. And thus by such little kindnesses they made working life bearable and at the same time I was able to provide food and clothing for my family. I was even able to supplement my earnings by making toffee apples and selling them to the children as they came out of school. I sold them two a penny and every penny I earned I had to spend. It was useless trying to save anything now Charlie was drinking more heavily and contributing next to nothing to the family income. Mum was boozing more too and causing more

335

quarrels as a result. I survived by closing my eyes and ears to what was happening and concentrating all my attention on the children and their needs.

It was too good to last, I knew, and sure enough one morning I arrived at work to find Mr Brain alone, packing his tools into a tea chest. I was too horrified to speak when in response to my shocked enquiry as to what he was doing he told me was being forced to close because of lack of orders. I stayed to help him pack his things away. Then he handed me my insurance card and three days' pay that was owing. He did say that if he should start up in business again I would be the first to know, but this was scant consolation to me now that I was out of a job again and penury was staring us in the face. There was no alternative: I would have to apply for relief again. Mum suggested we take in washing and ironing and I agreed since there was no other way of earning money. This arrangement was doomed, of course. After two weeks she demanded a larger share of what little we were able to earn and we quarrelled.

'Well, they're my tubs an' mangle, an' coal, yower usin',' she insisted.

After that the situation quickly deteriorated. Her constant nagging got on my nerves and the strain began to tell. One night it finally became too much for me to cope with any longer and I almost did a terrible thing.

I washed the children as usual and put them to bed. Katie and Johnny slept between Charlie and me. I could not bear him near when he was drunk, which he was every night now, and we had not made love for nearly a year. Jean's bed was a makeshift one in the wardrobe drawer. This particular night she wouldn't stop crying for me to feed her, but my milk was drying up and she got little satisfaction from my breast. Then as I was putting her back in her drawer cot, Mum began banging on the ceiling with a broom.

'Stop that babby cryin'. I want ter get some sleep!' she bawled.

'I'm doin' me best,' I shouted back from the top of the stairs.

'About time yow got 'er a dummy,' came the reply.

I'd never used a dummy because I'd seen too many little children drop them in the filth and then pick them up and put them back into their mouths. It was no wonder to me that so many children died of gastric diseases, diphtheria and the like. I returned to try to comfort Jeannie without resorting to a dummy but then the broom banged again. At that moment something snapped inside me. I flung my baby into the drawer and kicked it shut before collapsing on the bed exhausted. It must have been several minutes before I'd calmed down sufficiently to realise what I'd done. I jumped up and pulled the drawer out. It was just in time; another few minutes and she would have suffocated. I took her in my arms and wept. I could have fallen asleep and let her die. I might have been hung for murder, I thought, and thanked the Lord that I'd come to my senses.

I tried one more trick to quieten my wailing baby. I smeared condensed milk thickly over my nipple and gave her that, and for a wonder it worked. She lay contentedly sucking the empty breast and I thought with great relief that Mum could bang the ceiling as much as she liked; Jeannie was safe and if she cried we would both have to put up with it.

The next morning I went to see the doctor, Doctor Mackenzie, who had a front-room surgery in Arthur Place. His manner was abrupt but he could be kind and he listened sympathetically while I told him what had happened.

'How old are you?' he asked when I had finished.

'Twenty-four,' I told him.

'And how many children have you got?' he asked.

'Three now, doctor,'

'Any miscarriages?'

'Two.' Both had been brought on by doing heavy presswork.

After asking several more questions he gave me a bottle of 'Parish's Food' and told me to take two teaspoonsful at night and to return to see him in a week's time. I found that his prescription seemed to do me good and that I experienced a good night's sleep for a change. I must confess that I also put a teaspoonful in Jeannie's milk bottle and she seemed to thrive on it; so did Katie and Johnny. But instead of the medicine lasting a week it was gone in two days. It was like a drug: I wanted more. So I went back to the doctor and lied.

'You again,' he snapped when I entered the surgery. 'I said a week's time.'

'I'm sorry doctor. I had an accident and the bottle broke.'

'Very well, try not to break this one.' He handed me another bottle.

I went easier with that bottle and when I visited him again he gave me a panel note. This meant that I could draw sick pay, which wasn't much but enabled us to manage better with the little my husband was bringing in. It might be enough to tide me over until I was strong enough to work again. The rules about entitlement to sick pay were strict. You had to be indoors when the visitor called, otherwise your benefit would be stopped. You could only draw sick pay for six week; after that you had to submit to a means test and see the doctor again. When he re-examined me the doctor wrote out a letter.

'I want you to take this letter to 161 Corporation Street and have your chest X-rayed,' he told me as he wrote. This alarmed me.

'What's the matter with me chest?' I asked tentatively. 'Have I got consumption?'

'Nothing to be scared about. This is only routine and in the meantime I want you to take this medicine.'

I was hoping for some more Parish's Food but no such luck. I took the other stuff as directed, but two days later I developed a cough so decided to do as I had been instructed and go to be X-rayed. It was a bitterly cold morning as I readied myself to make the journey into the city centre. Mum and Charlie were out and I was glad I didn't have to tell them where I was going. Mrs Taylor agreed to look after Katie and Johnny and I wrapped Jeannie in my thread-bare shawl and hugged her to me; then off I went on the two-mile walk into town. When I arrived at Corporation Street I was exhausted and I flopped down on the dirty wooden stairs to catch my breath. As I sat there Jeannie began to cry and I wished that I had brought some condensed milk with me. There was only one thing for me to do to quieten her cries. I unbuttoned my blouse and took out my breast, praying that she would find enough milk there to satisfy her. She tried her best, dear little thing. Then I happened to look up and found a small, well-dressed man gazing down at me. I felt a rush of embarrassment and fumbled to cover my nakedness but he put his hand gently on my shoulder.

'Dont cover yourself, mother. You both make a lovely picture.' And with that he pressed a ten-shilling note into my hand before he walked past me up the staircase. I could scarcely believe my good fortune; that money was a godsend. All thought of the X-ray vanished and I set off for home to buy some food. I made my first mistake by telling Mrs Taylor of my luck.

'That's all right dearie, yow goo an' get yerselves summat ter eat an' collect yer kids when yer get back.' I thanked her and asked if I could get her anything for looking after the children. 'Yer can get me twopenn'orth o' snuff,' was the predictable reply.

I bought sugar, tea, bacon, lard, bread, some stewing steak and milk for the baby. I still had change and I slipped it into my purse, which I carried between my breasts. I returned and spread my purchases out on the table, then I put Jeannie in her makeshift bed and went for Katie and Johnny. I went into the yard to find Mrs Taylor gossiping with some other old women. I ignored them and gave Mrs Taylor her snuff, and as I did so I noticed the others looking down their noses at me. I had nothing to be ashamed of although I could imagine how they would be speculating about how I got my ten shillings. I left Katie and Johnny with the other kids playing in the yard and went in to prepare a meal. I was so happy that afternoon that I even sang a tune as I waited for the kettle to boil. Just then Mum came bustling in. She looked in amazement at the food laid out on the table.

'Where yer got all this grub from?' she asked and I gladly told her.

'Yer a liar,' she exclaimed before I had hardly finished.

'It's the truth, Mum,' I protested.

'Men don't give yer ten bob fer just lookin' at yer breast,' she sneered. 'Yer sure yer dain't let 'im feel yer up a bit?' she asked slyly. That did it. I flared up in a fury at her suggestion.

'Yer disgustin'! Men don't bother me that way. I've got enough with Charlie. I ain't Liza yer know', I yelled at her.

'Yow leave Liza outa this!' she bawled at the top of her voice. 'An' close that bloody dower. I don't want all the neighbours ter 'ear!' I had touched a sensitive nerve because Liza had always been her favourite; in all the years I'd lived under her domination I'd never found the courage to retaliate until that moment. I had bottled my resentment up but now I let the cork out and my temper with it. Funnily enough, now that I had plucked up courage to speak my mind I felt no inhibitions whatsoever.

'No! I won't shut "the bloody dower" as you call it. Let the neighbours 'ear a few home truths for a change!' I had my dander up now all right.

Suddenly she lurched at me as if to strike me.

'Yow dare!' I screamed, grabbing the iron saucepan from the

table. 'I'll bash yer brains out with this!' She could see that I meant it so she walked deliberately round the table and kicked the door to.

'Nosey lotta bastards!' she yelled through the closed door.

'One o' these days yer'll get summonsed fer yer language,' I told her.

''Ave yer finished?' She spoke more softly, sitting down on a chair.

'No! You've never loved me. Even before I was born yer never wanted me.' I was going to speak my mind now I'd started.

'Yer don't know what yo'er talkin' about,' she said, poking the fire with her back to me.

'I've bottled all yer secrets up fer years because I didn't want ter 'urt Dad while 'e was alive but now I'm goin' ter tell yer this. I know all about the 'ot baths you had an' the pikey pills and penny royal you took ter get rid of me.'

'That's a lie!' She shifted round to face me. 'Yer don't know nuthin',' she screamed.

'They're not lies. Mary told me when I was first married. You tried ter get rid of me an' you gave Mary the money ter give ter Mrs Taylor to get you all sorts of concoctions. My sister was only nine years old then an' she 'ad ter look after Jack an' Charlie an' the twins that died.'

''Ave yer done yet?' She subsided and resumed poking the ashes in the grate.

I continued with a few more home truths but I kept my distance because I wouldn't have put it past her to throw the poker at me.

'Mary told me the whole thing. I know Dad came home and found you in the bath with Mrs Taylor helping, and when he started to knock you about Mrs Taylor went for the police. He ran off an' didn't come back for a week.'

'Yer sister's got a lot ter answer for when I see 'er agen,' she yelled.

'I didn't want to talk about all this but now I 'ave I feel better. An' if you start on me again I'll let the neighbours know about how you an' Jack stole that pig!' I retorted. Then, just as she started up from the chair, Charlie walked in.

''Ave yer finished, you two?' he asked irritably.

'It's 'er,' Mum exclaimed.

'It's not all 'er Ma, I've 'eard every word,' he told her.

'Yoo bin listenin' at the dower then?' she asked sarcastically.

'I couldn't 'elp listenin'. I had to stand at the dower ter keep the neighbours from 'earin' what was goin' on.'

I started crying while he was speaking. I was drained by the effort of all this arguing.

'Wipe yer eyes luv an' collect up that food. We'll cook ours upstairs. I'll fetch the kids.'

I still hoped Mum and I could settle our differences and I turned on the stair and spoke to her.

'I'm sorry I 'ad to tell yer these things but yer asked for it.' But she just shrugged.

As I pottered about in the attic it occurred to me how like Mum I'd sounded when I lost my temper and I shuddered to think that I might become like her as I grew older. I just sat down and wept until I heard the children on the stairs. Then I pulled myself together and wiped my eyes. While I busied myself laying the table, Charlie lit the fire. As I waited for the kettle to boil I watched Charlie playing with the children on the floor. Katie had my old straw-filled golliwog, Topsey, that was made for me by Granny when I was a child. As she was doing so Charlie spoke to her.

'Katie, Daddy's goin' ter buy yer a real dolly one o' these days an' some lead soldiers for Johnny.'

I couldn't believe his thoughtlessness.

'There yow go again!' I flared up. 'Promising them things yow can't afford.'

'But we will when I start work tomorra,' he said smiling. I could hardly believe my ears as he added, 'I start at a factory an' there's a regular job if I keep good time. An' believe me, Katie, I'll keep it this time.'

I threw myself round his neck and as I kissed him I realised that it had been so long since I had done this that I'd almost forgotten how to do it. I couldn't remember being so happy as I was that teatime with a full table, my children, my husband and the prospect of a brighter tomorrow. Then when I'd put the children to bed and tucked Jeannie up in her drawer I sat down next to Charlie by the fire. He asked what we'd been quarrelling about and I told him about the ten-bob note.

'I already 'eard that,' he spoke softly.

'But you don't think I'd let a man do that to me, do yer?' I asked.

'No luv, but if it'd been Liza I would 'ave.' He chuckled. I had to stick up for my sister though, despite the fact that we didn't get on.

'Mum's to blame there. Liza'd have been a better woman today if

341

Mum hadn't encouraged her in her wicked ways.'

'Well we won't talk about 'er. What I want ter know is, what's this about a pig?'

I satisfied his curiosity and told him about Jack stealing the pig and Mum and the hop-pickers and the comical court proceedings. He burst into laughter and so did I, for we could both see the funny side of the story.

'An' when did all this 'appen?' he asked.

'Oh, years ago when I was a small girl. Now come on, take yer shirt off so I can wash an' dry it for the morning.'

I felt so happy washing that shirt and putting it in front of the fire to dry. I was that pleased Charlie had a job and things seemed suddenly much brighter, like a black cloud had lifted. I turned down the lamp, undressed and lay in my place at the foot of the bed. Charlie lay down beside me and took me in his arms and we made love; the first time we had in twelve months.

Mum and I seldom spoke in the months after our showdown, but I didn't mind. I was happy being a housewife, looking after my husband and children. I no longer had to go and humiliate myself before pompous relief officers. With Charlie earning full wages I could pick and choose when I went to the shops. I bought second-hand woollens, unravelled them and knitted them up into clothes for the kids. They looked like Joseph's many-coloured coat. John was attending St Paul's school at the top of Legge Lane where I had gone myself. Katie went to Nelson Street school and I had more time to myself, and for a few brief months everything seemed rosy. I breathed a sigh of relief and thanked God for my blessings. Life, however, had taught me that it was just when things were going well that disaster struck. Existence was at the best of times precarious, and people like us never crossed our bridges before we came to them.

I was not so much surprised as resigned when Charlie was put on short time. I knew what I had to do. The two eldest were at school and Charlie could look after Jeannie while I went out to work. It had to be a part-time job that fitted in with with my husband's hours, but luckily I found one at Canning's jam factory. My job was topping and tailing gooseberries, and sometimes sorting out the over-ripe strawberries. Unfortunately the job lasted no more than a month. I was sacked for helping myself to the fruit. I suppose I should have expected this, but the kids loved them.

Troubles do not come singly and no sooner had I lost my job than Charlie, whose health had never been good, was brought home from work ill. Then I thought the bottom had fallen out of my world. I helped him up to bed and sent for the doctor. He took one look at Charlie and ordered him to go to Dudley Road Hospital. Charlie wouldn't hear of this and he prevailed upon the doctor to give him some medicine. He got his medicine but the doctor warned him that if he became worse he must send for him immediately.

The few shillings of savings we had soon dwindled away, but I refused to go on relief again and concentrated on nursing Charlie back to health. My efforts were rewarded. After a month he recovered sufficiently to return to work. He couldn't keep good time though, and soon he was given the sack. He went downhill after that. His spirit was being sapped away. He was irritable with the children and snapped at me. I used to take them on long walks and often visited my brother Frankie and his wife, Nellie, who were very kind to me. They had their own problems though, and I didn't like imposing on their generosity. I dreaded returning home, knowing that I would find Charlie raving drunk or snoring on the bed.

I had no choice. I had to get a job if Charlie could not or would not. I was fortunate I suppose. At least I was skilled enough to find work; there were plenty who were not. I was taken on at B. H. Collins in Frederic Street and I was happy there, enamelling metal badges of all kinds. We were able to survive and if I didn't see much of my family at least I was able to put food on the table.

Each Friday night after we'd been paid for the week the girls I worked with went for a drink in The Rose Villa, a local pub. They were forever urging me to join them and couldn't understand why I always refused. I was tempted but I couldn't spare the money I would spend on drink. Then one Friday Harry from the toolshop repeated the offer.

'Why don't yer stay an' 'ave one? 'It'll doo yer no 'arm,' he said, laughing.

'It's not the drink I'm worried about 'Arry,' I told him. 'It's my 'usband. If my 'usband comes home drunk and finds I'm not there, I don't know 'what will 'appen. Anyway,' I added, 'I have three children to see to.'

'Just 'ave the one then, it'll do yer good,' he persisted.

And I relented: where was the harm in just one drink, I thought.

I joined them that payday and had a glass of stout before leaving. My mistake was making a habit of it. I went regularly and never thought that it was close enough to home for Charlie to get wind of it. He did and the next Friday night was waiting for me.

'So it's drinkin' in The Rose Villa now, is it? And with a married man as well!' He shouted so all the neighbours would hear. I tried to explain but he began raving, saying I'd been whoring, and he hit me several times. I don't know what he would have done if Mrs Taylor hadn't come running up the stairs to rescue me. When she appeared Charlie stamped off, still ranting.

I gave the job up. I was too ashamed to go back with my face bruised and my eyes blacked. Charlie was sorry when he'd sobered up; he promised to give up the drink, and he did for a time. He did his best to make it up to me and was kindness itself. I softened and forgave him that and other things.

I found another job the following week but this time it was not so pleasant. I was swinging a heavy press and it was heavy, dirty work, but the money was twice as good as I'd been getting. Now Charlie came to meet me from work and we walked home with the children. He was no healthier, however, and often complained about stomach pains. The doctor gave him tablets and they seemed to ease his pain for a while.

It was during this time that I noticed an advertisement in a shop window for a 'strong man to mend packing cases' at Gaunt & Sons, Warstone Parade. I was on my way to Frankie and Nellie's with the children and I hurried on my way. I was determined to get that job for Charlie, even if I had to beg. Strong man or not he needed a job and I had worked for this firm myself when I was sixteen. I left the children with their aunt and uncle and went along to inquire about the job and go down on my knees if necessary. I arrived breathless and pressed the bell hoping that the job hadn't already been taken. I didn't have to wait long. The forewoman I had known years before appeared. She recognised me at once.

'I seem to remember you, don't I? Didn't you work here before?'

'Yes, years ago. I'm married now, with a family,' I replied.

'Yes, I remember you. Your name was Katie Greenhill, wasn't it?' Nothing had ever escaped her beady eye. 'Well, if it's a job you've come for I'd be glad ter start yer,' she began, but I interrupted her.

'I'm sorry, Mrs Lane, it's not for me; I've come about the job for my husband,' I said in a rush. She looked surprised. 'Carn't 'e come 'imself?' she asked suspiciously, but I assured her.

'No, he's not, er, at home at the moment.' I nearly said he wasn't well, which would have lost him any chance of the job.

'Very well, you wait here an' I'll 'ave a word with Mr Booth. I'll do me best but remember, Katie, if you ever want a job yourself come an' see me.' With that she went away and I prayed she would succeed on her errand.

A minute or two later Mr Booth the manager appeared and asked how old my husband was and if he was strong.

'Oh yes, he's very strong,' I replied eagerly. I had to lie if he was to get the job.

'Very well, tell 'im to come and see me straight away, before five o'clock, and I'll see if he's suitable.' And with that he turned and went back into the workshop. I didn't wait around but made haste home, without collecting the children, I was so eager for Charlie to get that job. I fell into the kitchen and found Charlie talking to Mum.

'Charlie, I got you a job at Gaunt's, in the packing shop. You've got ter go an' see Mr Booth at once,' I told him, full of excitement. He didn't believe me at first until I'd spelled out the details.

'Now hurry yerself, before he changes his mind!' I was frantic at his apparent lack of concern. However, he had a quick shave and made himself presentable and went off without so much as a 'thank you' or a kiss.

'Come straight back an let me know 'ow you get on,' I shouted as he rushed out.

I returned for the children and after putting them to bed waited hours for Charlie to return with the news. I imagined all sorts of things had happened to him as it got later and later and still no sign of him. It was eleven o'clock when he eventually rolled in, drunk as a lord.

'I gotta start in the mornin',' he managed to say before I exploded with anger.

'An' a nice state you'll be in in the mornin'! An' where did yer get the money from for the drink?'

'I borrad it from me brother an' we've bin 'avin' a little celebration,' he mumbled.

'It's a pity 'e can't lend yer some food instead o' that lunatic soup you've bin drinkin.' I was furious by now.

I turned away in disgust as he fumbled to undress himself. Then he tried to put his arms round me and I pushed him away in a fury: I was not having him mauling me.

'Stay there yer drunken beast!' I screamed, pushing him over onto the foot of the bed where he collapsed in a heap and forthwith started snoring. I stood watching him sinking into his stupor then was about to go downstairs when I stopped and reflected that the last thing I wanted at that moment was a superior lecture from Mum so I returned to the bedroom. I was so bitter. He had to be up at seven o'clock in the morning and he had just selfishly gone out drinking with money he had yet to earn instead of thinking of me and the kids. Where would all this end, I thought, as I stripped off his shirt. I washed it and hung it over the chair to dry, then I undressed myself and lay down at the opposite end of the bed and hugged Katie and Johnny until I fell into a fitful sleep.

The next morning I was afraid to look at the foot of the bed in case he was still there but he must have got up early and left without disturbing us. He did keep the job for a few weeks too, and even brought part of his wages home to me but the rest he spent on drink. We quarrelled often and I refused to sleep with him.

'Yow'll be sorry one o' these days,' I remember Mum saying. ''E'll find another woman who will sleep with 'im,' she told me.

''E can sleep with a dozen bloody women! I don't care any more, as long as 'e brings 'is wages home instead of boozing 'em away!' I rounded on her.

Nevertheless we were both working now and I was able to put a little aside each week for the inevitable rainy day. And there were happier times. If Charlie was off the drink he could be very good company and although the first flush of love had passed long since we would go out together some Saturday nights visiting our old haunts around the Bull Ring markets. Mum even brightened up now she was receiving more rent money. Then a few months later I discovered that I was pregnant again and I was horrified. I didn't want another baby just as we were beginning to get on our feet. We still had no real home and were sleeping five in a bed. It was too much. I prayed to God for a miscarriage: an abortion was out of the question. I had to carry on for the children's sakes and couldn't risk anything that drastic. I continued working as long as I could but I knew that after the baby was born we would be back to square one and probably end up on parish relief again. I was more determined than ever that I would have no more children after this and that I would work as hard as I could to get us a place of our own, although I knew how difficult this would be when no landlord wanted to rent rooms to a couple with so many children.

As this pregnancy progressed Charlie became steadily more ill. I didn't appreciate it because he slept at the foot of the bed and I hadn't noticed how much stomach pain he suffered. Then one afternoon in April 1931 I became ill at work and two of the girls had to bring me home. We arrived to find Charlie being put into an ambulance and being rushed off to hospital. He'd been under the doctor and taking pills he had prescribed for about two weeks, but apparently one of the ignorant neighbours had tried an old wives' treatment on him that day. This consisted of putting a hot salt bag on his stomach and it had made him much worse. The doctor was called and after reprimanding the neighbour he'd sent for the ambulance.

When I heard from a neighbour what was happening I rushed upstairs just in time to see Charlie being laid on a stretcher. He was unconscious. With that I fainted and the next thing I remember was coming round to find that my labour had started. Mum and a friend of hers called Gert did what they could to make me comfortable and then went to call an ambulance to take me to Dudley Road Hospital where I had registered previously to have my baby. My pains were coming very fast by now and the ambulance was cancelled. I could hear the children downstairs crying for their Daddy and I felt totally lost.

Then Gert Wilcox stepped into the breach. She said she would take the children for a few days and come back later to see how I was. So she took them off to play with her kids and left Mum to look after me. I shall never forget that woman's kindness to me in that time of need. She lived nearby in Pope Street and her husband Harry, who was an old friend of Dad's, was a barman at The George and Dragon. She was 'a busy little body', always bustling about, cleaning and tidying. She always wore a starched white apron and although she was not a qualified midwife she was the next best thing. I decided to place my trust in her when she returned to help me. She'd telephoned the Hallam Street Hospital in West Bromwich where Charlie had been taken and they had told her he was comfortable. This eased my worries a bit but I was still in labour and experiencing very painful contractions. I didn't want this baby and that made it worse. Without doubt this was the most difficult birth I had ever undergone. I thought at one stage I was going to die and have never been so frightened in my whole life as I was then. I prayed that the child would be stillborn and that my mother or Gert would take it away and bury it somewhere, but that changed when it had been born and I'd seen Gert hold it up by the feet and slap it into life. When I heard those yells I knew my baby was alive and I breathed a sigh of relief.

'You've got a luvly baby daughter, Katie, and sure enough she's got a good pair of lungs,' she said smiling. She was as exhausted as I was and Mum had to do the tidying up. Gert washed the baby and put her on my breast. Then I knew she was here to stay. She was such a pretty little thing, with a mop of black hair, and as she sucked my breast I hugged her to me and thought how proud Charlie would have been to see her. But he never did see his daughter: three days later the news came that Charlie had passed away. That was 25 April 1931, our tenth wedding anniversary.

Thus, at the age of twenty-eight, I was left a widow with four young children to bring up now that Mary, two months premature, had arrived. I prayed for the Lord's guidance before and after Charlie's funeral. I had absolutely no idea how I would cope now. I wouldn't have had enough money for the funeral without my maternity money and the collection that the kind neighbours took up for me. I had no money and was too weak physically and emotionally to work. I applied for a widow's pension but was turned down because Charlie hadn't had enough insurance stamps for me to be eligible.

It seemed and still seems very cruel to me that I was forced back on the parish. There was, it goes without saying, no child allowance or supplementary benefit in those days. The good old days they may have been for some, but for me and plenty like me they were not good. It was pitiful to see the men and boys of all ages walking the streets looking for work or hanging around the yards idling away their time. Mum had had only her pension since Dad died and most of that went on drink. Now she said, 'If they won't pay yer a pension then the parish'll 'ave ter keep us.' So I went along to the Gospel Hall in Hockley Street where I had to queue outside for over an hour before being called in to state my case. I shall not forget easily the two stern-faced women who sat behind the table looking down their noses at everyone. While I waited to plead my case I remembered Mum's saying, 'God 'elps them as 'elps themselves but God's good but the devil ain't amiss'. I thought of the time I had considered gassing myself and the children but had had no money for the meter. I was sure that if I was refused help again I would start stealing or do something desperate. Then my name was called and I had to make myself humble. While I explained our plight to one of the women the other one shuffled through files.

'So you've had another child since you were here last?' She spoke coldly.

'Yes,' I replied, 'an' I've lost my husband too.'

'Have you applied for a pension?' she asked.

'I have but my application was turned down.'

'Turned down?' she asked in obvious disbelief. Then fixing me with her cold, emotionless eye she continued, 'But you say you were married or weren't you?'

'Of course I was,' I snapped. I explained the situation about the lack of insurance stamps and she wrote it all down.

'I see. So, you have four children and you are living with your mother? I see she is on our files too.'

'I 'aven't come about me mother,' I said, becoming angry. 'I've come for food for me children.' My impatience was showing now.

'I don't want any insolence. You sit over there and wait. I'll call you when we're ready.' She indicated a seat next to an old woman.

'That's tellin' 'er, but yer wanta watchit, luv, with that one or yow'l get nuthink,' she whispered to me.

I was past caring. I gazed blankly round the room at the drabs, old and young alike, resignedly waiting for their handouts. Then I silently said a prayer that if God gave me my strength back I would do something better for my children than sitting here being humiliated. Then I was called back to the table to be told they were sending a visitor to conduct a means test.

'But I'm desperate now! I want food for my children,' I insisted.

'You heard what she said,' the other woman chimed in. 'We can't give you anything until the visitor has called.' Then as I stood there dumbfounded, the other woman whispered, 'Some of these women shouldn't have children.'

'Are you married?' I demanded, losing my temper. 'No, I suppose you're a couple of old maids,' I continued when I received no reply. 'It looks as if it would do yer good ter 'ave a few ter keep yer occupied.' I turned and stamped out of the hall amid audible titters from the other women.

The visitor didn't call for two weeks, which I suppose was their way of punishing me for daring to speak out. In the meantime I'd pawned everything I had left of any value to buy food. Then when that was gone I went back to the relief office and threatened to leave my kids there with them if they didn't help me. There was a man there that time and he was more sympathetic. He asked me to sit quietly and he said he would try to help. Down came the files and we went through the same rigmarole again. It was all I could do to manage the children while I waited. Then he called me into an office. There he asked me about all the details of where Charlie had worked and about his illnesses and after he'd written every little detail down he eventually gave me a ration card to take to Baker's, the grocers. I thanked him. I was so happy to be getting anything. He told me to call once a week for food vouchers and in the meantime he said he would see about my pension although he couldn't promise anything. I thanked him again and told him I had every intention of starting back to work as soon as I was well enough. I might have saved my gratitude because when I found out what my ration was I discovered that it didn't amount to enough to feed me, let alone the children.

I wouldn't have survived at all if I hadn't taken the risk of trying to earn a few extra pennies doing odd jobs. I went into business making ginger pop for the kids. I worked with a neighbour, but after all the washing of bottles it was hardly worth it. Then I took in washing, but it was hopeless trying to get into the brewhouse because every day was somebody's washday. So when I heard about a job cleaning at Cullis's pawnshop I decided to investigate it.

I pushed the two youngest in a borrowed pram and set off. I went to the rear entrance and gave a girl who was hanging about a penny to look after the babies. I saw Mr Cullis in the back room where he lived and slept. It was filthy but I couldn't afford to turn my nose up at the money. It took me over an hour to scrub clean those bare old boards. When I told him the job was done he said I could clean the shop window. Before starting I popped out to see if the children were all right and found them fast asleep. Relieved, I fetched a bucket of soapy water and wet and dry rags and set to work. When I'd finished to my satisfaction I asked Mr Cullis when he wanted me again.

'Ye've done a very good job but I won't want it done agen for a long time now, so I'll let yer know.' And with that he handed me two shillings. I was livid and threw the bucket, dirty water and all, across the counter.

'Yer can do yer own cleanin' in future! Yer bloody skinny old Jew!' I shouted before leaving. As I stepped into the street I noticed an old woman collecting horse manure from the road with a bucket and shovel. I felt very inclined to daub that horseshit over his bright clean windows, but it was just as well I resisted the temptation because he would undoubtedly have called the police.

When I got back to the yard I couldn't find Johnny anywhere. I was beginning to become worried when I spotted a policeman bringing him down the yard.

'What's 'e bin up to now?' I asked, half scared and half angry.

'I found 'im beggin' outside the factory gates an' I'm warnin' yoo now, if this 'appens again I'll 'ave ter take 'im ter the station.'

By now I was surrounded by our nosey neighbours and all I could do was meekly say 'I'm sorry'. I could see Johnny was frightened too; he had filled his trousers so I didn't scold him when I got him indoors. I scrubbed him in the bath and sent him off to bed without his comic.

'Oh God,' I moaned to myself as I was washing his soiled trousers through. 'Where is this all goin' to end?' I was desperate, friendless and almost at my wits' end. In the weeks that followed I tried my best to make ends meet and even asked my sister Mary if she would take one of the children until I could get back on my feet. But she'd hardened since her second marriage.

'Sorry Kate, but I've got me own three. Anyway, me and Bill are thinking of selling up and going to try our luck in America.' That was that. It was a similar story when I went to Jack.

'Rosie's mother's livin' with us now an' we ain't got the room,' he said.

'But it's only for a few weeks while I get a job,' I pleaded but to no effect. I got nothing from him but a promise to try to help later; I saw neither hide nor hair of him for years after that.

Suicide was not far from my thoughts during that period, and I also considered becoming a prostitute. But I was too shy to talk to a stranger let alone lift up my frock for one. After all, I'd never undressed in front of Charlie even. I'd always insisted on blowing the candle out before going to bed. Charlie used to laugh at me but I didn't change my ways.

Then I was lucky enough to get a job cleaning at The George and Dragon. I had to start at six o'clock in the morning and work an hour lighting fires and scrubbing the bar. The ten bob the publican paid for this was very useful and the time was perfect for me. I could creep out before the children were awake and be back to get them off to school. I tried to keep this job quiet and told no one at all about it. The publican was well pleased with my work and gave me a cup of tea as well as bread and cheese and a bottle of stout to take home. It made me sad when I scrubbed that step. It was the same step I had sat on with my bum freezing while I waited for Dad to call for me to sing for the customers.

I might have realised that luck like this could not last. One morning when I'd finished the landlord called me into the smoke room.

'Mrs Flood, I've bin told you're on parish relief,' he began. 'Is this true?'

'Yes,' I admitted. It was no good lying.

'You should 'ave told me. I'm sorry, but I'll 'ave ter let yer go. We'll both be in serious trouble if they find out. But if you sign off, I'll take yer on again with pleasure.'

'I carn't do that,' I answered tearfully. 'What little they give and what I earn 'ere is the least we need. I'll 'ave ter find something else.'

I tidied away the brooms and brushes and was about to leave when he appeared with a parcel of bread and cheese and a bottle of stout as usual. I almost refused to take them but I thought twice. I could not afford pride in those days if it meant cutting off my nose to spite my face. I took the gifts and thanked him and he slipped a pound note in my apron pocket.

'I'm sorry,' he murmured as I opened the door to leave.

I realised that it was pointless trying to get a job on the quiet; there were plenty of wagging tongues to give the game away. However, I decided to try anyway. What could I do? I wasn't fit enough to work, and with four young children and no husband I couldn't have held down a full-time job. So it was back to chopping and selling firewood, and I found myself plodding round the streets till late at night touting my wares for a few pence.

Mum had a new drinking partner now. Her name was Bridget and she was short, fat and had three chins and beady eyes like boot buttons. She was Irish and very patriotic. She wore a long bright green dress, a green ribbon in her hair and usually sported a sprig of shamrock. This was her normal attire whether it was St Patrick's day or not, and when she'd had a few drinks she would sing the songs of her fathers. I remember her calling for Mum one evening at about this time.

As soon as they'd left I washed and fed the baby who was a few months old now and no longer being breastfed. She was another mouth to feed but I'm afraid the best I could do to fill it was to feed her stale crusts boiled to a mush with condensed milk. I made things easier for myself by lining her rag nappies with tissue paper before putting her down for the night in her drawer. I'd just done this and got Katie and Johnny to bed when Liza breezed in. She was the wild one in the family, was Liza. Although married with two children she was always gallivanting out to pubs and dance halls. Her men friends changed with the wind. As soon as I looked at her I could see she was out on the town.

Liza would have been a good-looker if she'd left the warpaint alone. She wouldn't have it though. She even shaved her eyebrows and pencilled them in with a thin line. She'd dyed her hair so many times it was multi-coloured.

'Where's Mum?' were her first words.

'Gone out with that Bridget woman,' I snapped. We'd never been close, now less than ever.

'Oh all right,' she snapped back, 'I'll find 'em. An' if Al asks yer if yow've seen me, tell 'im I'm workin' over,' she added.

'I'm not tellin' lies for yow. 'E'll find out in any case,' I shouted after her as she disappeared into the yard with a shrug of her shoulders. Albert was a good, hard-working man and I felt sorry for him. But that didn't prevent me thinking how foolish he was to close his eyes and ears to what was going on. He was used to coming home from work and seeing to the children but I wondered why he didn't put his foot down with Liza. Despite what Liza had said, though, he was the last person I expected to call, so I was surprised when he walked in not long after my sister had left. I greeted him and offered him a cup of tea.

'No thanks Kate. I thought Betty' (he always called her that) 'might be here.'

'The kettle's boiled, it won't take long,' I stuttered, not knowing how to answer him.

'No thanks all the same, Kate. I carn't stay but if Betty calls, tell 'er I've put the kiddies to bed an' she'll find me at me mother's. Goodnight Kate.' So saying, he left.

I must have dozed off after that because the next thing I remember is the door slamming and my looking up to see Mum, Bridget, Liza and a scruffy-looking individual Liza called Joe. They were predictably drunk.

Bridget began to sing 'Danny Boy' and I shushed her because the children were asleep. At that Mum flared up.

''Er can sing when 'er like. Oo's bloody 'ouse is it anyway?' she demanded. I didn't reply; I knew it was useless arguing with her. I turned instead to Liza.

'Albert's been 'ere for yow,' I informed her coldly.

''Ow long ago was that?' she asked, apparently unconcerned.

'Just after yer left.' To which she replied, 'I'd betta be goin' Mum. It's gettin' late. Yow comin' Bridget?' She didn't seem so cool now.

'Ah, twas a foine night we've 'ad Polly, but what about 'im?' she said, nodding at the still silent Joe.

'Yer betta goo with Liza, Bridget. I'll see ter Joe. 'E's missed the last tram an' it's rainin' now anyway.' I could see that the Irish woman was reluctant to leave but Liza took her arm and steered her out into the night, slamming the door behind her.

'An' where do yer think 'e's gooin' ter sleep?' I demanded when they'd gone.

'I'll mek 'im up a bed in my room.' I could guess what that meant. With that Joe heaved himself off the wooden sofa he was sprawled on and flopped in Dad's armchair. That was the final straw as far as I was concerned.

'Get yer bloody arse out of my Dad's chair. Yow ain't fit ter be 'ere,' I stormed, but he was either too stupid or too drunk to reply. Mum was neither, more's the pity.

'Yer forgettin' this is my 'ouse an' I'll 'ave ooever I want 'ere!' she bawled.

I knew argument was useless so I gathered up the children's clothes and went up to the attic to finish drying them by my small grate. I undressed and got into bed with the children and thought in despair of the pretty pass we'd come to. I wondered what Dad or Charlie would have done if they'd been alive. Next morning I knocked on Mum's door with her usual cup of tea but there was no answer, so I pushed the door open and to my surprise found the bed empty. In fact it hadn't been slept in at all and was just as I'd made it the previous afternoon. Mum didn't put in an appearance until the following day.

I didn't dare question her about where she'd been but I did wish sometimes that she would do a moonlight flit and never come back. People in the area often did a flit to avoid paying their rent arrears and the sight of chattels being loaded onto a handcart was not out of the ordinary. I would dearly have loved to leave the hovel we shared with Mum but there was no point simply moving to a similar house, and the idea of living in a better house in a pleasant district was a pipedream. I wanted above all to give the children a decent upbringing away from all the bad influences around them. They were always in and out of the neighbours' houses and came home repeating the bad language they'd heard. I hated having to correct them and it was a vain task trying to counter the combined force of the circumstances of our lives. Some children had been taken into homes and I came to believe that this was the best thing for them. Many times I'd considered allowing my own children to go into a home but I lacked the courage to go through with it, and as long as I could continue selling firewood we existed. I still hadn't notified the parish about this sideline but each week as I collected our ration I became more nervous.

Eventually the day of reckoning arrived. The visitor called one morning and told me I had to go to the office at once. I was terrified of what they would do to me but I had to go; if I didn't they would send someone to fetch me. When I arrived at the church hall I found there were several others there with equally worried expressions on their faces. I waited to be called to stand in front of the long wooden table behind which the inquisitors were seated. Finally my name was called and my heart sank to my boots.

'Come along, we have something to ask you.' The harsh voice echoed in the large hall and I crept slowly towards the speaker who sat there, hard faced and threatening. I have never felt so utterly humiliated and ashamed and defeated.

'It has come to our notice that you have been selling fire-wood,' the woman said loudly so that all could hear, and she wagged her finger at me so there could be no doubt to whom she was addressing her remarks.

'Yes,' I almost whispered, too scared to lie.

'And you haven't declared your earnings have you?' She did not look at me but glared round the room at the others. 'You know we can prosecute you for this deception, don't you?'

Then something inside me snapped and I forgot my fear in my frustration and anger.

'Earnings? You call it earnings! Sellin' a few sticks of fire-wood! What you lot dish out 'ere isn't enough to keep a sparra alive!' I shrieked at her.

'Stand back there, we'll deal with you later,' she said reddening, indicating with an irritated gesture that I was to move to the back of the queue. But I was not budging. I was determined to say my piece now I'd summoned up the courage.

'You stand back there an' beg for crumbs an' see 'ow yow feel! Anybody'd think it was your money that paid for our chickenfeed! We're entitled to it an' a good deal more!' By now all eyes were on me and you could have heard a pin drop when I stopped, breathless.

'You'd better leave now,' she hissed, suppressing her obvious fury, 'or, I'll call the police.' But she could not outface me that easily.

'Yow can send for the whole bleedin' police force, yer bloody ol' cow!' There were murmurs of agreement from amongst the audience. Then a young man left his place in the queue and, taking my arm, led me outside.

'I'm glad you spoke up for all of us. I'd have liked to back you up but I've got my own family ter think about an' I can't afford to offend them,' he said gently.

'Neither can I but I'm glad now I've got that off me chest,' I replied.

Then I turned and walked slowly away from that miserable place. It was only then when I had calmed down that I realised what I'd said and done, and when I returned home I sat on the sofa and wept bitterly. I expected little sympathy from Mum and I got none.

'I warned yer they'd find out! Now what yer gooin' ter do?' she snapped after I'd told her about my confrontation at the relief office.

'I'm goin' ter do the best I can,' I said defiantly and went upstairs out of her way, but when I was in the bedroom I collapsed on the bed and realised how hopeless our situation was. And it was then that I decided to send the children to the only place where they would be well fed and cared for. I would put them into a home before they were taken from me, which they would be if I was sent to prison. I fretted and cried sleeplessly all that night and the next morning made my final decision. I went down to Mum's bedroom to tell her of my intentions, but her bed was unslept in so after I'd sent John and Kathleen to school, I called on Mrs Taylor to keep an eye on Jean and Mary while I went off to make the necessary arrangements. I had to confide in someone so, trusting her to say nothing, I told her of my intention to put the children into a home.

'I promise I won't say a word, but are yer sure yer want ter do this, Kate?' she asked.

'Yes, my mind is made up, Mrs Taylor.' I began to sob. 'I may 'ave ter go ter prison for what I've done an' I can't leave the kids not knowing where they'll be. I love them too much.'

'But whatever'll yer Mum say when she finds out?'

'I'm not tellin' 'er till it's done. In any case, she'll probably not be back for a few days an' by then we'll be gone.'

'Mary, Mother of God!' she gasped, crossing herself. 'Whatever's goin' ter become of us all?' she wailed. I left her in this state to look after the children and went to get it over with.

It was a cold, wet morning and although I had pieces of cardboard in my shoes my feet were still frozen. I pulled my coat closer round me and made my way to the tram stop. I walked along in a trance, still not finally decided. In my heart of hearts I knew there was no other course for me. I was in a corner from which there was no escape. We would get no more parish relief, I couldn't take a job without neglecting the children and I couldn't earn enough from the firewood to feed and clothe them. I knew where to go, and without being really conscious of how I got there I found myself outside the gates of the Dr Barnardo's home in Moseley Village, which was almost in the country then but has now been swallowed up by Birmingham.

Nervously I knocked at the door, which was opened almost at once by a middle-aged, kindly looking woman who had on a long grey dress covered by a white starched apron with a matching bonnet on her head.

I was too choked with emotion to speak but she put me at my ease and said she was the matron as she showed me into a large room and indicated that I could warm myself by the fire. The room we were in was almost bare: just four leather chairs and a large oak table laden with cakes, jam, bread and butter. In a corner stood a bookcase with books and ledgers. The floor was bare but brightly polished and above the fireplace was a large portrait of an elderly gentleman who I guessed was Dr Barnardo. As I looked up at this picture she spoke.

'Would you like a cup of tea, my dear?'

'Yes please,' I murmured. She offered me a cake but although I was hungry I couldn't have eaten a thing. I was overwhelmed by emotion and on the verge of tears. We sat on chairs, or at least I perched on the edge, and tried to explain why I'd come. After I'd completed my tale of woe I could see by the look on her face that it wasn't going to be plain sailing.

'I don't know whether we can help you. This is only a home for orphans,' she said quietly.

'But I must find somewhere for them, matron. It's only for a short time, till I get work an' find a proper home.'

'Well, perhaps if you tell me all about yourself we can do something to help.'

So saying, she reached for a large sheet of paper and began to note down everything I told her about myself from the time of my marriage. After this she offered me another cup of tea and told me she would send two visitors round the next day. As I was about to leave she asked if I'd walked from Birmingham and when I told her I had walked part of the way she pressed a half crown into my hand.

'I shouldn't do this,' she said, 'but maybe it will help.' I would have kissed that matron if I'd dared. I thanked her profusely as she showed me to the door. As I walked down the gravel path I could hear the sound of children's laughter.

I boarded the tram, tired and hungry, and as soon as I alighted I headed for the first butcher's shop where I bought sixpenn'orth of stewing steak. I spent the rest of the money on vegetables, bread, margarine, tea, sugar, jam, a tin of Nestlé's milk and a few rusks for Mary instead of her usual sop. I busied myself preparing the meal until the children came home from school. I had to keep active to take my mind off my troubles. That day we had a meat dinner for a change and Mrs Taylor joined us. After the children had returned to school I put Mary to sleep on the sofa, and while Jeannie played in the yard Mrs Taylor and I set to work to scrub and clean the attic ready for the visitors' inspection the following day. I was glad Mum wasn't about because it would have been 'don't move that', 'leave that there', and 'I want my things where I can lay me 'ands on 'em'. When we'd finished, Mrs Taylor left.

A little later there was a loud knock on the door and when I peered through the curtain I saw a tall man and a woman standing there. My first thought was that it was the police come for me. I didn't know whether to hide or not, so I called out that Mum was out.

'We haven't come to see your mother. We've come to see you, Mrs Flood. We're from Dr Barnardo's,' the man's voice replied. I opened the door slowly to let them in and as I glanced round the yard I noticed the neighbours' nosy faces peering out of their windows.

'I'm Mrs Flood but the matron said I wouldn't have any visitors till tomorrow.'

'Yes, but the matron thought we had better call as soon as possible. May we look around and see the children?' the woman answered my question.

I picked Mary up off the sofa and hugged her to me and managed to say, choked with emotion, 'This is my baby; Jeannie is playing in the yard, and John and Kathleen haven't come home from school yet.' They inspected my two youngest and then went up to inspect the attic. Then they asked me all the same questions that I had already answered for the matron. Finally the woman asked if I really wanted to let the children go into the home.

'No, of course I don't, but there's no alternative for me, is there? We're living 'ere with my mother who don't really want us, we've no money for food, an' all I've got is what I earn sellin' firewood,' I answered in exasperation.

'Are you sure you can't get help from the parish?' the man asked again.

'Not now. They're goin' to prosecute me for not tellin' them I'd bin sellin' firewood,' I explained patiently. 'An' now if you refuse ter 'elp us I might end up doin' something desperate.'

'I'm sorry to have upset you, Mrs Flood. If you bring the children to the home tomorrow we can talk some more and make the necessary arrangements,' he said.

A weak 'thank you' was all I could say as I showed them out. Then as soon as they'd gone I collected all the children's clothes which, although well worn, I was determined would be clean. While I was hanging them on the line across the yard, Mrs Phillips came over to speak to me.

'I see yow 'ad a couple o' visitors, Kate. An' I can see yer 'avin' a good wash day' she said, inviting a reply.

'Yes!' I snapped at her. 'Do yer good, an' some o' yer kids, if yer'd do the same.' As she turned to go indoors I called after her, 'Yer nosy old sod.' She slammed her door and I continued with my task, wondering when I would wash my children's clothes again. I knew Mrs Phillips would tell Mum what I'd said and I hoped that we'd be gone by the time she returned. That night I gave the children a good wash ready for the morning.

'But Mum,' Johnny said when I fetched in the zinc bath, 'it ain't Friday night.'

'No, I know, but yer 'avin' a bath tonight anyway.'

'But why?' He was like all small boys, reluctant where washing was concerned.

'I'll tell yer in the mornin'.' I could hardly speak, I was on the verge of tears.

'But why carn't yer tell me now?' he persisted.

'All right I'll tell yer later then. Now get in that bath before the water's cold. An' don't ask questions.'

I helped him give himself a good scrub, then he took himself up to bed. Later when I went up to turn in, Jeannie was asleep but Katie and Johnny were sitting up waiting for me to read them the 'funnies' from the newspaper. I thought to myself, this is as good a time as any, so I steeled myself to get my secret off my chest. I settled down to explain where I was going to take them the next day. I didn't know where to begin until Johnny spoke.

'Mum, what yer tryin' ter tell us?'

'Well,' I began, 'you and Katie aren't goin' ter school tomorra, I'm takin' yer on a kind of holiday to a place where where there's lots of trees and flowers and a big lawn ter play on with other little children. There's a kind lady there too who'll look after yer an' give you cakes and nice things to eat.' I struggled to make it sound inviting but I really had no idea what life in the Barnardo homes was like; all I had to go on was their reputation and the few brief impressions of my visit.

'Are yoo comin' too?' they chorused.

'Yes, I'm takin' yer in the mornin' but then I'll 'ave ter leave yer but I'll come an' visit yer and bring yer treats ter eat too.' I soothed them as well as I could. 'Now lie down an' I'll read the funnies.' But as I tried to read to them I had to turn my face away to hide my tears. Bless them, they didn't seem to notice or to question that they were going on holiday but simply accepted what I had told them and soon they were fast asleep. Then I kissed their cheeks and tucked them in. I busied myself putting the bath away and eventually went back upstairs, undressed and climbed into bed beside them and quietly cried myself to sleep.

The children were up bright and early next morning, excited at the unexpected prospect of going on a long tram ride and having a holiday from school. I dressed them in their clean rags and after a breakfast of porridge we started on our journey.

The trams in those days had two long wooden benches facing each other on which the passengers sat. When we got on, there were only three vacant seats so I had to sit down with Mary and Jeannie on my lap. The people on the opposite seat seemed to stare at us as if they knew where I was taking the children. On the next tram it was the same. I imagined they must be thinking what a heartless mother I was to be parting with my children in this way, but I put these thoughts out of my mind with the thought that it would be for the best in the long run and at least the children were enjoying the ride, even if I was not.

When we arrived at the home the matron was ready waiting for us with warm milk for the little ones and a cup of hot cocoa for me. Then she sent the children out to play while she talked to me. She said they'd decided to take the children into the protection of the home until such time as I was in better circumstances and was able to provide a better home for them. When I thought that this time had come I would be visited by their inspectors who would, if they saw fit, recommend that I could have my children back. I remember thanking the matron and promising that I would work night and day to get back on my feet, and I really meant it. But I had no idea then how long this would take or how difficult it would be to get your children away from Dr Barnardo's once you had allowed them to take your children.

When we had talked for a while the matron got up and showed me through a glass door which led onto a large lawn where I could see Johnny and Katie playing and laughing with the other children. They didn't notice me; they were too absorbed in their game to see me standing there, but as I watched them I began to feel easier in my mind, seeing them settled down so quickly to their new surroundings. So despite my continued reluctance to part with them I was happier thinking that they were in good hands and would be well cared for until I reclaimed them. How they felt when it dawned on them that this was their home I do not know, but I can imagine. I hoped then and later that they wouldn't feel that they'd been abandoned by their mother, and indeed I was determined to visit them every Saturday afternoon as the matron had informed me I could. She also told me to tell the home immediately I had a change of address, and with that I thanked her and she called the children over for us to say our 'goodbyes'. I was choked with emotion and sorrow when I kissed them but they didn't seem to notice and ran off, eager to rejoin their new chums.

I returned in a trance to my mother's house, overwhelmed by feelings of loss and loneliness. Just how much I'd given up I realised when I went into the kitchen, empty now with no grubby little faces to greet me and none to greet for I had no idea how many months or years. It was then that I knew how lonely and single minded would be the furrow I must plough if I was to achieve my goal, a goal I was determined to reach at any sacrifice.

'Oh God, what 'ave I done ter deserve this?' I moaned selfpityingly, hunched in Dad's old armchair, but the mood passed and I pulled myself together. I must get away from this unlucky house and my mother as soon as possible, I thought. The warning from the parish inquisitors about setting the law on me was also in my mind. Suddenly I was galvanised into action. I crammed a few clothes into a shopping bag and went downstairs to leave, vowing that I would never return. I closed the door behind me and looked round the yard for what I thought was the last time.

These were the familiar sights and sounds of my entire lifetime, stretching back to before I could remember anything, but I was not sorry to be cutting myself off from them. All my troubles resulted from this poverty and degradation. Anything would be better than this. I saw the twin three-year old daughters of a neighbour sitting on a cold, wet step, frocks up over their knees so you could see they had no underclothes on and sucking grubby dummies. There were other girls and boys fighting and swearing while their mothers gossiped, oblivious. I was sad but also angry to think that these young drabs were fellow creatures who'd been worn out by the struggle, day in, day out, year in, year out, simply to survive in the web of penury and squalor that had trapped them. Chin up, I thought. You're young and still healthy and with luck and hard work you can make a better future for yourself and the children. As I struggled with my wordly possessions up the hill I was thankful that the Lord had given me the strength to go through with my resolve.

I might have known that I wouldn't escape so lightly. My mother must have heard on the grapevine about what I had done because as I neared the corner I heard her shout, 'Katie', in her too-familiar bray and I turned to see her and several neighbours bearing down on me.

'Yer oughta be ashamed o' yerself,' she started, 'tekin' me gran'chillun away. An' where d'yer think yer gooin' now?' She could see what I had in the bag.

'Away from this unlucky hole! An' yoo! An' I ain't ever comin' back either!' I yelled, near to tears.

'Yow'll be back, yow'll see,' she said triumphantly, looking around at her cronies for support; I didn't answer her. Instead I went on my way, but I could hear them muttering about how I was 'a terrible woman', 'the wust woman in the district', for putting my children into a home. It mattered not to them that I couldn't properly care for them. As far as they were concerned any kind of inadequate dragging up was better than allowing your children to be taken care of in an institution. I hurried away tearfully, cursing them for their ignorant prejudice and me for the terrible fortune fate had dealt me.

There was only one person in the whole world I could turn to now: my brother Frank. And, bless their memory, he and his wife Nellie welcomed me with open arms when I reached their door. I broke down and wept bitter tears as I tried to tell them what I'd done but they comforted me and told me I needn't explain to them. They understood, and in any case Mum had been there already. Nellie put her arm round me and sat me by the fire to warm up, and soon I had a cup of tea in my hand and we talked while she prepared the supper. I had no appetite for food but I drank two cups of tea. Then Frankie came back in and asked me why I'd let the children go and I found myself trying to explain again, but he cut me short.

'Yoo know if yer'd asked Nellie an' me, we'd 'ave taken two of 'em until yer got back on yer feet,' he said with regret in his voice.

'No, Frank, it wouldn't 'ave worked out. Yow an' Nellie 'ave enough on yer plate, what with two daughters an' another babby on the way. An' yoo on short time as well. No, I couldn't think of that.' I didn't want him to feel hurt that I hadn't turned to him in my hour of need.

My Struggles Really Begin

Next morning I came down to find Nellie, Frank and my two nieces sitting down to Sunday breakfast.

'We thought we'd let yer sleep in a bit longer, Kate,' Nellie greeted me.

'Thanks, Nellie,' was all I could bring myself to say although I was grateful for the extra rest: the last few days had been exhausting and now the immediate pressure was off, fatigue had hit me. I pulled a chair up to the table and joined them. When I saw the delicious-smelling bacon, egg and tomatoes on the plate I realised how hungry I was as well, and I tucked in with a will. I hadn't eaten for nearly two days.

'Thanks Nellie, this is really good of yer,' I thanked her between mouthfuls.

After breakfast was over and the breakfast crocks cleared away I gave Nellie a hand with the housework. While I was busy sweeping and dusting I found myself glancing up at my brother sitting in his armchair, smoking his pipe. It was then that it dawned on me how very like our father he was and tears welled up into my eyes.

A little later when the girls had left for Sunday school Frank asked me what I planned to do and where I was going to go.

'I'm gooin' ter look for a job first, Frank. Then I'll have ter look for lodgin's,' I replied. His immediate response was to ask me if I had any money. I had to admit that apart from the list of names I had no more than a few pence.

'But I'll 'ave ter let that goo, Frank. I can't face them people any more.' At that he jumped up.

'Yoo give me that book, I'll soon get it for yer,' he volunteered.

I was in two minds but I still went upstairs and brought it down for him. I handed it to him and after a quick glance he donned his cap and jacket and was off with a cheery 'see yer soon'. And, as good as his word, he was back in hour or two and, with the exception of a handful, they'd all paid up. When we counted it all up we found I was better off by over two pounds. My first thought was to offer to pay them for the food I was eating but Nellie wouldn't hear of it and told me to put it in my pocket. She looked offended.

'Yow don't 'ave ter pay us for anything. Me and Frankie'd loike ter 'elp yer more but yer know times are bad an' we ain't got much but while yer under ower roof yer welcome ter share what we've got,' Nellie said firmly.

'Thank yer both, very much. I've got ter find a job an' a place so's I can get the children back,' I replied.

'Well, yer welcome ter stay 'ere till yer find summat suitable,' Frank assured me.

When I thought it over I was grateful to stay where I was wanted although I decided that I couldn't let my brother give up his bed for me. I told him I would swap and take the sofa. Although he was on short time, on the days he was working he had to be up at five in the morning before leaving for a ten-hour day in the brass-casting shop where he worked. He needed his sleep and in any case I had no intention of letting the grass grow under my feet now my mind was made up. I wanted to get away from the district with its myriad of mostly sad memories. I confided my plans to Nellie in case she thought I wasn't grateful for their help and she understood my feelings perfectly. So it was decided that my stay with them would be as short as possible.

Escaping completely from the Jewellery Quarter was of course impossible. I would keep clear of the Camden Street area but this was the only place I knew, and more important the only place I could find work as an enameller. I was soon out tramping about on the lookout for something. I could have returned to Collins's in Frederic Street but I was well known to all the girls there and I didn't want to have explain to them what I had done. They would have been sympathetic, of that I had no doubt, but it was sympathy I could do without: I wanted to put that behind me and square up to the task I'd set myself. In any case, it was too near the streets I wanted to avoid.

After I'd been walking for what seemed like hours, I spotted a notice in the window of Canning's for 'a young woman to work press', and I hurried in to inquire how long the notice had been there. The lad who was serving said it had just gone in, and hearing that I dashed to the address he'd given me as quickly as I could in case anybody had got there before me. When I arrived at the factory in Vittoria Street I spoke through the trap to the boss, a Mr Gibbons, who told me that the job was still vacant. He asked me my name and age and then, asking me to wait, went to fetch the foreman who turned out to be a pleasant little fellow named Bingham.

'Well,' he said, looking me up and down, 'you don't look strong enough to work a press.'

'Oh, but I am,' I told him eagerly, 'I've worked a hand press before.'

'All right, if yer like ter give it a try, the wages are two pounds ten shillings a week, eight o'clock till six, an' one o'clock Saturday. Bring yer unemployment card and your insurance card an' yer can start next Monday.'

'But that's a week away. Could I start tomorra? I need the money, yer see.'

After a pause he said, 'Very well. Don't forget eight o'clock in the mornin'.'

I ran nearly all the way to Frank's to tell them the good news. They were as pleased as I was, and had also found me lodgings with a middle-aged widow who lived in Warstone Lane. Frank told me her name was Knight and the rent was a pound a week for my bed, which turned out to be poor, and my food. I moved into Mrs Knight's as soon as I could and started work at the foundry. During this period I was able to begin to sort myself out. I saved some money and got myself some new second-hand clothes. I treated myself to a hairdo as well: a Marcel wave which was all the rage then. The hair was curled tightly to the head with heated irons which waved the hair like corrugated cardboard.

Despite my change of fortune the job on the press was getting me down: I still aspired to something better, and when I asked the boss for a change he put me on an even heavier job. On that I had to use both hands and duck each time I swung the press handle round otherwise it would have laid me out. The grease and oil got in my hair and on my clothes and each night when I returned to my digs I had to have a thorough wash down. By the time I'd followed this with my supper I was too exhausted to do anything but drag myself off to bed.

Further up Vittoria Street, however, was an enamelling firm, J. A. Butler's, and when I saw they were advertising for learners and experienced girls I gave my notice at the brass foundry and went to work there. This time I was determined to learn everything there was to know about the business and complete my training. The job was a vast improvement on my previous one: it was clean work and so was the workshop, and after working there only a few days I went onto piecework and was able to earn four to five pounds a week with all the overtime I did. Naively I thought that if I could keep this up for a few weeks I would soon have saved enough to be able to afford to rent a house, buy some second-hand furniture and have the children back with me. At that stage I had still to discover how tenaciously Dr Barnardo's clung on to your children once they had their claws in them.

When my wages improved I offered Mrs Knight another five shillings a week, but she didn't need it because she'd taken in a gentleman lodger since I had taken up residence with her. Still, I made her accept it. I kept out of the way of the man and avoided meeting him, but one night when I returned he was already seated at the table eating his supper.

'This is Fred,' Mrs Knight introduced us, 'he's come fer a few weeks.'

'Good evening.' I greeted him formally and shook his hand. He turned out to be a rather nice-looking fellow, dressed in a dark suit, clean white shirt and dark blue tie. His dark, thick hair was brushed back from his open face and I noticed what a personable manner he had.

'So you're Katie. Very pleased ter meet you.' He spoke gently and all through supper I could hardly keep my eyes off him, but when he looked up and caught me looking at him I became embarrassed and, making excuses, left him talking to the landlady and went off to my bedroom to write a letter to the children.

A few days after this he asked me if he could take me to the pictures.

'Make a nice change for yer Katie, instead of stayin' up in yer room each night,' he said persuasively, but I was too tired to go anywhere and refused his offer. 'Some other night then, Katie?' he replied, taking my refusal well. 'Perhaps I will, one night,' I assured him, and after thinking it over on the tram to visit the children I made up my mind to accept his offer.

We went to the cinema, and after dropped in at The Vine in arver Street for a drink. He was quite the gentleman and showed me the sort of consideration I had not experienced for years, and when we got to our digs he wished me 'good night' with not so much as an attempt to kiss me. Although he was kind, he was also persistent, and took it for granted that I would go out with him again. When I refused he told me he would like to be more than a friend. I knew what he meant but feigned obtuseness, but then he came out with it and asked me to marry him.

'I'm sorry Fred,' I replied with difficulty, 'I like you very much but marriage no.'

'Well, at least say yer'll sleep on it an' think it over,' he insisted and held my hands tightly so that I couldn't turn away from him.

'I will Fred, but now let go of my hands an' I'll give yer my answer in the mornin'. Good night,' I added as I made my way up to bed. But I had no intention of reconsidering: my mind was made up. I was glad the landlady was out when I came downstairs the following day. I could face him alone and give him my answer.

'Good mornin' Kate,' he said, advancing towards me eagerly. 'Have you considered my proposal, dear?'

'Yes, I have Fred, and I'm afraid I don't want ter marry again. All I want ter do now is ter work 'ard an' get a home of me own,' I said firmly.

'You will, dear, if yer'll marry me, an' if yer want, I'll even take yer away from 'ere as soon as yer like.' He pleaded, trying to put his arm round me, but I brushed him aside.

'No. I won't go without my children. Anyway, if I did marry yer an' we went away I'd be startin' another family an' I don't want marriage or any more kids.' I began to weep and although he tried to comfort me I pushed him gently away and told him as well as I could between sobs, 'No, Fred, that's my final answer.'

I was relieved when at that moment the landlady walked into the room and I was saved from further difficult explanations. She wanted to know why I was upset, of course, but I left Fred to tell her and sat down to recover myself.

'Well, Katie, yer could doo worse,' was her first reaction. This was more than I could stand and I went straight up to my room without saying a word and waited for him to go out. I kept out of their way until I returned from work the following evening to find Mrs Knight in tears. When I inquired what was wrong she turned on me.

'He's gone!' she yelled.

'Who's gone?' I asked, perplexed at her behaviour, which was normally so polite.

'Fred, who do yer think? 'E's taken 'is clothes an' left. I put 'is supper in the oven an' while I was out he must 'ave took 'is things an' gone,' she wailed, upset more about her reduced income than anything else as far as I could see.

'Maybe 'e'll come in later an' explain,' I ventured weakly but I could sense that she blamed me for this unexpected turn of events. I had no desire to argue with her, so I washed and changed and took a walk to visit Frank and Nellie. I talked things over with them and Nellie advised, 'Yer know yer own mind best. Yer an attractive young woman but I know yer'll be careful.' I stayed a while with them, then wished them 'good night' and returned to my lodgings. When I got to the step the door opened and Mrs Knight dragged me inside and slammed the door.

'That bugger was married! An' 'is wife's lookin' for 'im fer maintenance!' she gasped breathlessly.

'Who?' I was thoroughly confused.

'That plausible bugger Fred, that's who!'

'How do yer know?' I could not believe this.

'The police 'ave bin 'ere asking questions. I knew he sounded too good ter be true,' she said, as if she'd known all along that her lodger was a conman. To me it was a complete shock when I realised how close I had been to being duped.

'Come an' sit down, Kate, an' I'll get 'is supper outta the oven. It'll still be all right an' we can 'ave a double 'elpin'. Open that bottla stout an' we'll 'ave that an all.'

I could think of nothing to say. I was still getting used to the idea of Fred being a total fraud and an attempted bigamist to boot.

'Yow was lucky to turn 'im down,' Mrs Knight confided in me when we sat down to our supper.

'Yes, an' ter think I might 'ave weakened when you said, "yer could do worse",' I said, mimicking her, and we both burst out laughing and continued until our sides hurt. When we'd calmed

1. Kate's mother (seated) and eldest sister Mary (standing right) with Mary's daughter and baby granddaughter in 1932

2. Kate's brother Jack (seated far left) in the army in 1914

3. Kate's father (standing fourth from right) outside the 'George and Dragon', Albion Street, 1921

4. Kate's brother Charles holding her first born son, Camden Street, 1922

5. Kathleen Dayus in 1933

6. The Bull Ring was, and still remains after recent redevelopment, the market where Brummies go for a bargain. This shows the view from the High Street looking towards St Martin's-in-the-Bull-Ring as it was in 1895, with the market stalls in the shadow of the church.

7. The heart of Joseph Chamberlain's remodelling of Birmingham was the Council House, seen on the left here. Colemore Row which stretches into the distance was cut through an area of poor housing and its inhabitants moved into areas like that Kate grew up in, immediately to the north and west.

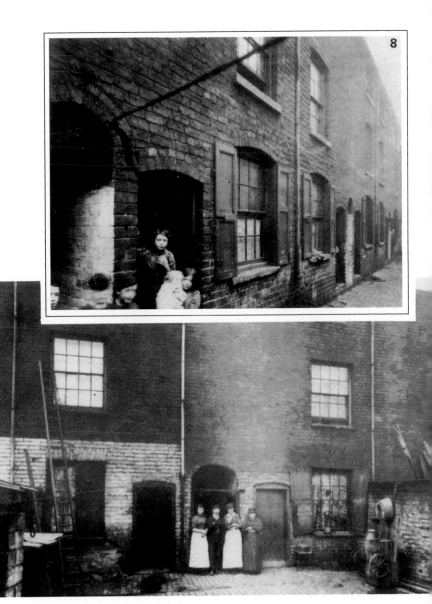

8

8. Number 1 Court, Camden Drive was identical in every respect to Number 4 Court where Kate's family lived. Five three-floor, three-room back-to-back houses faced the communal toilets and wash houses, across the brick yard.

9. This court at the rear of Holland Street was typical of thousands in the densely-populated central wards. The galvanised iron bath hangs on a hook and the milk churn and barrow suggest that the family had a small milk round.

 10

 11

10. The ground floor living room of a court house like Kate's. The sparse furnishings, small ornaments and pictures over the range are just as the author describes her own house. Ironically, this was probably taken to illustrate how a 'respectable' working-class family might live; few would have been able to aspire to this level of luxury.

11. Black Country hop-pickers at Little Witley, Herefordshire, in 1896. The photograph captures both the community spirit and holiday atmosphere of working excursions like those taken by Kate's family into the countryside.

12. & 13. These ragged, bare foot 'children of the poor' were photographed on an outing by the charitable Cinderella Club to Sutton Coldfield Park. Like Kate, they can have had few opportunities of a good meal or a sight of the countryside.

14. Two women in the Flower Market, one of Birmingham's central markets not far from the Bull Ring, photographed in 1900.

15. Whenever a Victorian or Edwardian photographer set up his cumbersome tripod a crowd of curious onlookers gathered to enjoy the experience of being photographed although they can rarely have seen the results. Here such a group of children and shop assistants are gathered outside shops in Great Hampton Street, one of the main thoroughfares which bounded the area of slums and workshops where Kate's family lived (1901).

16. Surprisingly few photographs of Birmingham's metal-working trades have survived. This one of brass bed-stead makers taken in 1905 shows the cramped work space and laborious nature of the job.

17. St Paul's churchyard, seen here at the end of the nineteenth century, was the 'titty-bottle park' of Kate's childhood. The church was designed by the Wolverhampton architect Roger Eykyn in 1777 when St Paul's Square was the fashionable home of merchants and manufacturers. However, long before Kate knew it, the area had declined socially and the houses had been converted to small jewellers' workshops, which they remain to this day.

down sufficiently she said she'd try to get a proper gentleman lodger next and at that point I decided that before that happened I too would leave for a quieter berth.

The same weekend I began answering adverts for rooms but they were all too expensive; some landladies wanted almost as much per week as I was earning. However, I was determined not to admit defeat but to keep on until I found some respectable digs in a better class of area than I was living in in the Jewellery Quarter.

Finally I found what I was looking for in the small-ads columns of the local evening paper, the *Evening Mail*. It was a notice for 'a young respectable woman' and the address was Soho Road, Handsworth. Handsworth was then a solidly middle-class district of quiet streets of large terraced houses. The houses had double bay windows and neat little gardens and it was a pleasure to walk along the streets. Unfortunately, this is no longer the case today and the area has steadily slid downhill and the appearance of the place has suffered, although I noticed recently that the urban renewal schemes have improved some of the streets. Be that as it may, it was a pleasant area when I first went there, *Evening Mail* clutched in hand, to find lodgings. I found the house and from its size and appearance I anticipated another disappointment, but since I'd walked all the way there I decided to inquire anyway; so I lifted the brass knocker and waited for my knocks to be answered.

I waited for several minutes but, becoming impatient, I eventually turned to walk away. It was then that I heard a woman's voice behind me say, 'Did you knock, dear?' When I turned round I found myself facing a neatly dressed middle-aged woman. She wore a white blouse, long black shirt and had pearl drop earrings in each ear, with a matching string of pearls around her neck. She was slim and about five foot six in height, and although she was an imposing figure she had a pleasant smile on her face. 'Y-yes', was all I managed to say in reply.

As she opened the door wider I saw how highly polished the hall was and caught sight of the richly patterned carpet. My heart sank: I was not going to ask about the room because I knew I'd be disappointed.

'I'm sorry, I must have come to the wrong house,' I apologised, but I noticed her eyes light on my newspaper.

'Have you come about the room?' she asked, and I had to admit that I had. 'But I'm afraid it'll be more than I can afford.' But she put me at ease immediately and brushed aside my protests and I agreed to look at the room, more out of curiosity than any serious hope that I would be able to take it. I followed my hostess into a beautiful room she called 'the parlour'.

'Sit down by the fire, dear, and I'll put the kettle on. Then while we're having a cup of tea I'll tell you about the room and you can decide if you want to see it or not.'

'Thank you,' I replied, making myself comfortable in a chair by the fireplace. When she'd gone to the kitchen I looked at the wonderful things the room contained. The round table was covered with a lace tablecloth. On it were three china cups and saucers – not the odd crocks I was used to at Mrs Knight's – places to match, a cut-glass jam dish and a cakestand laden with homemade scones. Against the wall stood a large oak dresser with several shelves full of china dishes and plates and glassware of every description. Against the opposite wall was a highly polished leather couch which matched four high-backed chairs. Around the fireplace were a low brass fireguard, brass fender, brass fire irons and a small bellows, all of which shone as if they'd just been polished. On the mantel stood silver-framed photographs. The whole room was spotlessly clean and all in all I was extremely impressed, never having set foot in such a palace of a house before. I was still trying to take it all in when the lady of the house returned with the tea. I made a mental note that I would have a room like this myself when I'd sorted my affairs out. Then I took the proffered cup of tea and in answer to her question told the lady my name was Mrs Flood.

'Oh,' she said, 'but I didn't see you wearing a wedding ring. I thought you were single.'

'I'm a widow,' I replied.

'Do you have any children?' was her next question.

I hesitated before answering, but I could see no harm in telling her, particularly since I wouldn't be taking the room in any case. She looked disappointed when I told her I had four children and said she was sorry that she had no room for them. This annoyed me. I was still very upset about their fate and I flew off the handle.

'I didn't ask yer to!' I made to get up, tears welling into my eyes. 'I only wanted the room for myself until I can get a home of my own and have them with me,' I blurted out.

'I'm sorry, I didn't mean to upset you, dear. Now sit down and have another cup of tea.' And while I drank my second cup I told her a bit of my story. Then I noticed the time and made my excuses and made to leave.

'But you haven't seen the room,' she said. 'Would you like to?'

I was curious to see the room so I agreed and I followed her up the red-carpeted stairs and into a well-furnished bedroom off a small landing. I was amazed at how sumptuous it was, right down to the rose-patterned bedspread. There was a bedside electric lamp that could be switched on and off. It was simply luxurious and I was glad to have seen it because it gave me ideas about what I wanted to do when I could afford a house of my own. As I was musing like this and absentmindedly looking under the bed the lady startled me.

'We have a bathroom down the corridor,' she smiled and I reddened.

'Well,' she said finally, 'do you like it, my dear?'

'It's lovely, but I couldn't afford to rent a room like this. But I would like to know how much it is. Just for curiosity's sake,' I replied.

'It's only twenty-five shillings a week all found,' she told me to my amazement. There must be a catch somewhere I thought.

'Did I 'ear you right?' I asked.

'Yes, Mrs Flood. You see, it's not the money I need. It's someone to keep me company, to talk to. I'm afraid I get very lonely by myself at night and I've got this spare room, so rather than keeping it empty I thought I'd let it. I've had several young women call to see it but I'm going to let you have it, if you wish.' She told me she'd taken to me at once and said I had an honest face and that I could move in as soon as I wished. I was still suspicious: it seemed too good to be true and besides if she lived alone, as she had said, why were there three places laid for tea.

'You say you live alone,' I said, and she nodded. 'Then who was the table laid for, then?' At this she smiled broadly.

'I was expecting George, my gentleman friend, but he can't come until next weekend. I have an old chap, too, who tidies up the garden once a week.'

'Oh, I'm sorry. I didn't mean to pry.' I was embarrassed by her forthrightness. Then to change the subject I told her about Mrs Knight's and why I had to find new lodgings.

'I understand your reasons,' she said kindly. 'But you're an attractive young woman. Do you think you'll ever marry again?' she asked.

'No. All I want is to work hard and save enough to rent a house with a garden and get my children back.'

'Well, I wish you good luck in your ambition. In the meantime I'll do my best to help, but be on your guard in case any more Freds come along.' She smiled and we shook hands and it was arranged that I should move in on Monday evening.

As I walked back down Soho Road I seemed to be floating on air. I thanked my lucky stars I'd found such a delightful berth and such a sympathetic confidante. Although I went straight back to work my boss reprimanded me for lateness so I had to tell him where I'd been. But all he said was, 'Well, yer betta keep regular hours or you'll 'ave yer cards. Now get on with that job yer left 'alf finished.' My workmates were more pleased when I told them about my good fortune after knocking-off time. I felt as if a great weight had been lifted from my mind and that I could settle down and plan my future and the children's.

When I returned to Mrs Knight's I was surprised to see her two new lodgers sitting down to their meal.

'I see yer 'aven't wasted much time.' I spoke sharply and she started up from the table and tried to introduce me. I must have seemed very rude when I snapped at her.

'There's no need for introductions now, Mrs Knight. I'm leaving on Monday.'

'Where yer goin'?' she asked, obviously taken by surprise.

'I'm going ter see my brother. I'll tell yer when I get back.' And I hurried out without another glance at the startled company.

Nellie and Frank were pleased to hear I had better digs. Then as I was telling them about the house, Frank interrupted to tell me Mum had been by and left a letter, which he handed to me.

'But it's bin opened,' I said at once.

'Yes, she said she opened it, thinking it was summat important,' he replied.

'But she can't read.'

'I know. She probably got one of the neighbours ter read it,' said Frank, stating the obvious.

'Bloody cheek. She thought there was money in it.' I was furious.

'Most likely,' Nellie agreed.

I looked at it and saw that it was a week old and had come from Barnardo's. I was to call to see the matron as soon as possible to discuss my children's welfare. This was worrying and my anger at Mum's lack of concern for the urgency of the matter increased. I decided that I must go first thing in the morning. It was Saturday, the day of my weekly visit anyway.

I stayed with Frank and Nellie and joined them in a bite of supper. I was famished for I'd not eaten all day, and after the meal, over a glass of stout, we chatted and Frankie told me Mum had reapplied for relief now I'd left her.

'But I thought she had a couple living with her.' I didn't see that it was my fault.

'She did, but they left after a row last week, so I was told. So the visitor asked her how many sons she had working and now Jack, Charlie and me have ter allow her two an' six each per week to 'elp maintain her,' Frankie continued.

This was typical of the meanness of the parish officers, but as Nellie pointed out it was better than having her there to live with them.

'She's got money hid away, if I know my mother.' I knew she wouldn't go short if she could help it. But by this time it was late and I had to leave to face Mrs Knight and postpone further discussion of Mum's plight until another day. I said good night and left, promising to let them know what happened when I visited the home the next day.

I was glad to find Mrs Knight alone when I entered but I could see at a glance that she was angry. She was taking it out on the fire with the poker as I explained about my new lodgings.

'That's the thanks I get fer tekin' you in, she snapped.

'But I told yer I wasn't settled when that Fred was 'ere. Surely you don't expect me to stay now yer've got another two lodgers? Anway where am I goin' ter sleep now?' I added.

'I thought being you're leavin' on Monday, yer could sleep with me,' she said slyly. But I couldn't bring myself to accept this offer, for although she was a kind woman in many ways she was not very particular in her personal habits. In fact I wondered if she were not deaf, she broke wind so thunderously on occasion.

'No,' I said simply.

'Why not?' she asked and I could only make the excuse that I'd arranged to stay with Frank and Nellie.

She didn't seem disappointed as I paid her what I owed. Then I went up to my room and found to my disgust that the lodger's suit-cases were already there at the foot of the bed. I hastily stuffed my clothes into my case and returned downstairs, hopping mad, to find Mrs Knight sitting staring glumly into the fire.

'You crafty old cow!' I screamed at her. 'You'd already planned this.' I didn't wait for her to reply but swept out, slamming the door behind me.

Now I had to rely on Frank and Nellie to let me stay for a couple of days, but I needn't have worried because they quickly offered me their sofa. Next morning I took Nellie up a cup of tea – Frank had left for work – and later I helped with the housework before leaving for the children's home and my interview with the matron. On the way I bought the usual basket of fruit and made for the tram. I was half an hour early, so I called in at a teashop for a snack and soon it was time to be on my way.

As I walked up the gravel path to the front door of the big house I was surprised that it was so quiet. There were no children's voices screeching in the background. I assumed they had been taken out for walks and thought no more of it as I lifted the knocker. Then, almost at once, it opened and I was confronted by a tall, elderly, stern-faced woman, dressed in the same uniform as matron.

'Well?' she asked sharply. 'What do you want?' I was very nervous but managed to stutter that I had come to see matron.

'Matron is not here anymore but you may leave a message,' she informed me snootily.

'But I've come ter visit me children,' I blurted out.

'Oh, I see. Matron and all the children have been transferred to the homes at Barkingside. Weren't you notified? This is only a receiving home for a few weeks.'

'But why wasn't I told? An' when will they be back?' I asked, unable to grasp the situation until she told me where Barkingside was. Barkingside, Ilford, Essex meant nothing to me until she explained. Then I was shattered. I couldn't understand why they'd taken the children away without my consent and I received little in the way of explanation from this cold-faced woman. Soon I found myself facing a closed door and all I could do was turn and retrace my steps down the gravel path to the street.

How I got back to my brother's house I cannot remember. I was broken-hearted. I imagined I would never see them again. I had only a few shillings in the world, but the next day I boarded a train bound for Essex. When I got off the train at my destination I found a policeman and asked directions to the homes, then after jumping on and off several buses I found myself outside an imposing institutional building that made me feel scared. But I'd come this far and was determined to see my children. I'd walked only a few steps towards the house when I was stopped by one of the 'mothers', as the women in charge were called, who asked me who I was looking for. I told her I had come from Birmingham to visit my children, and I was surprised that this seemed to displease her. She told me that all the children had gone to church, it being Sunday of course, and that I couldn't see them anyway without a pass, and then only once a month on Saturday afternoons. This was too much for me and I collapsed in tears.

'Please let me wait an' see them. I've come such a long way,' I pleaded.

All she said was, 'Wait here,' before turning on her heel and disappearing into the house. While I waited I kept a lookout, hoping to catch sight of the children but all I saw were a few older girls going from house to house. They were dressed in uniform grey, with white, lace-trimmed pinafores. Just then the house mother reappeared and beckoned for me to follow her and we made our way to an almost bare office where without another word she handed me a pass with the rules and regulations. I handed over the basket of fruit and sweets I had brought and read the paper through my tears. I pleaded with that woman to let me see the children but I could see that there was no melting her hard heart, and eventually I left. But I hung around for a long time in the hope of catching a glimpse of them until I was spotted and ordered off the premises with a warning not to return. I know if I'd seen them that day I would have run off with them. Anything to get them away from the prison I had inadvertantly handed them over to.

I was only just in time to catch the late train for Birmingham. I flopped into a seat and took a closer look at the pass and saw that it was only three weeks until the next visiting day, and that cheered me slightly. During that three weeks I had to work very hard to save the extra for the fare and the basket of treats. It was years later that I found out that my children received none of the presents I had taken for them. Whether the staff had them or they were added to the general food supply I do not know: all I know is that it was very cruel to leave my children thinking that their heartless mother never took them even the smallest gift. But then there was more heartlessness in the administration of Barnardo's than the public would have suspected if they'd judged by the favourable publicity the homes usually generated. I suppose that to the people at Barnardo's I was an inadequate mother who was incapable of looking after her children. But I felt that I was being treated like a criminal and I can't say they showed much sympathy for me and my circumstances. My efforts to improve my life were not regarded with much interest by Barnardo's, because in the eight years the children were with them they sent somebody to visit me only once.

Those three weeks seemed like years and when the time eventually came the train seemed to crawl. But at last I arrived outside the main gate where I found two elderly women and a young man waiting for it to be opened. We fell into conversation and I found that they had children there too. Some children were orphans and had no visitors at all. The man was of the opinion that it was good that such a place as this existed to cater for orphans but the women did not agree.

'It's a 'ard an' cruel place,' one insisted, 'an' if my ol' man 'ad bin alive mine wouldn't be 'ere now.' But I was hardly listening and it was years before I discovered how true that woman's words were.

I was led into an office where a stern-faced 'mother' faced us from behind a large oak desk strewn with files. She asked me whom I had come to visit and when I gave my children's names she reached for a hand bell and rang it loudly. In no time at all a young girl, aged, I would think, about twelve, appeared at the door. The child was thin and pale and dressed in the uniform grey and white pinafore of Barnardo's. She had thick stockings and heavy boots and her hair was cropped as if someone had put a basin over her head and cut round the edge. She bowed to the mother and stood waiting for her orders.

'Bring in the Flood children,' she snapped at the timid-looking girl.

I didn't have long to wait when Kate and Jean appeared, curtsied as well and stood there awaiting their instructions. They too were clad in grey and had the same prison-cut hairstyle. I went towards them and as I bent down to kiss them they forgot their drill and threw their arms round me and we embraced. Mary was only a babe in arms and too young to understand, and when I held her to me she seemed unused to affection and didn't respond. Soon we were all in tears, but this only provoked the mother to reprimand me for this show of emotion. But I kissed and hugged them and told them that they would only be there a few weeks while I got a home for them. I had no idea that it would take me eight years before I had them back with me. Then after a few minutes they were led away and I was informed in cold tones that if I upset them again I would have my pass revoked and would be prevented from seeing them. I had no time to reflect on the injustice of this and had no idea that any of this harsh regime could be challenged then or later. Today this kind of institution would be exposed publicly in the media but before the war nobody thought that the parents of Barnardo's children had any more rights than the poor children did themselves.

I asked where my son John was and I was told he'd been transferred to the boys' home in Kingston-upon-Thames. I visited him there later. He was there for nine months until he was eleven years of age, when he was sent to Watts Naval Training School at Elmham, Norfolk, and later, while still only eleven, was put on HMS *Ganges* at Shotley, where he was trained for warships and practised with live explosives and firearms and did bayonet practice. It is horrifying to think that Barnardo's had the right to force the youngsters in their care into the armed forces at such a tender age. Needless to say the life at HMS *Ganges* was even more strictly disciplined than in the homes and the men who were in charge were all hardened naval men. It seems clear to me that the Navy used Barnardo's to ensure a supply of young recruits who had no choice at all about whether they were pressed into service or not. When John was barely fifteen he was put aboard the HMS *Hood*, a battle-cruiser. When I found out I wrote to the Admiralty and to his captain explaining that I was a widow and that he was too young for active service, but they brushed my protests aside because he had signed on for the duration of the war. After that my letters went unacknowledged and I became very bitter. If I had had the right contacts I could have got him out but what could a poor widow like me accomplish when it came to the Navy's need for cannon fodder?

After he joined the *Hood* all I could do was pray that the Lord would watch over him and keep him safe from harm. He broke his arm while doing PT, however, and was given leave while his arm healed. It was during that period, in 1941, that the unfortunate ship was sunk with all bar two or three hands, so I suppose my prayers were answered. John was next sent to the HMS *Dorsetshire* where he was the youngest leading seaman as well as a torpedo man. He was aboard during the engagement with the *Bismarck* as well as seeing service against the Vichy French fleet off West Africa. The *Dorsetshire* engaged the battleship *Richelieu* which was fortunately out of ammunition. Later John saw service in the HMS *King George V* on Russian convoys before being based at Simonstown, South Africa, where his ship engaged in escort duties. Those war years were the most worrying of all my life.

While I was visiting the children regularly all my money was going on travel and I was unable to save enough to have any realistic hope of ever getting my own home. I used to lay awake nights thinking about the children and wishing I at least had Mary with me. Then one day on my way to the station I bumped into Liza who offered to go with me. I agreed; I could do with the company, I thought.

'I'd like ter see 'em too,' I remember her saying and when I told her I was going to try to take Mary back she replied, 'The best thing yow can do anyway.' Then she added with a wink, 'Just leave it ter me.'

I thought if we both pleaded the authorities would allow me to have my youngest child back, but it was a terrible mistake. For a start it was Sunday and when we arrived we were told we couldn't see the children on Sunday, only Saturday. I began to weep at this, but we were turned away.

'If they were my kids bloody 'ell an' 'igh water wouldn't stop me from takin' them away from this cold-lookin' prison,' Liza exclaimed angrily. 'Would yer like me ter try an' get Mary?' she added.

'Yes, Liza,' I said tearfully, not really thinking about what she intended.

'Well, you leave this ter me. Yow 'ide be'ind this wall an'as soon as I see 'er I'll call out, then you grab 'er quick an' run.'

We didn't have long to wait. All the older children were at church and the place was almost deserted when a few minutes later we spotted one of the housemaids coming across the yard with my daughter in her arms. Liza went over to her casually and engaged her in conversation, then I grabbed my baby and made for the gate. But Mary didn't know what it was all about and probably didn't recognise me, and she began to scream. Before I realised what was happening she was roughly snatched back from me by one of the staff whose attention had been attracted by the screaming and I was caught. I tried to explain but it was no good. I knew I should never have taken Liza's advice but I was desperate and hadn't stopped to think of the consequences. Now it was too late. We were ordered off the premises and were warned that if we were seen around the grounds again we would be dealt with severely. We left crestfallen and later that week I received the inevitable letter informing me that I would not be able to visit my children until further notice and should I attempt to contact them I would be dealt with by the law. My sister and I quarrelled before we parted that Sunday, and I didn't see her for many years after that.

My Dreams Are Realised

After my ill-fated attempt to snatch Mary away from Barnardo's I could do nothing except wait for replies to my letters and work at my one aim of saving as much money as I could, living in hope of my dreams being realised one day. However I seemed to be dogged by bad luck: often I was unwell and had to have time off work, and after three warnings I was given my cards and left Butler's. Then I had to take a job on a power press at Joseph Lucas's in Great King Street. I had had plenty of experience on a hand press but none on a power press, so when I applied I lied. The money was attractive so I had to try and I clocked on and the following Monday morning, received my brown overall and cap and, nervous as a kitten, made my way to the block where the power presses were. Then as luck would have it a young woman spoke to me.

'Don't be nervous,' she said, 'I'll show yer the ropes.' She was a real chatterbox and a jolly girl. I soon found out her name was Ada.

'I've only worked a 'and press before, Ada. I shouldn't 'ave started really, but I need the money.'

'Don't we all?' she smiled. 'But there's nothin' ter be afraid of. The noise from the presses gets on yer nerves but yer'll get used to it in time.'

Then the hooter sounded for everyone to get to their places. I took a three-legged stool like the other women and sat in front of the machine. When the motor started I nearly jumped out of my skin. Ada pushed me down onto the stool and showed me how the press was operated before the foreman had time to come down the block. Fortunately, I picked the job up in a minute or two.

'Yer OK now, Katie?' Ada shouted above the din. I stuck my thumb up and nodded. Ada was cutting out blanks which were passed to me to have holes pierced through them by the press. Then they were sent to the assembly shop where wires were threaded through them before they were sent to car plants to be fitted to dashboards. Ada and I could talk only in the canteen during breaks because talking was forbidden while the presses were in operation to cut the risk of accidents. She told me she'd only been there a month and I was sorry to hear that she was leaving soon to join a friend who was learning to be a dressmaker.

'Don't yer like it here, then?' I asked.

'Well, the money's good, but the bloody job's too dirty and greasy for my liking,' she replied and I had to agree. We chatted like this whenever we had the chance and became quite friendly. She promised to introduce me to her friend, which I looked forward to.

The following week everyone on the power presses had to go over to piecework. The rate fixers came with their stop-watches and stood over us. Every job was timed according to the Beddow system, the name of the organisation expert who dreamed the method up. As the reader might appreciate, this system was not devised for the benefit of the workers. It was real sweated labour and there was scarcely time to go to the lavatory. There was great pressure to cut corners to make sufficient money and one day my friend Ada did a very foolish thing. She tied back the safety guard to work more quickly. Suddenly I was startled by a scream which pierced the hubbub of the workshop. It came from the direction of Ada's machine and I went over immediately to see what had happened. I bent over Ada who was on the floor and blood spurted over me. I'm afraid I fainted at the sight of blood and when I came round I found myself lying beside my friend in an ambulance. She was unconscious and when I looked I saw she had lost several fingers; I vomited and passed out again.

The next thing I recall is coming round in bed in a hospital ward. I'd been washed and was lying between clean sheets. I enjoyed being waited on but I couldn't see why I had been kept in. I inquired of one of the nurses but all she could tell me was that I would have to wait until the doctor had seen me the following day. I didn't think there was anything wrong with me but I was enjoying the service, particularly when a boiled chicken dinner arrived followed by a mug of Ovaltine for supper. Later, in the middle of the night, I got up to use the toilet. I tiptoed down the ward to the lavatory but before I could switch on the light I felt something squelch under my bare foot. I was horrified when I flicked the switch and looked at the floor. There were dozens of cockroaches scuttling for the skirting. I screamed and fled back to my bed. This awakened some of the patients and brought the nurse running. She smiled when I told her what had happened and explained that although they 'tried to keep them down, the building was old.' I still wanted to go to the toilet though so I asked the nurse for a bedpan.

'You are a nuisance, aren't you?' she replied. 'You'll have to wait. Didn't you go when you went to the bathroom?'

'No. Not with them things running around me feet. An' I'm cold now,' I added.

She went away and returned in a few minutes with a hot-water bottle and a warm bedpan. Such kindness, despite my troublesomeness, was more than I had experienced for some time and I revelled in it. When the doctor examined me all over he gave it as his opinion that there was nothing wrong with me, simply that I was undernourished. I was told I was to be discharged the next morning and to call at the dispensary where I received tablets and Parish's Food. This brought back memories of the children.

I returned to Lucas's the following afternoon and gave in my notice, having decided to have another try at enamelling. I was determined to leave the heavy factory work alone; indeed, just the mention of a power press made me nervous. I often thought about Ada and wondered how she was. She would never be a dressmaker after her accident. I wished many times I had taken her address so I could have kept in touch.

My next job was in a small shop; 'Hart's, enamellers to the trade' it said above the door. I told Mr Hart I was fully experienced although I still wanted a lot of knowledge in the trade. There were ten other women beside myself, one of whom, a young woman called Rose, was in charge. She was a bit of a snob and very stern. She wasn't liked because she lorded it when the boss was not around. Sometimes he would be away for days 'on business', that is to say, at the races. We could tell when he'd lost and then we dared not say a word, but when he'd been lucky he would bring in cakes, strawberries sometimes, and then ask us to work over.

One day Mr Hart gave me a special job. I had to enamel a little white dog on a brooch. This was to be the sample for an order. I tried hard to get it right and the boss was pleased, as was the customer. It was to be a big order which would last for weeks, but when Rose found out I was in Mr Hart's good books she became very jealous. This was compounded when Mr Hart commented that I was turning out more than she was. Inevitably she had to have revenge.

A few days later I found I was having difficulty with the white enamel which kept bubbling up. I kept swilling the colour and used a clean cloth, but to no effect. Then Mr Hart saw what was happening. It must have been one of the losing days because he flared up a temper and started to rave. Then I noticed the smirk on Rose's face and realised something was wrong. So did he; he sat down and examined the frit. Then he exclaimed:

'I knew as much! There's salt in here.'

He sent for Rose in the little back room he called his 'office' and after a few minutes she emerged in tears. She'd been given the sack on the spot. This I thought a bit unfair, but later the girls explained that this had happened before when she'd taken a dislike to somebody. I felt a little less guilty when I heard them say 'good riddance'.

After this Mr Hart joined us in the work for a bit until a couple of weeks after Rose's departure he called me into his office and asked me to take charge and inspect the finished work. Then he went out 'on business'. He couldn't have taken so much time off if he hadn't had a reliable manager in the shop all the time.

I was able to get to know much more about the business side of the trade in my new position: the prices of every kind of enamel badge, invoicing and accounts. Then a few days later I ran out of paper to wrap an order so I tried the door to his private room off the office and found it was open. I went in and found a small room like a living room with carpeted floor, two red plush chairs, pictures on the wall and a table in the middle of the floor strewn with racing papers. Thinking he would not miss a couple I took them to wrap the work and closed the door behind me. When Mr Hart returned two days later we all went quiet: we could tell at once by his manner that he had lost. He stormed through the shop to his office and into his private room. Then all at once he came storming out.

'Who's been in my room?' he demanded.

'I did,' I told him. 'The door wasn't locked an' I wanted some newspaper to wrap some work in.'

'I never leave that door open!' he shouted.

'But it was open.' I was indignant. 'An' a customer's got yer racing paper now.'

He calmed down after this and replied more quietly, 'Very well, next time I'll leave you the key.' But he never did.

I was now chargehand enameller, viewer and office worker all rolled into one. However, I was not complaining; I knew the trade inside out and I was getting top wages with a promise of a bonus on our turnover. Some of the girls worked faster than others so we worked as a team and got on well, especially when Mr Hart was out. However, his unpredictable moods could be extremely trying, and in the end too much.

Late one afternoon he came bounding in, picked up a handful of badges, glanced at one and then threw them onto the floor in a temper.

'These are the wrong colour!' he bawled.

'But that's the colour we always do them,' I replied.

'You should have asked for the sample,' he yelled at me and before I could reply he'd disappeared into the office. When he came back he almost threw the badge at me.

'Now that's the one! Pick it up, I want you in the office!'

This was the final straw for me: I couldn't tolerate his tantrums any longer.

'Pick it up yourself. You should be 'ere to run yer own business instead of 'avin' it out of me when yer lose on the 'orses!' The girls stared at me, mouths open. So did he when I added, 'See if yer can get somebody else ter do the work I do. I'm leaving right now!' And with that I put my coat and hat on and left.

On the following Friday I had to fetch my pay and my unemployment card. Hoping he was not at a race meeting, I rang the bell and waited. I was ready with an answer if he started on me again. Almost at once the door opened and he asked me in. It must have been one of his good days.

'I've come for the few days' pay that's due to me and me cards,' I said before he could say anything.

'Won't you think it over and come back?' he asked very pleasantly.

'No, Mr Hart, I've got my old job back,' I told him.

'Enamelling?'

'Yes, just enamelling and more money.'

'Well, I can give you a rise.'

'No, I've made up my mind.' And so I had.

'Well, if you should change yer mind, you've only to ask,' he said. Never, I thought.

As he handed over what was due to me he said how sorry he was to lose me. I nearly told him he should have thought of that before now, but I buttoned my lip, seeing no further point in arguing with him.

I started back at T.A. Butler's the following Monday morning. I didn't intend to let the grass grow under my feet now I was saving hard and fast. I was still lodging with Mrs Green in Soho Road and enjoying being there. Each night we would chat about our respective days and we were on Christian-name terms.

Then one day the tide turned for me. My opportunity arrived at last. It happened that Mr Butler – Tom, we all called him – had a large order for different kinds of badges and motor plates but he couldn't employ enough experienced workers to cope. So one night I asked Nell, my landlady, if she would rent me her small empty back room to do some work at home. She agreed willingly and offered to help, to learn herself. It was easy to talk to Tom; he was like one of the workers, who would always find time for a friendly chat with his employees. My chance came to raise the subject with him and I offered to do some of the filing, a process prior to firing, at home. He agreed at once and let me take some Castrol badges and return them the next day. I laid the enamel on during the day and took three or four gross of the red and green badges home in the evening. Nell and I would sit up in her little back room after supper singing to the gramophone as we filed the badges with carborundum stones.

For me this extra work was worthwhile because I wanted to earn more and more and one day start my own business. In normal circumstances you had to work much harder then than today. There were no paid holidays except for Bank Holidays, and normal working hours were long – 8 a.m. to 6 p.m. – and included Saturday mornings as a rule. In the two years after I started doing homework I worked through, only taking off Christmas Day, Boxing Day and Good Friday. The only recreation I had was when George and Nell took me for a drink on Saturday nights or occasionally to the pictures. During those two long years I managed to save over a hundred pounds which in the 1930s was a considerable sum of money. However, it still was not sufficient to buy or rent a house and obtain furniture and all the things I needed for the children. I thought about what I was to do and decided to ask Tom Butler if he would supply outwork if I could find suitable premises and, bless him, he agreed.

After that I kept my eyes peeled for a workshop and it was on Good Friday 1937 that I happened to be walking along Spencer Street and paused outside a cake shop, in the window of which were hot cross buns. I went in and bought some to take back to Nell's. As I came down the steps with my purchase I glanced across the street and saw a notice which read, 'Top Floor Shop to Let. Apply Within'. Everything was closed for the Easter holiday so it was the following Tuesday when, hair newly Marcel-waved, in my Sunday-best hat, coat and gloves, I went to try my luck. The name of the principal occupier of the premises was 'F. Marson, makers of diamond rings, 90 Spencer Street'. I was interviewed by Mr Marson himself. His questions concerning my age, marital status and so on made me nervous, but I told him what I wanted the rooms for, who I worked for and what my boss's name was; but Mr Marson still said he needed references. I told him that Mr Butler would vouch for me and he said he would ring him and that I should hear from him in a few days.

Later in the week Tom Butler called me into his office to tell me he had given me a good reference, and when he handed me my wages that Friday I could've thrown my arms round his neck and kissed him. I didn't, though, because he had a reputation as a lady's man and I didn't wish to encourage him. But I thanked him sincerely. He told me to let him know when everything was fixed, and when I was ready to start he would send his errand boy round with badges and motor plates.

That weekend I was so excited I couldn't sleep in anticipation of going round the following Monday to see the rooms. Mr Marson took me up to the top floor and when I looked round I could see that it hadn't been used for years. There was rubbish everywhere and it was thick with dust, but I didn't mind the filth. That could soon be cleaned away and I was eager to start. Against one wall there was an old roll-top desk and there was some old machinery including a rusty old motor which was nevertheless in working order. In the corner was a cupboard that was supposed to be an office. All in all it was scarcely believable that such a place could exist, but when Mr Marson told me the rent was twelve shillings and sixpence a week I could have jumped for joy. I sealed the bargain by giving him a month's rent in advance and said I would be cleaning it out that week. He gave me the key and we shook hands.

When I got back I told Nell all about it. It had been a glue factory at one point, but with a little elbow grease would be just right. We set to and used just that. Frankie and a mate of his white-washed it for me the following weekend. Then I went to the bank and withdrew fifty pounds to buy materials. I purchased enamel from Hutton's in Great Hampton Row, carborundum files and wire panning from Harry Smith's, Key Hill, and several second hand three-legged stools and tables as well as pestles and mortars. Nell came the first week to help but when she found we had rats refused to come again. Frank had warned me that we had them but I was used to rats from childhood and carried on working alone until the council workmen arrived to poison them. However, they were tenacious creatures and the council men had to come back every few weeks.

When everything was cleaned and scrubbed I put a notice for experienced enamellers and learners on the wall outside and I was in business. During the next month I employed four experienced women and two learners. Later I took more girls on and a mixed bunch they were, but I worked beside them and we were quite a happy family. I was always first to arrive at seven thirty in the morning and last to leave after seven o'clock most nights. I'd always been a jack of all trades but now I had my own business and I was independent for the first time in my life.

The girls knew about the rats although they didn't come out during daytime, but each night before I left I would set a trap, baited with half a kipper, and in the morning there would be a rat, sometimes two, to be drowned in the bucket. The girls never knew about this.

I was still at Nell's in 1937, and weekends would sit with her and George who was very interested in what I was doing. It was during one of these evenings that they told me that they were getting married in a few months and that they would sell up and go abroad.

I was not surprised: I knew they slept together at weekends. I didn't comment: they'd been good to me and it was none of my business what they did. I would have loved that house and the furniture it contained but I couldn't afford to buy it, so I had to start looking for a house to rent.

I was extremely busy now. After paying the girls and taking care of all the overheads I was able to bank money each week. I was still able to visit the children more than I had when I was working all hours God made doing homework. Kathleen was still at Barkingside but Mary and Jean were fostered out to two maiden ladies they called 'aunties'. When Nell and George had sold up I rented a house in Albert Road near Handsworth Park. I was in seventh heaven furnishing the front room, sitting room, the kitchen and the three bedrooms. What was best was the large garden at the rear where the children could play. As soon as everything was ready I wrote to the offices at Ilford and told them about my business and the house and that I was now in a position to have my children back with me. Two weeks later I received a letter informing me they would be sending a visitor to inspect my business premises and my house as soon as they could. In the meantime the work from Butler's went slack and I had to look round for other customers. First of all I took down the sign outside and replaced it with one which read, 'K. FLOOD, ART. ENAMELLER TO THE TRADE, TOP FLOOR'. My first customer, the next day, was R. Gomm. He gave me a good price for the work I did and he supplied me with orders for years, and after I had retired I continued to do outwork for him. I obtained work from Munster's in Hockley Street as well. Often Mr Munster himself would bring the work. He was a well-dressed, elderly gentleman and rather thickset. He had silver-grey hair and I thought him very distinguished-looking. He was German but spoke very good English. He was quite the gentleman and had beautiful manners. So one day when he invited me out to lunch, I accepted even though he was old enough to be my father.

I had some happy times with him; he was wonderful company, very considerate and not an emotionally demanding man: each time we parted he would just kiss me on the cheek and say, 'good night'. Then one night after dining out he took me in his arms gently and asked me to marry him. This was both flattering and upsetting because I had to tell him that I could not marry him, not until I had my children with me. He knew about them and how they came to be at Barnardo's. He was obviously disappointed but said if I changed my mind he would take me to Germany and make a future for the children there. In the meantime he was going abroad on business. But, he said, he hoped I would say yes when he returned. Next day I saw him off on the train and when we embraced and kissed he said, 'Goodbye my dear, don't forget your promise.' However, I never saw Mr Munster again although sadly I heard some years later that he'd been interned for the duration of the war. If I had not had the children to think about and the business to pursue I believe I might have married him. I might have married several times in those years before the war; I had several proposals, but when I told them I had four children their ardour seemed to subside for some reason.

During these years I lost touch with most of my family – Frank and Nellie excepted, of course. Then one day when I was picking up some work from a customer in Albion Street I saw my brother, Jack. I tried to avoid him but he spotted me and approached.

'Ello Kate,' he called out. 'I dain't know yer in yer smart get up. An' 'ow's the kids?' he inquired cheerfully.

'No thanks ter you that they're all right!' I snapped, and made to walk away. But he grabbed me by the arm.

'Don't yer wantta know'ow yer Mum is?' he asked.

'No! Nor yow! An' yer know why.' I'm afraid I was still very bitter about how they had failed to help me when I needed them. Then he changed the subject.

'Yer know Mary's back from America, don't yer?' And I was willing to listen to what he had to say about my older sister who I hadn't seen for years.

'No, I didn't,' I answered more calmly. 'Where's she living now?'

'She's livin' in the Drive, in the top yard for the time bein'.'

'Oh, my God!' I exclaimed. 'What a comedown for her. If you see her will you tell her I'll come an' see her in a day or two. Thanks for telling me, I've got to be off now.'

As I turned away he said, 'I'm just goin' in The George an' Dragon to 'ave a drink. I'll buy yer one . . .'

'Don't bother, I don't drink!' I snapped in bitterness at him.

I decided I would look Mary up, and a few days later I was on my way there when by coincidence I bumped into Mrs Taylor's twin boys. They were in their mid-twenties now but unmistakable as the little tots I used to drag along in my gocart to Titty-Bottle Park all those years before. Joey was still bandy and Harry hadn't lost his squint. I still had a soft spot for them. Joey was pushing a basket carriage full of firewood and Harry was walking beside. I tapped Joey on the shoulder.

'Don't yer know me Joey?' I inquired jokingly.

''Ello Tatie,' they both replied in unison: they always called me 'Tatie'. 'Where'd yer spring from? An' where're yer gooin'?'

'To see my sister Mary, but I'm glad I've seen yer both. An' what are you two up to these days?'

Then they both looked sheepish and Harry replied, 'I'ope yer don't mind but when yer went away an' yer told ower Mum yer wasn't comin' back, we thought we'd take over yer customers, an' now we've got a good little business goin'. One day we'ope ter buy an 'orse an' cart, don't we Joey?' he added and gave a broad grin.

'Of course I don't mind Harry. I'm glad yer both doing well, but don't trust anybody on the slate.'

'No fear. We only sell for cash an' we put money in the post office every week.'

'Harry, will yer do me a favour?' I asked.

'Yes Tatie, anything fer yoo,' came the prompt reply.

'Would you go down the Drive an' see if my mother is about? I don't want ter see 'er if I can 'elp it.'

'Don't worry. I'll go. You mind the basket, 'arry,' said Joey before running off in the direction of the Drive. While he was gone I asked Harry how his mother was.

'She died a few weeks after yow left,' he answered sadly.

'Oh, I am sorry to hear that,' I replied shocked. 'I loved your Mum, she was good to me.'

'Yes, she always said 'ow kind you were to 'er an' us when we were little lads,' he said with a tear in his eye.

'Never mind, wipe your eyes, Joey's coming.'

Joey came hurrying back, all smiles. 'Yow don't 'ave ter worry, Tatie. The ol' battleaxe 'as gone away agen an' the door's locked.' He grinned. 'Yer know,' he added, 'when yer left she took in a coupla lodgers who 'ad a little lad. Poor little bugger was all skin an' bone. 'Is Dad was always beatin' 'im with 'is belt an' one night ower Mum 'eard 'im cryin' down the cellar among the bleedin' rats.

Well, she sent for the cruelty man an' when 'e see the bleedin' red weals on 'is arse 'e tuk 'im away. Then when yer Mum found out, she threw 'em out with all their things in the yard.'

'What 'appened then?' I'd not heard this before.

'They both scarpered cos the neighbours threatened ter beat them up.'

'An' yer know summat else,' put in Harry. 'We admired what yer did, an' some o' the neighbours said they wished they 'ad girls ter do what yow did.'

'Well, the children should be coming home soon an' when they do I'll bring 'em down ter see you.' I was pleased that I was not universally condemned for sending the children into a home. 'An' now I'll 'ave ter be on me way.' And I turned to go. Then Joey spoke shyly.

'Doo yer mind, Tatie, if we give yer a kiss?' he asked.

'No, course not. But hurry up; I don't want the people round 'ere to get the wrong idea.' And they each pecked my cheek and blushed. Then they hurried off.

I continued towards my sister's yard where I asked a small girl which house Mrs White lived in.

'In that one,' she told me, pointing to the fourth house. As I approached it I saw a tray of steaming doughnuts on the windowsill which made my mouth water. The door stood wide open. My sister was nowhere to be seen and when I looked round the place, I was surprised to see it was almost bare. It was clean enough, apart from flour all over the floor, but the only furniture was two wooden chairs and a deal table. There was a fire in the grate and on the green-mottled gas stove stood a bubbling pan of fat. As I stood taking this in my sister came bounding down the stairs with a large bag of flour in her arms. I could hardly believe my eyes; she'd put on so much weight. Round her ample waist she wore a hessian apron and she had men's boots on her feet and was covered from head to toe with flour. She gave an exclamation of surprise, dropped the bag on the table and flung her arms round me. We kissed and wept as you might imagine after such a long break.

'Oh Mary, I can't believe you've come down 'ere to live.' I was genuinely shocked because as the reader will remember Mary was always so disdainful of the yards. 'What a hole!'

'Oh, don't let that worry yer; this is only temporary,' she assured me.

'But I thought you were doing well in America,' I said.

'I was, at least at first, but the Americans don't live like we do an' ower money didn't last. But when I was there I did learn to make doughnuts an' now I've got a little business selling to neighbours an' supplying the shops. Carn't make 'em quick enough in fact.' She sounded cheerful enough.

'Does it pay?' I was unconvinced, having engaged in similar enterprises myself without much success.

'W-e-ll.' She hesitated. 'I'll let yer into my little secret; I know you'll keep it. I don't want Bill to know yet, but I've got quite a little nest egg now and Mrs Charles, 'er who 'as the draper's shop in Albion Street, is thinking of leaving soon an' she's given me the first chance to buy it.' She spoke confidentially.

'I wish you all the luck in the world, Mary. I'll keep yer secret, but mind 'e don't find out,' I replied.

'I'm past carin' about him now, Kate,' she said bitterly. I wondered at this because although Bill was a Casanova, a liar and a drunkard, I remember Mary would never have a word said against him. Anyway, we sat talking for a long time and I told her about my business and the house in Albert Road. She was pleased to hear that I was expecting a visitor to decide whether I could have the children back. She made tea and I sampled her doughnuts, which were delicious, and I bought two dozen for my workers. Then we kissed and I gave her my address.

'But don't bring 'im,' I warned her and she knew what I meant.

'I won't,' she replied, and as I hurried down the yard I noticed several customers arriving with bags ready for Mary's doughnuts.

I returned the next week to see how she was getting on and to purchase more doughnuts, but when I got near Mary's I saw several women eyeing me up and down. I gritted my teeth and ignored them. Mary was still the same, sleeves rolled up, perspiring as she dipped her doughnuts into the boiling fat and rolled the cooked cakes in sugar. Like me Mary wanted to better herself and neither of us had any reason to be ashamed of wanting to join the ranks of the employers. We'd been downtrodden, starving even, ourselves, and there was little chance that we would forget that in our dealings with our people. There were plenty of Brummies, born in poverty, who pulled themselves up by their own bootstraps. One, now a scrap-metal millionaire, had been sweet on Mary in the old days. Perhaps she should have encouraged him. There was Joe Lucas, who founded the famous engineering firm, who still lived in Carver Street in those days and who my Dad could remember selling tin bowls and kettles from a wheelbarrow. There were plenty more like these. I knew many like them. We didn't have parents who could give us a start in life, nor government grants, nor even social security when we were at rock bottom; just hard work and sink or swim. Unfortunately, Mary never really made it but it was not for want of trying. I haven't got any answers, but the grinding poverty of the old slums did breed some very determined people.

I was doing well enough now to think about getting a small car. Then as luck would have it I bumped into Freddy Jones, an old mate of Frank's, and he happened to mention he had an Austin Seven he wanted to sell.

'Why ask me?' I asked, my suspicions roused.

'Yower Frank ses yer might be interested. It's me own car, an' paid for,' he added in his salesman's patter.

'How much do yer want fer it?' I asked him, still not convinced by a long way.

'Well, I 'ave bin askin' thirty poun' but I'll let yow 'ave it for twenty-five.

'Why do yer want to get rid of it?' I thought it sounded too cheap to be any good.

'It's like this, yer see. I've bin put on the labour an' the kids ain't got any boots on their feet,' he explained.

'All right. When can I see it?' I asked, my doubts answered to some extent.

'I'll bring it round,' he said eagerly. As good as his word, five minutes later he appeared in a black Austin Seven. It was mud-splattered and full of junk but when Freddy saw the look on my face he cried out cheerfully, 'It only wants a good clean out an' it runs like a bird. Jump in an' I'll show yer 'ow ter drive it.'

There was no harm in having a demonstration drive, I thought, and if Frank had recommended him he must be all right. I climbed into the driver's seat full of trepidation. I listened carefully to the instructions and amazingly I set off successfully and did three circuits of the block. When I arrived at the starting point, excited after my first drive, I stopped to exchange a word and then made to set off again.

''Old on! Yow'll be usin' all me petrol an' yoo 'aven't said if yer'll 'ave it yet,' Freddy exclaimed.

'Right. Bring it round to 90 Spencer Street – you'll see my name on the door – an' I'll give you the money.' I had decided to take this opportunity to become mobile and I must admit that the thought of driving about in my own car had me in quite a state of anticipation.

'Thanks Mrs Flood. I'll get the missus ter gi' it a good clean out,' Freddy shouted as he drove off.

That night whan I got home I wondered if I'd done the right thing. It was a battered old banger and I knew nothing at all about motorcars. But it was too late to change my mind now I'd accepted his price, so I put any lingering doubts out of my mind. Freddy kept his promise and arrived with the car the following afternoon and when I went downstairs, there it was, shining black and well cleaned inside and out.

'I've filled 'er up with petrol, Mrs Flood,' he assured me as I climbed into the driver's seat and clutched the wheel again to savour that feeling of having made it that sitting there gives a new car owner.

'Yoo are gooin' ter 'ave it, ain't yer?' he asked.

'Yes, Fred. Stay 'ere while I slip up an' get yer the money,' I said finally.

I didn't have enough cash on hand so I wrote out a cheque to bearer. However, when Freddy saw this he wasn't pleased.

'I carn't tek that. I'll 'ave ter tek the car back if yow ain't got cash.' He sounded annoyed. He needn't have done though, because I'd fallen in love with the car.

'Jump in then,' I smiled, 'an' I'll draw some out of the bank.' We drove round to my branch and I took out twenty-seven pounds and I gave him a pound extra for the petrol and a pound for his wife for cleaning it up for me. He was pleased as punch with this and thanked me. He wanted a lift home so we set off, me needing no excuse to experience the thrill of being behind the steering wheel. On the way I asked what he was going to do with the money.

'First of all I'm goin' ter buy the kids some boots an' things an' then I'm gooin' ter buy vegetables with the rest so's me missus can open up the front room as a shop.' I was pleased to hear that he didn't intend to fritter it away on the horses, because I knew he liked a flutter. He kept his word too; a few weeks later I happened to pass that way and I saw the Joneses' front window full of fruit and vegetables. I stopped and parked and popped in more out of curiosity than anything else. There were several women waiting to be served but when Fred saw me he called his wife to serve me. Then someone piped up, "Er's gotta tek 'er turn, same as us.'

'That's all right, I can wait.' I knew the pecking order. But Freddy would have none of this and as he carried on I began to redden.

'Yoo serve 'er missus.' Then, looking at the other customers he continued, "Er's a good wench 'er is. 'Er 'elped ter start me gooin'.' I made an excuse and left but not before I gave him my address and asked him to deliver an order weekly, which he did on his pushbike. Freddy Jones prospered, bought a horse and cart and delivered door-to-door while his wife ran the shop. I always got choice goods and I never regretted buying my first car.

I went everywhere in that old banger. You didn't need a licence to drive in those days so I never passed a test. I could drive quite well considering. However, I made one mistake. I could drive straight and change gears correctly when turning corners but I couldn't reverse for the life of me. One Friday afternoon I went to draw the workers' wages and came out of the bank to discover that there was a dustcart in front and a motor behind so that I could only get out by reversing first. I sat there for nearly two hours and I dozed off. The next thing I knew I felt a hand on my shoulder and when I opened my eyes I saw a policeman standing by the open car door.

'You all right miss?' he inquired in a fatherly tone of voice.

'Y-yes, why?' I managed to say.

'I've been round the block a couple of times and seein' you still here outside the bank, I wondered . . .' His voice trailed off.

'I'm all right, thanks, Constable.' Now I could see the road was clear I was anxious to be off. He smiled when I added why I'd been parked for so long. No doubt a policeman today wouldn't have seen the joke or if he did he would still have to book me.

Not long after I'd bought the car, on a hot July day I decided to take Mary for a run and I must admit that I wanted Mum's neighbours to see I had a car and so show off a bit. I parked near the school that we had attended and went to fetch my sister. I found her putting out another tray of doughnuts to cool.

'Bleedin' doughnuts an' flower all over the place!' I heard Bill's voice from inside the house.

'They've 'elped ter keep us gooin',' Mary shouted back.

'An' where's me dinner?' he bawled again.

'In the oven! An' yer can get it yerself, yer big an' ugly enough!' Mary was capable of holding her own with her husband.

When they saw me they stopped quarrelling but Bill turned on me.

'An' what d'yoo want? Mrs High and Mighty!'

'You've got nothin' I want! An' if I did want anything, yer'd be the last one I'd ask,' I snaped back.

At that he stood up, put on his cap and made to go out, but when she saw what he was doing Mary questioned him.

'Well, if yer want ter know, I'm goin' tattin'. I've bought meself an' 'orse an' cart,' he replied triumphantly.

'An' where yer think yer gooin' ter keep it?' Mary sounded scornful.

'I've bought some straw an' I'll keep 'er in the brew' ouse.'

This provoked further argument which was brought to a dramatic halt by the intervention of the nag which it appeared Bill had already installed in the temporary stable. There was a loud clatter in the yard and when we'd dashed out to see what it was we found the tin tray on the bricks and the horse hungrily eating the remains of the doughnuts. In a rage Mary snatched up the tray and hurled it towards the luckless horse and although she missed her aim, the horse could see how the land lay and she turned and trotted down the yard and into the street. She was heading for Kiniver's stables, the same stables Granny had hired the horse from when she moved out of our house years before. Mary guessed where Bill had bought the nag and continued to vent her wrath about the ruined doughnuts on Bill.

'An' 'ow much did yer give for that bloody nag?' she screamed, to the amusement of the inevitable crowd that had gathered to be entertained.

'Two quid,' her husband answered defiantly.

'Two pound?' Mary yelled in disbelief, 'why, 'er's only fit fer the knacker's yard. Yer bring it back 'ere an' I'll throw yer both out.'

And with that she marched back indoors, for all the world the spit of our Mum. Bill turned on his heel and ran after his horse and I made excuses and left them to it. Later, I found out that Kiniver had refused to give the horse back because Bill hadn't paid for a bag of oats he had had and a fierce argument had ensued in the course of which the pair had almost come to blows; it was only settled when a bobby appeared on the scene, threatened to arrest Bill and ordered the horse to be taken to the knacker's yard. Thus ended Bill's foray into the rag and bone trade.

All's Well That Ends Well

It was during 1938, while I was waiting for Barnardo's to make up their minds to give me my children back that the fears about war were growing. These were fuelled after Hitler invaded the Sudetenland, and nobody was fooled by Mr Chamberlain when he returned with his scrap of paper and promises of 'peace in our time'. Everybody made jokes about Hitler and Chamberlain's paper but the reality of the situation made itself felt when we saw the young lads joining up and the Territorials parading the streets and strutting about pretending to be grown-ups in their ill-fitting uniforms. The sight of them made me feel sick and I became depressed thinking about life in wartime without my children by me. Then came the ultimatum and we were really at war with Germany.

My old banger eventually gave up the ghost in the spring of 1939 and I had to leave it by the side of the road and catch a bus. It was some time since I'd had to use one and I'd forgotten what it was like to travel home on a bus loaded with workers. The conversation was about air-raid shelters and ration books. One old woman was very agitated.

'Gawd 'elp us all. I remember the larst lot. Me 'usband was gassed.'

'Don't worry ma,' an elderly man reassured her, 'it won't larst long this time. It'll be over be Chris'mas, yow'll see.'

'It's the bloody gover'ment wot causes all these bleedin' wars!' exclaimed another old codger. 'But I don't see any of 'em goin' out ter fight. No! That lot live in the lap o' luxury while the young 'uns get theea 'eads blown away. I done me bit in the last bleedin' lot but they ain't gettin' me this time for the King's bloody shillin' an' two bob a day!'

'I was a conchie in the last war an' I 'ad an 'ell of a time with the neighbours. Called me a traitor they did,' ventured another, more forthright than prudent. 'But thank Gawd, I'm 'ere ter tell the tale now,' he continued.

At this a big burly fellow jumped up from his seat and made for the last speaker.

'Tell wot tales?' he yelled down at the unrepentant conscientious objector. 'It was yower bleedin' sort that stayed at um, werkin' an' gettin' rich while others 'ad ter goo ter the front an' fight fer the likes o' yow.' He getting red in the face.

'Somebody 'ad ter go ter the munitions,' the other said timidly.

'Yus! Young girls an' women who 'ad ter leave young babbies. Werked all hours they did, an' my mother was one of 'em,' put in a third.

I believe that they would have come to blows if the conductor hadn't appeared and pushed them back into their seats. This was typical of the sort of talk there was in the final months of 1939.

Production was going over to war work and I had to let some of my girls go because my work went slack as the demand for the luxury enamelled brooches I was making declined. Soon I had too little work to keep going and I had to look for some kind of war work myself. I was fortunate in spotting an advertisement for a contractor to enamel officers' pips. I had a regular order making these for years, as well as other orders for enamelling Auxiliary Fire Service badges, WVS badges and other enamelled items. I had to take on more workers and things were looking up, at least financially; but I was still depressed about the children. It seemed Barnardo's was determined to prevent me ever seeing them again.

Then one day in November 1939 I arrived home to find a letter marked 'Urgent'. I picked it up and tore it open when I saw the post-mark; London. It was to inform me that I was to meet the mid-day train from London the next day and that my children would then be handed over to me. I was so excited I couldn't eat or sleep that night. I kept looking at the clock, imagining that it was going slow and thinking that day would never break. Eventually it was time to get up and I went along to the shop, got together the urgent orders and then when the girls arrived I told them I was giving them the day off and why. I locked up the premises and hurried home to light a fire, warm the beds and tidy everything before going to meet the train.

It had been eight long, worrying years since I'd kissed the children goodbye at Dr Barnardo's in Moseley and the Second World War had just begun, not the most auspicious moment to resume a settled family life. In retrospect it seems likely that Hitler had as much to do with Barnardo's deciding I was a fit person to care for my children as anything else. However, I was not thinking about why they were returning that morning as I nervously prepared the house to receive them. I was more anxious about whether they actually remembered me still. Kathleen was now fourteen years old, Jean was twelve and Mary nearly nine. I knew Mary wouldn't know me because she'd been a mere babe in arms when she left, and she showed no signs of recognition on the few occasions I'd seen her since. She'd been fostered out with Jean for about eight years and we'd had no real contact in the interim. I had seen Kathleen more; she'd been there at the homes when I had visited, but these visits had been few in the last years while I had been so busy building up the business.

So mid-day found me waiting on the windy platform, stamping my feet to keep warm and scanning every train that arrived in case I should miss them. The porters got fed up with me inquiring which was the London train only to receive the same reply: 'It'll be 'ere at two.' Then finally it drew into the station, all steam and swirls of smoke. I surveyed the passengers disgorging from the carriages and for a terrible moment doubted whether they were on the train, but then I saw Kathleen step down from an open carriage door and as I ran along the platform towards her I saw two women, holding Jean and Mary by the hand, follow her out of the carriage.

'Hello, Mom,' Kathleen called out as soon as she'd spotted me. I threw my arms round her and we hugged each other. When they saw this the two stern-faced elderly women came towards us.

'Are you Mrs Flood?' one of them inquired.

'Yes,' I replied.

'Sign here,' the other said curtly, handing me a document. I'd been caught by Barnardo's getting me to sign things before and I wasn't going to put my name to this without reading it carefully. When she saw what I was doing the first woman intervened to say that it was simply to say that I had the children safely. She was anxious that I signed it quickly, she explained, because they had to get back aboard before the train continued on its journey as they had other children with them to take on to other destinations. So I did as she asked and without another word the women returned to their carriage, leaving me alone with the somewhat bewildered children.

Jeannie wasn't sure who I was, and Mary had no idea: that was clear from the puzzled expressions on their faces and their silence. Then Katie told them who I was and I kissed each in turn and we made our way back along the platform to the gates.

They were famished, not having had anything to eat since they had left, so I took them into a nearby cafe where they ate ravenously. They were excited and apprehensive and it wasn't until I got them home that they began to settle down.

I stoked the fire and took their coats and berets and while they sat round the fire, taking in their new home, I laid the table with cakes and other goodies I'd bought specially for them. When they'd eaten their fill I took them upstairs to show them their bedrooms and I was relieved to see they were pleased with what they saw.

We had lots to talk about after such a long time: they about their 'aunties' and me about the firm. When Kathleen heard about this she was excited about starting there herself and this is what she did. I taught her the skills involved, how to check the work for quality, how to make out orders, invoices and statements of accounts. She received a wage and was very happy. This suited me because now I had only to attend to the workshop in the mornings and had the afternoons free to be with the children.

Taking care of Jean and Mary was harder than I had imagined it would be. They seemed restless and couldn't settle down in their new surroundings. I suppose, looking back, that I was a stranger to them; they had been young when they'd left and although they had been well cared for by their 'aunties', they'd been deprived of a mother's affection. It must have seemed as if I had abandoned them to the not-so-tender mercies of the 'mothers' at Barnardo's; they were too small to grasp the situation and probably wouldn't have understood even if they could. Then, out of the blue, they were brought back and here was I lavishing all the care and attention on them I could, trying to make up for the years we'd been apart. Yes, it must have been extraordinarily difficult for them to adjust, especially for Mary, to whom I was literally a complete stranger. I was trying to buy their love and affection and I realised later that I rushed them in my eagerness to develop a maternal relationship with them. I gave them too much, too soon: that was my big mistake and they saw only the gifts and treats, not the love that prompted the giving of them. In short, I spoiled them.

We moved from the rented house into one I had bought, and it was just as well we did because the house in Albert Road was bombed not long afterwards. We fell into a routine of having tea, closing the blackout curtains, then listening to Radio Luxemburg before heading for the shelter to sleep. The problem was that Mary could not settle to life in a city, having been used only to the countryside, and when she came home one day in tears because she was not being evacuated like the other children in her class I relented and agreed to let her go. I was very upset because I was only just beginning to know her and it hurt that she was so keen to leave me, but she was more affected by the Blitz which was then at its height in Birmingham and I decided reluctantly that it would be for the best if she went. During the time she was evacuated I took Jean and Kathleen to see her and I could see that she was happier living in the country than she had been in bombed-out Birmingham.

But troubles with the girls were not over. Jean began to rebel. One night I heard her crying in bed and when I went to see what was the matter with her she turned on me.

'I hate you! I hate you!' she screamed at me as I stood helpless beside her bed. In truth I had missed out on a lot of motherhood and I didn't really understand the children. All I could do was to ask limply, 'Why?'

'I don't like this town, nor the bombing. I want to go back to my auntie's in the country,' she wailed.

'But Jean,' I answered, 'I wanted you home here because I thought we could start a new life and be happy together.'

'No! I don't like it here and one day I'm going to run away!' She spurned my attempts to break down the wall of resentment that she'd built between us. I attempted to reason with her and I even promised that I would buy a cottage in the country when the war was over, but she just pulled the bedclothes over her head. I was get-ting nowhere so I returned downstairs to make a cup of tea and think. I wondered if I'd done the right thing to bring them away from the country where they'd been happy with the two maiden sisters for eight years. Perhaps my ambitions for them were simply a reflection of my own selfish desire to have them with me. With the war at its height and Jean such an obviously self-willed child I was concerned lest she should take it into her head to run off one day while I was at the workshop. I didn't know what to do for the best so I decided to talk it over with Kathleen, who was now sixteen. She had a bright idea that I hadn't thought of: why not let Jean come to work with us where an eye could be kept on her? I put this to Jean and she jumped at the chance. I paid her a wage and she settled down there and really enjoyed it. Now she was happy I began to relax too.

We were still spending every night down the shelters. These were actually the large cellars under the shops along Soho Road which had been converted from storerooms and are no doubt still used for this purpose because many of the buildings are still there. During the war anything of use was conscripted into the war effort and these makeshift shelters were second home to us. Some people were Air Raid Wardens but there was a need for more to volunteer their services; I dearly wanted to do so, but what with my business and the children I couldn't find time to do a regular duty. However, I did the next best thing. I called on all the women who were neighbours of ours, except those who had young babies, and organised them to knock on people's doors and help the old and infirm to the shelters at the first sound of the sirens. Several of us organised ourselves into a patrol and we brought back the news that everyone wanted to hear, namely that their houses were still standing. We were given whistles to blow if we were in trouble and out we went amidst the falling incendiaries to keep watch.

One of my companions was a young woman named Phoebe. She was Black Country born and bred, a rough and ready sort who swore like a trooper. She had a heart of gold though and we became friends. Many's the time we patrolled the streets together and it was during these walks that we exchanged stories: she had had as rough a time as I had. One night as we walked along the darkened street we paused to light fags and she said, 'I wundeer wheea my olt mon is ternight?'

'Why don't 'e come down the shelter, Phoebe?' I asked.

'Not 'im!' she replied with a laugh. "E's too busy knockin' it off with some tart. 'E's an 'orny olt bleeda.'

I cannot say I was shocked exactly; such carryings on were all too common in my experience but I was curious as to why such a spirited lass as this should put up with that kind of treatment.

'If 'e's like that why don't you leave 'im?' I asked.

'Well, Kate, 'e brings 'is money um, that's one good fault 'e's got. But I wouldn't care if 'e dain't drink sa much,' she replied.

'Does he drink a lot then?'

'Drink a lot?' she repeated with a laugh. ''E soaks 'is bloody bread in it!'

As I began to laugh she nudged me and said, 'Yo ain't 'eard nothin' yet. One night I was in bed when 'e cum um drunk, it musta bin about two in the mornin' an' as soon as 'e got in bed – just in 'is shirt – 'e lit a fag an' fell asleep. It warnt lung afore I smelt summat bernin'. It was the flock bed smoulderin'. With thet I kickt 'im outta bed an' ran fer a bucket o' wata. Well, when I come back 'e was standin' in 'is short shirt with 'is cock in 'is 'and, pissin' over the bed.' At this we both burst into fits of laughter before I recovered enough to ask, 'What 'appened then?'

''E 'ad the bleedin' sauce ter arsk me ter get back in bed with 'im. "Cum on," 'e said, "it's wet but warm."'

'And did yer?'

'I 'ad ter, there wus nowhere else ter goo, but I did manage ter turn the mattress over an' sleep at the foot.' When I continued to laugh she said in mock seriousness, 'Yo'll larf yer bleedin' 'ead off one day when I got time ter tell yer some of 'is antics!'

Phoebe was a great tonic to me on those blacked-out nights and in later years we remained great friends and neighbours. She was dragged up, one of sixteen children, and her father a miner. In turn I told about my own childhood, little better than hers, about the theft of the pig when we went hoppicking, and about Granny. We amused each other for hours with tales about 'the old days', a habit that the reader can see I have not lost.

There was a spirit of camaraderie in the shelters; we had sing-songs to raise our hearts. There was a young woman named Rose Smith; her father owned the cut-glassware shop above, and each night she and her young man would play banjo and concertina while we sang our hearts out to drown out the sound of the bombing. They were a great bunch of characters; often they would slip across to The Freighted Horse for a nip and return tiddly, but who could blame them for trying to remain merry? None of us knew if we would see tomorrow.

While we were out on patrol one night, Phoebe and I called in to my house to fill flasks with cocoa to take back for the children. Suddenly a series of incendiaries rained down nearby. We dashed out to see what damage had been done but in the confusion I lost sight of my friend. I blew my whistle and a second or two later she appeared, tearing down the street carrying two dustbin lids.

'Put this on yer bleedin' 'ead,' she cried out to me over the din, 'while I get a bucket o' sand.' Being unofficial we had no tin hats like the regular Wardens. We looked like a couple of coolies that night, rushing about with buckets of sand, trying to quench the flames. It was real panic stations and no mistake.

I always left my door open, day and night. You could trust everybody in those days. I would leave a big kettle of boiling water on the stove and several cups, milk, tea and sugar on the table for the Wardens to go in and make themselves a cup of tea. There was also a drop of the hard stuff should any of them prefer that to the weaker brew. On quiet nights when there were no raids I would invite the neighbours in for a sing-song. Somebody would play the piano and I would start the ball rolling with one of my jolly songs or a story and soon I had the nickname 'The Merry Widow'.

During April 1941 we had the worst raids. They lasted from dusk to dawn and although we women did our best, the Wardens almost pushed us down the shelters, saying that it was not fit for us to be out. Then the shelters were really crowded with people from all over. Children would be crying and women weeping and all were praying to the Lord to bring us safely through the night. We sang 'The White Cliffs of Dover' and 'Pack up Your Troubles' to keep up our spirits until the morning when the 'All Clear' sounded and we emerged, blinking, into the cold grey light of dawn to survey the night's destruction. Several of our neighbours had been killed in their cellars. This was the nearest the reality of death had come to us so far but I was soon to discover to my shock the personal horror of the Blitz. A Warden came running up, breathless and asked for me by name. When I told him who I was he informed me that Camden Drive had been bombed and that Mary and Mum had both been killed.

The cold, damp walk to the Drive sticks clear in my memory even now. I prayed that the Warden had been mistaken or that it had been another house that had been hit. Although we'd never seen eye-to-eye, blood is thicker than water after all. I stumbled over bricks and rubble where bombs and incendiaries had destroyed buildings in the streets leading to the Drive. Then I came to the top of the hill and could see at once that my worst fears had been realised. There were dozens of people standing about looking dazed; some were weeping quietly. Parties of rescue workers were digging into the rubble for the bodies of victims. I pushed through the crowd until I found myself prevented from going further by an Air Raid Precaution Warden and a fireman. It was only after I'd explained why I was there that they let me through. When I got to the heap of bricks that had been my childhood home I found that Jack, Frank, Charlie and Liza were already there. I asked Jack if the Warden had been right and he nodded sadly. Frank said there was nothing we could do, which was true, but I wasn't satisfied with their explanation of what had happened. I wanted to know why they hadn't been in the shelter in the basement of Stern and Bell's warehouse. Jack answered that no one had had a chance because the bombs fell before the warning had sounded. A few survivors had been dug out but many had suffered the same fate as Mum and Mary.

I didn't stay long but made my way along the cobbled streets; I was angry that they'd died like rats without a chance. They were like plenty of others who struggled along for years through the Depression in the hope of a better tomorrow and this was it. They'd had a brief glimpse of prosperity when the war industries had taken on labour, and the same war had snuffed them out as if they had never been.

However, I had little time to brood because I had to go to check that my business premises were still intact. When I arrived I found that some of the girls had started work. They pointed out a hole in the roof and when I investigated I found an unexploded incendiary bomb under the slates and plaster that littered the floor. I screamed at them to get out at once. They hadn't noticed it there but now they needed no second bidding to collect their gas masks and evacuate the place posthaste. When we were outside I called to some firemen who were shoring up some nearby buildings. They came as cool as you like and carried the bomb out. Luckily for them it turned out to be a dud.

Mum's and Mary's funeral was a few days later. I followed the coffins and saw them buried in Warstone Lane cemetery nearby. It was another bitter April day and there were crowds of mourners.

This was not a private occasion. Dozens were buried that day. The coffins were lined up in rows outside the church, stretching back out through the iron gates into the street. The bell clanged all day long. I did not see what my Mum's and sister's injuries were and I was glad to remember them as they were when I last saw them. In fact I didn't visit the site of our yard again for forty years, and when I did the memories it brought back started me writing.

There is little left to tell of my story. The war dragged on for years after that, but the raids stopped and we were to settle down to an almost normal life; that is, if you don't count the rationing and shortages and news of casualties from the various theatres of war. These were far away, though, and I could take some comfort in having Kathleen and Jean with me, and I was in any case fully occupied with the war effort.

When peace broke out in 1945 I fetched Mary home from Wales and I put her in the workshop with her sisters, thinking she would settle down. She wanted to serve in a fruiterer's so I let her but she hopped about from one thing to another, never staying anywhere long. Eventually she entered nursing and I breathed a sigh of relief. She worked with tubercular patients at Selly Oak hospital for a time but she left and went on the buses! She tried hairdressing and later the Women's Royal Airforce. While she was serving in Singapore she met and married a Scotsman and eventually they settled in the USA and raised four sons there.

Jean has four daughters and four grandchildren herself now. She was a very attractive girl and when she was sixteen had the boys after her like flies round a honey pot. I had to keep my eyes open, especially where the Yanks were concerned. You don't need me to repeat the reputation they had. I dare say it was overdone, but I knew of girls who got more than they bargained for by going out with an American. I had no case to worry though; I knew I could trust my girls to take care of themselves and they didn't let themselves or me down. There were some incidents, however. Once I remember a travelling salesman calling with some samples. Kathleen said he'd been before but I hadn't seen him. I was making out an order and could watch as he walked over to the bench where Jean was working. They exchanged words and I saw Jean shake her head and blush. At this I intervened and asked him what he wanted.

'I only asked her if I could take her out for a ride in the car. May I?' he added.

'No yow may not,' I told him firmly, leaving him in no doubt.

'There'd be no harm,' he insisted smoothly. 'I'd have brought her back safe.'

'Maybe you would and maybe not. But she's scarcely sixteen and you're probably a married man.' I gave him the flea in the ear he deserved and he took his order and left. Later I discovered that he'd given Jean a gold chain and pendant but she'd been too scared to tell me and had flushed it down the toilet.

My son returned safe after the war and he married a Scots girl and they have four children and six grandchildren now. Kathleen is happily married and she and her husband now live with me, so you could say that all in all, despite some sticky patches, I've had a successful life. I have twelve grandchildren and ten great grand-children. My one regret is that I missed out on Kathleen, John, Jean and Mary's childhood but I can do nothing about that now. I have got lots to be pleased about. I have many dear friends and to cap it all I am an author whose work, I am told, has been enjoyed by many people. My original ambition that my people should not be forgotten has been achieved and now, a week away from my eighty-second birthday, I have only that one nagging regret: the loss of those years half a century ago when my children needed a mother's care and love so much.

ALL MY DAYS

Contents

Tales of Childhood

I am now in my eighty-fourth year, and I often find myself thinking of my childhood. I was born in Birmingham in 1903, and I grew up with people who, like my own family, lived in dire poverty, in disease-ridden slums. They had to bear hardships always, and tragedies often. But these people had a determination to survive, whatever the cost. It was this, coupled with a sense of humour, which enabled them to get through a life of existence.

The day I was five years old my mother registered me at the local school. I remember my teacher, who was a small, dumpy person, very stern and forbidding, with a weather-worn, wrinkled skin which made her look older than her years. She was never seen without a bamboo cane carried at the ready.

We were taught our ABC sitting on bare wooden floors which always smelt strongly of disinfectant. Many of us kids didn't even have bloomers or knickers, and if teacher happened to notice us with our legs apart, she would rap our knees with the cane.

'Disgusting,' she'd yell out for all the other kids to hear. 'Showing all you've got! It's disgraceful the way some of you girls are sent to school! Tell your mothers, aunts, or sisters, or whoever's in charge of you, to find you some kind of bloomers! Otherwise I shall send you back home next time you come.'

The kids who were lucky enough to own a pair of bloomers would titter and call after us:

> Maggie Brown's got no drawers
> Will yer kindly lend her yowers

When I got home one Friday afternoon, I told my mum that the teacher had said she would send me home if I came again without bloomers.

'Yer'll afta buy 'er a pair Polly,' I heard my dad say to Mum.

'Buy 'er a pair?' she yelled. 'Where do yer think the money comes from? It don't grow on trees, yer know.'

'Well, try an' mek 'er a pair out o' my old striped union shirt. It's beyond patchin', any'ow,' Dad replied.

'I was goin' ter cut that up fer towels,' she answered.

No more was said. Dad went out to fetch in the tin bath from off the outside wall, for Friday night was my bath night. As I sat splashing myself all over in the warm carbolic soapy water, I noticed Mum had already begun to cut up the shirt, and was trying to codge two legs together, as she sat by the fire facing me.

I remember wearing those monstrosities until they had gone too far to be patched any more. Sometime later, one of our neighbours was lucky enough to buy an old second-hand sewing machine. Soon after that all the neighbours pooled their pennies and bought some brown calico and made all us unfortunates new bloomers. But I was only allowed to wear these when I went to church, or Sunday School. For everyday school I had to wear my codged-together ones.

When we were a bit older we moved up off the floor to long dark oak forms, which seated four. Raised above each form was a lean-to ledge, with a slot for our wooden pens, and four holes which held our crock ink wells. Everything always smelt of disinfectant or paraffin.

Our teachers were very strict, and strong on discipline: but there was nothing they could do about how we lived or dressed, as long as we had clean heads, and bodies free from vermin.

One day at school I began to itch all over. My teacher noticed me scratching, and with a scowl on her face she called me out in front of the class. As I stood beside her, she said loudly, for all to hear, 'Have you got fleas? If you have, you had better sit in the back row.'

'No, miss. I just itch,' I answered nervously.

'Turn around, and face the class!' she said sternly.

Keeping me at arm's length, she lifted my hair with a pencil; when she'd had a good look, she gave me a hard poke with her thumb in the middle of my back.

'Now get back to your seat. And don't let me see you scratching again, or I'll send you to the clinic.'

I knew all the other girls' eyes were on me, as I held my head down and walked slowly back to my seat. I felt ready to cry. I was glad when I looked up at the clock that hung on the wall over the blackboard, and saw that it read a minute to twelve. That next minute seemed like an hour, until teacher took up the iron bell from her desk to let us know it was time to march in single file down the narrow dark corridor, and out into the street.

I was still tearful as I entered our house, hoping Mum was not at home. But she was standing black-leading the grate. As she had her back towards me I took the opportunity to give my back a good hard rub against the edge of the wooden sofa. Suddenly she turned round and saw me.

'What's up with yer now?' she yelled.

'I itch all over, Mum, an' now me back feels sore,' I whimpered.

When she had looked at my back, she said she was taking me to see the doctor.

'Can't 'e come 'ere, Mum, yer know I'm scared of doctors.' (Our neighbours often called a doctor a 'quack' or a 'butcher', or an 'old sawbones'.)

'No 'e can't,' she snapped. 'I ain't got coppers ter waste on visits.'

She grabbed my hand and hurried me along to see Dr Mackay, who lived in a bow-windowed shabby old house, just around the corner, with his wife and three children. He did all his consulting in his front room, and his back room was the dispensary, where his wife gave out bottles of medicine or whatever was needed. You didn't have a prescription to take to a chemist in those days. His visits were as low as sixpence, but even that was a lot for poor people to pay; you could get a couple of meals for sixpence in those days.

Mum and I sat on the long, hard form in the narrow corridor, which smelt strongly of disinfectant. There were several other women waiting their turn, with small children and babies in arms. When it was our turn, Mum stopped whispering to the woman next to her, and almost dragged me in. The doctor was a large, thick-set man, with unruly red hair and moustache. I began to tremble with fear, wondering what he was going to do or where he would send me. He frowned over the top of his spectacles, first at Mum, then at me, then, turning his gaze on Mum again, he snapped 'Well?'

'I've brought me daughter fer yer ter see, doctor. Yer see, she keeps scratchin' 'erself.'

'Take her behind the screen and take her clothes off,' he snapped impatiently.

Quickly Mum undressed me, taking off all but my threadbare shift. As I stood there shivering with fear and cold, she went to tell him that I was ready. As soon as he saw me he told Mum to take off my shift, and there I stood, naked. I looked away and closed my eyes. When it was my bath night, I always felt dirty when I looked down at my nakedness. Now here I stood, as naked as I was born, with this man staring down and prodding me. I couldn't for the life of me open my eyes until he'd stopped. Then I heard him say to my Mum, 'Get her dressed at once, and wait in the corridor until I bring you out some powder.'

'What's 'er got, then?' I heard Mum ask, as I hurriedly fumbled to get dressed.

'Chicken pox,' he snapped.

While we waited in the corridor again, one of the women asked Mum what was wrong with me. I expected her to say 'Mind yer own bloody business,' but she didn't for once. When she cried out 'Chickenpox' I saw everyone move away from us quickly.

When the doctor gave Mum the powder he told her to dab it on the chickenpox sores twice a day. For four weeks I stayed away from school, with Mum roughly dabbing my neck, back and chest. I was also kept isolated from the rest of the family. This meant I couldn't sleep in the same bed as my brother and sister, so I had a bed made up for me on the wooden sofa downstairs. During those four weeks my Mum had a regular jaunt to the school clinic for bottles of disinfectant to wash our clothes with, and use around the rooms.

When I got well again I started back to school. But three weeks later I was sent home with a sore throat. I was too scared to tell my Mum in case she took me to see the doctor again, but at school the next day I vomited all down my frock, and my teacher gave me the cane and sent me home.

As soon as Mum saw the state I was in, she cried out, 'What yer bin eatin' now?'

'Nothin', Mum, but me throat is sore. *Please*,' I pleaded, '*please* don't tek me ter that doctor again.'

'Open yer mouth an' let's look,' she shouted.

She blew some dry sulphur powder down my throat, then she

dragged in the tin bath from off the wall outside. I had a bath, then I was sent straight to bed.

'An' yer can stay theea, until I can find time ter see ter yer!' she yelled impatiently.

Although I cried as I climbed the attic stairs, I was pleased she didn't take me to see the doctor again. But I was still feeling sick and restless. I couldn't even swallow my spittle without it hurting me. Later that afternoon, I plucked up my courage and, regardless of what my mum would say or do to me, I got out of bed and went downstairs.

'Mum,' I cried, as I sat on the stairs, 'I think I'm goin' ter die, I can't swaller, an' my throat feels on fire.'

She soaked one of my dad's old woollen socks in camphorated oil and pinned it around my throat, then sent me back upstairs again.

During the night I tossed and turned. My throat was so hot and dry, I felt I must have a drink. But I was scared to wake my mum and ask her: waking her at any time was the worst thing any of us could do. So, not to disturb my brother and sister who slept in the same bed, I crept slowly and silently out of bed and reached for the piece of candle that was kept on the orange-box beside the bed. Barefoot and in my threadbare shift, I crept quietly down the stairs. When I reached the first floor landing I didn't feel quite so nervous, for I could hear Mum and Dad sending the pigs home to market. When at last I crept into the living room I got a piece of paper and from the hot embers I managed to light the piece of candle. I looked up at the mantleshelf at the alarm clock which only had one hand. I saw that it was pointing between twelve and one, so it was now about half past twelve. We didn't have water laid on in the house, so I tried the kettle on the hob, but it was bone dry. There was only one thing left for me to do. I slipped Mum's black shawl over my head and shoulders and, picking up a mug from the table, I went out to get some water from the tap in the yard. I didn't need the lighted candle now. It was a lovely moonlit night, and the gas lamp in the yard lit up all the houses and the yard. I drank three mugs straight down of that delicious cold water. I had just filled the mug again to take indoors, and was about to cross the yard, when I heard the sound of cartwheels coming down our narrow cobbled street. Scared, I hid behind the wall that divided the back-to-back houses, but as I peeped over it, I could see quite clearly two ragged individuals, a man and a woman, pushing a flat hand-cart with their few chattels: two wooden chairs, a table, two straw mattresses, an iron bedstead, and other odd utensils. Following close behind were a small boy and girl, who, I was to find out later were my age and were twins.

''urry yerselves, yow two kids,' I heard the man say. 'We ain't got all night.'

I realised that this family, like a good many more families in those days, were doing a moonlight flit. As I peeped from my hiding place, I saw the man and woman push the hand-cart into the next yard and enter the empty house at the back of ours. These people were to be our new neighbours.

Shivering with the cold night air, I hurried indoors. After throwing off Mum's old black shawl, I drank the other mug of water and quietly crept back upstairs again. By now my throat had cooled down a little, and it didn't seem to be quite so painful. I looked down at my brother and sister, and, glad to see they were still asleep, I snuggled down on the warm mattress beside them. Soon I fell asleep too. The next thing I knew, Mum was yelling up the attic stairs.

'Yow betta 'urry yerselves, yow three, fer school, afower I come up theea an' tip yer out.'

My sister and brother leapt out of bed first. I would never dress or undress in front of them, so I waited. Then as soon as they went down the stairs I jumped out of bed and began to dress quickly. When I was only half-dressed I happened to glance into the piece of looking glass that hung over the small fireplace. I got the shock of my life. Staring at me I saw another face with narrow slits for eyes. Quickly I looked around the room expecting to see someone there, but there was no one. When I looked into the mirror again and put my hands up to feel if it was *my face* I could see, I got scared. My face and neck were twice their normal size, and my puffed eyes were just slits. Screaming, and half-naked, I ran down the stairs.

'Mum! Mum!' I screamed, aghast. 'Look at me face!'

'Oh, my God!' she yelled out, 'Yow've got mumps!'

So, with another sock and a smothering of more of that vile-smelling camphorated oil, I was hurried back to bed again.

I couldn't settle to lie down in bed. The smell from the sock was so awful I could almost taste it. I needed air, so I got out of bed and pushed up the attic window, and as I looked down into the yard below, I saw my Mum with several of the neighbours. Through snatches of overheard conversation I discovered they were discussing our new neighbour.

I hadn't been standing there for long when Mum happened to glance up and see me at the window. Before I could fly back into bed she was in the room.

'Get yerself down in that bed at once!' she shrieked. 'An' if I catch yer out again yer'll feel the back of me 'and.'

Scared, I slid down underneath the bedclothes and stayed there until I heard her slam the window down and return downstairs.

I had to stay in bed for two whole weeks. But I was glad about one thing: I had the bed to myself. Liza and Frankie had to sleep in Mum's room, on a makeshift bed on a straw mattress.

Kind neighbours sent whatever titbits they could spare, and, with Mum's home-made concoctions, my face soon came back to its normal size. Although I was very pale and thin, I wanted to go back to school, for I was missing my playmates. But when I asked my mum, she snapped at me 'No! Yer can't go yet, yer can 'ave another few days 'elpin' me with the washin'.'

I followed her down the yard, where she handed me the bucket.

'Yer can start fillin' this, an' bring it in the brew'ouse.'

It was a heavy galvanised bucket, one my dad had brought home from somewhere. I'd got it half filled, and was about to carry it to the brewhouse when I dropped it quick, and ran behind the brewhouse door for cover.

'What's the matter with yer now? An' where's the bucket o' water?'

'Ssh, Mum,' I whispered. 'The school board man's knockin' our door.'

'Well, yer betta stop theea till 'e's gone.'

We both watched as he knocked several times on our door. Getting no answer, he walked away. He came back the following afternoon just as Dad was soaking his feet in a bowl of hot water. As soon as I saw him, I hid on the stairs. When he knocked, Dad called out, 'Come in.'

'I've come about your daughter,' he said at once. 'She's not attended school for three weeks, so I've come to warn you, if you don't send that child to school you'll be having a summons.'

'The missus couldn't send 'er, she's 'ad mumps,' was Dad's reply.
'Well, you have to send in a doctor's note,' he answered.

Dad said he hadn't got coppers to spare for a doctor's note, but he would see that I went next day. Mum and Dad quarrelled. In the end she promised him I would go next day. But she still kept me to help in the house.

A week later Dad received the summons. He was fined half a crown and given seven days to pay it. But the good, kind neighbours rallied round, and with their few pennies they were able to pay his fine.

After more quarrels I was happy to be back at school. But I found some of the girls kept their distance from me, afraid they would catch what I had lost. I snubbed them in return. Then, as I stood alone in the playground, a little red-haired girl came up to me.

'Yow 'ad mumps?' she asked at once.

'Yes,' I snapped, 'an' what's it ter do with yow? An' who are yow? I've never seen yer before.'

'Me name's Winnie Nashe, I live in the next yard.'

'Ooh, I remember, yer the new people come ter live in number nine.'

'Yes. Want a piece o' toffee?' she asked as she handed me a piece of treacle toffee.

'Thank you, but yer betta not let teacher see yer suckin' it or yer'll get the cane.'

'I'd like ter see 'er or anybody else lay a finger on me, an' they'll get what for.'

She was quite a little spitfire, but I liked her, and from then on we became good friends. We went almost everywhere together, and shared whatever we had. She was just three months older than me, and the same height. But, apart from that, we were as different in looks, as chalk is from cheese. I had long dark hair, and I was pale and thin. She was plump, with a round, rosy face covered with freckles. And she was very pretty.

I took her home one day to meet my mum. Mum usually didn't like the girls who called for me, but I was pleased to see she took to Winnie at once.

As we were walking up the hill, we met Winnie's twin brother, Willie. He was so much like Winnie, you couldn't tell them apart, only that he wore much too large ragged trousers, well below his knees.

When we left school the following day Winnie said she had to hurry home to help her mum. I didn't want her to. I said I wanted someone to talk to.

'Would yer like ter come 'ome an' meet my mum, then?' she asked.

'Will she mind?' I asked.

'Course she won't, I told 'er yesterday I'd bring yer sometime, so come on, don't be shy,' she said, as she took my hand.

As we passed our yard I told her I would have to call and tell my mum where I was going. There was only Frankie at home.

'Frankie,' I said, 'will yer tell me mum if she wants me I'll be round the back in Winnie's 'ouse.'

'All right, but mind what yer up to,' he replied.

'Who's that 'ansome lad yer spoke to?' Winnie asked.

'Me brother,' I answered.

'I could fall fer 'im,' she giggled. 'Come on if yer comin'.'

When we got to Winnie's I was surprised to see such an untidy house. Everything seemed to be cluttered about everywhere. There were old coats thrown over chairs, and strips of cloth strewn across the table. Squatting on the floor sat Winnie's mum and dad. They too had red hair. And when they both stood up they looked like Tweedle Dum and Tweedle Dee.

'Come an' sit down if you can find room, an' would you like a cuppa tea?' Winnie's mum asked.

'Yes, please,' I answered.

'Put the kettle on the fire then, Winnie, while I get the things in off the line.'

What I expected to see her bring in was a basket full of washing, but instead she had an armful of old grey, black and brown coats that she gave to her husband to cut into strips.

On the way home, I asked Winnie what her dad did for a living.

'Oh, 'e's in the rag trade,' she said.

'What yer mean, the rag trade?'

'Well, 'e's really a rag and bone man, but when anybody asks, we all say that, because it sounds better.'

'But what's yer mum and dad cut the coats into strips for?'

'Well, Mum makes peg rugs, and sells them fer a shillin'. Sometimes when she gets an order, I take one, or maybe two, and charge another tuppence, which I keep fer meself,' she added.

So that was why she always had plenty of sweets to share with me.

One day during the summer, I went with her to take two rugs to a woman who lived a few streets away. When Winnie knocked on the door she came out and said she was sorry, but she only wanted one.

'But me mum said yer wanted two.'

'I'm sorry, dear,' I heard her say, 'but my sister's changed her mind.'

'Yer can 'ave 'em both fer two an' tuppence,' Winnie said.

'I only want the one, or not at all,' she replied firmly.

'Very well,' Winnie replied, an' thank yer.'

She gave her the peg rug, and took the one and tuppence.

As she walked down the path Winnie dropped the two pennies down her stocking, and said she would try to sell the other one next door. She lifted the brass knocker. But the woman who came to the door shouted at us, 'Be off with yer or I'll set the bloody dog on yer.'

'Yer can 'ave it fer a shillin', Winnie said.

'I don't want it!' she yelled again.

When she tried to shut the door Winnie pleaded, and pushed the door wider. But as soon as we saw the bull terrier growling at us in the hall, we ran for our lives. When we glanced back we saw the dog was gaining on us. Now, Winnie wasn't able to run as fast as me, for she was carrying the rug. But as soon as the dog got near enough, she turned around and flung the rug at him and fled. When we got some distance away, we looked back to see the rug going around in circles with the dog beneath, trying to free himself. Then we hurried to explain to her mum what had happened.

'Never mind, as long as he didn't bite you,' was all she said.

The next day, Winnie told me her dad had found the rug lying in the gutter, so he brought it home in the cart.

A while later Winnie's mum had to go into the infirmary for an operation, and my mum said Winnie could stay with us until she came home again. Mum made up a makeshift bed so that Winnie and I could sleep together, and we had great fun telling stories and reading from the comic strips. We were both so happy – for a few days. Then the school nurse came to examine all our heads and bodies, and when she saw Winnie and I had scabies, we were sent home at once. Mum was furious. All the neighbours knew now from the other kids, so they kept their distance. When the health man came that afternoon, he said we and Mum too, would have to go to the clinic to be cleansed.

I shall never forget the humiliation we suffered that day. When we arrived, Mum was sent into one room and Winnie and me were taken into another. We were stripped naked, and all our clothes, and even our boots, were taken away to be fumigated. We were embarrassed, trying not to look at each other's naked bodies.

When the nurse came in, she took us into an almost bare whitewashed room which contained a large enamel bath full of steaming hot water. As we stood there, trying to hide our private parts with our hands, she poured disinfectant from a large blue bottle into the bath. We were fascinated by the way the disinfectant turned the water almost white, like milk. Then the nurse made us jump, calling out impatiently, 'Come on! Get in, yow two!'

But we jumped out quicker than we went in: the bath water was so strong, it almost burnt our flesh. However, there was no escape. With her two strong hands she pushed us roughly into the water, and with the hard brush she scrubbed us from head to foot. When she thought we'd had enough she lifted us out, and took us dripping wet into another room. This too was bare but for an iron pipe stove that was belching smoke. We gazed at one another. We had begun to weep, wondering what she was going to do to us next, when she came back into the room with a bucket of what looked like white-wash, a large brush, and a coarse calico towel.

'Dry yerselves with this, then follow me,' she called out as she threw the towel towards us.

As we followed behind her, we tried to cover our naked bodies by wrapping the towel around ourselves. But it was soon snatched away.

'Yer don't afta be shy in front of me! I 'ave lots more than this ter deal with. Now 'urry up, I ain't got all day!' she cried our impatiently.

This room too was bare as we entered. We were told to stand in the middle of the room, and, using the brush, she slapped the white paste all over each of us in turn. She seemed to be enjoying this job, smiling at each stroke. We were left again until the paste had dried. Then we were handed our clothes (which had been fumigated), and we got dressed. We met Mum in the hall. She was shouting and swearing at the nurse, and the attendants, about the state of our clothes that we had to walk home in.

The three of us felt ashamed to walk down our street, so Mum took us the long way round to avoid the nosy neighbours. When we got home, Mum told us to take off our frocks and she would iron out the creases. Later that same day, she went back to the clinic to fetch her supply of disinfectant for the home. This disinfectant was called Condy's Fluid. It was very powerful stuff, but Mum hid it away and only used it sparingly. Half a spoon in the washing, the same in the water used for cleaning the bedroom and attic, and a drop in the slop bucket we kept beside the bed, in case we were cut short in the night.

Growing Up

A s soon as Mrs Nashe came home from the infirmary, Mum
sent Winnie packing. Mum said it was their fault we had got
scabies, through the old coats they collected, and I was forbidden to
have anything more to do with Winnie, or go near their house. After
that Winnie never came to our house for me, and I never went to
hers. All the same, unbeknownst to Mum, I often met her outside
school hours. But a few weeks later I was upset to find that Winnie
and her family had left the district.

It was some months before I saw her again. Then one afternoon,
as I was busy scrubbing the stairs, there came a couple of taps on
the door. At first I was afraid to answer it. I asked myself, was it
someone for my dad for the debts he owed? For Mum had warned
me if anyone called while she was out I was not to answer, or if I
had to I must just say my dad had gone away, and I didn't know
where. But whoever it was this time wouldn't leave, they just kept
on knocking. Slowly I opened the door a little, and I was about to
ask who it was when I was surprised to see my old friend Winnie.
At first I hardly recognised her. She'd quite grown up. Where I was
still straight up and down and flat-chested, she had developed a bust
which seemed to burst through her too-tight faded brown velvet
frock. And her hair, which had been fiery red, had changed to a rich
auburn. I noticed that she still had plenty of freckles, though.

She cried out, 'Don't stand there gawpin' at me, don't yer know
me?'

'Yes, of course I do, Winnie, but my, how you've changed.'

'Ain't yer goin' ter call me in then?' she asked.

'Yes, Winnie, but I never expected ter see yer – not terday,
anyroad. Well, come on in, an' pull up a chair by the fire, while I
put me bucket away, an' mek a pot o' tea.'

Winnie told me that she was back living in the next street, and she would be coming back to our school on Monday. I told her that I was now in Standard Six, with a new teacher, Mrs Frost. I liked Mrs Frost. She was strict, but kind if you tried to do things right. The only trouble was, she tried to make us sound our aitches, and generally 'talk posh', as we called it. This was easy enough when you were repeating words in class, but as soon as you got home, with your mum and dad and all the neighbours talking Brummy slang, it became impossible. It was like speaking another language.

A while after Winnie returned, I was soaping my chest one bath night when I became scared. I felt two hard lumps around my nipples, and they were painful to touch. I couldn't tell my mum in case she took me to see the doctor again. But I had to tell someone. Winnie was my only hope. Next morning when she called for me to go to the park, I began to weep. When she asked why I was crying, I said, 'I can't go out with yer terday, Winnie, I've got these awful pains around me nipples.'

''ow long 'ave yer 'ad 'em?' she asked.

'Well, I only felt 'em last night when I 'ad me bath.'

'Yer betta let me 'ave a look,' she said.

I was too shy to show her, so I asked her if she knew what was wrong with me.

'I don't know, do I, unless I look at 'em!' she snapped.

'All right, I'll shut me eyes while yer look.'

When I pulled up my frock and she felt my breasts, I began to feel dirty, and cringed. But she put me at ease, when I heard her laugh out loud and say, 'Yer can put yer frock down an' open yer eyes. Yer silly little fool – yer know what's wrong with yer? *Nothin*'. It's the start of yer titties growin', but they're only lemon drops yet. You wait till they grow like mine.'

'Ooh, I don't want 'em to grow out like yowers,' I replied. 'I wouldn't know what clothes ter wear.'

'You will when the time comes. My mum tells me if I grow 'em any bigger, I'll afta wear a camisole an' a pair of stays.'

I was relieved to know it was only the beginning of my little 'lemon drops' or my 'titties' as she called them.

Some of the girls at school went to swimming classes, and one afternoon Winnie asked me if I'd ever been swimming.

'Never,' I said. 'Why do yer ask?'

'Well, we go to the public swimming baths on Wednesday afternoons.'

'I don't think my mum would let me go.'

'She wouldn't know if yer dain't tell 'er. Anyway, it's better than a tin bath, yer can't swim in a tin bath, an' teacher says it develops yer body muscles, an' Katie, yours sure needs developin', yer such a skinny little thing fer yer age.'

'But I can't swim, an' I ain't got a costume,' I replied.

'Yer can borrow my old one, it's too small for me now. It's only a penny. I'll treat yer. Say now yer'll come.'

'But I've told yer, I can't swim.'

'Yer can learn. There's always an instructor there with a long pole.'

Well, I thought, here goes. If Winnie could swim, it was about time I learned. So the following Wednesday afternoon I went with Winnie and the other girls to Northward Street baths.

Winnie paid my penny to the attendant, but when she handed me a towel she looked down her nose at me. 'Yer a new 'un, ain't yer? Well, see as yer scrub yer feet befower yer go in the baths.'

After Winnie and I scrubbed our feet in the large basin, we had to undress in a shared cubicle. It wasn't really large enough for one person, let alone two of us. There was hardly room to turn round. It had half a door that swung outwards and inwards, and it wasn't very private, anyone passing could see our faces, and our feet and legs. But we managed to undress.

When Winnie handed me the costume I was to wear, I was disappointed. It had dark brown and yellow wide stripes. Any other time I wouldn't have been seen dead in it. But Winnie had meant to be kind. I couldn't hurt her feelings by refusing to wear it, so I put it on, but it was too big.

'Don't worry, it'll cling ter yer when it's wet.'

We walked out of the cubicle together, but when I saw such an expanse of water I became nervous. I didn't even have the courage to go in the shallow end. I just sat on the side and was content to dangle my feet in the water, watching Winnie dive and swim in the deep end. But as I was sitting there someone came behind me and pushed me in. I panicked, went down like a brick, and hit the bottom. When I came up to the top, I almost choked. Foolishly, I began to clutch at the water, and went down a second time. The next thing I knew, I was being dragged towards the steps on the end of the pole. I then began to climb out. I didn't realise I was naked until I saw the attendant holding up what looked like a wet prehistoric bumblebee. I was overcome with shame. Putting one hand over my titties and the other to hide my private parts, I slid along the wet slabs to find the cubicle. In my confusion I turned into the wrong one. Someone swung the door out again, and I almost landed in the water once more. But Winnie came to the rescue and dragged me along into the next one.

She collected the 'bumblebee' while I dried and got dressed, and when she came back, she told me who it was that had pushed me in.

'Don't cry now,' she said. 'I'll push 'er in next week, an' 'old 'er down! Until she apologises ter yer,' she added.

'But I ain't comin' again,' I whimpered.

'Yer'll enjoy it when once yer've learnt ter swim.'

'I'll never learn, anyway I ain't wearin' that monstrosity again,' I said, throwing it on the floor.

'Well, will yer come an' watch me? Yer needn't get undressed.'

I agreed, but it was no fun just watching, and I was so eager to learn. A couple of weeks later, I told my dad that I wanted to learn to swim.

'All the other girls in our class go, Dad, but I ain't got a costume.'

'Well, if that's all that's worryin' yer, I'll buy yer one from the second-'and market.'

Sure enough, he bought me one which was made of some kind of black woollen material, with white polka dots and frills around the neck and the bottom of the skirt, and a cap to match. And they fitted. I threw my arms around his neck and thanked him. But when Mum saw it she said, ''ow much did that cost yer?'

'Only 'alf a crown,' he replied.

'I could 'ave bought food with that, instead of turnin' 'er 'ead on such silly folderols!'

He told her it was his baccy money he'd saved, and that I wanted to learn to swim. I remember she just shrugged her shoulders and walked out.

I thought, whatever happens, I'll pay him back for his kindness. I was now determined I was going to be the swimmer my Dad would be proud of. And so I made a nuisance of myself, pestering the attendant to teach me, at first with the pole. A few weeks later, I won my certificate for ten lengths of the bath. And I was very happy to see how proud my dad was of me, as he hung it on the wall next to my brothers' twenty-length certificates. In the coming weeks I became a better swimmer than Winnie. I even learned to dive, and I won my next certificate for twenty lengths.

But I was also determined that, whatever happened, I would manage to give my dad his half-crown back. He was still out of work, and it upset me when I used to see him splitting open nub ends of cigarettes for tobacco to put in his clay pipe.

Winnie was very kind, and each time we ran errands we saved our halfpennies. But this way it was taking too long for me to save the half-crown *and* the coppers to go swimming. Then one day, as we were walking along the Parade, we saw workmen digging up the tar blocks from between the tram lines. Winnie went up to one and asked if we could have some.

'No, yow can't! Bugger off, before I clout yer ear'oles!' he shouted. But we weren't to be put off. We hid ourselves and waited until the workmen moved further along the tram lines, then we came from our hiding place and helped ourselves to several blocks that we saw stacked up against the wall. These we sold, two for a penny and no questions asked, to some of the poor people several streets away, who couldn't afford threepence for a bag of coal, or a bucket of slack. We thought we could help ourselves regularly, but other people must have had the same idea. The next day the rest had been carted away.

Another afternoon I did a very foolish and wicked thing. My eldest sister, Mary, had come to visit my mum. As I sat on the stool by the fire I heard them having high words. Mum wanted Mary to lend her some money, but Mary was adamant. 'No! You've had the last off me. I never get it back.' In her temper she bounced out, with Mum following her. I noticed Mary had forgotten to pick up her purse, which was lying on the table. Quickly I opened it to look inside, and when I saw some loose change, including two half-crowns, temptation got the better of me. I took out one half-crown and closed the purse. Almost immediately I wanted to put it back, but it was too late, my sister had come back for the purse, and left again with it.

Now I was scared. As soon as I thought about it I knew I couldn't really give the half-crown to my dad, he'd ask questions where I got it from, and I couldn't ever lie to him – he always had a way of finding out. I would have to try to return it somehow. There was only one answer. When Mary called again, I'd try and slip it into her purse, or drop it in her coat pocket. Meanwhile I hid it inside one of my woollen stockings. I even went to sleep in my stockings, in case I lost the half-crown. The coin seemed to burn a hole in my leg with guilt.

Mary called again the next day, and as soon as I saw her, I went hot. She must have seen guilt written all over me.

'Katie,' she said at once, 'after I left my purse here yesterday, there was half a crown missing. Did you take it?'

I hid my face in my hands and began to sob.

She shook me several times. 'You little thief! I've a good mind to tell yer dad. Where is it?'

'It's down me stockin',' I managed to whimper. 'I'm ever so sorry, Mary, I won't do it again.'

'You won't get the chance! Anyhow, why did you take it?'

Between sobs I told her how Dad had gone without his baccy to buy me my swimming costume, and I wanted to pay him back.

'You little fool! Stealing isn't the answer!' she said. 'You know you can pay him back in other ways. He told me how proud he was when you won your certificates. That was payment enough. And remember he doesn't go short of a smoke when I'm about ... Do you understand what I've been telling you?'

'Yes,' I managed to answer.

'Now, dry yer eyes before Mum comes in, you know how she'll belt you if she finds out. But if you'll promise not to steal again, I'll not tell Mum, or Dad.'

I promised. But for months, each time she came to visit us, I always coloured up, still feeling ashamed to look at her.

Hard Times and Good Times

As far back as I can remember, when I was a child, there was always hardship and unemployment. I knew many a man spend his days from dawn till dusk searching for any kind of odd jobs that would bring in a few pennies to help feed a young family. And many a woman had to leave her children to roam the streets while she went out scrubbing someone else's house. In their desperation and despair, people would take on anything.

During one very cold spell, everyone in the yard was burning any kind of rubbish on the fire, to keep warm, or to cook. My dad chopped up the shutters from outside the window, which were hanging off anyway. And the neighbours followed suit. Mum, one afternoon, said I would have to take a sack and gather some branches that had blown off the trees down the lanes.

I called for Winnie and off we went. When we got as far as Wasson Pool, we could see other kids had been before us. We walked miles to try to fill that sack, until we came to a canal where there were more trees with low branches. As we went towards them we saw a flat hand-cart with a sack like ours strewn across it, and two men with their backs towards us, stripping off their clothes. At first glance we thought they'd come here to settle some argument, which we had often seen men do, but when we saw them strip themselves naked, we became scared, so we hid ourselves behind a large tree.

''ush,' Winnie whispered, 'don't move, or mek a sound. We'll afta wait 'ere now, till they go.'

'What they goin' ter do?' I whispered back.

'I don't know, we'll afta wait an' see.'

I didn't want to wait. I'd never seen any men naked before, and I was afraid and ashamed.

'Not me, Winnie, I'm off,' I said.

But before I could move one step, she pulled me down into the long grass beside her.

'Keep quiet,' she said. 'We can't go now, they'll 'ear us, an' yer know what that'll mean.'

I knew well enough. I didn't fancy a beating, or being tossed into that dirty, oily canal. Suddenly, we heard one of the men say, 'I think I 'eard some bugger movin' about out theea, Joe,' pointing towards where we were hiding. We became really scared.

'Don't be bleedin' daft,' was the other's reply.

'Well, I 'eard summat, do yer think it could be the rossers?'

'It can't be, they'd 'av arrested us afower now, so come on. It's about time fer the other two ter come up.'

All of a sudden there was a splash, as two more naked men rose up out of the water, each carrying a large lump of coal. When we saw who they were, we couldn't believe our eyes.

It was Winnie's father, and my dad.

We had to stay there now, and watch as the other two men dived in. This went on for about fifteen minutes, until the sack was full. After drying themselves down with their shirts, they put the sack of coal on the cart, and quickly dressed and away they went.

As soon as we felt safe to come out from our hiding place, we picked up our half-empty sack and began to laugh out loud.

'That was a near escape,' I giggled.

'Yes, an' did yer see what was danglin'?'

We tittered all the way home. But when we got to the end of our street and I said we'd meet the next day, she replied, 'Can't see yer termorra, Katie. I'll afta go ter confession.'

'What for?' I asked, as she tittered again.

'Well, yer know it was wrong fer us ter watch them naked bodies.'

'But we couldn't 'elp it.'

'I know, but I won't feel clean again, until I go.'

'Are you a Catholic then, Winnie?' I asked.

'No. Me and our Willie was born in Tipton. So was me dad. But me mum's Irish, and she's a Catholic, but she never goes ter Mass, she always ses *she* knows what's wrong, an' what's right, without bein' an' 'ypocrite.'

'But why do *yow* go? Is the priest nice lookin'?'

'Ooh no, 'e's quite ugly and shifty-eyed, and 'as a big purple bulbous nose, that sticks out like a ripe plum, ready ter burst. An' 'e drinks whiskey.'

''Ow do yer know that?' I asked.

''e come round to see me mum one day an' only me and me dad was in, and when me dad offered 'im a drop of Scotch, 'e said 'e only drank Irish. But 'e wasn't fussy the next day when 'e come an' me dad gave 'im some Scotch.'

'An' what do yer say when yer go ter confessional?'

'Well, when I go inter the box, 'e always seems to be waitin' fer me, an' 'e ses, "I see it's you again, and what have you to tell me this time?" When I tell 'im, 'e give me a kind of a lecture, then tells me I'm forgiven. So yer see it's easy when yer do things wrong, yer can start again after yer've been forgiven. See what I mean?'

No, I didn't see what she meant, but I nodded my head and said I'd call for her sometime.

When I got indoors, the first thing I noticed was a roaring coal fire, which I hadn't seen for years. Dad was naked apart from his trousers, with his bare feet resting on the fender, sitting in front of the fire, while Mum was drying his wet shirt on the back of the chair.

When I gave Mum the half-sack of twigs, he suddenly turned around. 'An' where 'ave yer bin till now?' he asked.

'Gettin' some broken branches fer Mum,' I replied nervously.

'I dain't ask yer what yer got!' he snapped. 'I asked yer where yer'd bin.'

I nearly blurted out 'by the canal', but checking myself in time I quickly said, 'By the . . . Wasson Pool.'

Just then Mum piped up. 'Yer better get yer 'ands washed and 'ave yer tea.'

I sat up at the table, but each mouthful I took I kept glancing up at Dad's bare back, thinking perhaps he already knew Winnie and I were there that afternoon, watching him in his nakedness. And each time he happened to glance across at me I felt guilty and ashamed.

Mum left the table to put more coal on the fire, but Dad suddenly yelled out: 'I dain't get nearly drowned fer yow ter waste it! Any'ow, yow'll afta go steady with it. I won't be able to go again fer some time.'

'Why?' she asked.

'Why? Because I *can't* go again, till there's nobody about. That's why. And Joe said somebody 'ad bin watchin' us this afternoon.'

'Ooh dear, who was it?' Mum asked.

'I don't know, it worn't the cops. Joe said it must 'ave bin some kids playing about. An' I don't want 'er goin' near that canal,' he replied, pointing his finger at me.

I went all hot. Did he really suspect me? Was he waiting for me to explain? Please, God, I prayed to myself, don't ever let him find out it was Winnie and me.

A week later Dad tried his luck again with Mr Nashe, but they came back with an empty sack, telling Mum it was too dangerous now, a man and a woman had been arrested.

Next time Winnie and me met, we quarrelled. She asked me if I would go along the canal again with her.

'No! I don't! I don't want ter go near it again, never,' I snapped.

'Why?'

'Because I think it's wrong an' dirty.'

'Oh, please yerself,' she snapped.

'An' I think my dad suspects me.'

''ow could 'e, *my* dad never said anything.'

'Any'ow, yow betta not go near again. The bobbies 'ave already arrested a man and a woman,' I said.

'Yes, I know, I saw 'em.'

'Yer saw 'em? When?'

'A few days ago.'

'Anybody we know?' I asked.

'Yes, it was Mr and Mrs Carter, from out of Sloane Street.'

'Oh dear. Ain't that the woman yer sold a rug to?'

'Yes.'

'Are yer sure it was them?' I asked.

'I went along the canal one afternoon with our Willie, when we saw Mr Carter strip an' jump in the water. While 'is wife was on the look-out, the cops came. She tried to warn 'im by shoutin' inter the water, but it was too late. When 'e come up, they were both arrested. Me an' Willie tried ter warn 'em, but we were too late. Any'ow we 'ad ter run an' 'ide ourselves, or they would 'ave arrested *us*.'

Listening to all this made me feel sick, for she seemed to be enjoying telling me. Suddenly I screamed at her, 'I think you're wicked, Winnie Nashe, an' Willie, ter go there ter watch naked men again. I suppose you'll go in the confessional box again too, an' ask the priest ter forgive yer again, so yer can do somethin' else yer know what's wrong . . . Yer know what yow are? . . . Winnie . . . bloody . . . Nashe . . . a bloody 'ypocrite! An' I never want ter speak to yer ever again!' I yelled.

And there I left her, standing with her mouth wide open gawping at me. We passed each other by like strangers for the next few days. A week later I said I was sorry, and we made it up.

During that year, my dad and Mr Nashe were the best of mates. They went everywhere together to look for work. People often used to turn and stare when Mr Nashe tried to keep up a pace with my dad. Often I thought, how comical. He was such a little man, where my dad was six foot tall and as strong as an ox; no one ever got the best of an argument when Dad was around.

Early one morning Mr Nashe called to tell Dad that there was a couple of porters wanted on Snow Hill railway station. Dad left a note on the table to tell Mum he'd be back soon. She waited all day, but when he returned she was pleased to hear that Mr Nashe and he had got the jobs as porters. He said it was only temporary until something better could be found. But it was better than being on parish relief.

He worked all hours, and the few coppers that passengers sometimes gave him when he carried their bags helped to give Mum a bit extra, which pleased her enormously. Each night he came home tired and dirty. But although we were very poor, Dad was a proud man. The clothes he wore were well patched, but he always kept himself clean. Each night, no matter how late, before he sat down to eat, he would strip to the waist and wash himself down, and if it wasn't too late, Mum would let me wait up and get his bowl of water ready to wash his tired, swollen feet.

In the middle of September we heard there was a fair at the Serpentine grounds in Aston (I think it was called the Onion Fair). The following Saturday I heard Dad ask Mum if she would like to go.

'Not me,' she replied. 'I've got too much to do. Any'ow, I don't know why yer want ter waste yer money on that place, it's only a catchpenny.'

'Can I go, Mum?' I asked eagerly.

'No, yer can't. I want yer ter fetch me half 'undredweight o' coal from the wharf.'

439

'Can I go Dad, when I come back?' I pleaded.

'No, yow 'eard what yer Mum said.'

'But Winnie's goin' with 'er dad,' I replied.

'I don't care who Winnie's goin' with, yow ain't goin', an' that's that. An' I've told yer befower, yer know what I've promised yer if I see yer with 'er again.'

But I did go.

As I was wheeling the coal trolley from the wharf, I happened to meet Winnie.

'Yer goin' ter the fair, Katie?' were her first words.

'No, me mum and dad said I wasn't ter go.'

'But I'm goin', why don't yer come with me?'

'I daren't, your dad'll tell my dad, and I'd get in trouble.'

'My dad ain't takin' me, 'e said I'd gorra stop an' 'elp Mum, but Mum said I could go as long as me dad dain't see me there.'

'Yer sure 'e won't see yer?' I asked.

'O' course 'e won't, they'll be crowds of people there, so 'e won't be able to see us if we look out.'

'Are yer sure it's safe ter go?' I asked.

'O' course I am, an' I've got a whole shillin' I've saved, an' we'll share it. See you two o'clock,' she added.

I was tempted, and I said that I'd do my best to meet her. But she was not to wait after a quarter past two, in case I couldn't make it.

After returning the trolley and giving back the penny deposit off the trolley to Mum, I asked if I could go out and play.

'No, yer can't!' she yelled. 'Yer betta light the candle, I want yer ter come with me down the cellar ter fetch up some slack fer the brew'ouse fire.'

We went down and I held the lighted candle while she sorted over slack and whatever rubbish she could burn under the boiler. I kept wondering how I could get away to meet Winnie. But Mum made it easy for me. As soon as we came up the cellar again, she said she didn't feel well and was going to lie down on the bed.

'Leave the bucket in the pantry an' don't mek a racket,' she said. 'An' tell yer dad ter wake me up when 'e comes in.'

Now was my chance. Should I ask again? Or should I just go, and not ask? But what if she refused, and found me another job to do? No. I'll go now, and suffer the consequences later. It was after two o'clock when I met Winnie. She told me she was just about to go without me. I was glad she'd waited.

'Come on, 'urry up,' she called out, grabbing my hand.

As we hurried along, I asked, ''ave yer been to a fair befower?'

'Yes, lots of times with me mum and dad, but not this one. An' it'll be better and more fun without them.'

'Why?' I asked.

'Well, we can go all over the place an' do what we want ter do.'

'I hope me dad, or your dad, won't see us.'

''e won't see yer if yer keep by me. Now come on an' stop yer worryin'.'

'All right, I'll try.'

I'd never been inside a fairground before. The music and the noise from the crowds of people of all ages was quite deafening, and as soon as we mingled with the crowd I lost my nervousness and began to enjoy the merriment. Winnie shared her shilling and we bought candy floss and popcorn. Then we tried to win a goldfish, but we had no luck, and Winnie said it was a catchpenny. Then we went on the swings. Now we only had tuppence each left.

'What shall we buy now?' I asked.

'Come on,' she said. 'Yer see that coconut shy over there? Well, let's 'ave a go at that.'

But as we stood there making up our minds, the big fellow who stood beside the stall shouted out at us.

'What yow two kids starin' at? Bugger off.'

'Walk up, walk up, three balls a penny,' he kept repeating. Then, 'If yer don't clear off, I'll put me foot be'ind yer.'

'But we want ter 'ave a go,' Winnie said.

'Yer gotcha money?' he snapped.

We both held our hands out, and showed him our last tuppences. He quickly helped himself to them and gave us three balls each. Winnie threw hers, and I thought I had to throw mine at the same time.

'Yer don't throw 'em together,' he bawled out. 'Yer throw 'em one at a time!'

He gave us the other three each and we tried again. But we walked away disappointed. We had no money left now, and we were hungry, dirty and disheartened, so we decided we'd go home. But when we saw and heard a crowd laughing and jeering, we stopped to see what it was all about. We managed to squeeze through the crowd and had full view of a crude open air boxing ring, with sawdust on the floor. Inside the ring were the prize fighter and his manager. The manager was calling out, 'Who dares ter come inter the ring ter pay 'alf a crown and win a golden sovereign?'

It frightened me even to look at the boxer with his nose flattened across his face, two red cauliflower ears, and thick lips. He was leaping backwards and forwards, and each time he came towards the ropes he waved his arms like some wild beast. 'Yow, yow! Yow! Or yow!' He kept pointing to the men, but no one would take up the challenge.

'Only three rounds and yer can win yerself a sovereign, *and* yer 'alf-crown back,' the manager kept calling out.

Winnie and I were about to move on away, when suddenly we heard a familiar voice say, 'Go on Sam, yow've done some fightin' in the Army. Yow can beat 'im.'

When we looked among the crowd, we saw it was our dads.

I didn't know whether to stay or run, but Winnie wanted to stay and see what was going to happen. So I had to stay too, hoping my dad wouldn't see me.

'Go on Sam,' I heard Mr Nashe repeat again. 'Yow can do *ten* rounds with 'im, let alone three.'

'Well, I could do with the money, but I ain't even got the price of a pint, let alone 'alf a crown.'

'I'll lend it yer, Sam, an' yer can pay me back when yer win.'

I heard the crowd cheering for Dad to take up the challenge. I felt now I had to stay and watch, and pray that he would win. But I was alarmed when someone called out, 'Yow don't wanta go in theea, mate, 'e'll slaughter yer.'

'I couldn't stand one round, an' it was me last 'alf-crown,' came from another man at the back.

But admist the cheers of the rest, Dad went beneath the rope. Almost before he could enter the ring the bruiser made a dive, but Dad was too quick for him and ducked. He swung again before he could strip off his shirt, but again Dad sidestepped, and as the bruiser stumbled there were cheers from all sides. Crowds of people from the stalls now came to watch the fight.

As soon as the first round was over I looked among the crowd for Winnie. When I saw her talking to her dad I got scared. I was about to run from the crowd when I felt Winnie pull me back.

'Yer don't 'ave ter go now, me dad's told me ter fetch yer where we can get a betta view.'

'But me dad'll see me.'

'O' course 'e won't, 'e'll be too busy fightin'. Now come on an' don't look so scared.'

'Mr Nashe,' I said, 'please don't tell me dad I've been 'ere.'

'Well, yer betta keep quiet if yer wanta stay.'

'Do yer think me dad'll win?' I asked.

'O' course 'e'll win, luv, an' when it's over yer betta 'urry off 'ome, the pair o' yer.'

The second round was now about to start. And as soon as the bruiser's manager (or rather, owner, trainer and referee, all rolled into one) rang the bell, Dad was on his feet.

'Come on yer bloody big ape,' he called out with his fists at the ready.

Dad landed heavy blows to the boxer's body. The bruiser, when he got closer, put his two long hairy arms around Dad and nearly threw him down on the wet sawdust. But when Dad managed to break loose, he caught the boxer a blow to his chin, and down he went. The cheers from the crowds were quite deafening. I was getting excited too. Suddenly the fighter's trainer threw a bucket of dirty water all over him. 'Get up, yer bleedin' fool. If yer lay there yer'll know what ter expect!' he yelled.

As he staggered to his feet the bell went. That was supposed to be the end of the round, but the crowd thought different. They hissed and booed, shouting that there was another minute to go. Everyone standing there knew Dad had beaten the fighter. When the third round began there were more cheers for Dad. I was now enjoying watching.

'Come on, matey!' someone shouted out. 'Yow can beat 'im. Keep away from 'is clutches.'

'We'll see yer get fair play,' others yelled out.

But Dad was not having it all his own way. When the bruiser landed Dad another blow, and I saw blood coming from his mouth, I went wild. Forgetting where I was, I shouted, 'Yer bleedin' varmint!'

Dad was startled by my voice and gave me a quick glance, and the bruiser, seeing his chance, gave Dad another blow, which put him flat on his back.

The referee didn't bother to count. Raising bruiser's hand, he declared him the winner. But by this time Dad had sprung to his feet and as the boxer was taking his bow, Dad gave him an uppercut that laid him flat out. The manager hurled another bucket of water over him, but when that had no effect he had to begin counting him out, very slowly.

At first the manager refused to pay out, saying the fight hadn't gone the full three rounds. But when the crowd said they would lynch him, he soon gave Dad the gold sovereign and the half-crown. I didn't wait for Dad to put on his shirt, I ran and hid among the crowd, but he soon found me. I burst out crying. I believe he would have hit me there and then if Winnie and her dad hadn't come on the scene. Pulling me towards him, he asked why I was there, but before I could manage to blurt out why, Winnie said, 'It's my fault, she didn't wanta come.'

'All right, but what I wanta know is, 'ow long 'ave yer bin swearin'?'

'I don't say it, Dad, only when I get mad, but I'm always 'earing Mum say it.'

'All right, wipe yer eyes an' yer can 'ave a tanner each ter spend on the stalls. When yer've spent that, yer can meet me an' Joe by the coconut shy.'

So off Winnie and me skipped, but instead of going to the stalls we had several rides on the roundabouts. Then we went back to the coconut shy to meet our dads. There we saw them trying their luck. Mr Nashe had already won a teddy bear for Winnie, and Dad was trying his best to win one for me, but no luck. It was then, when I looked up at him, that I saw his right eye was swollen, and almost closed. And a front tooth was missing. My own eyes filled with tears.

'I'm sorry, Dad,' I blurted out.

'It's me that's sorry, luv. I'll buy yer one next week.'

'I don't want one, Dad,' I whimpered. 'I said I was sorry because it was my fault. If I 'adn't 'ave shouted, an' swore when I did, you wouldn't 'ave been 'urt.'

'I was 'urt before I 'eard or saw yer, luv. Now, dry yer eyes an' you an' Winnie betta get off 'ome now, before it gets dark.'

'Dad, yer won't tell Mum I was at the fair, will yer?' I asked.

'Why? Don't she know?'

'She said she didn't feel well an' went ter lie down, an' I was to tell yer when yer come in ter wake 'er up. Then I went with Winnie.'

'Where's Winnie now?'

'Over there, with 'er dad,' I answered, pointing to one of the stalls.

'We'd betta go over to 'em, then yer betta get off 'ome.'

'Dad, please don't tell Mum I was at the fair, will yer?' I repeated.

'Not unless she asks me . . . But if she asks *you* yer must tell 'er the truth. Do yer understand? I won't be long after you,' he added.

'Yes, Dad,' I replied.

Winnie and I hurried home from the fair. When I got indoors I was glad to see that Mum was still upstairs. The fire was nearly out, but I set to, put some coal on, and hurried it along with the bellows. Then I set to tidy up the room, and to lay the table ready for Dad coming in.

'Is yer Mum still upstairs?' he asked as soon as he entered.

'Yes,' I answered.

'Come an' see what I bought 'er.'

He put his hand inside his waistcoat pocket and pulled out a small green cardboard box. Inside was a large gilt cameo brooch about the size of a half-crown.

'Nice, ain't it?' he said.

'Yes, that'll please 'er,' I said.

When she came downstairs and saw Dad's face, she yelled, 'Oh my God! What yer done ter yerself?'

'It's a long story, Polly, but first let me show yer what I've bought yer.'

As soon as she saw the gilt brooch, sure enough, her eyes lit up.

'Is it gold?' she asked.

'Well . . . it's near enough, but don't try an' pawn it.'

'Oh, no, Sam. I'll just wear it on me birthday.' (But knowing my Mum, I was sure she'd try to pawn it some day.)

I watched as she put it back in its box then dropped it in the vase on the mantleshelf, among the pawn tickets.

While we were eating, Mum noticed the gap in Dad's mouth.

'Where's yer tooth?' she asked.

'I don't know, Polly, I think I must 'ave swallowed it,' he replied, winking at me.

All that afternoon and evening, I was on thorns, wondering whether she would ask me any questions. But she never did. I believe she was too pleased about her present to question me.

Later, I asked my dad if he really had bought that cameo brooch. 'Why do yer ask?' he said.

When I told him I'd seen two or three like it at the fair, he said, 'Well luv, I tried ter win it, 'cause I knew yer mum would like it, an' when I did win it, I realised it cost me more than it was worth.'

'It's very pretty, Dad. Is it gold?' I asked.

'No luv, it's only gilt,' he replied.

A few weeks after that, as I was sitting on the wooden sofa, trying to finish knitting a scarf for my brother from odd scraps of wool, I saw my mum's eyes kept looking up at the mantleshelf.

Now, if ever she wanted anything, it was always me. 'Fetch this! Fetch me that!' Even when things were near at hand.

'Yer betta stand on the stool and reach me down that purse,' she said.

As soon as I saw her face, I knew she had found it was empty. And when she told me to reach down the vase and take out the little green cardboard box, I knew at once what she was going to do. She slipped on Dad's cap and put the box into her apron pocket. I said, 'Dad said yer wasn't ter pawn it.'

'Yer Dad won't know, an' I'm warnin' yer if yer dare tell 'im, yer know what ter expect.'

'Any 'ow,' she added, 'I've gorra buy summat to eat. I'll be able to get it back on Saturday. And yer can come with me an' call at the butcher's on the way back.'

The pawn shop had once been a dwelling house and it was very small, with a narrow entry at the side, where neighbours queued up with their bundles of washing under their arms, or whatever else they could find to pawn. Over the entry were the three brass balls and a rusty sign which read: S. J. Woolf, Pawnbroker. There was only room for two people at a time in the shop, everyone else had to stay in the entry until it was their turn.

My mum was called in at the same time as Mrs Ellis. Now, Mrs Ellis was one of the neighbours in the next yard, and Mum didn't like her. When Mum got near the counter, Mrs Ellis stared at her in surprise.

'Yow fetchin' summat out?' she asked.

'What yow want ter know for?' Mum snapped.

'Well, I don't see yer carrin' any washin'.' She snapped back.

Mum took out the box from her apron pocket, and slapped it down on the counter. 'Can yer lend me a couple of bob on this till Saturday?' she said.

But when the pawnbroker opened the box, he almost threw it back at her. 'This ain't no good to me, missus,' he snapped.

'Well,' Mum pleaded, 'lend me a shillin' on it. I'll fetch it back on Saturday,' she added.

'No. It ain't even worth the box it stands in.'

Mum picked up the box and as she dropped it back into her apron pocket she pushed past Mrs Ellis, almost knocking her over. When we got out into the street, I saw tears in Mum's eyes as she muttered, ''er would be theea, now it'll be all over the neighbourhood. But it'll be the last time I'll tek anything theea, the old skinflint.'

As we hurried along Albion Street she said I was to call in the butcher's. 'Ask 'im ter let me 'ave sixpennorth o' bits till Friday . . . I'll slip 'ome an' put the kettle on,' she said.

'I don't like to, Mum, 'e refused me last time. 'e said you owed enough for one week,' I replied.

'Oh, well, yer better go in an' ask 'im fer some lights for the cats.'

'But we've only one cat, Mum,' I said.

'Well, if yer say cats, 'e'll p'raps give yer mower. Now, 'urry yerself,' she snapped. 'I ain't got all day.'

When I went in to the butcher's, he just stared. 'If yer've come fer meat, tell yer mother she'll 'ave ter come 'erself, and pay a bit off what she already owes,' he said.

'I 'aven't come fer meat, Mr Underwood. Mum sent me fer some lights fer the cats.'

''ow many cats 'ave yer got?'

'Only one, but Mum shares it out to the neighbours' cats,' I pleaded.

'Very well,' he replied. 'But don't forget, I want ter see yer mother on Friday.'

As soon as I had thanked him for the lights I ran all the way home. When I got indoors I gave Mum his message, but she just shrugged her shoulders. I asked if I should put the brooch back in the vase, but she said she had already done it.

In those days, I often had to fetch a pennyworth of jam in a cup, or a pennyworth of dripping from Stoddard's, the pork butcher's at the corner of Icknield Street. 'An' don't forget ter tell 'im ter put plenty of dark jelly with it,' she would say. It was always a pennyworth of this, or that.

Each Saturday morning, my mum would send us to Houghton's, the butcher's in Broad Street. He was very kind to us kids, and always gave a little extra meat with our small order. Sometimes we'd take the little kids from our yard and give them a ride in the go-cart. Sometimes we went the long way round, down Camden Drive, along Arthur Place, down the Sandpits, then up Nelson Street. The reason was, there was a large fruit, vegetable and fish stall on the corner of Nelson Street, and the owner was another person who was kind to us. Whenever he saw us passing that way he would call us over, and put some bruised fruit, or a haddock, or a few herrings, in our cart. 'Cover 'em over an' take 'em straight 'ome to yer mum,' he'd say.

Sometimes, when he wasn't about, we'd carry on along Vincent Street, along Sheepcote Street, along the narrow passage called King Edward Place, and across the horse road to Houghton's. But before we crossed the horse road, we used to linger on the corner of the narrow passageway, where there was an ice cream parlour (I think the name was Devotis), hoping that someone would be kind enough to give us an ice cream, even if it was only a lick. But we were always shooed away.

When we called at the butcher's, it was always sixpennyworth of pieces. Sometimes he'd give us a large piece of hipbone steak, which had fallen off the chopping block into the sawdust, or a couple of pork chops and a breast of lamb. Or sometimes there'd be pork bones and a piece of belly draft. All of which Mum had to swill well to get the sawdust off. But she was always pleased when she saw what we'd bought for sixpence.

But one such Saturday, as we wheeled the little cart towards the ice cream parlour, I saw my brother Frankie take out a cracked cup from under the sack. When I asked him what it was for, he said, 'Don't ask questions, we're goin' in fer a pennorth of ice cream.'

'Not me,' I said. ''e'll only run us out. I'll wait on the corner.'

Soon he came out of the shop, grinning all over his face.

'Come on,' he cried out, 'before I eat it all meself.'

As we were taking turns scooping it out with our fingers, I asked him where he'd got the penny from.

'I ain't tellin'! Now, come on an' let's fetch the meat,' he snapped.

As soon as the cup was empty he hid it under the sack again.

We wheeled the little cart inside the butcher's, and as my brother stood against the counter I heard him say, 'Please, Mr 'oughton, me mum ses, can yer let 'er 'ave five pennorth today?'

I knew then he had used one of the pennies for the ice cream.

As the butcher was wrapping up our five pennyworth, I saw Frankie knock two udders off the end of the counter into the cart, covering them over with the sack. I was dumbstruck and scared, for I'd never known him to do anything like this before. Then, when we had received our parcel of meat and were on our way, I said, 'Frankie, you shouldn't 'ave done that. If Mum finds out, she'll skin yer alive.'

'Why? Yer goin' to tell 'er then? If yer do, yer'll know what to expect!'

Of course, I had no intention of telling Mum. But as soon as we got home and she saw what was in the parcel, she said, ''e ain't gid yer much. I'll tell 'im when I see 'im.'

When Frankie handed Mum the two udders she was suspicious. 'Where did yer get them from?' she asked. 'An' look at 'em, covered with dirt.'

When he told her Mr Houghton had given them to him she didn't believe him. 'Yow'll tek 'em back this minute!' she yelled.

He was scared now, and ran off down the street. When she asked me if I knew anything about them, I lied. I said I didn't know until I saw them in the cart. But she wrapped them up in newspaper and almost dragged me back with her to the butcher's. I knew at once that he'd missed them, for as soon as we entered, he waved the chopper at us and yelled, 'If them little buggers come anywhere near my shop again, I'll chop their bloody 'ands off with this chopper!'

Mum made all the excuses she could think of, and when she handed over the udders to him, he said, 'Yer betta take 'em now, I won't be able to sell 'em like that. But I'm warnin' yer! Next time I see 'em, I'll put the bobbies on to 'em.'

When we got home Frankie was nowhere to be seen, but when he did come in, later that night, she gave him the biggest caning he'd ever had. She was also mad we had lost such a good kind butcher, and had to try elsewhere. But I noticed she was pleased to clean the udders, and prepare them for our meals.

I was glad too, that she never found out about how we managed to buy that ice cream. Otherwise, Frankie would have had another belting off Dad, and maybe I'd have had one too.

When Dad's job as a porter came to an end, he told us we would all have to put our shoulders to the wheel. My brother Jack was now the only one who was bringing home his small pittance. My eldest sister, Mary, was already married and had a home of her own. And my brother Charlie was living with his two friends Billy and Albert Wynn and their widowed mother – though he always sent home whatever he could spare. Frankie, Liza and me were still at school.

Dad began to chop and sell firewood again. Frankie and me had to help, while my sister Liza, often grumbling, helped Mum. In the winter, as soon as there was a promise of snow, Dad'd wake Frankie. Before it was daylight, I'd hear him call up the attic stairs, 'Come on, Frankie, it's goin' ter snow.' And I'd see my brother, half-awake, almost tumbling down the stairs, trying to get dressed as he went. With the shovel and the broom over their shoulders, they'd go from door to door, knocking and asking if people wanted their paths and the pavements outside their houses cleared. Sometimes they'd be out all night long. In the streets near us people might just give Dad a hot bowl of soup, or Frankie a drink of hot cocoa. If they couldn't afford even as much as that, Dad would sweep their paths for nothing. But when they went round the posher quarters (as Dad called them), he would get a shilling, or one and sixpence, for each path. When they came home, tired, wet and hungry, Dad would tip out his pockets. After giving Frankie sixpence, he'd count the rest out and give it to Mum. I remember one night he brought home over two pounds, and before he went up to bed he prayed the heavens would open up and send down snow more often. 'Meks a bloody good business. Betta than workin' in a factory,' he'd say.

We weren't always little drudges, sometimes we had great treats, such as a ride along the canal. We called it 'up the cut in the coal boat'. And though we had no toys to speak of, we had plenty of fun with games like hopscotch, marbles and jackstones.

But the best time of all was bonfire night. At this time of year, everyone who could afford it would get a new straw mattress. You would hear the 'Pat Man' coming down the hill with his cart.

'Come an' get a clean straw mattress,' he'd call out. 'A bob each, or two fer one an' ninepence. Three fer 'alf a crown.'

The old mattresses went on the bonfires there were in almost every yard on the Fifth of November. People would throw their bedroom or attic windows wide, and mattresses would come flying through the air. You'd be lucky if you saw them in time to duck. We children would help drag them to the end of the yard, where, with other rubbish, they'd be piled high, ready to be lit when it was dark. We'd also go around with a go-cart, or a coal trolley, and collect whatever rubbish we could find, or beg – old boxes, old stools, old palings, anything that would burn. And, of course, we'd beg pennies for the guy, to buy sparklers or Catherine wheels. The bonfire was lit as soon as it was dark, and there'd be singing and dancing round the fire till the early hours of the morning. For us young ones there'd be baked chestnuts and baked potatoes, half-raw and with the skins burnt black, but we were glad to eat them. The grown-ups had gallon stone jars of beer.

And then, if you were lucky, there was for once in a way a clean straw mattress to sleep on.

War, Work and Workmates

———◦◦◦◦———

When war broke out in 1914, life changed for us all. My brothers Jack and Charlie joined up at once, without waiting for their call-up papers. Even Dad tried to enlist, but he failed his medical. Instead he got a job in a brass-casting shop, making shell cases. My sister Liza too got a job on munitions. There was plenty of war work for everyone, no scratching for pennies now.

I, too, yearned to leave school and be a grown-up woman, earning my own living. I shall never forget the day I left school. I was just fourteen. I hurried home all excited, feeling as free as a bird, and as I ran in the house I began to dance around the table. 'Rah, rah, rah!' I kept singing, 'Me schooldays are over, rah, rah, rah!'

My dad came and grabbed hold of me. ''old yer 'orses! 'ave yer gone mad, of a sudden?'

'No, Dad,' I replied. 'But I've said goodbye ter school terday, fer ever.'

'Well, yer betta tek yer pinny off, an' come an' sit on this chair, I want to talk ter yer, afower yer mum comes 'ome,' he said sternly.

'What 'ave I done now?' I asked.

'It's not what yer've done, it's what yer goin' ter do, luv,' he said more kindly.

'Yes, Dad,' I replied, as I sat facing him.

'Now, I want yer ter listen carefully, and remember what I'm goin' to say.'

'Yes, Dad,' I replied, and added quickly, all in one breath, 'Yes, Dad, an' I'm goin' ter work in a munition factory an' earn some money for you an' Mum.'

'That can wait, luv. What I want to say is this. Yer ter start work next Monday mornin'. Now, remember this, when yer work in a factory, it'll be strange ter yer at first, it'll be like another world.

452

Yer'll be mixin' an' workin' with all kinds of older men and women, boys too. Now, if yer ever get into any difficulties, or want ter know anything, I want yer always to come and tell me, or yer mum, first.'

'Yes, Dad, but nobody seems ter know I'm growin' up, an' there's lots of things I want ter know.'

'Well, what's troublin' yer?' he asked.

'I want ter know about marriage, an' love, an' babbies, but when I ask Mum about these things, she gets angry with me an' yells it's not right fer me to even mention these things yet.'

'She's probably right, Katie, but she'll tell yer sometime. But don't try ter grow up too soon, luv,' he added. 'Yer too young yet ter understand lots of things.'

'But I think I know about love, because I love yow, Dad.'

'I love yow too, Katie,' he said gently. 'But there are lots of other kinds of loves, which yer'll understand more as yer grow older. Any'ow, I'll 'ave a talk with yer sister an' ask 'er if she'll explain these things ter yer.'

I threw my arms around his neck, and as I hugged and kissed him, he said again, 'Remember what I say, luv. Don't grow up too soon.'

But I didn't see my eldest sister for months. Her husband was also in the Army, somewhere in the country where she had the chance to visit him several times before he went abroad. By the time I did see her, I had almost forgotten Dad's warning.

My first job was working a metal press, cutting out brass buttons for army uniforms. But I didn't think I was paid enough for the hours and the hard work I did, so I soon left. In those first years I flitted several times from one job to another. Once I was working, although most of my wages went to Mum, I had enough money left to buy myself extra food, and some second-hand clothes. And my mother let me have more freedom now I was earning, and bringing home my wages each week.

One of my early jobs was working in a small press shop with four women of about my mother's age. These women were very coarse, and swore like troopers, but this didn't bother me. I was used to bad language at home, and from our neighbours in the yard.

At lunchtime the women sat on three-legged stools around the coke stove in the centre of the workshop, eating whatever food they had brought with them or, sometimes, fish and chips which they got me to fetch for them. When I had to go out to get the fish and chips

I was always late going home for my own lunch. Using this as an excuse, I asked my mum if I too could have sandwiches to take, instead of coming home.

'Please yerself,' she said. 'But don't come back at nights sayin' yer 'ungry.'

So I stayed to have lunch with the women. I was pleased about this, mostly because I was dying to know what they talked about while they were sitting around the stove: I thought I might learn from them some of the things my mother wouldn't tell me. But whenever they saw me listening they would move closer to the stove, and lower their voices so I couldn't hear.

One lunchtime I was told to fetch their four tuppenny pieces of cod and four pennyworth of chips. 'An' 'urry yerself! We don't want 'em cold,' Florrie warned.

'We want 'em separate. An' put plenty of vinegar on,' Mabel called out as I hurried down the stairs.

But when I gave my order, and handed the money over the counter, the woman glared at me.

'Can't yer read?' she snapped, pointing to the notice on the wall.

As I turned around to read, she called out angrily, 'Cod's threepence now! An' chips are tuppence!'

'But I only 'ave a shillin',' I replied. 'I'll 'ave ter go back an' tell 'em.'

'Who they for?' she asked.

When I told her, she said angrily, 'Don't they know there's a war on? Food's gettin' scarce, an' there's talk o' rationin'. Yow tell 'em they'll afta tighten their belts soon.'

But when I told them how much the fish and chips were, Florrie yelled, 'I don't believe yer. Yer little liar!'

Suddenly I flared up. 'Well! Yer can go yerself!' I shouted. 'If yer don't believe me. Anyway, yer'll 'ave ter tighten yer belts!' I added, throwing the shilling across the bench.

'Don't yer come 'ere with yer bloody cheek!' Mabel piped up, 'or I'll clout yer bleedin' ear'ole,' she added, raising her hand. But she picked up the shilling, and hurried to fetch the fish and chips herself.

She came back with nothing.

''er said they've got no fish left, an' the taters 'ave gone up,' Mabel said. 'Yer'll afta go an' try in Branston Street,' she told me.

'I'm not goin'. I ain't ate my sandwiches yet, an' it'll soon be time ter start ter work again,' I shouted back at the four of them. But I was ready to cry when she shouted in my ear, 'Yer'll do as yer told!'

Just then the foreman came in and when he heard what all the noise and commotion was about he said I was there to work, not to fetch and carry for them.

This didn't help matters. During the next few days, as usual, I tried to listen when they were whispering together. As soon as they saw me listening, Mabel called out, 'Yer'd betta get yer grub down yer, or yer'll get splinters in yer ears.'

'Yes, an' yer'll 'ear mower than wot's good fer yer one o' these days. Yer nosy, cheeky little sod!' Florrie added.

I dragged my stool further from the fire, but I still kept my ears cocked. I should have taken their warning. The next day, as we sat by the coke stove, I was surprised to find that they were talking loud enough for me to hear. Foolishly I listened, and innocently I believed every word they said.

'Fancy that! That's terrible!' I heard Mabel cry out.

'Wot's that yer talking about?' Alice asked.

'Don't yer know, Alice? All the other workers know,' Florrie replied.

Now I was all ears to know who they were talking about.

'Yer know that young girl as used ter work 'ere, 'er 'ad ter go ter the 'orspital,' Florrie said.

'Whatever for?' Alice asked.

'Well, she 'ad 'air growin' in between 'er legs.'

'Yer mean on 'er fanny?'

'Yes, an' if she don't get it cut off, it'll grow, an' grow, like an 'orse's tail, an' she'll be a freak,' Maggie piped up, looking at me.

I was too scared now to listen any more. I kicked over the stool and fled down the stairs as quick as I could go. I was terrified. I too had hair growing there. I didn't want to be a freak, or grow a horse's tail. But what was I going to do? For I was afraid of hospitals too.

When I got home I was relieved to find no one in. I flung myself down on the sofa and wept. There was no one I could confide in, least of all my mum. I thought there was only one thing to do, and I must do it quickly, before anyone came home. I couldn't lock the door, for the key had been lost years before. We didn't even have a knob on the old door, just the hole where it should have been. But

I got some waste paper and plugged up the hole. Then I bolted the door and, taking the scissors Mum used for everything, I dropped my skirt, pulled down my drawers, and began to cut away the unwanted hair. But the scissors wouldn't cut butter hot, let alone my bum fluff. Suddenly I hit on using Dad's open razor from the table drawer. Just as I was about to make an attempt the door began to rattle. I started to tremble. The razor slipped and I cut myself. Quickly I threw the razor back inside the drawer, as the door rattled again.

'Who've yer got in theea? Open this dower at once! Befower I kick it down!' I heard my sister Liza yell. I unbolted the door, thinking how like my mum she sounded, as she yelled again, 'What yer got that dower locked for? Who've yer got in 'ere?' she added, as she looked around the room. 'I'm goin' ter tell Mum when she comes in.'

I couldn't speak. I just stood there, terrified at what I'd done. When she began to shake me, I stammered, 'Oh, Liza, I . . . I'm blee . . . bleedin' an' I . . . I'm scared.'

Before I could explain any more, she burst out laughing.

'That ain't nothin' ter be scared of. It's when yer don't see 'em, that's the time ter be scared,' she replied.

'It's not me monthlies, Liza,' I whimpered. 'I've cut meself with Dad's razor.'

'Yer done what? 'ow? Why?'

When I had managed to tell her why, she burst out laughing again. 'Yer bloody little fool, yow ain't a freak, everybody grows 'air theea, it's natural.'

When I said I didn't believe her, she stood up on the chair and brazenly pulled her skirt right up to her waist. She didn't have any drawers on.

'Look! If yer don't believe me!' she cried out, flaunting herself. 'I got a big bunch!'

Quickly I looked away. I felt ashamed to look, but I had to look again, before I could convince myself what I'd seen was true. When I took my eyes away, I was also curious to know why she wasn't wearing any bloomers.

'Why ain't yer wearin' any bloomers, Liza?' I asked.

'Oh, them?' she replied, as she jumped down off the chair. 'They're too much trouble ter pull down an' up.'

This didn't make any sense to me at the time.

'Come on, let's see what yer done,' she asked as she came towards me.

'No!' I yelled. 'It's not bleedin' now. It's stopped.'

I couldn't for the life of me show my nakedness to Liza.

'Please yerself,' she replied.

'Liza, I can't go back ter work at that place again,' I whimpered.

'Don't worry, I'll go an' collect yer wages, an' I'll mek some excuse ter yer gaffer. But it's worth a few coppers fer some fags,' she added.

'But what excuse am I goin' ter tell me mum?'

'Yow tell 'er nothin'. Just keep out of sight an' leave it ter me,' she replied.

'Promise yer won't tell her what's 'appened, Liza, yer know what 'er temper's like, she'll go ter that factory an' murder them women.'

'They'll very likely murder 'er, if they're like wot yow say they are,' she replied, smiling.

Although the bleeding had stopped, I felt very sore. After Liza left I bolted the door again, and reaching down some Fuller's Earth from the top cupboard, I sprinkled it between my legs. It felt easier for the moment, but when I sat down, I had to sit on the side of my bum.

'What's the matter with yow?' my mum yelled out, when she saw me trying to sit straight on the chair the following day.

'Noth . . . nothin', Mum,' I stammered.

'Yer gotta flea up yer arse or summat?'

'No, Mum,' I replied tearfully.

'Well, sit up straight, unless yer wanta grow up lopsided!'

'Yes Mum,' I replied painfully, as I tried.

'Any'ow, yer betta get the bass broom an' sweep outside the dower,' she added.

For once, I was grateful for her orders. I found it a relief to stand or walk about.

First Love

At the end of that week I had to dip down into my small savings to make my mum's money up. But I was grateful to Liza for keeping my secret – I hadn't really believed she would, for she often carried tales to my mother. I tried to buy her some Woodbines, which were scarce. There was talk now of food being rationed and, with more money to spend, people were also stocking up their cupboards in case of an invasion.

It was during the next week that I met my friend Winnie again, one evening as I was leaving my new job. I couldn't take my eyes off her. She'd grown into a pretty young woman, plump and shapely, but she'd dyed her red hair to blonde, which made her look older than her sixteen years. I was glad to see her again, and we got chatting at once.

I was surprised to find that she was working at the brass factory I had just left.

"'ow long 'ave yer worked there?' I asked her.

'Two weeks,' she answered.

'That's funny, I never saw yer. But I left last week. Any'ow, what part of the factory do yer work in?'

'In the machine shop, on the ground floor, on a turnin' lathe, with some men and other girls. But the foreman's movin' me next week. I'm to work in another part fer more money.'

'You take a warnin' from me, Winnie, don't let 'im move yer inter that press shop!'

'Why?'

'That's where I used to work, with four coarse women, an' believe me Winnie, they're four real tykes.'

'Yer still a modest little miss, Katie, yer want ter tek life as it comes, like me. I don't care what people say or do. If I don't like

458

what they say, it goes in one ear an' out the other. Any'ow, what's troublin' yer?'

'Come an' 'ave a cup of tea in the tea shop an' I'll tell yer all about it.'

It wasn't until I'd finished telling her all the things I'd done, that I saw the funny side. So did she. We both began to laugh out loud and almost choked on our tea.

I was really happy to have met her again. She was always fun to be with. But I was about to get into more trouble.

She said she had a young man to meet, from where she was working. 'Why don't yer come along, Katie? I'll introduce yer ter 'is friend,' she said.

'I don't know, Winnie. I've never been out with the opposite sex,' I replied.

'Yer don't 'ave ter to be nervous, or shy, 'e's quite a nice fellow. Any'ow, yer'll be all right. I won't leave yer. We'll make a foursome.'

She sounded convincing enough, so I agreed. I promised to meet her the following Saturday night at her mum's new address, in Edward Street, near the Sandpits.

I dolled myself up in a new satin blouse and long hobble skirt, and did my hair on top in a bun. With a dab of face powder and carmine on my cheeks, I felt the part of a grown-up miss. But when I was ready to go, I looked down at myself and noticed the neck of my blouse was too low, showing the top of my breasts. I thought of the cameo brooch my dad had won for my mum at the fair, I knew she always kept it in the vase, and I borrowed it to pin the top of my blouse together. When I arrived at Winnie's I was surprised to see the change in her mother. She looked much cleaner than I'd seen her before, when she used to make rag rugs for a living. Her red hair, which had always been untidy, was now well brushed and rolled into a bun at the back of her head, and she looked quite smart for such a dumpy little woman. As I stepped inside the room I noticed that that too was clean and tidy, and the table had a real white lace tablecloth spread with homemade buns, cakes, meat, even best butter and jars of different kinds of jams and pickles. Winnie's twin brother, Willie, was sitting with his feet up on the fender, smoking a cigar. As soon as Willie saw me, he said, ''ello Kate, any chance of tekin' yer out fer a walk some night?'

Before I could reply his mother yelled out at him. 'No you can't!

She's goin' out with a friend of Winnie's. An' take your feet down off that fender, before they come in.'

Trying to avoid looking at Willie, I concentrated on the display of food on the table. I wondered how Mrs Nashe had come by such an enormous amount of food, when everything was so short in the shops. I thought to myself, was she a hoarder? Or had she been lucky with some of the shopkeepers who had their own special customers? At this time, towards the end of 1918, most women were finding it very difficult to get enough to feed their families. Many, including those with babes in arms, would rise at six o'clock in all kinds of weather to be at the front of the queue when the shops opened at nine. The fortunate ones would get a bit of bacon, or cheese, or brown sugar, a lump of mutton fat or, sometimes, horse-flesh. But many were turned away disappointed, when the door was closed and a notice put in the window: 'SORRY, SOLD OUT', or 'TRY AGAIN TOMORROW'. In some shops it was 'CLOSED FOR THE DURATION'. Hoarding food was considered a great crime. Lots of poor people in our district were fined for hoarding. No sympathy was shown for the fact that many of these people had several young mouths to feed. But often I would hear my dad say, 'It's one law for the rich and one for the poor.' It was always the rich that got away with everything in those days.

Winnie was lifting the curtain every few seconds, to see if the boys were coming. Suddenly she dropped the curtain and called out, 'Katie! Come on, hide! Quick! On the stairs. The priest's comin' 'ere.'

'Good evening,' we heard him say as he marched in.

But Mrs Nashe sounded annoyed. 'An' what do you want this time, Father? There's no whiskey, if that's what you've come for.'

'I've called to see your good husband,' he replied.

'Well, you'll have a long journey if you want to see him. He's in France, doin' his bit for his king and country.'

'And when will you be joining up, my good lad?' he asked Willie. But Willie didn't answer. We heard the door slam behind him.

'He'll go when they're ready to call him up,' was his mother's reply. 'An' it would do some good to the likes of *you*, to take off your dog collars an' put on some khaki an' help them lads that's over there, instead of hidin' under that frock you're wearin'!'

'We cannot all go, some of us have to stay at home,' he replied calmly. 'But what I've really come about is to ask you if you'll come to Mass some time.'

'No!' we heard her reply angrily. 'I've got no time for to hear you breathin' hell fire an' damnation at every poor unfortunate sinner you happen to cast your eyes on.'

'Well, I'll call again. In the meantime, I'll pray for you, and your family. Good evening.'

'You'd do better to pray for them poor buggers out there, who need it,' she called out as he closed the door.

As soon as he'd gone, we came out from our hiding place. Pulling Winnie towards her, Mrs Nashe cried out, 'An' *you*, Winnie, don't you ever let me catch you or know you go in that confession box again!'

'No, Mum,' she replied.

Her mother had just about calmed down, when there came another knock at the door.

'Come in, lads,' she said, as she opened the door. 'The girls are here already, waitin' for you.'

While she was putting the kettle on the fire to boil, Winnie introduced me.

'Katie, this is Joe. Joe, this is Katie. An' this is *my* fellow, 'arry,' she said, putting her hand on his face and stroking it.

I thought Joe looked quite a handsome chap with his dark wavy hair. He was wearing a well-cut dark blue suit, and he sounded so polite, when he spoke, saying 'Very pleased to meet you, Katie.' Foolish me, I thought I had fallen in love for the first time in my life, and started to blush.

At that moment Willie came back in, and the three boys started chatting together.

Winnie said, 'Do yer like 'im?'

'Yes,' I whispered, feeling myself blush again.

'I knew yer would. I've been out with 'em both a couple of times.'

When we sat down to eat Joe was quite the gentleman, pulling out my chair for me to sit next to him. I felt very uncomfortable, as each time I looked up from the table I saw Willie's eyes on me. When he actually winked at me, I felt I could have got up and slapped his face. I was glad when it was time to go.

As I left, Willie whispered, 'See yer later, Kate.'

'Not if I can 'elp it!' I whispered back fiercely.

461

Winnie's mother called after us, 'Mind you behave yourselves, an' don't forget, I want you back by ten.'

It was now eight o'clock, and we were too late for the pictures. Harry and Winnie decided we should all go for a walk. It was a lovely moonlit night, you could almost read a paper.

'Do yer mind not goin' ter the pictures?' Joe asked.

'No,' I replied, 'I think I'd rather go for a walk.'

Winnie and Harry walked in front, with their arms around each other. And as we followed behind, Joe asked if I'd mind if he put his arm around my waist. I blushed, and said I didn't mind. As I felt him gently pull me closer and squeeze my waist, I got my first thrill. It was a wonderful sensation, one that I'd never experienced before.

We walked on and on. I didn't care where he was leading me. Eventually he stopped, and asked if I'd mind standing in a doorway while he lit his cigarette. As he lit up I asked where Winnie and Harry were.

'They'll see us when they pass by,' he replied.

I stood there, and as soon as he put out his cigarette, he hugged me close to him. 'I'm very fond of yer, Katie,' he said, as he placed both hands on my shoulders. 'Will yer be my regular?'

'Yes, Joe,' I replied. 'But I'll have to go now, it's getting late. I'll see yer termorra.'

But as he didn't answer, I looked up into his face and in the moonlight I saw his eyes staring at me. They were sort of glistening; his mouth too was wide open. He looked so funny, I could almost have laughed. But something inside me told me this was no laughing matter. Then, as he drew me closer, he said, 'Will yer let me kiss yer, Katie, just once?'

Like a silly young girl, I trusted him. But as I put my lips close to his, I felt his mouth all wet and his tongue trying to prise open my teeth. I pushed him away. 'Don't do that, Joe!' I cried out. 'It's dirty, an' I don't like it.'

'But I love yer, Katie. Only this once.'

'No!' I yelled, but as I pushed his hands away from my shoulders, he suddenly grabbed my right breast and squeezed it hard and began to rub himself up and down against me. With his other hand he tried to lift up my skirt. I felt humiliated, afraid, and angry, and with all the strength I could muster I pushed him away from me. While I was straightening my clothes, he asked me to forgive him.

'I'm sorry, please forgive me, I don't know what came over me, please forgive me, Katie,' he kept pleading. 'I promise this won't happen again.'

'Yer won't get the bloody chance!' I replied angrily.

At that moment I had the sudden thought that I might have lost my mother's brooch in the struggle. I put my hand on my breast and found, to my relief, that it was still there. He came closer to me and asked again if he was forgiven. I said 'Yes.' When he told me he wasn't going to touch me again, I dropped my hand down and suddenly I felt a clammy piece of flesh. It was his 'peter', hanging limp. All at once I went berserk. Not knowing what I was doing, I grabbed it with my two hands and gripped it tight, as I tried to pull it away from me.

'Let go! Let go!' I heard him scream.

When I did let go, I saw him double up. As he fell to the ground, I ran away, leaving him there.

I didn't realise the time until I heard the clock in the distance strike eleven. I kept running, thinking he would catch up with me. Several couples I ran past stopped to stare, but I was too scared to speak or tell anyone. When I got to the end of the Sandpits I was panting and I had to slow down to a walk. I had only walked a few yards when I noticed a steaming puddle on the pavement. When I looked up to see where it was coming from I got another fright. Coming out of a doorway was a dirty drunken old tramp, trying to put his peter back inside his trousers. When he saw me, he tried to bar my way. ''ello, me luv,' he managed to splutter.

Quickly I pushed him over, and as he fell down into his puddle I started to run again. When I reached our house I found the door was bolted. I flopped down on the step and broke down and wept. I knew what to expect, if I banged on the door. It would be another beating. But I couldn't stay there all night. I was afraid of the tramp too now, in case he knew me, or knew where I lived, and came after me. I thought of staying in the brewhouse till the morning, but that was out of the question. The neighbours would find me if I fell asleep, for some of them always rose at dawn to start their washing. I couldn't sleep in the closet, the stench would be too unbearable. There was only one thing to do. I'd go down our cellar, and hope for the best.

I walked back up the yard, and took off the wet, smelly piece of matting, and prayed the cellar grating was not padlocked. To my relief the rusty grating yielded. Slowly, not to make a noise, I lifted it up and slid down on my bottom, inside, among the rubbish. I stood there for a couple of seconds, but everything seemed quiet and still. Even the rats and cockroaches must have gone to sleep. When I climbed the steps and entered the pantry, I took off my shoes and quietly crept up the stairs. I was relieved when I stopped on the first landing, everything was still quiet. But when I reached the attic I saw my sister Liza sitting up in bed, reading her tuppenny romance book by the light from the candle.

I flopped down on the bed and sobbed.

'Where've yer bin?' she whispered. 'Yer know what time is it?'

I shook my head.

'It's nearly twelve o'clock! Come on, I want ter know where yer bin, an' what yer bin doin'.'

'It's a long story, Liza. I'm frightened, an' tired, let me tell yer all about it termorra,' I managed to say.

'Well, 'ow did yer get in the 'ouse, then? It was bolted.'

'I climbed down the cellar. But why did Mum bolt me out?' I whispered back.

'She dain't know yer was out, I 'ad ter lie fer yer. When she called up the stairs an' shouted if yer was in, I told 'er, yes, yer was fast asleep.'

'Thank yer, Liza, I'll treat yer termorra, or try an' get yer some more Woodbines. Now, move over, I'm tired. *Please.*'

'Not before yer brush them cobwebs out of yer 'air.'

As soon as I gave it a good brush, I undressed and quickly got in bed beside her, and while she began to read again, I tried to get to sleep. But suddenly there was a bang on the outside door. I sprang up in bed, trembling like a leaf.

'Oh, my God! It's 'im!' I cried out.

'I don't know what yer bin up to, but yer betta be quiet. They might go away if nobody answers it.'

But there was still more knocking, louder the second time, as we sat up to listen. Then we heard Mum's bedroom window open.

'Who's that down theea? Knockin' on my dower this time o' mornin'.' she yelled down into the yard.

'It's me.'

'Who's me?'

'Willie.'

'Willie who?'

'Willie Nashe.'

'I wonder what 'e wants, Liza?' I whispered anxiously.

''ush, an' listen,' she replied.

'Is yower Katie in?'

'O' course she's in! Fast asleep! Where yow should be! Any'ow, what yer wanta know fer?'

'Me mother wanted ter know if Katie 'ad seen our Winnie, I've looked everywhere, an' we can't find 'er.'

'Well, she ain't 'ere. Katie's bin in bed since ten o'clock.'

We heard the window slam down, but we also heard Mum's footsteps coming up the stairs.

'Get down the bed quickly, pretend yer asleep.'

Quickly Liza blew out the candle and lay down too, hiding her novel under the pillow. But Mum had already seen the light go out.

'What 'ave I told you about readin' in bed? Next time I see one o' them luv-sick books, I'll put it on the fire!' she yelled, as she lit the candle.

I was now more scared than ever. I thought, any moment now she's going to pull the clothes off me. Then I heard her say, ''ow long did yer say Katie's bin asleep?'

'Since about ten o'clock, Mum. Why?'

'Willie Nashe's bin bangin' on the dower, askin' if she'd seen their Winnie.'

''ow could she? She's bin with me all night.'

'Very well, but she'll be sorry if I ever do see 'er with 'er. That Winnie's too old in the 'ead fer 'er years. Now, blow that candle out, an' remember what I said about novels!'

'Yes, goodnight, Mum,' Liza replied.

But Mum went down the stairs without answering. As soon as I heard her bed creak, I sprang up. 'Thank yow fer lyin' fer me, Liza, but I don't want yer ter get inter trouble, if she finds out.'

'Yow leave that ter me, an' remember, I want an explanation termorra. Now, lie down an' let's get ter sleep.'

'Yes, Liza,' I yawned, for I felt safe now I was in my bed. And as soon as my head touched the pillow, I fell asleep.

My mother always let us sleep a little later on Sunday mornings, and when I awoke I saw Liza was reading her tuppenny paperback book. I quickly glanced at the title: *Mill Girl Marries Her Boss.*

When she saw me looking over her shoulder, she cried out 'Yer awake then?' and hid the book. 'Now! Come on, I want yer ter tell me what 'appened last night.'

I had hoped she'd forget to ask. I said it didn't matter now. But she was insistent. While I was telling her, I noticed she kept on smiling.

'What yer smilin' at? I can't see nothin' ter smile about. In fact I'm still scared to go outside now. I thought that knockin' last night was 'im, or the tramp, an' it could 'ave bin the police.'

'No need ter be scared, yer might not see 'im again.'

'But what if 'e's still there? An' e's dead?' I asked.

'Yer can't kill a bloke that way, yer silly. But yer very likely ruptured 'im,' she added.

'What's that mean? Ruptured?' I asked.

'Yer'll find out soon enough when yer older,' she replied.

Suddenly I lost my temper. 'Yer all the same in this bloody 'ouse!' I snapped. 'I'm near enough sixteen, and not one of yer'll tell what I should or shouldn't know about life, or sex.'

'Well, yer liked 'im, dain't yer? Or yer wouldn't 'ave gone with 'im.'

'Er . . . yes, an' I believed 'im when 'e said 'e loved me, an' wanted me ter be 'is regular.'

'What did yer feel like when yer first touched it?'

'I wanted to be sick. It felt like a limp wet sausage. I'll never trust another fellow as long as I live.'

'We all say that, Katie, but nature sometimes plays tricks with our feelin's.'

'Do yer think I should tell me dad, or Frankie, Liza?'

'No!' she snapped. 'Yer betta not! Best if yer try an' forget it.'

As I put on my camisole I felt my breast was sore where Joe had squeezed it. I shuddered, remembering it all again. And for weeks, no matter how many times I washed my hands, I could never wash away the thought, and the feel, of that clammy piece of flesh in my hands.

I stayed indoors all Sunday, and when Mum asked me why, I said I didn't feel well. I didn't go to work on Monday either, for I only felt safe when I was indoors. During the morning I heard the newspaper boy call out 'Special! Special! Read all about it!' I began to tremble with fear. Had they found him, and would the police come to arrest me? I had to buy a paper to read what was special.

As the newsboy came towards me I opened the door a little way, handed him a penny and snatched the *Birmingham Daily Mail* from him. I looked down at the 'latest' column and saw the words 'Two German U-Boats Sunk'. Then I scanned the paper all over. I was relieved to find nothing about the incident, but I wasn't satisfied till I had examined another paper, and another. After that I plucked up the courage to go out.

I thought I had better find out why Willie had been enquiring about his sister. Putting my fears to one side, I knocked on the Nashes' door. But when Mrs Nashe appeared, she yelled at me: 'What do you want?'

'Is Winnie in, Mrs Nashe?' I asked timidly.

'Yes, she is! An' it was one o'clock in the mornin' when she came home! An' she's had a beltin'. An' I've locked her in her room till she's ready to tell me where she's been.'

'But it ain't my fault, Mrs Nashe,' I replied. 'We were goin' ter stay together, but Winnie an' 'er fellow wandered off on their own.'

'I don't want to hear any more excuses. So you'd better not call again. An' she's not goin' with any more fellows, either, until I get the truth out of her. Now bugger off! And she slammed the door in my face.

I couldn't understand why Mrs Nashe had to blame me. It wasn't my fault Winnie had come home at one o'clock in the morning. As I walked back home I kept wondering where Winnie had been that night.

Two days later, as I was walking down Narstone Lane, someone tapped me on my shoulder. When I turned around and saw Joe standing there, I cried out, 'What yer want now?'

'I've been lookin' fer yer, Katie, each morning, to tell yer 'ow sorry I am,' he replied, as he put his two hands on my shoulders.'

'Too late fer that now! An' take yer 'ands off my shoulders!' I snapped.

As I went to walk away, he said, 'Don't go yet, Katie, *please*. I want yer to hear what I've got ter say, then yer can go.'

He looked so sad that I couldn't help but say, 'Very well, but I can only spare you a few minutes.'

'I really do love yer, Katie, please believe me, and I'm sorry for what 'appened on Saturday night.'

'I'm sorry too,' I replied, 'but now I must go.'

As I went to move away, he said would I see him again, and he would prove how sorry he was.

'Why?' I asked.

'I've had my calling up papers, an' I leave in two days' time. I'd like to see yer again before I go.'

'Very well. Where?'

'Can I see yer at eight o'clock tomorrow night, by Chamberlain clock?'

'Very well,' I answered.

As I walked away, I looked back. Seeing him still standing there looking all forlorn, I began to feel sorry for him. After all he'd tried to do to me, I still liked him. Suddenly, on impulse I ran back and kissed his cheek. Neither of us spoke, but when I hurried down the street again, I looked back, and saw him wave. I waved back. During that afternoon, while I was working, I kept thinking about him, wondering whether I should meet him or not. I asked myself, had I been foolish to promise to meet him? Was this a trick to punish me for what I did to him? I thought I'd ask Liza to advise me what I should do. When we sat up in bed that night, I told her all about it.

She yelled at me, 'After all 'e tried ter do ter yer? Yer want ter see 'im again? If yer tek my advice, Katie, yer'll keep away from 'im. In my opinion 'e sounds very plausible.'

'I don't think so, Liza, 'e's really nice when yer get ter know 'im.'

'Yer've only bin out with 'im once! Yer can't tell me yer know 'is ways by that! Do yer still like 'im?' she asked.

'Yes, Liza, but I don't know why. I feel I want ter see 'im an' yet I don't. I really don't know what ter do.'

'On second thoughts, would yer like me ter go an' see 'im?' she asked.

'Yes, Liza, an' tell him 'ow sorry I am, but I'm not too well.'

'Leave it to me, I'll find some excuse. I want ter see what 'e's like, any'ow.'

Next day I took the long way round to work and back, in case I should bump into him. So I was late getting home. When I walked in, I was surprised to see that Mum and Dad were dressed in their Sunday best.

'Where yer bin till now?' Mum snapped at once.

'I felt like some fresh air an' took the long way 'ome,' I replied.

'Very well,' my dad said, 'come an' get yer tea, luv. I want ter tek yer mum out, it's 'er birthday.'

Usually birthdays in our house just came and went. Our family were not ones to show any outward love or affection. Though sometimes my dad would tap my head, or stroke my hair, when I said goodnight.

Mum and Dad left, and my brother followed soon after to go courting his girl, Nellie. Then I watched as Liza put on her 'war paint' and her best hat, coat and gloves. I really didn't feel well now, I was so nervous, wondering if I'd done the right thing.

'Wake me up if I'm asleep when yer come in, Liza, an' tell me what 'e says.'

'Okay,' she replied, as she closed the door behind her.

Ten o'clock came, and Liza hadn't returned. I lay in bed, imagining all kinds of things that might have happened. I seemed to have been lying there for hours before I heard her climb the stairs.

'Where yer bin till now?' I cried out as I sat up in bed. 'I've bin worryin' meself sick about yer.'

'Yer know where I went!' she snapped.

'But it didn't afta tek yer all this time!' I replied angrily.

'I 'ad ter go ter see me own young man, didn't I? An' it was late. We 'ad a few words, 'e was going to leave me, but when I told 'im why I was late, we made up.'

'I'm sorry,' I said. 'I forgot you had to meet George. Are you both all right now?' I added.

'Yes. But, Katie, yer should really 'ave gone yerself to see 'im, 'e was really disappointed, when yer didn't come yerself.'

'What did yer say?' I asked eagerly.

'I made the excuse yer was poorly in bed. An' yer know what? 'e's a real nice, 'onest bloke.'

'Maybe 'e is, Liza, but there was no reason why 'e should try to molest me that night.'

'Katie,' she replied, 'they all try it once, an' if yer give way, yer never see 'em again. But if yer refuse, they really respect yer, that's why 'e wanted ter see yer again. Yer understand what I mean?'

'Yes, Liza, an' thank yer fer goin'. But perhaps I should 'ave gone ter meet 'im, Liza.'

'It's too late now, 'e catches the early morning train for France termorra. But I gave 'im our address an' 'e said 'e'd write ter yer, an' would yer wait fer 'im when 'e comes back 'ome again. The way 'e spoke, Katie, I believe 'e really, truly loves yer,' she added.

Tears began to flow now as I said, 'Yes, Liza. If 'e writes, I'll tell 'im I'll wait fer 'im.'

'Now, there's no need fer tears, by the time 'e comes back from the war yer'll be able ter mek yer mind up. Now let's both get ter sleep.'

But all through the night, off and on, I kept thinking about him, and for many more nights too. A couple of months later I received a beautiful lace-edged card from him. On the top right-hand corner was a picture of a young soldier, gazing down to a girl in the left-hand corner. Printed in gilt letters were the words 'You are always in my thoughts, my darling.' On the back of the card there were a few lines to say he would always think of me and when the war was over he would come to see me again. He ended, 'God bless you, Katie, all my love, Joe, xxxx.'

I treasured that card for years. But, sad to say, I never saw or heard from Joe again. I couldn't even write, for I had no forwarding address. I didn't even know his surname, or where he lived.

Winnie's Trouble

After the Saturday night we made up that foursome, I didn't see Winnie for weeks. Then I saw her in the fish and chip shop. She was muffled up in a scarf, but, when she turned around, I noticed that her face was swollen and bruised. She hurried past me, but I caught up with her.

'What yer done ter yer face, Winnie?' I asked, 'An' why yer bin avoidin' me?'

Suddenly, she began to weep. When I asked her what was wrong, she said, 'I can't tell yer now, I've got ter 'urry back 'ome.'

'Well, why is yer face all bruised?' I asked.

She drew the scarf closer around her face and wept.

When I asked her why she was crying, she said, 'I can't tell yow 'ere, but can I come to your 'ouse an' see yer, when yer mum's out, then I'll tell yer all about it?'

'Yes, Winnie,' I replied eagerly. 'I shall be by myself Saturday night, will that do?'

'Yes, I'll try,' she managed to say, through her tears.

'Say about eight o'clock, then you can tell me all about it, now don't cry any more, tek my 'anky.'

As she wiped away the tears, she said, 'I'll 'ave ter go now, before Mum misses me.'

For the next few days, until Saturday evening, I worried about her. Had she fallen down somewhere? Or had she been beaten? Or was it something more serious?

Eight o'clock. I waited. Half past eight. A quarter to nine. I had almost given up hope when she knocked on the door. 'Come on in, Winnie,' I cried out. 'The door's open.'

When she came in, I saw that her eyes were still red from weeping.

'Come an' sit down Winnie, by the fire, while I mek yer a nice 'ot cuppa tea.'

As we sat facing each other, drinking our tea, I asked, 'Why 'aven't yer bin ter see me before? It's been nearly two months now.'

'Mum won't let me out of 'er sight since that Saturday night,' she replied at once.

'Then 'ow yer come ter get out now?'

'She's gone ter see me aunt. But I can't stop long. I afta get back before she misses me.'

'She blames yow, Katie, fer keepin' me out that night.'

'But it wasn't my fault!' I cried, indignantly. 'Yow left me and Joe, and walked off on yer own! An' if it 'adn't been fer my sister sayin' I was in bed early I should 'ave bin in trouble too.'

'I told 'er it wasn't your fault, I told 'er we got lost. But she still didn't believe me.'

'Where did yer get to, then?' I asked, as I saw the tears run down her face again.

'I 'aven't told anyone. But I think I can trust you, Katie.'

I tried to comfort her by saying I'd always liked her no matter what she'd said or done, and as I wiped away her tears, she began to tell me.

''arry asked me ter go to 'is 'ome ter meet 'is dad, but when we got there, 'e was out. We sat on the sofa, an' while we waited, we kept drinkin' port. I don't know 'ow many glasses I had, but I was feeling drowsy. But I remember 'arry sayin' 'ow much 'e loved me, would I marry 'im when the war was over. Then, after we snuggled close together, we kissed, and made love. A little while after I began to feel ashamed fer givin' in to 'im. But 'e said again 'e loved me, and 'e'd save up an' we could be married an' would I wait ter see 'is father. But I wanted ter get 'ome. I 'ad no idea of the time. So I asked 'im ter see me 'ome. On the way 'e kissed me again an' we promised ter see each other next day. But when I got indoors, Mum was waitin' fer me, with the leather strap.'

'But I always thought your mum was a kind, gentle woman?' I said, surprised.

'A lot of people think that, but yer don't know my mum, she belted me, an' locked me in the attic, an' I 'ad ter stay there till she was ready ter let me out. A few weeks later I kept feelin' sick an' when she knew I couldn't eat my food she almost dragged me ter the doctor's. He examined me, an' told Mum I was in the family way. On the way back 'ome she kept callin' me bad names, an' when we got indoors she beat me again. Then she locked me in a second time, an' went to see my aunt, ter see what could be done about me. Then, ter make matters worse, a telegram came from the War Office ter say my dad was missin'. And when Mum read it, she flopped down in the chair an' began to cry. I felt shocked too when I read it, but when I went ter put my arms round 'er, ter try ter console 'er, she punched me in the face an' called me a dirty little slut. She was still 'ittin' me, when me aunt walked in. She screamed at Mum. I 'eard 'er say, "Yer can't knock it out of 'er that way." An' she said she knew of a woman who could give me an abortion. But Mum screamed back at 'er and said I was goin' into the work'ouse or the home fer fallen women. I'm scared now, Katie. I don't know what ter do.'

Tears filled my eyes too as I said, 'Why don't yer go an' see 'arry an' tell 'im? If 'e said 'e loves yer, surely 'e'll marry yer?'

'But that's the worst of it, Katie, 'e don't know. When I went to see 'im, 'is father said 'e'd joined the Navy, and when I told 'is dad I was goin' ter 'ave 'is baby, 'e said 'e didn't believe me, an' I was to find some other silly bugger ter put the blame on. I don't know what ter do now, Katie, Mum's took all my clothes away, an' I've got no money. I'd run away, but there's nowhere to go to, only my aunt's, and I'm even scared of 'er now.'

'I only wish I could 'elp yer, Winnie. Pr'aps in a few days when yer mum's got over 'er grief, she'll change 'er mind. But in the meantime if yer'll come an' see me termorra night I can let yer 'ave four pounds from my post office savings.'

'But I don't know when I shall be able to pay you back, or when I can get out ter see yer again.'

'You will,' I said, as I wiped away her tears. 'Yer'll find out later, when yer near yer time, she'll be sorry fer beatin' yer an' callin' yer names.'

'I'll pray each night an' hope yer right, Katie. I must go now, before she comes 'ome. An' thank yer fer listenin' ter me. I feel a bit better now I've told yer about it. But promise yer'll not say I've bin 'ere, or say anythin' about my condition to anyone.'

'Yer can trust me, Winnie,' I managed to say as I kissed her wet, swollen face.

As I watched her go down the street I went indoors and cried, and prayed to the Good Lord to forgive her mother, and to bring them closer together. And I thought how lucky I was. The same thing could have happened to me, that night.

I waited for Winnie the next night and for several nights, but she never came. The following Sunday I plucked up courage to go to her mum's house but when I got there I found the house empty. All the furniture had gone, and there was a notice stuck inside the window: 'THIS HOUSE TO LET. KEY AT NUMBER SIX, RENT 7/6 per week.

When I called at number six the woman said she didn't know much about them. She didn't even know they'd left, until the landlord gave her the key to let the house to the next tenant. It was several years before I saw Winnie again. But each night I would mention her in my prayers, and ask the Good Lord to watch over her in her hour of need.

Improving Myself

I'm afraid my romantic feelings for Joe didn't stop me being attracted to other young fellows. And Liza was right, the memory of my struggle with him didn't really make me wary.

One day the forewoman where I worked asked me to help sort out some files in the office. Writing at the desk was a young man so handsome I couldn't take my eyes off him. As soon as the forewoman left the room, I said, 'Yer new 'ere, ain't yer?'

'Beg pardon?' he replied pleasantly.

'I said, yer new 'ere?'

'Yes,' he replied, smiling.

I could see he wanted to say more, but when the forewoman entered he went back to his writing.

'That'll be all,' she said. 'Thank you for helping me out.'

'Oh, that's all right, I'll be glad to any time.'

As I went through the glass door, I looked back and saw him smile at me.

I saw him several times during the next two weeks, when he came through the workshop. Then one afternoon he came up to the bench where I was working.

'Excuse my asking, but I was wondering if you'd come for a walk with me on Saturday afternoon?'

All the girls' eyes were watching us, but I didn't care. In fact, I felt highly honoured. I agreed to meet him outside the corner tea shop in Victoria Street at two o'clock. As soon as the eagerly awaited afternoon came, I dressed in my best and put on a bit of 'war paint', then I had only to slip a perfumed 'Phul-nana' card down between my breasts, and I was ready to go.

As soon as he saw me coming around the corner, he came towards me, and as he raised his hat I thought he was the handsomest fellow I'd ever been out with.

'I'm glad you were able to come,' he said.

'Oh, I always keep me promise.'

We went inside and he ordered tea and cream cakes, and while we sat eating he told me his name was Richard Evans and he lived in Monument Road. (Oh dear, I thought, among the posh nobs.)

'My name's Kathleen,' I said.

But he said he already knew, from the clocking-in cards. I was glad he didn't ask where I lived.

After we had our tea he asked if I'd like to take a walk with him around St Paul's Church. He was so polite, not saucy like other fellows I'd met. After that we walked out together every Saturday afternoon for several weeks.

One lovely warm afternoon we walked along by Wasson Pool. I began to smile as I thought of the last time when I was here with Winnie, when I'd seen my dad and Winnie's dad rising up out of the canal naked, carrying coal above their heads. When he asked me why I was smiling I told him it was a long story, but maybe I'd tell him some time.

'Shall we sit down by this tree?' he asked, taking off his coat for me to sit on.

We sat there talking for a few minutes. Then he asked me if he could kiss me. I just nodded. But as soon as he had kissed me, he said, 'I think we had better be moving, Kathleen, it's getting late.'

'Yes,' I replied, as I handed him his coat. 'I've gorra go too, or I'll get in trouble with me mum.'

'Kathleen, I like you a lot, you're a very nice girl and very attractive but . . .'

'But what?' I asked.

'I hope you won't be offended, but I'd like you better if you didn't put that rubbish on your face.'

I lost my temper at once. 'If yer don't like me as I am yer know what yer can do!' I snapped, as I went to walk away.

'Don't go. I'm sorry if I offended you. I wanted really to help you. I could help you speak nicely and properly.'

'What yer mean, speak properly?'

'Not to say "gorra" when you really mean "got to", or "have to", and several other words you say. If you spoke correctly you'd go a long way, Kathleen, believe me,' he replied, as he took my hand.

'But I can't 'elp 'ow I speak!' I snapped.

'But you can, if you'll let me teach you.'

'It's all right for yow, p'raps yow've 'ad an education, but I ain't. My teacher did 'er best for me, when I was a young girl. I was gettin' along fine well, until I tried practisin' at 'ome, then when I tried talkin' as I'd been told ter my mum, she said "Don't come 'ere talkin' like that with yer bloody airs an' graces!" An' then I gave up. Yer see, Richard, it's 'ard when yer don't know any different, an' yer 'ear it all around yer, day in an' day out.'

'I understand. Next time we meet, I'll bring you a book and you can practise with me.'

'I'm not stupid, yer know!' I said, flaring up once more. 'I can read, an' write, an' add up, an' subtract!'

'But that's not everything. You see, I like you a lot, and I'd like to take you to meet my parents, but . . .'

'But what?' I cried out angrily.

'Until you let me teach you to speak correctly, I don't think they would approve, and you'd feel hurt.'

At that I really lost my temper. 'Well, if it's yer parents yer worried about, I won't bother ter see yer any more.'

As I walked quickly away, he came after me, but when he asked me again to try, I felt very hurt and angry. I slapped his face, and ran. When I went to work on the Monday morning I did my best to avoid him. He tried to speak to me several times, but I always turned away. And when I heard some of the girls say we'd had a lovers' tiff, and make some other remarks as well, I left that job to work at another firm.

I never saw Richard Evans again, but I often remembered what he had tried to tell me. As it happened, I found that the girls and women at my new firm were very kind and spoke very politely. I knew now that I wanted to speak correctly, and I tried to learn by listening to them, and copying the way they spoke.

I tried practising when I was at home, but it wasn't easy. My sister sneered, and my mother ranted. 'Yer bloody fool,' she'd shout. 'Yer know where that bloody talk'll get yer! On the road ter ruin, that's what!'

But I ignored them both. I was determined to learn to speak

correctly, and I kept up my efforts. Sometimes I'd hide in the brewhouse, or the yard lav, to practise. But I was too ignorant in those days even to know there was such a thing as a dictionary. It was only by listening to others that I was able to educate myself enough to adapt and get by.

The End of the War

One very cold, dark night, while Dad, Liza, Frankie and me were sitting at the table waiting for Mum to dish out our supper, we saw our brother Jack stagger inside the door, with his laden kit bag. As he flung it on the floor, we all rushed to welcome him home.

Mum threw her arms around him, saying, 'When do yer go back?'

Jack began to laugh. 'I've only just got 'ere, Mum.'

'Yer know what 'er meant ter say, son,' said Dad. 'Any'ow, 'ow long are yer 'ere for?'

'I've only got seven days furlough, Dad, I go back Sunday night. I've been travellin' all day, it was a slow train, and we were packed like sardines, sailors and soldiers. Lots o' poor, tired bleeders 'ad ter stand in the guard's van, an' in cattle trucks. I'm glad ter be 'ome, Ma, I'm tired, an' I'm clammed.

While Mum dished up some supper for Jack, Dad slipped out to get him a drink. When he came back, with a half-gallon stone jar of ale, he said. 'We're goin' ter celebrate when yer've 'ad yer supper, son, an' 'ave a few neighbours in.'

But Jack had other priorities. 'Not ternight, Dad. I'd like a bath, I'm lousy. Is there any place I could go?'

'I'm sorry, son, the public baths are closed ternight. But after you've 'ad summat to eat, I'll light a fire under the copper in the brew'ouse.'

Then Dad said Grace, and thanked the Lord for sending Jack home safely.

After we had eaten, we all set to, fetching and carrying water from the tap in the yard, to fill the boiler. When the water had heated up we had to ladle it out into the maiding tub, for Jack to stand in. Dad lit a couple of candles, hung an old blanket over the rusty iron window frame, to keep out the cold, then told us to stand guard outside in case any nosy neighbours or kids came near. But not a soul was to be seen, only us. It was even too cold for our moggy to go courting.

Mum handed Frankie a bottle of Lysol disinfectant and told him to slip it under the blanket. 'An' tell 'im not ter use it all. 'e'll find a piece of carbolic soap be'ind the mangle,' she added.

Next day was Sunday, which was supposed to be a day of rest. But when I heard my mum get up early, unfortunately I got up too and so I had the job of swilling out the brewhouse and filling the copper boiler ready for the Monday morning wash. After I'd finished, and come indoors, I watched my mum turn my brother's khaki tunic and trousers inside out and iron all the seams, to kill the lice and eggs. Next day she washed his shirt, long pants, vest and socks in Lysol.

Although Jack and my parents very seldom saw eye to eye, and they quarrelled frequently before he went in the Army, now Mum and Dad were proud to show him off in the pubs, in front of the neighbours. Mum didn't like it when Jack went to visit the widow he'd ben courting, though. And when he stayed two days and nights of his leave with her, Mum quarrelled with him. Dad said it was his own business and that he was old enough to make his own mind up what to do or where to go. When Mum began weeping he said, 'Let 'im enjoy what short time 'e's got. The Lord only knows when we shall see 'im again, Polly, so let's do the best we can, an' mek 'im 'appy befower 'e goes back ter France.'

Jack's last couple of nights our neighbours were invited to come in, to have a few drinks and sing songs. Jack brought his young woman in too, and while Dad and Jack were giving her plenty of attention, I could see by Mum's face she didn't like her. But there was nothing she could say or do, for Dad had already warmed her.

Sunday came all too soon. We all went to see Jack off at the station. The platform was crowded with hundreds of men in different uniforms with kit bags slung over their shoulders, and women and children were crying as they hugged and clung to their loved ones before being parted from them.

The rejoicing when the war ended was in contrast to this scene. There was dancing in the streets, the pubs flung open their doors to distribute free beer, and people gave away food that they had hoarded for years.

My mum, and the neighbours too, forgot all their grievances when she carried out our old gramophone, and we danced up and down the yard, with our skirts held well above our knees, singing:

Knees up Mother Brown,
Yer drawers are comin' down
Get a pin an' pin 'em up,
Before they come right down.

But through it all there were still many thousands grieving for the loved ones they knew would never come back. And when the fighting men were demobilised, bitterness and anger began to grow. The soldiers remembered those promises from politicians, that this war would be the war to end all wars, and England would be a place fit for heroes to live in. They hadn't long returned from the trenches, many with limbs missing, or worse, before they realised that there was only unemployment awaiting them. Nothing but war, it seemed, could provide employment for starving people, and now the war was over the people were starving again.

Those soldiers returned from the 1914–18 war would have been still more bitter if they had realised that the next generation, their sons and daughters, would also be gun fodder for war-mongering politicians.

Marriage and Children

O n Christmas Eve 1919 I met and began to fall in love with Charlie, who was to be my husband. We were married in 1921. Charlie happened to be one of the lucky ones who found employment after he was demobilised, but it was to be for only a short period. I too had work in a factory. Many firms employed women in preference to men: they would do the same work for less wages.

When we were first married we lived in a furnished room. But when my first son was only a couple of months old, and I was already pregnant with my second baby, the landlady gave us notice. I was still working, but Charlie was by then on short time (he was soon to be out of work altogether), and we were very hard up.

I tramped the district far and wide in search of a place to live, but everywhere I met with the same answer, 'No children allowed'. I humbled myself to visit the parish relief offices, but when I asked them if they could find us a place to live, their answer was 'We do not find accommodation for anyone.' Then they added, 'If you have nowhere to live, there is always the workhouse.'

As soon as I got back to the furnished room I broke down and wept. When Charlie came home late that night with the useful coppers he earned by selling sawdust, and I told him what those inquisitors had said, he went wild. 'The workhouse? They told yer the workhouse? After fightin' for a better life an' a place to live? They talk about the bleedin' workhouse. If I'd got me rifle here, I'd shoot the bleedin' bastards, and them in the bleedin' Government!'

By now we were really desperate, and though the last place I wanted to live was with my mother, when Mum and Dad said we could move in with them, to live in the attic I had slept in as a child, I had to agree. I promised myself that we would leave as soon as things got better.

Charlie and my dad whitewashed the attic walls, and when they had left to go for a drink in the George and Dragon, I laid my son down on the sofa and set to and scrubbed those worn, knotted boards. All that evening I longed for my mother to come up and help me, or talk to me, but she never came. I broke down and wept.

Until we could get some kind of furniture to put in the attic, my husband, my baby and myself had to sleep on a mattress on the floor in Mum and Dad's room. Later we were able to buy a second-hand double bed, two ladder-backed chairs, a well-worn kitchen table, and a large wardrobe with an oval front mirror. Later still we bought a couple of grey army blankets from the Army and Navy stores. And some of the neighbours who lived in our yard were very kind and helpful. Although they didn't have much to spare themselves, they gave me a few odd crocks, and lent me some of their utensils until we could afford to buy our own.

When my mother realised that the neighbours were helping to give us a start, she unbent a little. 'Yer can fetch a bit of coal up from down the cellar an' light yerself a fire in the attic grate,' I remember her saying. But I'd to pay for it. In more ways than one.

And so we had to live and sleep in that small attic from the end of 1921 onwards. It was 1931 before I left. And I will remember until the day I die the bitterness of those ten years.

In my ignorance, during this time I gave birth to five children, and had two miscarriages. My eldest son was only six years old when he was knocked down and killed on the way home from school. In that same year, 1927, my dad, whom I loved and was always proud of, died in the workhouse. Soon after, my mother turned to drink, which made our lives more unbearable. Often when she went away for long weekends I'd pray she would never return, but my prayers were not answered.

On 25 April 1931, our tenth wedding anniversary, my husband died. I was told I wasn't entitled to a widow's pension because he hadn't enough insurance stamps. I could only get parish relief, which was not enough for our needs. You weren't allowed to have any earnings while you were on parish relief, but I had to stretch it somehow, and so, after putting my children to bed, I would go out at night selling firewood from door to door. Then someone made it their business to tell the officer in charge of parish relief that I was selling firewood. I had to appear in front of a tribunal, where I was refused any further help, and warned that I would be prosecuted for not declaring my earnings. My children and I were now almost starving. Some of our kind neighbours offered their help with food they themselves could hardly spare, but I couldn't take it.

In total desperation I made a heartbreaking decision: I resolved to let my children go into a home where they would be fed and well cared for, until such time as I could provide a proper home for them, and give them the love and affection they needed. I went to see the matron of Dr Barnardo's home in Moseley, and asked if I could leave the children in their care for a short time, explaining that as soon as I got everything arranged for a better future I would have my children back with me again. I thought this would be a matter of a few weeks. And so it was arranged. But later I found I had made a terrible mistake, in not having it all in writing.

It was a bitterly cold day when I took my children to Moseley Village Home, and left them there in the charge of the matron. I hugged and kissed them and after giving them a few sweets I'd saved I walked away before they saw my tears. I don't remember anything about walking back alone to my mother's house that day. I only remember that when I climbed those dark, narrow attic stairs, and entered that room with so many memories, I broke down completely.

But after a while I pulled myself together. Now I was alone I had to think about the future. I had to get out of this house at once. I left almost everything behind. With a clean change of underclothes crammed into a hessian bag, and a few coppers in my purse, I came down those attic stairs for the last time. As I closed the door behind me I happened to glance down the yard and saw several toddlers playing in the gutters, and others sitting on their bare bums on the cold doorsteps, while their mums were either in the brewhouse or somewhere gossiping. Poor little half-starved mites, I thought; I made the right decision in parting with mine. And for the first time in years I began to relax. As I walked away, I never looked back. I vowed never to enter that unhappy place again.

For a few weeks after that I was able to visit the children every Saturday afternoon and, seeing them clean and happy, I was content that I had done the right thing for them. But after six weeks, without anyone notifying me, the children were transferred from Moseley, the girls to the cruel discipline of a Dr Barnardo's home in Barkingside, in Essex, and John first to a home in Kingston-upon-

Thames and later to Watts Naval Training School at Elmham in Norfolk. I fought desperately to get my children back, but all my efforts were useless. I realised eventually that all I could do was work as hard as I could to get together the sort of home that Barnardo's would approve of. What I didn't realise was that it was going to take me eight long, troublesome years to reach my goal.

Another War

During those eight years of hard work and determination, I managed to build up my own enamelling business and to get together enough money to rent a three-bedroomed house in Albert Road, Handsworth, which was then a very select area. Dr Barnardo's finally agreed to send a visitor to inspect my home, to see if I was in fit circumstances to have my children returned to me. The visitor came and looked over the house and workshop and details of my income, and left saying she was satisfied with what she saw, and that I would be receiving a letter from head office. Then one day in November 1939 a letter came to say I was to meet the midday train from London next day, and my children would be handed over to me.

Already another war had begun. And as I stood on the platform crowded with young men in uniform, and women of all ages kissing and weeping as they said goodbye to their loved ones, I thought about the 1914–18 war, and my parents and the rest of our family saying goodbye to my two elder brothers.

But when I saw the train coming into the station, I had no thought for anyone but my children. I pushed my way through the crowd, searching anxiously for their faces. Then I saw my eldest daughter, Kathleen, step down from the train, followed by Jean and Mary. Kathleen ran towards me.

'This is our mum,' she said to Jean.

I threw my arms around Kath and we hugged each other. But when I went to hug Jean and Mary they held back. I felt hurt, but I must have seemed a stranger to them. They had been so young when I parted with them. And though in the intervening years I had sometimes been able to see Kathleen in the home, Jean and Mary had been fostered out, and we had had hardly any contact.

As I began to explain who I was, two elderly women came up to me and one asked if I was Mrs Flood. I replied that I was, and asked her about my son, John. She said her instructions were only to deliver my daughters safely. But before she boarded the train again she wrote down the address of Watts Naval Training School, and said I should enquire about him there.

That night, after tucking the girls up in their beds, I wrote a letter to Watts, asking why my son hadn't been returned to me. A few days later I received a reply saying that my son was now serving on one of His Majesty's ships. After that I wrote several letters explaining that he was only fifteen years old, but I had no more replies. I also wrote to the War Office, but I had no reply from them either. John went all through the war in the Navy.

I did my utmost to make my three daughters happy, trying to make up for the lost years. Kathleen, who was now fourteen, settled in well. Soon she came to help me in my enamelling business. But Jean and Mary, who were twelve and nine, couldn't seem to settle at all. This was not surprising, in the circumstances, but at times it was very hard. I had scarcely got to know Mary when she wanted to be evacuated with the other children from her school. Although I was upset to part with her again so soon, it seemed best to let her do as she wished. I could only pray that the Good Lord would keep her safe and reunite us as soon as the war ended. Meanwhile, as often as we could, we visited her in Wales, where she seemed happy to be with her schoolfriends. Jean, too, was very restless for the first couple of years after she clame back to me. Then, at Kathleen's suggestion, I took her to work in the business as well. She enjoyed that, and began to relax.

Not long after the girls were returned to me, I left the rented house in Albert Road and bought a house in Waverhill Road, off the Soho Road, Handsworth. Only a couple of weeks after we moved, we heard that the house in Albert Road had been bombed. It was then that I realised that this was not only a war for the men in the forces, it was to be a war for the whole population of innocent men, women and little children. Later we were issued with identity cards, gas masks, ration books for food, and coupons for clothing.

Each night, as soon as Radio Luxemburg went off the air, Kathleen and Jean and I would put on our siren suits, so that we were ready to go down the air raid shelter when the warning sirens went. Our shelter was one of several underground storerooms under some little shops on the corner of our road. They were long nights in the shelters, and none of us knew whether we would be alive to see the dawn. But we had some good times. We did a lot of community singing, to the accompaniment of an accordion and a banjo, and as well we were all expected to do 'turns' to help keep our spirits up.

There was one wonderful character, who was a great contributor to the entertainment. Everyone called her 'Old Molly'. She was a small, round figure of a woman, who always wore a faded red scarf tied over her curlers, an old long brown frock, and a pair of men's boots which had seen better days. She had the job of cleaning out the public lavatories across the road, and you would often see her coming out of the pub opposite, carrying her mop and bucket, with a Guinness or a bottle of Mackeson's stout inside the bucket. When the raids were very bad she'd come down the shelter with her mop and bucket and its contents, ready to go across the street when the all-clear sounded. She would always give us a song, and we would encourage her by throwing pennies in her bucket. But she was artful enough to entertain us with only one chorus each night, knowing she'd be able to collect more coppers in the bucket when she sang to us the next night.

I would sing or tell stories. I remember one night, while there was a lull, I told them some stories about things that had happened when I was a girl: how my family and my granny and an assortment of neighbours went into the country, hop-picking, and how my brother came to steal a pig, and how my mum won her black eye.

While I was talking there was suddenly a screaming whistle outside and a nerve-racking clatter in the street above. All at once Molly yelled out, 'Them bleedin' 'cendiaries! If I 'ad that bleedin' 'itler 'ere, I'd ram this mop down 'is bleedin' throat!'

'Now, now, Molly,' Mrs Fray, one of my neighbours, said quietly. 'There's no use upsettin' everybody, yer must try an' calm yerself down, like the rest of us.'

'But I've gotta go out an' clean the urinals,' she cried out.

'Yer not goin' anywhere,' Mrs Fray replied, 'until them fire bombs 'ave finished droppin'.'

'They won't 'it me! I can put me bucket over me 'ead!'

'You'll stay where yow are!' Mrs Fray replied. 'Any'ow, there'll be enough water in them closets ter clean all of 'em at once themselves, if they do get 'it. Now sit yerself down, Molly, an' keep quiet, an' wait.'

After a lot of coaxing Molly took the bottle of stout from out of the bucket and drank it down, then toppled down on a bunker, making sure she held on to the mop and bucket, before she dozed off. Later, one of the wardens brought several large packets of chips and handed them around while Mrs Fray and I made tea for everyone. Although it went a bit quiet outside, we could still hear the thuds from the bombs in the distance and the fire engines racing down the street. Now and then we could hear one of our big guns (we called it 'Big Emma') firing at the bombers as they roared overhead. While we waited for the all clear, four men came into the shelter. I recognised two of them, our neighbours Mr Turner, the train conductor, and Mr Ellis, who worked at the Co-op; their wives and children had been evacuated. The four of them were covered from head to foot in debris. They told us they'd been in the thick of it, helping the wardens and firemen to put out the incendiaries.

After they had drunk their tea and lit their fags they squatted around an upturned crate and began to play cards. As soon as they heard a warden come in they snatched up the money and spread the crate with matches. But it was too late. He had already seen the money changing hands.

'I ain't 'avin' any gamblin' down 'ere!' he cried out as he came towards them.

'We're only playin' fer matches,' Mr Turner replied.

'Yer don't fool me!' the warden said. 'Yer'd do better if yer'd go outside an' see what yer can do ter help others.'

'Why, yer bloody old sod!' Mr Turner cried out. 'We've bin out theea all night, 'elpin' ter do your job.'

'Ah, an' we don't get paid fer it!' replied Mr Ellis, 'so sod off an' let us alone.'

But by now, the warden had lost his temper.

'Well, if that's yer attitude, if yer don't put them cards away I'll fetch a copper in, ter do it for yer.'

'Yer can fetch the 'ole bloody force in!' Mr Turner replied.

As he went out they began to play again, still playing with matches – but I heard one of them say quietly, 'One match equals a penny. We'll settle up later.' They hadn't been playing long when a policeman entered, followed by the warden.

'Now,' he asked as he walked towards the players, 'what's this I hear about you four gambling?'

'We're not gamblin', Constable,' Mr Ellis remarked. 'As yer can see, we're only playin' with matches.'

'Oh well, carry on lads, as long as you don't cause any trouble, there's nothing I can do.'

As soon as the officer left, the warden became fuming, and went out and brought in another policeman, who was not so easy-going. He didn't believe them, and he tipped the crate over and told them to clear off out. There was such a skirmish, the policeman's hat fell off.

'Leave 'em alone, they ain't been doin' any 'arm,' Mrs Fray piped up. 'Pity yow ain't got better things to do.'

'You keep out of this, missus,' he replied.

'She's speaking the truth,' I replied. 'We all saw them playing with matches.'

The Constable left the shelter, but as soon as he got up the steps outside we heard him blow his whistle. Another policeman arrived, and the gamblers were arrested and taken to the police station. Next morning they were carted off in the Black Maria to the law courts, where they were tried. Mrs Fray and I and several other women, including Old Molly with her mop and bucket, went to give evidence. But there was no need really for us to have gone; the magistrate just cautioned them and said they were to behave in future. After that night the warden was known around as 'Mr Nark'.

I often felt sorry for Old Molly and so did everyone else who knew her. But she was always very independent-minded.

One night I said, 'Molly, there's a widow who lives a few doors from me, she wants a cleaner, she'll pay you well, better than that stinking, messy job you're doing.'

'I'll thank yer ter mind yer own business!' she snapped. 'I like doin' me job. It's me life.'

I did my best to talk her round, but in the end I gave up. Then one night we missed her coming down the shelter to sing and do a knees-up. Later we were told she had been killed while on her rounds.

Mary and Mum

O ne cold day in February 1941, I happened to be standing in the queue outside the greengrocer's in Icknield Street. It was my birthday, and I was trying to buy some extra fruit to give my daughters a treat when they came home from work. I felt someone tap me on the shoulder, and turning around I was very surprised to see my eldest sister, Mary. We threw our arms around each other.

'I'm so happy to see you, Kate,' she cried out tearfully.

'Me too, Mary,' I managed to say as we hugged and kissed each other.

'How long has it been since I saw you last, Kate?'

'The last time was over three years ago. You were making doughnuts, and you threw the tray at Bill's old horse for eating 'em. Remember?'

We both began to laugh, and she added, 'Yes, and it was a pity they didn't put him in the knacker's yard with the old mare.'

'How are you getting on with him now?' I asked.

'Oh, it's a long story. Maybe I'll tell you all about it some day,' she replied. 'Anyhow, when you've got what you've come for, let's go over the road and have a drink. You don't know how glad I am to see you again, Kate,' she added.

I was very surprised, the way she kept chattering, for I'd always remembered her as a very quiet person, who kept herself within herself.

We went into the pub, and she had a gin and I had my favourite Mackeson's stout. While we sat drinking and chatting I happened to notice Mary's husband over in the bar.

'Bill's in there,' I pointed out.

'And he can stay there for all I care,' she replied bitterly.

'Are you two at loggerheads still?' I asked.

'We have been since we came back from America.'

'Why? Didn't you like it?'

'I did, and I made lots of friends, but he was such a bighead and so sarcastic to the people I met, they didn't get along with him. I kept making excuses for him, but it wasn't easy to convince them.'

When we left the pub, she asked if I had time to come over home with her. I said I would but couldn't stay long. She had a beautiful home. Everything was spick and span. I stayed long enough to have a cup of tea, then promised I'd call again.

She said, 'Will you try and come next Saturday? Bill's going to Slough to see his mother and sister for the weekend, and I'll be by myself. There's such a lot I want to tell you, and I may never get another chance.'

On the following Saturday afternoon I kept my promise and went to see Mary. As we sat drinking our tea, she told me that she had saved enough money to buy a small lock-up shop.

'I'm selling ladies' and children's dresses and underwear, and other kinds of odds and ends. But I'll be doing better still when the coupons come off the clothes. You'll have to come and have a look at it some time, and see if there's anything you'd like. And bring my nieces.'

'I don't think I'd have enough coupons, Mary, to buy what they'd like,' I replied.

'Don't bother about coupons, I can soon fix that,' she said. 'Anyhow, where are you living now?'

'Still in Handsworth, Mary, you'll have to come and visit me some time. I'm sure the girls would love to meet you.'

'I'll try, but Kate, don't you think you should go and see Mum? I think she'd like to see you after all these years. How long is it since you saw each other?' she asked.

'It's been over ten years now. But I don't want to see her. I can't ever forgive her the way she treated me and my children all those years ago,' I replied bitterly.

'Don't be too hard on her, Kate. You'll find she's changed a lot lately, wouldn't you like to come with me some time and talk to her?'

'No, Mary, I won't. If you can forgive her, I can't. Ever since I was a child, as far back as I can remember, she was cruel and unkind. Maybe, Mary, she never led you the life she led me.'

'Don't be too sure about that, Kate. It wasn't all honey for me. I'd like to tell you about my life as far back as I can remember, when I was only a small child, and when you've heard it, Kate, you may understand why our parents were like they were.'

During that visit, and several visits I made to her over the next few weeks, Mary told me a lot about the family in the days before I was born: about a brief period of prosperity, when Dad had a good job and he was able to rent a nice house, and how they lost all that and had to return to the slums; and about the little brothers and sisters who had died, especially her beloved brother Sammy, who died of consumption. Through what she said I did come to have a better understanding of Mum and Dad, and why my family was as it was.

I still couldn't bring myself to go and see Mum, but when Mary told me how hard up she was I arranged to give Mary five shillings a week for her, on condition she didn't know where it came from.

Then, one afternoon while I was home, busy laying the table for my daughters' teas, I heard the front doorbell. When I opened the door, who should be standing on the step but my mother. I couldn't believe my eyes. She hadn't altered a bit.

'Well!' she exclaimed. 'Ain't yer gonna call me in then?'

'Yes, come in,' I replied.

As soon as she sat down I said, 'How did you find out where I lived?'

'Mary told me. An' thank yer fer the five bobs yer sent me,' she replied sharply.

'Would you like a cup of tea, Mum? I'm just getting it ready for the girls when they come in.'

'ow are me gran'children?' she asked.

'They're fine.'

'But why ain't yer bin ter see me? Yer can go an' see yer sister, but I suppose yer too stuck up now ter come ter see me.'

I didn't answer. I thought it was best not to reopen old sores.

'Will you stay and have a bit of tea?' I asked.

'No, not now. It's openin' time. But don't yow forget ter send me gran'children down ter see me, even if yow don't wanta come,' she added, slamming the door behind her.

When I told Mary about this visit she was glad some contact had been made. She also said she would talk to our mother and make

493

arrangements for us to meet at her house. When the three of us met, later that week, I asked my mother if she would like to come and stay with me for a few days. She seemed all for it, and Mary too was pleased.

After that first visit Mum came to stay several times, but she always went back to her own house from Friday to Monday. I tried my best to make her feel wanted, but always towards the weekend I could see she was restless to be gone again. I realised she was eager to be back where she could be drinking with her neighbours. At the back of my mind I knew I'd made a mistake in asking her to stay. She was very bombastic towards me and my teenage daughters, and they didn't like her ordering them about. It was very hard to keep peace in the home while she was there. And she was a great worry during air raids. She would never go down the shelter when the sirens sounded, she just went upstairs with her bottles of beer and stayed in bed. ''itler ain't got me name on one fer me,' she'd say.

During the nights of April 1941 we had our worst bombing raids. The shelters were full to overflowing. But although many poor souls crouched in the corners afraid, many tried to keep up their morale by singing, to help drown the constant noise from the fighter planes above, the heavy gunfire and the falling bombs. We could hear the fire engines too, as their bells clanged, racing backwards and forwards along the streets, from dusk to dawn. When the bombing was not so heavy many of us voluntary workers would help the wardens to put out incendiaries, using buckets of sand, and dustbin lids.

There was one old dear who like my mother, didn't believe in going down the shelter. She always said she felt safer in her Anderson Shelter, which was only a piece of corrugated iron in the shape of a small igloo, covering a hole in the ground at the end of her garden. After the raids someone would always go and see if she was still safe. I remember very vividly one early dawn when I peeped down inside, to see her cat and little dog asleep beside her on the mattress. As I was going to give the message that she was safe, one of the wardens came running up. He told me that Camden Drive had been bombed, and that Mum and Mary had both been killed.

I tried to make my way to Camden Drive, past slimy, stinking mud, animal bodies and small fires from burning rubber, metal and rags, past buildings blown off their foundations, and men and women trying to salvage some of their treasured belongings. When at last I reached the top of the hill, neighbours from the district confirmed the bad news. But I still couldn't believe it, until I got half-way down the hill, and saw my brothers, Jack, Charlie and Frank, and my sister Liza, standing against the school wall weeping with many of Mother's neighbours. And there, lying on the floor with sacks covering them, were several bodies waiting for the ambulance to take them away. As I tried to look which ones were my mother and sister, the wardens quickly pushed me away and told me not any of them bodies were fit to be seen.

'Just remember how you last saw them alive, Kate,' my brother Jack said.

I was told that about twenty bodies had been dug up from cellars. One neighbour, who had a few cuts and bruises, said the bombing had taken them by surprise, before the sirens sounded. It was too late to go down the shelters, so people took refuge down their cellars. My brothers said there was nothing I could do now to help, but as soon as things were straightened out, they would get in touch with me.

The day of the funeral hundreds of people gathered from all areas beside the many coffins in Warstone Lane cemetery, where gravediggers were working day and night.

After the funeral I said goodbye to my brothers and my sister Liza, and walked home praying that my son John was still safe on the high seas. And that this was the last air raid we would witness. But there was a lot more to come, before that (never should have been) bloody war ended.

Fires, a Policeman and a
Wartime Christmas

———————⟨∘⬦∘⟩———————

E ach night, when the all clear sounded and we came up from the shelters, none of us knew what changes we would find to our homes. Many times I wondered, too, if my small workshop would be intact after the raids.

For most of the war my enamelling business was run by me and my daughters and ten young women. At one time my workers had to clock in before starting work. But when the war started in earnest I said they could forget it, I didn't mind how late they arrived for work, I quite understood their worries and sleepless nights. Some of the workers brought sandwiches to eat out at dinner times. But during the cold weather some of us would pool our rations. One would supply a few carrots, another a couple of onions, someone else some carrots or split peas, and whenever I could I brought a piece of meat. While the girls were working, and listening to 'Music While You Work' on the wireless, I'd prepare our dinner, put everything in the pot on the gas ring and let it stew away until it was time for us all to have a small basin full, with a piece of dry bread to mop it up.

That terrible morning after Camden Drive was bombed, I arrived at my workshop to see several firemen still putting out fires at the buildings across the street. I was scared to think what I would find as I climbed up those two steep flights of stairs, but when I entered the room, everything seemed to be in order. The girls were all busy doing their work, and listening to Tommy Handley on the wireless. Later that morning I prepared the meat and vegetables as usual, put them in the pot, and left them to simmer. Later, happening to go to the other end of the shop, I looked up and saw a gaping hole in the roof. At first I thought it must have been made by a piece of shrapnel. But then I looked around and saw another hole in a bench.

496

When I peered down I saw an incendiary bomb resting on a ledge beneath the bench. I screamed out, 'Leave everything, girls! And hurry down into the street!' We were all down those stairs like a flash. But before I could stop her, one of the girls suddenly rushed back up the stairs again. She cried out, 'I'm goin' back fer me tin "at an" gas mask.' A few seconds later she was back with them in her hand. But she was lucky, and so were we all, that the bomb turned out to be a dud. Often, later, we teased Lily about her attachment to her tin hat and her gas mask. But she never even smiled.

When the firemen said it was safe to go back upstairs, we returned to the workshop – to find it full of smoke. The dinner I'd left on the gas was burnt to a cinder, and so was the pot. But the kind woman at the tea shop nearby produced a makeshift dinner for us.

When we had an occasional rest from the bombing, usually all we wanted to do was catch up on our sleep. But one night during a lull, for a special treat, I took my daughters and two of their friends to see a show in town. It was late when the show was over, and we'd missed the last tram home, so we had to walk.

It was a lovely moonlit night, but the roads were icy. By the time we got as far as Hockley Brook we all wanted to pee. Looking around we couldn't see anywhere we could go. We were afraid to stoop down in the gutter, in case someone came along and saw us. But when we'd walked a little further, we noticed a low wall jutting out on the pavement. Dropping our knickers down over our ankles, we sat down on it. As we were giggling and peeing, from out of nowhere a policeman came towards us. We were all scared to move now, we could only sit there with our bare bums freezing and the steady stream trickling down the pavement for anyone to see. He said, 'You young ladies should be indoors at this time in the morning.' When I tried to explain we'd missed the last tram, he replied, 'Come along, then, I'll see you home.'

'Thank you, officer,' I answered quickly. 'I'm their mother, and we've only a few yards to go.'

I noticed he was smiling as he replied, 'Very well, mother, you'd better hurry along before you all freeze sitting there.'

As soon as we saw him stroll away, we quickly pulled up our wet knickers, but as we slid down from the wall we saw he was waiting and looking at us from the corner of the street. You couldn't see us for dust, as we fled up the Soho Hill. As soon as we got indoors we kicked off our wet knickers and made a mad dash towards the fire to thaw out our bums.

We laughed, later. But we suspected that policeman was probably laughing too!

One cold November day my brother Jack came to see me, and said if I'd lend him my old Austin Seven he'd give me some petrol coupons. When I asked him what he wanted the car for, he said he wanted to go to Henley-in-Arden market, where there were some live chickens for sale. I said he could take the car providing that I could come along too.

The old jalopy spluttered and rattled all the way, but eventually it got us there. Jack bought four hens and a cockerel, and I bought a turkey to fatten up for our Christmas dinner. I didn't know where I was going to keep the turkey. But when my brother suggested he'd take it home with him and bring it back on Christmas Eve, ready for the oven, I didn't trust him. I hadn't forgotten the pig he'd stolen when we went hop-picking when we were young, and I didn't think Jack had changed much meantime. So I refused.

I decided that the only place I could keep the turkey was in the coal-house outside. I moved what little coal I had, and set the turkey on some straw. My daughters named her Gertie, and grew very fond of her.

One bitterly cold night Jack borrowed the old car again and brought me back a sack of coke, which I mixed with the coal I had to make a roaring fire in the scullery grate. I almost forgot about Gertie until I went to feed her, when I suddenly noticed that the brick wall between the back of the fireplace and the coal-house was red-hot. Quickly I dragged poor Gertie into the kitchen, where she had to sleep that night, for otherwise she might have been cooked alive.

We were unable to risk lighting a fire in the scullery after that. A few nights later it was again freezing hard. So I put extra coal and coke on the living room fire and, as my daughters sat around warming themselves, I held a piece of newspaper up to the fire to help it along. Suddenly it was sucked alight by the draught and blown up the chimney. In no time at all, the chimney was on fire. Soot covered us like black snowflakes. We panicked and rushed outside. But the firemen arrived even before we had time to call the fire brigade; they had seen the flames and sparks shooting out of the chimney pot. The fire was so fierce, they had to go into the back bedroom and knock a hole in the breast of the chimney before they could put it out.

What a mess, and what a crowd of people we had outside looking in. And then, no sooner had the firemen done their job and left, when in walked a policeman. I recognised him at once. He was the same tall, handsome policeman who had seen us sitting on the wall, with our bums freezing. I felt so embarrassed. My only hope was that although I knew who *he* was, he might have forgotten who we were.

As he took out his note pad and pencil, he asked, 'When did you last have your chimney swept?'

'I never used this fireplace till tonight,' I replied.

While he was writing down all my answers to his questions, I saw him look up and smile at my daughters.

'And where's your husband?' he asked.

'I'm a widow,' I replied.

Suddenly he asked, 'Do I remember seeing you from somewhere?'

'No, I don't think so,' I answered quickly.

But he looked across at my daughters again, and he smiled more broadly as he said, 'Ah, I remember now. You were all sitting on the wall at the bottom of Soho Hill, late one night.'

I didn't answer yes or no, but tried to change the subject. 'Would you like a cup of tea, officer?' I asked.

'No, thank you,' he replied, 'but if you have a drop of something stronger I'd be very grateful.'

I hurried to the cupboard and brought out the remains of a bottle of Johnnie Walker that I kept for the wardens. I noticed that the girls had disappeared into the kitchen.

The policeman took off his helmet and sat down on the couch. He began to get very chatty, and asked how long I had lived there, how old my daughters were, and how long I had been a widow.

After he'd jotted it all down, he told me he had a wife and two young boys who were staying in Wales with his parents, until after the war.

'But you don't sound like a Welshman,' I said at once.

He didn't reply. He just stood up, and as he was putting his helmet back on my daughters came into the living room.

'Be good girls,' I heard him say to them, 'and don't let me see you out late at night again, doing what you shouldn't.'

They almost knocked one other over as they dashed back into the kitchen. And there they stayed until he had gone. I felt more embarrassed than ever now, and I was eager for him to go, before he asked any more questions. I was relieved when I saw him tear up his notes as he went down the path thinking all the time we'd been talking about how he knew what we had been doing that night as we sat on that wall, with our bare bums freezing as we giggled and piddled.

It was a few days before Christmas and snowflakes were falling fast when my brother came to see me again. As soon as he got indoors and took his wet overcoat off I said, 'Jack, I'm worried about Gertie.'

'Why, what's the matter with 'er?' he asked.

'I don't know, she hasn't eaten her food these last few days, and she sits in her corner all broody and looking so pitiful, as though she knows what's going to happen to her, and the children are upset too about having her killed.'

'Well, she's old, Kate, an' if I don't do it soon she'll die probably on yer later, then she'll be no good to eat, an' she'll 'ave ter be buried somewhere.'

'But you didn't tell me she was old!' I snapped.

'I didn't know till the other day. That must have been why she was so cheap,' he replied.

'Oh, well, you'd better start to do it now, before the children come home,' I said.

'I can't do it now, Kate,' he replied.

'Well, what have you come for?' I asked angrily.

'I was goin' ter ask yer ter lend me the car again.'

'Sorry, Jack,' I said, 'I've taken it to be overhauled and it won't be ready till after Christmas. If then.'

'Pity,' he replied sullenly. 'I could 'ave done yer a good turn.'

'What! Like the turkey you said was a good buy?' I said angrily.

'Sorry about that, Kate. Anyway, I'll come Christmas Eve morning and fix 'er fer yer,' he said, as he walked out of the house.

The next few days Kathleen, Jean and Mary (who was home for

Christmas) tried their utmost to make Gertie eat. They even talked to her like you would to a child. But she just sat in her corner of the coal-house, looking broody and all forlorn, as though she knew what was going to happen to her.

It was still snowing when my brother came on Christmas Eve. While he sat in front of the fire smoking his pipe, the girls came in. As soon as they saw their uncle, Jean ran up to him and asked, 'Have you really come to kill Gertie, Uncle Jack?'

'Yes, luv,' he said. 'She's old and she'll die if I don't do it now. Anyway,' he added, 'it'll be a nice change fer you all ter sit down ter turkey instead of a couple of sausages.'

At once there was a crying match. But my brother explained to them why it had to be done, and I thought they understood. Still, I didn't want them to be anywhere near the house to witness the killing, so I gave them some money and sent them off to the pictures. While I worked in the kitchen, busily washing up and preparing the vegetables for the next day, Jack went into the coal-house and did what had to be done. Then I plucked the bird and began to clean it. When I put my hand inside it I pulled out one large egg in its shell, another almost ready, three yolks, and dozens of small eggs the size of peas. I put them into a basin to be made into custard, for pouring over the Christmas pudding. When I'd finished cleaning the turkey, I hid it in the larder where the girls wouldn't see it, until the next day when it would be cooked.

I was determined to make this a happy Christmas, for in those days no one knew whether we would ever see another one. On Christmas morning, while the girls were still asleep, I slipped up to the bakehouse in Soho Road with the turkey and paid a shilling for it to be cooked. When I got back I set the table with all my best china and glasses, and added Christmas crackers and four paper hats I'd bought at a garden fête. Also a few goodies I'd collected over the past weeks, and a bottle of port wine my brother Jack had given me for the loan of my car. I took up the girls' breakfast and their small presents, and I said they should stay upstairs until I called them down. When I had fetched the turkey from the bakehouse, I drained off the fat into a basin, put the bird on a dish, and put it in the oven to warm. Then, as soon as all the vegetables were ready, I called the girls.

I was pleased as they sat at the table drinking their port, laughing and smiling. But as soon as I put Gertie on the table and began to carve, there was another crying match. 'We don't want any!' they cried out, and sprang up from the table.

I did my utmost to persuade them to eat, but it was a waste of time even to try. I did manage to get them back to the table again to eat their Christmas pudding, which I could see they relished. But if they'd known the custard had been made with Gertie's eggs, they wouldn't have eaten that either.

After they went out to see their friends, I began to weep. What a waste of time and energy and money, I said to myself. I was too upset now to eat any of Gertie, either. So I wrapped it up and gave it to one of my neighbours who I knew had a lot of mouths to feed. When they asked why, and I tried to explain, the old grandad said, 'The ungrateful little buggers, kids are terday. They'll be glad to eat "orse-flesh before they're much older." (Little did we know, we already had.)

When I got back home I sat down again and wept, and after clearing the things away I thought to myself if only my brother Jack or Charlie had come that Christmas morning they might have persuaded the girls to eat some of it. But I felt alone now, and it was Christmas Day. Suddenly I couldn't think of anything else, only to put the crackers and the paper hats on the fire and take the rest of the port and a glass of whiskey up to bed. It was night-time when I awoke, with a fearful headache. I hurried downstairs and just as I was making myself a cup of tea, my daughters came in. When they said they were hungry, I snapped, 'You can be bloody hungry! You can have some bread an' drippin', but you can get it yerselves!'

Little did they know it was Gertie's dripping they were spreading on their bread, and I wasn't going to tell them in case there'd be another crying match.

Later in the spring Jack brought a dozen little chicks for the girls. They were so delighted they kept them in a basket while it was cold. But one morning when we came downstairs they all lay dead on the hearth. That was another crying match. After that I said, 'No more livestock in this house,' and if they wanted a chicken or a turkey it would have to be a dead one from the butcher's.

But I understood really how my daughters must have felt that Christmas Day. I'd have felt the same when I was a girl – though I wouldn't have dared refuse anything I was offered.

Sooty and Sandy

I managed to stick to the 'no livestock' rule for a while, but it wasn't easy. My daughter Jean was very possessive where animals were concerned, and often she'd bring home some stray cat or dog. Then I'd have to sort out who owned it.

One night my daughters were in bed and I was sitting reading the newspaper, when all at once I heard a sound like a baby crying. It sounded as if it was coming from one of the bedrooms, and as I opened Jean's bedroom door, I knew it was coming from there.

When I turned the bedclothes back, I saw a black kitten lying in Jean's arms, mewing for all it was worth. I felt angry to think she had disobeyed me. Just as I picked it up and put it on the floor, Jean woke up.

'What have I told you!' I cried out at once. 'No more livestock!'

'He followed me, Mum,' she protested as she sat up in bed.

'I've heard that before! Like the other cats and dogs you tell me follow you!'

'But it's the truth, Mum, I tried to shoo him away but he wouldn't go. I thought if I gave him a drop of milk he'd go away.'

I knew then we'd never be rid of it.

'Now, I want the truth,' I said. 'How long have you had it in bed with you?'

'Only a few nights, Mum. Please let me keep him,' she pleaded, as the kitten jumped up on the bed. As soon as I saw her tears flow, I began to weaken.

'I'll think about it. But you can't have it sleeping with you in bed, it's unhealthy. It can sleep in the kitchen tonight, then I'll decide what you can do with it in the morning. Now, lie down and go to sleep.'

I picked up the black kitten and took him downstairs, where I gave him a drink of milk. Then I put him outside to do his business. At the back of my mind I hoped he'd go back to where he came from, but after a while he began to meow louder than ever outside the kitchen door, so I let him in. I found a discarded old woollen jersey, and as soon as I picked him up and laid him down on it he snuggled up and went to sleep.

Next morning I told my daughter she had to try to find out who owned the kitten, but if no one came forward she could keep him. But I warned her it was her responsibility to teach him to be clean. The next day I bought him a basket to sleep in. And Jean gave him the name of Sooty.

As Sooty grew older, he began to stay out late. By then I was as silly as Jean, and I wouldn't go to bed until he was indoors. One night he didn't come home until one o'clock. I scolded him for keeping me up late. But he just purred and rubbed against me.

The following night he stayed out again. I waited for a while and called him, but no Sooty came. 'Very well,' I said aloud, 'you can stop out,' and I locked the door.

It was early in the morning when I heard him meowing outside the back door. I couldn't sleep now, knowing he'd be almost frozen out there, so I went down and let him in. But I was still angry with him for disturbing my sleep.

This went on for a couple of nights more. Then one night there was a caterwauling session of toms and she-cats under our windows, and the neighbours'.

I couldn't sleep, and nor could the neighbours. I heard windows being pushed open and all kinds of oddments being thrown at the cats, and I heard somebody say, 'Bleedin' cats, I'll drown the bleedin' lot on yer if yer don't get away from under my winda.'

After a while it went quieter, but I still couldn't sleep until I knew Sooty was back. As soon as I heard his cry I went down and opened the door. There he sat, looking so pitiful, and soaking wet.

'It's yer own fault,' I said as I dried him before I went back to bed.

I knew it was Sooty's nature to go out courting, but I had to do something about him staying out late. So I decided to leave my kitchen window a little way open for him to come and go as he pleased, so that I could get some sleep. This worked until one late night I heard a great din coming from the kitchen, and I went down to find Sooty and his girl-friend, a ginger she-cat from down the road, making love. I got the broom and swiped at them, and they both fled through the window.

'That's the last time I leave my window open, or let you in again when you stop out,' I said to myself. There was only one answer to the night prowling, I would have to have him castrated.

The following day I put him in his basket, and while my daughters were out I took him to the PDSA (the People's Dispensary for Sick Animals) in the Soho Hill. As I sat waiting my turn with other people with their pets, I began to weep. How could I do this to Sooty? I was just about to take him home again when the vet called me in.

When a little while later, the vet laid the unconscious Sooty in my arms, he said to keep him warm and watch for him to wake up, and then to give him a drink. I thanked him and when I asked him the fee, he said, 'It's voluntary, but if you'd like to put whatever you can spare in the box.' I dropped a half-crown in the 'Sick Animals' box and put Sooty gently in his basket and carried him home. When I laid him down on the rug in front of the fire I began to weep again. He lay there so still, I thought he was going to die. I thought, what was I going to say to my daughters. I couldn't tell them the truth, things like this were never discussed in front of children in those days. I sat and waited, hoping he would come round before the girls saw him. And a few minutes later, I was pleased to see him come to. Soon he was on his feet and walking, and he seemed to be his usual self as he looked up at me and drank his milk. But as the weeks went by, and I noticed he wasn't so frisky as he used to be, I began to be sorry again that I'd taken his little pleasures from him.

Then one day Jean walked in with a little all-black kitten in her arms. I was furious, and shouted, 'You're not bringing any more cats in here!'

'I'm not, Mum,' she protested. 'I've only brought him to show you.'

'Well! You can take it right back again to where you've had it from.'

'Mrs Wilks says her cat's got four, and three of them are just like our Sooty.'

'I don't care if they're like King Kong!' I replied angrily. 'Take it back at once. And if you're not satisfied with Sooty, I'll give him away.'

'I still love Sooty, Mum. But he isn't playful any more.'

'Well, he's growing older now, you can't expect him to play like he did when he was a kitten. Anyway, love, I can't put up with any more cats. I must have my rest. What with the air raids and getting up half the night, and one thing or another, I don't get much sleep. You can have anything else, but definitely no cats.'

Tears began to fall, but she didn't miss her chance. 'Can I have a dog, then, Mum?'

'I'll have to think about it. Now, do as yer told and take the kitten back.'

A few weeks after, I heard that Mrs Wilks had given the kittens away, but kept her ginger she. Later, after her house was bombed, she went to live with her sister in another district, but she didn't take her cat with her, she left it to roam the streets. Day and night that cat would whine outside our back door. I couldn't see her hungry, so I used to feed her out in the yard. Then one night it poured in torrents, and Jean began to plead for me to take her in. When I dried her with a piece of cloth, she nestled up to me. After that I couldn't let her go out in the rain again. So I gave her a home, and we called her Sandy.

Sandy too had to go to the vet's, for I made sure I wouldn't have any more kittens in the house. And from then on Sooty and Sandy were content to sleep side by side, without any sign of lovemaking. They grew old together, and when they died I buried them beneath my kitchen window. Eventually Jean got her dog, but that was years later.

The Children Grow Up

My three teenage daughters were now growing up fast in mind and body. I knew I couldn't keep them under my wings all the time, but whenever possible I always took them out and about with me. I used to worry when they went out by themselves. There were lots of American troops in the district, and many young girls (and married women too) found them hard to resist, with their gifts of chocolates, cigarettes, silk stockings, and other scarce luxuries. Many a young girl was left holding his baby. I remember one of my neighbour's daughters had fallen this way. And I often think of how she said one day about her daughters, 'They make your arms ache when they're young, but they make your heart ache when they're older.'

One day I received a letter from my son, John, who was still serving in the Navy, to tell me that while he was on leave in Scotland he'd met a young Scots girl whom he wished to marry. I was very upset. I'd had other plans for John. I'd been hoping that as soon as the war ended he'd take over my business, so that I could care for the girls and the home. I wrote at once asking him to wait until the war was over, as they were both too young to think about marriage. But John wrote back to say that the banns had already been read. I went up to Scotland with my daughters, still intending to talk him out of marrying if I could, but when I got there I found I couldn't say anything disapproving. They looked so happy, and so much in love. After the wedding John had to go back to his ship. His wife stayed with her parents until he came   f the Navy when the war ended.

During 1944 my daughter Kathleen was married. I planned to give her a wonderful wedding, a better day than I had had. My one trouble was the food rationing. But again my brother Jack came to the rescue.

'If yer can lend me the old car again, I'll see what I can do,' he said.

So I lent him the old jalopy. He said he'd be back in an hour. I waited all that morning, getting more and more worried. All kinds of thoughts entered my head. Then about two o'clock in the afternoon he came in with another chap, both drunk, and laden with parcels of food.

Although I was pleased to see him, I was also angry. 'Where've you bin till now, our Jack?' I cried out. 'I've been worried stiff.'

As they dropped the parcels on the table, he managed to say 'It's all right, sis, but I got some bad news ter tell yer.'

'Well, sit down and tell me, before you fall down!' I replied angrily.

'When I drove back 'ere, the bottom of the old jalopy fell out and the grub fell inter the road. This chap 'ere,' he said, waving his hand towards him, ''elped me ter pick it up and bring it 'ere.'

'Where's the car now?' I asked.

'We dragged it on some waste ground an' 'ad ter leave it.'

'Oh, well,' I replied, 'I knew it would happen one day. As long as you're all right, that's all that matters.' I thanked the young chap for his help and asked him if he'd like a cup of tea, but he said he was in a hurry to get back to work. When he called again, a few days later I invited him to the wedding, which was to be in two months' time.

My next worry was we couldn't hire a hall for the wedding reception: every possible room seemed to be booked for ARP (Air Raid Precautions) meetings. But a friend of mine who was a builder talked me into having the wall between the front room and the dining room knocked down and made into one large room. I later called it the lounge.

And in the end everyone seemed to have a jolly time at the wedding. Piano-playing and singing went on far into the night, well after my daughter and her husband had left to start their honeymoon.

Later Kathleen and her husband, Jim, went to live in Scotland. After a while she wrote to say she wasn't very happy where she was living. I wrote back to say I was thinking of leaving the old house and buying another, and if she was still not settled they could come and take over the house in Waverhill Road. And when I bought my house in Landgate Road, and Jean and Mary and I moved there, Kathleen and Jim moved into Waverhill Road. A little later Kathleen came to work with me again. Then when Jim lost his job he came to work along with us. He didn't know the trade, but he was happy to do all kinds of jobs, and worked very hard.

It was of course a great pleasure to me that Kathleen and Jim had settled down so near. But many were the times I'd lie awake at nights thinking about my son John, on the high seas and perhaps in battle, and pray to the Good Lord above to keep him safe. There were now only my two younger daughters, Jean and Mary, at home with me. I dreaded the thought that some day soon they too would fall in love and leave me to be married. I knew I'd miss their love, excitement and laughter when I was left in this house alone.

I had had many offers of marriage over the years, but I hadn't been interested. All I had wanted was the love and affection and comfort of my children around me. But how foolish I was to think I could keep them by my side for ever.

My youngest daughter, Mary, was restless, always trying one job after another. One of her jobs was serving in a fruit and vegetable shop owned by a Mr and Mrs Hitchman in Hockley Street. Mrs Hitchman was kind to anyone really in need, but she was a very domineering woman, and very large, and I often felt sorry for her husband, Fred. He was so different, a weedy, hen-pecked little man.

Mrs Hitchman was sweet on my brother Jack, who was very plausible. And many times Jack would take her in her car to markets. She'd get all dolled up when she was going to see him. I used to hear customers whisper, 'Silly old cow! 'er's old enough ter be 'is mother.'

One day I told my brother how people were talking. But he said it was none of my business, or other people's. 'Let 'em talk,' he said. 'That's the only time I can get any black market off'er, when I give 'er what she wants.'

I was furious at his attitude, and we quarrelled. I didn't see him again for a few weeks after that, but I knew really that, as he said, it was none of my business. So when I did see him again I thought it best not to mention it.

Then one day Jack's wife heard about their affair, and threatened to leave him. He never went near the shop again, nor was he ever seen taking Mrs Hitchman about. Whether he met her secretly I couldn't say. But he always had plenty of black market food.

During that period my daughter Mary came home one afternoon and said she'd seen a notice in Mrs Hitchman's shop window for a young girl to serve behind the counter. I knew if I refused to let her go she would go anyway, for she was very self-willed. So, to save any arguments, I let her have her fad out. I went to see Mrs Hitchman and we agreed on the wage, and that Mary would have her meals free. As food was still on rations, it was a help for me to save the coupons. But she had only been there about three weeks, when she came home one day crying.

When I asked her what was wrong, she said she wasn't having enough to eat, and that she'd been helping herself to bananas and couldn't find anywhere to hide the skins. When I asked why she hadn't told me before, she said, 'I was too scared, Mum.'

'Well, what *did* you do with the skins?' I asked.

'There's a big vase on the top shelf and when I thought she wasn't looking I threw them inside the vase. But it's getting full, and I was scared, and when she asked me to go up the ladder and reach down the vase, I panicked.'

'What happened then?' I asked, as the tears flowed.

'I ran up the stairs. As soon as I heard her talking to a customer I crept quietly down, but half-way down I met Mr Hitchman coming up and . . . er . . .'

'Go on, and what?'

'He pinned me against the wall. I knew what he was after. So I punched his face and pushed him down the stairs, and ran away.'

'But why didn't you tell me about this before? And why didn't you tell her you had the bananas because you were hungry?'

'I was afraid, Mum, because she'd know I'd stole them.'

'Oh. You knew you were stealing, then?' I snapped.

'Yes, Mum,' she whimpered.

'Very well, dry your eyes, and any time you get into any scrapes in future, come and tell me at once.'

'Yes, Mum,' she replied, as she dried her eyes.

Next day I called to give Fred Hitchman a piece of my mind. But he was nowhere to be found, and after that he always avoided me when he saw me. In the end I thought it would be better to leave things unsaid, to save any trouble which it would cause between him and his wife. After Mary left the fruit shop she went to train as a nurse at the TB Hospital in Selly Oak. She got along fine there, until she became tired of working all hours and left to try her hand at a hairdressing salon. Soon after Mary left the hospital the matron came to see me. She spoke very highly of Mary, and asked if I could persuade her to come back again. I said I'd do my best. But no matter how I tried for her to see reason, it was hopeless.

When she got dissatisfied with hairdressing, she tried being a conductress on the buses. Later she joined the forces, and she met and married her husband in Singapore. After the war, she and her husband made their home in Scotland. Later I had a letter from her to say they were going to live in America. Now Mary has four sons: two I have never seen. And I have only seen my daughter twice in twenty-seven years. For years I never heard from her, although I knew she recieved my letters. And I felt very hurt. But recently she has telephoned me a couple of times, which has been a great joy.

Over the years I have often asked myself if Mary still hasn't forgiven me for parting with her, when I left her at Dr Barnardo's.

My Second Marriage

My daughter Jean stayed at home longest, but I knew I would lose her too some day. And when she began courting I was often very lonely. I really felt I needed a companion and friend, someone to talk to of an evening. One night, as I was reading the *Evening Mail*, a knock came. When I answered I was surprised to see standing on the doorstep my brother Jack. I hadn't seen him for several months.

'Hello, stranger!' I said, sarcastically.

'Anythin' troublin' yer, Kate?' he asked.

'No, I just feel a bit under the weather,' I replied.

'Yer know what's wrong with yer, Kate, yer want to get out more and find yerself a man friend. 'ow old are yer now, forty?'

'Forty-two. Maybe I will, one day,' I said.

'Yer know sis, yer a good-looking chick and yer dress smart and –'

'Oh, go on, flatterer,' I interrupted, smiling up at him, as he stood with his back towards the fire.

He said, 'Well, there's many a decent chap who'd be proud ter be seen walkin' out with yer. So take my advice an' don't leave it too late.'

'I won't,' I replied. 'Anyhow, what's brought you here? I haven't seen you for months.'

'I've bought a second-hand car and I thought you might like to accompany me and the missus on a ride out in the country, termorra afternoon.'

'Thanks, Jack,' I replied, eager for the treat. 'I'll be ready when you call.'

It was a beautiful run, and I enjoyed the company – until we called in a pub to have a drink. The smoke room was crowded, it being market day. And when my brother kept showing me off in front of everyone, I felt embarrassed. I was glad when we left. As soon as we got outside to the car I lost my temper and stormed at him.

512

'If I want a fellow I don't need *you* to find one for me. I'll find my own! Thank you very much.'

'She's right, yer know, Jack,' said Rose.

He turned on his wife. 'Nobody asked yow ter poke yer bloody nose in!' he snapped.

I didn't want to be involved in an argument, so when I saw them get into the car I hurried down the lane. All the same I was glad when I heard the car coming towards me, for I had no idea where we were. There were no road signs to tell me which way to go – they had all been taken away in case of invasion. I got into the car. But I never spoke a word, until he dropped me outside my house. I was still angry. 'Next time you try pairing me up, Jack, don't! I can do my own pairing up, thank you!' I snapped. Then I went in and slammed the door. The car had just driven away, when Mrs Morgan, my next-door neighbour, called with a message. 'Come in while I put the kettle on,' I called out to her.

She was a kindly person and she had been very helpful when I first came to live next door.

I liked her, and I was glad of her company when I was alone. But she had one fault, she was an awful gossip, and knew everybody's business. When I had given her a cup of tea, I asked her what the message was.

'Oh, yes,' she said. 'I almost forgot. A young man called about an hour ago, an Air Force sergeant, said his name was Joe, and he knew you years ago. I asked him to come into my place and wait for you, but he said he had somewhere else to call, and he'd be back in an hour. Do you know who he is? He was a handsome fellow,' she added.

'I'm not certain who he could be, Mrs Morgan, but thank you for telling me.'

'Would you like me to wait with you till he comes?'

'No, thank you, dear,' I replied. 'I think I'd better see him alone. But thank you all the same for coming to tell me.'

'Well, don't forget to give me a knock on the wall if you need me,' she said as she went out.

As I tidied myself up, I wondered who this handsome fellow could be. I was soon to find out. A few moments later the bell rang, and when I opened the door there he stood.

'Hello, Kate,' he said, as he put his hand out for me to shake. But

I didn't take it, I was too surprised he even knew my name.

'Sorry,' I said, 'I don't believe I know you. Anyhow, you'd better come inside.' (I was thinking of my nosy little neighbour, watching.)

He came inside and took off his Air Force cap, and I told him to sit down.

'Would you like a cup of tea? I've just made one. Then maybe you can enlighten me as to who you are,' I said.

He drank some of the tea, then he said, 'You sure you don't remember me?'

'I'm sorry, I don't,' I replied, still wondering.

'Well, we only met a couple of times. It was before you were married.'

Suddenly I remembered my first boy-friend, that I'd had such trouble with. He had been called Joe. Could this be him? But the stranger went on, 'You were about seventeen, and I asked your dad if I could take you to the Albion Picture Palace. And do you remember, you let me put my arm around you, but when I tried to kiss you, you slapped my face and ran out. I never saw you after that.'

Then I remembered. I began to smile, and he asked me what I was smiling about. I asked him, 'What became of the box of chocolates I threw at you when you tried to kiss me?'

'Oh, them? I gave them to the usherette.'

I knew then it had been a rotten thing to do, to throw his present at him.

We chatted for a bit, and I found that Joe had met my brother Jack, and that was how he knew where I was living. After a while he got up to leave. Suddenly I felt I didn't want him to go, in case I never saw him again, so I asked him if he'd like to see my garden. He agreed, saying he'd got a few more minutes to spare. I took him through the back of the house and around the small pool we shared with other neighbours.

'Any fish in?' he asked at once.

'There's a few tiddlers, but mostly tadpoles. The trouble is, part of the year we get frogs on the front lawn, but they don't really bother me. They fascinate me when I see them hop from one place to another.'

As we walked back down the path and entered the kitchen, he took my hand. 'Kate,' he said, 'I hope you don't mind my asking, but could I call and take you out one evening?'

'I'd like that very much, Joe,' I said.

'What about next weekend?'

I'd been hoping he'd say the next day. But I tried not to be too eager to see him again. 'Yes, Joe, that will suit me nicely.'

He took my hand to shake, but then he said as he gripped it, 'Would you mind, Kate, if I kissed you – just once, before I go?'

I didn't answer, but as I put my face close to his he kissed me and squeezed my hand. That was the first thrill I'd had in years, and I hoped then that it wouldn't be the last, and that this would be the beginning of a long friendship.

I wasn't the teenager he'd known any longer, I was a grown-up woman with a family. But I needed a man's love and companionship. As he walked down the front path and waved to me, I felt sorry to see him go. He closed the gate and waved again, and I saw Mrs Morgan coming down her path. I knew she wanted to find out who he was, but I didn't feel inclined to gossip. 'Not now, Mrs Morgan,' I called out sharply as I went inside and closed the door. I needed to be alone and sit down to think things over. I wanted to see him again. But I couldn't help wondering if he was married. I should have asked him straight out, but I'd been afraid the answer would be yes. Anyway, even if it was, I thought, we could still be friends.

As I sat there thinking, I said to myself, if he was a married man, what if my daughters should find out? Whichever way it was, I would have to come to that decision later. I climbed the stairs and got into bed that night with a feeling that my life now was going to change for the better.

For several weeks after that Joe and I kept company, going to the pictures or to the theatre to see a show. But each time he kissed me goodnight before leaving me I wondered if he had a wife. I was still afraid to ask him, but I couldn't go on like this without knowing. So one night when he brought me home, I asked him to come in for a while and have a cup of coffee. He sat down and I handed him his cup, then I picked up courage to ask him – dreading the answer.

'Joe, I, er – wanted to ask you – er – are you – married?'

'I'm glad now you've asked me, dear. I should have told you that first day we met, but I didn't think it mattered then. But now it does, darling, because I've fallen in love with you.'

Now I knew the truth, I began to weep, and as he handed me his handkerchief I managed to say, 'I'm in love with you, too, but we mustn't see each other again after tonight, Joe.'

'Listen, Kate love, wipe your eyes, and try to listen to what I have to say. My wife and I have been at loggerheads ever since I came back from India. We're divorced now. Your brother Jack knows all about it. I'm only waiting for the divorce to be made absolute, and then I want to marry you.'

'Are you still living with her?' I asked.

'No. I'm living with my dad and my sister. *Will* you marry me, Kate?'

'I can't give you my answer now, Joe. Let me have a few days to think it over.'

'Very well,' he replied. 'But I hope you'll say yes, because I do love you, truly I do.'

'Joe,' I answered, 'give me a few days to think it over, then I'll give you my answer, one way or another. You'll have to go now before Jean comes home – and I can hear my nosy neighbour coming up the path.'

'Goodnight, then, Kate darling. But don't forget, I'll be coming for my answer. And whatever you may decide, I'll try and understand.'

I kept my tears back as he took me in his arms and kissed me several times. But as soon as I heard the door close behind him, I broke down and sobbed. A few seconds later the doorbell rang. I knew at once who it was.

'I can't see you now, Mrs Morgan,' I called out through the door. 'You'll have to call another time.'

As I heard her footsteps go back down the path I felt relieved. She was the last person I wanted to confide in.

I don't know how I got through the next few days, as I went about my daily routine. I was missing his fondness for me, and his company, and the things he used to say to make me laugh. I knew I was in love. But how could I tell my daughters that I was in love with a married man? Yet I knew I had to tell them sooner or later.

My brother Jack called to see me, and he asked why I was looking so worried. As soon as I tried to explain, I began to weep.

'Yer old enough to make up yer own mind, Kate, and now's yer chance to make something o' yer life. When Jean's married yer'll be left all alone. So think it over carefully. They're not children any more.'

'But, Jack, I'm worried about what the girls will say when I tell them I'm in love with a married man.'

"e won't be married when 'is divorce papers come through. Now, listen to me,' he replied sternly, 'yer never 'ad a 'appy life with yer 'usband befower 'e died. So now's yer chance. 'e's a good bloke, sis, so make up yer mind before it's too late. An' if yer want me to talk to the girls and explain, yer've only ter say.'

'Thanks, Jack. I think it would be best coming from me,' I said.

'Well, remember, Kate, yer've put them first in everythin' fer years, and now yer've the chance to be 'appy with someone who really loves yer. Make up yer mind before it's too late.'

After he left I began to think over what he had said, and I decided that as soon as Jean came home from work I would try and explain to her what I intended to do.

But when she came home I was still on tenterhooks how to begin. After she'd had her tea, we both sat by the fire. But before I could begin, she said, 'Mum, do you mind if Sam calls for me tonight? He wants to take me to the pictures.'

'But, Jean, I wanted to talk to you about something that I've been trying to tell you for some time.'

I was taken aback when she answered at once. 'Is it about you and Joe? Because if it is, I know what you're going to tell me.'

'Very well,' I replied. 'If you know, I'd better tell you what my intentions are. Joe has asked me to marry him.'

'Are you going to marry him, Mum?'

'Yes, as soon as his divorce papers come through.'

'I already knew he was married,' she replied.

'How do you know?'

'I met Uncle Jack the other day, and he told me everything. But if you do marry him, Mum, does that mean that he will live here?'

'Of course. I've already made up my mind, Jean.'

'But why, Mum?' she asked.

'I've thought all this over carefully. When you and Sam are married I shall be left on my own, and I couldn't face that again.'

'But we'll come to visit you, Mum.'

'That's not the same. When you are older and have a family you will understand what I mean. Now there's no more to be said. So you better get yourself ready if you're going to meet Sam.'

As she went upstairs to the bathroom, I began to feel sorry I had spoken so sharply. But soon the doorbell rang. It was Joe. I was just letting him in when Jean came down the stairs. When he began to wish her good evening, she didn't answer, but pushed past him and walked out. I felt very angry with her.

That same night I told Joe I would marry him.

But no matter how we both talked to Jean and tried to make her understand, we had many quarrels. A few days later she came home to tell me she was going to live with her sister. And as she was packing her belongings, I said. 'Very well, Jean, if that's what you want. But remember, if you wish to change your mind your home is always here – and remember,' I added, 'whatever happens, I shall always love you.'

A few weeks later, in February 1947, Joe and I were married at the registry office in Edmond Street.

Life With Joe

———◇◇◇◇◇———

J oe and I had many happy years together. We had our disagreements (no one is perfect); but he was kind and considerate, and I loved him.

Some funny things happened as well. I remember one very bright moonlit night when we were first married and still living in Landgate Road. Something, perhaps the light, woke me, and I got out of bed to open the window wide to let in some air. As soon as I got back into bed I must have dozed off to sleep. But it wasn't long before I was woken again, by a kind of cooing sound. The light from the moon flooded the bedroom, so I didn't have to switch on the light. I was sitting up to see where the sound was coming from, when all at once I saw two large, bright eyes staring at me through the open window. Terrified, I slid down the bed beneath the bedclothes, and I pinched Joe's leg. 'Joe,' I managed to say, 'wake up! There's somebody staring through the window!'

Quickly he sprang out of bed, and as I held on to the tail of his shirt and followed him towards the window, we saw a large owl sitting on the window ledge, gazing at its own reflection in the glass. After Joe shooed him off and closed the window, we lay back in bed and laughed. My husband said that the owl, seeing its reflection in the glass, must have thought it'd found a mate.

But soon after that I got really scared. Ever since I'd come to the house, I'd been bothered by creaking noises in the bedroom at night. When I tried to explain to Joe he just laughed at me, saying I was imagining it.

'But, Joe,' I said to him one night, 'I can't sleep sometimes. It seems that there's someone in the room.'

'Yes,' he said, trying to put me off. 'It's us two.'

Then, one day while Joe was out, Mrs Morgan called to say the postman had left a parcel for me. I thanked her and, being glad of someone to be with me, I asked her in to have a chat and a cup of tea. As soon as we settled down together I began to tell her about the weird sounds I heard at night. But she just said, 'I'm surprised you've stayed here this long.'

'Why? What do you mean? I've only been here twelve months.'

'Well, didn't you know the house was haunted?'

'No, I didn't. But how do you mean, haunted?'

She asked me what bedroom we slept in, and when I told her the back bedroom, she said, 'Well, that's the room where a young woman murdered herself.'

'You mean she killed herself?'

'Yes, in that very room. And three families have lived there before you came.'

'And you told them what you've told me?'

'I didn't have to, they found out for themselves.'

Before she could tell me any more my husband came home, and when I told him what she had said, he forbade her to come near me or the house again.

Now I was more nervous than ever. I found it hard to sleep at night, and when I did drop off I awoke imagining all kinds of weird sounds. My husband said I was being foolish and superstitious, and we quarrelled. But I was now determined to look for another house. I walked for hours, until I saw one I liked that was for sale. I went at once to get the keys from the agent.

The house, which was in Uplands Road, was older than the one we were living in, but it was in good condition, and newly painted and decorated. It also had a long, well-kept back garden, where my husband could build a loft for his pigeons. Pigeon-racing was one of his favourite hobbies. After I had looked over the house, I asked the woman next door if she could tell me why the last people had left. She said they had been a very nice couple who had lived there for nearly thirty years, and had now gone to live in Canada with their son. I felt satisfied, so I went back to the agent, paid a deposit, and said I would call and make the necessary arrangements in a few days.

I hurried home, happy to think I would soon be leaving that house and those weird sounds behind me. But when I told my husband what I'd done, he flared up at me.

'The least you could have done was to tell me you intended to leave here. I like it here, and so would you if you hadn't listened to that bleedin' old busybody next door.'

One word brought up another. But I was adamant. We hardly spoke to each other for days, and when we did, we snapped at each other. I knew that I really should have discussed the situation with him, but I was desperate to move. The following week I made a start packing china and glass and other articles, which kept me busy during the day, but when night-time came, no matter how much my husband tried to convince me I was imagining things, I still couldn't sleep. Then something else happened. I had been awake for most of the night, as usual, but I dozed off just as dawn broke. Soon after, we both woke with a start, to find that the wardrobe door was wide open. Joe jumped out of bed and looked inside the wardrobe. He found that our savings had been stolen during the night. His wrist-watch had gone from the bedside table too. There didn't seem to be anything else missing. We pulled on some clothes and Joe went downstairs to phone the police, with me following very close behind him.

'I can't understand,' he said. 'I always make doubly sure that the doors and windows are locked before we go to bed.'

'I told you the house was haunted,' I cried out at once.

'Don't be foolish, Kate. Why would a ghost want a watch? And it couldn't spend money. It must have been somebody already in the house when I locked up.'

The police searched the house, but they found no clues to the intruder's identity. They left saying they would send someone to take fingerprints later.

As soon as it was daylight Joe went out into the back garden to feed his pigeons and, as I wasn't going to be left behind on my own, I went with him. But there another shock awaited us. Many of Joe's beloved birds lay dead on the lawn, and their eggs were strewn all over the path. Joe just went back into the house and wept. I too began to weep. Neither of us could understand why anybody would do such a cruel thing.

At least after this Joe too was pleased to get out of that house, and move to the villa in Uplands Road. But it took me a long time to get over my nervousness.

I'll never forget the first night we went to bed in our new home.

We were both very tired after arranging some of the furniture, and we fell asleep as soon as we went to bed. But during the night I woke up with a fright. 'Joe! Joe!' I screamed out. 'There's a tall man standing beside the bed!' He sprang out of bed and switched on the light. I covered my head over with the bedclothes, scared to look.

'Where? There's nobody here,' he exclaimed.

When I managed to point to the bedroom door he became angry.

'What have I told you, about imagining things! What you saw was my dressing gown hanging on the back of the door. Now, let's get some sleep.'

After he got back into bed, we both began to laugh at my foolish fancy, and cuddled up together and slept.

A while later, one cold night in November, I switched on the electric blanket before getting into bed. During the night I woke up feeling very hot. Joe was restless too, and he'd thrown off the bedclothes. I tried to cover him up, but as soon as I pulled up the bedclothes a waft of smoke hit me.

'Joe!' I screamed out as I shook him, 'wake up, quick, the bed's on fire.'

He was out like a shot, so was I. I ran downstairs for a bucket of water, and when I came back he had already thrown the smouldering feather bed through the window into the yard below. That night we had to sleep on a mattress. Next morning, when I went into the bathroom to put my false teeth in, they weren't in the mug. I couldn't understand, for I knew I'd put them in water before getting into bed. Joe wasn't very pleased when I woke him up to tell him my teeth were missing.

'Sure you ain't swallowed 'em?' he snapped.

'Of course I ain't! I put 'em in the mug of water on the bathroom shelf.'

'Well, I didn't see 'em in the mug when I threw the water over the bed. Anyway,' he added, 'if they were in the mug you'll find 'em among the feathers! So now I'm going back to bed.'

In my nightie, and with bare feet, I dashed downstairs and out into the yard. I searched among the wet feathers for a long time, but in the end I found the teeth.

I went back upstairs and scrubbed off the feathers which were clinging to them.

Joe was still angry with me. 'No more bleedin' electric blankets I want to see in this bed. Or you sleep on yer own.'

I began to sneeze. I felt ready to weep.

'Now get yerself back in bed before you catch cold.'

When I got in beside him and sneezed again, he forgot his anger and took me into his arms. As soon as we got up we went to a furniture shop to buy another bed, but it was a week before they delivered it. Still, we were happy and contented sleeping in each other's arms on that hard mattress.

For most of our married life, Joe worked as a bookmaker's clerk. At first he used to take bets on street corners, but later he got a job taking bets in a Conservative club of which he was a member. Off-course cash betting was illegal then, but luckily for Joe he was never caught. Still, I was always on edge until he came home.

Working on commission, he did very well. On the days of big races, such as the Derby, or the Oaks, or the Grand National, he'd earn twice as much as if he'd been working in a factory (which he couldn't have stood, anyway – he never liked people giving him orders). Sometimes his commission at the end of the week would be over £100 (that was very good money in the forties and fifties). I didn't ask him for much, because I still had my small enamelling business. Be he never hesitated to buy me something he thought I wanted. He was always kind and generous. Unfortunately, though, he was a habitual gambler himself. I used to get very worried when he lost heavily on the horses or the dogs, but he always seemed to come out on top in the following weeks. When I tried to tell him that he should be more careful, his job wouldn't last for ever, he would reply, 'You won't go short. And as long as I've got me fags, and a few shillings in me pocket, and you, I'm happy.' But I didn't know what he had in his pocket. I knew he wouldn't tell me even if I asked.

One day he brought home a television set he'd bought so that he could watch the horses running on Derby day. By the time of the big race he was very excited. He'd already won over £30 on the first two races, and he'd put it all on a horse called Devon Loch to win the Derby. As soon as the horses started he got down on his knees and pulled the screen nearer to get a better view. Devon Loch was winning easily. 'Come on, you little beauty!' Joe kept yelling at the screen. When the horse was nearly at the post, its legs splayed out and it dropped dead. Joe went berserk. He picked up the television and slung it across the room.

I knew then it was time for me to vanish. I didn't come home till late that night, and by that time he'd cooled down. But he never stopped talking about that Derby horse. He always swore it had been doped.

Every Friday morning Joe would do his Littlewoods football pools coupon and post it on the way to his club, and on Saturday nights he'd light up his fags and watch the results on television. Once he won a fourth dividend, but he knew it wouldn't be much because there were such a lot of draws. The following Wednesday the letter came and when he opened it out fell a postal order for 2s.6d. He looked disappointed. As he went to sling it into the fire I took it from him and put it in the desk. A couple of weeks later he had got up early to light the fire and bring me up my usual cup of tea, when I heard him call up from the bottom of the stairs, 'Kate, what did you do with that postal order?'

'It's somewhere in the desk. Why?' I called down.

'Where's the key?' he asked.

'In my bag. I'll be down in a minute,' I replied.

As I opened the desk and gave it to him, I said, 'Surely you're not that hard up!'

'Of course I'm not. I thought of using it on the last coupon of the season.'

He didn't even study it, just filled in eight draws and went out and posted it.

As a matter of fact we both forgot all about it, and we didn't even watch the television that Saturday night. The following Wednesday we had a letter, and a cheque for £1,400. As soon as I saw it, I took hold of it.

'You're not having this to gamble with,' I cried out. 'If you do, I'm leaving you . . . And I mean it.'

He stared at me hard. But I was absolutely determined. I knew I'd given him something to think about.

'Very well, then, I'll put it in the bank,' he said.

But I still couldn't trust him. So I replied, 'It's not going into your bank. It's going into mine.'

It didn't stay there long. Soon after, Joe had a windfall on the horses, and won over £200. With that plus the pools money and the money we got for our house in Uplands Road, we were able to buy a new house in Rookery Row. And we had enough left over for a fishing holiday in Ireland.

Holidays in Ireland

〜◇〜

O ur holidays in Ireland were the happiest of all the happy times we spent together. Joe was delighted by the plentiful coarse fishing, and we both loved the kind, helpful people.

One afternoon as we'd settled down to fish beside the River Shannon, two ragged little boys about the age of eight, with their bare bums showing through their trousers and no boots or socks on their feet, came running along the bank towards us.

'Ye want some worms, mister?' one cried out, as they came near us.

'No, thank you, sonny, we've got plenty,' Joe replied.

'English? They're no good for our rivers. Ye want our Irish worms if ye want to catch big fish, mister.'

'Yes, mister,' the other little lad piped up, 'we can go and fetch ye some, mister, and ye'll catch bigger fish, mister.'

We felt sorry for them the way they were persisting, so Joe said we could do with a few more worms, and off they ran. The two little artful dodgers must have had the worms already hidden behind the trees nearby. They hadn't gone but a few seconds before they came back with a tobacco tin full of fat worms, which we knew would be no different from our English worms.

Joe took the rusty tin and thanked them, and when he gave them a few coppers they were delighted. But as soon as they ran off we were pestered with several more ragged little urchins, all trying to sell us their tins of worms for a penny each. I thought then, those crafty little fellows must have made quite a nest egg for themselves, if other fishermen bought their Irish worms. But we didn't encourage them to pester us. We packed up our rods and moved to the other side of the river.

We sat down on a low bank where we had a long stretch of river to ourselves, and fished quietly for two or maybe three hours.

Then, as my husband was turning around to put another worm on the end of his line, he saw another little ragamuffin.

'Here's another one of 'em!' he called out to me.

When I turned to look I felt sorry for the little mite. He looked a poor, neglected little chap. I would say he was about six years old. He was barefoot, and he had no shirt or jersey, only an old grey check waistcoat that was too big for him, and home-made trousers that looked as if they'd been cut down from a man's old ones. As he walked slowly towards us he kept hesitating, whether to come on or go back to wherever he'd come from.

Neither of us spoke, until eventually he made his mind up to come and stand beside me. After he had been watching for a few minutes he said, 'What are yer fishin' for, lady?'

'Well,' I replied, smiling at him, 'just a few fish.'

'Do yer mind if I sit down an' watch?'

'No,' I replied. 'As long as you keep quiet.'

He sat there watching the rods and lines in the water. After a while my husband came over and opened up the creel where we kept our sandwiches. As he took the lid off the tin he said, 'There's not much food left, Kate, but there's a piece of cake here if the little lad would like it.'

'Yes, please, mister,' he replied at once, as his big brown eyes opened wider, eagerly watching the cake being unwrapped. We took a few steps back up the bank in view of our rods, and when I handed him the piece of cake he thanked me and came and sat beside us again, as though he belonged to us. Whoever he belonged to, the little chap had nice manners.

As soon as he finished eating, and we had given him a drink of tea from our flask, we moved back and sat beside the rods again, and he sat down on the grass beside me. When I asked what his name was he replied cheerfully, 'Me name's Sean Murphy.'

'But you don't speak like the other little Irish lads.'

'No, me an' me mam come from England to stay with me granny.'

'What part of England?' I asked.

'Dudley, near the Black Country.'

'We're from England, too,' I said.

'We 'ave lots of men fish 'ere who come from England. But I've never seen a lady fisherman before.'

'Does your daddy fish?' I asked, smiling at him.

'No, me dad ain't with us, 'es back in Dudley lookin' after me three brothers and sister.'

'And how old are you?'

'I'm nearly seven,' he replied.

He was quite a little chatterbox now I'd got talking to him.

He told us his dad had been a prisoner of war in Germany and only had one leg, and that when he grew up he was going to be a soldier like his dad.

I said, 'You'll change your mind, son, when you grow up, for there's better things in life than being in the Army.'

''ave you bin a soldier?' he called out to my husband a few feet away.

'No, sonny Jim. I was a recruiting officer in the Air Force. Now, just sit still, I can see my line moving,' he cried out.

'If yer catch a big one can I 'ave it ter take 'ome ter me mam, mister?'

'Yes. Now, sit quiet while I try and land it.'

But whatever it was my husband was trying to wind in, it broke his line and got away. The three of us were disappointed, but he soon fixed the line again, and the little chap and I moved a few paces further away, so that we wouldn't disturb him, for I knew he liked to be quiet while he was fishing.

As I watched Joe light another fag, the little chap began to tell me more about himself and his mam and his granny.

'Me mam came 'ere to look after me granny,' he said. 'But now me granny's died an' we're goin' back 'ome after the funeral.'

'Oh, I'm sorry to hear about your granny.'

'I ain't, she used to beat me when me mam went out.'

'And why, Sean, would she beat you? Were you naughty?'

'Oh, no. She was very deaf an' sometimes when she 'ad 'er temper up she'd shout at me to get out of the way, an' if I wasn't quick enough she'd 'it me 'ard.'

'Did you tell yer mam?'

'No, I was too scared, an' she only 'it me after me mam 'ad gone out. One night I went inter the bedroom an' put lipstick and rouge on my face, like I'd seen me mam do it, an' as soon as me granny came up and saw me she gave me another beatin' and made me scrub it off an' sent me to bed without anythin' to eat.'

'But you should have told yer mam, Sean.'

'She made me promise not to, an' I did. Afterwards she put her arms around me an' cried, then she went downstairs an' brought me up a mug of cocoa an' a plate of cake, an sat on the side of me bed an' cried some more, an' said she was sorry, an' would never 'it me again. After that night she never did, a few mornin's later when me mam came 'ome, she found 'er in bed an' she was dead.'

I'd heard enough to put two and two together, so I changed the subject.

'Do you like this country, Sean?' I asked.

'Yes, I like the rivers an' the green fields an' all the animals, an' sometimes I go along with the farmers an' talk to their dogs an' the sheep an' the cows, an' when I grow up I shall come back an' live 'ere,' he gabbled.

'You do that, Sean, if that's what you'd like to do. It will be better than being a soldier.'

But who was I to tell him what he was to do? I might never see him again. He was not my son, though I was beginning to wish that he was.

While I was sitting thinking, suddenly he cried out, 'Yes, that's what I'll be, lady, a farmer!'

As I kissed his cheek, my husband called out excitedly, 'Bring the keep net, Kate. I've got a big one here, and I don't want to lose it this time.'

It was a large pike. As he landed it into the net he took the hook from its mouth, and threw it on to the bank.

'Is that for me, mister?' little Sean cried out as his eyes lit up.

'I think it's too big for you to carry home, sonny Jim.'

'But you promised, mister.'

When I saw the disappointed look on his face, I asked my husband how heavy he thought it was.

'Must be seven pounds, at least,' he replied.

But the little chap said, 'I've got some string in me pocket, an' if I can't carry it I'll drag it. Can I 'ave it now, mister?'

I asked him, 'How far away do you live?'

'At the top of the bank along the lane.'

'Well, if you'll go and bring some newspaper we'll wrap it up and carry it home for you.'

'Yer mean it lady? Yer won't throw it back in the river, lady?'

'No, we'll keep it for you. Now hurry up, and don't be long.'

I watched as he ran up the few steps along the side of the bank and out of sight.

'Enjoy yer little chat?' my husband asked as I sat down on the grass beside him.

'Yes, Joe, he's a lovable little chap. I feel as if I could adopt him . . . You know, Joe,' I added, 'I'd love to take him back home with us for a holiday.'

'Well, if you feel like that, love, perhaps you could ask his mum . . . Where did he say he lived?'

'He said his dad and brothers and sister lived in Dudley.'

'Well,' he replied, 'that's not far from Handsworth, on the bus. But, again, I don't think it would be wise, love. What I hear the little chap say about his mother, I don't think we should get involved.'

'Maybe you're right, Joe. But I still feel sorry for him.'

Just then we looked up towards the steps and saw a middle-aged man holding Sean by the hand. The man was in his shirt sleeves, rolled up to the elbows, and as he came towards us I saw his round, very red face, and thick barrel chest and protruding stomach. Tied around his middle was a dirty apron. In his other hand he held a large paper bag.

'Good evening,' he greeted us at once. 'I bet that one give you a fight,' he added, as he looked down at the pike on the grass.

'It did that,' my husband replied.

As little Sean gazed admiringly at his fish, the man said, 'My name's Peter O'Connor, but everybody here calls me Pat.'

After my husband told him who we were, and shook hands, he told us that he kept the little pub a few yards away, at the top of the bank.

'But it's not seen from here. Little Sean says you're giving him the fish to take home to his mam,' he added.

The way he kept looking at the fish I had a feeling he wanted it for himself.

'Yes, we are,' I said sharply. 'We promised he could have it for his mum.'

'Now, now, don't get me wrong, missus,' he snapped back. 'I only came with the lad to carry it for him.'

Over his shoulder I saw oe frown hard at me, a warning not to say another word.

Then Pat O'Connor turned to Joe and asked where we were

staying. Joe mentioned the name of the place some distance away where we had taken a room, but added that we had stayed out too long and missed the train back, so we needed to find somewhere for the night.

'We haven't had time to look around for a place yet,' he added.

'I'm afraid you'll have a job to find a place around here, but if it's only for the one night me and the missus can put you up, bed and breakfast.'

'Thanks, Mr O'Connor, but . . .'

'Call me Pat, everybody else does.'

'Thanks again, Pat, but I really want to find somewhere we could stay for a couple of nights, I'd like to do some more fishing around here.'

'Well, I think we might be able to manage that. But we don't take anybody to stay as a rule.'

When I thanked him and tried to apologise for snapping him up, he said he understood, and asked my name. I said, 'Well, if I call you Pat, you can call me Kate.'

'Very well. If you'll both come along with me I'll try and fix you up with me missus.'

While we'd been busy talking, Sean had run towards the edge of the river. 'Look, mister! Somethin's pullin' yer rods in the river.'

Quickly Joe grabbed hold of the rod and landed another large pike, almost as big as the first one. As he took the hook from the mouth of the pike, Pat O'Connor cried out, 'Don't throw it back, I'll take it back to me pub. The missus likes to stuff 'em.'

And so, after collecting our tackle we followed him and Sean up the bank on to the road above. Little Sean looked so proud walking beside the publican as he carried both fish.

'I'll have to leave you here, Joe, to stay with my fish, while I take this little chap home to his mam, he said, as he laid the fish on the piece of grass beside us. 'He only lives around the corner. I'll be back in a tick.'

The little chap thanked us again, and asked if we would still be there the next day. I said I couldn't promise – Joe liked to move about to explore different waters. But as I hugged and kissed him I felt my tears begin.

While we sat at the top of the bank waiting for Pat, we looked along the narrow, cobbled village street and saw several whitewashed old houses, different shapes but all very small. To me, they all looked as if they were toppling sideways. I could hardly believe that people lived in them. On the corner stood the little whitewashed pub, with a sign over the door reading 'ALL ARE WELCOME INSIDE TO OUR HUMBLE DWELLING. P. AND M. O'CONNOR'.

There was not a soul to be seen, only a few stray cats who came sniffing at the fish. But I was scared by the odd look of everything, and was about to say, let's look for somewhere else, when Pat came towards us. Picking up the pike, he said, 'Come along, you must be starving, I know I am, let's go and see what the missus is cooking.'

We followed him across the cobbled path to the pub, where he took us through a large room which he called the tap room, then into another room which I supposed must be their kitchen. I stumbled a couple of times, swearing to myself as I caught my shin on the edge of an iron-legged table.

As soon as he lit the gas jets on the wall, I quickly glanced around. The place was old, but it looked clean and tidy.

'Sit yourselves down,' he said, as he pointed to a couple of horsehair chairs, 'while I slip upstairs and tell the missus.'

'Well, it ain't too bad, I've been in worse,' Joe said.

'Me too,' I said. 'If the bed's clean I don't mind.'

A few seconds later Pat entered with his wife.

'This is Maggie, my wife, and she says she can manage to put you both up for a couple of nights.'

'Thank you, Mrs O'Connor,' my Joe said at once as he took her hand. 'And this is my wife, Kate.'

'Pleased to meet you both,' she greeted us, smiling.

She was a large, buxom woman, with a round face, very big blue eyes and blonde hair which looked to me dyed, as it showed grey at the roots. She was very cheerful and asked if we would like a drink. Joe said, 'I don't drink myself, but I'd like a drink of lemonade, and Kate would like a stout.'

They bought in our drinks, with two glasses of whiskey for themselves, and sat by the table facing us. When Joe asked how much he owed, Pat said, 'That's all right, Joe, that's on us for the pike you give me and the lad.'

'Would you like to see the bedroom?' Maggie asked when we'd finished our drinks.

'Yes, please, Mrs O'Connor,' I replied.

'I'd like you to call me Maggie, everybody does, it sounds more friendly. If you'd like to go to the lav, it's on the landing next to your bedroom. And you'll find water and towel on the washstand.'

She lit the gas mantles on the landing and in the bedroom. The room was very small and almost bare, but clean.

'I'll leave you now to clean yourself up, then I'll have your supper ready.

When she'd gone I had a better look around.

There was an iron bed in the corner, and when I turned it down I was pleased to see it was clean and free from bed bugs. There was an old wicker basket chair beside the bed, a wardrobe which was very old and painted green, and a marble-topped washstand. Its legs too were painted green, and on it were a crock basin and jug (the jug filled with water), and a towel. There was no carpet of any description on the floor, just the uneven wooden boards with their knots protruding. Underneath the bed was a chamber pot. On the lime-washed brick walls there was nothing except a small oval mirror, and the gas bracket with the lighted gas mantle, which kept popping and hissing, throwing moving shadows across the room.

I stripped down and had a good wash. Unfortunately, I had nothing with me but my fishing clothes – a thick jersey and a pair of navy slacks – so I had to put them back on again. But after I spruced myself up and combed my hair I felt a bit more presentable.

When I went downstairs I found that the table in the kitchen was already laid out with cold mutton and vegetables, salad, hunks of bread and cheese, and a large jug of cider. While we ate, we chatted about who we were and where we came from, and got on quite friendly terms. When supper was over Joe went with Pat into the other room to have his fag, and I helped Maggie to wash up the supper crocks. After a while Joe came back to say he'd phoned through to the lodging house where we'd been staying, and he and Pat would be going early in the morning to pick up our cases. For that night Maggie kindly lent me a night shift which looked more like a bell tent, and Pat said Joe could use one of his nightshirts. And we went up to our bedroom.

I could have turned around three times without moving that shift. And I had to laugh when Joe slipped the shirt over his head – he looked like Marley's ghost. But soon I fell asleep. I woke in the night, to see Joe get out of bed, light the gas, and make his way across the room to the landing closet. Tripping along, lifting up his nightshirt with his hands, he looked so comical I couldn't stop laughing.

I was still smiling when he came back into the room. As soon as he lowered the gas, he snatched off the nightshirt and jumped into bed naked. When I began to giggle again, he snatched off my bell tent too. And that was the first time we ever made love together in the nude.

It was about seven o'clock the next morning when I woke again, to find Joe had already gone. It was a beautiful warm sunny morning. I washed and dressed quickly, picked up the night attire off the floor, and went downstairs. Finding myself in the front part of the pub, I looked around. This bit was more like a stores than a pub. There were groceries of every description. On the counter were weighing scales, cheese, tea, tobacco, soap, blacking, even bundles of firewood. You name it, they sold it. Walking a little further, I came to another small room with a bar, taps which drew the beer, and a small white crock barrel with a tap, and 'Irish Whiskey' on it in gilt lettering.

Then I found my way to the kitchen. Maggie soon came in from the yard, and she began at once to prepare breakfast on an open fire. She told me the men had left early, and would be back about ten o'clock.

While we were sitting having breakfast together, she began to describe what sort of people came into the shop.

'Does Sean's mum ever come in here?' I asked.

'No, not now. She's a bad 'un, that one, and when they bury her mother her and Sean'll be going back to Dudley.'

'Poor little chap,' I said, 'I felt very sad when he left us.'

'Yes, poor little feller. But he'll be better off when he goes back to his dad and the rest of the family.'

'I hope so, Maggie,' I said.

After breakfast I took a stroll along the village street. There were more people around this morning, and each and every one greeted me as I passed, some even coming out of their houses to say 'Top o' the mornin' to ye, mam'.

When I got back, Pat and Joe were waiting for me. Joe was ready and raring to go, with his rods already in his hand and his creel on his back.

'Can't miss the last few hours, Kate, get yer rods, I'm ready to be off,' he cried out.

'But what about some food, and a flask?'

'Maggie's put us up some bread and cheese, a piece of cake, and that bread and jam you liked.'

I got ready quickly, and we set off. Joe only had a few maggots left, but Pat said we would be able to get some bait from a friend of his, Paddy O'Leary, who had a boathouse at the other end of the village, so that was our first stop. The boathouse turned out to be just a corrugated covered shed. There was no one about, so we looked around. Over the wooden door was a sign which read, 'Paddy O'Leary, Carpenter. No jobs too large or too small'. Inside we saw new and old planks of wood and pieces of old furniture, and on a long, worn wooden bench there were nails, hammers, and a couple of hand-saws. Everything was cluttered up, and there was a thick layer of sawdust on the floor.

I was startled when a voice behind us said, 'Hello, there. Can I help ye?'

We turned to see a thick-set, elderly fellow, with sandy hair and a thick sandy beard. When Joe explained who we were, who had sent us, and what we were after, he said, 'I don't happen to have any maggots. I don't use 'em meself. But are you willing to have a piece of wasp cake? There's plenty of fat grubs, better than all your maggots. I won't fish with anything else.'

Joe thanked him and asked how much he was in his debt.

'That's quite all right,' he replied. 'But I'd be glad if you'd catch me a pike, or a nice fat chub.'

'I'll do that, and thanks again.'

Then as we went down the slope towards the river, he came after us. 'If you'll wait a few minutes, I'll get the old punt down and you can row where you want.'

He was so kind and helpful. The next thing we knew, he was wheeling the boat on an old rusty barrow towards the water's edge. We got in, Joe took up the oars and as we thanked Paddy again he gave the boat a push, and wished us good luck.

We found a peaceful, pretty spot in the middle of the river: green trees and wild flowers on the banks, not another soul about or any boats to disturb us, it suited us fine. When we had anchored, Joe said he would fix his rod up first while I got out the eats, and then he'd fix mine. I watched him take one of the grubs from the wasp cake, hook it on the end of his line, and drop the line in the water. Then we sat down, one at each end of the boat. But just as I handed him his sandwich, we heard a loud buzzing, and we looked up to see a swarm of wasps trying to attack us. I leapt up, dropping the flask and the sandwiches in the boat, and I nearly tipped us both in the river as I sprang over towards Joe. We must have looked as if we were trying to do some kind of a war dance. As the wasps flew at Joe he twisted and turned, and so did I. He took off his cap and as he swung a swipe at them the cap left his hand and floated down the river. I yelled to tell him two had settled on his bald patch, and he nearly tipped the boat over, jumping in the air.

As we were swinging around and waving our arms in all directions to swipe the wasps away, Joe suddenly turned and shouted, 'What's in them bloody sandwiches?'

'Only what Maggie put up. The bread and cheese and the cake and bread and jam,' I yelled back.

'Well, it must be that they're after. Throw it in the bloody river.'

I did as I was told. But still they dived down at us. Just as I was about to lift my hands to protect my face, I saw several swarm down on the wasp cake that lay on the floor of the boat.

'Look, Joe, look, Joe!' I screamed, pointing. 'That's what they've come after. Look!' I yelled again. 'There.'

Managing to get a piece of wet rag from his keep net, Joe covered his hand and slung the grubs as far as he could into the river.

'Well, we'd better make a move further up the river, before they decide to come back,' he said.

As soon as we settled down again, Joe asked for the sandwiches.

'There ain't any. You told me to throw 'em in the river.'

'I meant the bread and jam, not the bloody lot!' he snapped. 'Well, I'll have a drink of tea.'

When I said I'd thrown the flask in too, he began to bawl at me. I was almost in tears. When he said it was no use me blartin', I swore at him and told him I'd never come fishing again. But after he put his arm around me and said he was sorry he'd lost his temper, I sat quietly in the end of the boat while he began to fish again, using some of the few maggots he had left. But we had no luck. He said we'd have to go back and get something to eat, and after we might try the water where we'd fished the day before.

So we rowed back. As we tied the boat to the landing stage, Paddy came towards us. When Joe told him what had happened, he looked disappointed we hadn't brought him a fish.

'Didn't yer cover it over well out of sight?' he asked when Joe tried to explain.

'No, Paddy, I never give it a thought they'd swoop down on us like that.'

'No,' I piped up, 'and if I hadn't seen what they were after, we might have been swiping at them now, or I'd have jumped in the river.'

'Never mind,' Joe said. 'We'll know another time.'

'Not if I can help it,' I yelled at him.

I don't know what Paddy thought of me, but at the time I didn't care. I walked slowly away, leaving them talking.

As Joe and I walked back to the pub, he gave me a dressing down for loosening my tongue. I'd calmed down a bit by then, and, knowing that he had a worse temper than me, I thought better of making a sharp answer. We walked the rest of the way back to the pub in silence. But when we got back to our room he bent down and kissed me.

'Sorry I snapped at you, Kate,' he said.

'I'm sorry too. I didn't mean to be rude to Paddy after lending us his boat, either.'

'Oh, I think he understood. Anyway, let's hurry and get ready for something to eat.'

After we'd had our supper we went into the tap room, where we had a few games of crib with some of the locals. Then an old chap pulled out his tin whistle and played a tune, while another chap danced a jig. After which another sang 'Danny Boy'. Everyone in turn did something. When they asked me to sing, I was eager to burst forth. As I'd had a couple of glasses of whiskey and several of port, I was feeling very merry. I stood with my back to the counter and sang 'Kathleen Mavourneen', and then a song my brother had taught me when I was a child – 'Me little shirt me muvver made for me'. When I had finished, the men crowded around me asking for more. But I saw my husband frowning at me. 'No more, Kate, we've got to be up early in the morning to catch our train.' I was tempted to ignore him, but thought better of it. I didn't want to see him lose his temper among strangers. But I had the devil in me that night. I went over to everyone, and kissed them goodnight. Suddenly an old man put his arms around me and held me. He wouldn't let go, until my Joe came up to him and said, 'Now, now, grandad, watch yer blood pressure.'

When we got back to our bedroom I flopped down on the bed and began to giggle.

'I enjoyed myself tonight, Joe,' I managed to say.

'Yes, love, I could see you were, and I was watching that old man's hungry eyes on you!'

'Go on, yer jealous!' I giggled.

'Maybe I am. Now, get undressed and into bed.'

He helped me undress, and as soon as I crawled into bed I fell asleep. I didn't even feel him get in beside me.

The next day we had to get the train back to Dublin, where we were to catch the plane. We rose early and got packed ready to leave. Maggie was already cutting sandwiches in the kitchen when we went downstairs, while Pat was cooking our breakfast of ham and eggs over the open fire.

After breakfast Joe paid them, and we thanked them for their hospitality and promised to come again. I had just kissed them both, and we were turning to go, when we saw Paddy hurrying towards us with a parcel in his hand.

'I'm glad I didn't miss you, mam. I'd like to wish you luck on your journey home, and for you to accept this gift,' he said, as he handed me a cardboard shoe box. I began to smile, as I said, 'It doesn't happen to be another one of those wasp cakes?'

'No, it's something I've made for you to remind you of us all here in Arva.'

When I opened the shoe box I saw a wooden carving of the number of my house cut in an oval piece of dark oak. I threw my arms around him and thanked him, and as soon as I kissed him I felt the tears start, for they had all been so kind to us and I felt sad at leaving. But we had to go. They waved several times, and so did we, until we were out of sight.

Our next Irish holiday was the one we paid for out of what was left of Joe's pools win. I saw an advertisement in his angling paper, saying 'Come and stay at the Lakeside Hotel for plenty of good fishing.' It sounded just what we wanted. And we persuaded my eldest daughter, Kathleen, who had recently been widowed, to come with us.

The holiday didn't start too well. When we arrived in Dublin we found we had missed our train, so we had to find somewhere to stay for the night. Everywhere was dark, the streets were badly lit, and we didn't know where to begin looking for a place. But finally a local directed us to the Railway Hotel. When we got there we found it was a dilapidated old pub. It wasn't much to our taste, but we couldn't roam the streets till daybreak, so we decided to take pot luck. As we entered we saw it had no carpet on the floor, only wet sawdust. There was not a soul in sight, but we could see there must have been plenty of people there earlier, for the tables were strewn with empty and half-filled glasses of beer. The room which was supposed to be the bar smelt of stale beer and tobacco smoke.

As soon as Joe called out 'Anyone there?' a thick-set, middle-aged man popped up from behind the counter. With his flat broken nose and one cauliflower ear, he looked like an old prizefighter. His shirt was wide open at the front and showed a thick chest and protruding belly covered with sandy-coloured hair, and below his stomach hung a wet, greasy apron.

When Joe asked him if he had any rooms, he said that the place was almost full with a wedding party, but he could fix us up with a couple of rooms. Joe thanked him, and paid him, and a young lad appeared out of nowhere to show us upstairs.

We followed the lad up two gas-lit flights of stairs, almost tripping on the worn lino. He showed us a double room for ourselves and a small single room opposite, which was to be Kath's. The rooms were bare and shabby, but seemed clean enough. In our room there was an extra single bed, as well as our double one. We were tired from travelling all day, so we went straight to bed, and to sleep. However, I hadn't been asleep long when I heard the wedding guests had returned. They were running up and down the stairs, yelling and laughing. I was mad, and felt like jumping out of bed to tell them to be quiet. But I shook Joe instead. 'Wake up, wake up!' I kept repeating.

'Now what's the matter?' he cried out, yawning as he sat up in bed.

'This ain't a hotel! It's a bloody madhouse,' I yelled at him. 'Why don't you get up and put yer trousers on and tell them to have a bit more respect for people?'

'They probably don't know we're here. Anyway, let 'em enjoy themselves, they ain't bothering me.'

'But they are me. And I'm going to tell 'em so!'

As I went to get out of bed he managed to pull me back. 'You're mad. We don't know these people, they might be rough if you interfere with them. They'll soon get tired, and now let's lie down and get some sleep.'

We lay down again. Joe was soon snoring. I covered my head with the bedclothes, hoping I could drown his noise and theirs.

After a while the noises died down. I uncovered my head and looked at my wrist-watch. It was almost midnight. Soon I dozed off.

I hadn't been asleep long when I woke with a start, to hear loud rumbling noises in the distance. At first I thought it was thunder, but as it came nearer and louder, the whole room shook.

I screamed out, 'Joe, wake up! Joe, wake up!'

'What's the matter now?' he cried out angrily.

'I'm scared. There was such a loud rumbling noise, and the room shook.'

'Oh, go to sleep. You must be dreaming,' he said, as he began to yawn.

'Listen, there it goes again . . . you'd better put yer trousers on and go across the landing and see if Kath's all right.'

But he'd only just got his trousers on when the door was flung open, and in fell Kath in her nightdress. She slipped on a loose floorboard and it flew in the air, a chair going up with it.

'Whatever's happened?' I called out.

'Mum, there was such a terrible noise, sounded like a building falling down! Or thunder. But the second time I heard it, it was a train, come right past my window! I was so scared, I thought it was coming into the room. And I'm not going back there to sleep.'

Joe jumped back into bed, and covered his head over.

'Well, Kath, you'd better manage in that bed across in the corner, and mind you don't tread on that loose board again.'

I tucked her in and got back into bed myself, but we neither of us slept. Joe was snoring loudly. He must have had plenty of bruises the way I kept digging his ribs, but he'd still turn over and continue snoring.

We were all glad to see the dawn. We got up before five, and hurried to get dressed and away. I left Joe swearing as he was trying to shave in cold water, while I went across the landing to help my daughter pack her belongings.

In the daylight, that room looked so small. I hadn't noticed before that the head of the bed was against the window, which I saw had been nailed down. All I could see when I looked out was a brick wall a few feet away, and railway lines almost level with the window.

When we'd packed everything up we took all our luggage and went down to the dining room for our breakfast. Sitting near the counter there were four tough looking Irishmen, who kept eyeing us. When one of them came towards us, the proprietor stepped in front of him and said who we were. The fellow replied, 'Oh, I thought they were gate-crashers.'

We ignored them. But they still stared. Then the waiter brought in the breakfast. On each plate was a rasher of fat bacon, two fried eggs and some mushrooms, all floating in grease.

'Come on,' my husband whispered, 'let's go, we can't eat this.'

We picked up our luggage and got up from the table. The bar tender asked if there was anything wrong; any other time my husband would have kicked up a rumpus, but he just made the excuse we had to hurry or we'd miss our train.

As we walked towards the door I looked back and noticed the four men dash across to our breakfast and begin to devour it. They were welcome to it.

We had to eat somewhere though, the three of us were starving. We hadn't eaten since three o'clock the previous afternoon. Soon we came to a small tea room in a side street, and we were lucky, the man was just unbolting the door. As soon as we entered we ordered a large pot of tea and a dozen cakes. When he saw us eating hungrily, he asked if we had been travelling all night.

'No,' replied Joe, 'but I believe we would have been better if we had, instead of in the place we've just come from.'

'And where might that be, if I may ask?' he enquired kindly.

When Joe told him, he just stood and stared. 'You must mean Big Mike's. My God!' he exclaimed. 'But I didn't think anybody was put up there now. I heard someone tried to kill themself by going through the bedroom window on to a railway track.'

'That accounts for the windows being nailed down, then,' I said. 'And we hardly slept a wink for the racket. And the breakfast they brought us, we had to walk out and leave, it was just swimming in grease!' I added.

'You poor buggers! Just wait a few moments, I can hear my wife in the kitchen. I'll see if we can rustle up a breakfast.'

We never enjoyed a breakfast more.

When, later that day, dirty, weary and very tired, we arrived at the Lakeside Hotel, we found we had come from the ridiculous to the sublime. We had never expected it to be such a grand hotel.

Looking down at myself, in my travelling slacks and jersey, I said, 'We can't go in there, Joe, looking like this.'

'And why not?' he snapped. 'You answered their advert, and I sent the deposit. So come on!'

I fully expected we would be refused entrance, but we had only just stepped inside the lobby when an elderly gentleman dressed in plus fours came and wished us good afternoon. As soon as Joe said who we were, he replied, 'Oh, yes, you've come for the fishing. Just leave your luggage, I'll send the porter along to show you your rooms.'

I couldn't believe our luck. The hotel was fit for royalty. Joe and I had a beautiful room overlooking the garden, and Kath's room overlooked the lake.

We bathed and changed, and did our best to look presentable for dinner, but we hadn't brought anything at all suitable for a hotel like this. So next morning Kath and I left Joe to his fishing while we caught the bus to Limerick to do some shopping.

We visited several shops, and bought a mac, sandals and three dresses each. Then we bought some fruit to have for our picnics. On the way back we were pleased to find that the bus was only half full, so there were a couple of spare seats for our heavy parcels. And we sat back to enjoy the journey. But at a stop only about half-way, we were surprised to see all the passengers leave the bus. We still sat there, but then the driver called out to us. 'All off!' We looked at him dumbfounded.

'I said, all off!' he repeated.

'But we've paid our fare to go all the way,' I replied.

'Well, we only go this far. We have to go back and pick up the five o'clock passengers. So you'll have to wait here until we come back.' he replied irritably.

As we collected our parcels I snapped at him, 'Well, if this ain't Irish, tell me what is.'

'Irish, Scotch, Welsh or bloody English,' he snapped back, 'you'll have to wait here till I return.'

And there we stood in that lonely lane, with not a soul to be seen. There was only one little shop, which was closed. And next door to it a small whitewashed cottage. We were plaiting our legs for a toilet, but there was no sign of one, so I knocked on the door of the cottage to ask. A grey-haired old lady answered, and when I asked if there was a public toilet near she replied, 'You won't find any in these parts, my dears, but you're welcome to come inside and use mine.'

When we entered, Kath and I couldn't believe how small the living room was. She led us into an equally small space she called the kitchen, and pointed to a corner. 'In there, but mind you don't bump yourself.'

There was only room behind the door for one of us and once you sat down on the lavatory seat you couldn't close the door. As the little outhouse faced the street, anyone passing would have had a full view.

After we had been, we thanked her and went to pick up our parcels and the bag of fruit. But she said, 'Would you like a cup of tea, dears? I've got the kettle on the fire.'

We were very grateful and thanked her. While we waited for the tea I asked how often the buses ran.

'Buses?' she exclaimed. 'We only have one bus in these parts, and that only runs high days and holidays. It should be returning to pick you up in a few minutes,' she said as she looked up at the clock on the mantleshelf.

When we had finished our tea, my daughter asked how much we owed for it.

'You're very welcome,' she replied. 'It's not often anyone calls. But,' she added, 'I would like one of your oranges.'

As we picked up our parcels, my daughter gave her two oranges and a couple of apples for her kindness. Just then we heard the bus chugg-ing up the hill. The old lady kissed us both, and as we went towards the bus, she waved and called out, 'God bless you both, my dears.'

We waved back and climbed on to the old bone-shaker. This time there wasn't a seat to be had, people were packed like sardines, and we had to stand with our parcels all the rest of the journey.

As soon as we got to our hotel and up to our room, Joe greeted us with, 'Where the bloody hell have you two been till now? I've been waiting over an hour. And you'd better get yerselves cleaned up before the dinner gong goes,' he added as he walked out of the room.

'I'd better go and change, Mum, he's in one of his moods,' my daughter said as she left the room.

'Very well,' I replied. 'I'll get ready too, and let's put on our new dresses we've bought.'

I was ready before Kath, and as Joe was already so upset about our being late, I thought I'd better hurry down rather than waiting for her.

When I arrived in the dining room, he was sitting at the table, waiting.

'Well,' he asked more pleasantly, as I sat down, 'why were you late?'

I began to smile as I said, 'You won't believe this when I tell you, Joe. It's really funny now I come to think of it.'

'Try me,' he said.

When I told him our tale, he too couldn't help smiling.

'Well, I suppose you have to expect anything to happen in these villages. They still keep up their old traditions.'

'Did you manage to do a spot of fishing, Joe?' I asked.

'No,' he replied. 'I walked about half a mile along the river and got my rods ready to fish. But then I saw a couple of chaps fishing for salmon. I felt a bloody ninny. We should have explained when we wrote what kind of fishing we did. Anyhow,' he added, 'we'll have to move on and find another river.'

I tried not to look disappointed. I would have enjoyed a bit more of the comfort and kind hospitality this hotel provided, which I'd never been used to, not to mention the luxurious food and surroundings.

'But, Joe,' I said, 'Kath and I like it here. Let's stay a couple more days, please.'

I saw the look of disappointment on his face, so I didn't say any more until we had our coffee. He said then, 'Well, if you two want to stay for a couple more days, I'll see the manager and explain we'll be leaving at the end of the week.'

The next day we went playing crazy golf and putting, with some of the guests. But I could see Joe wasn't enjoying the games and I felt very selfish, for I knew what a fanatic he was about his fishing. However, after a while he happened to get in conversation with one of the guests who had been a prisoner of war, and he obviously found that more interesting. While they were talking, Kath and I took a stroll along the country lanes.

It was a beautiful warm sunny day, and we must have been walking for about an hour when we saw an old tramp coming towards us. His battered old trilby stood at an angle on his head, his grimy toes peeped out of his old boots, and his ragged coat and trousers were tied together with a piece of rope. His matted hair hung to his shoulders, and his face too was covered with hair. You could just about manage to see his eyes. But that was not all we saw. As he came nearer, we saw that his flies were wide open, and the end of the rope which held his trousers together was also twisted around his 'John Thomas'. We couldn't believe our eyes. We both began to titter, and my daughter managed to say, 'Is that what they call a shillelagh?'

'I don't know, but whatever it's called, he'd have a job carrying that thing under his arm.'

As he passed he must have known what we were tittering about. He turned around and winked. We never ran so fast in all our lives.

When I told my husband that night, he said he wouldn't let us wander alone again.

Next day the three of us were walking down another lane when we noticed a couple of cards lying in the path. We picked them up and saw they were racing cards.

'There must be some kind of horse-racing here,' Joe said. 'Come on, we'll go and enquire.'

Further along the lane we met a farmer, and when Joe asked him where the racing was he replied, pointing across a field, 'Over that stile yonder and across the meadow. You'll see it.'

So over the stile we went, and when we got into the field we saw it was a donkey derby.

I've never seen anything more comical than that donkey derby. There were eight donkeys of all sorts and sizes, some that could do with a good feed, others with pot bellies. Their jockeys were young lads who looked no more than twelve years of age. Each lad wore a well-worn white cow gown, three sizes too large, which almost dragged the floor, and on his back was a card with his name. Gordon Richards, Lester Piggott, Fred Winter, Harry Wragg, and other famous names, were in that donkey derby. After a hustle and bustle, the lads managed to get their donkeys into some sort of line. The rules were that no jockey was allowed to mount his donkey until the starter dropped his flag. Once the flag had been dropped there was absolute chaos as the lads tried to mount. Then they were off – or some of them were.

Two donkeys refused to budge, and were disqualified. Three more were already half-way down the field battling it out, when one decided he'd had enough: up went his hind legs, and off fell his rider. There were now only two donkeys left in the race. The one that was leading, seeing some blackberries in a hedge, decided he'd stop and have a feed. And when his jockey dug his heels in him and tried to pull him away, he kicked up his hind legs and the jockey went head first over the hedge. That left one pot-bellied donkey to plod along to the end of the field and back. Some people cheered, others catcalled, and Joe lost his half-crown. But it was well worth it for the fun.

Next day we heard there was some dog-racing nearby, so we decided to go to see that. The dog track was just a small field. There were ten dogs racing and each one was a mongrel, what we called the 'Heinz varieties'. There were long-haired, rough-haired, short-haired, wire-haired, and some with no hair at all. Each owner stood in front of a piece of canvas holding his dog firmly by the collar. Suddenly one owner called out, 'Black Beauty, where are you!' I looked down and saw the little black mongrel brush against my leg as he ran towards his owner.

'Kath!' I cried out, 'that's an omen, I'm going to back him.'

'Don't waste yer money,' I heard Joe snap. 'Anything can win. It's just a matter of luck.'

But I ignored him, and Kath and I hurried to put our couple of bob on Black Beauty to win. The man who was shouting the odds smiled at us. 'You're sure that's the one you want, missus?' he said.

We nodded. He gave us our tickets, and we went back to join Joe in the crowd and wait for the race to start. A piece of rabbit skin tied to the end of a piece of wire went around the field once, just to get the dogs keyed up. The second time it came around the owners let go of their dogs. Suddenly the dogs began to fight. Several flew up in the air, and there were balls of fur flung everywhere. A couple more just looked on. But there was little Black Beauty, running after the rabbit skin. He looked back once, as much as to say, 'You can all carry on, I'm all right.' He won the race and my daughter and I were the only two who walked up to that bookmaker to pick up our winnings, of five shillings each.

The next day was Saturday. We packed our luggage, said goodbye to everyone and started our travels again. We had decided to head for Athlone, where the coarse fishing was said to be good. Kath and I were sorry to leave the Lakeside Hotel, but Joe was pleased at the prospect of doing some fishing.

When we arrived in Athlone there was a bad thunderstorm, so we took shelter in a shop doorway. The owner of the shop, whose name was Mr Foye, invited us inside. When Joe asked him if he knew where there was a picture-house where we could go for a couple of hours, until the storm passed over, he replied, 'There's only the one next to the police office around the corner. I go meself sometimes. It's not much of a one, but it'll shelter you from the storm.'

'Would you be so kind as to let us leave our bags here until we come back?' Joe asked.

'I'm sorry,' he replied, 'I'm about to lock up. But if you like you can leave them next door, where I have my office. The old lady who lives upstairs never closes the front door, so you'll be able to pick them up when it suits you.

We thanked him for his kindness, and after putting the luggage next door we hurried from the rain around the corner, where we saw a large double-fronted house which seemed to have been converted into a cinema. Its windows had been bricked up and painted green, and in the glass fanlight above the door was written in black letters: 'Local Picture-House Prices four pence five pence and nine pence'. There were no posters outside to say what was showing. We took a chance and walked in. Sitting on a chair in the dim-lit hall was an old man who took our money: we paid nine pence, for the best seats.

The film was already showing when he directed us to our seats, which were hard and uncomfortable. I thought, if these were the best seats, what were the cheap ones like? I noticed too that the place was almost empty. To our disappointment, the first film was the Keystone Kops. However, we watched it through, hoping that the feature film would be a bit more up to date. But the next film was another silent, Charlie Chaplin's *The Kid*, which I had seen nearly forty years before. Joe fidgeted about, lighting one cigarette after another, until eventually he fell asleep. Half-way through the film he began to snore. I kept giving him digs, hoping to shut him up. After a while he opened his eyes and grunted, and then everyone in the house must have heard him, as he said loudly, 'Come on, I've had a bloody 'nough of this rubbish, let's go out and see if it's stopped raining.'

As we felt our way along the darkened gangway and out into the street we were glad to see the rain had stopped. But when we got to Mr Foye's office to pick up our luggage, we found the door locked. Joe went mad. He swore, he shouted, he banged and kicked the door, until a police inspector from the station next to the picture-house came to see what the noise was all about. When we explained who we were and why we were there, he said he couldn't understand why the old lady had locked the front door. 'It's always left open in case Mr Foye comes back late. Anyway,' he added, 'if you like to wait in my office I'll see if I can find him.'

We followed him inside, where there sat a very large, red-faced constable.

'Make these people a cup of tea, Tom. I'll be back in a minute.'

It took Tom a few seconds before he could ease himself out of the chair. 'Old achin' bones,' he said, as he shuffled to put the kettle on an old rusty pipe stove. We were just drinking our tea when the inspector came in with Mr Foye. He was all apologies when he saw us, and offered to drive us to our lodgings. But when we explained that we hadn't had time to look for a place, he drove us to some people he knew who put us up for the night.

Next morning after breakfast he brought our luggage and, apologising again, he offered us the use of his boat, if we wanted to fish the lake. We thanked him. In the end, Joe went out on the lake, with Mr Foye's son and another young lad to row him.

There wasn't room in the boat for five, so Kath and I stayed on shore. We thought we would clean up Mr Foye's boathouse while we were waiting, to show our appreciation of his kindness. The boathouse was really an old disused railway carriage that had been converted. All around the walls hung fishing rods, nets, and all kinds of fishing tackle. In the centre stood an old wooden table and two small wicker chairs, and against the wall was a marble-topped table where there stood a spirit stove, a tin kettle and an enamel teapot and some odd cups. Everywhere was thick with dust and grime. We got some water from the lake, and set about giving the place a clean, as best we could. We even went out and picked some wild flowers and put them in a cup of water in the centre of the table. Then we went for a walk. When we came back half an hour later we were surprised to see my husband and the two lads waiting for us. When I asked why they had returned so soon, Joe said he hadn't got enough bait to last any longer. He thanked the boys and gave them a couple of shillings each, and we went back to the digs to collect our belongings.

All the way Joe was sulking and swearing, saying all the time, 'I wish I'd gone back to Arva! At least the fishing was good. Yes, we should've gone back to Arva. My bleedin' holiday has been bleedin' spoilt. Waste of bleedin' money. Best we pack up and go home!'

I knew it was not for me to answer. On our way to Dublin to catch the plane back to England, he cooled down.

As soon as we arrived home and sat down, I said, 'Joe, next year, I think it would be better if you went to Ireland by yourself, and I'll take my holiday somewhere by the sea.'

'If that's what yer want, Kate. See what next year says, and we can make up our minds then.'

The following week I went with him to his fishing club, where we met his friend Jimmy Budd and Jimmy's wife, Elsie. Jimmy was a fishing fanatic, just like Joe.

'Enjoy yer fishin', Joe?' Jimmy asked as soon as he saw him.

Joe hadn't much to say about our last holiday, but when he started talking about the wonderful fish he'd caught in Arva, Jimmy was all ears. Soon we had made a plan that for our next holiday we would all go to Arva together, Jimmy and Elsie, and Joe, Kath and me. This pleased me. I knew Joe would enjoy his fishing more with someone like himself for company. I wrote to Pat and Maggie to ask if they could put five of us up for a week, and I had a reply to say that now they had two extra rooms, and we'd be welcome to come any time.

When we arrived in Arva we went straight away to the shop-fronted pub. Pat and Maggie met us on the doorstep, and as soon as we had introduced Kath and Jimmy and Elsie they took us into the tap room for a drink. It was too late to begin fishing, so the two men said they'd make an early start in the morning, and when we'd had supper we spent the rest of the evening playing dominoes with the old boys.

Next morning the men set off very early. Kath, Elsie and I decided we'd go back down the lanes and explore. As I remembered there was not much for us to see or do, but luckily we came across another donkey derby, and we were well entertained, watching and laughing at the capers the donkeys and the lads performed. It was a beautiful hot summer's day, and we stayed out till the early evening. When we got back to the pub we found that Joe and Jimmy were back before us. As we sat having our supper, Pat said, 'There's a fishing contest going out tomorrow morning if you're interested. It's only five bob, and the money prizes are good.'

'Where do they start from?' Joe asked eagerly.

'From the hall at the bottom of the village. But,' he added, 'it's only for fishermen, no women are allowed.'

'That's all right,' I said a once. 'The donkey derby's still on, we can go there till you come back, can't we?' Kath and Elsie agreed.

Early next morning we were all ready to see the men start from the village hall. I've never seen such an excited and happy assortment of fishermen. They all scrambled up on the farmers' hay-carts, hauling up their baskets, rods and wellies, and struggling to get the best sitting positions. Joe and Jimmy were up there with the rest, waiting for the shire horses to start. Then all at once from around the corner came an Irish bagpipe band, in their full regalia. And to the music of the bagpipes the hilarious procession started off. Everybody came out of the little cottages to wave and cheer.

Once they were out of sight we went along to watch the second day of the donkey derby, but we found it had been cancelled. So we decided to walk along the river instead. A little way along the bank I found I needed a pee. There wasn't a soul about, so while Kath and Elsie walked on in front I took down my knickers. But I'd only just begun to pee when I saw some cows coming down the lane. I'd always been afraid of cows (indeed of almost all four-legged animals except dogs and cats), and I took fright. Dragging my knickers (now wet) after me, I climbed over the hedge – and landed on my back. I looked up to see several goats coming towards me. I screamed for all I was worth. Luckily for me, the goats turned around and fled. Kath and Elsie, hearing my screams, came to the rescue and helped me back over the hedge. I laid my wet knickers on the grass and, while I was sitting there waiting for them to dry, my daughter asked me why I'd been screaming. When I told her she said, 'If you'd have waited you'd have seen the cows go over the footbridge.'

'But what about them goats in that field?' I asked.

'The way you screamed was enough to frighten a herd of elephants!'

No sympathy from that one, I thought.

That day we decided to go back to the pub and have our dinner. In the afternoon we went for another walk, and by the time we got back we could hear the bagpipes in the distance. The fishermen were returning with their bags of fish to weigh in. There was a lot of commotion and grumbling, as each one weighed his catch. My husband said he'd won the third prize, which was £2. But it was decided that locals had won first, second, third and fourth. Joe and Jimmy knew it was a fiddle, but as Joe said, 'Who were we to argue with a crowd of the locals.' They'd had a good day's sport. And Pat was pleased with the two pikes, four large bream and a chub that they brought back. Joe and Jimmy often brought fish to Pat, but we never saw any of it again. Whether he sold them or cooked them or stuffed them, we never knew.

The men went out very early the next morning. When we came down later we were puzzled to see that the shutters were still closed.

'Is it a storm we're having, Maggie?' I asked.

'No,' she replied. 'My shutters are still up because it's market day.' We thought no more about it until we went outside.

'Close the door after you, Kate!' I heard her call out after us. 'I won't be opening until this evening.'

Outside it was broad daylight and the sun was shining, with the promise of another warm day. As I looked up and down the narrow street. I saw that every little shop and cottage had its windows boarded up. Then I looked along the lane, and saw that coming my way were cows, bulls, horses, goats and sheep, all being led to the market.

I stood there petrified. My daughter and Elsie just laughed at me and walked away. Quickly I turned back and rang the bell, hoping Maggie would open the door and let me inside, but there was no answer. In terror, I crouched down between two low walls, afraid even to scream in case I drew the animals' attention. When they had passed by I came from behind the walls and rang the bell again, but there was still no answer. So, checking that the coast was clear, I made an effort to go and join the others by the river.

Every animal had freely left his load behind on the cobbles, and some had splashed up on the boarded windows. The stench was terrible. I had to pull up my skirts and hold my nose, as I goose-stepped to find a dry cobble to plant my feet on.

When I got to the river and explained, they just laughed. But I didn't see anything to laugh at, at the time.

Later, as we came back to our dinner, we saw people sloshing buckets of water over their boards, and others with water and brooms swilling down their front doors and the gutters.

In spite of the cattle problem, I was very sorry, and so was everyone else, when the day came to pack our luggage and get ready to leave, and catch our plane back to Brum. We wished Pat and Maggie goodbye, and we promised we would come again the next year. But Joe and I never saw Arva, or the friends we had made there again.

As we were walking towards the end of the next village, we saw four men lounging against the wall of another small pub, similar to the one we had just left. The priest was walking along the street too, and when they saw him coming towards them, they almost stood to attention as they raised their caps and said 'Good mornin', Father.' He just nodded in reply. As soon as he had passed on, a hand suddenly came from behind the door and beckoned them to come inside. How quickly they dashed in, almost knocking each other over.

A Working Retirement

In 1963 I was sixty, and I decided to sell my business and retire, so that I could stay at home and have more time with my husband. I put the money in the bank, and for a while we lived comfortably on the commissions Joe earned. But a few months later his employer sent for him to say that now off-course betting had been legalised she was going to open up a betting office where the punters could go and put on their bets and hear the results, so she wouldn't be needing his services in the club any more. She offered him a job working behind the counter, but he said he wouldn't work inside for no gaffer. Although I did my best to persuade him, he was adamant.

'I'll find something,' was all he said, when I asked him what he was going to do.

But when he came home late one night and said he'd got a job at Perry Bar Stadium, cleaning and feeding the dogs and taking them out for exercise, we began to quarrel.

'Can't you find a better job than that?' I snapped.

'Well, I ain't working in a factory, if that's what you mean!' he replied angrily.

Then one night he persuaded me to go and see the racing. I saw enough that night to know I didn't want to see any more. One young chap had put all his money on a certainty (so he was told). It came in last. I saw him kneel on the ground and punch it several times, shouting out 'It was doped! The bloody dog was doped!' People crowded around him, asking if he'd had a fit. I never went to the dog track again.

Each night Joe came home late we quarrelled. He'd got in with a gambling crowd and lost more than he earned. Foolishly I helped him out and paid some of his debts, but he just went on gambling. Until at last I made up my mind to do something about it.

During my retirement, several of my old customers had come to see me and asked if I would help out by doing some enamelling at home. It seemed to me that if I could persuade Joe to work with me it might keep him away from the gambling crowd. I put it to him.

'It's up to you, Kate, if that's what you want,' he said.

'It's not only up to me,' I replied angrily, 'I'm asking you! Would you help? And if we don't agree, we'll have to think of something else. But I'm telling you one thing now, Joe, you're to give up gambling or I'm selling up and leaving you.'

'Very well,' he said. 'I'll try.'

We built a workshop in the garden and had the gas and electric put in, and then we started to work together on the enamelling. Joe gave up going out gambling. I didn't mind him having a small bet once a week on the phone – I realised how miserable he would be if he couldn't have one little squander – but I knew and he knew how far he could go. We worked together happily each morning. In the afternoon, we went to Summerfield Park, where he taught me how to bowl. During the months that followed I won many trophies in prize money and we joined Handsworth Victoria bowling club, where later I was made Captain of the Women's Team. Later still I became Captain of the Warwickshire Ladies' Team.

These were happy years. Until I began to worry about Joe's cough. I knew he was almost chain-smoking, but each time I asked him to cut down, he became very irritable and bad-tempered. One day he complained about a pain in his chest and while he lay in bed I rang for the doctor. When he came he had Joe taken into hospital straight away. He'd had a heart attack.

I visited him in St Chad's Hospital the following day. But the next day while I was getting ready to visit him, he walked into the house, saying 'If I'm going to die I'll die at home.'

I was too shocked and upset even to answer him. After that he smoked more than ever. And one morning he collapsed on the floor. The doctor and the ambulance came at once, and Joe was taken to Dudley Road Hospital. When he began to improve, he phoned me each night, telling me he was now getting better and that I was to bring him some fags. I refused. But someone must have taken him some when they visited, and when the sister found out she warned him of the danger.

Late one night Joe phoned me, sounding very upset. When I asked him what was worrying him, he said 'Kate, you'd better bring my clothes.'

'Whatever for?' I asked.

'Never mind what for. Bring me my clothes. I want to get out of here!' he snapped. Then he added, 'What chance have I got when yer doctor drops dead in the ward?'

I rang the sister at once, but could get no reply. Next morning, after a sleepless night, I went to the hospital to visit him, and when he had calmed down he told me what had happened. Apparently the doctor had indeed had a heart attack and died while he was doing a ward round. Other patients too said the ward was all topsy-turvy when they took their doctor out on a stretcher.

Towards the end of the week Joe was discharged. He had been given some heart tablets to take, and I was pleased to see he was making an improvement. But he still smoked heavily. I knew it was useless now to try and persuade him to give up. A few weeks later I had to captain the bowling team in Manchester. When I asked him if he was coming with us, he replied, 'Not today, Kate, some of the chaps at the club have asked me to make up the team to bowl away. But I'll have yer tea ready by the time you come back home, love, and don't forget,' he added, 'I want to hear all about yer bowling.'

Then we kissed each other and waved goodbye. Those words were the last he ever said to me. That same evening when I arrived home from Manchester I was told that my husband had died while playing on the bowling green at Dudley.

It has now been over fifteen years. But I still miss him. More so than ever now. And I wish he were still here today.

Many times during the bowling season I watch the couples playing and think to myself how lucky they are that they still have each other, that they are able to talk to each other and share their worries and troubles. During many cold winter evenings I sit alone and think of those days and nights when we would pull up our armchairs close to the coal fire and make toast on the end of the fork. Sometimes later we would sit and play cards or dominoes, or do a crossword together until it was time for bed. Or he would pick up a detective story and read to me.

It all seems so sad, when you lose someone you love.

But I hope and pray, when the Good Lord opens up His book, and calls out my name, maybe I shall meet all my loved ones again. *Who knows?*

THE BEST OF TIMES

To my loving, caring daughter Jean
and her husband Sam Rainey

Contents

An Almost Forgotten Era

I believe today that many memories die hard, whether they are good, bad or indifferent. But as for me, I can never forget those bug-infested back-to-back hovels where I was born in 1903 and lived twenty-nine years in poverty and hardship, until I made heart-breaking decisions to leave all this behind me and to begin a new life for the better, for myself and my young family.

Often today, in my late years, I still find myself wandering around these old haunts, around the Jewellery Quarter, and recalling those once cobbled horse-roads and back alleyways, where I used to run to school with bare feet, in rags, with many other poor half-starved kids, begging for food outside factory gates. Many parents had no time to give us love or affection, which we needed, only strong discipline with the bamboo cane at the ready. Many times, too, old Vicar Smith would chase us with his walking-stick if he caught us playing in the churchyard of St Paul's Church, which we named 'Titty-bottle Park'.

And as I stroll along today, I notice how bright and clean this church and the surrounding district are. There are no more of those dilapidated back-to-back hovels where, I remember, people often begged and scratched for a crust of bread. Today you can see lovely flats and restaurants, where people live and dine in comfort, yet many of these surrounding buildings have only had a facelift. Also, many famous landmarks have gone now to make way for progress – but let us not forget our history, and who we are. Yet as I stroll around St Paul's Square and down George Street, I notice that the King Edward pub is still there, reminding me of the time I used to follow the hurdy-gurdy man around the square and along the 'Parade'. Many of us kids, when we came out of school, would hide up an entry and dance to the tunes he played, with our ragged frocks well above our knees.

Newhall Street had many little shops then. There was one shop I still remember well, where I used to fetch Mum's faggots and peas and dip my finger in, but not enough for Mum to notice. Once, she smelt my breath and I had the cane. But I didn't give her another chance – I always put my mouth under the tap in the yard before I took the basin in. But one day she sent me for a pint of milk. I knew she wouldn't be able to smell that, so after having a drink I added a drop of water, just about a tablespoon. As soon as I got indoors she asked, "Ave yer bin drinkin' any?'

'No, Mum,' I lied, as I began to tremble inside.

(But you could never lie to or deceive my mother.)

'Are yer sure?' she asked again, staring hard at me.

When I shook my head and replied no again, I felt my face colour up. She pulled me towards her and cried out, 'Well, if yer tellin' me the truth, let's see yer spit!'

As soon as I spat, she could tell I'd lied. I had that bamboo cane across my bare bum five times, and was sent to bed without my nightly cocoa.

Newhall Street was famous for cheap food. The shops sold almost everything: cow heels, tripe, chitterlings, pigs' trotters – you name them, they sold them, all piping hot. Leaving the shops that once were behind, I walk along Legge Lane, where I come to the old Camden Drive School, which I attended with my brother and sisters eighty-three years ago. I was then five years old. Yet many of these old buildings have now been renovated and turned into offices and workshops.

I recall the stories my granny used to tell me: how this district was always called the Jewellery Quarter. Many people with large families – like my mother and father, and their families – who once lived in these hovels had no prospects, just living from hand to mouth, and many who could not afford their rent let off their living-room to people who wanted to start a small business. They themselves moved to the upper floor to live. But Granny said as soon as the landlords or the agents found out, they raised the rent to a level they knew the tenants couldn't afford. So they were either turned out into the street or sent into the workhouse. This left the entire old houses to be let or sold to people who wanted to start up making jewellery. From then on, it grew to be what is still called the Jewellery Quarter today. There are still many alterations to be done to these buildings, yet many have only had a coat of paint and a facelift. There are still the back yards, brewhouses, and even old brick sheds where people used to keep pigeons, and did their washing ready for the pawnshops, yet people still ply their trades there.

As I walk on down the cobbled alleyway Camden Drive, where I was born, I am surprised to see the school wall and its playground, still just as Hitler's bombs left it. That was in the heavy raids on Birmingham in April 1941. Alongside the school wall, also, are to be seen the ruins of the iron foundry where my two eldest brothers once worked.

A lump comes to my throat as I think how sad and neglected and forgotten this place is today – just as we people were, who lived down that narrow cobbled alley many, many years ago.

It was a sad time for all of us that night the bombs came without warning.

Many of us lost loved ones, some to be buried in a communal grave in Warstone Lane Cemetery, just a few yards from where we once lived. This cemetery is neglected too, and I hope that one day it will have a facelift, to remind us not to forget our loved ones.

Just a few more yards I walk, and I come to the junction of Warstone Lane, Vyse Street and Frederic Street, where one of our famous landmarks, 'Joseph Chamberlain's Clock', stood with its ironwork painted dark green and gold, all faded and rusty. It has now been removed to be repaired and have a facelift too, but I'm told it will soon be restored to its original place. As I stand on the corner and look at that empty space, I remember the day my mother told me that when I was twelve months old she carried me to see that clock – which was erected in 1903, the year I was born – and to hear its chimes. Also, I think of the times when many of us kids leaving school at twelve midday would take it in turns to play around that monument, and look out for the Lodge Road tram making its way up to Warstone Lane, past the cemetery, round the clock, down Frederic Street, down Newhall Hill, and to the town terminus, and back again. That ride cost one penny. But today there are no trams, only buses, and you wouldn't get that same ride for less than £1.

Many years ago, I asked my teacher why the trams had holes in their slatted seats. She said they were for bugs, fleas and lice to drop through off dirty people.

As I stroll towards the city centre, near the Council House in Colemore Row, I notice that the statue of Queen Victoria is still there. Yet I can't understand why her son's statue is no longer standing beside her. I ask several people what has become of King Edward's statue – or Nelson's Column, which once stood in the Bull Ring, and many more famous statues – yet no one seems to know, or isn't interested any more.

Yet the fountain is still in the same place. That too has had a facelift, and as I stand and gaze up at it I think of the happy times we children had, dabbling our dirty sore feet in that cool, clear water. We weren't fussy, either, about having a drink afterwards. But we kept our eyes peeled for the 'bobby' coming along.

Often we had to make our own fun and games, which cost nothing, for our parents couldn't afford to buy us toys; we gave them every farthing or penny that was given to us or begged for. But we had many happy times sharing what other bits and pieces we had given us.

There was the loan of a whip and top; we'd spin it with one of Dad's borrowed leather bootlaces from his hobnail boots, or a skipping rope made from a discarded old clothesline; sometimes if neighbours were in a good mood they'd skip with us. We also played hopscotch, making the beds from pieces of slate that fell off the roof, or we drew with a piece of chalk if we were lucky enough to take a piece from the blackboard while teacher wasn't looking. And we girls made up many, many more games.

The boys would never be seen playing with the girls – they'd be called 'sissies', which often ended up in a fight. The boys found other games to play – sometimes they'd sort the ashcans over to find a Nestle[acute]'s milk tin, knock some holes in the side and tie a piece of string round it. When washdays came round they'd hide up the entry, then as soon as they saw a neighbour leave the brewhouse quickly they'd dash in, poke a few hot embers into the tin, then run off swinging it round and round their heads to keep warm.

'Tip Cat' was another game, but this seemed to fade out, as the lads got many a belting for breaking windows. Another game I remember them playing was football, but as they couldn't afford to buy a ball they would sneak into the dry closets, tear the newspaper (we called it bum paper) off the backs of the doors, soak it well, and when it was rolled into a hard ball tied with string, this was their football.

Often there was no more bum paper for people, so when they were caught short they took their own with them. Therefore the lads would search in other people's closets, or go to the rag-and-bone yard and beg for pieces of old strips of rag or cotton waste.

It cost us kids nothing to keep happy in those days. Yet I believe we were happier than kids today, who only have to ask and get everything: too much, too soon.

During the hot summer days we would dig up hot pitch beneath the cobblestones or the wooden blocks between the tramlines, roll it into balls and play five stones (jack stones they were often called).

Some of the worst times were our punishments with the cane, but we were used to the cane and expected it. But we never learnt our lesson; we were as bad as ever when the pitch wore off our hands.

There are many reasons why I like to stroll down Memory Lane: hoping to see some of the old haunts I used to visit, hoping also that I might meet some of the people I grew up with who still remember those days and the streets where we used to linger, thinking about our tomorrows and what they might bring.

One hot summer's day, during my travels, I found myself in Great Hampton Street, and as I came to Snape's the chemist's (that was) I stood looking up at the old sign hanging from its rusty hinges. I remembered that when I was about fifteen, and thinking of the boys I used to flirt with, I often used to call in and ask Mr Snape for a penny box of carmine, a twopenny box of Phul-Nana or Shem-el-Nisim face powder, and a threepenny tablet of Erasmic soap. And for each sixpence you spent he would give you a scented card. This was to push down between your breasts to make you smell nice. But I had only small titties then, if any at all, so I used to tear the scented card into two pieces and slip them down each leg of my drawers – or passion-killers, the boys used to call them, because they had elastic round the bottoms.

Many a time, when I couldn't afford to buy these so-called luxuries, I used to lift one of Mum's pictures from the wall, spit on my fingers and rub one of the red roses from the wallpaper into my cheeks and lips.

As I walked along, I came to Hockley Street. I was now very thirsty. I knew there used to be a little café once, but it was no longer there. I looked around for somewhere to have a cup of tea, then I decided to go into the Jeweller's Arms pub and a have a shandy.

This pub is still there today, on the corner of Hockley Street and Spencer Street, facing the small factory where I first started my enamelling business in 1931. It was crowded with young men and women factory workers having their lunch break.

The noise was deafening from the customers' chatter above the noise from the jukebox. But I managed to find my way to the bar, and while I ordered my pint of shandy I saw two elderly men staring across at me. I found a seat and ignored them. As they smiled across at me for the second time, I heard one of them call above the noise, 'You go over an' ask her, Harry.'

I felt everybody's eyes were now on me. My first thoughts were did they think I was a pick-up? Surely not – I was far too old; but you never know in this day and age!

I didn't wait to find out. I drank the rest of my shandy and left hurriedly.

I got only halfway down the street when I noticed they were close behind me. Quickly I turned round and asked why they were following me. All at once the taller one said, 'Excuse me, but we believe we know you.'

'But I don't know who *you* both are, and if you follow me any further, I shall call that policeman standing over there!' I replied angrily, pointing across the street.

Suddenly they both began to smile, so I cried, 'Well, if you say you know me, I'd be pleased to hear what you have to say!'

'We're sorry to have upset you, dear, but we want to know if your name is Mrs Flood, that used to live down Camden Drive.'

'Yes,' I replied. 'I'm the same woman that lived there, but who are you?'

'Don't you remember us? When we lived in the end house in your same yard?'

I couldn't believe my eyes, and as I stood staring up and down at these two well-dressed men, the taller one said, 'We're Harry and Joe Taylor, the twins you used to look after for me mum, when we all went hop-picking.'

'Well, well, I would never have known you. You're both

grown-up, and handsome too. The last time I saw you, you were both trying to sell fishboxes for firewood in a basket carriage. That must have been before the war.'

'We done better than that, Kate . . . er, Mrs Flood . . .'

'You can call me Kate,' I replied, smiling up at him, for they were two handsome, well-dressed men – nothing like the twins I knew when I was a young woman. 'Wonderful to meet you, and how you been doing?' I asked.

'We saved every farthin' we earned and later we bought an old horse and cart off Kinver, you remember old Skinflint Kinver, Kate, the one who kept the old stinking stables at the end of Camden Street.'

'Yes, Joe,' I replied. 'That must be the one who lent my granny the nag and cart when she left our house.'

'Kate,' Harry said, 'would you mind coming back to have a drink with us – we've only half an hour to spare and there's lots we'd like to talk about.'

'I don't think I'd like to go back there, everybody will stare and get the wrong impression, if yer know what I mean,' I replied, smiling.

'I see what yer mean; we'll go in the smoke room, where it's quieter,' Harry replied as he grinned and squeezed my hand.

How very happy I felt that day when we sat together in that smoke room!

Joe bought me a milk stout and Harry and Joe had a pint of mild and bitter each, and while we were drinking they asked if I would like a cigarette.

'I'm trying to give them up, but I'll have one today.'

'Where are you living now, Kate, not still around this old district?' Joe asked.

'No, Joe, I'm living in Handsworth with my family; you must come and visit us sometime.'

'Thank you, Kate, but I don't know when it will be. You see, we travel a lot.'

'Yes,' Harry replied. 'But we'll keep in touch.'

'What do you do, if you don't mind me asking?' I said.

'We travel the markets, Kate, going from town to town, and we're doing well. But we're honest,' they both replied, grinning at me.

'I'm pleased to hear you're both doing well, and I hope you'll always be honest. Anyhow, both, it's better than chopping up fishboxes and trying to sell them for firewood.'

'We dain't do too bad at that. We saved our little nest egg an' put it in the post office savings bank, and left it there when me and me brother went into the army. So when we was demobbed we had a few quid to start us off.'

'I'm so happy for you both,' I replied. 'But may I give you both a word of advice? Never be ashamed of your past, or who you are, or where you come from,' I added.

'We'll *never* be that, Kate. My mum always used to tell us that. And how kind you was to us, before she died in the bombing.'

'It was sad, too,' Joe replied, 'to come back from the war to hear our neighbours and your mum and sister was killed that same night.'

'Let's change the subject,' Harry replied, looking rather sad. 'What brings you around this district, Kate?' he added.

'I like to take a stroll around these old places where we were dragged up and to reminisce, hoping to find some of the people I used to know around this district, and you're the first two I've been happy to meet. You see,' I added, 'the reason for this is, I've written three books about the story of my life, and about the people who tried to exist in those days, and now I'm giving talks to schoolchildren and elderly people in homes and community centres, hoping to meet someone I know.'

'Have you mentioned *us* in your books, Kate?' they asked, like a couple of excited kids.

'I sure have, there's pages of you and all the people who lived in that bughole Camden Drive. *And* when we all went hop-picking – you were both only about three or four years old then – and I remember at my sister's wedding, you got lost and we found you in the brewhouse copper, draining the empty whisky bottles.'

Suddenly they burst out laughing. 'We don't remember that. Was we drunk?'

'I don't know about you being drunk,' I smiled, 'but you was too tiddly to be lifted out, until I called me dad.'

'But we do remember, don't we, Joe,' Harry replied, 'when our mum told us, before we went in the army, that your brother Jack stole a pig from the hop field and how your mum won her black eye.'

'Is that in the books, too?' Joe asked.

'Yes, Joe,' I replied. 'It's all there in black and white. There's photos, too, of the families and where we lived, and all the kids in the back yards.'

'What are they called?'

'The first one with the photos in is called *Her People*. The second one is called *Where There's Life*, and the third one is called *All My Days*.'

'We sure will get them, Harry,' said Joe. 'I'm sorry we have to be leaving now, and it's been lovely meeting you again, Kate, love, but we have a train to catch.'

'It's been lovely meeting you two, too, after so many long years. But I was thinking you could come home with me and meet my family, and have a good old chat about those old days. Perhaps another time.'

'I don't know about that, Kate. We're planning to make our home in Australia as soon as we sell everything. But we will certainly get your books to read, and will come and visit you before we go, and write to yer.'

I felt rather sad having to say goodbye to them, and as I was writing my address for them I felt I would never see them again, but as they both promised to write, I hoped they wouldn't forget. As we walked outside the Jeweller's Arms I shook hands with them both, when Joe said, 'Do yer mind, Kate, if we both kiss yer?'

As I held up my face, they both hugged and kissed me full on my lips. Every passer-by stopped to smile and stare, but I didn't feel a bit embarrassed when they both gave me an extra big hug and squeeze.

'The last time we kissed you, Kate, was when we was trying to sell the smelly herring-boxes for a living.'

How well I recalled those sad times, many years ago!

As I waved them both goodbye, my tears began to flow. They were the first two people I had met on my walks, only now to lose them again so soon. Yet I hoped they would keep their promise and that one day soon I would hear from them both, or meet them again.

Today, I am still hoping, and waiting.

My Mum

I never knew my mum's parents, yet often when she and Dad came back from the pub at night they'd sit talking by the fire. They didn't know I was in the room, so I used to hear snatches of conversation. One night I heard Mum talk about the workhouse where she was born and put into service when she was thirteen. Other times she'd say how cruel her mother had been. And I wondered if she was tainted the same, for when anyone was cruel people used to say, 'They can't help it, it's in their blood.' As a child, brought up in ignorance, this puzzled me somehow.

When I asked my brother Frankie, he said he didn't know either. Now my brother wasn't so nervous of Mum as I was, so he decided to ask her if we had any grandparents or uncles and aunts on her side. One night, as Dad and Mum came in from the pub, Frankie decided to do it then and there. As soon as they sat down, he piped up at once, 'Mum, where's our grandad an' gran'ma?'

'Why do yer wanta know that all of a sudden?' she cried.

'Well, all the other kids in the yard 'ave 'em, an' uncles an' aunts.'

Suddenly she got up out of the chair and slapped his face.

'Yo wanta know *too* much. Anyway, yo'll be none the wiser fer knowin'. Any'ow, they're in 'eaven, God rest their souls,' she added.

It would have been wiser if Frankie had left it at that, but he was sulking now. As soon as he saw Dad go upstairs, he cried, 'How do yer know they're in 'eaven, they might be in the other place stokin' up the fire fer yo.'

Suddenly Mum flew at my brother and gave him two more hard clouts across his face. 'That one's fer yer bloody cheek, an' the other's fer speakin' bad of the dead!'

Why our parents never talked to us about their parents we could never understand. When we asked any kind of question, we *should* have been told. It was always 'Yer know enough to goo on with', or 'Kids should be seen an' not 'eard.' But my brother and I, the first chances we got, we always cleared out of Mum's way, especially when things didn't go right. We had more fun and affection with our little school friends with whom we played in the side streets.

There's no climbing up a lamppost today.

Those iron posts were fun for us girls and boys, swinging a piece of rope over the iron arm that jutted out beneath the gas lamp. And if we couldn't manage to find a piece of rope, we would tie together plaited straw from empty orange-boxes and swing around backwards, forwards, backwards, forwards, ten times, then others in line took their turn. Or you would see the lads sitting on the edge of the pavement beneath the light from the street lamp, reading their swapped comics, or telling dirty stories, or skimming used tram tickets, to see who could skim the furthest.

Sometimes when our parents were out, the gas man would call to empty the pennies from the meter.

We would watch him tip the pennies on to the table and count them – sometimes there would be a penny or twopence over.

'Now give this to yer mum,' he'd say.

But this was *our* little treat – until we were found out.

I remember our gas meter was fastened to the wall, halfway down the cellar steps. I could never understand why our mum was the only one to put the pennies in the meter – other times she was too scared to go *near* the cellar. (Only by chance did I find out why.)

Some nights we would be sitting by the fire, when all at once we would see the gas light begin to flicker. Nobody would offer to go and put a penny in. But as soon as Jack, my eldest brother, came home, Mum would ask him if he could spare a penny, or sit in the dark.

'Wot, agen!' he'd cry. 'There must be summat wrong with that bloody meter. It must wait for me,' he added angrily.

'It only wants a penny in, Jack. I'll give it yer back later,' she replied.

'I've 'eard that befower! But it's funny ter me it wants feedin' wen I cum 'ome. Any'ow,' he added, 'I don't think yer gettin' enough gas for the pennies yer put in, yer betta see the gas man agen.'

'I will,' she replied. As she picked up the penny he'd slung on the table, she walked towards the cellar steps and dropped the penny in her black apron pocket. Mum knew Jack had been afraid to go down the cellar since he was bitten by a rat.

As soon as the gas flared up again she came into the room, all smiles.

Then one night, I happened to be alone in the house when all at once the light began to flicker. I knew soon I'd be in the dark and I was scared. Suddenly I thought of the rent money Mum always kept in the empty tea caddy on the mantelshelf. Quickly, I took a penny and went down to the cellar. But try as I could, I couldn't get that penny in the slot, until I heard several clicks and another penny that was already wedged in fell. I put the other penny in, then when I turned the knob again and heard it fall, I realised why Mum always went down to the meter. She'd put a penny in, turn it halfway, therefore she'd get only half the gas. Having pocketed Jack's penny, she'd finish the first penny already there.

I never told her how I found out. But that same night, as we sat round the fire, I was watching Mum looking up on the wall waiting for the gas to flicker, when all at once Jack said, 'Did yer tell the gas man about the meter, Mum?'

'No, I dain't. Why?' she replied, still glancing up at the gas mantle.

'Well, it's funny you don't ask me for a penny ternight.'

Suddenly I piped up, 'There's no need, Jack, *I've* put a penny in.'

Mum stared hard at me, daggers drawn, as she demanded, 'An' where did yer get yer penny from?'

'I was afraid to be in the dark, so I took a penny out of the tea caddy. But I couldn't get it in at first, because there was already one stuck in the slot.'

Mum never said another word, but next day she gave me a thrashing with the cane. When I asked what it was for, she said, 'That's fer tekin' a penny from the rent without askin'.'

But I wasn't all that green. I knew the real reason.

My Dad

During the whole of 1930 and even before, men talked of a war with Germany. Unemployed men who stood lounging on street corners were heard to say that if it did come they would be glad to join up, if only to get the King's shilling for a meal and a few fags. But little did they know that bad news was to come sooner than they expected. In fact, the streets and their lives would never be the same again, nor for millions of people throughout the world.

That dreaded morning came, as old men and young alike, who hadn't got the price of a pint of beer, crowded into the pub, the George and Dragon, to hear Churchill's voice over the wireless, announcing that we were at war with Germany.

'Hitler won't start on us, 'e's too scared,' old Joe Bishop cried out.

'Yer right theea, Joe me ole mate,' his friend piped up. 'The bleedin' Kaiser couldn't lick us, so wot chance 'as that bleedin' shot-up paper 'anger got?'

'But we gorra be prepared,' Billy Turner replied. 'Look what 'e's done ter Czechoslovakia, and Poland now 'e's got 'is bloody eyes on. Anyway, they ain't got nothin' ter stop 'im with, an' 'e knows it.'

'Neither 'ave we, Bill, unless our sleepy bloody government wakes up afower it's too late, an' if they don't do summat soon, we shall be in the same boat.'

'But dain't Hitler sign an agreement with old Neville Chamberlain?' Fred asked.

'Wot! A piece of paper! Wot good was that? An' now we're in it,' Billy replied.

As soon as Churchill had finished speaking, the boss of the George and Dragon, who had lost a leg in the first war, gave them all a free pint of beer.

'Drink up, me lads,' he cried out from behind the counter. 'The drinks are on the 'ouse.'

He was a jovial fellow, and as he and the barmaid pulled pint after pint, he told them, 'When yer join up, remember ter kill off a few German bastards fer me, an' yer can 'ave the loan of me wooden leg ter crack 'em with, in case yer run out of bullets. But don't forget ter bring it back,' he added.

Everybody laughed at the publican's humour. Yet little did they know that many would never see the George and Dragon again, or their cheerful landlord, for this was a war not only for men but for women and children too, and millions would lose their homes and loved ones.

I still recall those many years ago, when I was eleven, in 1914 when the First World War started. My brother Jack and my brother Charles couldn't wait for their call-up papers, like a good many lads who were unemployed. My dad too tried to enlist, but when he went to Thorp Street recruiting offices, he was told they wanted only younger men. Dad went wild. He told them he'd been a sergeant in the Boer War and knew more about the army than they would ever learn. But he did his bit to help in the war effort – he gave up chopping and selling firewood and went to work in Great Russell Street opposite St George's Church, where he worked in a casting shop making shell cases. I recall my dad had a scar about six inches long down the left side of his cheek. He never said how he got it, and we never asked. But I remember, one day, Mum telling the landlord one of the Boers gave it him, before he killed him.

I loved my dad. He was always kind and gentle, so different from my mother. I didn't grumble when she often made my brother Frankie and me take our dad's dinner to his works. When we left school at twelve o'clock, she would have a basin of stew already wrapped in a clean towel.

But Dad never let us see inside the yard where he worked, he always met us outside the wooden gates, and after taking from us the basin and the few coppers Mum supplied for his beer, he'd hand us yesterday's dirty empty basin to take back home.

'Now be off with yer or you'll be late for school,' he often used to say. But if we asked him if we could come inside the gates and watch him work, he would always reply that fumes from the sulphur would kill us.

But being two inquisitive kids, we decided that one day we would get in that yard and see for ourselves what he did.

That day came when we had a holiday, St George's Day. It was very warm, so off we went, Frankie and I, to explore. When we came to the big wooden gates, try as we might, they wouldn't budge. But as we walked away, disappointed, we spotted a horse and wagon loaded with sand. As soon as we saw the driver pull up outside those gates, we hid in St George's churchyard and waited. Soon we saw Dad open the gates wide, and in went the driver with the horse and his load. As we crept near the gates we noticed that Dad had left the driver to empty the cart. Now this was our chance. Quickly we crept into the yard and hid behind a big pile of brown sand and a mountain of coke. Soon the driver and the horse left, and as we looked around we saw that the yard was full of old wooden crates and broken riddles, and beneath the dirty iron-framed windows were three different kinds of sand – red, brown and white. And on the other side of the wall was burnt-out coke, still smouldering.

The smells were awful. I wanted to run away, but my brother pulled me back. 'No yer don't!' he managed to whisper. 'If Dad does catch us, we're in this together.' So I had to stay.

We had to wipe the dirt and sand off one of the small square panes of broken glass before we could see anything, and as we stood on a mountain of sand we managed to see inside: a long well-worn wooden bench, on one end an anvil, a large iron vice and several steel rasps. Everything was covered in sand, from the floor to the walls and ceiling. Brass castings and lumps of metal were strewn everywhere. We strained our necks to see further, but not until we noticed that a couple of the small windows were missing, so we could look through. The only other light was from a broken fanlight high up in the roof. As soon as we saw our dad at the other end of the room, we almost gave ourselves away as the smell of the fumes from the melting hot metal and sulphur wafted at us. But we still watched as he tied his muffler over his nose and mouth. He was clad only in his corduroy trousers; we saw his two large tattooed angels from the back of his neck to his waist sweating too, and as he bent over the hole in the ground, which was the furnace, we saw him grip a pair of long iron tongs and lift out what looked like a red-hot stone bucket. Beneath his feet was a wooden tray with patterns in sand, and as we watched him pour the boiling metal into the tray below, yellow, green and purple sulphur fumes wafted at us. We nearly choked. We slid down that mountain of sand and ran through the gates and into the street. We never went past those gates again. Although we still took Dad's dinner every day, he never knew we had seen him at work.

Often the doctor warned our dad about the sulphur fumes getting into his lungs. He still did his bit for his country and carried on until 1918. Then he was thrown on the scrapheap like thousands of other men as soon as the war ended, on the dole and the means test. A few years later my dad died in the Western Road Workhouse. When my daughter Jean was born, I often visited him. But sad to say, he lay in his bed, not recognising me. I often quarrelled with my mother and sisters and brothers for allowing him to die in such a horrible place.

The Mouse Trap

<hr>

My brother Frankie and I were always hungry and looked forward to going to school where each morning, before we started our lessons, we were given two slices of bread and jam and a mug of cocoa, which our parents could ill afford.

These were often supplied to all the poor children from the slum areas at St Paul's School in Camden Drive by our vicar, Canon Smith of St Paul's Church.

After leaving school at twelve o'clock, we would all rush home like little ants, hungry for our next feed, which might be scratching stew, or any other kind of food hashed up from leftovers from the days before.

My brother and I often begged for food outside the factory gates as people left. And each night before going to bed we had a piece of bread and dripping, while Mum and Dad sat down to bread and cheese and a Spanish onion.

Often our mouths would water at the very thought of it.

Dad also had his usual pint of beer, with a good head of froth on top. This was called 'The Long Pull', and in those days it cost twopence.

One night, while my mum and dad were out, my brother whispered, 'Katie, I'd luv some of that cheese.'

'An' me,' I replied. 'But Mum alwis locks it away in the chiffonier.'

'Ah, but I know 'ow ter get at it,' he replied, winking at me.

'But 'ow can yer? She keeps the key down inside 'er blouse.'

'I don't need the key, yer simply pull out the top drawer an' put yer 'and down inside an' lift the cheese out.'

'No, Frankie!' I cried. 'Mum's sure ter find out, an' if she does she'll kill us both.'

'If 'er does find out, I'll tek the blame, Katie, an' say it was me, but you'll 'ave ter put yower 'and down inside 'cause yer 'and's smaller than mine.'

I didn't feel so nervous when he said he'd take the blame.

But we didn't have the chance. Mum came back early that night. The following night, as soon as Mum and Dad were ready to go out, Mum told us to hurry ourselves and eat our bread and dripping and get off to bed. 'An' mind yer don't drop any of them crumbs on the flowa, we've got enough mice runnin' around the rooms.'

As soon as they left the house, we knew they wouldn't be back till after the George and Dragon closed at eleven o'clock. I stood and watched my brother pull out the top drawer. As he placed it on the table, he told me to feel down inside, where I'd find the chunk of cheese. After putting my hand down on to the ledge below, I just managed to lift the cheese out. As I placed it on the table, trembling all over in case Mum and Dad came home early, Frankie sorted in the drawer for a sharp knife, then carefully cut us each a thin sliver, and after I had put the rest of the cheese back, he pushed the drawer in.

This went on for three nights. Mum never said anything, so we felt safe.

Then one night, as we sat eating our meagre supper, we saw Mum unlock the chiffonier door, and as soon as she put the cheese on the table she yelled, 'Sam! You'll 'avta get me another mouse trap!'

'Yo've already got fower, wot yer want another one for?'

'Well, look at this piece of cheese! It seems ter be gooin' down very quick.'

'All right, all right,' replied Dad impatiently. 'I'll bring yer one from me work. Now let's 'ave no mower shoutin'! An' get me me supper, I'm clammed.'

While Mum was cutting the cheese and onion, I could feel her eyes on us both. Later, when I whispered to Frankie that I thought Mum knew it was us, he replied, 'Don't be daft, she still thinks the mice 'ave bin at it, any'ow she would 'ave said.'

We didn't try again until that piece of cheese had been used up. The following weekend Mum bought a larger piece, so we decided to try our luck again. But at the last moment I got scared: 'We betta not, Frankie. I've still a feelin' she knows it's us, the way she looks at us.'

''Ow can she, when she's got the key? Cum on, don't be scared, tell yer wot, we'll just 'ave a nibble around the edges an' when she sees teeth marks, she'll think the mice 'ave cum back agen.'

So out came the top drawer again and out came the cheese. I began to nibble one side and Frankie nibbled the other. But when he held the cheese and gazed at it longingly, I heard him say, 'It would be worth a beltin' from Dad to 'ave a good bite at it.'

'No, Frankie! No! Put it back, please,' I cried.

'OK. It was just a thought,' he replied, grinning at me.

Quickly I snatched the cheese from him and put it back where I'd found it. As soon as the drawer was pushed in, we went up to bed. That night I lay awake thinking he might go back downstairs and risk a thrashing by eating a lump. After hearing him get out of bed to use our makeshift bucket for a wee, I couldn't settle until I felt him crawl back to his place at the foot of the bed.

The following night we tried again, but as I felt around the ledge I began to scream – my finger was caught in a mouse trap. I pulled my hand out and ran around the room, screaming for all I was worth, with the mouse trap hanging from my finger.

'Frankie! Frankie!' I kept screaming. 'Pull it off! Pull it off!'

As soon as he released the spring I saw blood on the trap where my finger had been. After he had found a piece of rag and wrapped it, I began to weep.

'She'll know for sure now it's us, when she sees the trap,' I sobbed as my tears fell.

'Don't cry, Katie, I'll put it back an' if 'er does find out, I'll tek the blame, but try an' 'dle yer finger, an' if she does ask don't say nothink. I know wot ter say.'

Then came that Friday night, which was our bread, brimstone and black treacle night. (This was what Mum called our physic.) As we sat at the table, I tried my best to hide my finger beneath my pinafore. As soon as Mum began to open the chiffonier door, I began to tremble all over. Then I saw her throw the cheese and the trap across the table.

'Them bloody mice 'ave bin at it agen, Sam!' she yelled.

'Ain't yer caught them, then?'

'No! But wotever it was must 'ave bin caught, 'cause theeas the trap with the blood on it.'

Dad picked up his newspaper to begin reading. I wished the floor would open up and I could vanish as I saw Mum notice my finger.

'Wot yer bin up ter?' she cried.

Before I could open my mouth, Frankie said, 'It was an accident.'

'Wot yer mean, an accident?' she demanded.

'I 'it it with the 'ammer.'

Suddenly Dad glared at him over the top of his paper. 'Wot did yer say?'

'Katie was 'oldin' me fire can an' while I was knockin' a nail in the 'ammer slipped.'

'I'll knock a bloody nail in yow, me lad, if I see yer with another fire can – now get yer grub down yer! An' get up them stairs, the pair of yer!'

We didn't need telling twice.

Next day my finger began to throb and was very painful. I was too scared to tell my mum, or even show it to her, but I had to show it to someone. The only person was Mrs Taylor, our kind neighbour. I knocked on the door, and as she opened it and glanced down at that piece of filthy rag round my finger I began to weep.

'Wot's the matter, luv? Wot yer done? Yer betta cum in an' tell me.'

As she sat me down on an orange-box I cried, 'I've done a terrible thing, Mrs Taylor, an' I'm afraid me mum and dad's gooin' ter find out an' me finger's painin' me summat awful.'

'Now wipe yer eyes an' tell me all about it.'

When I told her she cried, 'Yer wicked, wicked wench! Ye'll both be punished as sure as God made little apples! Now stop yer blartin' an' let me get that filthy rag off an' see wot yo've done.'

I began to scream with pain as she tried to snatch the rag off, but the blood had dried up and it was stuck. I was ready to run out, but she held me firm, and when I'd calmed down she got some hot water and salt and after bathing the rag came off. As soon as she saw my finger all bruised and bent she suddenly exclaimed as she crossed herself, 'Mary Mother of God, the end of yer finger's broke!'

'Can yer mend it, Mrs Taylor? It's 'urtin' summat awful.'

'There ain't nothink I can do fer that! Yo'll afta go ter the 'orspital an' get it seen to.'

'Can yer cum with me, Mrs Taylor?' I pleaded. 'I'm afraid of 'orspitals an' doctors.'

'I can't, luv, I've gotta get me washin' finished ready for the pawnshop, but I'll get our Minnie ter tek yer.'

'If I goo, yer won't tell me mum what I've told yer or she'll kill me.'

'Yer poor wench, I understand. I won't say a word, now sit theea while I put a piece of clean rag on, then afta yer drink this 'ot cuppa tea I'll call me niece.'

I thanked her and waited while she went to call her niece. Minnie Taylor was twelve, two years older than me. I never had much to do with her because she was always swearing and telling lies. But I was glad she was coming with me, for I knew I was too scared to face a doctor on my own. Her aunt explained that I'd broken my finger, and I was pleased she hadn't told her how.

'Cum on, Katie, I'll tek yer, I ain't afraid of bloody doctors nor 'orspitals,' she cried as soon as her aunt was out of hearing.

We hurried up Spring Hill towards Dudley Road Hospital and came to the rusty wrought-iron gates. Minnie tried to push them open, but they were locked. Even the gates scared me. I was about to change my mind and turn back when I felt Minnie catch hold of my frock. Suddenly she pulled me towards the gates, just as a very tall elderly man dressed in a long white gown, looking very stern and forbidding, came down the path. As he made his way towards the gates he bawled out, 'Wot yo two kids want?'

I was too scared to answer, but I knew Minnie was scared of no one. She shouted through the bars, 'It's me friend 'ere, Katie. I've brought 'er ter see yer, Doctor.'

'I ain't a doctor! I'm the lodge-keeper. An' yer can't cum in 'ere!' he snapped.

'But we've cum a lung way, so yer betta open these gates an' let us in, 'cause me friend 'as broke 'er finger and the doctor's gotta mend it.'

'Yer can't cum in 'ere unless yer mother brings yer.'

'But I ain't got a muvver,' she replied.

'Well, tell yer friend ter tell '*er* mother ter cum.'

'She ain't got a muvver either,' she lied. 'So yo'll 'ave ter let us in.'

'Not until an adult cums with yer.'

'Adult? Adult? Wot's them?' shouted Minnie.

'Yo'll soon find out when I open these gates an' clout yer bleedin' 'ear'oles, now bugger orf the pair of yer!'

As soon as I saw him start fumbling for his keys, I was ready to run, but Minnie stayed to give him a bit more cheek. 'Bugger orf yerself, yer miserable old bleeda!' she yelled as she stopped to put her tongue out at him. We saw him put the key into the lock. We ran as fast as we could.

As soon as we got as far as Icknield Street we stopped to get our breath, and I managed to say, 'Minnie, yer shouldn't 'ave told 'im we ain't got a muvver. Wot if 'e finds out?'

'I don't care, but I 'ad ter tell 'im summat 'opin' 'e'd let us in.'

When Minnie told her aunt what had happened, she gave her a piece of bread pudding and told her that her mother was waiting for her. As soon as Minnie had closed the door behind her, Mrs Taylor said, 'Never mind Katie, luv, it'll 'eal up in time an' if you'll cum in every day after yer leave school I'll bathe and dress it for yer.'

After I had thanked her, I left to go home. As soon as Frankie saw me he asked how my finger was. I told him it seemed a bit better now Mrs Taylor had treated it. Suddenly he yelled, 'Yer dain't tell 'er wot 'appened, did yer?'

'Yes, Frankie, I 'ad to,' I replied, as tears ran down my cheeks.

'Now it'll be all over the street, an' Mum an' Dad will 'ear about it.'

'Nobody will know, she's promised not to tell anyone,' I whimpered.

I was glad I hadn't told him about Minnie and the hospital.

'Well, if they do find out I'll say it was only me, now wipe yer tears and let's go ter the rec and play Tip Cat.'

That following Monday morning while I was at school my teacher noticed the rag on my finger. When she asked what I'd done I replied, 'I think I've broke me finger, Miss.'

'Well, you'd better have a note and have it treated at the clinic,' she replied impatiently.

That afternoon I went reluctantly to the school clinic in Great Charles Street. This was where children went with all sorts of complaints, even to have their heads shaved for lice. But when I got to the door and saw a woman coming out holding a bloody rag to a little boy's mouth, my courage failed me. I turned back, and as I came down Great Hampton Street I called at Snape's the chemist's. With the few pennies I'd got hidden down my stocking I went up to the counter and asked for a finger bandage and some lint. While Mr Snape turned his back to reach down a box, I quickly pulled up the three pennies. 'That'll be fourpence,' he said.

'But I only got threepence, can I bring yer the other penny next week?'

'Sorry, me dear, I'll 'ave ter cut the lint in half,' he replied.

As soon as I got home I hid the lint and bandage until I was alone. Each night I bathed my finger in salt water, then wrapped it.

My teacher, glad to say, never questioned me when she saw my finger wrapped in a clean bandage.

As I grew older I was no longer scared of my mum. I remember the day I was eighteen – I thought now was the best time to tell her how Frankie and I stole the cheese. Imagine my surprise when she said, 'I knew it was yow two.'

'Yer knew? All them many years ago? An' yer never said a word?'

'No! Because I set the trap fer yer, an' thought you'd bin punished enough. Now you've got the end of yer finger broke ter prove it.'

Ever since I can remember my mother and I were never very close, but after she told me about that night I wondered how cruel she could be.

Often, when I'm trimming that fingernail, I remember how that mouse trap clung to it.

hundredweight of coal in a trolley, or going to the butcher's for
three ha'porth of bits (scraps of meat), or to the grocer's for two

My Grandma

M y Grandma Hannah was an eccentric, lonely old woman,
poor but very proud. She lived in a tumbledown old house
like ours. Although she was well known in and around the district,
she would never have anything to do with the neighbours. She
hated gossiping tongues.

Often she could be seen and heard smacking her lips as she sucked
a lozenge drop, or a pear drop, on her toothless gums. She knew,
too, how many were in a two-ounce paper cone. When she sent me
to the little sweet shop she always counted them, and gave me one.
'That's for bein' honest,' she would say.

Once or twice a week, she would be seen in her well-worn old
Salvation Army uniform and bonnet, shuffling towards our local
mission hall. Other times she would be wearing her old black alpaca
frock – which had seen better days and always swept the pavement
– with a black bonnet and knitted shawl. On her feet she wore
elastic-sided boots.

Apart from her uniform, I never saw her wear anything but black,
and she always carried a strong crooked stick. Many of the kids
from my school often called her an old witch, but if she happened
to hear them she'd curse and threaten them with the stick. God
knows what she would have done if she had caught one of them, for
she feared no one.

Whenever I saw or heard any of the kids shout after her, I would
await my opportunity and as soon as I saw my chance I would fight
like an alley cat. But sometimes I got the worst of these battles, for
I had my mum to contend with as well.

But she was my granny and I loved her. Many times when my
mum wanted me out of the way I used to go to Granny's and
run her errands and do little jobs, like fetching a quarter of a

hundredweight of coal in a trolley, or going to the butcher's for three pennyworth of bits (scrag ends), or to the grocer's for two pennyworth of bacon bones.

'An' tell 'im not ter shave all the bacon off the bones,' she used to say.

She was stubborn, too, and very seldom paid her rent. One day I happened to be there when the rent man knocked on the door, and as she made her way towards the stairs she whispered, 'Tell 'im ter call next wick an' I'll 'ave summat for 'im then.'

I don't know whether he saw her through a wide crack in the door, but as I gave the message he called out, 'And see that yer do, or it's the last chance!'

But Granny was not on her own – several neighbours got into arrears too. The rent in those days, during and before the 1914 war, was only 3s. 6d. a week, and if they couldn't pay something off the arrears, many had the bailiffs. Often I'd seen people bolt their doors on the inside and lie quiet until they passed. But at the first chance, the bailiffs would take off the door and carry it away.

I remember one bitterly cold foggy night, our door was taken away and my dad nailed up a piece of sacking, and when my brother Jack came home on leave he mistook it for the door and fell head first into the room, kit bag and all.

Later, Mum managed to make a bundle for the pawnshop, and with a loan from my married sister the door was soon back on again. But some were luckier than others – they did a moonlight flit. It often used to surprise me that my granny never lost her door; she was even more stubborn than my mum.

Whenever any bills were pushed under her door, she would tear them up and throw them in the dustbin. Other bills she would roll together and lay in the fender ready to put under the wood sticks to light the fire, and if some were soft paper she would fold them away, for her bum paper. She never wasted anything.

Sometimes on my school holidays I'd go and run her errands and sweep and dust the old well-worn furniture, which she didn't have much of. Often, I would see a mouse scurry down a hole in the wainscot. But I was never afraid of them, neither was my granny, for I was used to seeing both mice and rats, and many times I got into trouble when I put a few crumbs down by the hole.

One Friday afternoon I came home from school with a rash on

my face and arms. I couldn't stop my nose running, and I was feeling sick. No one was at home, so I made my way to my granny's house. As soon as she saw me she cried, 'Wipe your snotty nose!' I wiped it with a piece of rag she pushed towards me. But when she took a second look she asked, ''Ow long 'ave yer 'ad that rash on yer face?'

'Since yesterday, Granny,' I replied.

''As yer mum seen it?'

'Yes, she said it's a cold I've got.'

'Don't look like a cold ter me!' she answered. 'Anyway,' she added, 'yer betta come over by the winda where I can see yer betta.'

As I stood in the light, she told me, 'Pull yer frock up an' tek yer drawers down, while I 'ave a good look at yer.' After inspecting my bum, and then my back, she turned me round to inspect my belly. Suddenly she tut-tutted and announced, 'I thought as much! You've got German measles,' and as I began to cry she said, 'You can't goo back 'ome now in this cold night air, yer betta stay 'ere in the warm where I can keep me eye on yer.'

'But Mum will be wonderin' where I am,' I replied.

'If I know anythink about yer mum, she won't care, as lung as she knows I'm lookin' after yer. Now cum on, wipe yer nose, yer stayin' 'ere!'

I'd never stayed at my granny's for more than a couple of hours when I helped her and ran her errands, so I looked forward to staying. She made me a makeshift bed on an old horsehair sofa she kept in her bedroom.

After lighting the fire in the old iron grate, she gave me a cup of watered-down warm milk, covered me over with an old grey blanket, and as she tucked it round me she said, 'Now yo'll be all right. I shan't be lung, I'm gooin' ter the chemist an' get yer some saffron tea, then I'll call an' tell yer mum where yo are.'

That small bedroom became very warm; I quickly fell asleep, but soon I was awakened by my mum prodding me.

'Cum on! I knew I'd find yer 'ere! An' wot's them spots on yer face?' she added.

'Granny says I got German measles,' I managed to say as tears fell.

'Well, yer betta get dressed an' cum 'ome, an' I'll get the doctor.' Just then, Granny walked in.

'Yo'll leave 'er where 'er is, Polly! Yer wanta kill the child? Yo ain't tekin' 'er out of 'ere in this cold night air!'

'Very well,' I heard Mum reply as she went down the stairs, 'but if anythink 'appens to 'er I won't be responsible. Yer know yer spoilin' 'er,' she added.

'She'll be betta looked after in my care than in yowen!' I heard Granny reply before the door slammed.

During the day, Granny put a paper blind up to the window to keep the light from my eyes, and that half-light I had to contend with until I was better, except at night when she lit a piece of candle. Ever since I can remember I was always a nervous child with a very vivid imagination and, being undernourished, I wept at the least thing.

As I began to feel better and saw the rash was disappearing, I told her I wanted to go home and back to school.

Suddenly she stared hard at me. 'Yo ain't fit enough yet!' she snapped. 'Any'ow, we'll see wot the docta ses when 'e come!'

I could see she was angry as she added, 'Ain't I looked afta yer betta than yer mum?'

'Yes, Granny, but I'm missing my schooling,' I replied as the tears began to fall.

'Now, I don't want any blartin'! If you'll promise to lie quiet I'll tell yer some funny stories.'

I loved her when she didn't lose her temper with me, but she had changeable moods, like Mum.

Often when she sat on her bed facing me, telling me fairy stories, I would fall asleep. One night I asked her if she remembered her mum, when she was a little girl.

She replied, 'It's a lung story, Katie luv; when yer older I'll tell yer.'

'But didn't you ever go ter school?' I asked, for I knew she couldn't read or write.

'No,' she replied. 'I 'ad ter goo into service. Now goo ter sleep.'

But one night she did tell me that her mother used to hide her away in the attic when she heard the Mormons were about.

When I asked her to explain why, she said, 'They carried little girls away and took 'em ter Salt Lake City.'

I was just about to ask more questions when she shuffled her way down the stairs to make my nightly cocoa.

She seemed to be such a long time coming back that I wondered if she'd gone out and left me alone – everything seemed so quiet, and I was scared as I watched the flickering light of the candle making ghostly shadows on the bare whitewashed walls. My imagination got the better of me. Just as that small piece of candle burnt itself out, I began to scream.

As soon as Granny came into the room, she yelled, 'Now wot's the matter with yer?'

'The candle's gone out an' I thought you'd left me,' I whimpered. When she had lit another piece, she glared down at me.

''Ere's yer cocoa!' she cried as she slopped the cup down on the chair beside the sofa. 'Now,' she added, 'I want no mower silly screamin'! An' don't be such a big babby!'

As soon as I had finished drinking the cocoa she took the lighted candle, and as she shuffled her way towards the stairs I became scared of the dark again, but when I asked her to leave the candle she grew angrier.

'I ain't leavin' no light!' she shouted. 'Yo've slept in the dark befower, now get ter sleep!'

'But I'm frightened of the dark now, Granny, please leave the candle,' I pleaded.

'No, and I mean no!' she yelled over her shoulder. 'An' if yer don't lie down now, the bogey man will come an' get yer!'

That was the worst thing she could have yelled at me. When I heard her footsteps on the stairs, I covered my head with the old grey blanket and cried myself to sleep.

As soon as I was well again, I went back home and the next day I started back to school. But I never forgot my granny's warning – it was still there in the back of my mind. I wasn't afraid when I was back home, where I slept with my sister and brother. Nevertheless, I was still afraid to be out in the street when it was dark.

One afternoon, my mum sent me to the corner shop for two pennyworth of jam in a cup.

'An' 'urry yerself afower it gets dark,' I remember her saying.

I crossed the horse-road and entered the shop. Several women were waiting to be served. I knew that by the time it was my turn it would be dark. Boldly I walked up to the counter and asked Mr Baker to serve me.

'Yo wait yer turn! Any'ow, wot yer want?' he cried out for all to hear.

'Me mum wants two pennorth of jam,' I replied as I handed him the cup.

'Well, yer can goo back an' tell yer mum I don't run me shop on 'er two pennorths.'

Just as I was about to leave, one kind woman said I could take her turn. Although the others at the back began to sniff and grumble, the woman ignored them. But there were still two women to be served before me. As soon as it was my turn, Mr Baker stopped to light the gas jet on the wall. I knew now it must be getting dark outside. I began to get nervous. He took my cup and weighed it, then spooned the jam in from a large crock jar. As he took the twopence he cried, "'Ere's yer jam! An' tell yer mother this is the last two pennorth she'll get from 'ere until she pays some off the strap book!'

'Skinny old skinflint!' I thought. If only I'd been older, I would have told him where he could stick his jam.

When I got into the street it was nearly dark, so I began to hurry. Just as I turned the corner, I had the fright of my life as I came face to face with a black man. Suddenly, I thought this was the bogey man my granny had warned me about, for I'd never seen a black man before. I screamed, dropped the cup and ran for my life.

As I fell indoors, Mum wanted to know what was wrong.

'Mum, Mum, Mum,' I kept repeating. 'I've just seen the bogey man!'

'Wot yer mean, yer seen a bogey man?' she exclaimed.

'I *did*, an' 'e was black all over, an' 'e grinned at me!'

I could see she didn't believe me.

'But where's the jam I sent yer for?'

'I dropped it in the horse-road, and ran,' I replied, beginning to weep.

She still wouldn't believe me, until she took me back to the shop. But when we got there, we both saw the remains of the broken cup and two mongrel dogs licking the jam.

I was put to bed that night with a caning, and no piece of bread and jam.

That was the first black man I'd ever seen.

After school hours I still visited my granny and ran her errands, but I *never* stayed until it was dark. Although she was a funny old gran

– she made me both laugh and cry – I loved her at times. But when I was about ten years old she died. Often I wept, thinking only of the kindness and understanding she *tried* to give me.

I still think of her today and tell my great-grandchildren about her, and of some of the stories she used to tell me.

Scriptures and Safety Pins

---◦◦◦◦---

O ur living-room, like many rooms in our district, was not even large enough to swing a cat. So in very warm weather my mum, like the rest of the neighbours, would bring out one of the old backless wooden chairs, and peel and scrape potatoes into the tin bowl. These potatoes were a luxury for Sunday dinner. Other days we had fried leftovers. Some Sundays she would make believe she had a joint of meat to carve. She would bring out the carving knife and sing at the top of her voice for all the neighbours to come out and see her sharpening the knife on the window-ledge. Over the years that sandstone window-ledge, as well as the step, looked more and more like a half moon.

Mum would buy the cheapest and smallest potatoes she could find. She always said they stretched further, but many were too small even to scrape. They were tipped into a bucket of water, where I had the job of swishing them around with a broken brick until the skin came partly off, and whatever didn't come off they were put in the pot to cook. Also in warm weather, Mum would sit outside on the step shelling the peas. Once, and only once, did I sit on that step beside her, but when she caught me pushing a few peas into my mouth she knocked me flying.

Another time, she said I could have a few empty shells. Others she saved to put on the back of the fire. Nothing was ever wasted in our house. Those pods tasted delicious after you took the outer skin off, and some I saved.

Getting a piece of string and making a line tied from the lamppost to the tap, I hung each pea shell. Then I'd call out, several times, 'Pin a pick, pin a pick, one pod for a pin, and two for a safety pin.' Kids would find pins from somewhere and pick the ones they fancied.

Another time I would cut pictures from newspapers. I had a craze for saving pins, hairpins too, but I found that other kids had the same idea. So *that* didn't go down too well – until one day I stood on the orange-box from the corner of the attic and climbed into the loft, where I found lots of odds and ends. But there was nothing of any use, until I spotted a large old book covered in dust. When I blew the dust off, I saw it was a Bible. As I mooched around on my hands and knees, I came across a coloured picture book. This too was thick with dust. I knew my mum always threw unwanted rubbish in the loft, yet I couldn't ever remember seeing these before. I hid them under my bed. The first opportunity I had to be alone, I cut out all the coloured pictures and placed each one inside the pages of the Bible. I didn't have enough to fill each page.

Next day was Saturday, and while Mum and Dad were shopping in the Bull Ring, I took the old backless wooden chair outside. As soon as I was sitting down with the heavy Bible on my lap I began to cry out, 'Pin a pick . . . come and pick yer own coloured picture. Two for a safety pin.'

Soon there were several kids with their pins trying their luck – one brought a hairpin and another even brought me a hatpin.

Those who drew a blank were unlucky, but I'd let them have two tries. If they failed again, I would show them which page to stick the pin in to save any squabbles. That day I was doing a roaring trade. I had quite a large cocoa tin full – until little Rosie Pumfry, who lived opposite, came running towards me holding two safety pins up in the air. She was about eight, three years younger than me, very small but very podgy, with little red fat cheeks and corn-coloured hair. She was an only child.

As soon as I took the pins and showed her where the pictures lay, she ran down the yard as if someone would stop and take them from her. She had been gone only a few minutes when I saw her mum dragging young Rosie towards me. She was trying to stop her ragged drawers from falling down. I guessed then where the two safety pins had come from. As she came near me she yelled, 'Now, you can just give me back them safety pins befower I clout yer bleedin' ear'ole.' I was often scared of this hard-faced little woman, but I found enough courage to say, 'Well, Mrs Pumfry, yer can 'ave yer pins back if yer give me me pictures back.'

'I put 'em on the fire, an' I ain't gooin' from 'ere till I get my pins,' she yelled.

I was really scared now, and I knew that all the kids were gathing around to see what was going to happen. But someone must have run to tell my mum. As soon as she came and saw the commotion, and heard what was going on, she called all the kids together, then tipped the full tin of pins on the floor. I began to cry when she told them to help themselves. Suddenly there was a free-for-all as the pins began to vanish. Then, as my mum handed two safety pins to Mrs Pumfry, I saw her drag little Rosie home, with her dirty drawers falling about her ankles as she wept.

Some of the kids laughed and pulled faces as Mum snatched up the Bible and dragged me indoors. As soon as she had slammed the door she threw the Bible on the table, then flung me across the room. 'Werd yer gettit?' she yelled.

'I found it in the loft, Mum,' I managed to answer.

'You tellin' the truth?' she replied, glaring at me.

'Yes, Mum.'

'Whose is it, do yer know?'

'No, Mum, I don't know whose it is.'

'Um, could be yer granny's, 'er was always 'idin' things away from me, but if it is, she's gooin' ter haunt yer for stickin' pins in that Bible.'

Suddenly I shouted loudly, 'But I dain't stick pins in it!'

'Don't yer dare raise yer bloody voice ter me, yer cheeky little varmint!' she yelled as she slapped my face. 'An' now, yer can get that chair in what yo've left outside, an' yer can tell them pin-pinchers what's listenin' outside me dower if they don't clear off, I'll be cummin' out an' chuck a bucket of water over 'em, an' it won't be only dirty water I'll be chuckin', either!'

They must have heard the warning. As soon as I opened the door they fled.

As I pushed that old wooden chair under the table, she began to bawl again: 'Now! Yer can goo an' put that Bible back where yer said yer found it, till I'm ready ter call yer down! An' yer can stop yer blartin'.'

As I turned to go up the stairs, she caught me putting my tongue out. She was ready to hit me again, but I was too quick. Before her hand came down, I snatched the Bible and fled up the stairs before she could grab me. But I knew I'd get my punishment later, even if it was several days later – she never forgot.

After I had put the Bible back in the loft, I lay down on the flock mattress and cried myself to sleep. I didn't even feel my sister Liza get in beside me. But when morning came and we were on our way to school, Liza asked me why I'd been crying in my sleep. When I told her what had happened she said, 'I knew it was Gran's Bible, she told me to 'ide it away before she died.'

'But why did she want to 'ide it away?' I asked.

''Cause me mum always 'ated seein' anythink of me gran's lyin' about.'

'But why would Mum wanta get rid of it?'

'Yer don't know our mum, Katie. But yer gotta lot ter learn yet afower yer much older.'

How true! I remembered those words in the years ahead.

Rosie

Mrs Pumfry was a small woman in her mid-forties. Her greying hair was always pulled tightly over her ears and set in a bun in the nape of her neck. Her small dark eyes seemed always to stare out from her angular features and her thin lips drooped down at the corners, which made her look discontented and older than her years.

Whenever I happened to see her out in the yard, I would run back into the house and hide, for I was afraid of her since taking the two precious safety pins from Rosie.

But I hid once too often. When Mum asked me what was wrong I told her why I was afraid and what Mrs Pumfry might do to me.

'No need ter be afraid of 'er!' she exclaimed. ''Er bark's worse than 'er bite, so the best thing yer can do is ter knock on the dower an' say 'ow sorry yer are.'

As I stood wondering whether to go or not, Mum yelled as she pushed me outside, 'Goo on! An' do as yer told!'

When I knocked on the door, there was no answer. I was relieved in one way, but I knew that I had to get my message over. Quickly I knocked again – still no answer – but as I walked away I looked across the yard and saw Mrs Pumfry in the brewhouse, standing over the copper stirring the clothes over with the wooden boiler stick. As soon as she put the stick down in the sink she turned round, and as she wiped the hot steam from her face I blurted out quickly, 'Mrs Pumfry, I'm sorry I took those two safety pins off Rosie, but I didn;t know they 'eld 'er drawers up.'

'No 'arm done, love,' she replied. 'But if you would like to 'elp me with the wringer . . .'

I knew now I was forgiven. I also helped her to peg the washing out on the line across the yard.

Mum never asked if I'd given her the message, but later I told her

597

that Mrs Pumfry said I could call for Rosie any time. But whenever I did call, I could never understand why her mother always made me wait outside. Never once did she ask me in, nor any of her neighbours. They used to say she was stuck up because she owned a piano, yet no one ever heard it played. (People were lucky if they owned an old gramophone.) Plenty of gossip went around – people would say she wasn't married, a spinster left on the shelf with Rosie. But whatever she was she always ignored everyone, whether she heard them or not.

She went to church on Sunday mornings and evenings and sometimes of an afternoon to prayer meetings, and during these times Rosie was left alone to play with us children in the yard. This gave scope for more gossip. Talk went on – she must be meeting a 'fancy man'. Although there were plenty of Peeping Toms looking through their curtains, no one ever saw her bring anyone to the house.

One chilly afternoon I saw Rosie sitting on the doorstep crying. When I asked her why, she replied, 'I forgot to say me prayers last night an' me mum punished me.'

'Never mind, you go inside an' get warm, an' if yer want me to I'll come in an' stay with yer till yer mum comes 'ome.'

She stood up, nodded and wiped her eyes on her sleeve. I took hold of her hand and as we stepped inside, I realised that in all the three years they had lived there this was the first time I had entered her home. At once I noticed it was almost dark inside. The gas was going out.

'Do yer 'ave a penny for the meter?' I asked.

'Yes,' she replied. 'Me mum always leaves one on the shelf.'

After putting the penny in the meter, we came up the cellar steps into the living-room. I was surprised to see what a nice tidy room it was – not like our room, all cluttered up with everything in the wrong place. I noticed too that everything was old and well worn, but clean and highly polished. But what caught my eye most was the old piano against the wall facing the door. It had a roll-top lid, and two iron candle brackets jutting out from each side of the wooden music frame, and on the back of these was fretwork with faded red satin showing through. Also two rusty pedals. But for all that, I wished that I owned it. There was a piano stool beneath with an embroidered top, also faded and old.

'Does your mum play it?' I asked as I stared at it.

'No,' Rosie replied. 'She only opens it to dust and polish it.'

'Don't you play it neither?'

'No, I don't know 'ow to, any'ow Mum won't let me, even if I wanted to. She always keeps it locked.'

'But why does she keep it if it's never played?'

'She says she wouldn't part with it because it belonged to me Granny Pumfry. 'Ave you gotta piano?'

'No, we've only got an old gramophone with a brass trumpet. But that belongs to me brother Jack. 'E won't let us play it neither. But more often than not it's in the pawnshop, and Jack always carries the needles with him, and the sound-box. One day while he was out he forgot to take the soundbox. I looked everywhere for a needle, even a used one, but he must have put those away too. I was alone in the house, so I decided to get the chopper and chop a darning needle in two. With a bit of a struggle, Rosie, the needle snapped in two, so I put one half up the soundbox. I placed the soundbox on the record and as I turned the 'andle it gave a couple of moans and then the needle snapped and the soundbox fell on my brother's favourite record and cracked it. Me mum must 'ave been upstairs. Suddenly she came flying down. There was no time for me to run, so I got a walloping, and another when my brother Jack saw his favourite record in three pieces. After that, he always carried the handle and the soundbox with him, even if he was only going to the closet, to work, or out late at night, tomcatting.'

At that we both began to see the funny side and laughed together.

'But me and the rest of the kids in the street have lots of laughs when we put tissue paper over a comb and hold it to our lips and hum a tune. Sometimes we can't stop laughing when it tickles. We call it a jew's-harp,' I added.

The real jew's-harp is five thin bits of wire stretched across a small piece of plywood which cost threepence, which we couldn't afford, so that was our next best thing.

I left before Rosie's mum came home, but Rosie promised me she would try and find the key, then she would open the piano up and I could play.

One afternoon I was teaching her to play hopscotch, when all at once she stopped in the middle of the game and told me where her mother had hidden the piano key.

'Would yer like ter come and play a tune on it?' she asked.

'I'd love to, but what if yer mum comes 'ome and catches us?'

'She won't be back till five o'clock,' replied Rosie.

When we entered there was a bright fire glowing in the well black-leaded iron grate, and the kettle was already singing on the hob.

As soon as Rosie turned the key in the lock the piano lid rolled back with a few squeaks. But I was disappointed to see not black and white ivory keys but instead, staring at me, old and broken keys yellowed with age, like an old man's discoloured teeth – some missing too. But so as not to be too disappointed, I tried my one-finger exercise, 'God Save the King'. It was then that I realised also that some of the keys were dead, but after trying further up the scale I managed to finish part of the tune. When Rosie asked if I could play something else, I said I'd never had the chance. 'But I could if I 'ad plenty of practice,' I added.

'Well, if you'll come an' stay with me when me mum goes out you'd be able ter come an' practise.'

I'd always wanted to play a piano ever since my mum parted with the harmonium, but as this was now the only thing I could practise on I felt delighted. Each time the opportunity arose, I would go and play it while Rosie stood by to watch.

It wasn't long before I could play our national anthem with both hands.

Rosie and I were delighted, although it sounded out of key at times. Oh, if only some of the notes weren't missing – I'm sure it would have sounded better. Rosie made sure to lock it up and put the key back where she had found it, until the next time.

One Saturday afternoon I was very surprised when Rosie's mum knocked on our door and asked to see my mum. I was scared. Had she found out about me going into her house and opening up the piano? Guiltily I tried to hide, but it was too late. Mum had already called her in.

'Mrs Greenhill,' I heard her say, 'I was wondering if you could keep an eye on my Rosie for me. You see I 'ave to go to my brother's funeral today and I won't be back till about six o'clock.'

'Anything to oblige. Any'ow, Katie's 'ere, she'll keep 'er eye on 'er as well.'

After she'd gone, Mum said, 'Blimey, that's one out of the book.

Fancy 'er comin' ter ask me. Anyway, Katie, you can both 'elp me in the brew'ouse an' after that I don't see why yer can't both go to number fifteen and wait until 'er mum comes 'ome. An' then yer can tell me all about what 'er's got, an' that piana the kids are talkin' about.'

After we had helped Mum we left to go out to play, and Rosie suggested I should go and have more practice. There was still a good two hours before Mrs Pumfry was due home, so we had plenty of time. But when we got indoors Rosie couldn't find the key anywhere. We tried prising the lid open with a knife, but when the knife snapped that was the end of that. Suddenly I thought about the bunch of keys, all sizes, me dad kept in his toolbox, so while everyone was out I sneaked in and helped myself. I tried and tried every one, but none would fit. In the meantime Rosie was still sorting the drawer over where she last put it, then all at once I heard her cry out, "Ere it is, it was right at the back of the drawer beneath the knives an' forks.'

While I ran back home to put the keys back she already had the old piano open.

I was so excited now that I banged on those keys for all I was worth. Afterwards I opened up the piano stool and saw several faded pieces of music sheets. I took one out and tried to read the notes, but it was all Chinese to me. The only thing I could understand was it was a piece called 'Rock of Ages'. Another was 'Abide with Me', and another was 'Onward Christian Soldiers'.

I knew all these tunes off by heart, as we had sung them many times in Sunday School and church. But I made believe. I took each piece, propped it up on the music frame in front of me and pretended to play from the music, and as I began to play by ear I felt marvellous the way my fingers went over those keys, but making plenty of mistakes when I struck the dead ones. I was very excited, and so was Rosie – she even called in some of the kids who were playing in the yard to listen to me. But when the time for her mum to come home drew near, Rosie locked up the piano and out we went to wait. We were afraid the kids would tell on us, but Rosie said if they did she wouldn't let them come in her house again.

But now I was getting fed up of trying to play the same old tune, so one Saturday afternoon while Rosie's mum was out I started practising again. I know it must have sounded awful to some people, but I enjoyed it, so did Rosie and the kids. It seemed that all the kids in the street came that day to try and sing. But when they tried to dance they cried, 'Carn't yer play summat else, we carn't dance ter that!'

After a few more tries I managed to hit the keys, and found I could now play (after a fashion) 'Any Old Iron' and 'Knees Up Mother Brown'. All the kids began to sing and dance around the yard with Rosie. It was bedlam, with some kids taking turns looking out for Rosie's mum to appear and to warn us in time. But no one cared – even the 'looker-out' joined in, which was a mistake. As soon as someone shouted out that Mrs Pumfry was coming down the street the kids scattered, leaving Rosie to run in and warn me. But before she and I could close the lid, Mrs Pumfry almost fell into the room.

'You wicked, wicked pair!' she yelled as she snatched up the sheets of music and banged the lid down. I was trembling now with fear, and so was Rosie. As tears ran down her cheeks, her mother yelled again: 'An' what 'ave I told yer about that piano! Never ter be opened! An' where did yer find the key?'

'In the back of the drawer, Mum,' whimpered Rosie.

'Well, in future it goes in my pocket. And as for you!' she added. 'I don't want ter see you in my 'ouse again! Now clear off!'

I didn't need telling twice. I fled.

I never did enter that house at number fifteen again, but Rosie and I were still friends.

When I told my mum later, she just scolded me and said that Rosie could come in our house any time. I was pleased about this, but it wasn't the same, for I loved any kind of musical instrument, and I vowed when I was old enough to get married the first thing I would buy would be a real piano.

But my big ideas never materialised until 1950, after my second marriage. Then I had two!

The Facts of My Life

From the early age of three, I knew what I wanted from life. First, I wanted to grow up quickly and leave the godforsaken place where I was born and lived with my parents and family. I wanted love and affection (which I never got from my parents). I wanted to be married and have lots of babies, to be rich and independent. But these hopes never turn out the way you wish when you're a child! When you reach middle age, or before, you often wish you were young again, and could do the things you had forgotten to do.

But no one can turn back the clock – although many would wish to. I know *I* don't, because *my* happiness is now, in my late years, and I have my independence. However, it wasn't until I was seventy-two years old and began to write the story of my life that I found *real* happiness and independence.

Looking back now and remembering those awful years, I know it was a mistake trying to grow up too soon.

I left school when I was fourteen, and started work. The older girls at the factory used to laugh and tell jokes about me because I wore stockings that were always falling down, old shoes that were much too big for me, and a short frock which had seen better days and showed my pink flannelette bloomers. I grew envious of how nice and tidy each of these young women looked, so after a few weeks I determined to leave.

Jobs were easy to find for young learners in my day, and with a few shillings I'd saved I made up my mind to go to the rag market in the Bull Ring and buy myself some cheap clothes to make myself look older, then get another job. I often smile to myself when I think about those years, and tell my grandchildren and great-grandchildren about my narrow escapes and the funnier side of my life.

I pinned my long black hair on top and put on a long hobble skirt, a bright-green blouse and a pair of second-hand high-heeled shoes, much too big for me. I also wore a pair of grey whalebone stays, which I had to pack with pieces of cotton waste to fill myself out. I really had no dress sense, but I thought I was the cat's whiskers.

On the way back from the Bull Ring market (which was then in Moat Row) I called at Snape's to buy Phul-Nana face powder and a lipstick. To make myself smell extra nice, I pushed the scented card Mr Snape gave me between my titties.

Often I tried to find hiding-places for my 'war paint', as Mum called my make-up, and when she did find it she put it on the fire. 'Only tarts an' cheap women use that stuff!' she would yell. 'An' if I find any mower, it'll goo on the bloody fire, an' yo with it!'

So I shared with Sally, the girl next door, but I always managed to wash my face clean in the brewhouse before I went indoors.

My parents and neighbours often said Sally was a bad girl, always seen with a different feller out late at night, yet I never saw any wrong in her. She was my friend, a little older than me, and always kind to me. Often we would arrange to meet each other on the Soho Road – called the 'Monkey Run' – where we would flirt with older boys. I had many narrow escapes trying to keep them at bay.

I was never told the facts of life, but I was a virgin until I was nearly eighteen. Then, in my foolish ignorance, I got myself pregnant and had to get married. That was in the Depression year 1921. I remember all those many years during my unhappy married life, it was hard for my husband to find employment. We had no real home, only my mother's attic, where we lived and slept six in a bed.

During the next ten years I had two miscarriages and five children, losing my eldest son as he came home from Nelson Street School – a shock I thought my husband and I would never get over. In 1931 my husband died and I was left with four young children to bring up, clothe and feed.

Before my husband died, I had to turn my hand to anything to earn a few shillings to pay my mother rent and to buy food. Although sometimes my husband would leave a few shillings on the shelf when he sold bags of sawdust, more often than not he went out drinking. Often we quarrelled, but he never changed, and when he became bad-tempered the children and I kept out of his way.

One Saturday night my eldest sister Mary, who was a part-time barmaid at the Vine Tavern a few yards from where she lived in Carver Street, came to see me. Often she would bring me a glass of milk stout when my husband wasn't about, for he always objected to me having so much as one glass, or even going into a pub.

'I don't wanta see yer like yer mother!' he used to say.

I had bathed my children and put them to bed, and after I had put a patch on my little son's trousers, Mary arrived. When she asked if my husband was about, I said I didn't know where he was or when he'd be back. As she took the bottle of stout from her bag I got out a couple of glasses, and as I was drinking she said, 'Kate, would yer like to earn ten shillin'?'

'Ten shillin'? Are yer kiddin'?' I exclaimed.

'No, I ain't kiddin',' she replied, and began to smile.

When I asked what I had to do she said, 'There's an old white-haired couple comin' to the Vine tonight to celebrate their golden weddin', and the missus at the pub asked me if I knew anybody who could sing a few old songs for them and –'

'Why ask me?' I asked before she had time to finish.

'Well, the woman she engaged 'as let 'er down, and I mentioned you.'

'But Mary, I've never sung in a pub before, only when I was about ten years old when me dad sat me on the counter and I sang for his beer money. Any'ow, Charlie would kill me if I went an' he found out.'

'Charlie won't find out unless yer tell 'im, an' I know you ain't that daft! Any'ow, you'll only be away about an hour, you'll be back home in plenty of time before he returns. Knowin' 'im, he won't be back till they throw him out!'

'I'll think about it, Mary.'

'I must have me answer now, or she might get somebody else.'

'But I ain't even got a decent frock to wear!'

'That's no trouble, you can wear my blue taffeta one. It's too tight for me now, I know it will fit yer. So if you'll say you'll come, I'll give it yer.'

I always envied her that dress and ten shillings seemed a fortune to me in those days so, knowing I would be the owner of the blue taffeta dress, I agreed to go.

First I tiptoed up the attic stairs and, seeing that my children were fast asleep, tiptoed down again.

Mary had already got the curling irons in the fire for my hair, and after she had brought in the dress and I slipped it on she put a little powder on my face and neck. As she made my lips up with her lipstick, she said, 'Now look at yerself in the mirror.'

I couldn't believe my eyes – how different I looked, and what an improvement on my old blouse and skirt that I had to wear all the time and wash weekly to try to make myself look presentable wherever I went!

As I stood admiring myself, I heard my sister say, 'Why, yer look ten years younger. Anyway, if yer stand admiring yerself much longer you'll crack the mirror.'

Then we both laughed.

Before we left the house I listened once again at the bottom of the attic stairs, satisfied that all was quiet. We made our way towards the Vine. I was still very timid, but my sister put her arm in mine and said I would be OK once I got inside the smoke room. I felt as if everyone's eyes were on me as I looked around. In the far corner was a long table with all kinds of eats laid out, and bunches of flowers. I was told later that evening that kind neighbours had had a door-to-door collection for Mr and Mrs Wright's anniversary. In another corner of the room was an upright piano – its lid was open and as I looked at it I thought: I hope it plays better than the one I tried to practise on when I was a young girl.

Flo, as everyone called the missus of the pub, was no stranger to me; often she used to serve me in the Bottle and Jug Department when I fetched my dad's beer. She was a small dumpy woman with black frizzy hair which came down to her shoulders. To me she always seemed overdressed, and that night she wore a long flowing red velvet dress, long red dangling earrings, several rows of different-coloured beads and several rings on her fingers.

I thought, too, that she wouldn't have looked so loud if she hadn't had too much war paint on her face and lips. But as the missus of the pub, I supposed she had to look and be different to the rest of her customers. As she walked towards me and put her arm round my shoulders she said, 'I'm glad you could come, my dear, your sister has told me all about you. So sit down, and don't look so nervous.'

Suddenly I heard Mary say, 'She won't afta stop long, Flo, as soon as she's sung a couple of numbers I'll 'ave to go 'ome with 'er before 'er 'usband comes back.'

'Very well,' replied Flo as she turned to me again. 'Now, sit yourself down. We're not ready to begin yet, so would you like a drink? Whisky or gin, or –'

'Oh, no, no, thank you,' I answered quickly. 'But I would like a glass of stout.'

The old barman brought over the glass of stout and a gin for Mary, who was to accompany me at the piano.

While I was waiting to be announced, I still felt nervous, for I'd never sung in front of a lot of people before. But after another couple of stouts and a sip of Mary's gin I had plenty of Dutch courage to sing my numbers.

I knew I had a good singing voice. When I followed my sister towards the piano and she started to play, everybody in the room applauded. Then, when it was my turn to sing, I sang my favourite, 'Home Sweet Home', which was the song I learnt at school. Everybody applauded for the second time. I felt then that I could have gone on singing all night. But as I walked away from the piano, the old white-haired gentleman came towards me and asked if I would sing again.

'That was lovely, me wench, but could you please sing "When Your Hair Has Turned to Silver" for me an' me wife?' he asked. I stood beside the piano again and as Mary struck the first notes, I began to sing:

> 'When your hair has turned to silver,
> I will love you just the same.
> I will always call you sweetheart,
> That will always be your name.
> Through a garden filled with roses,
> Down a sunset trail we'll stray.
> When your hair has turned to silver,
> I will love you as today.'

I don't know how I sounded, for all the time I was singing tears filled my eyes as I saw the white-haired old couple kiss and embrace like a pair of young lovers. The applause was deafening – not only for me but for the old couple, who were still hugging each other.

'Mary,' I managed to whisper, 'it's getting late, I'll have to go.'

'Can't you stop an' do another number?' she asked.

'No! Yer know I've got ter get back 'ome, I've stayed too long as it is.' I didn't stay even for a sandwich.

'Oh, all right. I'll go over an' speak to Flo.'

But the missus was already walking towards me with a large bunch of flowers and the ten-shilling note. As she gave them to me she asked if I would come again.

'I'll 'ave to think about it,' I replied. 'But I'll let my sister know.'

She thanked me again and as Mary and I walked out into the street I put the ten-shilling note down inside my frock and, hugging those lovely flowers to me, I said, 'Mary, I think you better have these flowers, or me 'usband or me mum will start askin' questions an' I wouldn't know what to say. Any'ow,' I added, 'I've got what I want and the money will come in useful.'

But while we were laughing and saying what a wonderful night we'd had, I happened to glance across the street.

Suddenly I stood there scared, as I saw my husband standing beneath the light of the street lamp watching me.

'Kate,' I heard my sister say, 'don't be scared. I'll come 'ome with yer an' explain.'

But there was no time. Before we got a few steps further he suddenly dashed across the road. The next thing I knew, he snatched the flowers out of my arms and threw them across the street, then as he struck me across my face I saw stars, then as he tore the frock almost from my back I called out for my sister, but she had already fled.

Crowds were now gathering around, and as he turned to answer some of the women who were yelling at him I saw my chance and ran home.

But there was Mum, sitting by the fire ready to greet me. 'Serves you bloody well right, an' I 'ope 'e gives yer some mower!' she cried out when she saw my eyes swollen and my lovely frock all torn.

'But I've done no 'arm,' I began to whimper. 'I was only singin' an' I needed the money.'

'But yer know 'e's ferbid yer gooin' in a pub!'

I knew it was useless to try to explain to her, or to expect any help. So I went upstairs, and as I sat on the foot of the bed weeping, I heard Charlie come up. I was now scared stiff, expecting him to give me a belting. But when he pulled me up off the bed and saw what he had done, he just said he was sorry and walked back down the stairs. I didn't see him until the early hours of the next morning. Then he took me in his arms and said again how sorry he was for what he'd done.

After that, he began to change. He found a part-time job in a tatter's yard sorting out old clothes and pieces of copper, brass and iron. Things began to get smoother, but after a few weeks he kept coming home feeling sick. One morning he collapsed. I ran for the doctor and when he came and examined Charlie, he said he would have to go into hospital. But he was stubborn and refused to go. Eventually his pains got worse. I didn't know what to do, as I was expecting my fifth baby any day. Then a couple of days later, when I came home from work and saw an ambulance outside the house, I knew the worst.

Charlie was taken to Hallam Street Hospital, where he died of a perforated gastric ulcer. That same night I gave birth to my baby daughter, whom I later christened Mary, after my sister.

That was the 22nd of April 1931. My husband was only thirty and I was only twenty-eight, left penniless with four young children to care for and a drunken mother to contend with.

Now that I was left a destitute widow with no pension but four young dependants, I tried going out cleaning – I even got a part-time job in a jam factory. But that didn't last long – I got the sack for eating the strawberries and bringing some home for the children. When I did eventually find a job working on a heavy press, my mum wanted half my pay to look after her grandchildren. But when I came home unexpectedly one afternoon, I found my youngest baby still lying in her cot with her nappy caked hard to her bottom. I was livid to see how she had been neglected. I picked her up, bathed her and gave her a feed, cleaned the cot out, and after asking one of my neighbours to keep an eye on her, I went to find my mother. I didn't have to look – I was told she was in a neighbour's house round the back yard.

I knew my mother drank, but I never expected to see her drunk. There was a gramophone playing and I could hear singing when I knocked on the door of number seventeen. No one heard my knock, so I kicked the door for all I was worth. Suddenly an old man opened it. 'Who yer want?' I heard him splutter.

'Tell my mother to come out now!' I shouted through the open door.

'Sod orf, yer mother ain't 'ere!'

'I know she's in there, I've been told! And I ain't going till she comes out, or she'll be sorry.'

Neighbours gathered outside the door when they heard me shouting. I was about to call out again when Mum stumbled out, looking all fuddled with drink. As the door slammed behind her I cried out for all the neighbours to hear, 'You drunken sot! Leavin' my babby all day lying in her cot all caked in her mess! An' you takin' me money to look after her! You should be ashamed of yerself!'

Suddenly she raised her hand to strike me, but she was too fuddled even to see where she was. I went back down the yard, and as soon as I had collected my baby from Mrs Taylor I went indoors and found my mother lying stretched out on the sofa fast asleep.

She had never been like this when my dad was alive – how I wished he'd been there that day!

The next morning when I sent my other two children to school, I asked Mrs Taylor if she would look after Jean and Mary while I went to work. When she refused, I told her I would pay her the same as I had always given my mum.

'It ain't the money, Kate – God knows I could do with it! But yer know what yer mum's like, she'd 'ave the 'ole street up in arms, sayin' I took 'er job off 'er, an' them bein' 'er grandchildren an' all.'

'Do some of you neighbours good ter stand up to 'er! Yer seem to let 'er get away with everything!' I replied angrily.

'I don't know why *you* can't 'old yer own to 'er,' she exclaimed, 'instead of come bawlin' ter me.'

'I'm sorry to lose me temper. I understand, and I wish I could, Mrs Taylor, but livin' with 'er is different, and I 'ave to curb me tongue at times, otherwise she'd turn me an' my children out. Then where would we go? Anyway,' I added, 'I've got other plans now, I'll go to the parish an' let them keep us.'

But what little they gave us wasn't enough even to feed one hungry mouth, let alone five of us.

A Bitter Struggle

During the following months I tried to struggle on, with only parish relief and the firewood I was selling from door to door. Often it would be late at night before I could call at the little local shop in Albion Street and buy food. One night, after feeding my children and putting them to bed, I started to gather up their dirty underclothes ready for the brewhouse the next day, then I saw my son tossing and turning in his sleep. As we slept five in a bed, I tried to calm him down in case he woke his sisters up. But as soon as I felt his forehead, I knew at once he was sickening for something. I crept quietly down the attic stairs and as I came back with a bowl of cool water and a flannel, I heard my mother shout from her bedroom.

'Wot are yer doin' up this time a mornin'?'

'John's feverish.' I replied. 'An' I'll 'aveta get the doctor to 'im in the mornin'.'

As she came out on to the landing she said, 'I 'eard yer up an' down, carn't sleep meself with this stiflin' bloody weather,' and closed the bedroom door.

As soon as I went up the attic stairs I saw John sitting up in bed with his eyes wide open.

'Mum, I'm thirsty an' I feel 'ot.'

'Please God,' I said to myself, 'don't let him be ill.'

I gave him a drink of my home-made ginger beer, then took off his little shirt, sponged his naked body and looked for any spots, but there were none to be seen. I lay down beside him until he went to sleep, and stayed awake in case he got worse.

Just as dawn broke I was looking through the attic window, which I had propped open with a brick, when I heard my mum moving about. I was hoping she would come up to look at John, but I heard her go downstairs. Later that morning I woke my three girls, and after washing them and getting Kathleen ready for school, I took Jean and Mary to our nextdoor neighbour to keep an eye on them while I went for the doctor. But as soon as I went back indoors my mother cried, 'I don't know why yer wanta doctor, I don't believe in 'em, they kill more kids than they can cure. Any'ow,' she added, 'give 'im a dose of castor oil, it's betta than all yer doctors give yer, an' while yer think about it, if yer can afford a doctor, don't forget I want me rent!'

All I had in my purse that day was 6*s*. 6*d*., but I ignored her -- whatever happened she could wait for her rent.

I slung my coat over my shoulder and ran for the doctor. Dr McKenzie, the local doctor, lived only two streets away.

Luckily for me, I was first to arrive at his small surgery. As soon as I explained what was wrong, he said he would call in an hour's time and to keep John warm.

When I arrived back, I was met by one of the neighbours who said my mother was in the brewhouse chatting. But I wasn't interested in where she was or what she did – at times I felt I hated her.

As soon as I entered the attic I noticed my son was still asleep but didn't look so flushed.

I took Mary and Jean towards the small fireplace and washed and fed them, and while they sat on the mat playing with little blocks of wood I sponged John down again and made him comfortable, while I waited for the doctor.

When Dr McKenzie came and examined my son, he asked if any of my other children had had measles or chickenpox.

'Only measles, Doctor,' I replied anxiously.

After examining John for the second time, he said, 'I can't see any spots, or a rash.'

'But what is wrong with him, Doctor?' I asked anxiously.

'I believe he's labouring under a nervous fever,' he replied. 'I'll give you a prescription to take to my surgery, where my wife will make up a bottle of medicine. Give him a teaspoon three times a day, then when he's finished the dose bring him to see me.' Just as he was writing out the slip of paper, I saw my mother enter the room.

'Wot's wrong with 'im?' she cried.

'Just a feverish cold, but he'll be all right in a day or two,' the doctor replied.

'I don't know why 'er sent fer yo! I could 'ave gid 'im summat betta than yo alwis prescribe!' bawled Mum.

Suddenly Dr McKenzie turned to face her. I saw his face go red as he shouted, 'Leave the room at once! If I need your advice, I'll call you!'

As he turned his back on Mum and gave me the slip of paper, I saw her leave, and as she went down the stairs I heard her mumble, 'It's my 'ouse an' nobody tells me when or wot ter doo!'

As soon as we heard the door slam behind her, I offered the doctor his five-shilling fee for the visit and the medicine, but to my surprise he refused to take it.

'You need it more. Buy some milk for the little ones. But', he added, 'don't tell my other patients, otherwise no one will want to pay.'

"E will get better soon, Doctor?' I asked as I thanked him.

'Yes, with care. But that fever is due to this unwholesome air and this damn place, and unless you can find a healthier place for you and your children, they'll never grow up strong.'

I thanked him again, and after I had fetched the medicine I sat down and wept. The doctor's words had alarmed me. Where were we to go? I'd tried for years to move from this vile place, but who would take me and four young children when everybody in the district was overcrowded?

I had even asked my married sisters and brothers to take them into their homes until I could go out to work and save enough money to rent a house or other rooms, but with no result. I still remember their answers: 'Sorry, but we don't 'ave the room. 'Ow can we look after them when we 'ave ter goo out ter work?'

I was now both destitute and desperate.

Several weeks later things began to get worse. People didn't want to buy smelly fishboxes for firewood. I could no longer see any future ahead for me and my children.

I tried hard to claim a widow's pension (which was then only ten shillings a week) but I was refused – there weren't enough stamps on my husband's insurance card – neither could I claim any sick pay (or panel money). There were no social services in those days, nor citizens' advice bureaux, nor children's allowances. There wasn't even the Pill, only backstreet abortion. But I was scared. I'd heard of girls being found out and prosecuted, or even dying. I was left with a means test or parish relief. Like many others in similar circumstances I did odd jobs on the sly to help feed our children. But if we were found out, we were brought before the tribunal and got nothing. The only help I got was boots and clothes from the *Daily Mail* Fund. But you couldn't eat these, or try pawning them. We were almost starving, and when I saw my children begging for food outside the same factory gates I had begged at as a child, I was heartbroken. I didn't want them to grow up as I had been dragged up.

There was only one heartbreaking decision: I had to let my children go into a Dr Barnardo's Home, until I could leave that bug-infested attic and find work and rent a house for them to come home to.

I worked hard night and day and got a home together. Then eventually, after eight years, I succeeded in getting them back to Birmingham, but they were no longer babies. Mary was nine years old, no longer the baby I knew. Jean was twelve, Kathleen was fourteen and my son John was fifteen. John was sent into the navy before I could get him home, and was on the high seas in many major battles during the war. Not until my daughters came home did they tell me how cruelly and harshly they were treated, yet how different those Homes are in this day and age!

But I knew that if I hadn't persevered to get them away from there, they would have been shipped off to Canada, and I might never have seen them again.

I often wonder if people of this generation who read my books condemn me for parting with my children. Let them think again. What would they have done in my place?

If we had stayed in that godforsaken hole in Camden Drive, my children and I would not be what we are today.

Turning Point

The day I left my children at Dr Barnardo's I had only about eight shillings in my pocket. I decided it was now time to make a break from that unlucky attic and my mother's house.

It was a bitterly cold day when I finally pushed a few clean underclothes into a brown paper bag, and with the shabby clothes I stood up in I walked from that house and vowed never to return. As I went down the yard I saw several little children with whom my children had once played games – some younger ones sitting on the cold steps sucking their dirty dummies, others fighting and swearing as their mothers stood gossiping with folded arms.

I gazed around for the last time and thanked the Lord that my children were away from all this squalor. I had no idea where I was going until I found myself opposite the gates of Warstone Lane Cemetery, where my brother Frank, his wife Nellie and their family lived in an open yard, in a one-room-down-and-one-up old house similar to my mother's.

I had no intention of calling on them, but crossed the road and went through the cemetery gates. I sat down on a stone bench, then I saw, coming slowly along the gravel path, our old Vicar Smith walking in front of someone's coffin, carried by six bearers. I began to weep when I remembered my son Charles, and his father, my husband, buried here under the earth with no headstone to say who they were or where. Suddenly I began to feel tired, and I closed my eyes. I must have dozed off.

Now, I don't believe in supernatural powers or ghosts, yet I heard a voice whisper, 'Don't sit here in this morbid place feeling sorry for yourself. Leave now and speak to your brother.'

Suddenly I began to feel shivers going through me. I thought: was it my husband's voice I heard? Or have I been dreaming? Yet the voice was so real.

I got up off the bench. The next thing I did was to cross the road. When my brother opened his door, he was surprised to see me. He greeted me with open arms, and so did Nellie.

I still recall that wonderful warm greeting, as they made me sit by the fire. As soon as Nellie had given me a hot cup of tea, she asked me why I had come to see them.

I explained about the voice I'd heard, and my brother began to laugh: 'Yer musta bin dreamin'.'

'Don't laugh, Frank. It was no dream,' I replied seriously. 'I'm sure it was my 'usband's voice I 'eard.'

'You remind me of Mum with your superstitions,' replied Frank, still smiling.

'Don't yer mention yer mother in this 'ouse, Frank!' Nellie piped up. 'Anyway, Kate,' she added as she turned to me, 'we've already 'eard the gossip, an' we know 'ow yer feelings are.'

'I had to do it, Nellie, there was no other alternative I could think of,' I replied as I thought of my children so very far away from me.

'We understand, don't we, Frank?' said Nellie.

'Yes, Kate. I'm sorry to hear what 'as 'appened,' my brother replied. 'Now dry yer eyes an' after yo've thawed out we'll get yer a bitta supper.'

As soon as my brother left the room Nellie said, 'I'm sorry too, Kate, and if we could 'ave 'elped yer we would 'ave. It's a pity you 'ad ter live there, I'm glad me an' Frank dain't goo when yer mum asked us. Although this place ain't much, it's our 'ome, an' we're 'appy, an' if yer like ter mek shift sleepin' on the sofa, yer welcome ter stay until yer find summat betta.'

'Thanks, Nellie, but I've got ter find a place ter live and find work so that I can get me children back.'

'I understand,' I heard her reply as she went into the small kitchen.

After my first meal since the day before, Frank began to make me up a bed on the sofa. But Nellie would insist that my brother could sleep there and I could share her bed.

My sister-in-law said I could go up when I was ready, and I went after thanking them for letting me stay and wishing them both good night. Later she came up with a stone hot-water bottle to make me comfortable.

It wasn't long before I fell into a restless sleep. I didn't feel Nellie get in beside me, nor did I hear her get up the next morning.

It was late when I awoke. I guessed they had both decided to let me sleep on. As I got out of bed and began to dress I glanced at myself in the wardrobe mirror, and noticed how sallow my face was. My eyes too looked and felt tired; even my mouth was drooping at the corners. My hands were rough and chapped and my fingernails were broken and dirty.

I knew then that if I was to get a job or lodgings I had to clean and smarten myself up a bit.

As soon as I went downstairs, I washed myself at the sink. Then, after breakfast, I helped Nellie with the washing-up. My brother was already getting ready to go to work when I said I too would have to be looking for work, also lodgings. When he asked me what I was doing about money, I told him I still had a few shillings.

'But that ain't gonna tek yer far!' he exclaimed. 'Yer betta tek this two quid.'

As he pushed the two gold sovereigns into my hand, I cried, 'No, Frank, you'll need it yerself. Any'ow I don't know when I'll be able ter pay yer back.'

'Tek it,' Nellie replied. 'An' get yer 'air done an' a bit of paint an' powder on yer face, an' yer can leave that ragged coat yer wearin'. There's one of mine upstairs in the closet, it's better than yours.'

I felt very tearful, for they were so kind to me. I also knew that if they had had room I could have stayed. But I was too near Camden Drive and its sordid surroundings and too many sad memories. I knew that if I was to make a future for my children and myself, I had to make a move as soon as possible. I thanked them both for their kindness and promised that as soon as I got on my feet I would come and see them again. And wearing Nellie's good coat, I carried the brown paper bag which still held my clean underclothes and a few sandwiches she had put inside. I made my way down the yard, but they both insisted they should come and see me to the corner of Vyse Street, where I was to wait for the Lodge Road tram. As we stood waiting we kissed each other goodbye, and as the tram slowly came up Warstone Lane and stopped near Chamberlain's clock, I felt sad that I had to leave them.

As soon as I had boarded the tram and we waved to each other,

I heard my brother call out, 'Best of luck, Kate, an' don't ferget if yer need us, yer know where we live.'

I still remember those words and the tears in their eyes as they waved.

I got on top of the tram and when I had found an empty seat and the conductor had taken my fare, I began to weep again. All I had in the world was the two sovereigns and eight shillings, and the contents of the paper bag.

As I got off that tram in Edmund Street, I began to plan what I was going to do.

That day, in the late autumn of 1931, was the turning point of my life.

As I walked along Edmund Street and down Colemore Row and made my way towards the Bull Ring, I stopped to look in several stores and shop windows. And as I admired all the pretty dresses, shoes and other brand-new garments, I almost said aloud, 'One day I'm going to be able to buy some of those, not left-off garments from the rag market' – where I was now heading.

Little did I realise that in the years ahead I would be independent, have money in the bank and a small business. But I had many worries and heartaches, too, in those years.

As soon as I was inside the rag market, which was then in Moat Row, I looked around at each stall to see what I could buy. What I needed now was a cheap second-hand frock or a blouse and skirt, a pair of shoes and a hat. On one of the stalls I went to I happened to see a pretty blue taffeta dress. It looked similar to the one my sister had given me. I nearly bought it, but I changed my mind. It would have reminded me too often of the night my husband tore it from my back.

I went to the next stall and saw, hanging from the rail, a good second-hand dress. It was navy-blue serge with a white lace collar and cuffs. It also had pearl buttons down the front. On the stall lay a pair of patent shoes and a blue pillbox hat with a veil. I knew if I bought it it wouldn't leave me much change in my purse for other things.

The frock was marked 12s. 6d., the shoes 5s. 6d., and the hat 3s. 6d. Plucking up courage, I asked the old woman who owned the stall if she would take a little less.

'I'm sorry, me dear,' I heard her mumble. 'I bin sittin' 'ere all mornin' freezin', an' I ain't bin able ter sell a thing! So yer betta try somewhere else! Any'ow me clothes are better-quality than the others they sell on their stalls,' she added.

'P'raps yer prices are too 'igh,' I replied as I walked towards the next stall.

As I was still looking for something cheaper, I hoped she'd remember what I said and call me back. She did.

'Come on, dearie,' I heard her call out, 'I've changed me mind. I wanta get 'ome early any'ow, an' I can see yer in need of 'em. So what if I let yer 'ave 'em a bit cheaper without the 'at?'

I didn't need the hat anyway, for I had made up my mind to have my hair bobbed and marcel waved. She knocked a shilling off the frock and sixpence off the shoes. I still had a bargain.

I paid her the 16s. 6d., put the clothes in the brown paper carrier with my clean shift bloomers, underskirt and stockings, and thanked her. Then as I walked away she called out to me, "Ere yar, dearie, I'll give yer the 'at.'

'Thank you,' I replied, 'but I won't need it. I'm gooin' to 'ave me 'air cut.'

'Well, yer can 'ave it any'ow, it might come in useful one day. An' I'm closin' me stall anyway.'

I took the hat and thanked her again, then I heard her call out, 'Don't forget ter come agen, dearie, you'll alwis get a bargin orf old Aggie.'

I began to smile. I hoped not. I hoped one day I would be in a better position to rig myself out in new clothes, not somebody's cast-offs.

As soon as I came out of the rag market, it began to rain. I thought: that pillbox hat will come in useful after all. When I took it out of the bag and placed it on my head, I realised it was too large and fell over my eyes. I didn't intend to carry it about with me. Then, just as I thought of throwing it over somebody's wall, I happened to see an old woman standing on the pavement trying to sell flowers.

She only had a shabby black shawl round her shoulders and I noticed that she wasn't wearing anything on her head. As I took the hat from my carrier, I walked across the road towards her.

"Ere you are, Gran'ma, put this on yer 'ead, it's too big for me,' I said.

'Oh thank yer, luv,' she replied. 'But would yer like ter buy a bunch of flowers from me?'

'Sorry, Gran'ma, but I wouldn't know what ter do with them.'

But as I felt sorry for her standing and calling the price of her flowers in that pouring rain, I opened my purse and gave her sixpence. She thanked me. Then as I walked away, I looked back to see that she was wearing that pillbox hat.

The rain began to ease off, although there was still a cold wind. I was glad when the sun came out.

I then made my way towards Northwood Street public baths, paid my threepence for a tablet of soap and the loan of a corporation towel and made my way towards the cubicle, and while I lay soaking myself in that hot soapy water, I remembered the last time I was there. It was many years before, when our schoolteacher took us once a week – it was only one penny then. And I hadn't had a good soaking since. It was always a wash-down in the copper boiler, in the communal brewhouse, or the zinc bath in front of the fire on Friday nights.

As I lay there that day, I felt I could have soaked myself for hours, until I heard the attendant shout through the door, 'You in theea! Are yer all right?'

'Yes,' I replied.

'Well, 'urry yerself! Yer can't stay in there all day! Somebody else is waitin' to get in!'

I dried myself quickly and changed into my clean under-clothes. I put on my stockings and the frock and shoes I'd bought, and after putting my old dirty clothes I didn't want into the brown paper bag I felt clean and refreshed.

As I handed the wet towel over to the attendant she cried as she snatched it from me, 'Next time yo come, Mrs, I'll time yer!'

I didn't stop to answer, but smiled to myself as I thought: I hope there won't be a next time I have to go to public baths.

I still carried the bag with my dirty old undergarments in, also my old frock and well-worn-down shoes. I didn't need them any longer, yet I couldn't carry them about with me. I had to get rid of them somehow.

As soon as I heard the rag-and-bone man coming down the street I dropped them in the gutter for him to collect, and hurried away.

My next call was at a small-fronted shop, which said hair-cutting and waving. But when I walked in the woman said I had to make an appointment, which was in an hour's time, and the cost was 4s. 6d. for a cut, shampoo and marcel waves. I paid a 1s. deposit and told her I would come back in an hour.

As I walked around to kill time I came to a little house where they sold home-made cakes and tea. I went in and bought a cup of tea, then I realised I felt hungry. But when I felt in my paper bag for the sandwiches Nellie had put in, I realised I must have left them amongst the garments I'd dumped in the gutter. I bought another cup of tea and a plate of cakes, and then it was time to have my hair done.

It was the first time I had ever had my hair done professionally and when I was finished and stood up to look in the mirror, I couldn't believe it was me. I felt flattered. My hair had been cut below my ears and marcel waved with hot iron crimpers, which looked like large paper clips. I thought I looked like one of the flappers you saw in advertisements. That style was all the rage then.

Although I had only about a pound left in my purse, I was glad I'd had my hair done, and now my next move was to find somewhere to sleep for the night.

Ellen

❦

I knew if I went back to my brother and his wife they would gladly give me shelter. But I also knew I wouldn't get anywhere if I changed my mind, and I couldn't take advantage of their kindness. It was now late in the afternoon, and it began to get chilly. I wrapped my coat closer around me, and as I walked along Great Hampton Street looking to see if there were any rooms to let, I happened to see a notice in a newpaper-shop window, advertising a room. But when I hurried inside and asked, I was told it was already taken.

Further down the street I came to a little tea shop. I was about to buy myself a cup when I saw another notice: 'Furnished room to let, suit young lady or gentleman'. I almost fell inside that tea shop. There were several customers waiting to be served. The woman behind the counter didn't look very pleased when I cried, 'Could yer please tell me if that room's been taken what's advertised in the winda?'

'Yo'll afta wait yer turn, I got customers ter serve!'

'But I must know now,' I replied eagerly. 'Will yer write the address down? I 'aven't got a pencil,' I added as I stared at her.

'Yo'll afta wait!' she shouted again as she went on serving a customer.

I nearly yelled 'Grumpy old bugger!' But I knew that wouldn't get me anywhere.

I began to tap my fingers impatiently on the counter, then I saw a young man take a pencil from his pocket.

'Now come on, Maggie, let's have it,' he said pleasantly.

''Er won't get it, a young feller come arfta it an hour agoo.'

'But it might not be suited for 'im – I can try!' I replied.

'It's 5A Soho Road,' she snapped. ''Er name's Mrs 'Ands.'

As the young man gave me the name and address he smiled and whispered, 'Old Maggie must have got out the wrong side of the bed

622

and forgot to take her little liver pills. Anyway, dear, good luck.'

I thanked him and ran out of the shop and down the street towards Soho Road. I knew the road from years before when we teenagers used to call it the Monkey Run – we did our flirting there. Yet I never knew then where number 5A was. Up one side of the street and down the other I hurried, but still I couldn't find it. I was now cold and hungry, and the cheap shoes I bought that day were beginning to pinch my toes.

'If I don't find it soon,' I said to myself, 'there's only one alternative: I'll have to state my case at the Kenyon Street police station and ask the inspector to give me shelter for the night.'

I was just about to despair when I saw, a few feet away, five small houses which lay almost hidden in a cul-de-sac, and there was number 5A at the end. Each house, I could see, had two rooms up and down, each house was painted brown and cream, and each house looked the same, only there were clean white lace curtains at their windows, draped differently. Everywhere looked fresh and clean, even the narrow pavement. I hurried to the end house and lifted the bright brass lion's-head knocker, but there was no answer. I tried again, only louder. Soon I saw a woman peep her head round the door. When she saw me standing on the step, she opened the door wider.

She was rather a tall, upright woman with greying hair, wearing a long brown leg-o'-mutton-sleeve dress that almost hid her feet. She wore no jewellery, only a fob watch pinned to her chest. As I looked up at her I thought she looked severe. This made me feel very nervous, but just as my courage began to desert me I saw her smile as she asked, 'Have you come about the room?'

'Er . . . er . . . yes,' I stammered. 'I've bin sent by the woman from the . . . er . . . tea shop.'

'Oh yes, Maggie,' she replied, smiling. 'Everybody knows Maggie – her bark's worse than her bite; she's a good old soul really. Anyway, you better come in out of the cold.'

As I followed her through the narrow hall I noticed two rooms, one each side of the hall, and stairs led off the kitchen, where I saw a blazing fire roaring in a bright black-leaded range. I couldn't resist walking up to it to warm my hands. She told me to draw up a chair and sit by the fire, and while she went into the scullery to make a cup of tea I gazed round the room. There were several framed pictures of scenes on the walls and photos in silver frames on the mantelshelf, an old dresser with odd crocks that might have been antique. There was also an oval polished table, four leather chairs and an armchair, and a threadbare rug. Everything in the room was old and well-worn, but highly polished and clean. I couldn't see a bit of dust anywhere, only the few ashes in the hearth.

As I sat looking around the woman came in with two cups of tea on a tray and half a dozen biscuits.

'As soon as you've drunk your tea and had a warm, I'll show you the room,' she said pleasantly.

'Then it's not been taken by the young man Maggie said she'd sent?'

'No, he wasn't suitable.'

I didn't ask why in case she thought I was being too nosy, but I did ask how much the room was.

'You must see it first, dear, then we can come to some agreement.'

No more was said until we had drunk our tea and eaten our biscuits.

I followed her up the threadbare carpeted stairs – I counted eleven – and on each side of the landing was a bedroom.

As she walked into the one on the left, I followed. She turned and said, 'There isn't much furniture, but it's clean and comfortable. I'll leave you to look around, and when you come downstairs you can let me know what you decide about the rent.'

Before I could answer she was gone.

Although the room was scantily furnished, it seemed a palace to what I had left behind. There was a single bed with brass rails and well-patched clean bedcovers and a pillowslip with embroidered pansies on the corner, a tall oak wardrobe, a marble-topped dressing- and wash-stand with a crock bowl and a jug, a towel and a piece of soap, a wicker chair beside the bed and a hand-pegged rag rug beside the small fireplace. The rest of the floor was well-scrubbed bare boards. The walls were bare, but there was no sign of bugs. Everything was old but clean.

Thousands of people would have turned their nose up at this, but to me it was heaven.

After looking in the wardrobe I looked under the bed where I saw what I expected to see, the crock po.

When I went downstairs to tell the woman I would take it, I saw her sitting by the fire with an open Bible. As I entered she looked up and asked if the room was suitable.

'Yes, thank you,' I replied, 'but I would like ter know 'ow much yer askin' for the rent.'

'It's 7s. 6d. a week bed and breakfast, but other meals you will have to buy out unless you wish to have supper in, then you will have to put a few coppers in the meter. That will be a week in advance, dear.'

'Thank you, Mrs Hands,' I replied.

'Now sit down and tell me your name.'

As I opened up my purse and gave her three half-crowns, I told her my name was Mrs Flood and I was a widow. I hoped she wouldn't ask too many questions in case she changed her mind about letting the room. But when she said I looked too young to be a widow I told her it was a long story, and that I would tell her about my life and where my children were. But this was not the time or the place, and I was pleased she didn't ask, for I didn't feel I wanted her pity, otherwise I would have broken down and wept.

'When can I move in?' I asked quickly, hoping she would say now.

'As soon as you wish, dear,' she replied.

'I would like to stay tonight if yer wouldn't mind.'

'But you haven't brought any luggage with you – why do you wish to stay?'

'Me an' me mum had a big row and I walked out an' left an' I said I'd never go back there agen, that's why I was lookin' for a room ter stay.'

As soon as she saw my tears she said, 'Very well, dear, you can bring your luggage tomorrow. But what about your nightdress? Anyway,' she added, 'you may borrow one of mine tonight.'

After thanking her I said, 'Do yer mind if I go up to bed now, Mrs Hands? I'm so tired.'

'Very well, dear, but first I'll fill you a bottle to put in your bed.'

As she handed me the stone bottle filled with hot water and the long pink flannel nightdress, I could have broken down and wept. I had never known such kindness. As she sat down in her chair she opened up the Bible again then, turning to me, she whispered, 'Good night and God bless you, my dear.'

'Good night, Mrs Hands, and thank you,' I managed to answer.

As soon as I had kicked my shoes off I sat on the side of that bed and wept. Thinking about my children, I imagined that now they would be tucked up in bed and fast asleep. I hoped and prayed that they were clothed and well fed and didn't miss me too much, and that soon we would be together again. After asking God to take extra care of my children, I got undressed, slipped the flannel nightie on and lay down to think about tomorrow.

I now had only a few shillings left in my purse. I knew I had to buy a nightdress and a few extra clothes – any old things, even if I didn't wear them – before I could get a job.

I lay down planning what I intended to do until I fell into a restless sleep. When I awoke the next morning I saw that all the bedclothes had slipped on to the floor. I got out of bed, washed in the basin, and when I was dressed I went downstairs.

In the kitchen I saw my landlady frying bacon on the fire. As soon as she saw me she said, 'Good morning, dear, did you sleep well?'

'Yes,' I replied. 'But I must have been a bit restless during the night.'

'It often happens the first time in a strange bed. Anyway,' she added, 'you may wash at the sink in the scullery, and while I finish cooking breakfast you will find the lavatory through the scullery door and down the yard.'

She had her own private back yard, with a small wash-house with a copper boiler and a wooden mangle, and next to the wash-house I saw the lavatory, all whitewashed, old but clean. Although it had a square wooden seat it also had a long iron chain to flush water. It wasn't like the dry communal closets we shared where we used to live. And as I sat there that morning, I remembered that was the only place I could try to educate myself with my dictionary, away from my mum and sisters and brothers, who always criticised me for what they said was a waste of time.

My dictionary helped me to talk a lot better, but I still drop my aitches and when I get excited or lose my temper I still come out with the 'Brummie' accent.

After breakfast I helped to wash up the greasy dishes, then went up to make my bed. When I came down the stairs my landlady was sitting with the Bible on her lap.

'I'll 'ave to be off now, Mrs Hands, I'll be back later tonight.'

'I think you may call me Ellen,' she replied.

'Thank you, Ellen, and my name's Kate.'

'Very well, Kate,' she answered, smiling across the room at me.

I felt so pleased that I had found such a kind and friendly person, I felt like throwing my arms around her and kissing her, but I didn't want to seem too familiar.

Into Business

As I walked down the street I made my way to town and the rag market again. I knew that I had only a few shillings left. The first things I had to get were a nightdress and a few undergarments, until I could find work and buy better. I was looking around for the cheapest stall when I saw old Aggie pop her head around beneath a pile of old clothes. ''Ello me dear, come ter buy yerself some of me old clothes agen?' she called.

'Sorry, Aggie, yer too dear, I'm lookin' for something cheaper.' As I walked away I heard her shout, 'Goo ter the others, then, but yer won't get nothin' cheaper or better! They'll do yer, you'll see!'

I began to smile to myself as I crossed over to another stall, where I found what I wanted. The garments were old but looked clean – anyway, I would ask Ellen later if I could wash them. Now, with only a few coppers left, I had to find work.

I walked up one street and down another, carrying my garments in a paper carrier. I was getting tired and hungry, but I had to find a job.

Before and during my married life I had worked at several firms learning enamelling and polishing motor plates, badges, also jewellery. I was an experienced enameller, but I didn't want to go to the firms where I had learnt my trade. Although many of the people I used to work with were very friendly, I knew they would ask about my life, so I decided to go to other firms. But when I enquired at Fattorini's, I was told they wanted only girls to learn. I knew they didn't want to pay the wages I asked for. I called at Fray's in Tenby Street. Same answer. I was beginning to get depressed when I tried my last call at Butler's in Victoria Street. The money was twice what the other firms wanted to pay, and when I told the foreman that I knew all the processes of the trade I was given a trial to start the next morning. Things seemed to go well, and I felt very happy.

As I walked down Branston Street I smelt fish and chips. I looked in my purse, which now contained only 3s. 3d., which had to last until I could pick up my first week's wages. I bought three pennyworth of chips and ate them from the paper as I walked towards my digs.

As soon as I got there and lifted the knocker, I could smell something nice cooking. When Ellen opened the door to let me in, I made straight for the kitchen and squatted down on the sofa. As I clutched my paper carrier, I heard her say, 'Are you all right? You look very pale.'

'I'm just tired, Ellen. I've been walking about all day lookin' for work. Now I've found what I want – I'm to start tomorrow mornin' at eight o'clock.'

'I'm so pleased for you, and I must get another key cut for you, Kate. Now if you will put your things upstairs and have a wash, I'd like you to sit down with me and have a bit of supper.'

'Oh thank you, Ellen. I 'aven't 'ad time really to buy meself anything, only a few chips,' I said.

I couldn't tell her I had only a few coppers in my purse after buying the clothes.

I took the carrier bag up to my room and put it in the wardrobe with my coat. I washed my face and hands in the washbowl, and after combing my hair (which was losing its waves) I hurried downstairs. Ellen was already serving the stewed meat and vegetables in the dishes on the table, and as we both sat down to eat I felt very awkward when she bent her head and closed her eyes to say grace. I did likewise.

Each time I took a mouthful I thought about my children, wondering if they were happy and having good meals. I hoped too that they were not missing me as much as I was missing them. 'It won't be long', I said to myself, 'before I pay them a visit, and later when I find a real home I shall bring them back where I can love and care for them.'

I started my new job and worked hard for many long hours, yet I was turned down when I asked for a rise. I was dissatisfied, knowing I was worth more than two pounds a week. A few weeks later I heard that Mr Butler had too many orders to cope with and was advertising for outworkers. As soon as I asked about this, he refused, but when I asked for my cards he changed his mind. With all the knowledge I had stored away in my memory, I knew I could run my own business.

I was now feeling ambitious. During that Easter week I found an empty dilapidated top-floor room which I was able to rent for 12s. 6d. a week. But first I had to buy the tools of the trade. I knew firms had tools on approval, but I hadn't enough money to start. I had big ideas and wanted to be independent and have young girls working for *me*. I prayed that I could make it a success. So with hard work, scrubbing and cleaning those old wooden benches and several three-legged stools, I started my trials, but little did I think how many hurdles I would have to jump before landing on my feet in success.

I knew where to buy all the tools and enamels I needed, but I didn't have money in the bank. I couldn't ask there. So I took a chance. Sink or swim. I began to push my luck. I went to see Harry Smith, who owned the ironmonger's shop on the corner of Hockley Street and Key Hill. When I explained to him what I was going to do, and what tools I needed, he said I could have them on a weekly basis and he would send one of his workmen to deliver. But I had to have a guarantor, my landlord of the premises at 90 Spencer Street, Hockley.

The tools came two days later. That same afternoon I tried my luck at Hutton's in Great Hampton Street, who already supplied enamels to different firms. They were pleased to hear I was starting out on my own, and said I could hold an account (whatever that was – it was all double Dutch to me). But I signed the paper and had some enamels on approval.

Now I was halfway there. I had Carborundum files, iron panning, a mortar and pestle to grind the enamel down (today it is sold in powder form), a pair of old patched foot-bellows and a blowlamp. For the first two weeks, when the work started to come in, I sat for many hours at the workbench alone, and felt very lonely. I was receiving more work than I could cope with, but I was afraid to refuse the orders in case I lost them altogether – I didn't want to be a flop. Later I put a notice on the wall outside asking for young girls to learn the trade and a cleaning woman, also a pumice polisher. A few days later I employed two young sisters and during the following months I had twelve girls working with me at the long bench, side by side.

Now I was prospering, I had to have a car to fetch and take the orders and the heavy crates of motor plates. I bought a little second-hand Austin Seven. My brother Jack taught me to drive, but the first time I took the driving seat the wheels were so narrow I got stuck in some tramlines.

You didn't need a driving test, neither did I have a licence. When the Whitsun holiday came I closed my small business for a few days and drove off to see the Matron at the Homes. It was then that I got a shock: I was told my children had been moved to Dr Barnardo's Homes in Barkingside, and if I wished to see them I was to go there – where another disappointment awaited me.

Dr Barnardo's

I had made up my mind now that whatever happened I was determined to visit my children on the following Sunday.

On Saturday morning I went to the market and bought a basket of fresh fruit, and during the afternoon I made a large fruit cake to take the next day. Later that evening, my brother Jack called to ask me to lend him the car.

'I'm sorry, Jack, but I need it meself to go to visit the children in the Homes.'

'But yer carn't drive all that way on yer own!'

'Well, I had thought of asking you to drive me down.'

As soon as I saw him hesitate, I said, 'Well, if you can't manage to come, I'll go on me own.'

'But it's miles away! You'd never manage to drive all them many miles!'

'Well, I've made up me mind, even if I have ter push it!'

'No need ter lose yer temper. But if I can borrow the car for tonight, I'll bring it round early tomorra an' I'll promise yer ter tek yer. What time yer thinkin' of leavin'?'

'About seven o'clock in the morning.'

'Very well, be ready, I'll fill 'er up with petrol an' we'll tek it in turns to drive.'

'Thanks Jack, I'll be ready,' I replied.

I was pleased he'd be coming with me, as I wouldn't have known what to do if the car broke down.

Although my brother had given me driving lessons, I had never taken that old Austin Seven anywhere out of the district, yet I had plenty of confidence to drive her anywhere.

On Sunday morning I was up early, had my breakfast and got dressed ready. Six o'clock came. I kept gazing up at the alarm clock, waiting for it to point to seven. Yet that hour seemed like an eternity. As soon as the alarm went, I sat down and waited for Jack to walk in. Quarter-past seven. Then half-past seven. But still he hadn't arrived. I began to wonder if he would keep his promise, or if the old jalopy had broken down? I was thinking how foolish I had been to trust him. I was almost in tears when I heard the car come rattling along the cobbles and pull up outside.

As soon as I rushed outside and saw him at the wheel I yelled, 'Where've yer been? I've been waitin'! Since seven o'clock!'

'Sorry, Sis, I overslept. Any'ow, jump in if yer ready.'

I fetched the fruit and the cake and a bag of boiled sweets, put them in the back seat and sat beside my brother, who stopped to light his Woodbine, then we were off.

How well I remember how that old car went! After a few miles of rattles and shakes, Jack said it was time for me to take the wheel and give him a break. But I was enjoying sitting back and didn't want to drive, so I made the excuse that I felt safer if he drove.

'Why are yer afraid ter drive now, when I taught yer all yer wanted ter know?' he snapped.

'But Jack, that was only around the district, not all the rest of the miles we've got ter go.'

'Well, we'll take it in turns,' he replied. 'Get out.'

We changed over and I took the wheel, after he had given me directions. As I drove past Banbury, Jack told me not to do more than thirty on the clock. 'Otherwise the bloody thing will fall to pieces!' he cried.

I took it steady for a while, between twenty-five and thirty, then I saw that my brother was nodding off.

I thought it was a pity to wake him – anyway, by now I was enjoying driving, with little traffic on the roads apart from a few horses and carts. But after a while I too was getting tired, and I hit the kerb. Suddenly the car shook. Jack woke up with a start, grabbed the wheel and steered it into the tram tracks. Those wheels and tyres were so narrow and well-worn, we got stuck in the tramlines. I saw a tram approaching, got scared and jumped out. Several people on their way to church were staring at us.

'Get back in there!' Jack shouted, 'an' steer while I push the bloody thing!'

I tried and tried but the old thing wouldn't budge, and when I looked behind and saw the tram coming I began to get scared and jumped out again and stood on the pavement holding my breath. What if that tram driver couldn't stop? I thought. Jack could be killed.

But I was relieved when I saw him put his arms up in the air to wave the driver to stop a few feet away. When the conductor came to see what the trouble was, he began to smile. 'Well I never,' I heard him say. 'Where do you think yer gooin' in that ol' boneshaker?'

'It's a long story, mate,' Jack replied, 'but if you'll 'elp me ter get it out of the tramlines we'll be on our way.'

Jack called me back into the driving seat, and as he and the conductor pushed from behind we got out on to the road again, and as the tram passed us the driver and conductor smiled and waved.

I was glad when Jack said he would drive the rest of the way.

After stopping at little tea shops for cups of tea and a bite to eat, and to cool the engine down, we arrived at Dr Barnardo's Homes in Barkingside at about two o'clock.

Seeing the big wrought-iron gates wide open, Jack drove straight in. The outside of that grey stone building was like the outside of a prison. As my brother parked between two large cars, I thought my old boneshaker looked like something from Noah's Ark. Yet it had served its purpose.

As we approached that tall, grey, dismal-looking stone building, we saw an elderly woman dressed in a shabby, faded grey frock. Later I was to find out she was one of the Homes' helpers, who were called Mothers.

She looked very nervous and when she asked who we were, I told her I had come to see my children. 'But this is Sunday, I'm afraid they won't let you see anybody on a Sunday,' she said, rather sadly.

'But I've come a long way – from Birmingham – and I must see my children!'

'I'm so sorry, dear, if it was left to me I'd take you, but then I should get into more trouble than I'm in now. But you can try knocking on the door.'

As she walked hurriedly away she called out, 'I wish you luck, dear.'

As soon as she was out of sight, my brother remarked how scared she looked. 'P'raps she's one of the inmates,' he added. 'Anyway, come on, Kate, let's knock and ask.'

I lifted that iron knocker and dropped it on the big oak door for all I was worth. I heard its echo, but no one came, until Jack made two more attempts. We heard the bolts being drawn back and the door opened. We were faced with a very large, buxom, severe-looking Matron in a long grey dress and a stiff white starched pinafore, a white bonnet tied beneath her double chin. She cried, 'What do you want? Go away!'

When I told her who I was and why I had come, she replied, 'There's no business done on Sundays, you call on Saturdays between two and four o'clock!'

She was about to close the door on us when my brother explained the miles we had travelled to see my children and that we weren't going until we got some kind of satisfaction.

'Well, you'd better both step inside while I make some enquiries.'

I shall never forget that large, cold, dismal-looking room with its dark-green-painted brick walls. All it contained was one oak high-back chair and a large oak writing-desk with inkwells and pens and several ledgers. In the opposite corner of the room was another oak door.

Everywhere seemed so quiet – not a sound or sign of either adults or children.

When the Matron had asked my name and address and the names of my children, she began to open up the ledger. It was then that I was told my son John had been transferred to Watts Naval Training School, and that Jean and Mary were soon to be fostered out to King's Lynn, Norfolk. Kathleen, being the eldest, would be staying.

'But can I see my children now, if only for a few minutes, *please*?' I begged.

But when that hard-faced Matron said 'No visiting on Sundays!' I broke down and wept.

'Please, please,' I pleaded again. 'I must see them, I've come such a long way!'

'Those are the rules!' she replied sharply. 'Have you a pass?' she added.

When I shook my head she said, 'Well, you'll have to wait here while I get you one. Then you can visit on Saturdays only, two till four.'

'But what about my nephew John?' asked my brother.

'That is another matter. You will have to get in touch with the Training School.'

She went through the other door, and we heard her turn the key behind her. As soon as she'd gone, I sat down on the chair and wept.

'Never mind, Sis, it won't be long before next Saturday, we'll see 'em then,' comforted Jack.

'P'raps she'll change her mind, Jack, and let me see 'em, even if it's only for a few minutes,' I replied.

'I can't see that bloody old battleaxe bendin' even a little!' he growled.

I was still hoping, but she came through that door with only the pass in her hand.

'Take this,' she told me, 'and remember: without it you will *not* be admitted!'

As I handed her the fruit cake and sweets to give to my children, I remember her saying, 'I will see that they receive them. Good day.'

(Years later they told me they never did receive them.)

Suddenly Jack glared up at her and cried, 'It's a bloody pity yo ain't got a few of yer own kids 'ere!'

'We don't ask them to come!' snapped the Matron as she slammed the door against us.

My brother drove us all the way home. I sat in the back seat and cried myself to sleep.

That next Saturday morning couldn't come quickly enough, but when it did Jack came to say he was sorry, but his boss wanted him to work over to move some machinery.

It was then that my sister Liza and I decided we'd travel by train. We arranged between us that if I should happen to see one of my children I would get them to come along with me through the gates, away to the railway station and on to the train. As soon as we arrived, I happened to see one of the Mothers in the grounds carrying my youngest child. As I tried to grab her, she screamed. The next thing I knew, my pass was taken from me and I was ordered off the premises.

Although I made several attempts later, I never saw my children again for the next eight years. Although I wrote to them, I never got any reply to my letters, and it was not until they came home that they told me they never received any presents or letters.

During those years from 1931 to 1939 I worked hard day and night saving every penny I could spare to put into the bank to buy a house for my children to come home to.

The Vicar

When I first applied for outwork enamelling, some firms actually laughed at me. They had never heard of a young woman wanting to start up a business on her own, enamelling badges and motor plates. But my twelve employees and I worked together side by side. The large motor plates I did myself. I would also fetch and carry back the finished work.

One day, as I was carrying a large heavy crate of badges, I happened to meet my brother Frank. As he helped me, he remarked how pale and thin I'd become.

'I'm all right, Frank,' I replied: 'But I can't afford a man's wages yet.'

'Well, let me know if yer want any 'elp, an' don't work so hard or you'll be killin' yerself. The trouble with you is you're feeling too independent,' he added.

'Frank,' I replied as I smiled at him, 'hard work will never kill me. Anyway, I'm thriving on hard work and determination.'

When he carried the crate up the stairs and dropped it on the floor, all the girls looked up at him and smiled.

Before he went he turned and said, 'I wouldn't mind bein' in charge of these pretty wenches.'

Frank was a nice-looking chap in a rugged kind of way. He would have looked handsome if he'd had the right kind of clothes to wear.

I have never forgotten my brother's kindness.

One Easter holiday he came and whitewashed the shop. When I offered to pay he said, 'Just buy me a few fags, I'll be satisfied.' But later I did other kindnesses for him and his wife, for I could never repay them for all the help they gave me during those years of struggle.

Seeing my brother Frank more often, and working at the bench besides my workers, I didn't feel so depressed. Night-time was worst, when I closed the business and went home to a lonely house. It was then that I would think of my children and wonder if they were happy and well fed.

They had been away from me for over three years now. I hadn't seen or heard from them. So I decided to write again to the Matron of the Homes and tell her I had a well-furnished home and a business. I was now in a position to care for them. I also bought a new car.

Several weeks went by – still no reply.

When I told my brother, he said, 'Why don't you go and see the vicar – p'raps 'e can 'elp.'

'But I don't go to church, Frank,' I replied.

'That won't mek any difference – any'ow 'e knows you and our family. There ain't much 'e don't know,' he added.

'Frank, if he asks me to pray I shall walk away.'

'But why?'

'Because I don't believe there's a God above! I've prayed and prayed too many times and He's never answered *my* prayers!'

'But Kate, God moves in very mysterious ways and . . .'

'Don't start preaching to me, Frank!' I replied bitterly. 'He's never give *me* any signs of help!'

'Well, will you go if I go with yer?'

'I'll have to think about it.'

A few weeks later I thought it over, then one afternoon while there was no service on Frank and I went to see the vicar at St Paul's Church.

The churchwarden asked us our business, and when I told him he told us to take a seat and the vicar would see us.

While we were waiting, I whispered, 'Frank, what shall I say?'

'Just tell 'im the truth about 'ow the Homes are ignoring your letters and could he help. An' stop fidgetin', he won't eat yer.'

As soon as I saw the vicar I began to get nervous. He greeted us and asked why we wanted to see him. I began to stammer, and I was glad Frankie did most of the talking. Every minute I thought the vicar was going to ask us to kneel and pray, but he didn't, and when he took us into the vestry he said he knew my children were in the Homes. He asked why I had allowed them to go, and I replied, 'It's a long story, Vicar; I feel I cannot explain all the details now, but I was wondering if you could help me to get my children back.'

'Did you sign any forms to consent to them being taken into care?'

'No, Vicar, I took them to Moseley Village Homes for a few weeks, on the understanding that I should have them back when I got a proper home for them, and when I went back there a few weeks later I was told they'd been transferred to Barkingside Homes. Now I've had my pass taken away I can't see them, and they won't even answer my letters or let the children write to me.'

'I don't think there's much I can do, my dear. But I will write to them and see what can be done. You say you are now in a position to have them home?'

'Yes,' I replied.

As soon as I told him about the house I'd bought and my business, he wrote it all down and said he'd do what he could. In the meantime he would get in touch with me. As we came out of the vestry, I was scared in case he asked me to kneel and pray. But he just wished us both good day. As I stopped to put two half-crowns in the box, I saw him whispering to my brother.

As soon as we were outside the church, I asked Frank what he had said to him.

'He said he would pray for you and I was to try to get you to come to some of the services.'

'I'm sorry, Frank,' I replied. 'I don't wish to be a hypocrite, but I see enough of them people as do go pulling people to pieces with their gossip as soon as they leave the church.'

'I know, Kate. But they ain't all bad,' he replied.

'Maybe they're not, but I don't have to go to church. *I* know what's right and what's wrong.'

'Will you go if he has some good news for you later?'

'I'll think about it, Frank.'

As my brother put his arm round my shoulders, my eyes filled with tears.

'OK,' he replied. 'I know what yer mean and how yer feelin'.'

'I hope yer don't think I'm wicked, Frank, just because I don't go to church. But inside that place depresses me. Even when my children were all christened there, and the services I had to hear when my young son was killed and my dad died and my husband died all in the space of four years. Even weddings make me weep, and now I've got this dreadful feeling that my children will be shipped away to Canada or Australia, and I shall never see them again.'

'Yer mustn't think like that, Sis! Them places are only for orphans, or children whose parents don't want 'em. Anyway, they'll have to consult *you* first.'

'Consult *me*! Consult *me*!' I flared up at him. 'They dain't consult me when they removed them from Moseley Village!'

'Well, Kate, let's wait and see if the vicar can help, and in the meantime I'll have half a day off work next Saturday and we'll go and see this Matron you've mentioned.'

After thinking over what he said, I agreed.

I said I was sorry I'd flared up at him. He reminded me so much of our dad, who was also very placid and understanding. Many times during my grief I wished he were still here to give me advice.

My brother came to see me the following Saturday morning, and as promised we caught the early train. But as bad luck would have it, the train was two hours late.

When we arrived at the Homes, we saw parents and relatives just leaving.

'We're too late again, Frank,' I cried. 'What am I going to do?'

'Well, we can't go back now, we're here, so come on, we'll try and see this Matron.'

We hurried along the gravel path and when we knocked on the door, the same strong-faced Matron opened it and stood staring down at us. As soon as I told her I was sorry we were late visiting my children, and the reason why, she replied very severely, 'Rules are rules, not to be broken.'

'But I've come a long way, it isn't my fault the train was late. Please let me just see them,' I pleaded.

'You'll have to come next visiting day!' she snapped.

But when I lost my temper and tried to push my way past her, she called to two of the gardeners to put us outside the gates.

'Come on, Sis, I can see we shall get nowhere here, we'll wait until our vicar gets in touch.'

As we were roughly escorted outside those large rusty wrought-iron gates, Frank called the Matron a fat old cow. But that didn't help any.

Our last resort now was to leave it to our vicar, hoping his influence could help.

The following Sunday evening I stood in St Paul's churchyard and waited until all the congregation had left. As soon as I was sure no one would see me, I entered the church. It was very dark inside; only the odd light bulb lit up the altar. I was somewhat relieved that neither the churchwarden nor the vicar was anywhere in sight, and I had a queer feeling inside me. But now I had got this far, I made up my mind not to go back out without a prayer. I knelt down in front of the altar, and prayed quietly to myself to ask God to watch over my children and to bring news soon from them, also from our vicar.

As I walked slowly outside, I felt better for praying. Some people might wonder why I never attended the church services and sat among the congregation, but everyone knew me around the district and if some of our neighbours saw me they would begin their gossiping again. That's one thing I couldn't stand, nor being stared at.

But I went alone three nights running. Only the warden and the cleaner ever saw me as I knelt to pray.

Then one evening the vicar called to tell me he had spoken to the Matron, and I would be having a visitor in a few days' time.

When I asked him if he had seen my children, he said he had and that they were happy and well taken care of. I plied him with all sorts of questions, but he seemed reluctant to say any more, only that I would hear more when my visitors called. And I was to have patience and pray.

Several weeks passed, but still no one came, so I lost faith in going to church to pray. As soon as I told my brother Frank the news, he said, 'You must have patience, Sis.'

'Patience! Patience!' I cried. 'I've even been to church and tried to pray, but God ain't answered my pleadings. It all seems to me a waste of time. If only He would give me some sort of sign, I'd be satisfied. I think I'd do better going to the chapel and asking Father O'Brien if he'll help,' I added.

'How do yer think he can help? He's a Catholic priest. I don't think he'd even listen to yer, and if he did he'd have yer in his confessional box to rake up all yer past.'

'But I've got nothing to hide or be ashamed of, Frank. If parting with my children was a sin, then God help me.'

'Well, Kate, be advised by me: *don't* go to that Catholic priest, you'll only get more upset, so just wait a bit longer until you hear from the vicar again. Now let's have a cuppa tea.'

While we sat drinking our tea, he began to change the subject by talking about when we were young children and begged orange-boxes for our makeshift bed and a buginfested flock mattress to lie on.

'And you remember the factories where we used to stand with bare feet and in rags, begging for food?' he added.

'Yes, Frank, I remember those days all too well.'

Just as he was about to carry on talking, I heard a knock on the door. My brother answered – there stood an elderly man and a middle-aged woman, both with briefcases under their arms.

I guessed at once who they were when the man asked if I was Mrs Flood.

'Yes,' I replied. 'Will you come in?' I added, as I saw nosy neighbours staring across the street.

'I'll be off now, Kate,' Frank said. 'I'll see you later.' As he kissed my cheek and said 'ta-ra', the woman stared at us both and asked who he was.

'He's my brother,' I replied sharply. I wondered who she thought he was.

'We have come from the Homes about your children and details of your circumstances. We would like to look around the house.'

'You also have a business?' the man asked.

'Yes,' I answered as I began to show them round my home.

The two inquisitors looked around every room – they even turned the bedclothes down from the beds I had kept well aired ready for when my children came back.

After saying they were satisfied that everything seemed in order, they asked to see my small business.

I sat in their car (different from my old boneshaker I had to get rid of) and after looking around and taking notes, they told me they were satisfied and would send in their reports, and I should have my children back in due course.

But although I waited anxiously for two more long years, it wasn't until 1939 that my children came home to me. And then the war had started.

My Daughter Jean

$$\longleftarrow\hspace{-4pt}\Longleftarrow\hspace{-4pt}\Diamond\hspace{-4pt}\Longrightarrow\hspace{-4pt}\longrightarrow$$

While my children were at Dr Barnardo's, Mary and Jean were transferred to live in the country: King's Lynn, Norfolk. But my daughter Kathleen, being the eldest, was kept at the Homes to do heavy chores. One of their punishments was that if they didn't eat what was put before them it was served up at the next meal, and the next, until they were so hungry they were glad to eat it. Sometimes cold mutton set hard on the plate. Jean also told me that she had cake once a week, when a visitor called, but she didn't like caraway-seed cake and wouldn't eat it. For her tea the following Sunday she had to sit down to a plate of caraway seeds, which she was forced to eat in front of all the other children.

When I brought my daughters back home they were no longer the babies I almost lost, but young girls. They had no understanding of the world outside the Homes. I had to try to make them understand that I was their real mother, yet it was hard for me to explain why I had parted with them. I was determined to give them the love and affection they had missed, but I found it hard to understand their ways at times, and they mine.

Soon after I had enrolled my youngest daughter Mary at the school in Soho Road, she was evacuated with the other children and their teachers to Wales. I didn't want to lose her again, but I thought it would be best for her to be away from the bombing.

I tried not to let her see my tears as I stood watching her standing with other children on the railway platform, holding her small attaché case and clutching her teddy bear, and with her name on a card and her gas mask tied round her neck. I felt very sad. I was only just getting used to her ways, and now I was parting with her again. But we visited her several times, and I was pleased to see she was quite happy with other evacuees.

Yet I didn't know Jean was missing her sister. Later, she began to rebel and cried often. She too couldn't understand why I had brought her home from the country to live in Birmingham, full of noise, bombing and sleeping down in airraid shelters. Often she used to say she was going to run away, yet I couldn't keep my eye on her all the time. I had my business to run.

After a few tantrums, she asked if she could go to work and learn enamelling with her eldest sister. Everything went smoothly for a while, until Kath became very bossy. They began their little squabbles.

I knew I was giving more attention to Jean, in case she decided to run away. Kath became jealous, and the two of them never could see eye to eye. Often Kath carried tales to me. At times, I foolishly believed her.

But my three daughters were never angels. Although they brought me no disgrace, they had their faults, like all teenagers, and many times I used to get exasperated.

On VE Day, 1945, everybody in the streets for miles around began celebrating, singing and dancing.

Jean and my sister-in-law, who was living with me at the time, were working for me in my enamelling business in Spencer Street, which is still in the Jewellery Quarter. As usual, I left early to go home and get their teas ready, but they were late coming home, and I began to get worried.

It was two hours later when I saw Jean stumble into the room, looking very pale. My sister-in-law was trying to hold her up. I cried, 'Jean! Whatever's the matter?'

'I wanta be sick,' she managed to say as she put her hand to her mouth.

As I reached for a bowl, Nellie replied, 'She'll be all right, I'll take her up to bed.'

'No you won't! Help me to lift her on to the settee, while I run for the doctor.'

Dr Arthur, our family doctor, had his practice in a small old house in Soho Road.

As soon as he had examined her, he began to stare hard at me. 'How old is this child?' he snapped.

When I told him she was nearly sixteen, he began to bawl out at me: 'Nearly sixteen! You should be ashamed to let her get into this state! This child is drunk! Give her a good drink of salt water, that's all she needs!' and he stormed out.

When I asked Nellie how Jean had got into this state, she replied, 'We all heard it was VE Day over the wireless, so we all downed tools and went across to the Jeweller's Arms to celebrate.'

Next day, when I made enquiries, I was told that my sister-in-law and Jean had drunk a bottle of whisky between them, and were later seen banging on dustbin lids and singing.

Jean was ill for days, but she had learnt her lesson. She never drank alcohol again. Yet my worries were renewed when she began to smoke. However, I was no good example: I too smoked during those war years, but I noticed she never inhaled the smoke.

Today she is a wonderful caring daughter with a loving husband, four lovely daughters, and grandchildren.

I often recall the day when Mary was evacuated with hundreds of other young schoolchildren. I felt very sad about parting with her again, yet as the train began to move out of the station and I waved goodbye, she began to smile as she too waved from the open window. 'Goodbye, Mum,' she called. 'See you and Jean when the war's over.'

'Yes!' I shouted loudly. 'We'll come and visit you soon.'

As I sat on the platform bench, wiping my eyes, I overheard two women beside me talking to each other. Thinking they knew this place where the children were going, I stopped to listen, and I heard one of them say, 'I don't think our lads or us women are goona stand them Germans invadin' England, Betty.'

'Well, I'm glad my three kids will be safer evacuated in the country, Sarah.'

''Vacuated, my foot! I don't know wot yer wanta send the little buggers away for, it looks ter me as if some of 'em wanta get rid of 'em,' the other woman replied. 'Any'ow,' she added, 'we never sent our kids away in the last war, an' we 'ad the Zeppelins then, like great big floatin' sausages in the air. An' one dropped a bomb on Kynocks.'

'Yes, we know,' replied Sarah. 'But it warn't the same in the 1914 war, everything was different. Now we've got big guns an' aeroplanes, airmen, a navy, and an army.'

'Some bloody army! Them lads won't stand a chance. I remember my two sons had ter train in the streets like thousands of others, up and down the country, with wooden rifles slung over their shoulders, because we 'adn't enough guns!'

'It's no good yer dwellin' on that, them days are gone. An' now we've got more modern equipment *and* we're getting more every day. Any'ow, we've all got to put our shoulders to the wheel, old and young alike, an' 'elp in the war effort.'

'I still think yer should 'ave kept yer children with yer, yer don't know wot they'll be gettin' up to in the country, an' God knows wot'll 'appen to 'em if *we* get invaded.'

'You always look on the black side. Good job we ain't all like you. Any'ow, 'ow's yower Benny, 'ave yer 'eard from 'im yet?'

'No, not yet, 'e ain't bin away long enough ter write, but 'e will. Any'ow, I 'ope Benny wears them warm socks and underpants I've knitted 'im, he feels the cold night air summat awful.'

'Knowin' yower Benny, it won't be long befower 'e finds 'imself a nice little WAAF ter keep 'im warm at nights. Yo and yower Benny! Yer mek me sick. It looks ter me as if yer wanta think about yer old man a bit mower! Any'ow, I can't sit 'ere all day listenin' about yower Benny. Anybody would think 'e was the only pebble on the beach!'

I could see they were both losing their tempers, so I got up and walked away. When I looked back, they were still going at each other.

As soon as I was indoors, Jean asked if Mary had got off all right. 'Yes,' I replied as tears filled my eyes. 'But I still wonder if I've done the right thing, Jeannie.'

'She'll be all right, Mum. Mary's used to living in the country. She'll love it. And we'll go and visit her when she's settled in. Now sit down while I put the kettle on, and we'll have a nice cup of tea.'

Phoebe

During 1940 young men of all ages were no longer seen queuing for their dole money or miserable hand-outs from parish relief. Nor did you see barrow boys from that once-famous Bull Ring, shouting their wares along the side of the open fish market. But to keep up their tradition, old men who had fought in the 1914 war took over their places – their mothers and wives too.

Many families looked forward to a Saturday night out in the Bull Ring, bargaining around the barrows before going into the overcrowded pubs to have a few drinks and talk about the war or the young lives that had been lost.

Many a man or boy sent money home to their loved ones, whatever they could spare. But often some would grumble; you'd hear them say, 'What's the use of bloody money when meat an' vegetables an' clothes are rationed?'

Even soap was rationed, yet there was always the black market. But these traders, who were called 'spivs', were often fined or put into prison. I remember one such fellow, who lived in Graham Street, was a conscientious objector – people called him a 'conchie'. He was in Winson Green prison for a while, but never was he in the forces. He used to say he didn't believe in killing humans, and still sold on the black market.

During those war years I saw my mother only about three or four times. She was a very domineering woman – stubborn too. Often we quarrelled over my children and domestic matters, and she would never go down to the shelters. When the sirens sounded she would always go to bed. My friend Phoebe and I collected everyone from our yards and took them down to the air-raid shelter, but we had several false alarms in Birmingham.

Although I had my small enamelling business in Spencer Street, I

647

gave my services many nights. But we were happy to stay at home when there were no sirens or bombs falling. One night I was invited to a party at the Bridge Tavern in Hunters Vale, owned by Gladys and Arthur Glover. I'd had a few drinks and everyone was merry, until we heard the sirens. Thinking about my two eldest daughters, Kath and Jean, whom I'd left in bed, I fled up Soho Road and down Waverhill Road. But in my hurry I'd forgotten to pick up my handbag with my keys in. I banged and banged, and kicked that door, but my daughters never heard me. There was only one thing left to do: I picked up a brick and smashed the window. As soon as I had climbed through, I flew up the stairs, and when I entered the bedroom I saw that my daughters were sleeping peacefully. But I had to get them downstairs. 'Wake up, wake up!' I cried. 'The sirens have gone!' As soon as we got downstairs, the three of us went into the larder, where we always kept a mattress in case of an emergency. I kept awake while my daughters slept on. It seemed hours as we lay there, yet everywhere seemed so quiet. As soon as dawn broke, I went into the street. When I saw the warden, I said, 'I wonder when the all clear is going to sound?'

'All clear, Mrs?' he replied, staring at me as though I was mad. 'The all clear went about eleven o'clock last night.'

What I'd thought was the warning was the all clear! We had many a laugh over that night, and the hours we spent in that cold larder. But it cost me thirty shillings to have that window and frame mended.

I would have loved to join the ARP, but I didn't have the time, working all day. But I spent many nights helping the wardens with fire-watching.

Mr Smith, who owned the glass shop just round the corner from where we lived, was one of the wardens, and beneath his shop was the shelter. I remember he asked me if I'd marry him as soon as the war was over. But although I liked him as a friend, I refused him. I didn't feel I wanted to get married again. Anyway, I had my independence now, and my daughters to think about.

We had all kinds of people down in that shelter – which used to be a storeroom – that ran underneath the front shops. There were men home on leave, women and children – even babies in arms. We even had men and women tramps, whom we would have passed by at any other time, but everybody helped everybody else in those days, whether they were rich, poor or indifferent. I noticed now that my neighbour, Phoebe, spent more time in pubs. One night I asked her why.

'Yo wanta try it, Kate, it 'elps yer ter ferget wot's 'appenin' around yer.'

Although I liked a glass or two of stout, I knew when I'd had enough.

Phoebe was really having trouble with her husband, yet it wasn't for me to pry. So as long as we got along well together, I knew she would tell me all in good time.

Many times we went fire-watching together, putting out incendiaries with sand from bins on the pavement. Phoebe had a sense of humour, and often when we lit a fag she would tell me funny stories about her family life, and how her husband set fire to the bed and what he put it out with. When I said I didn't believe her, she said, 'It's true. But I'll leave yer to guess. We had no water in the 'ouse!' she added.

'He never did!' I cried, laughing.

''E did, Kate, 'e pulls it out an' pisses anywhere, even in the entry, can't even wait till 'e gets up the yard ter the closet.'

I often smiled at the many stories she told me as we patrolled the streets, and one night I asked her about her three young children.

'Have you ever thought of having your children evacuated?'

'No, if we do get bombed I'd like us ter goo all together.'

'But Phoebe, that's bein' selfish.'

'Selfish or not, while they're 'ere, I want 'em where I can see wot they're doin' any'ow. 'Ow's your young Mary doin' in Wales?'

'She's fine. She loves the country and we go to visit when we can. But I still miss her, Phoebe. I've only had them back from the Homes fifteen months, and I'm still finding it hard to do what's best for them. I love 'em, but sometimes Jeannie rebels.'

'But why? She's such a nice kid.'

'Well, she was brought up in the country with Mary after leaving the Homes, and misses her. And neither of them couldn't understand why I brought them back to Birmingham and the bombing. And Jeannie worries me when she won't go down the air-raid shelter when the sirens start.'

'Where's yer son John, then, can't 'e do summat to 'elp?'

'My John's in the navy – that's where the Homes sent him – and he was only just fifteen and now he's in the midst of it all, and I pray every night to the good Lord to keep him safe. Now come on, Phoebe,' I added, 'it's time we took the cocoa down the shelter before it gets cold – they'll all be waiting.'

That very same night we could hear the thud of the bombs being dropped and the gunfire in the distance. Many of us would pray they wouldn't come nearer. But as they were heard to get louder and louder, almost overhead, old and young alike soon crammed into the shelter. My one thought was my two daughters, whom I'd left in bed. But as I looked among the crowd I was relieved to see them sitting on an empty crate.

Suddenly the lights went out, and as we lit some candles we heard the bombs falling nearer. We could hear fire engines clanging their bells as children began to wake up and scream, while mothers tried to pacify them by singing to them.

All at once, as I stood near one of the bunks, someone nearly toppled over me. When I shone my torch on to the floor, I could see it was an old drunken tramp who had crept in later. She had rolled off the bunk on to the floor still half awake, and with help from Phoebe I picked her up and laid her back on the bunk, where she closed her eyes and began to snore again.

All through that night, until dawn, the Germans were dropping their bombs and incendiaries – anywhere.

Phoebe and I offered to go out to help the warden put out some smaller fires, but he was adamant. 'You stay where you are!' he cried out. 'You'll be more help trying to calm the children down.'

That night will live in my memory for ever. So will the dawn. One bomb hit Woolworth's, next to the bank. Many fools ran out when they saw slips of paper flying through the air, which they thought were pound notes from the bank; two boys were killed.

As soon as daylight came and the all clear sirens sounded, everyone rushed out to see if their homes were still there, but many had been badly damaged. Kind neighbours took them in. Just as I was leaving with my two daughters, the warden came towards me.

'I'm sorry to tell you this, Mrs Flood, but I think you had better try and make your way down Camden Drive. It's had a direct hit.'

That was in April 1941 – my mother and sister Mary were killed, with many neighbours and friends.

I shall never forget the day of the funerals. There wasn't a dry eye in the Lane, and as we entered the cemetery I saw men and women alike still digging to make room for those communal graves.

As I stood there and wept, with my brothers and sister Liza, I thought only of the harsh words my mother and I had often exchanged. And the saddest thing of all: it's too late to withdraw them – but they still live in my memory.

If only my mother had come to live with me when I pleaded with her to leave Camden Drive! She wouldn't have been lying there in that communal grave with my sister Mary and the many neighbours on that fatal night in April 1941.

Phoebe, too, was at that same graveside weeping with many other people who had lost loved ones, for she had lost a young brother and her dad, whilst fire-watching.

After that terrible night of bombing there was a lull, and I saw less and less of Phoebe. The only times she came was when she wanted to borrow.

As everything was now on ration it was hard for everyone to manage. Queuing up for hours outside different shops, you would be lucky if you got three sausages. Other times, after waiting, when it was at last your turn, as soon as you got to the door, you'd see the butcher put a notice in the window: 'Sorry. Try again tomorrow.'

It was on a morning like this that I saw Phoebe at the end of the queue.

'He's sold out, Phoebe, let's try some of the other shops – we might be lucky for a few scrag ends,' I said.

''E ain't sold out! I know 'im, the crafty ol' bleeda! 'E keeps 'is best pieces under the counter, ter sell on the black market. Somebody oughta shop 'im!' Phoebe shouted for all to hear.

'Why don't *you* shop 'im?' cried one of our neighbours, who already had her three sausages.

'You shut yer gob, you ol' bag!' yelled Phoebe. 'I see you've got yower three sausages, an' it's not only sausages 'e lets yer 'ave. It's p'raps a feel of '*is* sausage, if I know 'im.'

Everybody began to laugh, and the neighbour, Mrs Reeves, suddenly screeched, 'I'll wrap these bleedin' sausages around yer bleedin' ear'ole, yer saucy bleeda!'

'Goo on then!' Phoebe shouted back. 'I could do with a feed.'

As Mrs Reeves was about to dash across the way, she stopped and seemed to have second thoughts, for she knew Phoebe was a tough customer. As Phoebe stood waiting for her next move, crowds of bystanders were listening, expecting to see a rough-and-tumble.

'Come on, Phoebe,' I said, pulling her coat sleeve. 'Let's go before the coppers come.'

'All right, all right!' she replied angrily. 'But I'll see that butcher closes down. Anyway,' she added, 'I know where I can get a piece of meat, without any trouble.'

'But where?' I asked.

'There's a bloke I know who's got a butcher's shop.'

'Where?' I asked again.

'It's in Aston, near the House that Jack Built.'

'But I can't go now, Phoebe, I've already spent three wasted hours trying to get three sausages I dain't get, and my daughters will be waiting for their tea.'

'Got summat nice, then?' she asked.

'Well, no, we got to make do with yesterday's leftover mutton, tough as an old horse,' I added.

'I 'ad some 'orse flesh last week off Alf, an' it was better than a piece of steak,' she replied.

'Who's Alf?' I asked.

''E's this friend of mine who's the butcher – now are yer cummin' or not?' she cried impatiently.

'All right, but I'll have to leave a note where I'm going.'

'Whatever yer do, Kate, don't tell 'em where we're gooin', I'm supposed to keep quiet about him.'

'All right, I'll just say "I won't be long".'

Off we hurried. But as soon as the butcher saw me, he asked, 'Who's 'er?'

'She's me friend,' replied Phoebe.

'Is she all right?' I heard him whisper.

'Yes, she won't say anything.'

'All right, me old cock, but where yer bin 'idin' yerself these days?'

'I'll explain later, but can yer manage to let me 'ave a bit of liver an' a few chops?'

'Anything for you, me darling,' I heard him whisper. I saw him pinch her bottom and put his hand up her skirt. She burst out laughing.

I blushed all over, and wished I hadn't come. I was beginning to feel embarrassed.

As soon as he had given her a parcel and we were outside, I said, 'Why did yer let him do that?'

'Do what?' she asked.

'Pinch yer bottom,' I replied. 'And let him put his hand up yer skirt, and what was yer whispering about?' I added.

'Oh, nothing that would be of any interest to you, Kate. Any'ow, there's no 'arm done, 'e's only me cousin.'

I'd heard that one before, and I wasn't as green as she thought I was.

But I was grateful for the liver, and next day we sat down and enjoyed our fried liver and onions, and no questions asked. Later, Phoebe came to say Alf had had to go in the army. As everything was rationed, it was hard to manage.

I hadn't seen Phoebe for a couple of weeks, then one day I was surprised to see her knock on my door.

'Can I cum in?' she called through the letterbox.

As soon as she came into the front room, I saw that her eyes were all black and blue.

When I asked her how they got that way, she replied, 'It's a long story, I ain't got time ter tell yer now, but could yer let me 'ave a bit of sugar?'

As I didn't take sugar myself, I gave her what was left in the basin. She said she'd return it later, but she never did. Another day it was a bit of lard, or margarine, then I never saw her again until a week later. And as I opened the door to let her in, she flopped down on the chair. I noticed that her eyes were still discoloured. All at once she asked if I could let her have a bit of tea.

'I'm sorry, Phoebe,' I replied, 'but I only have my two ounces a week and you know how far that goes; you'll have to stew the leaves up.'

'I've got no leaves ter stew up now, Arthur teks 'is two ounce an' shares it with 'is mates at work, an' sometimes I can't even find me ration books, 'e even teks the coupons out and changes 'em for Player's Weights, *an'* some of me clothes coupons,' she added.

'But can't you hide the books?' I replied.

''E'd find 'em any'ow, an' if I don't give 'em to 'im, 'e starts beatin' me. But as soon as this bleedin' war is over, I'm goin' ter leave the drunken bastard, an' the kids.'

As soon as I saw the tears, I felt sorry for her.

'Here you are then, yer better have half of what I've got. But that'll have to be the last.' I gave her half what was in the caddy, and as she went to go out she said, 'Kate, could yer lend me ten shillin'?'

'No, I can't! What yer want ten shillings for anyway?'

'Well, I can get a bit of black market off that bloke in Graham Street.'

'I'm sorry, Phoebe, but I don't encourage people in the black market.'

With that she left, but I remember I was glad of a bit of black market when my daughter Kathleen got married later.

Mrs Hickman, who had a fruit and vegetable shop in Hockley Street, supplied everybody, as long as she could see their money. I knew it was wrong, but it was a temptation – you could get a fine or imprisonment or both. Many times I was worried in case I was found out. But many of us didn't care, for we never knew if we would be alive from one day to the next.

Yet often, if I got an orange or a couple of bananas, I'd give them to a neighbour for her hungry baby. And they never asked how I came by them. No doubt they guessed.

Once I gave Phoebe some tomatoes. When she asked me where they came from I replied, 'It's very hush-hush.'

She was the last person to tell, otherwise I could see her going to that shop and making a nuisance of herself.

The next time she called she walked in and as she sat down on the settee, she asked at once, 'Kate, I ain't cum ter borra any of yer rations, but I was wonderin' if yer could lend me yer fox-fur stole? Yer see, I've bin invited to this birthday party.'

'What party's this?' I asked.

'It's a young woman I used ter work with – lives in Nursery Road,' she added.

I'd always had a soft spot for her, for she hadn't many clothes and often I gave her what I could spare and liked to see her wearing them. I hadn't worn my furs for a couple of years. I'd never liked them anyway, they were still in the wardrobe.

As soon as I brought them down and handed them to her, she cried at once, 'They're lovely, Kate. Wanta sell 'em to me?'

'No, Phoebe, but see as you bring them back – remember, I'm only lending them to yer.'

I would willingly have given them to her, but I could see now I was only encouraging her to come borrowing.

Three weeks later she never came, so I decided this was the last time I would believe or trust her. Therefore, I made up my mind to call at her home and fetch them back.

I had never been inside her house, but as I stood outside I noticed that the place didn't look very wholesome. As I stepped over rubbish, broken bricks and slates, and broken windows, some still holding together with sticking plaster from previous bombings, I wondered then if anyone still lived there. But I had to find out. As soon as I knocked on the door it suddenly flew open wide, and there stood Phoebe's husband, a tall, thin, sallow-faced man. At once I noticed several days' growth of grey stubbly hair sprouting from his chin and upper lip, where hung a half-broken fag. The sleeves of his grubby shirt were rolled up to his elbows, his arms were covered in blue and red tattoos. His trousers were greasy and tied round his waist with his braces. And as he stood there in his stockinged feet, staring at me, he shouted, 'Wot do you want? If yer cum ter see Pheeb, she ain't 'ere!'

'But can I come in and wait?' I asked.

'Yo'll 'ave a lung bleedin' wait then! She's left me, an' me kids!' he bawled.

Just then I saw two grubby little girls, about three or four years old, staring at me as they came and stood beside him.

'Lizzie!' he bawled. 'Cum and fetch these kids in!'

But they seemed scared and ran into the room.

'I'm sorry,' I replied. 'I'll call again.'

I was about to go, when he yelled, 'Wot yer cum for any'ow?'

'Could you tell me if she's left my furs here? If so I would like them back,' I replied.

'No, 'er ain't!' he snapped. ''Er p'raps took 'em with 'er, ration books an' all!' he added. ''An' if yer *do* see 'er, yer can tell 'er from me, I ain't ever 'avin' 'er back!'

I could see I was getting nowhere, and as I went to go he slammed the door in my face.

I didn't bother about the furs now; all I kept thinking about was those two unwashed, neglected children.

A few days later I opened my door to a loud knock. When I opened it, a young woman stood on the step. I noticed she was overdressed, with well-rouged cheeks and painted lips; also her eyebrows had been shaved and pencilled over. Her hair, I could see, she had attempted to dye blonde, with the black roots showing. She wore long dangling red earrings, a long green dress and a short rabbit-skin fur coat (we used to call them bum-freezers). As soon as I asked who she was, she replied, 'I'm Pheeb's sister, an' I've brought yer furs back.'

I couldn't believe she was Phoebe's sister, she hadn't even mentioned she had one. She wasn't anything like her. As she handed the parcel to me she cried as she looked across the yard, 'I see yer got plenty of nosy neighbours.'

I would have invited her in, then I saw Mrs Carter turn her nose up at her as she passed.

'But why couldn't she come herself?' I asked.

'That's 'er bloody business!' she snapped. 'Any'ow,' she added, 'I'm only 'ere ter look after Arthur's kids!'

I took the furs and as I said 'thank you' I closed the door. As soon as she'd gone I peeped through the curtain to see several women across the street whispering together.

She didn't look the type of person to care for children. Yet, I thought, if she *was* telling the truth, then it was none of my business.

Later that same evening I was to find out from neighbours. She was the barmaid from the Globe Tavern, also Arthur's fancy woman.

A couple of days later, when I opened up the parcel, I found that one of the tails was missing. I took the furs upstairs, pushed them into the wardrobe, and forgot about them – until I decided to have a clear-out. Then I saw that moths had decided to have a loan of them. I put them in an old basket for my daughter Jeannie's cat, Sooty.

I never saw or heard what became of my fire-watching friend Phoebe. Nor her family. I knew only that they had moved before their house was bombed.

Sal

Many kind neighbours would help each other as best they could in the war years, and often we called each other by our Christian names. Except children. No matter how poor, they were always taught their manners by addressing their elders by their surnames or whatever, and it was always 'Yes please' or 'No thank you'. But often you would get the odd cheeky, but harmless ones. They were always disciplined by their parents or schoolteachers.

Mrs Briggs – Sal, as I often called her – was one of my neighbours. She had two daughters, Florrie and Annie, who were in the land army. She also had three sons, who were too young to enlist with their father. Two of them were working on munitions; the youngest lad, Georgie, was nearly six. He was a lovely little lad who often reminded me of my son John.

Early one morning, Sal came knocking on my door. As soon as I opened it she cried, 'Oh, Kate! Kate! I've just 'ad a telegram from the War Office ter tell me me 'usband is missin'. Wot am I gooin' ter tell me lads?'

When I saw the tears streaming down her face, I said, 'You better come in, Sal, and sit down.'

As she flopped down on the sofa, she began to sob into her apron.

'I'll put the kettle on and make you a cuppa, Sal,' was all I could say, for she was sobbing and crying aloud.

'It's little Georgie, 'e'll break 'is little 'eart when 'e knows.'

I didn't know what to say to console her, but I said how sorry I felt.

I knew she liked a drop of whisky. As I handed her the cup of tea I asked if she'd like some, and she nodded. As I poured it into the cup, I told her I couldn't spare much as it was for the wardens when we had a bad night. As she drank it down she was still sobbing. I said, 'Look, Sal, it could be a false alarm, and you might have another telegram to say he's safe. Then you'll have all yer worry for nothing,' I added, trying to console her.

'But I don't know 'ow I'm gooin' ter tell me lads,' she managed to say.

'Well, Sal, if you think it's best, tell your two eldest, but I should spare little Georgie's feelings until later, as you know he's too young to understand. Anyway, Sal, as I say, it could still be a false alarm.'

After finishing her tea, she said, 'Little Georgie's six termorra an' I promised ter mek 'im a cake, an' 'is little friends 'ave bin invited. But now I feel too upset ter even think about it.'

'Try not to worry, Sal. I know it's easy for me to say don't worry, but if I can help in any way, I will. Anyway, *I'll* make him a cake. I ain't got much as regards ingredients, but if I ask one or two of the neighbours, I'm sure they'll help.'

As she thanked me I hoped she would understand what I had been trying to say, for she was still sobbing as she left.

As soon as the door closed, I found a recipe I had cut out of a newspaper – 'How to make a wartime cake'. It read something like this:

> 6 oz self-raising flour
> 2 oz margarine, lard, or dripping
> 2 teaspoons powdered milk
> 5 saccharin tablets or black treacle
> 1 large carrot, scraped and diced small

> Put in mixing bowl, add half teaspoon of bicarb.
> Mix well with one teacup of water.
> Grease tin and put in oven mark four and leave
> for one hour.

As soon as it was baked I took it from the oven, but I was scared to think what it would taste like. Anyway, it looked nice and brown.

When I called Sal indoors to see it, she remarked how nice it smelt. 'Wot yer mek it with, Kate?' she asked at once.

'Ha,' I replied, smiling. 'It's a secret, but I did manage to scrounge some of the ingredients off the neighbours. There was only one who refused, and I don't have to tell you who that skinny old skinflint was,' I added.

It was a warm, sunny spring day, so we decided to take a couple of kitchen tables out into the yard, and with the help of whatever the neighbours could spare, we set the tables with bread and jam, bread and treacle and bottles of homemade ginger pop. I decorated the cake I'd made with silver paper and six candles I'd found in a drawer, also a small paper Union Jack in the centre, and placed it in the middle of the table.

After we had set the six odd cups for the pop, the six little lads, including Georgie, were seated. We adults stood by to watch them enjoy their so-called feast. But when it came to the cake, I wondered what it would taste like.

I watched Sal cut six pieces, one for each lad, and it was decided we should all sing 'Happy Birthday' to Georgie.

I was pleased to see that the lads were enjoying the cake, but all at once little Freddy Carter threw his across the table. 'I don't like that!' he cried out. 'It's got carrots in!'

Suddenly his mother gave him a hard slap across his face.

'Yo'll bloody well eat it, or I'll ram it down yer throat!' she cried out as she picked it up.

'But I don't like carrots,' he whimpered.

'Yo 'eard wot I sed! Yo'll eat it an' be grateful!' she replied.

I watched his tear-stained face as he tried. But after the first swallow, I was pleased to hear him ask for another slice. The other kids seemed to enjoy it too.

After the feast was over, Mrs Freer decided to bring out the old gramophone, and as she put on a record and turned the handle, we all began to sing to the old cracked record:

> 'Oh yes, we have no bananas,
> We have no bananas today.
> We've got broad beans, and bunions,
> Carrots, and onions,
> And all kinds of things they say.
> But yes, we have no bananas,
> We have no bananas today.'

A few days later little Georgie came and thanked me for his birthday cake and asked when was I going to make another.

'I don't know, Georgie. Everything's on ration, and we can't keep asking for food, that's hard to come by.'

'But I can get some carrots off the farm, an' Freddy is six on Sunday. Could you mek 'im one so we can 'ave another party?'

'Is that the lad who said he didn't like it?' I asked.

'Yes, but 'e did after 'e ate it, an' 'e's asked me to ask yer.'

'I'm sorry, Georgie, but I'll give his mum the recipe, then she'll be able to make it. Anyway, when the war's over we'll have a *big* party, and I'll make you a *real* cake with currants and cherries, and it will have real sugar in. Now be off, or you'll be late for Sunday School.'

Now, in 1944, the war had taken a turn for the better. News was coming over the wireless every hour to say how our planes were bombing Germany. But there was still fifteen months before peace would be declared, and food was still on ration well after the war was over.

Everyone made the best of their troubles and losses, and whenever someone lost their home there was always a helping hand ready and willing to take them into *their* home, which resulted in many being overcrowded. But people still had a real sense of humour.

Often you would hear them singing dirty little ditties and slogans about Hitler and his mistress Eva Braun. In pubs or clubs and even inside the factories where they worked, and wherever you walked, you would see posters stuck to ruined walls, even outside munitions factories. Many of the slogans were there for everyone to read. One poster that was stuck on the outside toilet walls read:

> When Hitler couldn't get his Braun,
> He'd use old Goebbels with the horn,
> But often Goebbels cried with shame,
> Even he couldn't stand the strain.

Slogans like this were there for everyone to read and joke about. But if little kids were heard to repeat them, many would get a spanking – which did *some* good, yet never did them any harm.

Since I never saw or heard any news from my fire-watching friend Phoebe, I found more time for talking and listening to my neighbours' gossip. Yet there was quite an assortment who lived in our district. Some I liked, but to those I didn't I would only say good morning or good evening, whatever the time of day, and walk away.

But I missed my friend Phoebe, and several nights on my rounds I used to get very lonely. I wasn't too brave either. When I told Mr Smith, the warden, that I was thinking of giving it up, he said he would ask one of the other women to accompany me. But it so happened nobody wanted the job, without pay. Then one night, as I left the air-raid shelter to go home to make the usual jugs of cocoa for the kids whose mothers were afraid to have them evacuated, someone tapped me on the shoulder. When I turned round I saw it was Sal.

'Kate, would yer like me ter 'elp yer mek the cocoa?'

I was glad of her offer, and as I thanked her she replied, 'Yer know summat, Kate, I think yer very brave ter do that fire-watchin'.'

'Thank you,' I replied. 'I didn't mind doing it when Phoebe was here to help, but I don't feel so brave now on my own, so I'm thinking of giving it up.'

'Well, Kate, now me sons are on night shift p'raps I could cum with yer.'

'But you know it's only voluntary. There's no pay, and I don't have to do it. But it's better than staying down that stuffy air-raid shelter, and you can feel safer in the street.'

'That's if yer lucky, Kate,' she replied.

'Anyhow, when yer time comes, no matter where you are, that's it,' I added.

As soon as we got indoors we put both the kettles on the gas stove. While we were waiting for them to boil, she said, 'Your 'ouse, Kate, it's nice, an' it's tidier than mine. Anyway yer must cum an' 'ave a cuppa with me some time, an' a chat.'

'I'd love that, Sal, but wouldn't your sons mind?' I asked.

'No, they always talk about yer and say 'ow kind you are an' little Georgie thinks an' ses yer lovely. Tells all the kids in the school too about that cake yer med fer 'is birthday.'

As soon as we had made the two large enamel jugs of cocoa and were on our way to the shelter, she said, 'When Ted and Wilf cum 'ome in the mornin', I'm goin' ter tell 'em I'm gooin' fire-watchin' with yer.'

'Thank you, Sal, but if they object I shall understand.'

'They can't stop me! If once I mek me mind up ter do summat, I do it!'

I smiled and thanked her. From then on we became firm friends. As soon as we entered the shelter, the sirens sounded the all clear for the second time. But no one was in a hurry to leave when they saw us with the cocoa; children and parents stayed to finish it.

The following night Sal came to tell me that she'd told her sons, and she was to please herself. 'But I must be in when they cum 'ome fer their breakfast.' Although I was grateful for her offer, I thought about her youngest, who was only six. 'But what about Georgie?' I asked.

'Georgie will be all right down the shelter, Kate, 'e'll be with 'is friend Jimmy an' 'is mum ses she'll keep 'er eye on 'im.'

We enjoyed a drop of whisky and a fag together – when we could get any.

On quieter nights, when my daughters were tucked up in bed, we would go into each other's homes and talk for hours about when we were young, and about our families. The first time I entered Sal's house I noticed how gloomy it was, with its dark wallpaper and sombre paintings. The furniture was old but highly polished; every corner of the room was very clean, but untidy.

As soon as Sal saw me looking around, she cried out, 'It ain't alwis like this, Kate, but me lads are very untidy, it ain't like your place.'

'I quite understand, Sal. You want to see it when my daughters come in – everything's thrown about and they expect yer to hang everything up after them,' I replied.

'It's betta than the place where we used ter live, but one of these days we're gooin' ter move, no more one down and one up,' she said.

'I know how you feel, Sal. I came from the same district before I made a break.'

When I told her where we used to live, she replied, 'Well, I never! An' I alwis thought yer cum from a posh area.'

'No, my mum had thirteen children, and it must have been a blessing that seven of them died of childhood complaints. The rest of us lived in one living-room, one bedroom, and an attic,' I replied, remembering those hardship years.

'My mum 'ad six before she 'ad me, an' I was seven when she told me they all died young. But I'm not ashamed, Kate, ter tell yer 'ow I was dragged up.'

'I'm sorry, Sal, but do yer feel yer want to tell me?'

'Yes, Kate,' she replied. 'I've never told anyone, not even my sons or daughters, and they've never asked.'

So we lit another fag and drank the remaining whisky, then she began to relate her childhood. And as I sat by the fireside facing her, I listened.

The Facts of Sal's Life

<hr />

'W hen me mum an' me dad died of TB, Kate, I was left an orphan, an' I never 'ad any schoolin'. I can't even read or write, an' ever since I can remember them many years ago I was 'ungry, ragged, dirty, 'air lousy, an' after me mum an' dad was buried by the parish, I 'ad nowhere ter turn to, I even walked miles ter find the 'ouse where me Auntie Maggie lived. But when I did find it, she said I 'ad ter goo an' see me dad's sister, Auntie Maud, who lived in the next yard. When I knocked on the door, an' she saw me, she dragged me inside quick, ashamed the neighbours would see me. She 'ad a man lodger, an' when 'e sat there starin' at me, me aunt cried out, "Look wot the cat's dragged in".

'She sheltered me for a while, but I was knocked from pilla ter post; but I was grateful for the leftovers she fed me, also the flock mattress where I slept in the attic. But I 'ad ter slave like a lackey to earn that.

'I was really scared of Maud's lodger. I knew she slept with him some nights, other nights I used to 'ear 'er snorin' in 'er own room. Sometimes I used to see 'im with a lopsided grin on 'is ugly face, watching me every movement. I could even feel 'im undressin' me with them eyes of 'is. One night when me aunt was out, I saw 'is hand begin to unfasten the buttons on 'is flies. I got scared, then all at once 'e cum grinnin' towards me an' pushed me up against the pantry door, an' when 'e pulled me frock up an' I felt 'is hand inside me drawers, I began ter kick an' scream for all I was worth. As soon as 'e let go of me, I bit 'is 'and an' scratched 'is face. Then 'e slapped me across the face an' threatened ter kill me if I told me aunt. But as soon as she came in, I *did* tell 'er, but she wouldn't believe me, an' yer know what she did, Kate? She said I was a brazen trollop, an' that I must 'ave encouraged 'im. Then she beat me an' said she was sorry she took me in. The next day she took me to an orphanage. Wot an awful place that was! I was deloused an' bathed in 'ot disinfectant, an' me rags were took away an' burnt, an' after they shaved all me 'air off, I stood naked on that cold stone floor until they decided ter bring a pair of old leather boots, a pair of red flannel drawers, an' a dark-grey smock fer me ter wear. Then I was pushed roughly into a room full of other young girls, dressed an' scalped like meself. After we were lined up we was given a stale crust of black treacle and a mug of warm weak tea. Then after we'd eaten, we was led into another room ter pray fer our blessin's.'

'My God!' I replied. 'Some blessings!'

Then she went on to say, 'I didn't mind the punishments that were dished out ter me. It was when several older girls got together an' often called me lousy. I felt so ashamed, an' I was punished fer fightin'.'

'But having a dirty head was nothing to be ashamed of in those days, Sal. I remember many girls and boys who had dirty heads, but even if you was clean you always used to catch them. But *we* had a nurse who came once a week to our school to inspect us and if she found any nits you was sent home with a note, and I had one once.'

'I can't imagine you to 'ave a dirty 'ead, Kate.'

'I sure did,' I replied. 'It happened one day. Once a year girls who were clean were given a party ticket, called Pentlands Royal Robins. I remember my sister had one; when I asked her why I hadn't got one she said I'd better ask me teacher. I said, "But what if she don't give me one?" Then she said I was to start crying an' to make sure to yell loud. When I did, all I got was the bamboo cane, but teacher said she would find one for me later. And that's the first time I knew I had nits, a few days later, when my teacher gave me a note sealed in an envelope. I thought it was a party ticket. I ran all the way home, and as soon as I saw me mum in the brewhouse doing her washing with the other neighbours, I waved the envelope in the air and shouted, "Mum, I've got a party ticket, look!" As soon as she opened the envelope, she went wild. She caught hold of my hair, and dragged me indoors. "Wot have I done now?" I managed to yell out. She said, "Yo've only showed me up in front of the neighbours! Now I'll be the talk of the street!" She said that wasn't me party ticket, it was a note from the nurse to say I got nits, and when she told me to get her the steel toothcomb and I bent over a piece of newspaper, there was the truth. And after painful tuggings, she washed my hair in Derbac Soap. After that, she cut my hair, which looked like two small fat sausages tied with string. So yer see, Sal, everybody gets 'em, some time or other,' I said.

'But when me 'air started ter grow agen, I still 'ad 'em, an' that was when I tried ter run away. That was when I was fifteen, Kate. But before that, there was another girl – many called her "Tin Ribs" because she was so thin; I never knew 'er real name, an' she never used to say. When we 'appened to speak to each other, I used ter call 'er Lizzie, and she seemed pleased enough. She was an orphan too, an' every mornin' we 'ad ter be up at five o'clock cleaning boots, emptyin' slop buckets, while the elders looked over us. We even had to empty the ashes an' black-lead the grates until yer could see yer face in 'em, Kate. I could talk for hours about 'ow cruel the people was in that orphanage.'

'And did yer manage to get away?' I asked.

'Yes, me an' Lizzie planned it together. But she was a nervous girl, an' kept makin' excuses. But eventually, one night, we escaped through the dormitory winda. It was a pitch-black night, an' we'd only gone a few yards, and Lizzie believed in ghosts. She began to scream, an' said she saw one, so she ran back an' left me. I ran on, but it wasn't long before one of the keepers shone 'is torch on me. We were both punished and beaten an' sent ter bed. Next mornin' me an' Lizzie 'ad ter sit an' watch the other inmates eat their porridge. There was none left for us two. Later that night we were given an 'ard crust of bread an' a cuppa warm watered-down tea. A few weeks later, I saw me chance ter run away agen. I didn't tell Lizzie, I was afraid she'd see ghosts agen an' let me down. So then I was on me own.

'It was while I was marching with the other inmates on our way ter chapel. One of the sisters in charge told us to follow on quietly. As I was the last one left behind to enter the chapel, I saw my chance. I slowly tiptoed backwards – lucky for me no one saw me an' I knowed I wouldn't be missed fer the next hour or more. So I 'ad plenty of time ter run.'

'Wasn't you afraid of being caught again, Sal?' I asked.

'Oh yes, but yer couldn't see me arse fer dust, when once I got outside them chapel gates,' she replied, smiling.

We both began to laugh. Sal lit a cigarette, and when I got up from the chair I asked if I should make a pot of tea.

'Yes, Kate, but I ain't finished tellin' the 'alf of it yet.'

I could see she was now eager to tell me the rest of the story. I too was eager to listen.

As soon as we finished our cigarettes and drank our tea, she said, 'Yer sure yer want ter 'ear the rest?'

'Oh yes, Sal,' I replied eagerly.

'Well, where was I?'

'Yer couldn't see yer arse for dust,' I replied, smiling.

'Well, I dain't know 'ow long I'd bin runnin', until I dropped down exhausted an' fell asleep in an 'edge. I don't know 'ow long I slept when I felt somebody shakin' at me with a stick. When I opened me eyes I saw an old ragged woman bent almost double. She was still pokin' the stick in me when she asked who I was an' where I'd cum from. I was too scared ter tell 'er, so I just said I was on me way 'ome an' was lost. But when she stared down at me she said "Yer tellin' lies, now ain't yer!" She must 'ave noticed wot I was wearin'. When I got to me feet, she said, "Yo ain't lorst at all, yo've run away from them theea orphanages, ain't yer!" An' when I pleaded with 'er not ter send me back, she replied, "Why yer poor 'arf-starved little bugger, I wouldn't send a dog ter die in one of them places. I know, I was brought up in one meself. But that was a long time agoo." Well, any'ow, she told me ter follow 'er ter the cottage, an' when we got inside she put some more logs on the fire and made me sit down while she made me a basin of hot broth. An' while she was makin' it in the corner of the room, I glanced around to see that the place was cluttered up with old clothes, an' there was spider webs 'angin' from the ceilin', and even cockroaches an' rats, but it was a shelter an' somewhere ter 'ide. Yer know summat, Kate, I was fifteen an' a 'alf before I ever knew wot kindness was. That dear old woman looked after me, fed me, an' give me a warm straw mattress ter sleep on, an' in return, all I 'ad ter do was keep 'er cottage clean an' do 'er washin' an' cookin'. It dain't tek me lung ter get rid of them spiders, an' them cockroaches an' rats. She was like an old lost lovable granny I'd found.'

'Didn't anyone find out where you were?' I asked.

'No, that tumbledown cottage was miles away from anywhere an' everybody. An' yer know wot, she kept me 'idden away till I was seventeen. She 'ad one son who used ter cum ter visit 'er in an old truck. That was only once a month. But 'e brought us vittles an' was kind to me too. But she was very old an' I cried for days after she died. An' when the son came an' said I 'ad ter leave, I got into a terrible state. But when I told 'im I 'ad nowhere ter goo, 'e said I could stay on a bit longer until 'e sorted things out.

'After a while 'e said 'e was comin' ter live there, an' if I would still take over the chores, I could stay. When I put me arms around his neck an' kissed 'im and thanked 'im, 'e just smiled. 'E was ten years older than me. After a while 'e came to live there. 'E was very kind to me, Kate, an' I liked 'im, an' one night we slept together an' med luv, that led ter more luvmekin'. When I got pregnant an' me first babby died only two days old, 'e asked me ter marry 'im. After we married 'e sold that old cottage. That's where we cum to terday, an' where me two daughters an' me three sons were born, an' I don't think anybody 'as gone through the mill like I 'ave.'

'We all have a cross to bear, Sal. I too had a hard life when I was young and suffered too, only under different circumstances. I wasn't an orphan, but I had a very cruel mother. Maybe, one day, I'll tell you about my family and how hard and cruel my mother was. I hated her at times, Sal. But when we grow older and have a family of our own, it's not until then we realise what our parents have gone through to rear us, or even *try* to, in a back-to-back dilapidated house full of fleas, and bugs, and no money coming into the household. Everybody in the district had sad moments and heartbreaks, but time heals all wounds, and *my* happiest days was when I attended school.'

'If I'd 'ave gone ter school p'raps I would 'ave 'ad a better life,' she replied.

'Anyway, Sal, we got to live for today and our children. We never know what tomorrow will bring while this war's on, and we can't see into the future, otherwise we'd plan our lives to suit ourselves.'

'I suppose yer right, Kate. But I feel better now I've told you. An' yer know summat,' she added, 'you're the first one I've felt like talkin' to. I ain't ever spoke about me life before, not even ter me sons an' daughters.'

'Have they ever asked?'

'No. I'd feel ashamed, an' they already know I can't read or write.'

'You've nothing ter be ashamed of, Sal, but one day, when they get married and have a family of their own, they may ask, or their grandchildren will, so believe me, don't be scared – or ashamed – to tell them. I'm sure they'll understand.'

'I 'ope so,' she replied.

After we had wished each other good night, I called out, 'See yer tomorrow, Sal – that's if we don't hear the sirens wailing.'

We didn't. That was one of the good nights and we enjoyed a welcome night's sleep.

Florrie Comes Home

S al had very bad arthritis in her hands, and often when I found time I would help her to do her washing and ironing.

One Saturday morning, as her three sons were sitting down to breakfast, I called and gave the boys their shirts I'd ironed. They were always grateful, and so was I for the kindnesses they did for their mum and me. Fetching coal from the wharf and cleaning our windows – nothing was too much trouble for them. Sal was very proud of her sons. I was about to leave when Ted said, 'Georgie, move off that chair and let Mrs Flood sit down.'

I thanked Georgie and sat down. Sal handed me a cup of tea and Georgie cried, 'Yer cum ter mek me another cake?'

'Not this time, Georgie, but I've promised you the big one when the war's over,' I replied as I smiled at him.

Yer won't forget then, will yer?' he asked, smiling back.

'Now yo goo out an' play!' his mother told him, 'an' stop yer mitherin'.'

As soon as he'd gone and the two elder boys had finished eating their breakfast, and helped me and their mum to wash and wipe the crocks, they went into the other room to play dominoes, leaving me and their mum to sort over the dirty clothes ready for the brewhouse on Monday morning. And as we were chatting together, the door suddenly flung open and in came Sal's daughter, Florrie.

It seemed only yesterday when she came to me and told me she was joining the forces, away from her drunken bad-tempered father. She was a lovely-looking girl, and very smart she looked in her WAAF uniform.

As soon as her mother saw her, tears fell as she flung her arms about her. And as Florrie picked up Georgie and hugged him, Sal called out, 'Ted, Wilf! Cum an' look who's cum 'ome!'

As soon as they came into the living-room and saw their sister, Wilf cried out, 'I thought it was me dad!'

'That's a nice greeting, I must say!' Florrie replied. 'I thought you'd be over the moon to see me.'

'We are, we are, Sis,' Ted replied excitedly. 'But we 'ad news from the War Office ter say our dad was missin', and we never expected it ter be you.'

'Well, come and give me a kiss, then,' she exclaimed.

While they were embracing, I thought it was about time I left them to enjoy their meeting. But as soon as I said I was going, Florrie replied, 'You don't have to leave, Mrs Flood. I'm pleased to see you, and I wish to thank you for doing what you can for me mum.'

'That's all right, Florrie. It's nothing really, but what are neighbours for – only to help in these wicked times.'

'Mum's never mixed with any neighbour before, and Ted has written to me often telling me how she's took up fire-watching with you.'

'It's quite fun at times – that's when we get a quiet night,' I exclaimed. 'And when we *do* have to go down the shelter it's better than being at a variety show. The different people we meet with their sense of humour,' I added.

'Yer carn't beat the British for that,' Wilf piped up. 'Any'ow, why dain't yer send us word yer was comin'?' he added.

'I suppose your answer would have been "I'd 'ave med yer a cake." Any'ow,' she added, 'I only got forty-eight hours' leave.'

'Well, let's all sit down,' her mum replied, 'an' tell us 'ow yer bin.'

As we all sat, I asked Sal if I should make a pot of tea.

'I was wondering when you was going to make one. Yer know something? I ain't had a decent cuppa since I left here, only canteen bloody swill, and that tasted like maid's water.'

Suddenly little Georgie, who had been standing in the background listening, cried out, 'Maid's water? Wot's that?'

His sister just smiled at him, but felt she couldn't explain. But she opened her bag and pulled out a small bar of chocolate. 'Here you are, Georgie, now go out and play.'

He didn't need telling twice. Off he ran to find his playmate Jimmy.

As soon as the kettle boiled I made a fresh pot of tea, and when Florrie had drunk hers and asked for a second cup, Ted began to tease her. 'I betcha 'ad a good time, Sis, with the men in uniform.'

'If yer call it having a good time, our Ted – you'd be surprised. There's nobody *I* fancied in that camp, they're quite a mixed bunch. There's the tough ones we all call guys since the Yanks came, then there's the comical guys, who only brag about the good times they'd had outside the camp, and then there's the quiet ones, who never make any effort to have a conversation, and most of them are married, and them as wasn't had a heyday with some of the WAAFs, who couldn't refuse them. And many danced with two left feet,' she added.

'Well, any'ow, love,' said her mum, who had been listening quietly, 'we're all glad to see yer safe an' well. Wot about another cuppa, love? Do yer mind mekin' another pot, Kate?'

I didn't mind in the least, for I was eager to hear more.

'We'll tek yer down ter the local, Sis, ternight, and buy yer a drink,' Ted piped up.

'Oh, an' we'll show the lads wot a smashin' looker we've got fer a sister,' Wilf added, smiling and winking at her.

'Go on with yer. I bet yer say that to all the girls you meet,' replied Florrie, smiling across at her brothers. 'Anyway, ain't my brothers started courting yet, Mum?'

'I don't think they bother about anybody yet, love. I suppose they will when the right ones cum along, or p'raps when yer dad cums back from the war. That's if 'e cums at all,' she continued, as the tears filled her eyes.

'What yer mean, Mum, if he comes?' exclaimed Florrie.

But when Sal tried to explain more about the sad news, Florrie didn't seem a bit disturbed to hear that her dad was missing. She only replied, 'He won't be missing long, Mum, if I know him. As soon as the war's over he'll turn up like a bad penny.'

'We've told 'er that, Sis,' both lads replied, for they remembered – and so did I – the sort of life he led Sal and his family before he joined the army.

As soon as Florrie saw her mother's tears, she quickly changed the subject. 'Don't forget to write and let me know when you two start courting,' she said, turning to her brothers and smiling.

'There's nobody around 'ere we fancy,' replied Wilf.

'But yo've forgotton, yer fancy old "Vinegar Tits"!' Ted began to tease.

'What did yer say, Ted?' asked his sister.

'Old Vinegar Tits,' he replied, grinning all over his face.

'And who's she?'

'She's that fat old bag across the yard,' answered Ted.

'Yer wanta keep clear of 'er,' his mother piped up.

Florrie was now all ears. 'And why do yer call her Vinegar Tits?' she asked.

'Well,' Ted replied, as both lads started to smile, 'the other day it was very 'ot, an' everybody sat outside on their doorstep ter get cool, when we saw Fanny Green come out and stood on 'er doorstep an' we noticed she 'ad 'er blouse wide open ter keep 'er tits cool, an' as . . .'

'That's enough of that, Ted! Yer sister don't wanta 'ear any mower about that brazen trollop! Nor 'er daughters,' she added.

'It's all right, Mum,' said Florrie. 'We hear and see a lot more than that where we're stationed – some of the talk and carry-on would make your hair curl. So go on, Ted, you was saying . . .?'

'Well, she was standin' theea where all the neighbours could see, almost showin' 'er belly button, when a wasp, thinkin' it was a nice place to settle, landed on one of her tits. Then, all at once, we saw 'er run down the yard shoutin' "Pull it orf! Pull it orf! Somebody pull it orf!" And when she managed to tear off 'er blouse, and came runnin' terwards me screamin' an' swearin', I dain't know wot ter do fer laughin', an' so was everybody else who saw the performance.'

'Did yer knock it off?' his sister asked, as she too began to smile.

'Not on yer nelly, Sis. Now if it 'ad been a young pretty wench like yourself, we might 'ave,' Wilf replied. 'Anyway, as soon as everybody saw 'er dirty tits 'angin' like shrunken bladders, nobody would tek any notice.'

Suddenly we all began to laugh out loud as Wilf then tried to demonstrate.

'Only Mrs Freer, she came runnin' towards 'er with a bottle of vinegar an' poured it all over 'er tits. And that's why we all calls 'er Vinegar Tits.'

'But what will happen if she hears yer call her that?' Florrie asked.

''Er knows,' her mother replied. 'Yer can call 'er whatever you'd a mind ter, she's too thick-skinned ter bother.'

'P'raps she's deaf, Mum.'

'Not 'er, she can 'ear when she wants to.'

That evening we all went down to the local pub, The Stores, on Soho Road, for more stories about the men and girls in Florrie's camp.

Florrie Goes Back

Monday morning came all too soon for Florrie's mum and her three sons. Before Florrie was ready to leave, she came to see me and wish me goodbye.

I'd already made up a small packet of tea and sugar and some biscuits I'd been saving, also a couple of laundered hankies. She was reluctant to take them at first, but I made sure she did, and as she thanked me she said, 'Mrs Flood, I'm pleased my mum has a friend she can talk to – you see, she never has mixed with any of the neighbours much.'

'Well, Florrie, your mum keeps herself much to herself.'

'I know,' she replied. 'But I notice she speaks well of you, and so do me brothers.'

'I think your mum thinks all the neighbours are a bad lot, but they're not all bad, not when you get to know them. Only the one your brothers call Vinegar Tits – she's also got two daughters about your age, an' they're nothing but trouble and their mother ain't any better. All the neighbours steer clear of 'em, they give the place a bad name when they bring the Yanks home, and now one of 'em is in the family way an' believe me, Florrie, it won't be long before the other daughter's the same.'

'But what's their dad do about it all?'

'That weedy little sponger! I don't think he bothers. He can't always be seen in the Frightened Horse, with the Yanks buying him booze and fags.'

'I often wonder about our Annie; my brothers say she hasn't written since she moved up to Scotland and joined the Wrens. I know me mum worries over her too. I wish this bloody war was over, then we could all settle down again!' she exclaimed bitterly.

'But what about your dad? Do you think he'll settle down?'

'I hope so, Mrs Flood,' she replied. 'But if he don't, and he begins his old tricks agen, the lads are older now to deal with him, so I hope he'll think twice before he starts his drunken brawls agen. That's if he does come back!' she added bitterly.

'Don't feel too bitterly about him, Florrie – after all, he is your dad and the war years may change him, and many more like him, for the better.'

'I hope so,' she replied. 'It's been nice having you to chat to, and thanks for helping Mum and the lads,' she added.

'Think nothing of it, Florrie. I like your mum and your brothers; I only wish I had three sons like them. But I have only my three young daughters, and my son John is in the navy, on one of the big battleships on the high seas, and I pray every night for our Good Lord to keep him safe.'

'Well, it's been nice talking to yer, but I have to be going. I've still one or two bits to pack.' She added, 'Mum says she'll leave the washing for another day. But if you wouldn't mind, I'd like you to come with me mum, to see me off at the station.'

'Will the boys be there?' I asked.

'No, they're on day shift. But I've already said my goodbyes.'

The railway station was packed with soldiers, sailors and airmen. Nurses and young women in uniform, too, stood sadly waiting for the train, and as it slowly puffed its way into the station everyone began to kiss and wave their loved ones goodbye, and after Sal had hugged and kissed her daughter, Florrie threw her arms round me and whispered, 'Look after me mum for me, and will you write and let me know how things go?'

'I will,' I replied, as she kissed her mum and me again.

As she managed to squeeze her head through the window and wave, our tears began to fall. Everyone cried – I don't believe there was a dry eye on that platform the day that overcrowded train pulled out of New Street Station.

Sal was very upset after saying goodbye to her daughter that Monday morning, so I thought it best that I should stay with her until her sons came home from work.

As soon as I had seen my two young daughters off to work, I went into her house and made a pot of tea. When we had drunk it Sal seemed to be more herself, yet I could still see she'd been crying. I knew she always cheered up after a drink of whisky, so I went back indoors and helped myself to a drop from what the warden had left.

'This will have to be the last, Sal,' I said, 'otherwise Mr Smith will want to know who's been helping themselves, and I can't lie to him.'

'But I thought it was yowers,' she replied.

'No, Sal, we had the last of that the other night. Anyway, I wish we *did* have a drop more; the way I feel I could drink a whole bottle.'

'Well, if yo'll look in me cupboard yo'll find half a bottle of Scotch in there.'

'You crafty old bugger, and there's me sneaking a drop from the warden's bottle!'

As I put the half-bottle on the table, she said, 'I won't 'idin' it, Kate. I was savin' it fer when Tom cums 'ome – if 'e does cum back. Any'ow, 'im bein' a Catholic 'e only likes Irish, so 'ere goes, pour it out, Kate.'

I poured out two little tumblers and we drank it up neat. Now that I felt the whisky was loosening our tongues, I said, 'I didn't know your husband was a Catholic, you never said.'

'It's only 'im that's Irish, but 'e wanted me an' me children ter change our religion an' become Catholics, but we're Protestants an' alwis will be. And that was the beginnin' of our troubles, an' when 'e wanted me in bed 'e often used ter say, "Sal me darlin', you'd mek a foine good Irishwoman," but I never did believe any of 'is blarney, an' yer know what, 'e was very lustful an' all, 'e'd 'ave 'ad it anywhere, mornin' noon an' night – that's if I'd 'ave let 'im; an' when I wouldn't sleep with 'im, that's when 'e started ter knock me about, an' many times 'e'd come 'ome drunk and swear at me.'

'But what did your sons say about him?'

'They worn't born then. It was just after 'e sold that old cottage what belong to 'is old mum, an' soon after, we came ter live 'ere. 'E wouldn't give me any money fer food or rent so I found meself a job in a rivetin' factory. After a while 'e began ter alter 'is ways, an' 'e said if I dain't let 'im 'ave 'is oats 'e'd turn me out an' get another woman in. So I eventually slept with 'im to cause peace. But when I found I was pregnant agen, I dain't know what ter do, an' when the girls in the factory said 'ow pale I was, I wouldn't say why. But when they found out, one of them said, "Yer wanta goo ter the chemist an' ask 'im ter mek yer up a box of the four Ps." When I asked what she meant, she said I must be green. They was called Dr Williams' Pink Pills for Pale People.'

Suddenly Sal began to laugh: 'I can laugh now, Kate, when I think about the time I took them pills. But I dain't laugh at the time. They nearly finished me off. Any'ow I was so desperate, after tekin' two, four times a day, they made no effect. So I bought another box and swallowed the whole lot.'

'Oh my Lord, you never did!' I exclaimed.

'I did,' she replied. 'But they only gave me the shits, an' I 'ad ter run down the factory yard ter the outside closet every few minutes, and when the foreman saw me 'e 'ad me in 'is office an' when I told 'im, 'e give me the sack. I was ill in 'ospital for over a week, but all the sympathy I got off Tom, bein' a Catholic, was if I'd 'ave bin a Catholic I could 'ave gone ter confession an' 'ad me sins forgiven by Father O'Murphy. But the worst of it was, I was still pregnant, an' when I told Tom, 'e forgive me. But while I was in the 'ospital, I lost the babby, an' Tom was frightened then that 'e'd lose me too.'

'You ain't had a very happy life even from the beginning, Sal. But why did yer marry him?' I added.

'I 'ad no other choice, Kate. When 'is old mother died, it was either be thrown out or sleep with 'im, an' I've regretted it ever since.'

'But you must have loved him to marry him later.'

'I dain't luv 'im, Kate, but 'e was good ter me at times and I thought it was fer the best – yer see I dain't want *my* children to grow up to be called bastards.'

'I understand, Sal. I could never say I really loved the father of my children. But it was a way out for me too – so I thought at the time. I was a drudge and a lackey when I was only a schoolgirl, I did everything to please my mum, but she was cruel and unkind to me, and in later years I found I wasn't wanted, even before I was born. She liked the sweets, but never liked the sours, if yer know what I mean,' I replied, smiling.

'Even when I was at school I had big ideas, and wanted to grow up quickly and get married and have lots of babies. I thought that was the only way to be happy. But like an ignorant fool, I met my handsome feller at a party, we'd had a few drinks, then one night we made love in an entry. I was then nearly eighteen and knew nothing of the facts of life, and when I found out I was pregnant, I was glad. Foolishly I thought, now he had to ask me to get married, I would have a home of my own, away from my mum and the squalid surroundings we lived in. But this was not to be – my first disappointment was when I went to live with him in Bath Row, before we got married, but when the landlady turned us out we went to live in a furnished room, and when I was three months pregnant my husband lost his job. Times were bad for almost everyone in the district in 1921, I couldn't pay the rent that was overdue. There was only one alternative. When I asked my mother if I could come to live back home until my baby was born she said, "No! Yo've med yer bed, so yer lie on it!" But after my dad discussed the situation we were in, she changed her mind. Believe me, Sal, that was the last place I wanted to go, but beggars can't be choosers. And that's where all my future hopes collapsed. My husband lost his job – as yer know, jobs were hard to find – and when he started to sell sawdust to the butchers and the pubs, he often came home drunk, and when he came home the worse for drink and wanted me in bed, I refused to even sleep beside him. He never came near me for months after we quarrelled. When he was sober, I longed for him to make love to me, but after walking the streets all day looking for work he was too tired even to have a conversation. One night while he was out, I dragged the zinc bath indoors and as I lay in the hot carbolic soapy water, I was scared in case the water got into my navel and drowned my baby. I was ignorant regarding childbirth. So I got a piece of sticking plaster and stuck it over my navel. As soon as I got out of the bath, I stood wet and naked in front of the long mirror, and when I removed the plaster, I felt wonderful and happy about this little life that was growing in my little swollen belly, and as I put my hand there I hoped to feel it move, then I suddenly saw my husband looking at me. I wanted him so badly, then, to take me in his arms and make love to me. But as he stared at me, you know what he said? "Yer betta put some clothes on, before yer catch cold", and he walked out.

'That was many years ago, Sal, and God knows how often I'd pray for things to change so that I could get away from that squalid district and rapidly increasing families. But my prayers were never answered, until ten years later in 1931 when my husband died.'

As I was telling her some of my life story, I noticed Sal was becoming *too* inquisitive. It was then that I realised my tongue had run away with me. 'I'll have to be going, Sal,' I replied at once. 'It's getting late and my daughters will be home for their tea.'

I had previously told her that I was leaving Waverhill Road to my eldest daughter Kathleen, as I had already bought a house in the select district of Handsworth. No doubt when I had gone she would find time to gossip with her other neighbour, Mrs Freer. I had nothing to hide or be ashamed of, yet I didn't like neighbours' gossip, and I don't know why I should have talked as I did. Therefore when she did ask questions, I would say, 'When we have more time' until she got tired of asking. But we were still neighbourly, and I felt sorry for her at times, so I did many kindnesses for her. But it wasn't until a few days before I was leaving the district that I realised she had been taking advantage of my kindness in little things she asked me to do, and I never refused.

Georgie's Superstitious Accident

O ne day Sal came to ask if I'd keep an eye on her little son
    Georgie, as she'd heard there was some extra sausages to be
had at the butcher's. 'I'll bring yer some, Kate, if they ain't sold out
afower I get there,' she replied.

'Thanks, Sal,' I replied. 'Don't bother if yer can't get me any, but
you can bring Georgie in.'

Georgie sat down, and as soon as Sal hurried away, I asked
him if he'd like a game of dominoes. We had a happy half-hour
together. He was a loveable little chap but when I saw the
disappointment on his face when he lost the first game, I let him win
the other two.

'Me bruvvers said I don't know 'ow ter play properly, but wait till
I tell 'em,' he gloated, smiling all over his face.

As soon as we started the next game, there was a knock on the
door. When I opened it, little Jimmy from down the street cried, 'Me
mum ses Georgie's in your 'ouse, can 'e come out an' play?'

When I told Georgie his friend had come for him, he said, 'Can I
goo now? 'E wants me ter play with 'is trains.'

'Very well, but you must be here when yer mum comes back.'

Jimmy was the little lad across the street, and I'd heard that no one
knew who his father was, not even his mother. And in that close
community, everybody knew everybody else's business. She was
known to go away, leaving him to roam the streets for weekends at a
time, and when the boy was born everyone knew he was a bastard.
Many neighbours used to shun her when the Yanks came to town,
yet some fallen girls had mothers who understood when their
daughters were left holding their babies. Other mothers just could
never find time to forgive. Yet today, thousands of children are born
out of wedlock, and couples just live together without marriage.

Sal came back two hours later with no sausages, in quite a temper. 'Two bleedin' hours I stood in that queue. An' when it cum ter my turn 'e said 'e'd only some scratchin's left. I told 'im where 'e could stick 'is scratchings – where the monkey sticks 'is nuts, up 'is arse!'

I began to laugh, then she said, 'An' yer know what 'e said – if I'd goo round the back 'e'd push 'em up mine! Saucy bleeder!' she exclaimed.

When she asked where Georgie was, I told her he was playing with Jimmy. Later that same afternoon, it had been raining heavily when Sal came knocking on my door, dragging little Georgie behind her. As soon as they entered I noticed that his knee was covered in blood and there was mud all over his face and hands, and he was sobbing.

'Whatever have you done?' I cried as I gazed down at him.

''E won't say, Kate. I carn't get a word outa 'im!' yelled Sal as she shook him. 'All as I can get out of 'im is 'e fell down.'

'Well, Georgie, let me have a look an' see what you've done.'

I sat him down on a chair, and got a bowl of water and some salt. When I bathed the mud and blood from his knees, I saw that on his left leg there was quite a deep cut.

When I asked how he'd done it, he replied, 'I fell over.'

'Georgie,' I replied, 'you're not telling the truth, are you?'

'I am, I fell over in the mud,' he replied as he began to sob.

'Trouble, trouble!' his mum cried out. 'I don't know what I'm gooin' ter do with 'im.'

'You'll have to take him to the hospital, Sal,' I snapped. 'It's a bad cut he's got there.'

'I carn't tek 'im, Kate, I'm scared of 'ospitals.'

'So am I!' I replied angrily. 'Anyway, I'll take him to see Dr Arthur first and let him have a look at it.'

When she said she would come along too, I replied, 'No need for the two of us, it may not be all that serious. Anyway, if my daughter Jean comes home before I get back, just tell her where I've gone.'

As soon as the doctor saw Georgie he said, 'Now come along, young man, and let me sponge them dirty tears away, then when I've looked at your knee you can tell me how it happened.'

'I fell down,' he whimpered.

'But that's not all, is it, Georgie? Have you been fighting?' he asked.

'Oh no, I worn't fightin' an' that's the truth, Doctor.'

Suddenly he began to cry again.

'Now wipe your eyes and tell me how you cut your knee.'

'I told yer, I fell down in the mud, an' that's the truth.'

The doctor, like me, was getting nowhere, but after he'd cleaned the cut, he said I was to take the boy to the hospital.

Georgie was a brave little chap. He had two stitches in that cut and never murmured, and the doctor said I was to report back to him. As soon as we left the hospital, I took him to my home before taking him to his mum, and after giving him a drink of warm milk I said, 'Now Georgie, if you'll tell me what really happened, I'll get the dominoes out and we'll have a game.'

'Will yer promise not ter tell me mum or me bruvvers?' he asked.

'Why?' I asked.

'Becuss they'll belt me.'

'No they won't, Georgie,' I replied. 'Anyway, if you tell me what really happened, I'll keep it a secret, but I can't promise until you tell me.'

As soon as I handed him a hanky to wipe his tears, he said, 'Yer know Jimmy, well, 'e tells lies.'

'Do you tell lies, Georgie?' I asked.

'No, Mrs Flood,' he replied, 'only little white fibs, but Jimmy does.'

Now I'd got him talking. I sat and listened.

'When it stopped rainin' we went for a walk alung the canal bank and 'e told me ... er ... er ...'

'Go on, Georgie, he told you what?' I asked, smiling at him.

''E told me, if yer stared at a cross-eyed woman it was bad luck, but if yer stared at a crossed-eyed man it brought yer good luck, an' then yer could wish for anythink an' it would come true, but Jimmy told me a lie and, and ... er ...'

'Yes, go on, and what else did Jimmy say?'

'As we was walkin' along the bridge we saw this cockeyed woman, an' Jimmy ran away and left me.'

'And what did you do?' I asked.

'When she cum nearer I got frightened an' run away.'

He didn't seem to want to tell me any more, for I could see he was beginning to cry again.

I wiped his eyes. 'Now, Georgie,' I said, smiling down at him, 'you don't want to cry. I only want you to tell me how you came to cut your knee, then we can have a game of dominoes like I promised.'

And so he went on telling me. He was on his way home when he met a cross-eyed man. 'So I went straight up to him and stared at 'im, then when 'e asked me what I was starin' at, I told 'im that my friend Jimmy said it was lucky ter stare up at a cockeyed man. Then 'e said, "Well, yer can 'ave this fer luck," then he hit me twice across me face, then knocked me down in the mud an' I fell on some broken glass. An' I'll never believe anythink Jimmy tells me again.'

'Well, Georgie, they're all silly superstitions and if anyone tells you anything you don't understand, just ask your mum or your brothers to explain, they're the ones to put you right. Now come along, we've got to go back and report to the doctor. Then we'll come back and play dominoes.'

I took hold of his hand and off we went. On the way he said, 'Please don't tell me mum nor the doctor.'

'I won't,' I replied.

A few days later, when I called to see the doctor about my chest cold, he asked if the lad had confided in me. I saw no reason why I should *not* tell him, and when I did, he began to smile.

'The things these lads say and do surprises even me. Anyway,' he added, 'he's maybe learnt his lesson.'

Superstitions die hard as they're handed down from one generation to the next.

I remember my mum was very superstitious. If there was a storm brewing and lightning about, she was like a woman demented. She'd jump up from wherever she was sitting and face the mirror to the wall, and knives and forks would be suddenly snatched up from the table, whether you were having your dinner or not, and slung underneath, also the steel poker from the fireplace.

'Don't you dare open that umbrella in the 'ouse!' she'd yell.

And to crack the mirror was seven years' bad luck. There are a thousand and one silly superstitions – if you walked under a ladder, that was said to be bad luck, but it was bad luck if you stepped off the pavement and got knocked down by a horse. You could also hear people swearing every day, but not on a Sunday, otherwise the Devil would be with you the rest of the week.

I also recall my mum would never wear green, nor have it anywhere in the house. I didn't know about this until one

Christmas. I'd tried to save up a few shilling to buy Mum a present. When the 'pat man' (the hire-purchase man) came to the door and showed me a green chenille tablecloth, I hadn't got enough money, but he said I could have it on the 'strap' for sixpence a week, and with the promise to pay sixpence I gave him the first instalment. I thought it would look lovely on our scrubbed wooden table – make a change from the pages from the *News of the World* (so I thought), but as soon as I gave the parcel to her and she saw what was inside she went wild and threw it on the fire.

I was shocked, but before I could say a word she yelled out, 'If yo ever bring anythink green in this 'ouse again, it'll still goo on the fire!' Then all of a sudden the room lit up, as we saw the chimney had caught fire. Balls of soot came rolling down, and the room was full of smoke. Just then my dad came running with bags of salt to push up the chimney, but we hadn't had it swept for years. The old chimney was alight – flames, sparks and smoke were belching out into the yard below as we ran outside. We heard the pot crack. The firemen came and a couple of policemen, but all Mum could do was tell the neighbours and swear as she helped to drag in the washing off the lines.

Later, Mum was fined half-a-crown, and I still had to pay that sixpence a week to the 'pat man', until four and elevenpence three farthings was paid.

I swore after that episode I would never buy her anything green. In fact, I never bought her anything else either.

Yet today green is one of my favourite colours.

It was during the spring that the landlord decided to have all the doors painted in the yard (which he did once in a blue moon). My mum happened to be out at the time, and when she came back later and saw the door painted green, she went wild. She rushed over to the brewhouse and helped herself to a bucket of warm soapsuds from the boiler, and as she got the bass broom all the neighbours came out to see her perform. But try as she might with that broom, the paint wouldn't budge. Suddenly she lost her temper and threw the rest of the suds against the door. Next day, when the landlord came for his rent, she yelled out, 'Yow'll get no bleedin' rent off me, till yer get that green paint off me dower an' put another colour on!'

She meant it, too. But when he threatened her with the bailiffs,

Dad said he'd paint it over. Dad was no painter, but he managed to beg a tin of brown paint, and after thinning it down he too lost his temper and slapped it anywhere. And our door was the only one in that street that had smudgy brown and green streaks. Often I used to imagine I could picture figures and faces where that paint had dried, and it was left like that from when I was only a young girl until Hitler decided he didn't like it either and destroyed it in 1941.

Lambs to the Slaughter

During May 1945 the war was nearing its end and there was less bombing, if any at all, over Birmingham.

During these times we could go to our beds and try to catch up on the many hours of sleep we had lost during the heavy raids. I was still living in Waverhill Road with my daughters, but I had every intention of leaving for a better house in a much quieter district as soon as the war was over.

I remember that my kitchen was very small and the door opened inwards, so it always banged against the wall. I thought if I could get someone to rehang it so that it opened outwards, that would give me a bit more room in the kitchen.

A friend of mine said he could do the job for me, but that I would have to have a new door as the old one was warped. He also said it would be a long time before he could get a new one as he would have to get a priority note, but he could get one from a bomb site. He got a very heavy door, made of oak. After he had planed it down it fitted, and after a lot of hard work and strong language he managed to make it swing outwards, and I had a bit more room. We didn't realise it was now going to be a tight squeeze to get outside between the door and the wall in the entry, yet my two daughters and I managed somehow. It was more of a squeeze for me – I was then twelve stone. But we said that now the door was up it could stay until such time as we left.

A few weeks later, I was surprised to see my brother-in-law Bill. He worked for a butcher in Handsworth, fetching and carrying meat from the markets in his van.

'Hello, stranger!' I cried as I opened the front door and saw his meat van outside. 'Come in.'

'I can't stop long, Kate,' he replied. 'But I happened to be passing, so I thought I'd call and see if yer wanted a bit of lamb.'

'Thank yer, Bill, but I ain't got any coupons to spare,' I said.

'That's OK. I've got some to spare if yer want the meat.'

'All right, bring it in then,' I answered eagerly.

'I ain't got any with me now, but I'll drop yer some in a day or two. So long, I've gotta 'urry now,' he added as he went out.

After I had thanked him and watched him drive away, I wondered if I'd done the right thing by accepting the lamb he'd promised. On second thoughts, I said to myself, if he did bring some it would only be maybe a few chops.

A couple of weeks went by. No Bill came with any lamb, so I forgot about it. I was glad really, I knew it was on the black market, but I made up my mind that if he did come now I wouldn't accept it, for I was scared I would be found out.

A few nights later I was awakened by noises which sounded like bombs being dropped, a long way off. Half asleep, I sat up in bed waiting for the sirens to wail. I heard a loud thud, then another, and another, which seemed to sound much nearer. I sat up in bed now, wide awake, thinking the sirens would sound any time, but there was no more noise, so I lay down and tried to go back to sleep. But I was too restless. It was almost dawn when I decided to go downstairs. As I slipped my dressing-gown on and lit the gas stove to make myself a cup of tea, I looked up at the clock. It was five-thirty.

It was very stuffy and warm as I stood waiting for the kettle to boil. I thought I'd unbolt the door and let in some air. When I tried to push the door outwards it wouldn't budge. I put my shoulder to it, but still it wouldn't budge. I knew then that something was blocking it. Suddenly I became scared in case it was a delayed bomb, but I had to get outside to see. I went out through the front door and round the back towards the passageway, hoping and praying that someone would be walking along the street, and would come with me to see who or what was lying there. But there wasn't a soul in sight; everywhere seemed deadly quiet.

Warily I crept up to the back of my house, and when I got almost to the back door I couldn't believe my eyes. Wedged between my kitchen door and the wall were three whole lambs. I had to step on them and push them against the wall before I could get the door open.

I was relieved to see that none of my neighbours was about, but had to hide those lambs somewhere. I managed to drag each one into the kitchen, and after closing the door I sat down exhausted. I had to get them into the cellar somehow and hide them from my daughters. After drinking my welcome cup of tea, I went to my peg bag and found an odd piece of rope. I tied it round each lamb's neck and dragged them towards the cellar steps. As soon as I reached the edge of the steps I unfastened the rope and pushed them down.

I had expected that Bill would show himself with a few chops, or a half a leg, not *three whole bloody lambs*! Whatever was I going to do with them? I was more scared now than if they had been a dud bomb.

But as luck would have it, half an hour later my brother Jack called.

When I told him about my brother-in-law and what he'd left me with, he began to laugh.

'It's no bloody laughin' matter, Jack!' I yelled. 'What am I goin' ter do with 'em?'

'Well,' he replied, still grinning all over his face, 'I'll tek 'em away, I'll soon get rid of 'em.'

I didn't care what he did with them as long as they were out of the house. So it was arranged that the three lambs would stay where I had pushed them until after dark, when Jack would take them away in his car.

When he came later that night, he said he had room for only two and he'd call later to pick up the other one. Soon after he left, my brother-in-law called. As soon as I opened the door I yelled out 'Yer better come in and explain yerself!'

He looked around and asked, 'Wot yer done with 'em?'

'What yer think I've done with em!' I replied angrily. 'I had to throw 'em down the cellar.'

Smiling, he said, 'Well, I'll tek the two and leave yer the other one.'

'I don't want it! And if yer think yer can use me or my house for any of yer dirty deals, you've got another think coming!'

Suddenly his smile changed when I told him my brother had taken two of them away and was coming back later for the other one.

''E won't, yer know! Not if I can 'elp it. I'll tek the one 'e's left fer now, an' I'll see '*im* later!'

He was fuming as he made his way down into the cellar. As soon as he had put the lamb into a sack and began to throw it into the van, I shouted, 'This is the first an' last time yer try ter use me for your black-market deals!'

Later my brother came, expecting to take the other lamb away, but when I told him what had happened he replied, "'E won't bother me, Kate, 'e knows we're in the same boat. But', he added, 'if yer want a few chops, I'll ...'

'Yer know what yer can do with yer chops! You and 'im! Keep away from my house. I never wanta see you nor 'im again!' I bawled as I slammed the door behind him.

I never saw my brother-in-law again, and only very seldom did I see my brother Jack.

Sweet William and the Copycat

Ration books were more precious than identity cards. Clothes, food and vegetables were still rationed years after the war was over. Many people who were lucky enough to own a garden made good use of it by growing their own vegetables. Children, too, would help to dig and carry buckets of water after school hours. When my two brothers came back from the war they rented their houses, dug up the soil and grew their own too. Prizes were given by the Co-op Corporation Society for the best-laid-out gardens.

We were all proud when my brothers won first and third prizes. I don't know where they got their knowledge from.

As far back as I remember when we were children, we had only a cobbled yard. The only green we ever saw were the weeds between the blue bricks and pitch between the cobbles. Many of us young kids in our district walked miles to see trees and flowers, even a patch of grass.

Often I used to wish my mum would have the bailiffs and go to another house with a garden, but this was not to be. For I loved plants and flowers, and still do in my old age. When I was about five years old, I had this crazy notion that I could grow anything in a bit of soil. Once I planted a brown marble in the corner of the yard, hoping it would grow into many. After a few weeks I dug the soil over, but all I could see was that it had perished. Next I decided to pull up one of the bricks in the corner of the yard. I had a few bluebells I'd picked while out walking. I turned the dirt over, buried them and poured water on them every night. But one day, when I went to look, there was nothing there, only bits of dead leaves. Often my brother would tease me and laugh and tell me I must have planted them upside down. When he saw my tears, he said, 'Never

690

mind, Katie, one day when yer rich and yer goo to Australia, you'll find they've med their way and shot up there.'

Often on my walks I would still pick bluebells or buttercups and put them in jars of water, but they never lasted more than a couple of days before they too drooped and died on me.

Yet I had my reward. One day, as I stood gazing in the window of a flower shop, I couldn't take my eyes away from the beautiful plants and flowers arranged in pretty vases. As I stood there, wondering if I would ever be able to own a shop like that, the old flower-seller beckoned me to come inside. I was scared at first, for I had no money to buy even a leaf. But as soon as I stepped inside the shop, he said, 'You've been standing there for a long time, my dear, do you want to buy your mum something?'

'No,' I replied at once. 'I ain't got any money, but I love to look at your lovely flowers,' I added nervously.

He said he was sorry, but he couldn't afford to give me any. But as I went to walk out of the shop, he called me back. 'Well, dear,' he said kindly, 'would you like a packet of seeds? Then you can grow your own.'

'But I ain't even got a penny,' I replied.

'Well, dear, I'll give you a packet and you can bring me the penny another time.'

'Thank you, sir, thank you, sir,' I cried as I took the packet and ran out of the shop before he changed his mind.

When I got home, I didn't tell my mum – I hid the seeds in case she threw them away or on the fire. Yet I had no idea where I was going to plant them, and I didn't want them shooting up in Australia. So I thought the best thing was to give them to my dad, who might give them to somebody to grow for me.

Then one day I told him about the kind man at the flower shop and when I showed him the packet of seeds, he said, 'Well, luv, I don't know where yer gooin' ter grow 'em, any'ow leave 'em with me an' I'll see what I can do.'

A few days later, I saw him making a long narrow wooden box for the window-ledge, and when it was finished he not only gave me the penny to pay the flower-seller, he also bought a bag of compost.

As he planted the seeds into the soil and watered them down, I hugged and kissed him as he stood back to admire his handiwork. How proud I was now to have my own private little flowerbox! Just as we were admiring it, Mum happened to come back from her cleaning job. I was afraid she'd take it down. As soon as she set eyes on it, she cried, 'What's that monstrosity you've nailed on theea?'

'Yer won't call it a monstrosity', Dad replied, 'when yer see the sweet williams shootin' up.'

'Well, as lung as yer don't paint that box green,' she said, as she shrugged her shoulders and went indoors. Dad smiled and winked at me, for we both remembered the commotion when she tried to scrub the green paint off the door.

Every day I used to peer down into that soil to see if any little shoot had broken through. But when my mum caught me, she said, 'Yer must be barmy! Starin' at nothin'! Get in the 'ouse, where I can find yer summat betta ter do!'

I knew she didn't want that flowerbox on the windowledge. She never encouraged me at any time to do something *I* wanted to. Only my dad had patience with me.

One morning I was very happy to see several little shoots peeping through the soil, and when my dad saw them he too was proud to see what a success he'd made. From then on I had my own private little flowerbox, which I called *my* garden.

When the flowers began to flourish and show colour, all the neighbours who passed our door admired them, except the one neighbour at the end of the yard. Her name was Maggie, but everybody called her Moggy, because she had lots of cats. Mum never liked her and she didn't like our mum, especially when her mangy cats kept coming into our house – Mum would kick them out. But there was one big old ginger tom whose mangy fur would bristle and stand on end and defy her. Mum had to get the steel poker to *that* one, before he turned tail.

Whenever Maggie saw Mum take the curtains down to wash, she had to do the same. Even when Mum swilled out the dry wooden closets, or the yard, out would come *her* broom and bucket, and each Saturday morning Mum would whiten our well-worn-down step with a ball of whitening, and when any of us came in or out of the house, we were given our orders *not* to tread on the step, but to stride over it. This too Maggie copied. Yet when the rest of the neighbours did theirs, Mum seemed pleased to see that it improved the look of the yard.

One morning Mum got me out of bed very early, just as dawn was breaking. When I asked why, she replied, 'I wanta get inta that brew'ouse! Afower that bleedin' Moggy wakes up!' But while we were filling the two buckets from the standpipe in the yard, Mum happened to look up. As soon as she saw Maggie staring down at her from the open window, she cried out for all the neighbours to hear, "Ave yer bin standin' theea all night, yer nosy old cow?'

Suddenly the window shook as Maggie slammed it down. Mum went into the house and slammed the door, leaving me to shiver in the cold morning air.

There was no washing done that day by either of them, none until later that week.

There was only one brewhouse for all five back-to-back houses, so neighbours had to do their washing in pairs. Mum hated to do her washing standing beside Maggie. Often she would ask a neighbour if they would change over, but they always refused. They didn't get along with Moggy either. And when Mum had to do the washing standing beside her, neither spoke a word – they were like a couple of deaf mutes as they banged away with the 'dollies' at the washing in the maiding tubs.

Every time I saw Maggie stop to look at my flowers growing in the windowbox, I would see her sniff and shrug her shoulders.

A few days later I saw her dragging a wet fishbox down the yard. Being an inquisitive child, I stood to watch her. Other times she would shoo me off, but she took no notice of me as I watched her pull it apart and try to codge four pieces together with a few nails and a hammer. As it took shape I realised she was trying to make a windowbox. As soon as it was finished, she placed in on the window-ledge and filled it with some kind of dirt and soil. When Mum came out of doors and saw her sprinkling seeds into it, she cried, 'What yer think yower growing in theea, Moggy?'

'Not sweet williams!' she yelled back. 'Mine will be sweet peas!' she added, tossing her head.

Suddenly Mum burst out laughing and yelled, 'The only sweet peas yo'll grow in theea will be the sweet pees from yower mangy tom cats!'

True enough, a few weeks later she pulled it down. After throwing the dirt in the dustbin, she chopped the box up for fire-wood. She never made another attempt.

Joe

M y first place that I rented in Albert Road was 12s. 6d a week. I was in my seventh heaven when I began to furnish it ready for my daughters to come home to.

We were all happy together for a while, and now my business was thriving. I felt I wanted a better house, yet I couldn't make up my mind until the bombing started. Then I bought an old house in Waverhill Road, and as soon as we moved in, I heard that the house I had rented was bombed.

Kath and Jean soon settled into our new home, and after leaving work they would go out with some of the girls who worked for me. Yet I always had the feeling (like all mothers do) that they were growing away from me. Sometimes they would ask me to accompany them and we would have friends and neighbours in for parties and share our food rations. Yet as soon as they began to grow up during those teenage years, my trials began, for I now had to cope with a grown-up family. Although I gave them love and affection I believe I gave too much, too soon. I didn't stop to think that one day they would leave me to get married and have a home and children of their own. I thought the time to worry would be the time when they left me.

Then one day I had a letter from my son John, who was on leave in Scotland, to say he'd fallen in love with a Scots girl and was going to get married. He was only young. He knew no other life than the time he was at Watts Naval Training School, and he was only fifteen years old when he was shipped out to sea.

I went to see them both married in Scotland, taking my two elder daughters with me.

A couple of visits later, while we were there, my eldest daughter fell in love with a Scotsman. Later they were married from my home and went back to live in Scotland.

Mary, my youngest, was still evacuated, which now left only Jean and me at home, and sometimes life together was difficult.

Nothing ever seemed to go the way I had planned it. The war was at its height, more or less every town had its share of bombings, and later, when I heard that my mother and eldest sister had been killed in an air raid, I began to have feelings that this old house was unlucky. But then I thought maybe it was my silly superstition and I was being foolish.

Nevertheless, when I had a letter from Kathleen and her husband Jim to say they wanted to come back to Birmingham, I decided to leave the house in Waverhill Road to them.

The next house I bought was a semi-detached with a garage, a front lawn, and a large garden at the back. There was also a large pool that ran at the back of the houses and many frogs on the lawn, but these didn't bother me. Jean and I settled down and we grew closer together – until she too started courting. I was left alone at night in this house, where I had foolishly thought I'd never be alone again. I imagined all kinds of strange noises and creaks, especially when I slept alone in my bed. I began to think: was it mice – I could hear scratching – or was the house haunted? Later I had my doubts.

During those war years I had become very nervous and imagined all kinds of things when I was alone. Often, lying awake at night, I used to think: would I feel better with a man around the house? Should I advertise for a male lodger? But on second thoughts, my next-door neighbours knew I was a widow, and knowing how they loved to gossip, I thought it wouldn't be a good idea; anyhow, I knew my Jean would object.

A few nights later, as I sat knitting and waiting for my daughter to come home, I glanced up at the clock and saw it was almost half-past ten. She had gone to the pictures with her boyfriend, Sam. Although I knew I could trust him to bring her home safely, I still worried until she was indoors.

It was while I was waiting that I heard the front doorbell ring. I knew it couldn't be Jean, she had her own key. I thought it must be one of my neighbours, asking if we had seen their cat, for Jean was a lover of any kind of animal and always picked up a stray and brought it home, saying it had followed her. If I had given her the chance, our house would have been a menagerie.

When I opened the door, I was surprised to see a young man

dressed in sergeant's air force uniform. I peeped outside to see if my nosy neighbour was about before I invited him inside. I didn't recognise him at first, but as soon as he told me his name I knew him at once. He was the young man who had taken me to the Lyric picture house when we were teenagers, many years before.

'Sit down, Joe – would you like a cup of coffee or tea?' I asked as I began to smile, remembering that night.

'Tea, thank you, Kate,' he replied.

I was still smiling as I handed him his cup. When he asked me why, I answered, 'I still remember the night you took me to the pictures, and bought me a large box of Rowntree's chocolates. And do you remember when you pulled me towards you and tried to kiss me?'

'Yes, I still remember – you slapped my face and threw the box at me and ran off,' said Joe, smiling.

'Did you finish eating them?'

'No, I gave them to the usherette and went to find *you* to say I was sorry, but you seemed to vanish, and I never saw you again.'

'But how did you find me now?' I asked.

'I met your brother and he gave me your address. I hope you don't mind, Kate.'

'No, Joe, I'm glad to see you again,' I replied.

'Anyway, I'll have to be going, I've got to see my dad. Would you mind if I call again, Kate, and take you out for a drink and a meal?'

'No, Joe, I'd love that,' I replied eagerly.

As he said good night and left, I didn't know that this meeting was going to be the beginning of a long friendship.

He had been gone only a few seconds when I heard the key turn in the lock and Jean came in. Almost at once she cried, 'Who's that air force man I just seen leaving here?'

'It's a long story, Jean,' I replied. 'Just someone I met when I was a young girl.'

'But what brought him here? Did you invite him?' she asked, staring at me as though I had kept a secret from her.

'No I did not! Even if I did, I don't see why you have to question me about who I see. Now get your supper, I'm waiting to go to bed.'

'I don't want any supper,' she snapped, and bounced her way upstairs.

I could see she was in a mood and I put it down to a lovers' quarrel.

No more was said. Next night she got herself ready to meet Sam. When he called I greeted him, and not long after they left Joe came to take me out for a meal.

I remember I had a wonderful time. I met his dad and his sisters, and when we had said our goodbyes Joe brought me home. As we sat talking about my family and his family, time seemed to fly.

Before he left he took me in his arms, and we were kissing just as Jean came into the room.

'How long 'as this been going on?' she cried.

Before I could answer she shrugged her shoulders and went up to her room.

'I'm sorry, Joe, Jean feels this way, she thinks I shouldn't have anyone in the house when she's not here.'

'I understand, Kate, don't let it bother you. One day when she gets wed she'll come to realise how lonely life can be for you without her.'

Jean and I never spoke to each other for days. When Joe asked me to marry him, I agreed.

As soon as I told my daughter she yelled, 'But yer can't, Mum! He's already married!'

'I know, Jean, he's only waiting for his divorce papers, then we're going to the registry office to get married.'

'Don't ask me to be there when you do get married!' she replied quickly.

'I'm not asking *you* to do anything you don't want to do, Jean, but remember this: I don't want to hear any more about what I should do or not do, from you or anyone else,' I said angrily.

As soon as she went out I began to weep. If only she could see my point of view and know the lonely hours I spent alone in that house!

I was surprised to see her come home early that night with Sam, who left her to talk with me. As soon as I looked at her, I could see she'd been crying. Before I could say a word, she threw her arms around me and cried, 'I'm sorry, Mum, I've been angry with you. Sam has explained everything to me, and made me feel ashamed.'

'There's nothing for you to be ashamed of, Jean. I shall always love you no matter what happens. But you must realise that I have always put you, Kath, John and Mary first. I could have married again years ago but I was too busy building a home and getting a business together for all our comforts. But fate intervened in other ways. Now wipe your eyes – you're a pretty girl, you don't want to go to work with red swollen eyes.'

We kissed and as I put my arms around her she said, 'I'm sorry, Mum, but I do love you. It's only because I want to see you happy.'

'I'm sure I will be, Jean. But you must understand, when you and Sam get married I should have been left alone again, and you . . .'

'But we'll always come and visit you, Mum, and bring you anything you need.'

'I know you will, love; now let's have a nice cup of cocoa and tell me all about your plans for the future.'

'We haven't made any yet, Mum. But we'll tell you when we do. Anyway, Sam sends his love and I'm glad, Mum, he made me see sense.'

A few weeks later, Joe and I were married at the old registry office in Edmund Street, near the famous fountain where I used to paddle my sore bare feet as a child.

Joe was usually kind and considerate, and although we had many disagreements, I still loved him.

'Sheila'

─────◦○◦◦○◦─────

I realised that my husband was often mean, and at times he was not very easy to get along with. Yet despite meanness he had a sense of humour, which was one of the things I liked about him.

There was one thing I was grateful for: he didn't drink beer, or any kind of alcohol. Tea was his favourite drink.

We had our differences of opinion, as many couples often do, but when he was in one of his *good* moods I only had to ask and he'd give me the money to buy whatever I needed. While we were living in Handsworth, my husband became acquainted with a bookmaker who employed him. But taking bets and staying at his club late at night to pay money out to punters was not my idea of life. It meant I had to be left alone in that house until he came home.

Sitting alone, waiting, I was always nervous, wondering if this old house was haunted, like the previous one we had left. Sometimes I was scared of my own shadow. I'd switch on all the lights, but as soon as I heard him coming down the path I ran and switched them all off.

We had a front room, a dining-room, a small kitchen, and three bedrooms. This house was not centrally heated – our hot water came from the boiler at the back of the fire grate, which supplied us only with hot water from the tap in the kitchen sink. One day, we quarrelled about having central heating installed, but I was adamant.

I filled in all the usual forms, and while I was waiting for the men to come, I decided to turn the spare room (which was on a level with our bedroom) into a bathroom. The other spare room I kept furnished ready for when my youngest daughter Mary came home from the forces.

When the men came they delivered the washbasin, bath and toilet, but we still had to wait until the plumbers came, which meant we still had to go downstairs to the kitchen sink for a wash, and across the yard to the lavatory. The public baths in Oxhill Road were just round the corner from our house, which was very convenient for the time being.

I was always active, and I seldom felt the cold weather, but my Joe was always complaining about his cold feet. One week we had rain, snow and ice continually, non-stop. Joe decided to buy himself a rubber hot-water bottle. As soon as I saw it I cried, 'Thinkin' of yerself agen – why couldn't yer buy me one?'

'Yer tell me yer never feel the cold,' he replied, smiling across at me.

'Well, I do! When yer come up to bed late and put yer freezin' legs an' feet against me.'

'No need now, I've got me bottle,' he answered, grinning. I knew it was a waste of time to argue.

Every night he was last to come up to bed. Then one night, when I thought he was asleep, I pushed my feet down the bed. I grasped the bottle between my feet and as I smiled to myself I kicked it over to my side. But I felt his hand slide down the bed and fail to find the bottle, then I felt it sliding up my bare thigh.

Suddenly I shot up and shouted at him, 'No yer don't! If yer too mean to buy *me* one, you ain't goin' to use me to get warm!'

'All right, I'll sleep downstairs,' he replied.

It was no use arguing any more.

But he didn't stay long – back he came with a hot refill. I thought: one of these days he'll get that water too hot and the bottle will burst.

Sure enough, I woke up to find the foot of the bed wet – the bottle was leaking.

I screamed at him and threw the bottle on to the floor. 'Now look what's 'appened!'

'Oh, shut up!' he yelled back. ''Tain't my fault the bottle's leaked.'

'Is that all you can say? Well, this is the last time you 'ave a bottle in my bed,' I yelled. I picked up the dripping bottle and, opening the window, I threw it out into the yard below, and went downstairs.

The following night he was very late. I looked at the bedside clock – it was nearly one-thirty and he still hadn't come up to bed.

Surely, I thought, he can't still be sulking! I crept downstairs, but he wasn't in his chair or sitting on the couch. I began to get worried. I went into the kitchen, and there I saw him trying to fix a piece of sticking plaster on that bottle.

'How mean can you get!' I cried as I snatched it from him. 'This time it's goin' into the ashbin and if yer want ter get warm I'm going to buy an electric blanket.'

'What for? They're dangerous! You can get electrocuted with one of them!'

'Not if you switch 'em off!' I replied.

'Well *I* ain't buyin' one, I'm quite satisfied with a bottle and if you aren't I'll buy *you* one too.'

'If you do, I'll sleep in the spare room, where I can get a proper night's sleep.'

'You wouldn't, would yer, Kate?' he grinned. 'You always say you're scared to sleep on yer own.'

'What do you care?' I replied angrily. 'Yer come up late and wake me up, trying to lift me nightie, so yer can put yer cold feet on me belly. Even when I turn over yer try pushing 'em up me back. So now I'm going up ter bed an' I'm goin' ter sleep in the spare room, so good night!' I replied angrily.

I snatched up a couple of blankets and left.

As I tried to settle down to sleep, I heard him creep into the room.

'Are you awake, love?' I heard him whisper.

'Yes! Go away and leave me alone!'

'I've brought you up a nice hot cup of tea.'

'I don't want it!'

'Well, come back in the other bed where we can cuddle up an' keep warm.'

'No! I know your cuddle ups.'

'If you'll come back, I'll even do without me water bottle. I *promise*. I only want for us to cuddle up together. I'm cold.'

I suddenly began to feel guilty at the way I had behaved. I drank the tea and followed him back to bed. As we cuddled up close, he broke his promise and we made love.

Next day he gave me the money to buy a blanket. I called at Lewis's Stores in town and bought a full-sized one, before I changed my mind.

On the way home with my purchase, I began to smile to myself, thinking how possessive he'd been with his water bottle. But there won't be any more squabbles about whose side *this* would be on, I said to myself.

I called the blanket 'Sheila', a name I gave to most things I possessed. Joe often used to laugh at me, saying I was crazy.

The first night I put it in the bed, I was pleased he took to it straight away.

I could have said 'I told you so.' But I thought: let sleeping dogs lie. The trouble was, it was a hard job to wake him up in the mornings. He was always first to bed and last out.

One night a few weeks later, we had a terrific storm. It was lightening, thundering and raining all through the night. For once Joe was already fast asleep when I went upstairs, and the last thing I did after getting undressed and into my nightdress was to take out my teeth, put them in a pint jug of water with a pinch of salt and leave them on the bathroom shelf. Joe knew I had false teeth, but I never let him see me take them out – I would have felt embarrassed.

As soon as I got into bed I heard him snoring like a contented pig. After a few digs and a couple of grunts, he turned on to his side and went quiet.

I picked up my book and tried to finish reading it, but after a while I lost interest. I switched off the bedside lamp, and it wasn't long before I fell asleep.

I don't know how long I'd slept, when a loud clash of thunder woke me up. I shot up in bed and switched on the light. I felt so hot I thought I was suffocating, and as I slung back the bedclothes, a waft of smoke hit me.

Suddenly I flew out of bed. 'Joe, Joe!' I screamed as I shook him. 'Wake up, wake up!'

'What the bloody hell's the matter with yer now?' he cried, glaring up at me. 'Seen a few mower ghosts?'

'No Joe, look!' I shouted, pointing to the foot of the bed. 'The bed's smoulderin'.'

Suddenly he too flew out of bed. 'I told yer what would 'appen as soon as yer bought that bloody "Sheila", as yer call it! Yer run downstairs and bring some water up, while I try to smother it afore it gets alight.'

When I came back with a bowl of water, I could see he had already opened the window and thrown the feather bed into the yard below – 'Sheila' too.

After a few sharp words, we went to sleep in the spare bed.

Early next morning, when I awoke, it was still dark and still raining heavily. I decided to leave Joe asleep and go downstairs to make myself a cup of tea. I was still dithering in my nightie, but first of all I went into the bathroom to put in my teeth. As soon as I looked inside the jug, I saw there was no water – nor my teeth. I was certain I remembered putting them there. I began to think: had somebody or something come in the night and stolen them? I suddenly became frightened. I began to panic, and as my tears fell I ran back into the bedroom and tried to yell through my toothless gums.

'Joe, Joe! Me teef 'ave gone! Somebody's took me teef!'

'What yer mumblin' about now?'

'Me teef, me teef, they've gone!'

'What yer mean, yer teef 'ave gone!' he mimicked. 'You ain't swallowed 'em, 'ave yer? Anyway, where did yer put 'em?'

'In a jug a water in the baffwoom,' I managed to say.

Suddenly he burst out laughing. 'Then they must be still in amongst the feathers when I used that water for the bed.'

I fled downstairs, hoping and praying they hadn't melted. It was still raining when I bent down, put my hand in and felt among the wet feathers. I couldn't feel them anywhere, then suddenly I gave a sigh of relief – I saw my teeth clinging to 'Sheila'.

Apart from a few wet feathers clinging to them, I was pleased to see that my teeth were intact.

It was still thundering and lightning in the distance as I hurried back upstairs. Shivering and sneezing, I managed to brush the wet feathers off my teeth and put them in a fresh jug of water. After changing my wet nightie for a dry one, I decided we had to sleep in the other room. Joe had already had a cup of hot cocoa waiting for me. 'Come on, love, drink this and get into bed before yer catch yer death of cold.'

After drinking the cocoa I got into bed beside him. He put his arms round me, and as we cuddled up close to get warm, he whispered in my ear, 'You and yer teef!' We both saw the funny side and burst out laughing.

Next morning, when I went into our bedroom to clean up the mess, I knew at once: it wasn't 'Sheila's' fault the bed nearly caught fire. I realised I must have forgotten to switch it off before falling asleep.

When I told my husband, he surprised me by saying, 'Never mind, love, I've remembered it's your birthday tomorra. I'll give yer the money to buy another one. But', he added, 'I'll have the switch my side, then I'll be sure to take the plug out. But first, *you'll* have to buy another feather bed.'

The bed would cost *me* several times more than a blanket would cost *him* – I thought how mean he was.

But I didn't argue, in case he changed his mind.

Married Life

J oe had been a sergeant in the air force during the war. He
was stationed in India and South Africa. Often he used to show
me his album and tell me about some of the places he visited. He
said that one day he would save enough money to take me to South
Africa, but he never got round to it.

When he came back to Birmingham, he could never settle down to
work inside a factory. He loved giving orders, but couldn't take them.

He had several outdoor jobs, where he could earn himself a bit of
extra money on the side, for he loved handling money. At one
period he worked on a milk cart delivering milk. When he wasn't
able to straighten the books, he told the manager money was still
owing from bad payers. Later he was sacked.

The next job was hulking hundredweights of coal around the
streets from a horse and cart. That job didn't last long either.

His other job was at Perry Barr Dog Tracks exercising the dogs.
One day he brought home 'Hopwas Reward', one of the grey-
hounds, to show me. It was his favourite, but when I saw its ribs
showing through its skin I asked, 'What do yer feed 'em on to win
a race? Starve 'em?' I added.

'No, they have to be on a special diet.'

'I don't know about callin' 'im "Hopwas Reward". The name
would suit him would be Tin Ribs,' I replied.

Often Joe would leave the dog with me for a couple of hours
while he went to see his dad and brother-in-law to give them a
tip-off. While he was out I felt so sorry for that animal sitting in
front of the fire shivering, I gave him a roll of pig's pudding. He was
ravenous – another day I gave him lumps of cheese and buttered
toast and meat gravy soaked in bread. Each time Hopwas was left
with me I would feed him up.

The trainer saw he was putting on weight, but he couldn't understand why. Hopwas was never entered in another race. A few weeks later, I was told he had died. I was glad Joe never found out that in my ignorance I had overfed him with the wrong kind of food.

While my husband was still at the dog track, he came in contact with one of the bookmakers, Jimmy Budd. Jimmy asked Joe if he would like a part-time job collecting a few bets. As Joe loved the feel of money, this job went well for a while. On bad nights when betting was slack, Jimmy didn't want to pay much. They argued, and when Joe helped himself to his wages, that was the end of that job.

One night as we were on the way to the Elite picture house, Joe slipped into the betting shop owned by Jim and Joe Smith, to have a bet. As soon as he came out we walked towards the Elite in Soho Road. He said, 'Kate, I've had a word with Jim and Joe. They've asked me if I'd like a job collecting bets on our street corner.' As this was illegal, I was worried. 'But what if the police catch yer?' I said.

'That'll all be arranged. They'll put another dummy runner in my place, while I'm hurrying away to take in the bets. Anyway,' he added, 'I'll be workin' on commission.'

'Please yerself, if that's what yer want to do, but don't come to me to bail yer out if yer get caught!' I replied angrily.

'Come on,' he replied, 'or we'll be late for the pictures.'

Joe and I loved to see a cowboy film. But when we fumbled in the dark to find two seats, we noticed the film had already started. It wasn't until we found two empty seats in the front row, six seats away from each other, that we discovered the programme had been changed. They were showing Gracie Fields in *The Queen of Hearts*.

We were both disappointed, but watched it for about ten minutes until all of a sudden I heard Joe call out, 'Kate, come on! I ain't watchin' no mower of this bleedin' rubbish!'

I felt so embarrassed as I got up and followed him out. On the way home we had our usual quarrel, yet our arguments never lasted long. Often Joe would change the subject and make me smile with his sense of humour.

A few days later, Joe Smith called at our house to make all the necessary arrangements.

Soon he had punters come from all districts, for my husband was well known and well liked, especially amongst the women. He would often be seen with his hands in his pockets whistling some kind of ditty while waiting for bets on the street corner.

He was also known as 'The Bookie's Runner'. Often he would have pieces of toffee or a penny ready to give to some little urchin to keep a watchful eye out and warn him when he saw a 'bobby' coming.

He'd be seen standing beside a low wall, laughing and joking to some of the people who handed him the bets. Yet he was always on the alert to scale the wall and hide in someone's back entry or in their attic. When the all clear came, women would hand over their threepenny and sixpenny each-way bets, and when anyone asked him to tip them a horse or a dog, he used to say, 'Do yer think I'd be standin' 'ere if I knew any certainties? Yer betta try stickin' a pin in, yer might be lucky.'

Often the police disguised themselves in slouched trilbys and long shabby raincoats, but Joe was no fool – he knew them all and was over that wall and out of sight before they ever caught him.

One morning as I walked down the street, I saw Mrs Jenks, one of our neighbours, having an argument with my husband. When she saw me she came towards me. I asked her what the trouble was, and she said, 'Yer know, Mrs Dayus, I like yower Joe, until he tries ter pay me out short. I know I can't read but I know 'ow ter reckon up to a farthin'.'

'Oh well, Mrs Jenks,' I replied pleasantly, 'we all make mistakes,' and I walked away.

My husband didn't take only threepenny, fourpenny or sixpenny bets – men came from factories all around the Jewellery Quarter with large sums of money and large bets which earned him his commission.

During the Oaks, St Leger, November Handicap and other such important races, my husband's commission more or less came to £1,500 a week. He gave me most of it to save in my bank account. We now had quite a nice little nest egg.

During the winter months we'd sit beside a roaring fire and play cards or dominoes. He taught me all kinds of games, but he was a poor loser and often grumbled when I beat him. 'Beginner's luck' he used to say, and he said red cards were unlucky for him. When he had another-coloured pack he'd say, 'Let's have a shilling on who wins.' But when I won he wanted to double up. I knew he'd win in the end, so I gave up and put my winnings in my pocket.

Some nights he would read to me from one of his cowboy books, and if I felt tired and closed my eyes he'd ask me if I'd been listening.

'Yes,' I'd reply. 'I'm only restin' my eyes.'

But when he asked me what the last chapter was about and I couldn't tell him, he'd say, 'Never mind, I'll continue tomorrow night', and put the book away.

Later, Joe built himself a loft at the end of the garden for his pigeons. And after getting rid of all the builders' rubbish, he dug a garden where later I grew my own vegetables.

I felt now that I wanted to sell my business and retire. As soon as everything was sold, I had a couple of customers ask me to help them out with home work. Several weeks later Joe built me a workshop facing the back garden. Later I taught him how to do the enamelling and for several years we worked together doing outwork for T. A. Butler and R. E. V. Gomm. During those years we were very happy together.

Then one day my eldest daughter brought us the news that her husband had died tragically. She was a bundle of nerves and scared to go back to her own house. After my husband and I had made all the funeral arrangements, we talked things over and suggested she come to stay with us until such time as she could make up her mind to go back to her own home. But later she decided to sell the house and everything it contained and make her home with us.

While she was living with us, Joe and I took her on our fishing holidays in Ireland. We never left her to be lonely. He also taught her to drive the car and play bowls, and in the evening he would read to us or play cards or dominoes.

Winnie

It was during 1955 – I remember it well. One lovely sunny afternoon, I went to Handsworth Park for a bowling match, but as I was too early I sat down on the bench outside the pavilion and waited for the other members. As I did so I thought: how different that bowling green is now – I remember it as it was years ago! Then it was always kept in tiptop condition, yet today it's been neglected; nobody seems to care when they see young lads and even grown men abusing it. It was only a few years ago that Handsworth Park had two bowling greens, some of the best greens in the Midlands. It also had one of its best teams. Some of the ladies still meet in their club house to have a roll-up, but sad to say, they don't have a team any more.

As I sat on that bench, wiping my woods and getting ready to give my partner a game, I happened to glance across the green and noticed a poorly clad elderly woman sitting on the far side. I noticed she kept staring across at me. Playing beside her were two ragged children, a boy and a girl, about four years old, pushing an empty dilapidated pram.

Just as Annie, my opponent, and I began to start our match, the children ran across the bowling green. Suddenly we saw the boy pull out his little willie, and as the little girl scratched her head and watched, he began to piddle. Suddenly, Annie cried out, 'Yer dirty little bugger! Sod off!'

Quickly the little boy fumbled to push his willie back. As the remains of the piddle ran down his legs, he began to cry.

This held up our game as the other players began to laugh, and we were getting annoyed.

'Look at 'er, their mother!' Annie cried out. 'She ain't even botherin' about 'em, an' if they don't clear off, I'll goo over meself an' clout their ear'oles!'

'No need for that, Annie,' I replied. 'I'll take 'em over to their mum.'

Annie still stood there fuming as I held their grubby little hands. When I asked their names, the little boy replied 'Georgie'. 'An' my name's Jenny,' the little girl whispered.

As soon as I reached the woman, I asked, 'Are you their mum?'

'No,' she replied. 'I'm their grandmother.'

'Well, will you please keep the children off the green?'

As I began to walk away I heard her call out, 'Don't yer know me, Kate?'

'I'm sorry, I'm afraid I don't,' I replied. 'But if you're still here when the match is finished, I'll come back to yer.'

All at once, I heard Annie yell out, 'Cum on! Yer 'oldin' up the bloody game!'

'All right! All right!' I yelled back. 'I'm coming!'

All through our game I kept wondering who she was, and why she said I should remember her, which made me lose my concentration. I lost my game, twenty-one nil. That was the first time I ever lost with such a score, and I never lived it down. But I was pleased to know that the team had won.

I was still thinking and wondering who she was as I made my way with the players for tea, and as I looked through the window I could still see her beside the pram.

I was eager now to know who she was. I didn't wait for my tea, I took my cakes and some tea on a tray to give them. As the children stuffed the cakes into their mouths, their granny said, 'Where's yer manners?'

'Thank yer, Miss,' they managed to reply.

As soon as she had drunk the cup of tea, she said, 'Yer sure yer don't know me, Kate?'

'No, but if you'll tell me yer name, I might.'

'Me name's Winnie Nashe, we grew up together in Camden Drive.'

Suddenly I remembered. I couldn't believe my eyes. Although I remembered that she was my age, she looked old and worn. Her face was well lined and her once beautiful red hair was now turning grey.

Suddenly I flung my arms around her and kissed her. All in one breath I cried out, 'Oh Winnie, Winnie, I'm ever so happy to see you again after all these years. Where are you living now?'

'I live in one of the side streets in the All Saints district near the coal wharf.'

'Why haven't yer tried to get in touch before?'

'I didn't know where yer was livin' and it was only by talkin' ter one of me neighbours about yer, that she told me yer was playin' 'ere.'

'Well, I'm glad you found me, anyway. Come home with me and we can talk about old times,' I said.

'I'd like that, Kate, but I've gotta get back 'ome, George will be waitin' for 'is tea.'

'Who's George, yer husband?' I asked.

'No, 'e's the children's father,' she replied.

'Well, do you mind if I come home with you? I don't want to lose you again.'

'Yes, I'd like that, Kate, that's if yer don't mind the place we're livin'.'

'I ain't coming to see yer place, only you. Now stay there while I fetch me coat.'

As soon as I took the empty tray back to the club house, everyone asked who she was.

'A long-lost school friend I haven't seen for years,' I replied as I put on my coat and left.

Winnie had already put the twins in the pram and was wheeling it towards the park gates when I caught up with her. It was almost twenty minutes before we reached her home. This place, where they lived, was no better than the bug-infested hovels where we lived and played when we were children, many long years ago.

These back-to-back slums were a reminder of those forgotten years, with damp green slime clinging to the outside brickwork. There was still the familiar cry from the rag-and-bone man, and smells of urine drifting into the air from the gutters, and all kinds of rubbish littered those pavements. Today it's a different place; many of these old hovels have been pulled down to make way for tower blocks (monstrosities, I call them).

I'm no snob, for hadn't I too been dragged up in bug- and rat-infested slums? Yet as I looked around these godforsaken places these people called their homes, I felt I didn't want to be reminded of the past, or to go inside. But I couldn't hurt her feelings by making some excuse.

As Winnie pushed the old pram up a side entry, the children climbed out and joined their playmates in the yard.

As we entered the living-room, I saw an elderly thickset man in his none too clean shirtsleeves. His square chin sprouted grey stubble. When he stared at me as he sat up to the table, I noticed he had a flat nose and a cauliflower ear. I thought he must have been a prizefighter. I could see he'd had plenty to drink, for as he got up from the table he stumbled and just glared at me.

'I've brought me friend 'ome with me, George,' Winnie said.

As he made his way towards the stairs, the children ran in.

'Daddy,' the little boy cried out, 'can I cum up an' watch yer fly the pigeons?'

'Very well,' he mumbled, 'but watch yer sister don't fall down the loft this time.'

After they had gone up to the attic, Winnie closed the door.

'Is that yer daughter's husband, Winnie?' I asked.

When she nodded, I couldn't help but say, 'Whatever could she see in him – he must be old enough to be her father?' And so ugly, I thought.

'Yes,' replied Winnie. 'He was forty an' Alice was only sixteen when they got married. She 'ad ter get wed, she was four months in the family way. But 'e was good an' kind ter me an' Alice. He ain't always bin like this, an' 'e was a goodlookin' bloke until 'e went in the war, an' when 'e cum back from the army 'e looked different. It's shrapnel,' she added. 'But me daughter couldn't bear the sight of him near 'er. She used to go off with other men and leave the twins for hours, and when George found out, 'e used ter belt 'er. I tried talkin' some sense into them both and things seemed a bit better for a while – until George got a job on nights, then she'd go out an' never cum back until the early hours. Then one mornin' as I was givin' the twins their porridge, she told me she was packin' 'er things an' leavin' in a few days' time.'

'What happened about the twins – did she say she was taking them with her?' I asked.

'No, Kate, she asked me if I'd take care of them until she got settled elsewhere. I was afraid to tell George she was leadin' a bad life an' was thinkin' of leavin' us. I couldn't stand any more fights and rows. So, as long as there was peace, I kept my mouth shut. I prayed often she would cum to 'er senses. Then, to make matters worse, she told me she'd tried to 'ave an abortion, an' when I asked why, she said she didn't want another babby, because it wasn't George's. When I asked 'ow she knew it wasn't, she replied, "Well, we ain't slept together or med luv for six months an' I'm over three months now." That same night she packed 'er bags and left.'

'Where is she now?' I asked.

'I don't know, Kate, and I don't think I care any more, an' I don't believe George cares, either. He gives me wot 'e can ter look after the twins, but 'e ain't over-generous.'

'But how do you manage?'

'Well, I used ter mek peg rugs like me mum an' dad showed me. But there ain't much call for 'em today. I almost 'ave ter give 'em away.'

'But why don't you try and move away from here?'

"Ow can I? This is my 'ome. Anyway, I can't leave me gran' children to the mercy of 'im, 'e's all right till 'e gets the booze down 'im, then I puts on their 'ats an' scarves an' we leave 'im to it. That's why I came to find you at the park.'

'I'm glad you did, Winnie. But ain't their dad got any sisters or relations that can take *their* share?'

'They don't want ter know us, but I've got plenty of kind neighbours.'

'Well, Winnie, I'll have to be going now or my Joe will be wondering where I am. But will you promise to come next Tuesday when my husband has gone to the races and we'll have a good old natter about when we were kids?'

'I'd love that, Kate.'

'Very well, you know where I live – Uplands Road. Now promise me you'll come. Don't forget, next Tuesday.'

'I won't forget,' she replied, smiling.

As she stood on the step, several neighbours eyed me up and down, wondering who I was, but I left Winnie to explain. As I flung my arms around her again and kissed her, I called out, 'Don't forget!'

When I got home I felt very sad to think that Winnie hadn't tried to make something better of her life.

The following Tuesday, I made a large cake and laid the table with bread and jam and beef sandwiches. What they couldn't eat, I would wrap up for them to take home. About three o'clock there was a knock on the door. As soon as I opened it I asked Winnie where the twins were. She said one of her kind neighbours was looking after them.

'It don't do for 'em to 'ear too much these days,' she added.

As she came into the room I could almost see what she was thinking. As she glanced around she exclaimed, 'Wot a nice place you 'ave, Kate!'

'Never mind the place, you come and sit down and have something to eat with me.' I wasn't going to show her around the house – not because I didn't want to, but I had so much more than she had, I didn't want her to feel out of place.

But all the while we were having our tea I could see her eyes wandering around everything in the room, taking everything in. To distract her mind from her surroundings, I said, 'You're very quiet, Winnie.'

'I was thinking what I could do if I 'ad a place like this.'

'Well, it's not too late, maybe some day you will, but first you have to get out of that rut you're in.'

'How can I, with me gran'children needin' me?'

'But Winnie, you've got to think of yourself as well, and try and make a new life for yourself. Did you ever get married?' I added.

'No, Kate, I did go with a young chap but when he found out I'd had a love child, I never saw him again.'

'But you're still nice-looking, Winnie, and I'm sure you'll meet the right man one day.'

'Yes, the neighbours are always telling me that. But 'ow can I leave the twins? I luv 'em like they was me own, an' if I left 'em, who's goin' ter look after 'em?'

I knew now how she felt. I still remember it was a bitter blow for me, when I had to part with my four young children – but under very different circumstances. That was in 1931, during the Depression.

To cheer her up, I thought it best to change the subject.

'Winnie, do you remember how hungry we was when we were kids, and I raided my mum's cupboard and stole a piece of fat bacon? And as we sat on the step I told you to suck it slowly to make it last?'

'Yes, I remember. It slid down our throats before we could even chew it, an' we nearly choked.'

As soon as I saw her smile, I said, 'And do you remember when I told you about my brother Jack, stealing the pig from the farm where I went hop-picking, and how the court case ended?'

'Yes, Kate, but did 'e really steal it? It wasn't proved,' she replied.

'Yes, Winnie, he did steal it, but I don't believe he took it back to the farm; for the next few weeks we ate nothing but pork, pork and more pork. Mum even boiled the pig's trotters with all the leftover bones. We ate that much pork, we began to feel like pigs.'

She began to look more cheerful, but I still carried on talking.

'Winnie,' I began again, 'do you remember when all the kids and us two had whooping cough and our mums dosed us with castor oil, and Mrs Turner said the only thing to cure us was fumes from hot tar, and while the navvies was laying the wooden blocks between the tramlines, we were all marched down the Parade, where we had to bend over that cauldron and inhale the fumes?'

'Yes, Kate, an' we nearly choked, but we still 'ad to 'ave our dose of castor oil.'

'And still have our chests rubbed with hot tallow candles,' I replied.

'An' don't forget the old socks, Kate, soaked in camphorated oil an' fastened round our necks, when we caught mumps off the ther kids in the yard.'

I felt then that I didn't want to talk about our sad experiences, but over another cup of tea Winnie began to remind me of the one night I wanted to forget.

'You remember that night, Kate,' she began, 'when we 'ad that foursome, when we was fifteen?'

'Yes,' I replied. 'But let's talk about something else.'

But she was persistent in reminding me.

'But I must tell yer, Kate, I 'aven't seen yer since that day me mum beat me an' turned me out, when I was in the family way. It took a lot of years ter forget 'Arry, but time 'eals wounds.'

'We were two silly foolish girls then, Winnie. I'd almost forgotten that night,' I replied.

'Not me, I 'ad something to remind *me*.'

'How long has it been, then?' I asked.

'Well, Alice would now be twenty, so it's gotta be over twenty years when I fell for 'er.'

As soon as I saw her tears, I quickly changed the subject: 'You'd never believe the struggle I had with that other chap, that same night. I can smile now, when I think back, but not then. He pushed me in a doorway, and when I felt his John Thomas come out I got a fright and pulled it for all I was worth, and when he screamed and rolled into the gutter I ran for my life. I thought I'd killed him. Next day I kept buying newspapers to see.'

'Did yer see 'im after?' she asked.

'Yes. But he said how sorry he was, and when he had his call-up papers, he asked me if I'd wait for him. I said I would. Some time later he sent me a birthday card with lovey-dovey words written on the back, but I never heard or saw him again.'

When it was time for Winnie to leave, I made her promise to come again and meet my second husband, Joe. She said she would. After wrapping the rest of the cake for the twins, we said the usual ta-ra.

But she never kept that promise. I wondered why. I went to her home a few days later, but as soon as she saw me she said she wished I hadn't come.

'But why?' I asked.

'Well, Kate, I feel ashamed of this place for yer ter see.'

'That's nonsense, Winnie. If you'll come and see me next week, I'll see what I can do to help you.'

She promised, but she never kept her promise. I waited two whole weeks before I called again, hoping to give her some good advice. But it was too late. When I called and found the house empty, neighbours said they'd done a moonlight flit.

Sad to say, I never saw Winnie again. Yet my childhood memories of her still live with me, and I pray and hope that one day I shall meet her.

never believe the struggle I had with that other chap that same
night. I can smile now, when I think back, but not so

Trespassers Will Be Prosecuted?

O ur fishing holidays in Ireland were the best of times for Joe and
me. One evening after eating our supper we went across the
yard to the bar, where the landlord (after a fashion) introduced us
to the locals.

'These are our two boarders. An' this 'ere is Micky, Rolly, Mike,
Paddy' . . . and many more.

When I saw them all staring at me, I asked the landlord why.

'They ain't used ter see any young woman in 'ere.'

'That's OK,' Joe replied. 'My wife will 'ave a Guinness and I'll
'ave a shandy.'

Later that night we got very friendly with a couple who asked us
to play a foursome at cribbage. Joe and I knew the game well, and
enjoyed it.

Afterwards, a couple of Irishmen asked where we'd come from
and if we'd enjoyed the fishing.

'No, not yet, Paddy,' Joe replied.

''Ow's that? Plenty of big fish in these waters of ours.'

'I'm told there is,' Joe replied, 'until some little buggers started
throwin' stones in the water.'

Suddenly I saw Paddy wink, and as he burst out laughing Joe said,
'It was no laughin' matter, mate.'

'No offence meant,' Paddy replied, still smiling. 'But that'd be our
Mickie an' little Pat – did they try to sell yer sum of them Irish
worms?'

'Yes,' Joe replied, smiling back at Paddy. 'But I'd rather 'ave 'ad
Irish maggots.'

'If them's what yer want, mate, we've plenty of them – an' I mean
Irish,' he added.

I was glad Joe saw the funny side; he knew it was best to be on the right side of these big burly Irishmen. But I dreaded to think what would have happened to both of us if he *had* caught one or other of those mischievous little urchins.

After Joe had bought Paddy a couple of pints of Guinness he told him the best water to fish and where there were plenty of maggots to be had free.

'Just take a bucket an' the slaughterers will fill it for yer,' Paddy said.

When Joe asked where this place was, Paddy replied, 'Yer go along over the bridge and when yer turn ter the right yer see an old wooden buildin' where they slaughter the 'orses an' goats. It's what you English call a knacker's yard. Tell Rory Paddy Magee sent yer.'

After Joe had bought him another pint, we wished everyone good night. We retired to bed, but before we went, on the way across the yard to the lavatory I met the landlady coming out.

All at once she said, 'If I was you, me dear, I wouldn't go fishin' near theea.'

'But why?' I asked. 'I always go where my 'usband goes.'

'I understand – please yourself,' she replied pleasantly. 'Good night, my dear,' she added.

As I came back across the yard I heard the landlord say to my husband, 'Yer don't wanta believe all the blarney Paddy tells yer. But yer *will* get plenty of maggots. Any'ow, whether yer fish near there, yer please yourself.'

After wishing us both good night he went to bed.

I was too tired to ask Joe any questions, and once we were undressed and in bed we were too tired even to kiss each other good night.

Next morning, we were up at the crack of dawn and ready to go. After Paddy had greeted us with the usual 'Top o' the mornin', off we went with our paraphernalia strapped to our backs.

We walked some distance, then we saw two heavy-set Irishmen coming towards us. They had splashes of blood all over their clothes. At first glance, I thought they must have been in a fight. Later I was to find out that they were the men from the slaughter-house, which we were heading for. When they stopped to raise their hats and to greet us with their usual 'Top o' the mornin', Joe asked them the way and told them we'd come to do some fishing.

'You'll find it around the bend, it's the large wooden buildin' on the right,' one of them said.

'The best fishin' part of the river you'll ever find in Ireland,' the other fellow replied. 'But I wouldn't take yer missus near theea,' he added.

Joe thanked them and we hurried along. I asked, 'Why did he say I shouldn't go?'

'I suppose he thought it would smell too much. But knowin' you,' he added, 'you'll come whatever 'appens.'

I always did have an inquisitive nature, but I never realised what I was going to smell and see that morning. When we were a little distance away, we saw a large old wooden shed. Propping it up were three stout tree trunks.

As we drew nearer, I saw smoke coming out through the rafters and the stench was awful. I'd never smelt anything like it. As we got closer, we saw a big hefty fellow making his way to the doorway carrying a heavy iron cauldron full of maggots. He was dressed in an old well-worn cowgown covered with blood; his leather apron and wellington boots were covered with congealed blood too. Even his hands and arms were splashed with blood. While I was staring at him, Joe gave him Paddy's message. While they were talking, I peeped inside the shed, then wished I hadn't. The smell of burning flesh wafted out, and hanging from the low rafters was bloody wool, skin and hide; I also saw parts of dead animals strewn across a wooden bench, even on the floor.

I felt I wanted to be sick, and as I walked away I vomited into the river.

As soon as my husband saw me he sat me down on the bank.

When I had pulled myself together, I cried, 'I ain't gooin' in there!'

'But there's no other way we can get to the river, only through the slaughter'ouse, love.'

Suddenly I lost my temper. 'Joe!' I cried out angrily. 'If yer think I'm goin' through that bloody shed, with all them dead carcasses lyin' about, yer can think again!'

'But, love, it's only a few paces to the river, yer can 'old yer nose, an' if yer shut yer eyes, I'll lead yer.'

'Lead yer bloody self!' I cried out angrily. 'I'm gooin' back to the inn.'

'Very well,' he snapped. 'Please yerself. I'll see yer later.' And off he went.

After wiping my tears away, I thought: what a waste of time to go back and sit in my room on such a lovely warm day!

With my creel and rod still strapped on my back, I decided to explore the other side of the river, where I could settle down and fish.

I must have walked about two miles, around several bends of the river, until I came to a lovely stretch surrounded by trees. I looked around – not a soul was in sight, but as I glanced up at one of the trees I saw a notice: PRIVATE FISHING WATERS.

I said to myself: if anyone should come along and see me I'll say I haven't seen the notice. I undid my tackle, put one of the few worms I had left in my tin on the hook, and settled down to fish. I had the time of my life – within a couple of hours I caught four dace, three trout and a grayling. I put the trout and grayling inside the basket. The dace I threw back into the water. I had no more worms left, so I thought it was time to leave.

When I got back to the inn and entered our room, Joe stood facing me.

'Where the devil 'ave yer bin?' he cried at once.

'I went for a walk along the river.'

I wasn't going to tell him then what I had caught.

'Well, did yer catch anything?' I asked.

'Catch anything?' he cried, 'I threw in me first 'andful of maggots and they kept jumpin' up fer more. I couldn't get 'em out quick enough, great big bream they was.'

'Well, let's see 'em,' I replied anxiously.

'I threw 'em all back – I couldn't put 'em in me basket, they smelt to the high heavens.'

When he'd finished talking I said, 'Now Joe, shut yer eyes and open 'em when I tell yer.'

While his eyes were closed I opened up the basket, then showed him what I'd caught.

His eyes nearly popped out of his head. He cried, 'Wherever did yer fish them from?'

When I told him, he asked if anybody had seen me. When I told him nobody had, he made me promise not to say to the missus nor the landlord where I had been. But if they should ask, I was to say further along the river. Joe had one trout, the missus and the gaffer had one each and I had the grayling, which she cooked in wine. It was delicious.

I was surprised they never asked where I got them from, yet said that any time we brought any more she would cook them for us.

Next morning I promised to take Joe there. As soon as we arrived, he saw the notice, climbed the tree and hid it among the bushes.

While he'd gone to dig up a few worms, I got everything ready to start. As soon as he returned we stuck a worm on the end of our hooks, sat down on our fishing baskets and threw in our lines. Fifteen minutes later Joe caught a large trout, a few minutes later another, and so did I. We were very excited and about to thread another worm when we saw a well-built fellow coming through the trees towards us. We knew at once he was the water bailiff. A black-and-white sheepdog walked beside him. 'Hide them trout, quick, behind the bushes, and sit quiet, while I go on fishin',' hissed Joe.

There was no time to hide them anywhere – only in the basket. Then I sat down on it. As the man stood beside my husband, he asked, 'Have you a permit to fish here?'

'No, sir,' Joe replied.

'Did you know these are private waters?'

'No, sir, I didn't,' Joe lied.

'Surely you've got eyes to read the notice on the tree,' he replied.

'I'm sorry, but I didn't see any notice.'

As the man turned to show him, he cried, 'If I catch any more of them bloody gypsy kids around here, and up these trees again, I'll put me gun up their arse. Anyway,' he added, 'have you caught anything?'

'Only a few roach,' replied Joe.

I began to shake in my wellies when he asked to look inside the basket.

Stupidly I tried to put him off and change the subject – I began to stroke the dog. 'What a lovely coat 'e's got – what's 'is name?' I asked, smiling up at him.

'Never mind what his name is, I want yours! And I still want to look inside that basket!'

Joe, still thinking the fish were safely hidden in the bushes, said he could open it up and look with pleasure. Sure enough, as soon as he lifted the lid there was the evidence, eyes and mouth open, glaring up at him.

'Do you know these are trout?' he said.

'No, sir,' Joe lied again. 'I've never seen a trout. I thought they was roach.'

'Well,' he replied as he took out his notebook, 'you had better give me your name and address and I'll take the fish for evidence. Now you better pack up and leave.'

After we had given the bailiff our names and home address, he added, 'Next time I see you anywhere near these waters I shall confiscate your rods.'

As he took the trout and walked away he said we would hear from him later.

As soon as he'd gone and we were packing up to leave, Joe called me all the fools he could think of. 'Why dain't yer 'ide 'em in the bushes?' he snapped.

'There wasn't time. I dain't think he'd look in the basket,' I snapped. 'The dog would 'ave sniffed 'em out, any'ow.'

When he saw my tears he said he was sorry he'd lost his temper.

As soon as we arrived back at the inn, the landlord asked if we had brought some more trout. 'The missus 'as the pan on ready, Joe,' he added, rubbing his hands together.

'Sorry, mate, we dain't 'ave any luck terday.'

I noticed the landlord looked disappointed, but my husband wouldn't tell him why.

After our usual supper of bread and cheese, beef and pickles, we went across the yard to the bar, where we heard some of the locals singing.

'What's the celebration in aid of?' I asked the landlord.

'Oh, me lads always sing on Saturday nights, but ternight they're singing their numbers for you and yer missus,' he replied, turning to my husband.

I had heard Irishmen sing in our local pub at home, and when I was a child, but I'd never heard such lovely lilts and words to their songs as I did that night. As we sat among them, I thought: what a waste of talent! We saw and heard each Irishman in turn sing a number.

'Come on, Pat, let's 'ear from you.'

But when Pat began to sing 'Mountains of Mourne', the big fellow they called Mike cried out, 'Sit yerself down Pat, that's too sad, let's 'ave "Paddy McGinty's Goat".'

We laughed as we tapped our feet to the rhythm. Then it was Rolly's turn, and everybody joined in as he sang 'Abdul baba Amare'. It was a song I'd never heard before, but the words and the lilt of that tune set us all off tapping our feet. The landlord, I noticed, never objected to the noise, as several of the locals did an Irish jig.

By this time I had drunk a couple of whiskies and three Guinnesses, and was feeling merry myself. I wanted to sing a number, so I stood up and asked if I could.

I saw my husband warn me with a scowl, but I was determined to sing at least one song. But after I had finished 'Klondike Kate' and heard the loud applause, I began to sing 'That Little Shirt Me Muvver Made For Me'.

I felt so merry I could have sung all night, but when an old Irishman pulled me on to his lap I was pleased Joe came to the rescue.

'Come on, Grandad,' I heard him say. 'Enough's enough, so watch yer blood pressure.'

This caused more laughter amongst the locals.

It was now time to retire as we had to catch an early plane the next day, but Mike, the one with the lovely baritone voice, asked the landlord if he could sing one more number.

'Very well, then you must all go to yer 'omes.'

Turning to Joe, he asked, 'Do yer mind if I sing this last song for yer missus?'

Joe put his arm round me and as we sat down again the fellow gazed down at me and sang 'Kathleen Mavorneen'. Tears filled my eyes – not only because he sang it so beautifully, but I remembered back so many many years ago, when I was just sixteen, and my first husband sang it to me when we were courting.

After wishing everyone good night and saying we would come back to Ireland, we retired to our room, when Joe asked why I had wept.

'It was such a sad song and it brought back many sad memories, Joe.'

'The trouble with you, you 'ad too much to drink and . . .'

'It wasn't my fault if they asked me to 'ave one,' I replied.

'One? I counted three,' he said.

'Oh, you was jealous because I was 'avin' too much attention paid to me,' I replied as I began to weep.

Suddenly he took me in his arms and as he kissed my wet tears away he said, 'Yes, I was, love.'

As soon as we had undressed and got into bed he put his arms round me and hugged me to him. That was the last time we made love in that clean but rickety old bed. We had enjoyed our fishing holiday, and after saying our goodbyes to all the local people we promised to come back the next year.

Next morning we took the train to Dublin, where we caught the plane. After the stewardess had brought our cups of tea, I sat thinking about that water bailiff. When Joe asked me why I was quiet, I replied, 'You know, we shouldn't have given that bailiff our real address – what if we're put into prison?'

'I don't think so,' he replied, with a smile. 'He could 'ave had us arrested then and taken our rods. No, forget it, I don't want yer spoilin' yer 'oliday we've 'ad.'

As soon as we arrived home, there in the letterbox were bills and a letter with an Irish stamp on the envelope. When my husband opened it he cried, 'That crafty ol' bleeda, he must 'ave kept them trout and cooked 'em for 'imself!'

'But what's the letter say?' I asked eagerly.

'Just a warning to tell us not to fish there again. No address, an' no signature. Any'ow I still think we were lucky, Kate. It could 'ave been a real bailiff.'

The following year, 1961, we made plans to go to Ireland again, but cancelled it for two weeks at the seaside in Weymouth, where Joe had been stationed during the war. But it rained every day. It was disastrous. While we were on our way home my husband said we'd take a short cut down Rookery Road. As we walked a little way down the hill I noticed several workmen building six new houses. As soon as we got closer I thought how lovely it would be to own a newly built house where people haven't lived before.

'Joe,' I cried out at once, 'wouldn't it be nice to live in one of them?'

'Surely you ain't thinkin' of movin' again,' he replied.

'But Joe, I promise yer it'll be me last move, an' I won't get nervous any more, thinkin' about ghosts an' people committing suicide in them other 'ouses.'

'Well, wait till we get 'ome an' I'll think about it.'

'But Joe, why don't yer go an' ask one of the workmen now if they're for rent or to be sold?'

'They won't know,' he replied.

'No 'arm in askin'.'

'I've said I'll think about it,' he replied.

'All right, I'll ask meself.'

As I began to walk over loose planks of wood and piles of sand he pulled me back and made his way towards one of the workmen, who told him to enquire at the head builder's shed. After a while, he came back to tell me the houses wouldn't be finished until October but if we were interested we could go and see the estate agent. The first house in the row had a large frontage and a larger garden than the others – it was also detached.

Joe was as eager as I was now. Off we went to the address the builder had given us, and after giving him all the details we paid our deposit. In a few weeks we had everything signed, sealed and delivered, and soon we were the proud owners of 29 Rookery Road.

Maggie

I look forward with pleasure to my visits and talks to the elderly people of my generation – also to the young people I now come in contact with in schools and libraries. Yet I find it much easier to talk to the elderly who understand about the old slums and back-to-back hovels in those Edwardian Birmingham days. It is also a tonic to me to see their faces light up as they too recall their childhood memories, and the many they had almost forgotten.

And as I begin to talk to them as they sit or lie back in their chairs, I notice that many look younger or older than me, and I thank the Good Lord that I am one of the most fortunate ones who can get about and not have to stay where these people are from day to day, year to year. I know and feel that many of them would still prefer to go back and spend the rest of their lives in their own homes – although several tell me they would rather be where they are than live with their relatives.

Many of these ladies would not be in these homes if there weren't many kind people who dedicate their services and patient care to give warmth, comfort and pleasure to the elderly.

After my talks and readings from my books, I show them the video of the old and the new Birmingham, and the story of my family and of my life.

During one of these engagements I happened to notice a small white-haired lady very cheerfully wheeling a trolley with cups of tea and cakes, handing them out to the patients. All at once she came across, smiled at me and said, 'Excuse me, but I believe I know yer, and I've bin lookin' forward ter meeting yer, and when I knew yer was comin' 'ere I was ever so pleased. I've already read yer books, that's 'ow I remembered who yer was. Would yer like a fresh cup of tea?' she added.

'Yes thanks,' I replied, smiling back.

'I'll bring you a nice china cup, not one of these thick ones,' she said.

Before she moved away I asked how she knew me, as I couldn't remember who she was. She replied, 'I used to live in Pope Street with me mum an' dad an' me sister Becky. Me name's Maggie Brown, we used ter goo ter the same school.'

Suddenly I smiled and so did she – I whispered so that no one else could hear, 'Are you the Maggie Brown the other girls called after when we had no drawers to wear?'

'Yes, an' I still remember them words,' she whispered. 'Maggie Brown's got no drawers, will yer kindly lend 'er yours.' We began to laugh.

'Now I remember you, and your sister, and how we used to get the cane for helping each other with our sums. But we never went crying to our mums like the kids do today. I only ever ran home crying to my mum once and she said I must have deserved it, and if I didn't behave myself she'd give me some more.'

'Yes,' she replied. 'We was taught discipline in them days, ter respect our teachers an' our parents.'

'When I moved up into standard four I believe you and your sister left?'

'Yes,' she replied, 'we had to do a moonlight flit and went to live in Summer Lane, near the Salutation Pub. They was worse slums than the ones we'd already left – two rooms down and one up an' the front door cum on to the edge of the pavement.'

As we were still whispering our thoughts, we noticed the warden making her way towards us. She didn't look very pleased.

'Come on, Maggie!' she called out loudly. 'You're already behind, and there's the cups to be collected and put away.'

As Maggie took my empty cup she whispered, 'That sourfaced ole bugger! I wish the other warden was back. She was kind an' understandin'. We all liked 'er, but not this one. Can yer wait an' see me after I've finished?' she called as she hurried away.

I didn't have to wait long, and when we hurried outside towards the taxi that was waiting to drive me home, I told the driver I would be catching the bus instead. Maggie and I agreed to have tea and cakes in a little tea shop round the corner. As soon as we were sitting at the table and the waitress had served us, Maggie said, 'I ain't a patient at that community 'ome, I only goo theea ter mek teas an' goo errands to 'elp the old dears, who can't 'elp themselves. But we're blest, you an' me, we *can* get about, Kate – yer don't mind me callin' yer Kate?'

'No, not at all, Maggie,' I replied as I smiled across the table to her. She was quite a chatterbox, but then so was I. Yes, she was a nice pleasant person to listen to, and I was an eager listener as we chatted together as though we were old friends.

'I don't 'ave ter do this job, Kate, but it keeps me busy an' I like it, an' the little money I earn ekes out me pension an' me social security.'

As I watched her light a cigarette, I noticed the front of her silvery-white hair was almost yellow from the nicotine smoke. As soon as she asked if *I* smoked, I replied, 'No, Maggie, I gave them up over forty years ago.'

'I wish I could, Kate, they're so expensive now. I remember when me Woodbines cost me only twopence a packet, an' a couple of matches inside free. But I am tryin' ter cut 'em down, me doctor's alwis tellin' me ter give 'em up, but I'm too long in the tooth now ter change me 'abits. Anyway,' she added, 'they 'elp ter soothe me nerves. Any'ow, 'ow did you give 'em up?'

'It was very hard at first, Maggie,' I replied. 'I used to smoke anything, whatever was cheapest. One day I happened to have a fit of coughing and thought I was going to die. It was then I threw them all into the fire – whole packets too, which I'd bought on the black market. I swore that day I'd never smoke another one. That next morning when I woke up I sat on the side of the bed gasping for one. I kept saying to myself, "No! No! I *must* break myself from 'em." A few minutes later, when I went downstairs and walked into that stale-smelling smoky room, that started me off again, wanting one all the more. If it was only one, I said, I'd promise it would be the last, and no more. I searched all the drawers and cupboards, and even turned all my pockets inside out to find a nub end. Still craving, I put the kettle on the fire to make a pot of tea, then suddenly my eyes nearly popped out of my head – staring at me from the hearth was a small nub end. Now, Maggie, you'll laugh when I tell you what I did. It was so small and dry, I stuck it on the end of a pin. I lit it and dragged on that nub till it burnt my lips. I remember that first drag tasted like nectar, until I began to cough.

Again I thought I was going to die. I swore I would never smoke again.'

'But dain't yer ever get the cravin' for 'em agen?'

'Oh yes, Maggie, for days and weeks. But with perseverance, determination and willpower I managed to give them up. Also with help from a young woman I once worked with. She was always chewing on the end of a pencil, and when I asked her why she told me it stopped her from smoking, and if I ever wanted a cigarette I was to put a pencil between my lips and pretend. I did just that too, Maggie, which stopped the craving.'

'I'll try that, Kate, an' see if it'll 'elp.'

We both enjoyed chatting to each other, and as she ordered another two cups of tea, I went on to say, 'One day, as I walked along the Parade, I came towards a tobacconist's shop on the corner of Congreve Street, and in the window, surrounded by thousands of cigarettes, sat an old man rolling them on a small hand machine. As soon as I felt the craving come back I walked quickly past, took out me pencil and as I put it to my lips and pretended to puff away the imaginary smoke, I saw several people stop and stare. They must have thought I was crazy! But I didn't care – I knew I was cured. Now that's another habit I have – whenever I'm concentrating I always put my pen to my lips, but it's the better habit of the two.'

As I got up to go after tea, she said, 'Would yer like ter come ter my 'ome one afternoon an' 'ave tea? I'd luv ter tell yer about my young life.'

As soon as I promised, she wrote down her address and I gave her my phone number to ring me when it was convenient. We kissed each other, then waved as she got on the bus. As it was a lovely warm afternoon, on my way home I strolled through the park, where I saw two young girls about ten years old sitting on the grass, playing a guessing game with a stone held behind their backs. And as I stood for a few seconds to watch, I remembered my young days when I used to sit on the pavement with my brother Frankie and other boys playing at marbles and five stones. As I stooped down to watch, I asked, 'Do you ever play five stones?'

'What's them?' the little girl asked.

'Would you like me to show you?'

When they nodded, I picked up five very small stones from the gravel path, and after wiping the dust from them I sat down beside them and showed them how to play. As soon as I could see they had got the idea of the game, I left, but when I looked back I was pleased to see that other children were sitting round to watch. Sad to say, we don't see many children play the games we did when we were young. There was skipping with our mothers' washing lines, Whip and Tops, marbles, hopscotch, and many other games, which cost little or nothing in those days but amused us and kept us out of mischief.

Maggie and Harry

A few days later I had a phone call from Maggie asking me to come to her home to tea on the following Monday, and she would meet me at the King's Standing bus terminus.

I looked forward to seeing her again, and to more talks about those old days. That Monday as I waited in that bus queue, it started to rain heavily. There was no shelter anywhere. Even if there had been, I didn't want to miss my turn in the queue.

When the bus came I noticed it was full, and it drove on. Everybody started to grumble and swear, and I was in two minds whether to go back home, yet I didn't want to disappoint Maggie. So I stayed grumbling with the rest until the next bus came fifteen minutes later, and I was lucky to find standing room. As soon as I arrived at the terminus, I saw Maggie waving to me from the shelter.

'I'm sorry I'm late, but the first bus was full,' I said.

'Never mind,' she replied, opening up her umbrella for me to share. Then as she took my arm we hurried to a nearby cul-de-sac, where I saw six houses each side of a grass verge. I noticed how clean and well kept they were. As Maggie put the key into the lock, and closed her umbrella, I began to wipe my feet on the hallway mat, just as two neighbours hurrying past called out 'Good afternoon' to her.

'I've got some good, kind neighbours,' she said. 'They always keep an eye on me 'ouse or call to see if I want anythink.'

'Sounds like the old times,' I replied.

'Yes, Kate, but yer can't leave yer door unlocked now like we used to, too many break-ins around here.'

'Yes, I've had my home broken into twice, in the daytime too, and Bobby, my dog, beaten up. If ever I'd have caught them, Maggie, I believe I would have killed 'em, whether I was wrong or right,' I replied bitterly.

'We 'ad nothing to fear, Kate, not in that way – I suppose because we 'ad nothing worth pinchin' anyway,' she added. 'Let me 'ave yer wet 'at an' coat.'

As I handed them to her she made me sit by the fire and take off my wet shoes and stockings. After giving me a towel she handed me a pair of her warm slippers. I sat by that welcome fire with my feet resting on that shining brass fender and looked around the room, while she went into the kitchen to make some tea.

The table was laid with a white lace tablecloth and homemade sandwiches, cakes and bread and butter. Everything looked well worn but homely, clean and highly polished, even the black-leaded range you could see your face in.

As soon as she came in from the kitchen with the teapot and saw me gazing around, she asked, 'Do yer like me place, Kate?'

'Yes,' I replied. 'How long have you lived here?'

'Since we was bombed out in Summer Lane.'

We had our first cup of tea, then drew our chairs up to the table. As we sat eating, we often stopped to talk.

'When I read your books,' she began, 'I remembered all those streets and dark alleyways and some of the people who lived there near Pope Street where we lived. An' do you remember an old pub called the Lion an' the Lamb?'

'Yes,' I replied. 'When it closed down it was taken over by the Salvation Army, and my sister-in-law and her young daughter dished out to us poor free basins and jugs of stew and a piece of bread.'

'Was that your sister-in-law? I remember 'er ever so well, 'er name was Rose. She was alwis kind to the poor unfortunates, an' everyone liked Rose an' spoke well of 'er. She lived in Pope Street opposite Morton Street near us.'

'She was married to my brother Jack. Her real name was Rhoda, but everybody called her Rose. They both gave me away in 1921 at my wedding at Saint Thomas's Church in Bath Row, but we don't see any of them old-fashioned weddings any more, where all the neighbours celebrated too, and had the old gramophone in the yard or booked the hurdy-gurdy man, so everybody could have a knees-up to the tune from the old barrel organ.'

'Yes, Kate, them were some of the happy times. But I've known several young girls who ran away from 'ome who was pregnant an' gave birth to babbies born out of wedlock. My sister Becky was one of those unfortunates, but me mum put 'er pride in 'er pocket an' ignored the neighbours' gossip, an' between me an' me mum we managed to rear that lovely little girl until she died with whoopin' cough, an' she was only three, Kate. Our Becky was always out gooin' ter dance 'alls an' when she come 'ome late, me dad would be waitin' with 'is leather belt. But that seemed to 'arden 'er all the more an' she ran away from 'ome. The next time we saw 'er she was standin' by the graveside at me dad's funeral, all painted an' dolled up, but as soon as she saw all the neighbours staring at 'er an' whispering to each other, she left. We never saw 'er agen, until me mum was dying with that deadly disease, consumption.'

'Is your sister alive now?' I asked.

'Yes, she lives not far from 'ere, but since I buried me mum I don't ever wish ter speak to 'er again,' replied Maggie bitterly. 'She's livin' with a married man now old enough ter be 'er grandad, an' 'e knocks 'er about, so I 'ear from neighbours. She also 'as a son, my nephew, who is now 'appily married with a lovely wife an' three young children. 'E never goes ter visit his mother, yet 'e always cums ter see me every Saturday afternoon when there's a football match. 'E's rough an' ready but 'e's gotta 'eart of gold.' But when she spoke of her sister I noticed she became very bitter.

'Maggie,' I said. 'You shouldn't feel too badly towards your sister. Maybe if she hadn't fallen for that child, she might have been a different person. Women like us were brought up in squalor and ignorance, but children today are taught the facts of life and know what life is all about.'

When I was ready to go, Maggie seemed reluctant for me to leave. Then there was a knock at the door and in walked a tall, handsome young man in shabby dark-blue overalls.

''Ello, 'Arry!' Maggie cried, as she reached up to kiss him. Turning to me, she said, 'This is me nephew, Kate, and 'Arry, this is me friend I used ter goo ter school with, the lady who wrote them books yer bought me.'

'I'm very pleased ter meet yer, Mrs Dayus. I've 'eard such a lot about yer an' I've read yer books, me an' me wife, an' when me daughters grow up they too will 'ave ter read 'em.'

'What brings yer 'ere today, 'Arry?' asked Maggie.

'Will yer loan me a couple of quid till termorra, yer see I've cum without me wallet, an' I wanta goo ter me club straight from work.'

As she handed him the two pounds he kissed her and said he'd call the next day.

After shaking my hand he said, 'Keep up the good work, dear.'

After closing the door behind him, Maggie said, 'E's a good lad, always pays me back, an' although I'm only 'is auntie, 'e always brings me flowers on Mother's Day, an' other times 'e does odd jobs for me. I've only gotta ask.'

I gave her my address and phone number again and told her to ring me when it was convenient.

She saw me to the bus, then we waved each other goodbye.

A few days later I heard from her – she was already in town shopping and would I meet her outside the Kardomah Café?

When we met she said she was sorry to have kept me waiting but she had been kept waiting at the shops.

'Never mind, Maggie,' I replied, 'you're here now, so let's finish our coffee and catch the bus.'

Seeing the bus coming we hurried to catch it, and luckily the kind driver waited for us.

As soon as we got off the bus and arrived at my house, I said I'd already got the table laid for tea. As we walked up the front-garden path she said, 'You've got a nice 'ouse, Kate, do yer live 'ere all alone?'

'No, my eldest daughter and her husband live with me. Anyway they're away on holiday at the moment, and I'm happy to have the house to myself.'

When she asked how long I had lived in Handsworth, I told her that Joe and I had bought the house in 1961. 'But Handsworth's not like it used to be when we first came to live here. There was always those lovely old small familiar shops, where the people served you across the counter and always found time to have a friendly chat while measuring and weighing whatever you asked for. But we don't get that today. Food's already wrapped and your money taken and you never know what you've really bought until you unwrap it. It's the attitude you get from some of these supermarkets: "Take it or leave it".'

'Yes, Kate, I know wot yer mean – give me the old friendly corner shops any time.'

As we sat at the table and began our tea, I said, 'But I wouldn't like to see those poverty days again.'

'Nor me, Kate, nor live in them back-ter-back slums agen. It was a good thing in one way that Summer Lane came under the bombing, otherwise I think I would still be there terday. Yet it's sad when yer think of all them people who were killed. Did yer ever know Summer Lane, Kate?' she added.

'No, but I'd heard of it and was warned not to go near it when I was a kid.'

All at once we both began to laugh like a couple of teenagers, then Maggie cried, 'It was a street where men threw corks at each other with the bottles on the end. Police often paraded four abreast, an' many a man was frogmarched ter Kenyon Street Police Station for disturbin' the peace, women too dragged out of the pub. Some women were afraid of no man – often on Saturday nights, even Sunday dinner-time, you'd see an' 'ear a man an' wife fightin' over their kids, even over other people's cats an' dogs.'

'Talking about cats, Maggie, I remember a woman who lived in the end house in our yard – her name was Mrs Taylor, she had several cats and when they had kittens she used to drown them in the maiding tub, under the tap. And when the corporation men came she used to cover 'em over with ashes and hide them in the dustbin. Then our dry closets were demolished and we had the flush ones, but still the same wooden seats. Then one day we saw Mrs Bumpham come out of the end closet with her drawers hanging down over her boots, screaming her head off, shouting she'd heard a baby cryin' down in the basin. Somebody fetched the police and when they investigated they found it was another place where Mrs Taylor drowned her kittens. Do you know, Maggie, how superstitious people were in them times? Nobody would use that closet in case one came up and clawed at their bum. It was nailed up until the day Mrs Taylor died.'

'Are you superstitious, Kate?' she asked.

'Yes, I believe I am in many ways.'

'So am I,' replied Maggie, 'especially when I tek a walk in the cemetery – I never walk on the grass in case I walk on somebody's grave. I'm told it's bad luck. An' the people cum an' 'aunt yer.'

'I don't believe that one, Maggie,' I said, smiling.

'I do, Kate; there was a neighbour of ours who lived in Summer

Lane, she an' 'er husband were alwis fightin' an' when 'e died she said she wanted 'im cremated ter mek sure 'e was dead. Yet people couldn't understand why she kept 'is ashes in a vase on the kitchen shelf. When the neighbours found out and told 'er it was bad luck, she wouldn't believe 'em until a few nights later she began to 'ave nightmares. Somebody told 'er if she got rid of 'is ashes the nightmares would goo. A few days later, when we saw 'er sling 'is ashes through the winda, me nor none of our neighbours would walk on that part of the pavement until the rain cum an' washed 'im away. She's also cum ter live in King's Standin' not far from 'ere. Yer see there's no pawnshops now, near 'ere, but there used ter be a special bus laid on every Monday mornin', called the Jenny Brigton Bus, for these women ter tek their bundle of clothes or whatever, ter the Jenny Brigton's pawnshop in Summer Lane.'

'Yes, Maggie,' I replied, 'I was glad when *I* could find something to pawn, it was better than going to the loan sharks.'

We laughed and cried as we talked about the many things that happened those long years ago. And when she asked me why I didn't talk the lingo like the Brummies, I replied, 'I do – you should hear me when I lose me temper, Maggie!'

I also told her about the different boyfriends I had, and how I came to educate myself.

'I remember when I was about twelve I became one of my teacher's favourites. Her name was Miss Frost. She tried hard to teach me how to pronounce words properly, and when I did, all the kids in our street used to make fun of me. When I was fourteen and left school, I was determined to teach myself to talk better. It was not until I started work that I began to listen to the office girls and try to pronounce words as they did. And when I was about fifteen, still ignorant and innocent, I met a boy from the office. We often went for walks together, he too spoke very nicely, yet I could never break myself of the Brummie lingo. Then, one Sunday afternoon, as we strolled through the park, he stopped to put his arm round me and kiss me. Although I liked that sensation, Maggie, I was scared of what it might lead to. As I pushed him away I cried out, "Goo away! I ain't one of yer sort yer can tek yer way with, wot werks in yer office." Do you know, Maggie, after he said he was sorry, I still felt I wanted him to take me in his arms and kiss me, really passionately. But being dragged up and not knowing the facts of life,

I was scared. Then one day, as we strolled through that same park, he began to say I was a nice girl and if I would let him teach me to speak properly I could go places; he also said he'd bring a dictionary and teach me. I didn't even know what a dictionary was until he explained. But when he told me he'd like to take me to his home to meet his parents, but I had to learn to pronounce my words properly, I suddenly felt ashamed and embarrassed. I lost my temper and slapped his face as hard as I could and ran off. He still pestered me to go out with him, but after the girls I worked with began to talk and get the wrong ideas about us, I left. But I always remembered his words, and that he wanted to educate me. Then one day, a few weeks later, I did buy a dictionary. Although it seemed all Chinese to me I studied it hard, and when I did try to speak properly my brothers and sisters made fun of me and my mum said talking that way would be the ruination of me, and if any time she saw it she would put it on the fire. So I had to hide it away under the floorboards. And do you know how I began to learn, Maggie? Apart from listening to other people's conversations, I used to sit for hours on our wooden-seated closets and study and talk to myself, until somebody banged on the door and asked how long I was going to be. Then I'd quickly push the diary down inside my passion-killers.'

'Passion-killers? Wot are them?' Maggie asked at once.

'That's what the lads used to call our baggy bloomers,' I replied, smiling.

'Oh yes, I remember now, they was fleecy-lined with 'lastic round the legs!'

After we had talked some more about life, Maggie said she would have to be going before it got dark. And as she put on her hat and coat, she said, 'I could tell yer stories, Kate, that would mek yer 'air curl. P'raps when I cum agen, but I must 'urry now, I don't like ter goo under them underpasses, yo 'ear of too many muggin's.'

I offered to call a taxi for her, but she said she'd left a note for her nephew to say when she would be back. Just as we went along the hall and opened the front door, I saw her nephew get out of his car. As soon as she saw him she cried, 'Wot brings yer 'ere? I left yer a note ter say I'd be 'ome by five o'clock.'

'That's OK, Auntie, I thought I'd pick yer up any'ow, get in.'

She kissed and thanked me and got into the car. Her nephew said she looked forward to seeing me, but he hoped she hadn't talked me to death.

'No, she can come any time, we both enjoyed our reminiscences.'

As I waved them both goodbye, I felt so alone. So I went indoors, put Bobby's lead on and took him for his usual walk before it got too dark.

I couldn't understand why Maggie never kept her promise to visit me that following week. I had a premonition that something was wrong when I saw her nephew at the door. As soon as I called him in, he sat down and wept. When I asked what was wrong, he managed to tell me that his Auntie Maggie had been standing on a chair, hanging up some curtains, and had fallen off.

'I don't know 'ow long she'd been lyin' on the floor, but one of the neighbours saw 'er through the winda, an' phoned me at work. She was unconscious. I dain't know wot ter do, I couldn't wait for the ambulance, so I managed to get 'er in the car and drove to the hospital. The doctors said she'd broken 'er arm in two places an' she 'ad a broken 'ip.'

When I asked if I could go and visit, he said she had died the following day.

'If only she had waited an' asked me to 'ang 'em. But she was so independent, always sayin' "If yer want things done right, do 'em yerself".' As he sobbed, he managed to say, 'I shall miss 'er so much, Mrs Dayus. She was betta than a mother ter me, she brought me up like a son when my mother left me ter roam the streets.'

I was very upset too, I didn't know what to say to comfort him. So I made him a cup of strong coffee and after pulling himself together and wiping away his tears, he asked if I would like to see her when they brought her home in her coffin.

'I'm sorry, Harry,' I said at once, 'but I would rather remember Maggie as I last saw her.'

'I understand,' he replied. 'But p'raps yer would like ter cum ter the service?'

'Yes, I'll do that, Harry. Just phone and tell me when.'

A few days later I bought a wreath and went to the service, and as I stood by the graveside I saw Harry and his wife, also several neighbours weeping. I looked among the faces to see if I could see Maggie's sister Becky. Although I'd never met her I expected she might be among the crowd. And as I glanced around again, I saw an old woman dressed in a shabby black coat and straw hat, standing well back from the graveside and weeping. I could tell she was Harry's mother – their features were almost identical. Yet no one spoke to her or went near her. Then as soon as the coffin was lowered into the grave, I watched as Maggie's sister walked away.

As soon as I arrived home, I broke down and wept. I felt I had lost a very dear friend and companion.

Fred

When I married Joe Dayus in 1946, it was mainly for companionship. Although he had a wonderful sense of humour, in later years he became very moody, but I didn't have to be dependent on his moods. Often when we had sharp words over money matters, I got the feeling that he wished I wasn't so independent and would ask his advice on various matters. But over the years I had become too hardened in my ways to humble myself or to ask anyone's advice. I also realised that he was becoming very jealous of anyone talking to me. He would ask, 'What did they say? And who were they?' And when I bought a new dress he would say, 'I don't know why yer keep buyin' new frocks for, wastin' yer money.' Maybe I was a bit extravagant at times.

Whenever Joe took me to his fishing club and any of his friends looked at me, I could always feel his eyes on me.

Then, one day, one of his fishing mates called. I was surprised when I answered the door and saw it was a fellow that had been sweet on me some years before I was married.

'Hello, Kate, long time no see, remember me?'

'Yes,' I replied. 'What do you want?' I asked him nervously.

Although I had nothing to be ashamed of, I was afraid that if Joe knew he was one of my cast-offs, there'd be more questions and more quarrels.

When he asked if Joe was in, I invited him in. Joe was up at the top of the garden, feeding his pigeons. As soon as I went to the back door to call him, I felt Fred come too near me for comfort. I pushed him away, hoping my husband hadn't seen him, but I could see by the way he spoke he was annoyed.

'What brings you here? I told yer I'd meet yer at the club.'

'I was passing, I thought I'd call and look at yer birds.'

'How long have yer been interested in pigeons?' he asked sharply.

'Me dad used to have them to train, years ago.'

I could see by the look on my husband's face that he didn't believe a word. 'Well, come on then, Fred,' he replied as he quickly grabbed his hat and coat, and after giving me orders to feed the rest of his birds and lock them up, he gave me a quick peck on the cheek and they were gone.

Fred didn't call again until a few weeks later. He must have known I was alone, for in his hand was a large box of chocolates. I didn't like to refuse, or to hurt his feelings. I thanked him and told him not to call again when my husband wasn't at home, as he was very jealous of anyone calling to see me.

'No harm done, Kate. I happened to win 'em an' my wife can't eat chocolates, so I thought of you. Anyway, I expect I'll be seeing you at the club.'

'Thank you, Fred,' I replied nervously as I placed the box on the table, hoping Joe wouldn't walk in at the same time.

After Fred had gone, as I picked up the two-pound box, my mouth began to water. I wanted to open them, but I was afraid Joe would come home unexpectedly and ask questions, so I hid them away. Later I thought: what if he should find them? I didn't want to make excuses to avoid more quarrels. The next day I gave them to the woman next door to share amongst her children. I told her they had been won in a raffle and I couldn't eat them.

The following week Fred came again with a beautiful bunch of carnations. I had always loved flowers, so I couldn't refuse them – and I had no intention of giving these away. 'Why should I?' I thought to myself. As I arranged them in a vase of water, we chatted for about ten minutes. He spoke about his wife and his allotments and the flowers he grew. When I asked him if he'd stay and have a cup of tea he said he was pushed for time, but if I didn't mind he'd call another day. I thanked him again for the flowers and as soon as he left I knew that when Joe saw them he would ask me where they came from. I wasn't going to lie, and I didn't want to give them away.

Sure enough, as soon as he came through the door the first thing he saw on the table were the flowers. I was glad to see he was in a good mood. 'Them are beautiful carnations, where did yer buy 'em from?'

'I didn't,' I replied. 'Fred brought 'em for me from his allotment.'

I wondered if he knew about the chocolates when he suddenly became very angry: 'This has gotta stop! I ain't havin' him bringin' yer flowers or anythin' else – if yer want any it's up ter me ter buy 'em fer yer!'

I was afraid. I'd never seen him so angry. Suddenly he snatched the flowers from the vase and hurried out of the front door with them in his hand.

I don't know what he did with them, but we never spoke to each other for the rest of that day.

The following day he came home all smiles, carrying a large bunch of red roses. I glared at him as I said, 'If yer think that yer can buy me over by bringing flowers, you've time ter think agen.'

I didn't speak to him again for days. It was only that I felt sorry for him when he developed a bad cold. But in the meantime I felt sad to see those lovely roses left drooping beside the sink. Then as I put the kettle on the fire to make some tea I saw him put them into a vase of water, and each morning when he came downstairs the first thing he did was to change the water. I never knew what became of those lovely carnations, but Fred never called at my house again, and if I ever saw him out shopping with his wife I would avoid him.

A few weeks later, I happened to see him going towards the club. As soon as I caught up with him, I asked why he never came to see me again.

'I thought it best not to call again, Kate, after Joe made such a fuss about those flowers I brought you. We nearly came to blows the way he carried on. Bad-tempered bugger,' he added.

'What did he do with the flowers?' I asked.

'He gave 'em to the barmaid.'

'I'm sorry, Fred, about the quarrel, but Joe hasn't been well lately and he gets so short-tempered and irritable at times.'

'Yes, Kate, we've all noticed that even when he's playing snooker and he loses, he throws his cue down on the floor. He was never a bad loser until these last few weeks. Anyway, I'm sorry to say the gaffer here will refuse him if he don't change. But the incident is forgotten as far as I'm concerned.'

'Thank you, Fred. I'll try and have a talk to him.'

But I knew it would be hopeless. As soon as I got home, I found Joe fast asleep in his armchair. He was also now a chain smoker, and

often complained of a pain in his chest. But no matter how much I talked to him and even nagged him at times, it made no difference. I began to worry when he refused to see the doctor.

One day, whilst he was in the garden flying his birds, I cleaned and dusted the front room where he always sat. I also gave an extra polish to the hearth, which was often covered with cigarette ash. After putting a lump of coal on the fire, I left to do some shopping. When I arrived back the room reeked of stale smoke and more nub ends were strewn in the hearth. As I opened the window, Joe came in.

'What yer wanta open that bloody winda for?' he bawled. 'Want me ter catch me death?'

Suddenly I lost my patience. 'It ain't fresh air that's goin' ter kill yer, it'll be them bloody fags yer keep smokin'! An' look at me hearth agen!'

I felt sorry that I'd lost my temper when he replied, 'Yer won't have me here much longer to nag when I ain't here ter make yer a mess.'

I knew he wasn't in good health, but through all these years I still remember those words.

A couple of days after I was on to him again, to see the doctor about his cough. My daughter Jean visited us with my young granddaughter Chrissie (whom we often called 'Cookie'), who was about eight years old. As soon as Joe saw her he said, 'Would you like to play a game of dominoes, Cookie?'

'Yes, please, Grandad Dayus.'

'I don't like yer callin' me Grandad, I ain't yer real grandad, so yer can call me Uncle Joe.'

'OK, Uncle Joe,' she replied, smiling up at him.

She didn't tell him she already knew how to play, and when he drew up the coffee table by the fire he shuffled the dominoes and began to play seriously.

Jean and I left them to sit and play while we went into the kitchen to talk and make a cup of tea. Whilst we were there, Chrissie won the first two games. 'Beginner's luck' we heard Joe say. As we watched, she also won the next. But when she won the fourth game, he lost his temper and as he tipped the table up, the dominoes fell into the hearth. I had to rescue the double six from the fire. My young granddaughter was so scared, she never came again while Joe was there. I felt so ashamed and embarrassed. I still have those dominoes, with the double six which is all scorched.

As the days went by he became worse, his temper frayed and he became very irritable. At times he would say things that made me laugh, but you knew you could laugh with him but never at him.

Some days he was better than others, but little did I think I was going to be a widow for the second time so soon.

One night, as we lay in bed, he sat up fighting for his breath. I ran downstairs and phoned for the doctor. As soon as he came and examined Joe's chest, he said he would have to be moved to the hospital. Joe refused, but the doctor was adamant. 'I'm not asking you, I'm telling you!' he snapped. 'You've had a bad heart attack!'

The ambulance came and he was in St Chad's Hospital for two weeks. As soon as he came back home he began to smoke worse than before. When I had to call the doctor in again, and told him about the coughing and smoking, he called me into the hall and told me Joe had an enlarged heart and a thrombosis. There was nothing more he could do, he said, only get him to take his tablets regularly. Often he refused to take them, he said they made him feel worse. A few days later he was taken to Dudley Road Hospital. As soon as he was discharged he took up bowling again at his club.

As I was captain of the bowling team, my daughter and I had to go to Manchester to play an away match. My husband was sorry he couldn't come with us, as he had promised his club members to join their team on the same day. But he said he would have our teas ready for us when we came back.

During that afternoon I had a premonition that something was going to happen. As soon as I arrived home I received the sad news that my husband had died whilst playing on the bowling green.

I thought I would never get over my loss, but I pulled myself together and after the funeral I still carried on with my enamelling at home, also going to my bowling matches.

After a few months my daughter married again, but bowling trips, Christmas and holidays were never the same for me again.

Although Joe died many years ago, I still miss him and I think only of the happy times we had together. Yet I am not lonely any more – I have my meetings and visits to the elderly, and visits from my family. But life doesn't seem the same without a partner to confide in and share your troubles with. Although my Joe had many faults I still loved him and understood him, and often wish he were here today for us to grow old together. Now it's too late. But that's life.

Kathleen Dayus was born in Hockley, Birmingham in 1903. Her first book, *Her People* (1982), won the J.R. Ackerly Prize for autobiography. This was followed by *Where There's Life*, *All My Days* and *The Best of Times*. Kathleen Dayus lives in Birmingham still and spends much of her time visiting old people's homes where she reads from her autobiography. In 1993 she published *The People of Lavender Court*, inspired by the stories told to her by Annie Green, a Birmingham woman whom she met in a community home. In recognition of her contribution to the writing of Birmingham's history, Kathleen Dayus was awarded an honorary Master of Arts degree by the University of Birmingham in December 1992.